CCDE Study Guide

Marwan Al-shawi, CCDE No. 20130066

Cisco Press

800 East 96th Street

Indianapolis, Indiana 46240 USA

CCDE Study Guide

Marwan Al-shawi

Copyright© 2016 Pearson Education, Inc.

Cisco Press logo is a trademark of Cisco Systems, Inc.

Published by:
Cisco Press
800 East 96th Street
Indianapolis, IN 46240 USA

Printed in the United States of America 1 2 3 4 5 6 7 8 9 0

First Printing October 2015

Library of Congress Control Number: 2015949761

ISBN-13: 978-1-58714-461-5

ISBN-10: 1-58714-461-1

Warning and Disclaimer

This book covers various possible design options available while working across multiple places in the network. As part of the evaluation process, the book stays focused on various technical requirements, business requirements, constraints, and associated implications rather than on providing best practice recommendations.

Every effort has been made to make this book as comprehensive and as accurate as possible. The book does not attempt to teach foundational knowledge. Please supplement your learning and fill in gaps in knowledge by reviewing separate technology-specific publications as part of your journey to become a Design Expert.

The information is provided on an "as is" basis. The authors, Cisco Press, and Cisco Systems, Inc. shall have neither liability nor responsibility to any person or entity with respect to any loss or damages arising from the information contained in this book or from the use of the discs or programs that may accompany it.

The opinions expressed in this book belong to the author and are not necessarily those of Cisco Systems, Inc.

Feedback Information

At Cisco Press, our goal is to create in-depth technical books of the highest quality and value. Each book is crafted with care and precision, undergoing rigorous development that involves the unique expertise of members from the professional technical community.

Readers' feedback is a natural continuation of this process. If you have any comments regarding how we could improve the quality of this book, or otherwise alter it to better suit your needs, you can contact us through email at feedback@ciscopress.com. Please make sure to include the book title and ISBN in your message.

We greatly appreciate your assistance.

Trademark Acknowledgments

All terms mentioned in this book that are known to be trademarks or service marks have been appropriately capitalized. Cisco Press or Cisco Systems, Inc. cannot attest to the accuracy of this information. Use of a term in this book should not be regarded as affecting the validity of any trademark or service mark.

Publisher: Paul Boger

Associate Publisher: Dave Dusthimer

Business Operation Manager, Cisco Press: Jan Cornelssen

Executive Editor: Brett Bartow

Managing Editor: Sandra Schroeder

Senior Development Editor: Christopher Cleveland

Project Editor: Mandie Frank

Copy Editor: Keith Cline

Technical Editors: Andre Laurent, Denise Fishburne

Editorial Assistant: Vanessa Evans

Designer: Mark Shirar

Composition: codeMantra

Proofreader: Laura Hernandez

Americas Headquarters
Cisco Systems, Inc.
San Jose, CA

Asia Pacific Headquarters
Cisco Systems (USA) Pte. Ltd.
Singapore

Europe Headquarters
Cisco Systems International BV
Amsterdam, The Netherlands

Cisco has more than 200 offices worldwide. Addresses, phone numbers, and fax numbers are listed on the Cisco Website at **www.cisco.com/go/offices.**

CCDE, CCENT, Cisco Eos, Cisco HealthPresence, the Cisco logo, Cisco Lumin, Cisco Nexus, Cisco StadiumVision, Cisco TelePresence, Cisco WebEx, DCE, and Welcome to the Human Network are trademarks; Changing the Way We Work, Live, Play, and Learn and Cisco Store are service marks; and Access Registrar, Aironet, AsyncOS, Bringing the Meeting To You, Catalyst, CCDA, CCDP, CCIE, CCIP, CCNA, CCNP, CCSP, CCVP, Cisco, the Cisco Certified Internetwork Expert logo, Cisco IOS, Cisco Press, Cisco Systems, Cisco Systems Capital, the Cisco Systems logo, Cisco Unity, Collaboration Without Limitation, EtherFast, EtherSwitch, Event Center, Fast Step, Follow Me Browsing, FormShare, GigaDrive, HomeLink, Internet Quotient, IOS, iPhone, iQuick Study, IronPort, the IronPort logo, LightStream, Linksys, MediaTone, MeetingPlace, MeetingPlace Chime Sound, MGX, Networkers, Networking Academy, Network Registrar, PCNow, PIX, PowerPanels, ProConnect, ScriptShare, SenderBase, SMARTnet, Spectrum Expert, StackWise, The Fastest Way to Increase Your Internet Quotient, TransPath, WebEx, and the WebEx logo are registered trademarks of Cisco Systems, Inc. and/or its affiliates in the United States and certain other countries.

All other trademarks mentioned in this document or website are the property of their respective owners. The use of the word partner does not imply a partnership relationship between Cisco and any other company. (0812R)

About the Author

Marwan Al-shawi, CCDE No. 20130066, is a lead design with British Telecom Global Services. He helps large-scale enterprise customers to select the right technology solutions for their business needs and provides technical consultancy for various types of network designs and architectures. Marwan has been in the networking industry for more than 12 years and has been involved in architecting, designing, and implementing various large-scale networks, some of which are global service provider-grade networks. Marwan has also worked as a technical consultant with Dimension Data Australia, a Cisco Global Alliance Partner; network architect with IBM Australia global technology services; and other Cisco partners and IT solution providers. He holds a Master of Science degree in internetworking from the University of Technology, Sydney. Marwan also holds other certifications such as Cloud Architect Expert (EMCCAe), Cisco Certified Design Professional (CCDP), Cisco Certified Network Professional – Voice (CCNP Voice), and Microsoft Certified Systems Engineer (MCSE). Marwan was selected as a Cisco Designated VIP by the Cisco Support Community (CSC) (official Cisco Systems forums) in 2012, and by the Solutions and Architectures subcommunity in 2014. In addition, in 2015, Marwan was selected as a member of the Cisco Champions program.

About the Technical Reviewers

Andre Laurent, CCDE No.20120024, CCIE NO.21840 (RS, SP, Security) is a Technical Solutions Architect representing Cisco's Commercial West Area. He has been in IT engineering and consulting for his entire career. Andre is a triple CCIE and CCDE, joint certifications held by fewer than 50 people in the world. Outside of his own personal development, Andre has an equal passion about developing others and assisting them with the certification process. Andre is recognized by the Cisco Learning Network as a subject matter expert in the areas of routing, switching, security, and design. Although he wears a Cisco badge, Andre takes a neutral approach in helping clients establish a long-term business and technology vision covering necessary strategy, execution, and metrics for measuring impact. He spends a great deal of time conducting customer workshops, developing design blueprints, and creating reference models to assist customers in achieving quantified and realized business benefits. Andre has built reference architectures in numerous industries such as banking, retail, utilities and aerospace. He also works closely with some of the largest gaming and hospitality companies in the world.

Denise "Fish" Fishburne, CCDE No.20090014, CCIE No.2639, is an engineer and team lead with the Customer Proof of Concept Lab (CPOC) in North Carolina. Fish is a geek who adores learning and passing it on. She works on many technologies in the CPOC, but her primary technical strength seems, however, to be troubleshooting. Fish has been with Cisco since 1996, CPOC since 2001, and has been a regular speaker at Networkers/Cisco Live since 2006.

Dedication

I would like to dedicate this book to my wonderful mother for her continued support, love, encouragement, guidance, and wisdom.

And most importantly, I would like to thank God for all the blessings in my life.

—*Marwan*

Acknowledgments

A special and big thank you goes to the Pearson-Cisco Press team, especially Brett Bartow and Chris Cleveland, for the support and suggestions that made this book possible. It is a pleasure to work with you. I couldn't have asked for a finer team

I'd like to give special recognition to Andre Laurent for providing his expert technical knowledge and experience as a technical editor of this book. Andre's suggestions and feedback from his real-world practical experience as a technical solution architect with Cisco helped to shape and optimize the quality of the content in multiple areas.

I also want to give special recognition to Denise Fishburne for her valuable contribution and input. As usual, she's not afraid to tell you when you're wrong. In addition, the technical accuracy and insight regarding the technologies and design considerations provided by Denise from her long and extensive experience with Cisco POC helped to enhance the accuracy and quality of the content across multiple sections.

In addition, special a special thank you to Elaine Lopes (CCDE and CCAr Program Manager) for her continued encouragement ever since this book was only an idea.

Also, a special and big thank you to the following experts for their valuable time and their expert perspectives about some chapters and sections in this book, which added a significant value to optimize the contents:

Russ White, Orhan Ergun, Diptanshu Singh, and Ivan Pepelnjak.

Contents at a Glance

Contents

Icons Used in This Book

 Layer 2 Switch

 Layer 3 Switch

 Modular Layer 3 Switch

 Frame-Rely/ATM WAN Switch

 Router

 MPLS Router

 Layer 2 WAN/SP Aggregation Switch

 SAN Switch

 Router with IP Tunnel

 Firewall

 Satellite

 Host with Virtual Machines

 Load Balancer

 Fabric Switch

 IP Phone

 Workstation

 Server

 Remote or Regional Site

 Radio Tower

 Optical Ring

 Virtual Machine

 Ethernet Link

Legacy Link-Serial, Frame-Rely, ATM, TDM

Cloud-Routed or Switched Domain

Introduction

The CCDE certification is a unique certification in the IT and networking industry and is considered one of the most if not the only recognized vendor-neutral network Design Expert level certification. When it comes to design, it is like art: It cannot be taught or covered entirely through a single book or a training course, because each design has different drivers, philosophy, and circumstances that collectivity create its unique characteristic. Therefore, this book uses a comparative and analytical approach to help the reader answer the question why with regard to design or technology selections, and to think of how to link the technical design decisions to other influencing factors (technical, nontechnical, or combination of both) to achieve a true and successful business-driven design. In addition, multiple mini design scenarios and illustrations are included in the chapters to explain the concepts, design options, and implications.

This book is the first book to target the CCDE practical exam. Also, It is the first book that consists of diverse design aspects, principles, and options using a business-driven approach for enterprise, service provider, and data center networks.

This book covers the different design principles and topics using the following approach:

- Covers (that is, highlights, discusses, and compares) the different technologies, protocols, design principles, and design options in terms of cost, availability, scalability, performance, flexibility, and so on (along with the strength of the various designs and design concerns where applicable)

- Covers the drivers toward adopting the different technologies and protocols (technical and nontechnical) (whether intended for enterprise or service provider networks depends on the topic and technology)

- Covers the implications of the addition or integration of any element to the overall design, such as adding new applications or integrating two different networks

The design topics covered in this CCDE Study Guide aim to prepare you to be able to

- Analyze and identify various design requirements (business, functional, and application) that can influence design decisions.

- Understand the different design principles and their impact on the organization from a business point of view

- Understand and compare the various network design architectures and the associated implications on various design aspects of applying different Layer 2 and Layer 3 control plane protocols

- Identify and analyze design limitations or issues, and how to optimize them, taking into consideration the technical and nontechnical design requirements and constraints.

- Identify and analyze the implication of adding new services or applications and how to accommodate the design or the design approach to meet the expectations

This book references myriad sources, but presents the material in a manner tailored for conscientious network designers and architects. The material also covers updated standards and features that are found in enterprise and service provider networks. In addition, each chapter contains further reading suggestions pointing you to recommended documents that pertain to the topics covered in each chapter.

Therefore, you can use this book as an all-in-one study guide covering the various networking technologies, protocols, and design options in a business-driven approach. You can expand your study scope and depth of knowledge selectively on certain topics as needed.

Whether you are preparing for the CCDE certification or just want to better understand advanced network design topics, you will benefit from the range of topics covered and the practical business-driven approach used to analyze, compare, and explain these topics.

Who Should Read This Book?

In addition to those who are planning or studying for the CCDE certification, this book is for network engineers, network consultants, network architects, and solutions architects who already have a foundational knowledge of the topics being covered and who would like to train themselves to think more like a design engineer rather than like an implementation engineer.

CCDE Practical Exam Overview

The minimally qualified CCDE must have expert-level knowledge, experience, and skills that cover complex networks design (ideally global-scale networks) by successfully demonstrating the ability to translate business requirements and strategies into functional and technical strategies. In other words, CCDEs are recognized for their expert-level knowledge and skills in network infrastructure design. The deep technical networking knowledge that a CCDE brings ensures that they are well qualified to address the most technically challenging network infrastructure design assignments [1]. Therefore, to test the CCDE candidate skills, knowledge, and expertise, the CCDE practical exam is divided into multiple design scenarios, with each having a different type of network and requirements. In addition, each design scenario is structured of different domains and tasks that CCDE candidates have to complete to demonstrate expert-level abilities when dealing with a full network design lifecycle (gather business requirements, analyze the requirements, develop a design, plan the implementation of the design, and then apply and optimize the design).

Job Tasks

The CCDE exam is designed to cover different use cases, each of which may be integrated in one or multiple design scenarios in the exam. The following are the primary use cases at the time of this writing:

■ **Merge or divest networks:** This use case covers the implications and challenges (technical and nontechnical) associated with merging or separating different networks (both enterprise and service provider types of networks). This domain, in particular, can be one of the most challenging use cases for network designers because, most of the time, merging two different networks means integrating two different design philosophies, in which multiple conflicting design concepts can appear. Therefore, at a certain stage, network designers have to bring these two different networks together to work as a one cohesive system, taking into consideration the various design constrains that might exist such as goals for the merged network, security policy compliance, timeframe, cost, the merger constraints, the decision of which services to keep and which ones to divest (and how), how to keep services up and running after the divestiture, what the success criteria is for the merged network, and who is the decision maker.

■ **Add technology or application:** This use case covers the impact of adding technology or an application to an existing network. Will anything break as a result of the new addition? In this use case, you must consider the application requirements in terms of traffic pattern, convergence time, delay, and so on across the network. By understanding these requirements, the CCDE candidate as a network designer should be able to make design decisions about fine-tuning the network (design and features such as quality of service [QoS]) to deliver this application with the desired level of experience for the end users.

■ **Replace technology:** This use case covers a wide range of options to replace an existing technology to meet certain requirements. It might be a WAN technology, routing protocol, security mechanism, underlying network core technology, or so on. Also, the implications of this new technology or protocol on the current design, such as enhanced scalability or potential to conflict with some of the existing application requirements, require network designers to tailor the network design so that these technologies work together rather than in isolation, so as to reach objectives, such as delivering business applications and services.

■ **Scale a network:** This use case covers different types of scalability aspects at different levels, such as physical topology, along with Layer 2 and Layer 3 scalability design considerations. In addition, the challenges associated with the design optimization of an existing network design to offer a higher level of scalability are important issues in this domain. For example, there might be some constraints or specific business requirements that might limit the available options for the network designer when trying to optimize the current design. Considerations with regard to this use case include the following: Is the growth planned or organic? Are there issues caused by the growth? Should one stop and redesign the network to account for growth? What is the most scalable design model?

Exam Job Domains

In each of the CCDE exam use cases described in the preceding section, as part of each CCDE design scenario the candidate is expected to cover some or all of the following job domains:

- **Analyze:** This domain requires identification of the requirements, constraints, and risks from both business and technology perspectives. In this task, the candidate is expected to perform multiple subtasks, such as the following:

  - Identify the missing information required to produce a design.

  - Integrate and analyze information from multiple sources (for example, from e-mails or from diagrams) to provide the correct answer for any given question.

- **Design:** In this domain, the CCDE candidate is usually expected to provide a suggested design by making design choices and decisions based on the given and analyzed information and requirements in the previous task. Furthermore, one of the realistic and unique aspects of the CCDE exam is that there might be more than one right design option. Also, there might be optimal and suboptimal solutions. This aspect of the exam is based on the CCDE candidate's understanding of the requirements, goals, and constraints in making the most relevant and suitable selection given the options available.

- **Implement and deploy:** This domain contains multiple subtasks, such as the following:

  - Determine the consequences of the implementation of the proposed design.

  - Design implementation, migration, or fallback plans.

Note No command-line interface (CLI) configuration is required on the CCDE practical exam. The general goal behind this point is more about how and where you to apply a network technology or a protocol and the implications associated with it, and how to generate a plan to apply the proposed design.

- **Validate and optimize:** Here the CCDE candidate is required to justify the design choices and decisions in terms of the rationale behind the design's selection. The candidate's justifications should evidence that the selected design is the best available. Justifications are typically driven by technical requirements, business requirements, and functional requirements, considered either in isolation or in combination.

Exam Technologies

As a general rule for the CCDE practical exam technologies, consider the written exam (qualification) blueprint as a reference (see Figure I-1). However, remember that this is a scenario-based design exam, in which you might expect expansion to the technologies covered in the CCDE written blueprint. In other words, consider the blueprint as a foundation and expand upon it to a reasonable extent; it is not necessary to go deeply into technologies that are not used in real-life networks.

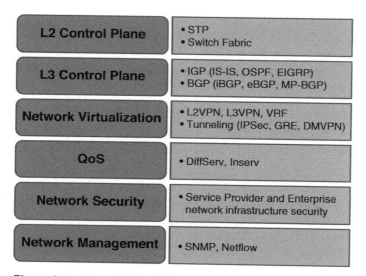

Figure I-1   *Exam Technologies*

Note   The above technologies include both IP versions (version 4 and 6) as well as unicast and Multicast IP communications.

PPDIOO Approach and the CCDE Job Domains

With regard to IT services, businesses usually aim to reduce total cost of ownership, improve its service availability, enhance user quality of experience, and reduce operational expenses. By adopting a lifecycle approach, organizations can define a set of methodologies and standards to be followed at each stage of the IT network's life. With this approach, there will be a series of phases that all collectively construct a lifecycle. With most lifecycle approaches, the information and findings of each phase can be used to feed and improve the following phase. This ultimately can produce more efficient and cost-effective IT network solutions that offer IT more elasticity to enhance current investments and to adopt new IT technologies and justify their investment cost.

The PPDIOO lifecycle (see Figure I-2) stands for Prepare, Plan, Design, Implement, Operate, and Optimize, which is Cisco's vision of the IT network lifecycle. This vision is primarily based on the concept that understanding what is supposed to happen at each stage is vital for a company (or architect, designer) to properly use the lifecycle approach and to get the most benefit from it.

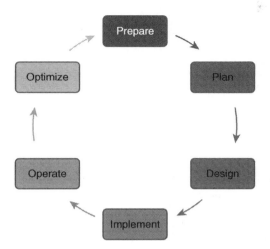

Figure I-2 *PPDIOO Lifecycle*

Furthermore, this approach offers the flexibility to have a two-way directional relationship between the phases. For instance, during the monitoring phase of the newly designed and implemented network, issues might be discovered that can be fixed by the addition of some features. This is similar to when there are issues related to design limitations. Therefore, each phase can provide reverse feeding, as well, to the previous phase or phases to overcome issues and limitations that appear during the project lifecycle. As a result, this will provide an added flexibility to IT in general and the design process in particular to provide a workable design that can transform the IT network infrastructure to be a business enabler. Figure I-3 illustrates the PIDDO lifecycle with the multidimensional relationship between the lifecycle phases.

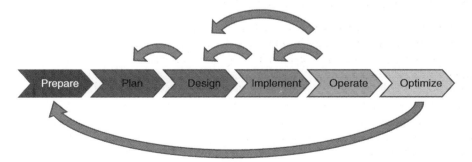

Figure I-3 *PPDIOO Multidimensional Relationship*

PPDIOO and Tasks

In fact, the PPDIOO lifecycle is applicable to the CCDE job domains, just like any other design project:

- The CCDE candidate needs to analyze the provided information (Prepare).

- Use this information to make design choices and decisions (Plan).

- Generate, propose, or suggest a suitable design (Design).

- Apply the selected design (for example, an implementation plan) (Implement).

- Collect feedback or monitor (Operate) for optimization and enhancement (Optimize).

Final Thoughts on the CCDE Practical Exam

Understanding the various domains and tasks expected in each of the exam's design scenarios can help CCDE practical exam candidates shape their study plans. This understanding can also help those who have the opportunity to practice it in their work environment. If they are working on a design and architecture project, they will have a tangible practical feeling and understand how the different stages of the design process can be approached and handled.

How This Book Is Organized

Although this book could be read cover to cover, it is designed to be flexible and allow you to easily move between chapters and sections of chapters to cover just the topics that you need more work with.

This book is organized into six distinct sections.

Part I of the book explains briefly the various design approaches, requirements, and principles, and how they complement each other to achieve a true business-driven design.

- **Chapter 1, "Network Design Requirements: Analysis and Design Principles"** This chapter covers how the different requirements (business, functional, and application) can influence design decisions and technology selection to achieve a business-driven design. This chapter also examines, when applicable, the foundational design principles that network designers need to consider.

Part II of this book focuses on the enterprise networks, specifically modern (converged) networks. The chapter covers the various design options, considerations, and design implications with regard to the business and other design requirements.

- **Chapter 2, "Enterprise Layer 2 and Layer 3 Design"** This chapter covers different design options and considerations related to Layer 2 and Layer 3 control plane protocols and advanced routing concepts.

- **Chapter 3, "Enterprise Campus Architecture Design"** This chapter covers the design options applicable to modern campus networks. The chapter also covers some of the design options and considerations with regard to network virtualization across the campus network.

- **Chapter 4, "Enterprise Edge Architecture Design"** This chapter covers various design options and considerations with regard to the two primary enterprise edge blocks (WAN edge and Internet edge).

  Part III of the book focuses on service provider-grade networks. It covers the various design architectures, technologies, and control protocols, along with the drivers toward adopting the different technologies (technical and nontechnical).

- **Chapter 5, "Service Provider Network Architecture Design"** This chapter covers the various architectural elements that collectively comprise a service provider-grade network at different layers (topological and protocols layers). The chapter also covers the implications of some technical design decisions on the business.

- **Chapter 6, "Service Provider MPLS VPN Services Design"** This chapter covers various options and considerations in MPLS VPN network environments, focusing on L2VPN and L3VPN networks. The chapter also examines different design options and approaches to optimize Layer 3 control plane design scalability for service provider-grade networks.

- **Chapter 7, "Multi-AS Service Provider Network Design"** This chapter focuses on the design options and considerations when interconnecting different networks or routing domains. The chapter examines each design option and then compares them based on various design aspects such as security and scalability.

  Part IV of the book focuses on data center networks design for both traditional and modern (virtualized and cloud based) data center networks. This part also covers how to achieve business continuity goals.

- **Chapter 8, "Data Center Networks Design"** This chapter covers various design architectures, concepts, techniques, and protocols that pertain to traditional and modern data center networks. In addition, this chapter analyzes and compares the different design options and considerations, and examines the associated implications of interconnecting dispersed data center networks and how these different technologies and design techniques can facilitate achieving different levels of business continuity.

  Part V of this book focuses on the design principles and aspects to achieve the desired levels of operational uptime and resiliency by the business.

- **Chapter 9, "Network High-Availability Design"** This chapter covers the different variables and factors that either solely or collectively influence the overall targeted operational uptime. This chapter also examines the various elements that influence achieving the desired degree of network resiliency and fast convergence.

Part VI of the book focuses on network technologies and services that are not core components of the CCDE practical exam.

- **Chapter 10, "Design of Other Network Technologies and Services"** This chapter briefly explains some design considerations with regard to the following network technologies and services, with a focus on certain design aspects and principles and without going into deep technical detail or explanation: IPv6, multicast, QoS, security, and network management.

Final Words

This book is an excellent self-study resource to learn how to think like a network designer following a business-driven approach. You will learn how to analyze and compare different design options, principles, and protocols based on various design requirements. However, the technical knowledge forms only the foundation to pass the CCDE practical exam. You also want to have a real feeling for gathering business requirements, analyzing the collected information, identifying the gaps, and producing a proposed design or design optimization based on that information. If you believe that any topic in this book is not covered in enough detail, I encourage you to expand your study scope on that topic by using the recommended readings in this book and by using the recommended CCDE study resources available online at Learning@Cisco.com

Enjoy the reading and happy learning.

Business-Driven Strategic Network Design

Chapter 1

Network Design Requirements: Analysis and Design Principles

Designing large-scale networks to meet today's dynamic business and IT needs and trends is a complex assignment, whether it is an enterprise or service provider type of network. This is especially true when the network was designed for technologies and requirements relevant years ago and the business decides to adopt new IT technologies to facilitate the achievement of its goals but the business's existing network was not designed to address these new technologies' requirements. Therefore, to achieve the desired goal of a given design, the network designer must adopt an approach that tackles the design in a structured manner.

There are two common approaches to analyze and design networks:

- **The top-down approach:** The top-down design approach simplifies the design process by splitting the design tasks to make it more focused on the design scope and performed in a more controlled manner, which can ultimately help network designers to view network design solutions from a business-driven approach.

- **The bottom-up approach:** In contrast, the bottom-up approach focuses on selecting network technologies and design models first. This can impose a high potential for design failures, because the network will not meet the business or applications' requirements.

To achieve a successful strategic design, there must be additional emphasis on a business driven approach. This implies a primary focus on business goals and technical objectives, in addition to existing and future services and applications. In fact, in today's networks, business requirements are driving IT and network initiatives as shown in Figure 1-1 [6].

For instance, although compliance (as presented in Figure 1-1) might seem to be a design constraint rather than a driver, many organizations today aim to comply with some standards with regard to their IT infrastructure and services to gain some business advantages, such as compliance with ISO/IEC 27001 Information Security Management,[1] will

---

1. http://www.iso.org/iso/home/standards/management-standards/iso27001.htm

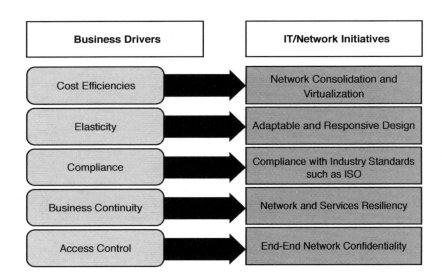

Figure 1-1 *Business Drivers Versus IT Initiatives*

help businesses like financial services organizations to demonstrate their credibility and trust. This ultimately will help these organizations to gain more competitive advantages, optimize their operational uptime, and reduce operational expenses (fewer number of incidents as a result of the reduced number of information security breaches).

Throughout this book and for the purpose of the CCDE exam, the top-down approach is considered as the design approach that can employ the following top-down logic combined with the prepare, plan, design, implement, operate and optimize (PPDIOO) lifecycle:

- Analyze the goals, plans, and requirements of the business.

- Define application requirements from the upper layers of the Open Systems Interconnection (OSI) reference model that can help to identify the characteristics of an application.

- Specify the design of the infrastructure along with the functional requirements of its components, for the network to become a business enabler.

- Monitor and gather additional information that may help to optimize and influence the logical or physical design to adapt with any new application or requirements.

Design Scope

It is important in any design project that network designers carefully analyze and evaluate the scope of the design before starting to gather information and plan network design. Therefore, it is critical to determine whether the design task is for a green field (new) network or for a current production network (if the network already exists, the design tasks can vary such as optimization, expansion, integration with other external networks, and so on). It is also vital to determine whether the design spans a single network module or multiple modules. In other words, the predetermination of the design scope can influence the type of information required to be gathered, in addition to the time to produce the design. Table 1-1 shows an example of how identifying the design scope can help network designers determine the areas and functions a certain design must emphasize and address. As a result, the scope of the information to be obtained will more be focused on these areas.

Table 1-1 *Design Scope*

Design Scope	Detailed Design Scope Example
Enterprise campus network and remote sites	Rollout of IP telephony across the enterprise, which may require a redesign of virtual LANs (VLANs), quality of service (QoS), and so on across the LAN, WAN, data center (DC), and remote-access edge
Campus only	Add multi-tenancy concept to the campus, which requires design of VLANs, IPs, and path isolation across the campus LAN only
Optimize enterprise edge availability	Add redundant link for remote access, which might require redesign of the WAN module and remote site designs and configurations such as overlay tunnels

Note Identifying the design scope in the CCDE exam is very important. For example, the candidate might have a large network to deal with, whereas the actual design focus is only on adding and integrating a new data center. Therefore, the candidate needs to focus on that part only. However, the design still needs to consider the network as a whole, a "holistic approach," when you add, remove, or change anything across the network (as discussed in more detail later in this chapter).

Business Requirements

This section covers the primary aspects that pertain to the business drivers, needs, and directions that (individually or collectively) can influence design decisions either directly or indirectly. The best place to start understanding the business's needs and requirements is by looking at the big picture of a company or business and understanding its goals, vision, and future directions. This can significantly help to steer the design to be more business driven. However, there can be various business drivers and requirements based on the business type and many other variables. As outlined in Figure 1-2, with a top-down design approach, it is almost always the requirements and drivers at higher layers (such as business and application requirements) that drive and set the requirements and directions for the lower layers. Therefore, network designers aiming to achieve a business-driven design must consider this when planning and producing a new network design or when evaluating and optimizing an existing one. The following sections discuss some of the business requirements and drivers at the higher layers and how each can influence design decisions at the lower layers.

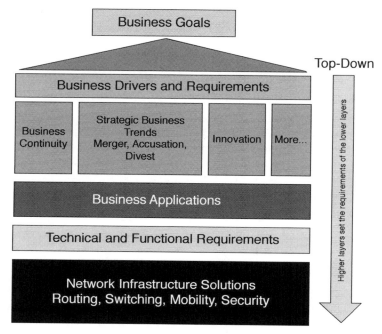

Figure 1-2   *Business-Driven Technology Solutions*

Business Continuity

Business continuity (BC) refers to the ability to continue business activities (business as usual) following an outage, which might result from a system outage or a natural disaster like a fire that damages a data center. Therefore, businesses need a mechanism or approach to build and improve the level of resiliency to react and recover from unplanned outages.

The level of resiliency is not necessarily required to be the same across the entire network, however, because the drivers of BC for the different parts of the network can vary based on different levels of impact on the business. These business drivers may include compliance with regulations or the level of criticality to the business in case of any system or site connectivity outage. For instance, if a retail business has an outage in one of its remote stores, this is of less concern than an outage to the primary data center, from a business point of view. If the primary data center were to go offline for a certain period of time, this would affect all the other stores (higher risk) and could cost the business a larger loss in terms of money (tangible) and reputation (intangible). Therefore, the resiliency of the data center network is of greater consideration for this retailer than the resiliency of remote sites [17].

Similarly, the location of the outage sometimes influences the level of criticality and design consideration. Using the same example, an outage at one of the small stores in a remote area might not be as critical as an outage in one of the large stores in a large city [11]. In other words, BC considerations based on risk assessment and its impact on the business can be considered one of the primary drivers for many businesses to adapt network technologies and design principles to meet their desired goals [5].

Elasticity to Support the Strategic Business Trends

Elasticity refers to the level of flexibility a certain design can provide in response to business changes. A change here refers to the direction the business is heading, which can take different forms. For example, this change may be a typical organic business growth, a decline in business, a merger, or an acquisition. For instance, if an enterprise campus has three buildings and is interconnected directly, as illustrated in Figure 1-3, any organic growth in this network that requires the addition of a new building to this network will introduce a lot of complexity in terms cabling, control plane, and manageability. These complexities result from the inflexible design, which makes the design incapable of responding to the business's natural growth demand.

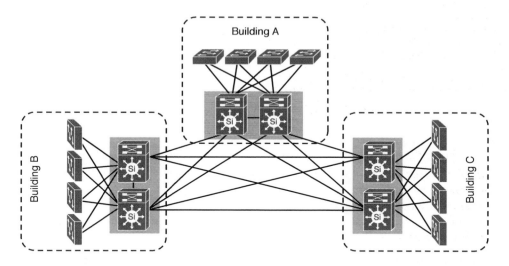

Figure 1-3 *Inflexible Design*

To enhance the level of flexibility of this design, you can add a core module to optimize the overall design modularity to support business expansion requirements. As a result, adding or removing any module or building to this network will not affect other modules, and does not even require any change to the other modules, as illustrated in Figure 1-4. In other words, the design must be flexible enough to support the business requirements and strategic goals. If network designers understand business trends and directions in this area, such understanding may influence, to a large extent, deign choices.

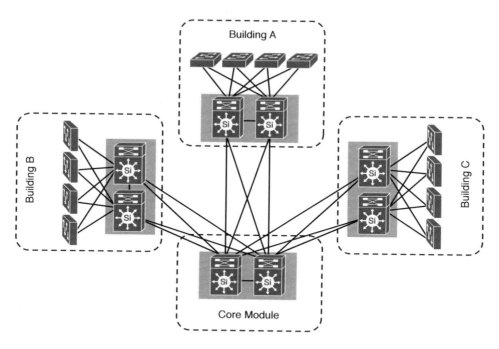

Figure 1-4   *Flexible Design*

Similarly, a flexible network design must support the capability to integrate with other networks (for examples, when mergers and acquisitions occur). With mergers and acquisitions, however, the network can typically grow significantly in size within a short period of time, and the biggest challenge, in both scenarios (mergers and acquisitions), is that network designers have to deal with different design principles, the possibility of overlapping IP address space, different control plane protocols, different approaches, and so on.

IT as a "Business Innovation" Enabler

In today's market, many businesses understand how IT technologies enhance their services and provide innovation to their customers. Therefore, when a certain technology can serve as a business enabler that can help the organization to compete in the market or increase its customers' satisfaction, the adoption of that technology will be supported by the business [17].

For example, nowadays, cloud-based data centers are opening new opportunities for hosting service providers to generate more revenue for the business. To offer good cloud-based services, there must be a reliable, flexible, and high-performance data center infrastructure to deliver this service. Consequently, this engenders the initiative and will drive the business to build a high-performance, next-generation data center network.

This network, by acting as a basis for cloud services, will be the enabler of the business's revenue-generation solution.

The Nature of the Business

Classifying the industry in which the business belongs or identifying the business's origins can aid in the understanding of some indirect requirements, even if these are not mentioned explicitly. For example, information security is almost always a must for a banking business whenever traffic crosses any external link. So by default, when planning a design for a business based in the banking industry, the design must support or offer security capabilities to gain acceptance from the business. In addition, industry-specific standards apply to IT infrastructure and services need to be considered. (For instance, healthcare organizations may consider complying with the IEC-80001-1 standard.[2])

Business Priorities

Each business has a set of priorities that are typically based on strategies adopted for the achievement of goals. These business priorities can influence the planning and design of IT network infrastructure. Therefore, network designers must be aware of these business priorities to align them with the design priorities. This ensures the success of the network they are designing by delivering business value. For example, company X's highest priority is to provide a more collaborative and interactive business communication, followed by the provision of mobile access for the users. In this example, providing a collaborative and interactive communication must be satisfied first before providing or extending the communication over any mobility solution for the end users. In sum, it is important to align the design with the business priorities, which are key to achieving business success and transforming IT into a business enabler.

Functional Requirements

Functional requirements compose the foundation of any system design because they define system and technology functions. Specifically, functional requirements identify what these technologies or systems will deliver to the business from a technological point of view. For example, a Multiprotocol Label Switching (MPLS)-enabled service provider might explicitly specify a functional requirement in a statement like this: "The provider edge routers must send VoIP traffic over 10G fiber link while data traffic is to be sent over the OC-48 link." It is implied that this service provider network needs to have provider edge (PE) routers that support a mechanism capable of sending different types of traffic over different paths, such as MPLS Traffic Engineering (MPLS-TE). Therefore, the functional requirements are sometimes referred to as *behavioral requirements* because they address what a system does.

---

2. http://www.iso.org/iso/catalogue_detail.htm?csnumber=44863

> **Note** The design that does not address the business's functional requirements is considered a poor design; however, in real-world design, not all the functional requirements are provided to the designer directly. Sometimes they can be decided on indirectly, based on other factors. See the "Application Requirements" section later in this chapter for more details.

Technical Requirements

The technical requirements of a network can be understood as the technical aspects that a network infrastructure must provide in terms of security, availability, and integration. These requirements are often called *nonfunctional requirements*. Technical requirements vary, and they must be used to justify a technology selection. In addition, technical requirements are considered the most dynamic type of requirements compared to other requirements such business requirements because, based on technology changes, they change often. Technical requirements include the following:

- Heightened levels of network availability (for example, using First Hop Redundancy Protocol [FHRP])

- Support the integration with network tools and services (for example, NetFlow Collector, or authentication and authorization system "RADIUS servers")

- Cater for network infrastructure security techniques (for example, control plane protection mechanisms or infrastructure access control lists [iACLs])

> **Note** The technical requirements help network designers to specify the required technical specifications (features and protocols) and software version that supports these specifications and sometimes influence the hardware platform selection based on its technical characteristics.

Application Requirements

From a business point of view, user experience is one of the primary, if not the highest, priority that any IT and network design must satisfy. The term *end users* can be understood differently according to the type of business. The following are the most common categories of end users:

- **Customers:** Customer can be individuals, such as a customer of a bank, or they can be a collective, such as the customers of an MPLS service provider. From a business point of view, customer satisfaction can directly impact the business's reputation and revenue.

- **Internal users:** In this category, the targeted users are internal users. Productivity of these users can translate to business performance efficiency, which has a direct relation to business success and revenue.

- **Business partners:** Partners represent those entities or organizations that work together to achieve certain goals. Therefore, efficient interaction between partners can enhance their business success in the service of strategic goal achievement.

Therefore, a network or a technology that cannot deliver the desired level of the users' expectation (also known as *quality of experience*) means a failure to achieve either one of the primary business goals or failure to satisfy a primary influencer of business success. Consequently, networks and IT technologies will be seen by the business as a cost center rather than as a business enabler.

On this basis, networks design must take into account how to deliver the desired level of experience. In fact, what influences users' experience is what they see and use. In other words, from a user's perspective, the quality of experience with regard to applications and services used by different types of users is a key deterministic factor.

Deploying network applications or services without considering the characteristics and network requirements of these applications will probably lead to a failure in meeting business goals. For example, a company providing modern financial services wants to distinguish itself from other competitors by enabling video communication with its customer service call center agents. If the network team did not properly consider video communication requirements as a network application, the application will probably fail to deliver the desired experience for the end users (customers in this example). Consequently, this will lead to a failure in achieving the company's primary business goal. In other words, if any given application is not delivered with the desired quality of experience to the end users, the network can simply be considered as not doing its job.

Furthermore, in some situations, application requirements can drive functional requirements. For instance, if a service provider has a service level agreement (SLA) with its clients to deliver Voice over IP (VoIP) traffic with less than 150 ms of one-way delay and less than 1 percent of packet loss, here VoIP requirements act as application requirements, which will drive the functional requirements of the PE devices to use a technology that can deliver the SLA. This technology may include, for example, a Class-Based Tunnel Selection (CBTS) MPLS-TE protected with fast reroute (FRR) to send VoIP traffic over high-speed links and provide network path protection in case of a failure within 50 ms. In addition, network designers should also consider the answers to the following fundamental questions when evaluating application requirements:

- How much network traffic does the application require?

- What is the level of criticality of this application and the service level requirement to the business?

- Does the application have any separation requirements to meet industry regulations and corporate security policies?

- What are the characteristics of the application?
- How long does the application need after losing connectivity to reset its state or session?

Design Constraints

Constraints are factors or decisions already in place and cannot be changed and often lead to a direct or indirect impact on the overall design and its functional requirements. In reality, various design constraints affect network design. The following are the most common constraints that network designers must consider:

- **Cost:** Cost is one of the most common limiting factors when producing any design; however, for the purpose of the CCDE practical exam, cost should be considered as a design constraint only if it is mentioned in the scenario as a factor to be considered or a tiebreaker between two analogous solutions.

- **Time:** Time can also be a critical constraint when selecting a technology or architecture over another if there is a time frame to complete the project, for example.

- **Location:** Location is one of the tricky types of constraints because it can introduce limitations that indirectly affect the design. For instance, a remote site may be located in an area where no fiber infrastructure is available and the only available type of connectivity is over wireless. From a high-level architectural point of view, this might not be a serious issue. From a performance point of view, however, this might lead to a reduced link speed, which will affect some sensitive applications used by that site.

- **Infrastructure equipment:** A good example here is that of legacy network devices. If a business has no plan to replace these devices, this can introduce limitations to the design, especially if new features or protocols not supported by these legacy platforms are required to optimize the design.

- **Staff expertise:** Sometimes network designers might propose the best design with the latest technologies in the market, which can help reduce the business's total cost of ownership (TCO) (for example, in the case of virtualization in the data center and the consolidation of data and Fibre Channel [FC] storage over one infrastructure Fibre Channel over Ethernet [FCoE]). This can be an issue, however, if the staff of this company has no expertise in these technologies used to operate and maintain the network. In this case, you have two possible options (with some limitations applying to each, as well):

  - **Train the staff on these new technologies:** This will be associated with a risk, because as a result of the staff's lack of experience, they may take a longer time to fix any issue that might occur, and at the same time, data center downtime can cost the business a large amount of money.

  - **Hire staff with experience in these technologies:** Normally, people with this level of expertise are expensive. Consequently, the increased operational cost might not justify the reduced TCO.

> **Note**   In some situations, if the proposed solution and technologies will save the business a significant amount of money, you can justify the cost of hiring new staff.

Crafting the Design Requirements

This section demonstrates how different types of requirements collectively can lead to the achievement of the desired network design, which ultimately will facilitate achieving business goals. This demonstration is based on an example that goes through the flow of information gathering (the top-down approach, as illustrated in Figure 1-5) to build up the requirements starting from the business goals (top) to the technical requirement level, such as the required features (bottom).

A national retail company is currently expanding their business to add several international sites within the next 12 months. However, with their current IT infrastructure, they face a high number of expenses in managing and maintaining their two current data and voice networks. In addition, the business wants to invest in technologies that offer enhancements to business activities and increase employee productivity.

The following is a typical classification of the requirements, some of which might be provided directly and some of which can be implied or indicated based on other requirements and goals:

- **Business goals:**

    - Reduce operational cost

    - Enhance employees' productivity

    - Expand the business (adding more remote sites)

- **Business requirements:**

    - Reduce the cost of maintaining multiple networks for voice and data

    - Improve employee productivity by enhancing and integrating internal communications through video and mobile devices, without compromising the company's security policy

    - Support the business expansion (the rollout of the new remote sites)

- **Functional requirements:**

    - A unified infrastructure that supports voice, video, data, and wireless

    - Ability to provide isolation between the traffic of guests and internal staff (for both wired and wireless) to comply with the standard security policy of the organization

    - Capability to support introducing new remote sites to the network without any redesign

■ **Application requirements:** In this particular example, we assume that no specific application requirements were given. In fact, they do not need to be provided because it is obvious that this organization is going to add VoIP and video as applications or services. The network must provide the required level of network efficiency, performance, and availability to meet VoIP/video requirements (real-time, delay, and jitter sensitive) to achieve one of the business goals.

■ **Technical requirements:** To achieve the above network's functional and application requirements considering the ultimate business goals, the design must cater to the following:

  ■ **High availability:** Increase high availability to support critical traffic such as voice (for example, redundant nodes, control plane tuning, FHRP)

  ■ **Quality of service:** Improve users' quality of experience by introducing QoS to achieve high-quality voice and video services (for example, queuing, traffic shaping)

  ■ **Security:** Optimize the network security to accommodate the new design, including voice and wireless security (for example, access control with 802.1X authentication)

  ■ **Traffic isolation:** Provide traffic isolation to meet the information security requirements (for example, tunneling such as generic routing encapsulation [GRE] with MPLS/VRFs [virtual private network routers/forwarders])

  ■ **Scalability:** Scalable network (WAN) design to support the projected business growth during the next 12 months (for example dynamic multipoint VPN [DMVPN] versus point-to-point GRE)

Figure 1-5 *Design Requirements Flow*

Table 1-2 summarizes the mapping between the technical requirements, business priorities, and technical implementation planning priorities.

Table 1-2 *Design Requirements Mapping*

Technical Requirements	Features/Tools to Enable the Technical Requirement	Business Priority Level, 1–5 (1 = highest, 5 = lowest)	Implementation Priorities
High availability	Modular and hierarchal network design. Network node and path redundancy. Tune control plane for fast convergence.	1	1
QoS	Traffic marking, classification, and prioritization to provide QoS.	2	3
Security	Add stateful firewalls with filtering to control communications between networks.	3	2
Traffic isolation	Use network virtualization techniques.	3	2
Scalability	WAN design must be scalable enough to support the business expansion such avoiding point-to-point mesh types of connectivity over the WAN.	1	1

Note that in Table 1-2 there are two levels of priorities:

- **Business priority level:** This level reflects the priority from business point of view.

- **Implementation priority level:** This level reflects the priorities from a technical implementation point of view. Although business priorities must always be met first, sometimes from a technical point of view there may be prerequisites to enable services or features across the network first to achieve a specific requirement. In the preceding example, from a technical design and implementation point of view, the network first needs to be designed and connected in the desired way (for example, hierarchical LAN, hub-and-spoke WAN). Following, the network designer can apply virtualization techniques to meet traffic separation requirements. At the same time, security appliances and functions must be integrated (holistic approach not siloed approach). Finally, QoS can be applied later to optimize traffic flows over both the physical and logical (virtualized) networks. In other words, the described sequence of the implementation plan in the preceding example was driven by both the business and technical priorities, considering that the business priorities must always be given the preference when technically possible.

Planning

There is an enduring adage: "If you do not have a plan, you are planning to fail." This adage is accurate and applicable to network design. Many network designers focus on implementation after obtaining the requirements and putting them in a design format. They sometimes rely on the best practices of network design rather than focusing on planning: "What are the possible ways of getting from point A to point B?" This planning process can help the designer devise multiple approaches or paths (design options). At this point, the designer can ask the question: Why? Asking *why* is vital to making a business-driven decision for the solution or design that optimally aligns with the business's short- or long-term strategy or objective. In fact, the best practices of network design are always recommended and should be followed whenever applicable and possible.

However, reliance on best practices is more common when designing a network from scratch (greenfield), which is not common with large enterprises and service provider networks.

In fact, IT network architectures and building constrictions and architectures are quite similar in the way they are approached and planned by designers or consultants.

For example, five years ago, an investment company built a shopping mall in one of the large cities in Europe, which was architected and engineered based on the requirements at that time. Recently, the stakeholders requested the design to be reviewed and optimized to overcome the increased number of people visiting this shopping mall (tourist and locals), because this increase was not properly projected and planned for during the original design five years ago.

Typically, the architects and engineers will then evaluate the situation, identify current issues, and understand the stakeholders' goals. In other words, they gather business requirements and identify the issues. Next, they work on optimizing the existing building (this may entail adding more parking space, expanding some areas, and so forth) rather than destroying the current building and rebuilding it from scratch. However, this time they need to have proper planning to provide a design that fits current and future needs.

Similarly, with IT network infrastructure design, there are always new technologies or broken designs that were not planned well to scale or adapt to business and technology changes. Therefore, network designers must analyze business issues, requirements, and the current design to plan and develop a solution that can optimize the overall existing architecture. This optimization might involve the redesign of some parts of the network (for example, WAN), or it might involve adding a new data center to optimize BC plans. To select the right design option and technologies, network designers need to have a *planning approach* to connect the dots at this stage and make a design decision based on the information gathering and analysis stage. Ultimately, the planning approach leads to the linkage of design options and technologies to the gathered requirements and goals to ensure that the design will bring value and become a business enabler rather than a cost center to the business. Typical tools network designers use at this stage to facilitate and simplify the selection process are the decision tree and the decision matrix.

Decision Tree

The decision tree is a helpful tool that a network designer can use when needing to compare multiple design options, or perhaps protocols, based on specific criteria. For example, a designer might need to decide which routing protocol to use based on a certain topology or scenario, as illustrated in Figure 1-6.

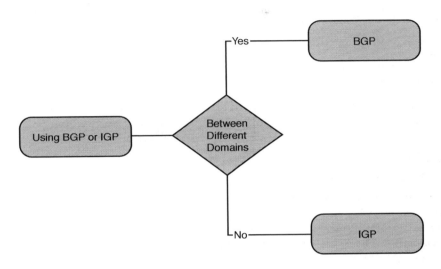

Figure 1-6 *Decision Tree*

Decision Matrix

Decision matrixes serve the same purpose as decision trees; however, with the matrix, network designers can add more dimensions to the decision-making process. In Table 1-3, there are two dimensions a network designer can use to select the most suitable design option. In these two dimensions, both business requirements and priorities can be taken into account to reach the final decision, which is based on a multidimensional approach.

Table 1-3 *Decision Matrix*

Business Requirements	Priority	Design Option 1	Design Option 2
Cost savings	4	Moderate	Low
Scalable	1	High	High
Secure	2	Low	High

When using the decision matrix as a tool in the preceding example, design option 2 is more suitable based on the business requirements and priorities. The decision matrix is not solely reliant on the business requirements to drive the design decision; however, priorities from the business point of view were considered as an additional dimension in the decision-making process, which makes it more relevant and focused.

Planning Approaches

To develop a successful network design, a proper planning approach is required to build a coherent strategy for the overall design. Network designers can follow two common planning approaches to develop business-driven network designs and facilitate the design decisions:

- **Strategic planning approach:** Typically targets planning to long-term goals and strategies. For example, a service provider needs to migrate its core from legacy (ATM) to be based on MPLS instead. The design decision in this approach has to cater to long-term goals and plans.

- **Tactical planning approach:** Typically targets planning to overcome an issue or to achieve a short-term goal. For instance, an enterprise might need to provide remote access to some partners temporally (for example, over the Internet) until dedicated extranet connectivity is provisioned. Design decisions in this approach generally need to provide what is required within a limited period of time and are not necessarily required to consider long-term goals.

Strategic Balance

Within any organization, there are typically multiple business units and departments. Each has its own strategy, some of which are financially driven, whereas others are more innovation driven. For example, an IT department is more of an in-house service provider concerned with ensuring service delivery is possible and optimal, whereas the procurement department is cost driven and always prefers the cheaper options. The marketing department, in contrast, is almost always innovation driven and wants the latest technology. Consequently, a good understanding of the overall business strategy and goals can lead to compromise between the different aims of the different departments. In other words, the idea is that each business unit or entity within an organization must have its requirements met at a certain level, so that all can collectively serve the overall business goals and strategies. For instance, let's consider a case study of a retail business wanting to expand its geographic presence by adding more retail shops across the globe with low capital expenditure (capex). Based on this goal, the main point is to increase the number of remote sites with minimal cost (expansion and cost):

- **IT point of view:**

  - The point of sales application used does not support offline selling or local data saving. Therefore, it requires connectivity to the data center to operate.

  - The required traffic volume from each remote site is small and non-real time.

  - Many sites are to be added within a short period of time.

  - **Optimum solution:** IT suggested that the most scalable and reliable option is to use a MPLS VPN as a WAN.

- **Marketing point of view:** If any site cannot process purchased items due to a network outage, this will impact the business's reputation in the market.

  - **Optimum solution:** High-speed, redundant links should be used.

- **Finance point of view:** Cost savings.

  - **Optimum solution:** One cheap link, such as an Internet link, to meet basic connectivity requirements.

Based on the preceding list, it is obvious that the consideration for WAN redundancy is required for the new remote sites; however, cost is a constraint that must be considered as well.

When applying the strategic balance (alignment) concept, each departmental strategy can be incorporated to collectively achieve the overall optimum business goal by using the suboptimum approach from each department's perspective.

In this particular example, you can use two Internet links combined with a VPN overlay solution to achieve the business goal through a cost-effective solution that offers link redundancy to increase the availability level of the remote sites, meeting application bandwidth requirements while at the same time maintaining the brand reputation in the market at the desired level.

Network Design Principles

Network design can be defined as the philosophy that drives how various components, protocols, and technologies should be integrated and deployed based on certain approaches and principles to construct a cohesive network infrastructure environment that can facilitate the achievement of tactical or strategic business goals. Previous sections in this chapter described the end-to-end process of a network design (PPDIOO) and the approaches that you can use to tackle different network designs (top down and bottom up).

This section, however, focuses on the design principles that network designers must consider when designing a network and translating business, functional, or application requirements into technological requirements. It is important to understand that these principles are not independent of each other. Therefore, to generate an effective design and achieve its intended goals, network designers should consider how each of these principles can integrate into the overall architecture; however, not all of these principles may be applicable or required by every design. By following the top-down approach, network designers can evaluate and decide what to consider and focus on.

Reliability and Resiliency

A reliable network delivers nearly every packet accepted by the network to the right destination within a reasonable amount of time [2]. In today's modern converged networks, maintaining a highly reliable network is extremely important because modern businesses rely heavily on IT services to achieve their business goals. For these businesses (especially service providers and modern financial institutions), it can be even more critical that their network is considered as a revenue-generating entity. For example, a five-minute network outage that might affect x number of customers can cost the business hundreds of thousands of dollars. Therefore, having a highly reliable and available network architecture that can survive during any network component failure without any operator intervention (also known as *resiliency*) is a key design principle. It is considered a top priority of most of today's modern businesses. For the network to achieve the desired level of resiliency, a redundant component must exist to take over the role of the failed component following a failure event.

Note   In spite of the fact that network availability is considered a "top priority of most of today's modern businesses," not every network needs high availability, and not every part of a network requires the same level of availability considerations. For more information about high-availability considerations, see Chapter 9, "Network High-Availability Design."

Modularity

Modular design is commonly used in software development, where an application can be built from multiple blocks of codes that collectively integrate to form the desired application. These "building blocks" of modular structure enhance and simplify the overall application architecture. For example, if an issue exists in one block or module of that software, it can easily be isolated from the other modules and fixed separately without impacting other parts. Furthermore, from the perspective of ongoing enhancements, it is easier to add additional modules or blocks to this structure if new features are required. This makes the overall application architecture more structured and manageable.

Similarly, modularity is one of the fundamental principles of a structured network. In a structured network, the network architecture can be divided into multiple functional modules, with each module serving a specific role in the network and represented by an individual physical network. The individual physical network is also known as the places in the network (PIN), such as the enterprise campus, WAN, or the data center.

Consequently, these functional modules are easy to replicate, redesign, and expand. Studies show that when building an IT network, about 20 percent of the budget goes to acquiring the hardware, and 80 percent goes to operational costs [9]. For instance, if a network is designed in a way (for example, flat) that cannot isolate security breaches, system upgrades, or failures in certain parts of the network, it will not be "responsive enough" to adapt to future business requirements such as scalability and fast network convergence.

Whereas with the modular design approach, if any given module faces an issue such as a security breach or the addition or removal of modules, there should be no need to redesign the network or introduce any effect to the other modules. Furthermore, breaking complex parts in the network based on a modular approach into manageable blocks will optimize the overall network manageability. In other words, from a network design point of view, modularity can promote design simplicity, flexibility, fault isolation, and scalability, as shown in Figure 1-7 [10]. At the same time, modularity reduces operational costs and complexities.

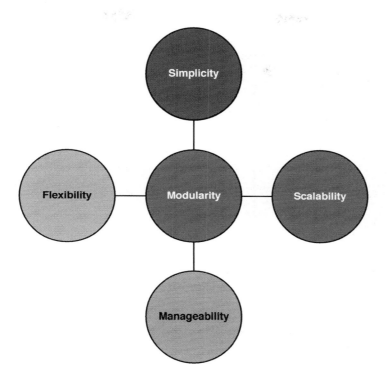

Figure 1-7   *Modularity*

Reliable and Manageable Scalability

Designing for scalability is one of the most important aspects that a network designer should consider. In fact, what can be considered as a successful scalable network is not only measured by the network size factor but also by how stable and reliable the network is and how easily this network can be managed and troubleshot. For example, a network may be designed in a way that can expand to thousands of routers, but at the same time, a failure in one link or device can introduce a high degree of processing and CPU utilization across the network, which may lead to instability. This design cannot be considered a successful scalable design, even though it can grow to a large number of routers. Similarly, a network may be designed to grow to a large scale while at the same time being difficult to manage and troubleshoot, with any issue potentially taking a long time to be fixed. This network cannot be considered a successful scalable design either.

Therefore, a successful scalable design must offer a manageable and reliable network at the same time. In other words, the added complexity of the configurations and troubleshooting with the increased size to an unmanageable scale will outweigh any advantage of the ability to expand by the size factor only, as shown in Figure 1-8 [8].

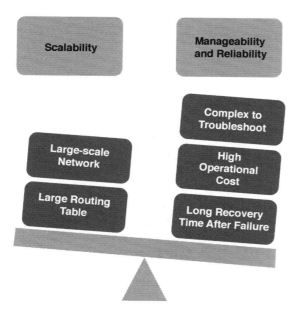

Figure 1-8   *Scalability Versus Manageability and Reliability*

Fault Isolation and Simplicity

Fault isolation boundaries are usually designed to provide fail-stop behavior for the desired fault model. The term *fail-stop* implies that incorrect behavior does not propagate across the fault isolation boundary [3]. In other words, network design must take into account how to prevent a failure in one domain from being signaled or propagated across all other domains in the network. This is necessary to avoid any unnecessary processing and delay across the entire network due to a link or device failure in one domain of the network. For example, in routing design, you can use summarization and logical flooding domains to mitigate this issue, where it is always advised that complicated networks (either physically or at the control plane layer) be logically contained, each in its own fault domain [10]. Consequently, you will have a more stable, reliable, and faster converging network.

Furthermore, this concept introduces simplicity to the overall architecture and reduces operational complexities. In general, fault isolation prevents network fault information from being propagated across multiple network areas or domains, which facilitates achieving more stable network design and optimizing network recovery time after any network failure event. For instance, with regard to the design in Figure 1-9, if any failure occurs on any network node or link, its impact will be propagated to all devices across the campus network. A high amount of unnecessary processing can occur after this failure.

In contrast, with regard to the design in Figure 1-10, if there is any failure at any network node, there will be limited impact (typically contained within one fault domain). This limited impact is facilitated by the separation of the "fault domains" principle, which normally can be achieved by logical separation (for example, hiding reachability and topology information of Open Shortest Path First [OSPF] between the flooding

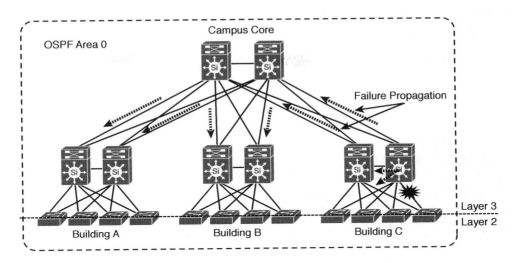

Figure 1-9 *Single-Fault Domain Design*

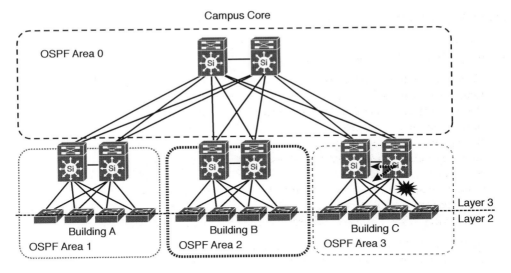

Figure 1-10 *Multi-Fault Domain Design*

domains or blocks). Consequently, the design will be able to offer a higher level of scalability, stability, and manageability.

Hierarchy

Adding hierarchy to the overall network design and within each domain or block can significantly simplify the design and enhance its flexibility to introduce more efficient places to isolate fault domains, because the network designer will have more chokepoints to aggregate traffic, topology information, and reachability information, which will facilitate the logical (functional) or physical isolation. For instance, Figure 1-11 shows a typical service provider network constructed of two tiers (core and POPs). Each POP is built from multiple tiers as well. This hierarchal structure provides the ability to control and minimize failure propagation between POPs over the core and between the different layers within each POP. Therefore, this design offers a level of stability (fault isolation) and control (chokepoints between the different tiers) to this service provider that makes it more responsive to any future growth requirements (scalable) without adding complexity to the overall design.

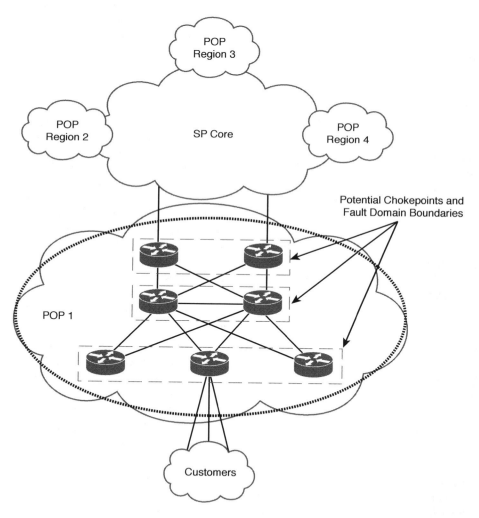

Figure 1-11   *Hierarchal Architecture*

Responsiveness

The term *responsiveness* refers to the set of design characteristics where a flexible architecture needs to respond to the changing business, application, and functional requirements. For example, the design should have the capability to support the rollout of secure mobility for internal staff and guests as well. In this case, a flexible architecture is required to respond to this new requirement and support rapid deployment and integration with different systems without any major change to the overall design. A modular and resilient design combined with the right forwarding and control plane architectures can collectively achieve this goal from the network point of view. When the overall architecture offers a high degree of flexibility, this will significantly facilitate the adoption and integration of the new business and technology requirements in the future, along with more simplified implementations to enable across the network. As a result, the network will be seen as a true service delivery entity from the business point of view.

Holistic Design Approach

A holistic design is a common design principle that considers a system being designed as an interconnected "whole" entity while at the same time potentially being part of something larger [4]. In other words, the holistic design approach emphasizes the big picture of any system, such as an enterprise network. Throughout this book, there are many design options and considerations of different types of networks, whether an enterprise network or service provider network, where each can fit a different set of requirements or solve certain issues. It is important to always consider the big picture using the holistic design concept before applying any of the designs discussed in this book in any given part of the network. Otherwise, you will be approaching the design using a siloed approach that will deal with the network as "communication islands." The result will possibly be a suboptimal architecture with lower performance, higher costs, and less flexibility. Most important, communications between these islands will probably be inefficient to a large extent because of the limited vision of this approach (not to mention the added complexity to manage networks that were not engineered as a single architecture).

To illustrate the importance of the holistic approach, consider the network in Figure 1-12. This network belongs to a manufacturing company that has a requirement to provide traffic separation between the internal staff and contractor staff from the remote sites across the WAN. A network designer suggested using two VRFs per site with a GRE tunnel per VRF across the WAN network. At the time of the design, there were only five remote sites. After six months, the number of remote sites doubled, and the company's IT staff started facing many complexities and traffic engineering issues. In addition, there was a requirement to extend this traffic separation to the data center services.

Technically, this is a valid design, and it does provide traffic isolation as per the business requirements; however, this design did not consider the big picture using a holistic design approach. Instead, it was designed based on communication islands (siloed approach), which probably will lead to a nonscalable and inflexible design.

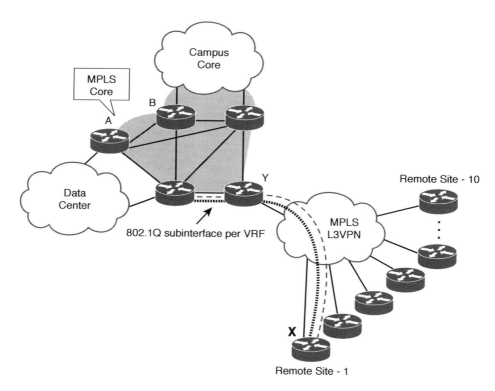

Figure 1-12 *Holistic Approach*

In this particular example, the holistic approach could have helped the designer to consider the business growth requirements. It could have also helped the designer to consider how this traffic isolation can integrate and work as a whole interconnected system with the "MPLS-enabled enterprise core" for optimal and smooth end-to-end communications and integration. Instead, the designer focused only on how to meet this requirement between point X and Y. However, with the holistic approach, the designer can look at the entire architecture to see how point X and Y can optimally communicate with point A and B as well. If the number of remote sites increases, the designer can determine how this may affect the manageability and scalability of the entire network architecture, rather than focusing on only one side or block of the network.

Physical Layout Considerations

In building construction, the foundation carries the load of the structure on top of it, in addition to any future anticipated loads, such as people and furniture. Everything goes on top of the foundation. In other words, a solid and reliable foundation can be considered the basis of everything that comes after. Similarly, in network architectures, the foundation of the network (which is the underlying physical infrastructure) is where the entire traffic load is handled. It can be a critical influencer with regard to the adoption of certain designs or goals. An example of this is the interconnection of the service provider's core nodes over a physical fiber infrastructure in a ring topology. On top of this physical ring, there is a full mesh of Multiprotocol Border Gateway Protocol (MP-BGP) peering sessions between the PEs at the service provider edges (POPs), as illustrated in Figure 1-13.

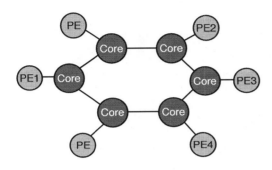

Physical

Figure 1-13   *Network Physical Layout View*

From the control plane and logical architectural point of view, these PEs are seen as directly interconnected, as shown in Figure 1-14.

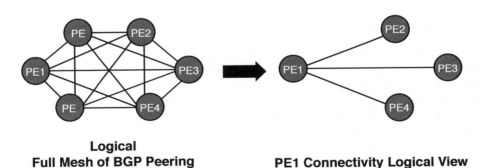

Logical
Full Mesh of BGP Peering   **PE1 Connectivity Logical View**

Figure 1-14   *Network Logical Layout View*

However, the actual traffic load and forwarding is handled by the physical core ring network, which means if any core router in the path has a congested link, it can affect all the POPs/PEs communicating over this path.

Consequently, it is important that network designers understand the foundation of the network to evaluate the load, traffic flow, and other aspects that sometimes cannot be seen from a protocol and the logical design point of view. In addition, understanding the underlying physical infrastructure can help network designers to steer traffic over the desired links based on different criteria such as expense of a given link, bandwidth requirements, and reliability of a given link to recover from a failure. (For example, protected fiber links can be more reliable than nonprotected links.) Throughout this book, the implications of using different Layer 2 and Layer 3 control protocols and overlay technologies are covered, considering the physical layout (the foundation of the network) when applicable. In other words, the logical layout of a network should never be designed in isolation of the underlying physical topology.

Note   Sometimes it is impossible, and unreasonable, to have visibility of the physical topology, such as routing or tunneling over the Internet.

Table 1-4 provides a summarized comparison between the most common physical network layouts.

Table 1-4   *Physical Topologies Comparison*

Topology Layout	Scalability	Cost	Manageability	Flexibility	Redundancy
Ring	Limited	Low	Moderate	Limited due to the high level of dependencies	Limited
Fully meshed	Limited (introduce limitations on higher layers [for example, control plane])	High	Complex	Limited	Very high
Partially meshed	Moderate	Moderate	Moderate	Moderate	Moderate
Multiplane core	High	High	Simple	High	Moderate
Leaf and spines	Can offer a high degree of scale-out capability	Moderate	Simple	High	High
Hierarchal	Can offer high scale up	Moderate	Simple	High	High
Hub and spoke	Limited	Moderate	Moderate (depends on the number of spokes)	Limited	Moderate

Note *Redundancy* in Table 1-4 refers to the nature of the topology to support redundancy. Network designers must decide on the level of redundancy and in which areas redundancy is to be placed, based on the design requirements and goals.

No Gold Plating

Gold plating in software engineering or project management (or time management in general) refers to continuing to work on a project or task well past the point where the extra effort is worth the value it adds (if any)[4]. This concept is 100 percent applicable to network design and can be considered one of the critical principles of network design. In fact, overengineering or adding more features and capabilities that go beyond the requirements (whether business, functional, or application) can be a double-edged sword. In other words, a network designer might think that adding extra features to the design will make the customer more satisfied. However, these extra features may lead to additional implementation time and cost (for example, higher end-product prices or more licenses), whereas the design without these features still meets the requirements. Therefore, network designers must produce a design that focuses on how to meet the requirements and become a business enabler rather than add unnecessary features, which can lead to a negative impact.

Note Requirements (business, functional, or application) define what is necessary (and what is not). As discussed earlier, the requirements can take different forms, such as fixing a current limitation or providing a design that will align with the business's future vision.

Summary

To achieve a network design that delivers value to the business and aligns with its goals and directions, network designers must follow a structured approach. This approach must start from the top level, focusing on business needs, drivers, and directions, to generate a business-driven design. In addition, with the top-down approach, network designers and architects can always produce business-driven network architecture that facilitates, at later stages, the selection of the desired hardware platforms and technology features and protocols to deploy the intended design. This makes the network design more responsive to any new business or technology requirements. Furthermore, considering the different design principles discussed in this chapter and considering the different requirements (business, functional, and mission-critical applications) can help network designers to plan and make the right design choices that ultimately will make the network be seen as a "business enabler."

Part II

Next Generation - Converged Enterprise Network Architectures

Many businesses today rely on technology to achieve their strategic goals. Therefore, today's enterprise networks are evolving to be more like a "service delivery" mechanism for different business services and applications, in particular real-time enterprise applications and services, over one converged infrastructure. Traditionally, these services used to be provisioned over a separate physical infrastructure, such as voice and video. In contrast, a converged network logically consolidates these physical networks into one unified physical network with multiple logical networks and allows for optimal connectivity between these various logical networks.

The typical question network designers may ask, "Is there any difference in how converged networks are designed today?"

In fact, this question is one of the key design questions. However, let's first review the applications that today's converged enterprise networks are carrying and the requirements and level of criticality of these applications.

Enterprise Application Requirements

Network Requirement	Collaboration Applications				Data Center Applications		Multicast-Based Apps	
	Today's Apps	Voice Bearer	Video Bearer	WebEx	Storage	VM, Live Migration	Live Video	Market Feeds
Latency	< 500 ms	< 250 ms	< 250 ms	< 250 ms	5 ms (S) 100 ms (A)	< 200 ms	< 15 ms	< 20 ms
Jitter	< 200 ms	< 50 ms	< 50 ms	< 100 ms	< 100 ms	< 100 ms	< 100 ms	< 10 ms
Bandwidth per flow or instance	Various	40 Kbps (G729A)	4 Mbs (1080p)	300 Kbps (15 fps)	Various (4/6/8 Gbps)	Various 25000 pps	Various (10 Gbps plus)	Various > 80 Mbps per feed
Convergence	< 10 sec	< 1 sec	< 1 sec	< 10 sec	< 500 ms (A) < 100ms (S)	< 2 sec	< 2 sec	< 2 sec

It is obvious from the preceding table[6] that most of these applications are critical to the daily business activities. However, these advanced applications and technologies bring aggressive requirements from network performance and resiliency perspectives. Traditionally, the network used to be seen by the business as a cost center. Today's converged network has been transformed from being seen as a cost center to being seen as a business enabler. As a result, the requirements to design a converged enterprise network are changing, as elucidated upon in the following examples:

- Converged critical applications on one shared network (voice, video, and data).

- High availability and fast converging. The downtime cost of a converged network is very high compared to a traditional network.

- Low latency/low jitter for real-time communication services.

- Scalable (hundreds of nodes, global scale).

- System virtualization.

- Mobility.

- Integrated infrastructure security.

- Maintenance with minimal impact (ideally zero).

The requirements of a today's converged enterprise networks are driving the transformation of network design considerations and approaches.

Note   For the purpose of the CCDE exam, you must consider only the business drivers and requirements that are provided to you in each scenario. For example, do not assume cost saving, scalability, or high availability are always required if not mentioned as a requirement, design goal, or possible solution to optimize the design to overcome an existing issue or limitation.

This section discusses the various design principles and aspects of the next-generation converged enterprise network architectures. These network architectures use a modular design approach to divide the network into multiple functional areas that are referred to as *modules* or *blacks* (interchangeably). The modularity that is built in to the architecture allows flexibility and scalability in network design and facilitates the future deployment and operation of the network.

There can be different types of functional modules introduced as part of this architecture based on the business needs, size, and industry. This book discusses the most common and vital modules that can be found in almost every large-scale converged enterprise network. These modules are as follows:

- Enterprise campus

- Enterprise edge (WAN and Internet Blocks)

■ Enterprise data center (The data center is discussed in Chapter 8, "Data Center Network Design.")

Chapter 2, "Enterprise Layer 2 and Layer 3 Design," starts by discussing Layer 2 and Layer 3 network design considerations. It specifically discusses the implications with regard to the different infrastructure topologies that collectively construct the overall Layer 2 and Layer 3 converged enterprise network architecture. The subsequent chapters focus on the design considerations and options of each module of the enterprise network without compromising the holistic design approach. In other words, although each enterprise module is discussed separately, the best design option must always be selected based on both the top-down and holistic approaches. This avoids the designing of the enterprise network modules in isolation and ensures that the design is always driven by the business and application requirements.

Chapter 2

Enterprise Layer 2 and Layer 3 Design

In network design, it is common that a certain design goal can be achieved "technically" using different approaches. Although, from a technical deployment point of view this can be seen as an advantage, from networks' design perspective on the other hand, almost always one of the most challenging parts is, which design option should be selected? (To achieve a business driven design that takes into considerations technical and non-technical design requirements.) Practically, to achieve this, network designers must be aware of the different design options and protocols as well as the advantages and limitations of each. Therefore, this chapter will concentrate specifically on high-lighting, analyzing, and comparing the various design options, principles, and consider-ations with regard to Layer 2 and Layer 3 control plane protocols from different design aspects, focusing on enterprise grade networks.

Enterprise Layer 2 LAN Design Considerations

To achieve a reliable and highly available Layer 2 network design, network designers need to have various technologies in place that protect the Layer 2 domain and facili-ties having redundant paths to ensure continuous connectivity in the event of a node or link failure. The following are the primary technologies that should be considered when building the design of Layer 2 networks:

- Layer 2 control protocols, such as Spanning Tree Protocol

- VLANs and trunking

- Link aggregation

- Switch fabric (discussed in Chapter 8, "Data Center Networks Design")

Spanning Tree Protocol

As a Layer 2 network control protocol, the Spanning Tree Protocol (STP) is considered the most proven and commonly used control protocol in classical Layer 2 switched network environments, which include multiple redundant Layer 2 links that can generate loops. The basic function of STP is to prevent Layer 2 bridge loops by blocking the redundant L2 interface to a level that can provide a loop-free topology. There are multiple flavors or versions of STP. The following are the most commonly deployed versions:

- **802.1D:** The traditional STP implementation

- **802.1w:** Rapid STP (RSTP) supports large-scale implementations with enhanced convergence time

- **802.1s:** Multiple STP (MST) permits very large-scale STP implementations

In addition, there are some features and enhancements to STP that can optimize the operation and design of STP behavior in a classical Layer 2 environment. The following are the primary STP features:

- **Loop Guard:** Prevents the alternate or root port from being elected unless bridge protocol data units (BPDUs) are present

- **Root Guard:** Prevents external or downstream switches from becoming the root

- **BPDU Guard:** Disables a PortFast-enabled port if a BPDU is received

- **BPDU Filter:** Prevents sending or receiving BPDUs on PortFast-enabled ports

Figure 2-1 briefly highlights the most appropriate place where these features should to be applied in a Layer 2 STP-based environment.

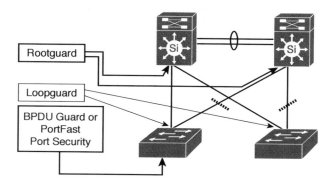

Figure 2-1 *STP Features*

Note   Cisco has developed enhanced versions of the STP. It has incorporated a number of these features into it using different versions of STP that provide faster convergence and increased scalability, such as Per-VLAN Spanning Tree Plus (PVST+) and Rapid PVST+.

VLANs and Trunking

A Layer 2 virtual local-area network (VLAN) is considered as a type of network virtualization technique that provides logical separation with broadcast domains and policy control implementation. In addition, VLANs offer a degree of fault isolation at Layer 2 that can contribute to the optimization of network performance, stability, and manageability. *Trunking*, however, refers to the protocols that enable the network to extend VLANs across Layer 2 uplinks between different nodes by providing the ability to carry multiple VLANs over a single physical link.

From a design best practices perspective, VLANs should *not* span multiple access switches; however, this is only a general recommendation. For example, some designs dictate that VLANs must span multiple access switches to meet certain application requirements. Consequently, understanding the different Layer 2 topologies and the impact of spanning VLANs across multiple switches is a key aspect for Layer 2 design. This aspect (applicability and its implications) is covered in more detail later in this chapter (in the section "Enterprise Layer 2 LAN Common Design Options").

Link Aggregation

The concept of link aggregation refers to the industry standard IEEE 802.3ad, in which multiple physical links can be grouped together to form a single logical link. This concept offers a cost-effective solution by increasing cumulative bandwidth without requiring any hardware upgrades. The IEEE 802.3ad Link Aggregation Control Protocol (LACP) offers several other benefits, including the following:

- An industry standard protocol that enables interoperability of multivendor network devices

- The optimization of network performance in a cost-effective manner by increasing link capacity without changing any physical connections or requiring hardware upgrades

- Eliminate single points of failure and enhance link-level reliability and resiliency

Although link aggregation is a simple and reasonable mechanism to increase bandwidth capacity between network nodes, each individual flow will be limited to the speed of the utilized member link by that flow, based on the load-balancing hashing algorithm used unless the flowlet concept is considered[1].

> **Note** In addition to LACP (the industry standard link aggregation control protocol), Cisco has developed a proprietary link aggregation protocol called Port Aggregation Protocol (PAgP). Both protocols have different operational modes, which the network designer must be aware.

---

1. "Dynamic Load Balancing Without Packet Reordering," IETF Draft, chen-nvo3-load-banlancing, http://www.ietf.org

There are two primary types of link aggregation connectivity models:

- **Single-chassis link aggregation:** The typical link aggregation type of connectivity that connects two network nodes in a point-to-point manner.

- **Multichassis link aggregation:** Also referred to as mLAG, this type of link aggregation connectivity is most commonly used when the upstream switches (typically two) are deployed in "switch clustering" mode. This connectivity model offers a higher level of link and path resiliency than the single-chassis link aggregation.

Figure 2-2 illustrates these two link aggregation connectivity models.

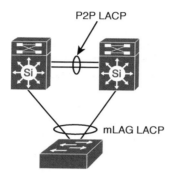

Figure 2-2   *Link Aggregation*

First Hop Redundancy Protocol and Spanning Tree

First-hop Layer 3 routing redundancy is designed to offer transparent failover capabilities at the first-hop Layer 3 IP gateways, where two or more Layer 3 devices work together in a group to represent one virtual Layer 3 gateway. Hot Standby Router Protocol (HSRP), Virtual Router Redundancy Protocol (VRRP), and Gateway Load Balancing Protocol (GLBP) are the primary and most commonly used protocols to provide a resilient default gateway service for endpoints and hosts.

Table 2-1 summarizes and compares the main capabilities and functions of these different FHRP protocols.

Table 2-1   *FHRP Protocols Comparison*

	HSRP	VRRP	GLBP
Standard	Cisco proprietary	IEEE	Cisco proprietary
IPv6 support	Yes (v2)	Yes (v3)	Yes
Authentication	Yes	Yes	Yes
Load sharing techniques	Multiple HSRP groups per interface	Multiple VRRP groups per interface	Native support (implicit)

Table 2-1 *continued*

	HSRP	VRRP	GLBP
Default hello timer	3	1	3
Virtual IP VIP	Different from interface IP	Can be different or same to the interface IP of the master router	Different from the interface IP
BFD support for subsecond convergence	Yes	Yes	No

One of the typical scenarios in classical hierarchal networks is when FHRP works in conjunction with STP to provide a redundant Layer 3 gateway services. However, some Layer 2 design models require special attention in terms of VLANs design (extending Layer 2 VLANs across access switches or not) and the placement of the demarcation point between Layer 2 and Layer 3. (For example, if the interswitch link between the distribution layer switches is configured as Layer 2 or Layer 3 link.) The aforementioned factors can affect the overall reliability and convergence time of the Layer 2 LAN design. The following design model (depicted in Figure 2-3) is considered one of the common design models that has a proven ability to provide the most resilient design when FHRP is applied to an STP-based Layer 2 network (such as VRRP or HSRP). This design model has the following characteristics:

- The interswitch link between the distribution switches is configured as Layer 3 link.

- No VLAN spanning across switches.

- The STP root bridge is aligned with active FHRP instance for each VLAN.

- Uplinks from access to distribution are both forwarding from STP point of view.

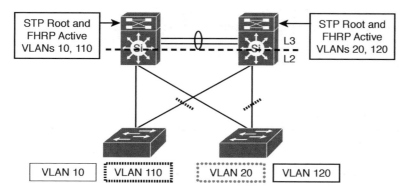

Figure 2-3 *FHRP and STP on Loop-Free U Topology*

Note   In the design illustrated in Figure 2-3, when GLBP is used as the FHRP, it is going to be less deterministic compared to HSRP or VRRP because the distribution of Address Resolution Protocol (ARP) responses is going to be random.

Enterprise Layer 2 LAN Common Design Options

Network designers have many design options for Layer 2 LANs. This section will help network designers by highlighting the primary and most common Layer 2 LAN design models used in traditional and today's LANs, along with the strengths and weaknesses of each design model.

Layer 2 Design Models: STP Based (Classical Model)

In classical Layer 2 STP-based LAN networks, the connectivity from the access to the distribution layer switches can be designed in various ways and combined with Layer 2 control protocols and features discussed earlier to achieve certain design functional requirements. In general, there is no single best design that someone can suggest that can fit every requirement, because each design is proposed to resolve a certain issue or requirement. However, by understanding the strengths and weaknesses of each topology and design model (illustrated in Figure 2-4), network designers may then always select the most suitable design model that meets the requirements from different aspects, such as network convergence time, reliability, and flexibility. This section highlights the most common classical Layer 2 design models of LAN environments with STP, which can be applied to enterprise Layer 2 LAN designs.

Note   All the Layer 2 design models in Figure 2-4 share common limitations: the reliance on STP to avoid loss of connectivity caused by Layer 2 loops and the dependency on Layer 3 FHRP timers, such as VRRP to converge. These dependences naturally lead to an increased convergence time when a node or link fails. Therefore, as a rule of thumb, tuning and aligning STP and FHRP timers is a recommended practice to overcome these limitations to some extent.

Figure 2-4 summarizes some of the design concerns and lists suggested usage of each of the depicted design models in this figure [5].

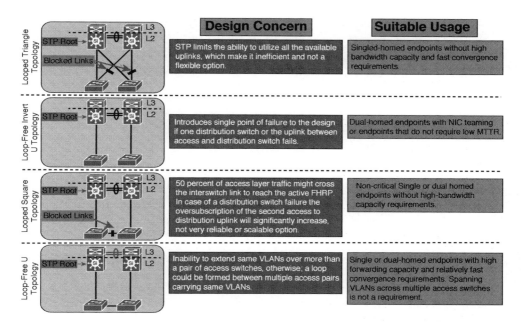

Figure 2-4 *Primary and Common Layer 2 (STP-Based) LAN Connectivity Models Comparison*

Layer 2 Design Model: Switch Clustering Based (Virtual Switch)

The concept of switch clustering significantly changed the Layer 2 design model between the access and distribution layer switches. With this design model, a pair of upstream distribution switches can appear as a one logical (virtual) switch from the access layer switch point of view. Consequently, this approach transformed the way access layer switches connect to the distribution layer switches, because there is no reliance on STP and FHRP anymore, which means the elimination of any convergence delays associated with STP and FHRP. In addition, from the uplinks and link aggregation perspective, one access switch can be connected (multihomed) to the two clustered distribution switches as one logical switch using one link aggregation bundle over multichassis link aggregation (mLAG), as illustrated in Figure 2-5.

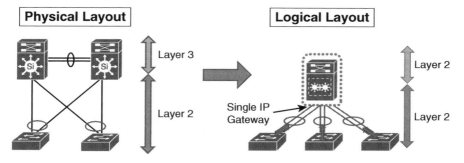

Figure 2-5 *Switch Clustering*

As Figure 2-5 shows, all uplinks will be in forwarding state across both distribution switches from a Layer 2 point of view. There will be one virtual IP gateway that should permit the forwarding across both switches from the forwarding plane perspective. It is obvious that this design model can enhance network resiliency and convergence time, and maximize bandwidth capacity, by utilizing all uplinks. In addition, this design model supports the extension of the Layer 2 VLAN across access switches safely, without any concern about forming any Layer 2 loop. This makes the design model simple, reliable, easy to manage, and more scalable as compared to the classical STP-based design model.

Layer 2 Design Model: Daisy-Chained Access Switches

Although this design model might be a viable option to overcome some limitations, network designers commonly use it as an interim solution. This design can introduce undesirable network behaviors. For instance, the design shown in Figure 2-6 can introduce the following issues during a link or node failure:

- Dual active HSRP

- Possibility of 50 percent loss of the returning traffic for devices that still use the distribution switch-1 as the active Layer 3 FHRP gateway

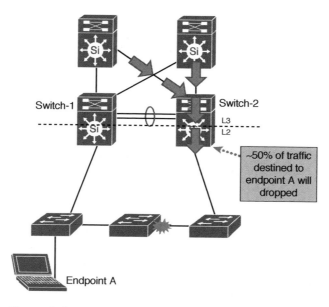

Figure 2-6   *Daisy-Chained Access Switches*

When suggesting an alternative solution to overcome a given design issue or limitation, it is important to make sure that the suggested design option will not introduce new challenges or issues during certain failure scenarios. Otherwise, the newly introduced issues will outweigh the benefits of the suggested solution.

Layer 2 LAN Design Recommendations

Table 2-2 summarizes the different Layer 2 LAN design considerations and the relevant design recommendations.

Table 2-2 *Layer 2 LAN Design Recommendation*

Design Considerations	Design Recommendations
Flexibility and scalability	Use switch clustering at the distribution layer when possible. Consider using link aggregation or mLAG between the different LAN layers. Avoid spanning L2 VLANs across multiple access switches.
Resiliency and Fast convergence	Design with triangles and not square topologies when possible. Always use switch clustering with mLAG when possible. Align the STP root with FHRP active when using the traditional L2 design model. Tune STP and FHRP timers. Use Unidirectional Link Detection (UDLD). Always interconnect the upstream distribution switch.
Control and security	Always enable STP, even with switch clustering. Use BBDU Guard, filtering, and Root Guard. Use an unused VLAN as the native VLAN. Use port-level security features such as Dynamic Host Configuration Protocol (DHCP) snooping, IP Source Guard, and ARP. security where applicable

Enterprise Layer 3 Routing Design Considerations

This section covers the various routing design considerations and optimization concepts that pertain to enterprise-grade routed networks.

IP Routing and Forwarding Concept Review

The main goal of routing protocols is to serve as a delivery mechanism to route packets to reach their intended destination. The end-to-end process of packets routing across the routed network is facilitated and driven by the concept of distributed databases. This concept is typically based on having a database of IP addresses (typically IPs of hosts and networks) on each Layer 3 node in the packet's path, along with the next-hop IP addresses of the Layer 3 nodes that can be used to reach each of these IP addresses. This database is known as the *Routing Information Database* (RIB). In contrast, the Forwarding Information Base (FIB), also known as the *forwarding table*, contains the destination addresses and the interfaces required to reach those destinations, as depicted in Figure 2-7. In general, routing protocols are classified as either link-state, path-vector, or distance-vector protocols. This classification is based on how the mechanism of the routing protocol constructs and updates its routing table, and how it computes and selects the desired path to reach the intended IP destination.[2]

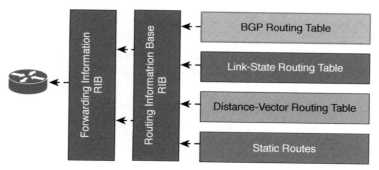

Figure 2-7   *RIB and FIB*

As illustrated in Figure 2-8, the typical basic forwarding decision in a router is based on three processes:

- Routing protocols

- Routing table

- Forwarding decision (switches packets)

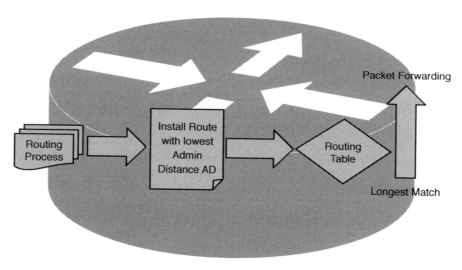

Figure 2-8   *Router's Forwarding Decision*

---

2. IETF draft: (Routing Information Base Info Model "draft-nitinb-i2rs-rib-info-model-02")

Link-State Routing Protocol Design Considerations

Open Shortest Path First (OSPF) and Intermediate System-to-Intermediate System (IS-IS) protocols as link-state routing protocols have a common conceptual characteristic in the way they build, interact, and handle L3 routing to some extent. Figure 2-9 illustrates the process of building and updating a link-state database (LSDB).

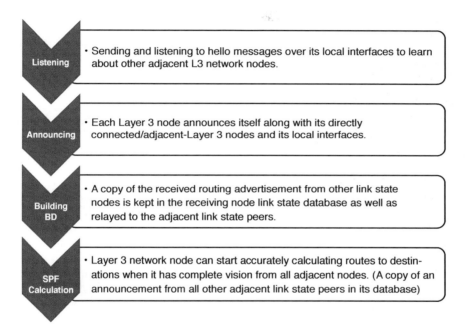

Listening
- Sending and listening to hello messages over its local interfaces to learn about other adjacent L3 network nodes.

Announcing
- Each Layer 3 node announces itself along with its directly connected/adjacent-Layer 3 nodes and its local interfaces.

Building BD
- A copy of the received routing advertisement from other link state nodes is kept in the receiving node link state database as well as relayed to the adjacent link state peers.

SPF Calculation
- Layer 3 network node can start accurately calculating routes to destinations when it has complete vision from all adjacent nodes. (A copy of an announcement from all other adjacent link state peers in its database)

Figure 2-9 *Process of Building an LSDB*

It is important to remember that although OSPF and IS-IS as link-state routing protocols are highly similar in the way they build the LSDB and operate, they are not identical! This section discusses the implications of applying link-state routing protocols (OSPF and IS-IS) on different network topologies, along with different design considerations and recommendations.

Link-State over Hub-and-Spoke Topology

In general, some implications should be considered when link-state routing protocols are applied on a hub-and-spoke topology, including the following:

■ There is a concern with regard to scaling to a large number of spokes, because each spoke node typically will receive all other spoke nodes' link-state information, because there is no effective means to control the distribution of routing information among these spokes.

■ Special consideration must be taken to avoid suboptimal routing, in which traffic can use remote sites (spokes) as a transit site to reach the hub or other spokes.

For instance, summarization of routing flooding domains in a multi-area/flooding domain design with multiple border routers requires specific routing information between the border routers (Area Border Routers [ABRs] in OSPF or L1/L2 in IS-IS) over a nonsummarized link, to avoid using spoke sites as a transit path, as illustrated in Figure 2-10 [13].

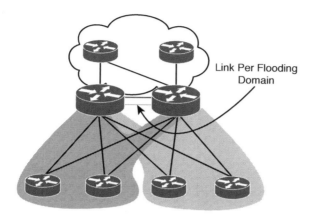

Figure 2-10   *Multi-Area Link State: Hub and Spoke*

So, for each hub-and-spoke flooding domain to be added to the hub routers, you need to consider an additional link between the hub routers in that domain. This is a typical use case scenario to avoid suboptimal routing with link-state routing protocols. However, when the number of flooding domains (for example, OSPF areas) increases, the number of VLANs, subinterfaces, or physical interfaces between the border routers will grow as well, which will result in scalability and complexity concerns. One of the possible solutions is to have a single link with adjacencies in multiple areas. (RFC 5185) [13]. For instance, in the scenario illustrated in Figure 2-11, there is a hub-and-spoke topology that uses OSPF multi-area design.

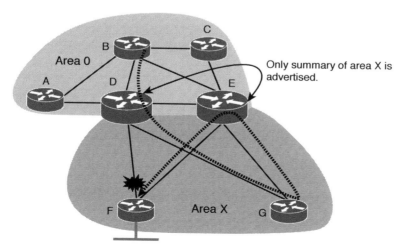

Figure 2-11   *Multi-Area OSPF: Hub and Spoke*

If the link between router D and router F (part of OSPF area X) fails, any traffic from router B destined to the LAN connected to router F going toward the summary advertised route by router D will traverse across the more specific route over the path G, E, then F.

To optimize this design during this failure scenario, there are multiple possible solutions, and here network designers must decide which solution is the most suitable one with regard to other design requirements such as application requirements where delay could affect critical business applications:

■ Place the inter-ABR link (D to E) in area X (simple and provide "north to south" optimal routing in this topology).

■ Place each spoke in its own area with link-state advertisement (LSA) type 3 filtering. (May lead to complex operations and limited scalability; "depends on the network size.")

■ Disable route summarization at the ABRs; for example advertise more specific routes from ABR router E. (May not always be desirable because this means reduced scalability and the loss of some of the value of the OSPF multi-area design.)

Note   The link between the two hub nodes (for example, ABRs) will introduce the potential of a single point of failure to the design. Therefore, link redundancy (availability) between the ABRs may need to be considered.

If IS-IS is applied to the topology in Figure 2-11 instead, using a similar setup where IS-IS L2 is to be used instead of the area 0 and IS-IS L1 is to be used by the spokes, the simplest way to optimize this architecture is to put the links between the border routers in IS-IS L1-L2 (overlapping levels capability), where we can extend L1 to overlap with L2 on the border router (ABR in OSPF), as illustrated in Figure 2-12. This will result in a topology that can support summarization with more optimal routing with regard to the failure scenario discussed above.

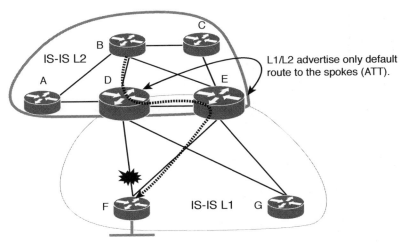

Figure 2-12   *Multilevel IS-IS: Hub and Spoke*

Note   OSPF is a more widely deployed and proven link-state routing protocol in enterprise networks compared to IS-IS, especially with regard to hub-and-spoke topologies. IS-IS has limitations when it works on nonbroadcast multiple access (NBMA) multipoint networks.

OSPF Interface Network Type Considerations in a Hub-and-Spoke Topology

Figure 2-13 summarizes the different possible types of OSPF interfaces in a hub-and-spoke topology over NBMA transport (typically either Frame Relay or ATM), along with the associated design advantages and implications of each [13].

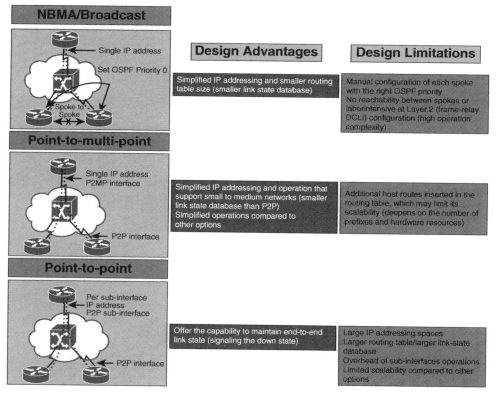

Figure 2-13   *OSPF Interface Types Comparison: Hub and Spoke*

Link-State over Full-Mesh Topology

Fully meshed networks can offer a high level of redundancy and the shortest paths. However, the substantial amount of routing information flooding across a fully meshed network is a significant concern. This concern stems from the fact that each router will receive at least one copy of every new piece of information from each neighbor on the full mesh. For example, in Figure 2-14, each router has four adjacencies. When a router's link connect to the LAN side fails, it must flood its LSA/LSP to each of the four neighbors. Each neighbor will then flood this LSA/LSP (link-state package) again to its neighbors. This process will culminate in a process like a broadcast being sent, due to this full-mesh connectivity and reflooding [13].

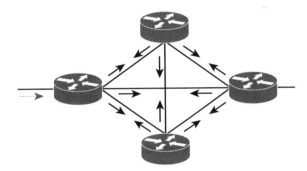

Figure 2-14   *Link-State: Full-Mesh Topology*

With link-state routing protocols, you can use the mesh group technique to reduce link-state information flooding in a full-meshed topology [23]. However, with link-state routing protocols in failure scenarios over a meshed topology, some routers may know about the failure before others within the mesh. This will typically lead to a temporarily inconsistent LSDB across the nodes within the network, which can result in transient forwarding loops. Even though the concept of a loop-free alternate (LFA) route can be considered to overcome situations like this, using LFA over a mesh topology will add complexity to the control plane.

> **Note**   Later in this chapter, in the section "Hiding Topology and Reachability Information," more details are provided about flooding domain and route summarization design considerations for link-state routing protocols, which can reduce the level of control plane complexity and optimize link-state information flooding and performance.

> **Note**   Other mechanisms help to optimize and reduce link-state LSA/LSP flooding by reducing the transmission of subsequent LSAs/LSPs, such as OSPF flood reduction (described in RFC 4136). This is done by eliminating the periodic refresh of unchanged LSAs, which can be useful in fully meshed topologies

OSPF Area Types

Table 2-3 contains a summarized review of the different types of OSPF areas [21, 22].

Table 2-3   *OSPF Area Types*

Area Type	Advertised Route
Stubby	All routes except type 5, external routing information
Totally stubby	Internal area routes + default route (both type 3 and 5 LSAs are suppressed.)
Not so stubby (NSSA)	All routes with the ability to inject/originate external routing information (type 7 LSA)
Totally NSSA	Internal area routes + default route, with the ability to inject/originate external routing information (type 7 LSA)

Each of the OSPF areas allows certain types of LSAs to be flooded, which can be used to optimize and control route propagation across OSPF routed domain. However, if OSPF areas are not properly designed and aligned with other requirements, such as application requirements, it can lead to serious issues because of the traffic black-holing and suboptimal routing that can appear as a result to this type of design. Subsequent sections in this book discuss these points in more detail.

Figure 2-15 shows a conceptual high-level view of the route propagation, along with the different OSPF LSAs, in an OSPF multi-area design with different area types.

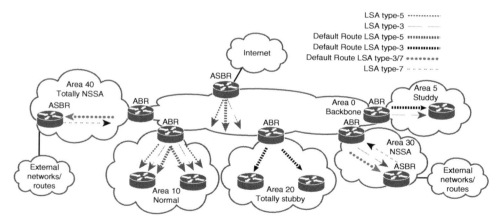

Figure 2-15   *OSPF Route Propagation in Multi-Area Design*

The typical design question is this: Where can these areas be used and why?

The basic standard answer is this: It depends on the requirements and topology.

For instance, if no requirement specifies which path a route must take to reach external networks such as an extranet or the Internet, you can use the "totally NSSA" area type to simplify the design. For example, the scenario in Figure 2-16 is one of the most common design models that use OSPF NSSA. In this design model, the border area that interconnects the campus or data center network with the WAN or Internet edge devices can be deployed as totally NSSA. This deployment assumes that no requirement dictates which path should be used [15]. Furthermore, in the case of NSSA and multiple ABRs, OSPF selects one ABR to perform the translation from LSA type 7 to LSA type 5 and flood it into area 0 (normally the router with the highest router ID, as described in RFC 1587). This behavior can affect the design if the optimal path is required.

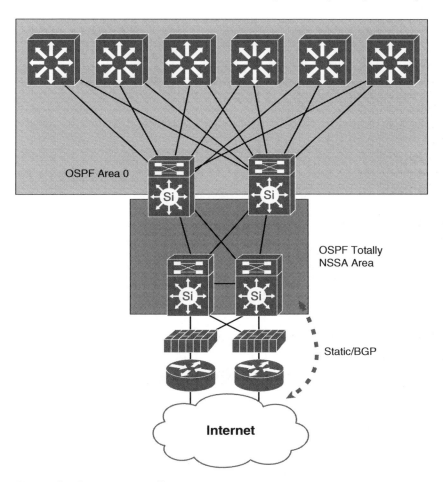

Figure 2-16   *OSPF Totally NSSA*

> **Note**   RFC 3101 introduced the ability to have multiple ABRs perform the translation from LSA type 7 to type 5. However, the extra unnecessary number of LSA type 7 to type 5 translators may significantly increase the size of the OSPF LSDB. This can affect the overall OSPF performance and convergence time in large-scale networks with a large number of prefixes [RFC 3101].

Similarly, in the scenario depicted on the left in Figure 2-17, a data center in London hosts two networks (10.1.1.0/24 and 10.2.1.0/24). Both WAN/MAN links to this data center have the same bandwidth and cost. Based on this setup, the traffic coming from the Sydney branch toward network 10.2.1.0/24 can take any path. If this is not compromising any requirement (in other words, suboptimal routing is not an issue), the OSPF area 10 can be deployed as a "totally stubby area" to enhance the performance and stability of remote site routers.

In contrast, the scenario on the right side of Figure 2-17 has a slightly different setup. The data centers are located in different geographic locations with a data center interconnect (DCI) link. In a scenario like this, the optimal path to reach the destination network can be critical, and using a totally stubby area can break the optimal path requirement. To overcome this limitation, there are two simple alternatives to use: either "normal OSPF area" or the "stubby area" for area 10. This ensures that the most specific route (LSA type 3) is propagated to the Sydney branch router to select the direct optimal path rather than crossing the international DCI [13].

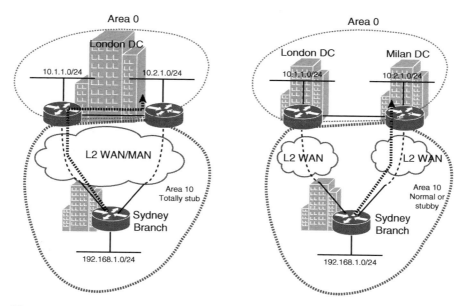

Figure 2-17   *OSPF Totally Stubby Area Versus Stubby Area Design*

In a nutshell, the goal of these types of different OSPF areas is to add more optimization to the OSPF multi-area design by reducing the size of the routing table and lowering the overall control plane complexity by reducing the size of the fault domains (link-state flooding domains). This size reduction can help to reduce overhead of the routers' resources, such as CPU and memory. Furthermore, the reduction of the flooding domains' size will help accelerate the overall network recovery time in the event of a link or node failure. However, in some scenarios where an optimal path is important, take care when choosing between these various area types.

Note In the scenarios illustrated in Figure 2-16 and Figure 2-17, asymmetrical routing is a possibility, which may be an issue if there are any stateful or stateless network devices in the path such as a firewall. However, this section focuses only on the concept of area design. Later in this book, you will learn how to manage asymmetrical routing at the network edge.

OSPF Versus IS-IS

It is obvious that OSPF and IS-IS as link-state routing protocols are similar and can achieve (to a large extent) the same result for enterprises in terms of design, performance, and limitations. However, OSPF is more commonly used by enterprises as the interior gateway protocol (IGP), for the following reasons:

- OSPF can offer a more structured and organized routing design for modular enterprise networks.

- OSPF is more flexible over hub-and-spoke topology with multipoint interfaces at the hub.

- OSPF naturally runs over IP, which makes it a suitable option to be used over IP tunneling protocols such as generic routing encapsulation (GRE) and dynamic multipoint virtual private network (DMVPN), whereas with IS-IS, this is not a supported design.

- In terms of staff knowledge and experience, OSPF is more widely deployed on enterprise-grade networks. Therefore, compared to IS-IS, more people have knowledge and expertise.

However, if there is no technical barrier, both OSPF and IS-IS are valid options to consider.

Note Some Cisco platforms and software versions do support IS-IS over GRE.[3]

Further Reading

OSPF Version 2, RFC 1247: http://www.ietf.org

OSPF for IPv6, RFC 2740: http://www.ietf.org

Domain-Wide Prefix Distribution with Two-Level IS-IS, RFC 5302: http://www.ietf.org

"OSPF Design Guide": http://www.cisco.com

"How Does OSPF Generate Default Routes?": http://www.cisco.com

---

3. "Cisco IOS XR Routing Configuration Guide for the Cisco CRS Router, Release 4.2.x," http://www.cisco.com

"What Are OSPF Areas and Virtual Links?": http://www.cisco.com

"OSPF Not So Stubby Area Type 7 to Type 5 Link-State Advertisement Conversion": http://www.cisco.com

"IS-IS Network Types and Frame Relay Interfaces": http://www.cisco.com

EIGRP Design Considerations

Enhanced Interior Gateway Routing Protocol (EIGRP) is an enhanced distance-vector protocol, relying on the Diffusing Update Algorithm (DUAL) to calculate the shortest path to a network. EIGRP, as a unique Cisco innovation, became highly valued for its ease of deployment, flexibility, and fast convergence. For these reasons, EIGRP is commonly considered by many large enterprises as the preferred IGP. EIGRP maintains all the advantages of distance-vector protocols while avoiding the concurrent disadvantages [16]. For instance, EIGRP does not transmit the entire routing information that exists in the routing table following an update event; instead, only the "delta" of the routing information will be transmitted since the last topology update. EIGRP is deployed in many enterprises as the routing protocol, for the following reasons:

■ Easy to design, deploy, and support

■ Easier to learn

■ Flexible design options

■ Lower operational complexities

■ Fast convergence (subsecond)

■ Can be simple for small networks while at the same time scalable for large networks

■ Supports flexible and scalable multi-tire campus and hub-and-spoke WAN design models

Unlike link-state routing protocols, such as OSPF, EIGRP has no hard edges. This is a key design advantage because hierarchy in EIGRP is created through routes summarization or routes filtering rather than relying on a protocol-defined boundary, such as OSPF areas. As illustrated in Figure 2-18, the depth of hierarchy depends on where the summarization or filtering boundary is applied. This makes EIGRP flexible in networks structured as a multitier architecture [19].

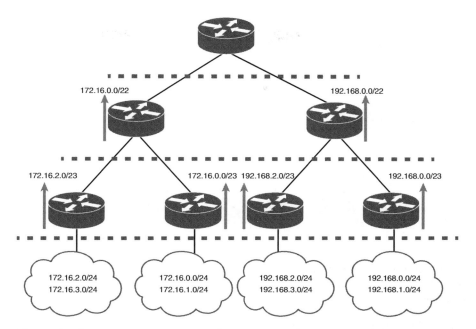

Figure 2-18 *EIGRP Domain Boundaries on a Multitier Network*

EIGRP: Hub and Spoke

As discussed earlier, link-state routing protocols have some scaling limitations when applied on a hub-and-spoke topology. In contrast, EIGRP offers more flexible and scalable capabilities for the hub-and-spoke types of topologies. One of the main concerns in a hub-and-spoke topology is the possibility of a spoke or remote site being used as a transit path due to a configuration error or a link failure. With link-state routing protocols, several techniques to mitigate this type of issue were highlighted. However, there are still scalability limitations associated with it.

However, EIGRP offers the capability to mark the remote site (spoke) as a stub, which is unlike the OSPF stub (where all routers in the same stub area can exchange routes and propagate failure and update information). With EIGRP, when the spokes are configured as a stub, it will signal to the hub router that the paths through the spokes should not be used as transit paths. As a result, there will be significant optimization to the design. This optimization results from the decrease in EIGRP query scope and the reduction of the unnecessary overhead associated with responding to queries by the spoke routers (for example, EIGRP stuck-in-active [SIA] queries) [19].

In Figure 2-19, router B will see it has only one path to the LAN connected to router A, rather than four paths.

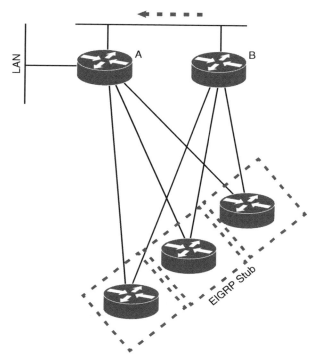

Figure 2-19   *EIGRP Stub*

Consequently, enabling EIGRP Stub over a "hub-and-spoke" topology helps to reduce the overall control plane complexity as well as increases the scalability of the design to support large number of spokes without affecting its performance.

Note   With EIGRP, you can control what a stub router can advertise, such as directly connected links or redistributed static route. Therefore, network operators have more flexibility to control what is announced by the "stub" remote sites.

EIGRP Stub Route Leaking: Hub-and-Spoke Topology

You might encounter some scenarios like the one depicted in Figure 2-20, which is an extension to the EGRP stub design with a backdoor link between two remote sites. In this scenario, the HQ site is connected to the two remote sites over an L2 WAN. These remote sites are also interconnected directly via a backdoor link. Remote sites are configured as EIGRP stubs to optimize the remote sites' EIGRP performance over the WAN.

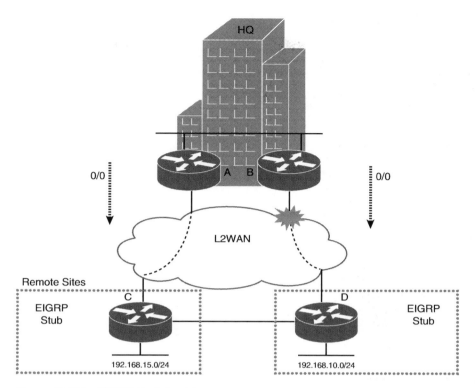

Figure 2-20 *EIGRP Stub Leaking*

The issue with the design in this scenario is that if the link between router B and router D fails, the following will result as a consequence of this single failure:

■ Router A cannot reach network 192.168.10.0/24 because router D is configured as a stub. Also, router C is a stub, which will not advertise this network to router A anyway.

■ Router D will not be able to receive the default from router A because router C is a stub as well.

This means that the remote site connected to router D will be completely isolated, without taking any advantage of the backdoor link. To overcome this issue, EIGRP offers a useful feature called *stub leaking*, where both routers D and C in this scenario can advertise routes to each other selectively, even if they are configured as a stub. Route filtering might need to be incorporated in scenarios like this, when an EIGRP leak map is introduced into the design to avoid any potential suboptimal routing that might happen as a consequence of routes leaking.

EIGRP: Ring Topology

Unlike link-state routing protocols, EIGRP has limitations with a ring topology. As depicted in Figure 2-21, the greater the number of nodes in the ring, the greater the number of queries to be sent during a link failure. As a general recommendation with EIGRP, always try to design in triangles where possible, rather than rings [20].

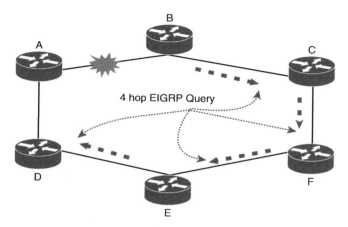

Figure 2-21   *EIGRP Queries on a Ring Topology*

EIGRP: Full-Mesh Topology

EIGRP in a full-mesh topology (see Figure 2-22) is less desirable in comparison with link-state protocols. For example, with link-state protocols such as OSPF, network designers can designate one router to flood into the mesh and block flooding on the other routers, which can improve the topology. In contrast, with EIGRP, this capability is not available. The only way to mitigate the information flooding in an EIGRP mesh topology is by relying on route summarization and filtering techniques [19]. To optimize EIGRP in a mesh topology, the summarization must be into and out of the meshed network.

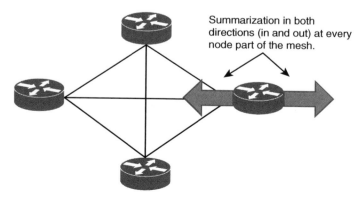

Figure 2-22   *EIGRP on a Mesh Topology*

Note As discussed earlier, link state can lead to transient forwarding loops in ring and mesh topologies after a network component failure event. Therefore, both EIGRP and link state have limitations on these topologies, with different indications (fast and large number of EIGRP queries versus link-state transient loop).

EIGRP Route Propagation Considerations

EIGRP offers a high level of flexibility to network designers, which can fit different types of designs and topologies. However, like any other protocol, some limitations apply (especially with regard to route propagation) and may influence the design choices. Therefore, network designers must consider the following factors to avoid impacting the propagation of routing information, which can result in instable design:

- **EIGRP bandwidth:** By default, EIGRP is designed to use up to 50 percent of the main interface bandwidth for EIGRP packets; however, this value is configurable. The limitation with this concept occurs when there is a dialer or point-to-multipoint physical interface with several peers over one multipoint interface. In this scenario, EIGRP considers the bandwidth value on the main interface divided by the number of EIGRP peers on that interface to calculate the amount of bandwidth per peer. Consequently, when more peers are added over this multipoint interface, EIGRP will reach a point where it will not have enough bandwidth to operate over that dialer or multipoint interface appropriately. In addition, one of the common mistakes with regard to EIGRP and interface bandwidth is that sometimes network operators try to "influence" a best path selection decision in EIGRP DUAL by only tuning the bandwidth over an interface where the interface with the lowest bandwidth will be the least preferred. However, this approach can impact the EIGRP control plane peering functionality and scalability if it is tuned to a low value without proper planning.

  Therefore, the network designer must take this point into consideration and adopt alternatives, such as point-to-point subinterfaces under the multipoint interface. In addition, with overlay multipoint tunnel interfaces such as DMVPN the bandwidth may be required to be defined manually at the tunnel interface when there is a large number of remote spokes.

- **Zero successor routes:** When EIGRP tries to install routes in the RIB table and it is rejected, this is called *zero successor routes* because this route simply will not be propagated to other EIGRP neighbors in the network. This behavior typically happens due to one of the following two primary reasons:

  - There is already the same route in the RIB table with a better administrative distance (AD).

  - When there are multiple EIGRP autonomous systems (AS) defined on the same router, the router will typically install any given route learned via both EIGRP autonomous systems with the same AD from one EIGRP AS, while the other will be rejected. Consequently, the route of the other EIGRP AS will not be propagated within its domain.

Further Reading

savage-eigrp-xx, IETF draft, http://www.ietf.org

"Introduction to EIGRP," http://www.cisco.com

"Configuration Notes for the Implementation of EIGRP over Frame Relay and Low Speed Links," http://www.cisco.com

"What Does the EIGRP DUAL-3-SIA Error Message Mean?" http://www.cisco.com

Hiding Topology and Reachability Information Design Considerations

Technically, both topology and reachability information hiding can help to improve routing convergence time during a link or node failure. Topology and reachability information hiding also reduces control plane complexity and enhances network stability to a large extent. For example, if there is a link flapping in a remote site, this might cause all other remote sites to receive and process the update information every time this link flaps, which leads to instability and increased CPU processing.

However, to produce a successful design, the design must first align with the business goals and requirements (and not just be based on the technical drivers). Therefore, before deciding how to structure IGP flooding domains, network architects or designers must first identify the business's goals, priorities, and drivers. Consider, for example, an organization that plans to merge with one of its business partners but with no budget allocated to upgrade any of the existing network nodes. When these two networks merge, the size of the network may increase significantly in a short period of time. As a result, the number of prefixes and network topology information will increase significantly, which will require more hardware resources such as memory or CPU.

Given that this business has no budget allocated for any network upgrade, in this case introducing topology and reachability information hiding to this network can optimize the overall network performance, stability, and convergence time. This will ultimately enable the business to meet its goal without adding any additional cost. In other words, the restructuring of IGP flooding domain design in this particular scenario is a strategic business-enabler solution.

However, in some situations, hiding topology and reachability information may lead to undesirable behaviors, such as suboptimal routing. Therefore, network designers must identify and measure the benefits and consequences by following the top-down approach. The following are some of the common questions that need to be thought about during the planning phase of the IGP flooding domain design:

- What are the business goals, priorities, and directions?

- How many Layer 3 nodes are in the network?

- What is the number of prefixes?

- Are there any hardware limitations (memory, CPU)?

- Is optimal routing a requirement?

- Is low convergence time required?

- What IGP is used, and what is the used underlying topology?

Furthermore, it is important that network designers understand how each protocol interacts with topology information and how each calculates its path, so as to be able to identify design limitations and provide valid optimization recommendations.

Link-state routing protocols take the full topology of the link-state routed network into account when calculating a path [18]. For instance, in the network illustrated in Figure 2-23, the router of remote site A can reach the HQ network (192.168.1.0/24) through the WAN hub router. Normally, if the link between the WAN hub router and router A in the WAN core fails, remote site A will be notified about this topology change "in a flat link-state design." In fact, in any case, the remote site A router will continue to route its traffic via the WAN hub router to reach the HQ LAN 192.168.1.0/24.

In other words, in this scenario, the link failure notifications between the WAN hub router and the remote site routers are considered as unnecessary extra processing for the remote site routers. This extra processing could lead to other limitations in large networks with a large number of prefixes and nodes, such as network and CPU spikes. In addition, the increased size of the LSDB will impact routing calculation and router memory consumption [8]. Therefore, by introducing the principle of "topology hiding boundary" at the WAN hub router (for example, by using OSPF multi-area design), the overall routing design will be optimized (different fault domains) in terms of performance and stability.

A path-vector routing protocol (Border Gateway Protocol [BGP]) can achieve topology hiding by simply using either route summarization or filtering, and distance-vector protocols, by nature, do not propagate topology information. Moreover, with route summarization, network designers can achieve "reachability information hiding" for all the different routing protocols [19].

Note Link state can offer built-in information hiding capabilities (route suppression) by using different type of flooding domains, such as L1/L2 in IS-IS and stubby types of areas in OSPF.

The subsequent sections examine where and why to break a routed network into multiple logical domains. You will also learn summarization techniques and some of the associated implications that you need to consider.

Note Although route filtering can be considered as an option for hiding reachability information, it is often somewhat complicated with link-state protocols.

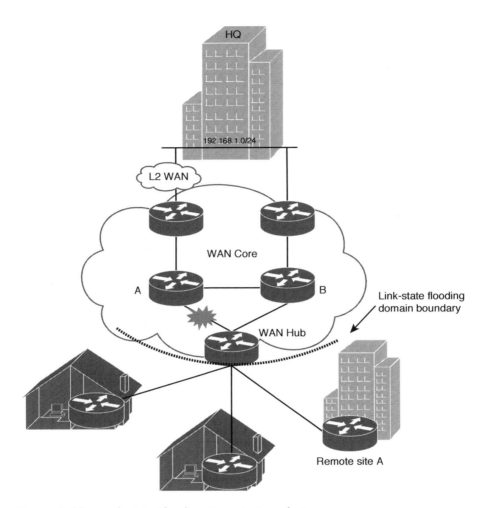

Figure 2-23   *Link-state Flooding Domain Boundaries*

IGP Flooding Domains Design Considerations

As discussed earlier, modularity can add significant benefit to the overall network architecture. By applying this concept to the design of logical routing architectural domains,
we can have a more manageable, scalable, and flexible design. To achieve this, we need
to break a flat routing design into one that is more hierarchical and has modularity in its
overall architecture. In this scenario, we may have to ask the following questions: How
many layers should we consider in our design? How many modules or domains is good
practice?

The simple answer to these questions depends on several factors, including the following:

- Design goal (simplicity versus scalability versus stability)
- Network topology
- Network size (nodes, routes)
- Routing protocol
- Network type (for example, enterprise versus service provider)

The following sections covers the various design considerations for IGP flooding domains, starting with a review of the structure of link-state and EIGRP domains.

Link-State Flooding Domain Structure

Both OSPF and IS-IS as link-state routing protocols can divide the network into multiple flooding domains, as discussed earlier in this book. Dividing a network into multiple flooding domains, however, requires an understanding of the principles each protocol uses to build and maintain communication between the different flooding domains. In a multiple flooding domain design with OSPF, a backbone area is required to maintain end-to-end communication between all other areas (regardless of its type). In other words, area 0 in OSFP is like the glue that interconnects all other areas within an OSPF domain [22]. In fact, nonbackbone OSPF areas and area 0 (backbone area) interconnect and communicate in a hub-and -spoke fashion, as illustrated in Figure 2-24.

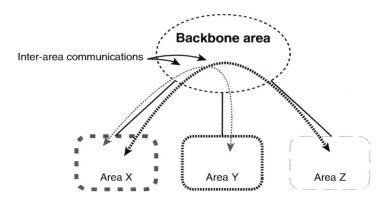

Figure 2-24 *OSPF Area Structure*

Similarly, with IS-IS, its levels chain (IS-IS flooding domains) must not be disjointed (L2 to L1/L2 to L1 and vice versa) for IS-IS to maintain end-to-end communications, where the level 2 can be seen as analogous to area 0 in OSPF.

The natural communication behavior of link-state protocols across multiple flooding domains requires at least one router to be dually connected to the core flooding domain (backbone area) and the other area or areas, where an LSDB for each area is stored along with separate shortest path first (SPF) calculations for each area. Moreover, the

characteristic of the communication between link-state flooding domains (between border routers) is like a distance-vector protocol. In OSPF terminology, this router is called
the *Area Border Router* (ABR). In IS-IS, the L1/L2 router is analogous to the OSPF ABR.

In general, OSPF and IS-IS are two-layer hierarchy protocols; however, this does not
mean that they cannot operate well in networks with more hierarchies (as discussed later
in this section).

In addition, although both OSPF and IS-IS are suitable for two-layer hierarchy network
architecture, there are some differences in the way that their logical layout (flooding
domains such as areas, levels) can be designed. For example, OSPF has a hard edge at the
flooding domain borders. Typically, this is where routing policies are applied, such as
route summarization and filtering, as shown in Figure 2-25.

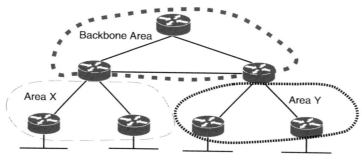

Figure 2-25   *OSPF Flooding Domain Borders*

By contrast, IS-IS routing information of the different levels (L1 and L2) is (technically)
carried over different packets. This helps IS-IS have a softer edge at its flooding domain
borders. This makes it more flexible than OSPF, because the L2 routing domain can
overlap with the L1 domains, as shown in Figure 2-26.

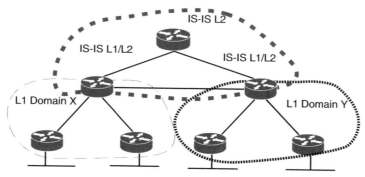

Figure 2-26   *IS-IS Flooding Domain Borders*

Consequently, IS-IS can perform better when optimal routing is required with multiple
border routers, whereas OSPF requires special consideration with regards to the inter-
ABR links (for example, which area to be part of, or in which direction is optimal routing
more important).

Recommendation: With both OSPF and IS-IS, the design must always reflect that the backbone cannot be partitioned in case of a link or node failure. Although an OSPF virtual link can help to fix partitioned backbone area issues, it is not a recommended approach. Instead, redesign of the logical or physical architecture is highly desirable in this case. Nevertheless, an OSPF virtual link may be used as an interim solution (see the following example).

The scenario shown in Figure 2-27 illustrates poorly designed OSPF areas. It is considered a poor design because the OSPF backbone area has the potential to be partitioned if the direct interconnect link between the regional data centers (London and Sydney) fails. This will result in communication isolation between the London and Sydney data centers. However, let's assume that this organization needs to use its regional HQs (Melbourne, Amsterdam, and Singapore), which are interconnected in a hub-and-spoke fashion, as a backup transit path when the link between the London and Sydney sites is down.

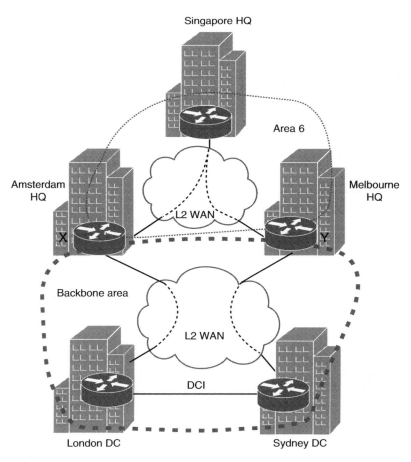

Figure 2-27 *OSPF Poor Area Design*

Based on the current OSPF area design, a nonbackbone area (area 6) cannot be used as a transit area. Figure 2-28 illustrates the logical view of OSPF areas before and after the failure event on the data center interconnect between London and Sydney data centers, which leads to a disjoint area 0 situation [22].

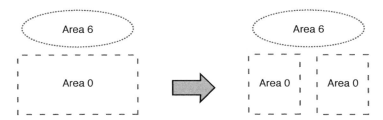

Figure 2-28   *Partitioned OSPF Backbone Area*

The ideal fix to this issue is to add redundant links from the London data center to WAN backbone router Y and/or from the Sydney data center to WAN backbone router X or to add a link between WAN backbone routers X and Y in area 0.

However, let's assume that the provisioning of the links takes a while and this organization requires a quick fix to this issue. As shown in Figure 2-29, if you deploy an OSPF virtual link between WAN backbone routers X and Y in Amsterdam and Melbourne, respectively (across the hub site in Singapore), OSPF will consider this link as a point-to-point link. Both WAN backbone routers (ABRs) X and Y will form a virtual adjacency across this virtual link. As a result, this path can be used as an alternate path to maintain the communication between London and Sydney data centers when the direct link between them is down.

Note   The solution presented in this scenario is based on the assumption that traffic flowing over multiple international links is acceptable from the perspective of business and application requirements.

Note   You can use a GRE tunnel as an alternative method to the OSPF virtual link to fix issues like the one just described; however, there are some differences between using a GRE tunnel versus an OSPF virtual link, as summarized in Table 2-4.

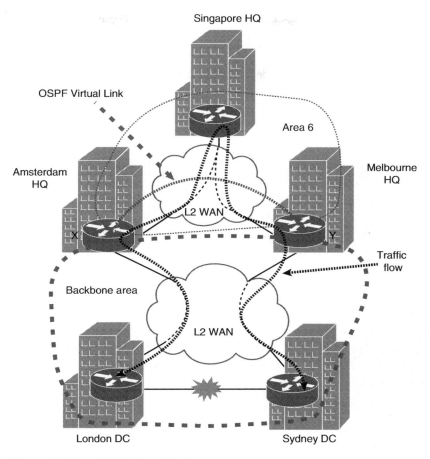

Figure 2-29 *OSPF Virtual Link*

Table 2-4 *OSPF Virtual Link Versus GRE Tunnel*

GRE Tunnel	Virtual Link
May add tunnel overhead as all traffic is tunneled and encapsulated by the tunnel endpoints.	The routing updates are tunneled, but the data traffic is sent natively without tunnel overhead.
May add operational overhead for example, IP addressing need to be configured if not deployed as "unnumbered" and the tunnel interface/IP need to be assigned manually to OSPF area 0.	Simplified operation for example, no IP addressing need to be configured manually, also it's under OSPF area 0 by default.
OSPF stub area can be used as a transit area for the tunnel.	The transit area cannot be an OSPF stub area.

Link-State Flooding Domains

One of the most common questions when designing OSPF or IS-IS is this: What is the maximum number of routers that can be placed within a single area?

The common rule of thumb specifies between 50 and 100 routers per area or IS-IS level. However, in reality it is hard to generalize the recommended maximum number of routers per area because the maximum number of routers can be influenced by a number of variables, such as the following:

- Hardware resources (such as memory, CPU)

- Number of prefixes (can be influenced by routes' summarization design)

- Number of adjacencies per shared segment

Note The amount of available bandwidth with regard to the control plane traffic such as link-state LSAs/LSPs is sometimes a limiting factor. For instance, the most common quality of service (QoS) standard models followed by many organizations allocate one of the following percentages of the interface's available bandwidth for control (routing) traffic:[4] 4-class model, 7 percent; 8-class model, 5 percent; and 12-class model, 2 percent. This is more of a concern when the interconnection is a low-speed link such as legacy WAN link (time-division multiplexing [TDM] based, Frame Relay, or ATM) with limited bandwidth. Therefore, other alternatives are sometimes considered with these types of interfaces, such as passive interface or static routing.

For instance, many service providers run tens of hundreds of routers within one IS-IS level. Although this may introduce other design limitations with regard to modern architectures, in practice it is proven as a doable design. In addition, today's router capabilities, in terms of hardware resources, are much stronger and faster than routers that were used five to seven years ago. This can have a major influence on the design, as well, because these routers can handle a high number of routes and volume of processing without any noticeable performance degradation.

In addition, the number of areas per border router is also one of the primary considerations in designing link-state routing protocols, in particular OSPF. Traditionally, the main constraint with the limited number of areas per ABR is the hardware resources. With the next generation of routers, which offer significant hardware improvements, ABRs can hold a greater number of areas. However, network designers must understand that additional areas to be added per ABR correlates to potential lower expected performance (because the router will store a separate LSDB per area).

---

4. "Medianet WAN Aggregation QoS Design 4.0," http://www.cisco.com

In other words, hardware capabilities of the ABR are the primary deterministic factor of the number of areas that can be allocated per ABR, considering the number of prefixes per area as well. Traditionally, the rule of thumb is to consider two to three areas (including backbone area) per ABR. This is a foundation and can be expanded if the design requires more areas per ABR, with the assumption that the hardware resources of the ABR can handle this increase.

In addition to these facts and variables, network designers should consider the nature of the network and the concept of fault isolation and design modularity for large networks that can be designed with multiple functional fault domains (modules). For example, large-scale routed networks are commonly divided based on the geographic location for global networks or based on an administrative domain structure if they are managed by different entities.

EIGRP Flooding Domains Structure

As discussed earlier, EIGRP has no protocol-specific flooding domains or structure. However, EIGRP with route summarization or filtering techniques can break the flooding domains into multiple hierarchies of routing domains, which can reduce the EIGRP query scope, as depicted in Figure 2-30. This concept is a vital contributor to the optimization for the overall EIGRP design in terms of scalability, simplicity, and convergence time. In addition, EIGRP offers a higher degree of flexibility and scalability in networks with three and more levels in their hierarchies as compared to link-state routing protocols [19].

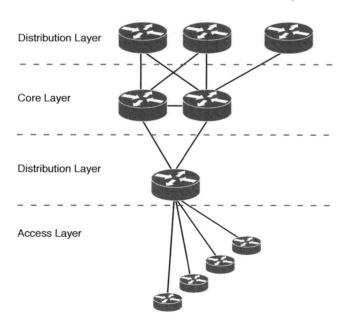

Figure 2-30   *EIGRP Domain Boundaries*

Routing Domain Logical Separation

The two main drivers for breaking a routed network into multiple logical domains (fault domains) are the following: to improve the performance of the networks and routers (fault isolation), and to modularize the design (to make it become simpler, more stable and scalable). These two drivers enhance network convergence and increase the overall routing architecture scalability. Furthermore, breaking the routed topology into multiple logical domains will facilitate topology aggregation and information hiding. It is critical to decide where a routing domain can be divided into two or multiple logical domains. In fact, several variables influence the location where the routing domains are broken or divided. The considerations discussed in the sections that follow are the primary influencers that help to determine the correct location of the logical routing boundaries. Network designers need to consider these when designing or restructuring a routed network.

Underlying Physical Topology

As discussed in Chapter 1, "Network Design Requirements: Analysis and Design Principles," the physical network layout is like the foundation of a building. As such, it is the main influencer when designing the logical structure of a routing domain (for example, a hub-and-spoke versus ring topology). For instance, the level of hierarchy held by a given network can impact the logical routing design if its structure includes two, three, or more tiers, as illustrated in Figure 2-31.

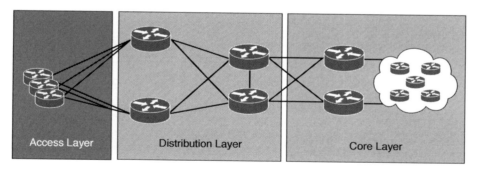

Figure 2-31   *Topology Depth*

Moreover, the points in the network where the interconnections or devices meet (also known as *chokepoints*) at any given tier within the network are a good potential border location of a fault domain boundary, such as ABR in OSPF [19]. For instance, in Figure 2-32, the network is constructed of three-level hierarchies. Routers A and B and routers C and D are good potential points for breaking the routing domain (physical aggregation points). Also, these boundaries can be feasible places to perform route summarizations.

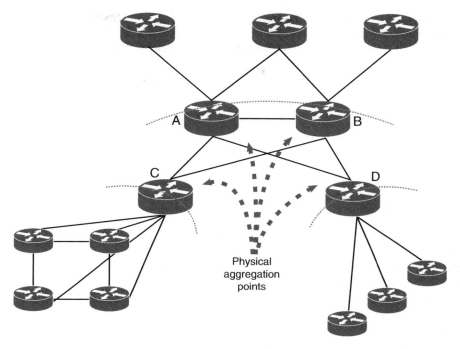

Figure 2-32 *Physical Aggregation Points*

The other important factor with regard to the physical network layout is to break areas that have a high density of interconnections into separate logical fault domains where possible. As a result, devices in each fault domain will have smaller reachability databases (for example, LSDB) and will only compute paths within their fault domain, as illustrated in Figure 2-33. This will ultimately lead to the reduction of the overall control plane design complexity [8]. This concept will promote a design that can facilitate the support of other design principles, including simplicity, modularity, scalability, and topology and reachability information hiding.

The network illustrated in Figure 2-33 has four different functional areas:

- The primary data center

- The regional data center

- The international WAN

- The hub-and-spoke network for some of the remote sites

From the perspective of logical separation, you should place each one of the large parts of the network into its own logical domain. The logical topology can be broken using OSPF areas, IS-IS levels, or EIGRP route summarization. The question you might be asking is this: Why has the domain boundary been placed at routers G and H rather than router D? Technically, both are valid places to break the network into multiple logical domains. However, if we place the domain boundary at router D, both the primary data center network and regional data center will be under same logical fault domain. This means the network may be less scalable and associated with lower control plane stability because routers E and F will have a full view of the topology of the regional data center network connected to routers G and H. In addition, routers G and H most probably will face the same limitations as routers E and F. As a result, if there is any link flap or routing change in the regional data center network connected to router G or H, it will be propagated across to routers E and F (unnecessary extra load and processing).

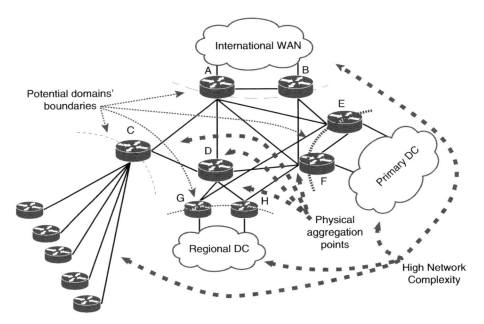

Figure 2-33   *Potential Routing Domain Boundaries*

Traffic Pattern and Volume

By understanding traffic pattern (for example, south-north versus east-west) and traffic volume trends, network designers can better understand the impact if a logical topology were to be divided into multiple domains on certain points (see Figure 2-34). For example, OSPF always prefers the path over the same area regardless of the link cost over other areas. (For more information about this, see the section "IGP Traffic Engineering and Path Selection: Summary.") In some situations, this could lead to suboptimal routing, where a high volume of traffic will travel across low-capacity links or expensive links with strict billing that not every type of communications should go over it; this results from the poor design of OSPF areas, which did not consider bandwidth or cost requirements.

Similarly, if the traffic pattern is mostly north-south, such as in a hub-and-spoke topology where no communication between the spokes is required, this can help network designers to avoid placing the logical routing domain boundary at points likely to using spoke sites as transit sites (suboptimal routing). For instance, the scenario depicted in Figure 2-35 demonstrates how the application of the logical area boundaries on a network can influence the path selection. Traffic sourced from router B going to the regional data center behind router G should (optimally) go through router D, and then across one of the core routers E or F, and finally to router C to reach the data center over one of the core high-speed links. However, the traffic is currently traversing the low-speed link via router A. This path (B-D-A-C-G) is within the same area (area 10), as shown in Figure 2-35.

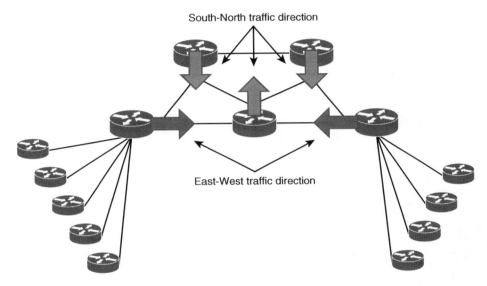

Figure 2-34   *Traffic Patterns*

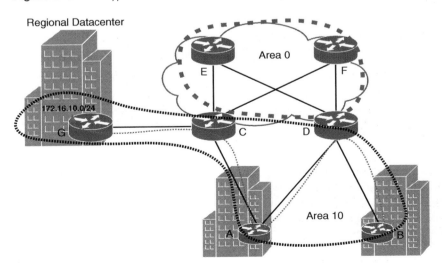

Figure 2-35   *OSPF Suboptimal Routing*

No route filtering or any type of summarization is applied to this network. This suboptimal routing results entirely from the poor design of OSPF areas. If you apply the concepts discussed in this section, you can optimize this design and fix the issue of sub-optimal routing, as follows:

- First, the physical network is a three-tier hierarchy. Routers C and D are the points where the access, data center, and core links meet, which makes them a good potential location to be the area border (which is already in place).

- Second, if you divide this topology into functional domains, you can, for example, have three parts (core, remote sites, and data center), with each placed in its own area. This can simplify summarization and introduce modularity to the overall logical architecture.

- The third point here is traffic pattern. It is obvious that there will be traffic from the remote sites to the regional data center, which needs to go over the high-speed links rather than going over the low-speed links by using other remote sites as a transit path.

Based on this analysis, the simple solution to this design is to either place the data center in its own area or to make the data center part of area 0, as illustrated in Figure 2-36, with area 0 extended to include the regional data center.

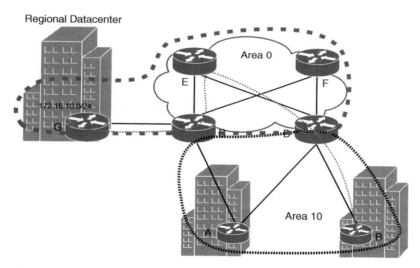

Figure 2-36   *OSPF Optimal Routing*

Note   Although both options are valid solutions, on the CCDE exam the correct choice will be based on the information and requirements provided. For instance, if one of the requirements is to achieve a more stable and modular design, a separate OSPF area for the regional data center will be the more feasible option in this case.

Similarly, if IS-IS is used in this scenario as illustrated in Figure 2-37, router B will always use router A as a transit path to reach the regional data center prefix. Over this path

(B-D-A-C-G), the regional data center prefix behind router G will be seen as IS-IS level 1, and based on IS-IS route selection rules, this path will be preferred compared to the one over the core, in which it will be announced as an IS-IS level 2 route. (For more information about this, see the section "IGP Traffic Engineering and Path Selection: Summary.") Figure 2-37 suggests a simple possible solution to optimize IS-IS flooding domain design (levels): including the regional data center as part of IS-IS level 2. This ensures that traffic from the spokes (router B in this example) destined to the regional data center will always traverse the core network rather transiting any other spoke's network.

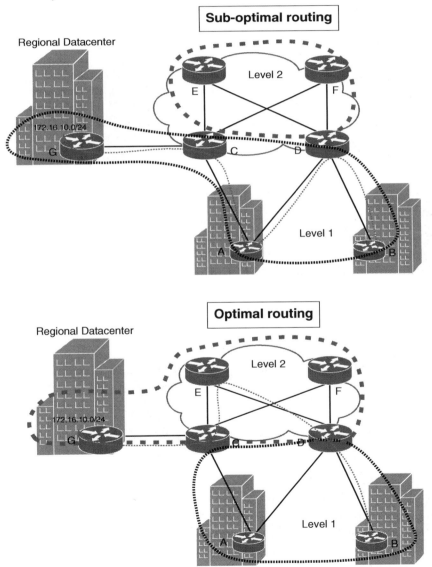

Figure 2-37 *IS-IS Levels and Optimal Routing*

Route Summarization

The other major factor when deciding where to divide logical topology of a routed network is where summarization or reachability information hiding can take place. The important point here is that the physical layout of the topology must be taken into account. In other words, you cannot decide where to place the reachability information hiding boundary (summarization) without referring to what the physical architecture looks like and where the points are that can enhance the overall routing design if summarization is enabled. Subsequent sections in this chapter cover route summarization design considerations in more detail.

Security Control and Policy Compliance

This pertains more to what areas of a certain network have to be logically separated from other parts of the network. For example, an enterprise might have a research and development lab (R&D) where different types of unified communications applications are installed, including routers and switches. Furthermore, the enterprise security policy may dictate that this part of the network must be logically contained and only specific reachability information needs to be leaked between this R&D lab environment and the production network. Technically, this will lead to increased network stability and policy control.

Route Summarization

By having a well-structured IP address align with the physical layout with reachability information hiding using routes summarization, as shown in Figure 2-38, network designers can achieve an optimized level of network design simplicity, scalability, and stability.

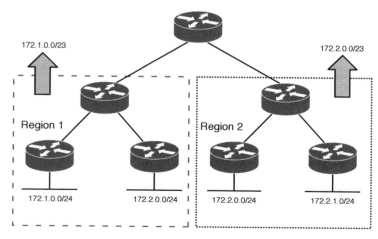

Figure 2-38 *Structured IP Addressing and Physical Connectivity*

For example, based on the routes' summarization structure illustrated in Figure 2-38, if there is any link flap in a remote site in region 2, it will not affect the remote site routers of region 1 in processing or updating their topology database (which in some situations might cause unnecessary path recalculation and processing, which in turn may lead to service interruption). Usually, route summarization facilitates the reduction of the RIB table size by reducing the number of route counts. This means less memory, lower CPU utilization, and faster convergence time during a network change or following any failure event. In other words, the boundary of the route summarization almost always overlaps with the boundary of the fault domain.

However, not every network has a structured network IP addressing like the one shown in Figure 2-38. Therefore, network designers must consider alternatives to overcome this issue. In some situations, the solution is "not to summarize." For instance, Figure 2-39 illustrates a network with unstructured IP addressing, and the business may not able to afford changing their IP scheme in the near future.

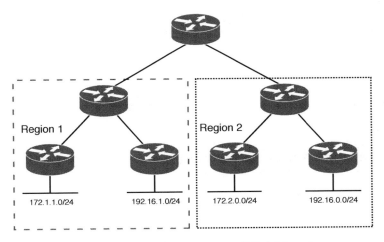

Figure 2-39 *Network with Unstructured IP Addressing*

Moreover, in some scenarios, the unstructured physical connectivity can introduce challenges with route summarization. For example, in Figure 2-40, summarization can lead to forcing all the traffic from the hub site to always prefer the high-cost and low-bandwidth link to reach 172.2.0.0/24 network (more specific route over the high-cost nonsummarized link), which may lead to undesirable outcome from the business point of view (for example slow applications' response time over this link).

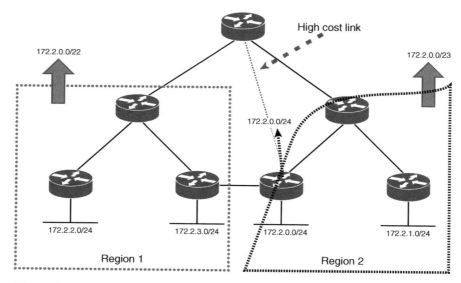

Figure 2-40   *Unstructured Physical Connectivity*

As a general rule of thumb (not always), summarization should be considered at the routing logical domain boundaries. The reason why summarization might not always be considered at the logical boundary domain is because in some designs it can lead to suboptimal routing or traffic black-holing (also known as *summary black holes*). The following subsections discuses summary suboptimal routing and summary black-holing in more detail.

Summary Black Holes

The principle of route summarization is based on hiding specific reachability information. This principle can optimize many network designs, as discussed earlier; however, it can lead to traffic black-holing in some scenarios because of the specific hidden routing information. In the scenario illustrated in Figure 2-41, router A and B send the summary route only (172.1.0.0/21) with the same metric toward router C. Based on this design, in case of link failure between router D and E, the routing table of router C will remain intact, because it is receiving only the summary. Consequently, there is potential for traffic black-holing. For instance, traffic sourced from router C destined to network 172.1.1.0/24 landing at router B will be dropped because of this summarization black-holing. Moreover, the situation can become even worse if router C is performing per-packet load balancing across routers A and B. In this case, 50 percent of the traffic is expected to be dropped. Similarly, if router C is load balancing on a per-session basis, hypothetically some of the sessions will reach their destinations and others may fail. As a result, route summarization in this scenario can lead to a serious connectivity issues in some failure situations [18], [19].

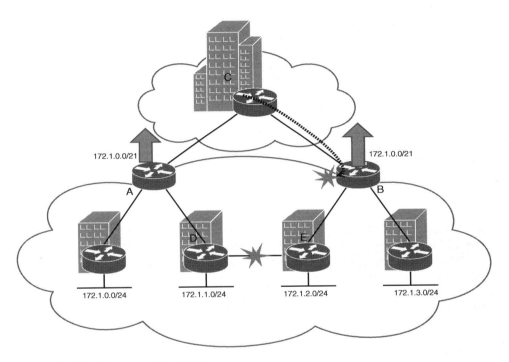

Figure 2-41   *Summary Black Hole*

To mitigate this issue and enhance the design in Figure 2-41, summarization either should be avoided (this option might not be always desirable because it can reduce the stability and scalability in large networks) or at least one nonsummarized link must be added between the summarizing routers (in this scenario, between routers A and B, as illustrated in Figure 2-42). The nonsummarized link can be used as an alternate path to overcome the route summarization black-holing issue described previously.

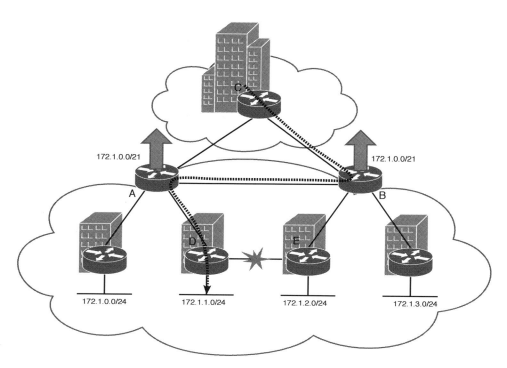

Figure 2-42   *Summary Black Hole Optimization*

Suboptimal Routing

Although hiding reachability information with route summarization can help to reduce control plane complexity, it can lead to suboptimal routing in some scenarios. This suboptimal routing, in turn, may lead traffic to use a lower-bandwidth link or an expensive link, over which the enterprise might not want to send every type of traffic. For example, if we use the same scenario discussed earlier in the OSPF areas, we then apply summarization on the data center edge routers of London and Milan and assume that the link between Sydney and Milan is a high-cost link that has a typically lower routing metric, as depicted in Figure 2-43.

> **Note**   The example in Figure 2-43 is "routing protocol" neutral. It can apply to all routing protocols in general.

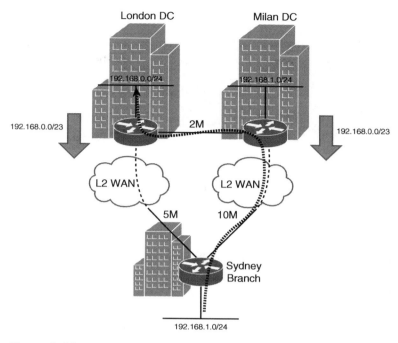

Figure 2-43 *Summary Route and Suboptimal Routing*

As illustrated in Figure 2-43, the link between the Sydney branch and Milan data center is 10 Mbps, and the link to London is 5 Mbps. In addition, the data center interconnect between Milan and London data centers is only 2 Mbps. In this particular scenario, summarization toward the Sydney branch from both data centers will typically hide the more specific route. Therefore, the Sydney branch will send traffic destined to any of the data centers over the high-bandwidth link (with lower routing metric); in this case, the Sydney-Milan path will be preferred (almost always higher bandwidth = lower path metric). This behavior will cause suboptimal routing for traffic destined to London data center network. This suboptimal routing in turn can lead to an undesirable experience, because rather than having 5 Mbps between Sydney branch and London data center, their maximum bandwidth will be limited to the data center interconnect link capacity, which is 2 Mbps in this scenario. This is in addition to the extra cost and delay that will from the traffic having to traverse multiple international links.

Even so, this design limitation can be resolved via different techniques based on the use of the routing protocol, as summarized in Table 2-5.

Table 2-5 *Suboptimal Routing Optimization Techniques*

OSPF	IS-IS	EIGRP	BGP
Using a normal OSPF area combined with LSA type 3 filtering at the ABRs to send /23summary route from Milan side and the more specific route along with /23 summary route from London ABR where the optimal path needs to take place	Using route leaking from L2 to L1 (RFC 2966); in this scenario, leaking the more specific route from London L1/L2 router	Send two summary routes containing the more- and less-specific routes from the router that needs to be used for the more-specific routes (London) Route leaking with summary to send more specific routes from the desired router for optimal path (London router).	By sending the summary along with the more-specific route (for example, using **unsuppress-map** with the BGP summary at the London router

Figure 2-44 illustrates link-state areas/levels application with regard to the discussed scenario and the suggested solutions, because the different areas/levels designs can have a large influence on the overall traffic engineering and path selection.

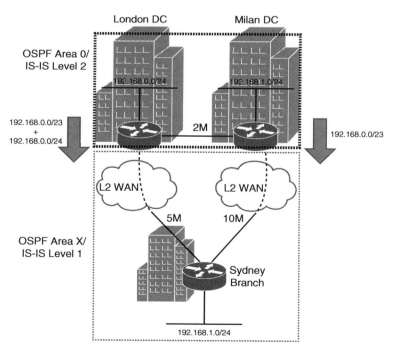

Figure 2-44 *Link-State Flooding Domain Applications and Optimal Routing*

> **Note**   with IS-IS, L1-L2 (ABR) may send default route toward the L1 domain and the route leaking at the London ABR will leak/send the more specific local prefix for optimal routing.

Based on the these design considerations and scenarios, we can conclude that although route summarization can optimize the network design for the several reasons (discussed earlier in this chapter), in some scenarios summarization from the core networks toward the edge or remote sites can lead to suboptimal routing. In addition, summarization from the remote sites or edge routers toward the core network may lead to traffic black holes in some failure scenarios. Therefore, to provide a robust and resilient design, network designers must pay attention to the different failure scenarios when considering route summarization [19].

IGP Traffic Engineering and Path Selection: Summary

By understanding the variables that influence a routing protocol decision to select a certain path, network designers can gain more control to influence route preference over a given path based on a design goal. This process is also known as *traffic engineering.*

In general, routing protocols perform what is known as *destination traffic engineering,* where the path selection is always based on the targeted prefix and the attributes of the path to reach this prefix. However, each of the three IGPs discussed in this chapter has its own metrics, algorithm, and default preferences to select routes. From a routing point of view, they can be altered to control which path is preferred or selected over others, as summarized in the sections that follow.

OSPF

If multiple routes cover the same network with different types of routes, such as inter-area (LSA type 3) or external (LSA type 5), OSPF considers the following list "in order" to select the preferred path (from highest preference to the lowest):

1. Intra-area routes

2. Inter-area routes

3. External type 1 routes

4. External type 2 routes

Let's take a scenario where there are multiple routes covering the same network with the same route type as well; for instance, both are interarea route (LSA type 3). In this case, the OSPF metric (cost) that is driven by the links' bandwidth is used as a tiebreaker to select the preferred path. Typically, the route with the lowest cost is chosen as the preferred path.

If multiple paths cover the same network with the same route type and cost, OSPF will typically select all the available paths to be installed in the routing table. Here, OSPF performs what is known as *equal-cost multipath* (ECMP) routing across multiple paths.

For external routes with multiple Autonomous System Border Routers (ASBRs), OSPF relies on LSA type 4 to describe the path's cost to each ASBR that advertises the external routes. For instance, in case of multiple ASBRs advertising the same external OSPF E2 prefixes carrying the same redistributed metric value, the ASBR with the lowest reported forwarding metric (cost) will win as the preferred exit point.

IS-IS

Typically, with IS-IS, if multiple routes cover the same network (same exact subnet) with different route types, IS-IS follows the sequence here "in order" to select the preferred path:

1. Level 1

2. Level 2

3. Level 2 external with internal metric type

4. Level 1 external with external metric type

5. Level 2 external with external metric type

Like OSPF, if there are multiple paths to a network with the same exact subnet, route type, and cost, IS-IS selects all the available paths to be installed in the routing table (ECMP).

EIGRP

EIGRP has a set of variables that can solely or collectively influence which path a route can select. For more stability and simplicity, bandwidth and delay are commonly used for this purpose. Nonetheless, it is always simpler and safer to alter delay for EIGRP path selection, because of some implications associated with tuning bandwidth for EIGRP traffic engineering purposes discussed earlier in this chapter, which requires careful planning.

Like other IGPs, EIGRP supports the concept of ECMP; in addition, it does support "unequal cost load balancing," as well, with proportional load sharing.

Summary of IGP Characteristics

As discussed in this chapter, each routing protocol behaves and handles routing differently on each topology. Table 2-6 summarizes the characteristics of the IGPs, taking into account the used topology.

Table 2-6 *IGP Characteristics Summary*

	Link State	**EIGRP**
Hub-and-spoke scalability	Moderate scaling capability.	Excellent scaling capability.
Hub-and-spoke considerations	Care must be taken with summary black holes. Consider stub areas with filtering to prevent transiting traffic via remote sites and large RIB tables.	Consider route leaking or specific routes to address summary black holes. Consider stub remote routers with filtering and summarization to prevent transiting traffic through remote sites.
Full-mesh scalability	Acceptable scaling capability, to a certain extent.	Acceptable scaling capability, to a certain extent.
Full-mesh considerations	Manually designate flooding points and increase scaling through a full mesh. A potential of a temporary routing loop following a network failure event.	Summarize into and out of the full mesh. Increased number of EIGRP queries following a network event failure.
Summarization	Only at border routers (ABR).	At any place.
Filtering	Only at border routers (ABR).	At any place.
Load balancing	Equal-cost load balancing.	Equal and unequal-cost load balancing.

Note In Table 2-6, *link-state ABR* refers to either OSPF ABR, ASBR, or IS-IS L1-L2 router.

Note As you'll notice, the full mesh in the preceding table has no excellent scalability among the IGPs. This is because the nature of full-mesh topology is not very scalable. (The larger the mesh becomes, the more complicated the control plane will be.)

BGP Design Considerations

Border Gateway Protocol (BGP) is an Internet Engineering Task Force (IETF) standard, and the most scalable of all routing protocols. As such, BGP is considered as the routing protocol of the global Internet, as well as for service provider-grade networks. In addition,

BGP is the desirable routing protocol of today's large-scale enterprise networks because of its flexible and powerful attributes and capabilities. Unlike IGPs, BGP is used mainly to exchange network layer reachability information (NLRI) between routing domains. (The routing domain in BGP terms is referred to as an autonomous system (AS); typically, it is a logical entity with its own routing and policies, and is usually under same administrative control.) Therefore, BGP is almost always the preferred inter-AS routing protocol. The typical example is the global Internet, which is formed by numerous interconnected BGP autonomous systems.

There are two primary forms of BGP peering:

- **Interior BGP (iBGP):** The peering between BGP neighbors that is contained within one AS

- **Exterior BGP (eBGP):** The peering between BGP neighbors that occurs between the boundaries of different autonomous systems (interdomain)

Interdomain Routing

Typically, the exterior gateway protocol (EGP) (eBGP) is mainly used to determine paths and route traffic between different autonomous systems; this function is known as *interdomain routing*. Unlike an IGP (where routing is usually performed based on protocol metrics to determine the desired path within an AS), EGP relies more on policies to route or interconnect two or more autonomous systems. The powerful policies of EGP allows it to ignore several attributes of routing information that typically an IGP takes into consideration. Therefore, an EGP can offer more simplified and flexible solutions to interconnect various autonomous systems based on predefined routing policies.

Table 2-7 summarizes common AS terminology with regard to interdomain routing concept and as illustrated in Figure 2-45.

Table 2-7   *Interdomain Routing Terminologies*

Term	Description
Stub AS	An AS that has one connection to one upstream AS
Stub multihomed AS	An AS that has connections to more than one AS, and typically it should not offer a transit path
Transit AS	An AS that connects two or more AS to provide a transit path for traffic sourced from one AS and destined to another AS

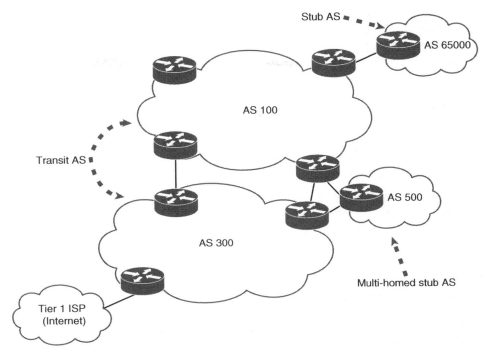

Figure 2-45 *Interdomain Routing*

Furthermore, normally, each AS has its own characteristic in terms of administrative boundaries, geographic restrictions, QoS scheme, cost, and legal constraints. Therefore, for the routing policy control to deliver its value to the business with regard to these variables, there must be a high degree of flexibility in how and where the policy control can be imposed. Typically, there are three standard levels where interdomain routing control can be considered (inbound, transit, and outbound):

- Inbound interdomain routing policy to influence which path egress traffic should use to reach other domains

- Outbound interdomain routing policy to influence which path ingress traffic sourced from other domains should use to reach the intended destination prefixes within the local domain

- Transportation interdomain routing policy to influence how traffic is routed across the transit domain as well as which prefixes and policy attributes from one domain are announced or passed to other neighboring domains, along with how these prefixes and policy attributes are announced (for example, summarized or nonsummarized prefixes)

As a path-vector routing protocol, BGP has the most flexible and reliable attributes to match the various requirements of interdomain routing and control. Accordingly, BGP is considered the de facto routing protocol for the global Internet and large-scale networks, which require complex and interdomain routing control capabilities and policies.

BGP Attributes and Path Selection

BGP attributes, also known as *path attributes*, are sets of information attached to BGP updates. This information describes the characteristics of a BGP prefix, either within an AS or between autonomous systems. According to (RFC 4271):

> BGP implementations MUST recognize all well-known attributes. Some of these attributes are mandatory and MUST be included in every UPDATE message that contains NLRI. Others are discretionary and MAY or MAY NOT be sent in a particular UPDATE message.

Thus, BGP primarily relies on these attributes to influence the process of best path selection. These attributes are critical and effective when designing BGP routing architectures. A good understanding of these attributes and their behavior is a prerequisite to produce a successful BGP design. There are four primary types of BGP attributes, as summarized in Table 2-8.

Table 2-8 *BGP Attributes*

BGP Path attribute	Characteristic
Well-known mandatory	Must appear in every update and must be supported by all BGP speakers (for example, ORIGIN).
Well-known discretionary	May not be included in the update message but must be supported by all BGP speakers (for example, LOCAL_PREFERENCE).
Optional transitive	May be supported by BGP speakers, and they should be maintained and passed to other BGP AS peers whether or not they are supported (for example, COMMUNITY).
Optional nontransitive	May or may not be supported BGP speakers. If an update is received that includes an optional transitive attribute, it is not required that the router pass it on (for example, MULTI_EXIT_DISC).

The following list highlights the typical BGP route selection (from the highest to the lowest preference):

1. Prefer highest weight (Cisco proprietary, local to router)

2. Prefer highest local preference (global within AS)

3. Prefer route originated by the local router

4. Prefer shortest AS path

5. Prefer lowest origin code (IGP < EGP < incomplete)

6. Prefer lowest MED (from other AS)

7. Prefer eBGP path over iBGP path

8. Prefer the path through the closest IGP neighbor

9. Prefer oldest route for eBGP paths

10. Prefer the path with the lowest neighbor BGP router ID

Note   For more information about BGP path selection, refer to the document "BGP Best Path Selection Algorithm," at http://www.cisco.com/c/en/us/support/docs/ip/border-gateway-protocol-bgp/13753-25.html.

BGP as the Enterprise Core Routing Protocol

Most enterprises prefer IGPs such as OSPF as the core routing protocol to provide end-to-end enterprise IP reachability. However, in some scenarios, network designers may prefer a protocol that can provide more flexible and robust routing policies and can cover single and multirouted domains with the ability to facilitate a diversified administrative control approach.

For example, an enterprise may have a large core network that connects different regions or large department networks, each with its own administrative control. To achieve that, we need a protocol that can provide interconnects between all the places in the network (PINs) and at the same time enable each group or region to maintain the ability to control their network without introducing any added complexity when connecting the PINs. Obviously, a typical IGP implementation in the core cannot achieve that, and even if it is possible, it will be very complex to scale and manage.

In other words, when the IGP of large-scale global enterprises network reaches the borderline of its scalability limits within the routed network, which usually contains a high number of routing prefixes, and a high level of flexibility is required to support "splitting routed networks" into multiple failure domains with distributed network administration, BGP is the ideal candidate protocol as the enterprise core routing protocol.

BGP in the enterprise core can offer the following benefits to the overall routing architecture:

- A high degree of responsiveness to new business requirements, such as business expansion, business decline, innovation (IPv6 over IPv4 core), and security policies like end-to-end path separation (for example, MP-BGP + MPLS in the core)

■ Design simplicity (separating complex functional areas, each into its own routed region within the enterprise)

■ Flexible domain control by supporting administrative control per routing domains (per region)

■ More flexible and manageable routing policies that support intra- and interdomain routing requirements

■ Improved scalability because it can significantly reduce the number of prefixes that regional routing domains need to hold and process

■ Optimized network stability by stressing fault isolation domain boundaries (for example, at IGP island edges), where any control plane instability in one IGP/BGP domain will not impact other routing domains (topology and reachability information hiding principle)

However, network designers need to consider some limitations or concerns that BGP might introduce to the enterprise routing architecture when used as the core routing protocol:

■ **Convergence time:** In general, BGP convergence time during a change or following a failure event is slower than IGP. However, this can be mitigated to a good extent when advanced BGP fast convergence techniques are well tuned, such as BGP (PIC).

■ **Staff knowledge and operational complexity:** BGP in the enterprise core can simplify the routing design. However, additional knowledge and experience for the operation staff is required because the network will be more complex to troubleshoot, especially if multiple control policies in different directions are applied for control and traffic engineering purposes.

■ **Hardware and software constraints:** Some legacy or low-end network devices either do not support BGP or may require a software upgrade to support it. In both cases, there is a cost and possibility of a maintenance outage for the upgrade. This might not always an acceptable or supported practice by the business.

Enterprise Core Routing Design Models with BGP

This section highlights and compares the primary and most common design models that network designers and architects can consider for large-scale enterprise networks with BGP as the core routing protocol (as illustrated in Figure 2-46 through Figure 2-49). These design models are based on the design principle of dividing the enterprise network into a two-tiered hierarchy. This hierarchy includes a transit core network to which a number of access or regional networks are attached. Typically, the transit core network runs BGP and glues the different geographic areas (network islands) of the enterprise regional networks. In addition, no direct link should interconnect the regional networks. Ideally, traffic from one regional network to another must traverse the BGP core.

However, each network has unique and different requirements. Therefore, all the design models discussed in this section support the existence or addition of backdoor links between the different regions; remember to always consider the added complexity to the design with this approach:

- **Design model 1:** This design model has the following characteristics:

  - iBGP is used across the core only.

  - Regional networks use IGP only.

  - Border routers between each regional network and the core run IGP and iBGP.

  - IGP in the core is mainly used to provide next-hop (NHP) reachability for iBGP speakers.

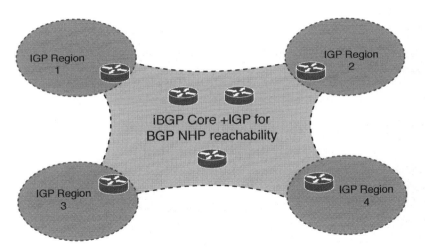

Figure 2-46 *BGP Core Design Model 1*

- **Design model 2:** This design model has the following characteristics:

  - BGP is used across the core and regional networks.

  - In this design model, each regional network has its own BGP AS number (ASN) (no direct BGP session between the regional networks).

  - Reachability information is exchanged between each regional network and the core over eBGP (no direct BGP session between regional networks).

  - IGP in the core as well as at the regional networks is mainly used to provide NHP reachability for iBGP speakers in each domain.

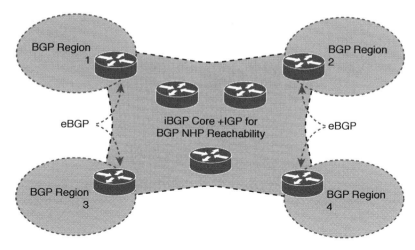

Figure 2-47   *BGP Core Design Model 2*

- **Design model 3:** This design model has the following characteristics:

    - MP-BGP is used across the core (MPLS L3VPN design model).

    - MPLS is enabled across the core.

    - Regional networks can run either static IGP or BGP.

    - IGP in the core is mainly used to provide NHP reachability for MP-BGP speakers.

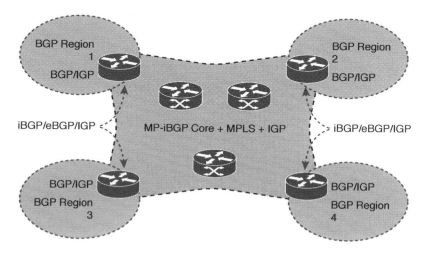

Figure 2-48   *BGP Core Design Model 3*

■ **Design model 4:** This design model has the following characteristics:

■ BGP is used across the regional networks.

■ In this design model, each regional network has its own BGP ASN.

■ Reachability information is exchanged between the regional networks directly over direct eBGP sessions.

■ IGP can be used at the regional networks to provide local reachability within each region and may be required to provide NHP reachability for BGP speakers in each domain (BGP AS).

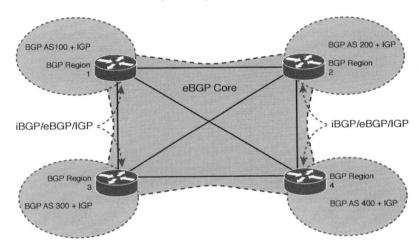

Figure 2-49   *BGP Core Design Model 4*

These designs are all valid and proven design models; however, each has its own strengths and weaknesses in certain areas, as summarized in Table 2-9. During the planning phase of network design or design optimization, network designers or architects must select the most suitable design model as driven by other design requirements, such as business and application requirements (which ideally must align with the current business needs and provide support for business directions such as business expansion).

Table 2-9   *Comparing BGP Core Design Models*

Design Models	Core	Branches/Regions	Design Model Attributes
Design model 1	iBGP	IGP only	This design model offers the least administrative domain control as compared to other models. Can be suitable in large-scale environments to overcome IGP complexities in the core, and offers more control between regions compared to IGP-based only. Moderate operational complexity.

Table 2-9 *continued*

Design Models	Core	Branches/Regions	Design Model Attributes
Design model 2	iBGP	iBGP + IGP	This design model offers moderate administrative domain control between routing regions. Can be suitable for environments under multiple admin domains and large-scale (global) enterprise WANs. Low operational complexity.
Design model 3	MP-iBGP + MPLS	iBGP/eBGP/IGP or eiBGP + IGP	This design model offers the highest administrative domain control between routing regions, combined with the ability to control multiple routing islands in different places with end-to-end path isolation. Can be suitable for environments under multiple admin domains and large-scale (global) enterprise WANs. Offers the highest flexibility and simplicity to introduce new capabilities across the entire enterprise or for specific regions only (for example, IPv6, multicast, and end-to-end traffic separation). High operational complexity.
Design model 4	eBGP	iBGP + IGP	This design model offers high administrative domain control between routing regions. Can be suitable for merging networks scenarios and environments under multiple admin domains (global organizations). Moderate operational complexity.

Note   IGP or control plane complexity referred to in the table above is in comparison to the end to end IGP based design model, specifically across the core.

BGP Shortest Path over the Enterprise Core

BGP as a path-vector control plane protocol normally prefers the path with the smallest number of autonomous systems when traversing multiple autonomous systems when other attributes such as local_preference are the same (classical interdomain routing scenarios). Typically, in interdomain routing scenarios, the different routed domains have their own policies, which do not always need to be exposed to other routing domains. However, in the enterprise core with BGP scenarios, when a router selects a specific path based on the BGP AS-PATH attribute, the "edge eBGP" nodes cannot determine which path within the selected core or transit BGP core AS is the shortest (hypothetically, the optimal path). For instance, the scenario in Figure 2-50 depicts design model 2 of BGP enterprise core. The question is this: How can router A decide which path is the shortest (optimal) within the enterprise core (AS 65000)?

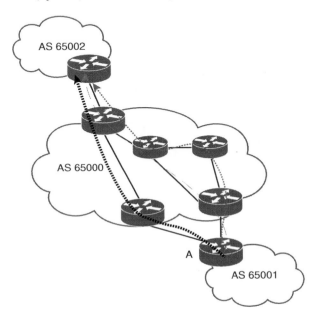

Figure 2-50 *BGP AIBGP*

Accumulated IGP Cost for BGP (AIBGP) is an optional nontransitive BGP path attribute, designed to enhance shortest path selection in scenarios like the one in the example, where a large-scale network is part of a single enterprise with multiple administrative domains using multiple contiguous BGP networks (BGP core routing design model 2, discussed earlier in this section). Therefore, it is almost always more desirable that BGP consider the shortest path with the lowest metric across the transit BGP core. In fact, AIBGP replicates the behavior of link-state routing protocols in computing the distance associated with a path that has routes within a single flooding domain. Although the BGP MED attribute can carry IGP metric values, MED comes after several BGP attributes in the path selection process. In contrast, AIBGP is considered before the AS-PATH attribute when enabled in the BGP path selection process, which makes it more influential in this type of scenario:

1. Prefer highest weight (Cisco proprietary, local to router)

2. Prefer highest local preference (global within single AS)

3. Prefer route originated by the local router

4. **Prefer lowest AIGP cost**

5. Prefer shortest AS path

6. Prefer lowest origin code (IGP < EGP < incomplete)

7. Prefer lowest MED (from other AS)

8. Prefer eBGP path over iBGP path

9. Prefer the path through the closest IGP neighbor

It is obvious that AIBGP can be a powerful feature to optimize the BGP path selection process across a transit AS. However, network designers must be careful when enabling this feature because when AIBGP is enabled, any alteration to the IGP routing can lead to a direct impact on BGP routing (optimal path versus routing stability).

BGP Scalability Design Options and Considerations

This section discusses the primary design options to scale BGP in general at an enterprise network grade. Chapter 6, "Service Provider MPLS VPN Services Design," extends these concepts and discusses the control plane and BGP scalability design considerations of service provider grade networks.

The natural behavior of BGP can be challenging when the size of the network grows to a large number of BGP peers, because it will introduce a high number of route advertisements, along with scalability and manageability complexities and limitations. According to the default behavior of BGP, any iBGP-learned route will not be advertised to any iBGP peer (the typical BGP loop-prevention mechanism, also known as the *iBGP split-horizon rule*). This means that a full mesh of iBGP peering sessions is required to maintain full reachability across the network. On this basis, if a network has 15 BGP routers within an AS, a full mesh of iBGP peering will require (15(15 − 1) / 2) = 105 of iBGP sessions to manage within an AS. Consequently, it will be a network that has a large amount of configuration associated with a high probability of configuration errors, and is complex to troubleshoot and has very limited scalability. However, BGP has two main proven techniques that you can use to reduce or eliminate these limitations and complexities of the BGP control plane:

- Route reflection (described in RFC 2796)

- Confederation (described in RFC 3065).

BGP Route Reflection

Route reflection is a BGP route advertisement mechanism based on relaying the iBGP-learned routes from other iBGP peers. This process involves a special BGP peer or set of peers called *route reflectors* (RRs). These RRs can alter the classical iBGP spilt-horizon rule by re-advertising the BGP route that was received from iBGP peers to other iBGP peers, also known as *route reflector clients*, which can significantly reduce the total number of iBGP sessions, as illustrated in Figure 2-51. Moreover, RRs reflect routes to nonclient iBGP peers as well, in certain cases.

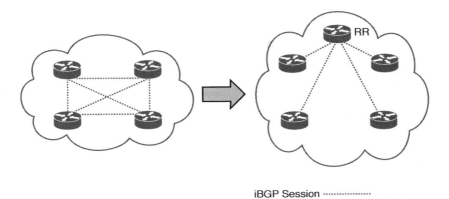

iBGP Session ················

Figure 2-51 *iBGP Session With and Without RR*

Figure 2-52 summarizes RR route advertisement rules based on three primary route sources and receivers in terms of the BGP session type (eBGP, iBGP- RR-client, and iBGP - non-RR-client).

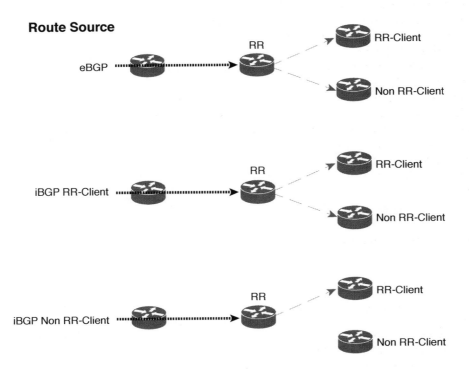

Figure 2-52 *RR Route Advertisement Rules*

It is obvious from the figure that the route(s) sourced from an iBGP non-RR client peer(s) will not be re-advertised by the RR to another iBGP non-RR client peer(s) [24].

As a result, the concept of RR can help network designers avoid the complexities and limitations associated with iBGP full-mesh sessions, where more scalable and manageable designs can be produced. However, BGP RR can introduce new challenges that network designers should take into account, such as redundancy, optimal path selection, and network convergence. These points are covered in the subsequent sections, as well as in other chapters throughout this book.

Route Reflector Redundancy

In BGP environments, RRs can introduce a single point of failure to the design if no redundancy mechanism is considered. RR clustering is designed to provide redundancy, where typically two (or more) RRs can be grouped to serve one or more iBGP clients. With RR clustering, technically, BGP use a special 4-byte attributes called *CLUSTER_ID*. If any pair of RRs has the same CLUSTER_ID, this means that they are part of one RR cluster. Each route exchanged between those RRs in the same cluster will be ignored and not installed in their BGP routing table if this route identified by the receiving RR has the same CLUSTER_ID attribute that is being used. However, in some situations, it is recommended that two redundant RRs be configured with different CLUSTER_IDs for an increased level of BGP routing redundancy. For instance, the RR client in Figure 2-53 is multihomed to two RRs. If each RR is deployed with a different CLUSTER_ID, the RR client will continue to be able to reach prefix X, even after the link with RR 1 fails.

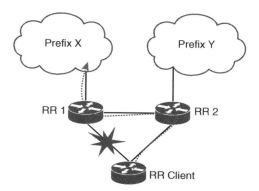

Figure 2-53 *RR Clustering*

In contrast, if RR 1 and RR 2 were deployed with the same CLUSTER_ID, after this failure event the RR client in Figure 2-53 would not be able to reach Prefix X. This is because the CLUSTER_ID attribute mechanism will stop propagation of a route from RR 1 to RR 2 with the same CLUSTER_ID.

Furthermore, two BGP attributes were created specifically to optimize redundant RR behavior, especially with regard to avoiding routing information loops (for example, duplicate routing information). If the redundant RRs are being deployed in different clusters, the two attributes are ORIGINATOR_ID and CLUSTER_LIST.

RR Logical and Physical Topology Alignment

As discussed earlier in Chapter 1, the physical topology forms the foundation of many design scenarios, including BGP RRs. In fact, with BGP RRs, the logical and physical topologies must be given special consideration. They should be as congruent as possible to avoid any undesirable behaviors, such as suboptimal routing and routing loops. For example, the scenario depicted in Figure 2-54 is based on an enterprise network that uses BGP as the core routing protocol (based design model 1, discussed earlier in this chapter). In this scenario, the data center is located miles away from the campus core and is connected over two dark fiber links. The enterprise campus core routers C and D are configured as BGP RR (same RR cluster) to aggregate iBGP sessions of the campus buildings and data center routers. Data center aggregation router E is the iBGP client of core RR D, and the data center aggregation router F is the iBGP client of core RR C.

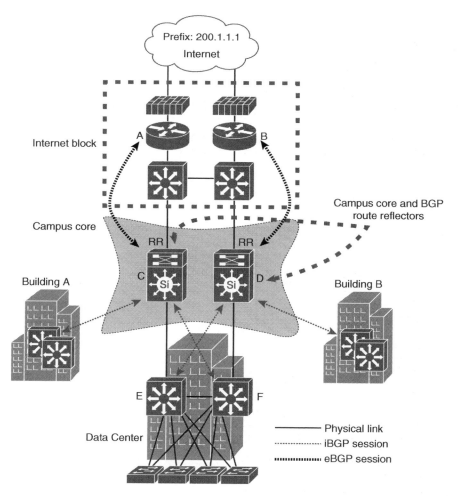

Figure 2-54 *BGP RR Physical and Logical Topology Congruence*

If the prefix 200.1.1.1 is advertised by both Internet edge routers (A and B), typically router A will advertise it to core router C, and router B will advertise it to core router D over eBGP sessions. Then, each RR will advertise this prefix to its clients. (RR C will advertise it to data center aggregation router F, and RR D will advertise to data center aggregation router E.) Up to this stage, there is no issue. However, when routers E and F try to reach prefix 200.1.1.1, a loop will be formed, as follows:

Note   For simplicity, this scenario assumes that both campus cores (RR) advertise the next-hop IPs of the Internet edge routers to all the campus blocks.

- Based on the design in Figure 2-54, data center aggregation E will have the next hop to prefix 200.1.1.1 as Internet edge router B.

- Data center aggregation F will have next hop to prefix 200.1.1.1 as Internet edge router A.

- Data center aggregation E will forward the packets destined to prefix 200.1.1.1 to data center aggregation F. (Based on physical connectivity and IGP, the Internet edge router B is reachable via data center aggregation F from the data center aggregation E point of view.)

- Because data center aggregation F has prefix 200.1.1.1, which is reachable through A, it will then send the packet back to data center aggregation E, as illustrated in Figure 2-55.

This loop was obviously formed because there is no alignment (congruence) between iBGP-RR topology and the physical topology. The following are three simple possible ways to overcome this design issue and to continue using RRs in this network:

- Add a physical link directly between E and D and between F and C, along with an iBGP session over each link to the respective core router. (It might take a long time to provision a fiber link, or it might be an expensive solution from the business point of view.)

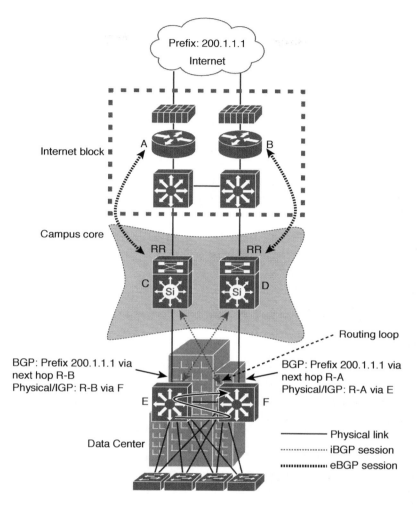

Figure 2-55 *BGP RR and Physical Topology Congruence: Routing Loop*

■ Align the iBGP-RR peering with physical topology by making E the iBGP client to RR C and F the iBGP client to RR D (the simplest solution), as illustrated in Figure 2-56.

■ Add a direct link between core RRs, place each RR in different RR cluster along with direct iBGP session between them. (This might add control plane complexity in this particular scenario to align IGP and BGP paths without alignment between the physical topology and iBGP client to RR sessions.)

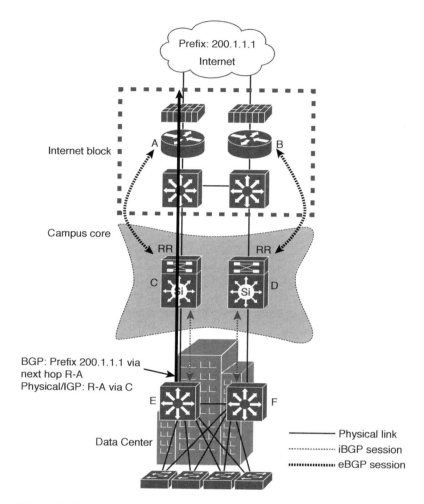

Figure 2-56 *BGP RR Alignment with the Physical Topology*

> **Note**   One of the common limitations of the route reflection concept in large BGP environments is the possibility of suboptimal routing. This point is covered in more detail later in this book.

Update Grouping

Update grouping helps to optimize BGP processing overhead by providing a mechanism that groups BGP peers that have the same outbound policy in one update group, and updates are then generated once per group. By integrating this function with BGP route reflection, each RR update message can be generated once per update group and then replicated for all the RR clients that are part of the relevant group, as depicted in Figure 2-57 [25].

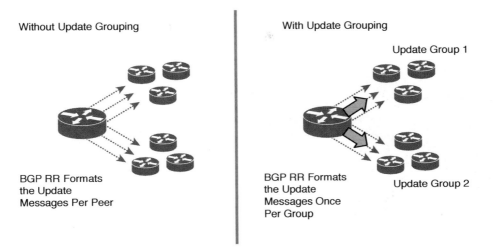

Without Update Grouping

With Update Grouping

Update Group 1

BGP RR Formats
the Update
Messages Per Peer

BGP RR Formats
the Update
Messages Once
Per Group

Update Group 2

Figure 2-57   *BGP Update Grouping*

Technically, update grouping can be achieved by using peer group or peer template features, which can enhance BGP RR functionality and simplify the overall network operations in large BGP networks by

■ Making the configuration easier, less error prone, and more readable

■ Lowering CPU utilization

■ Speeding up iBGP client provisioning (because they can be configured and added quickly)

BGP Confederation

The other option to solve iBGP scalability limitations in large-scale networks is through the use of confederations. The concept of a BGP confederation is based on splitting a large iBGP domain into multiple (smaller) BGP domains (also known as sub-autonomous systems). The BGP communication between these sub- autonomous systems is formed over eBGP session (a special type of eBGP session referred to as *intra-confederation eBGP session*) [24]. Consequently, the BGP network can scale and support a larger number of BGP peers because there is no need to maintain a full mesh among the sub-autonomous systems; however, within each sub-AS iBGP, full mesh is required, as illustrated in Figure 2-58.

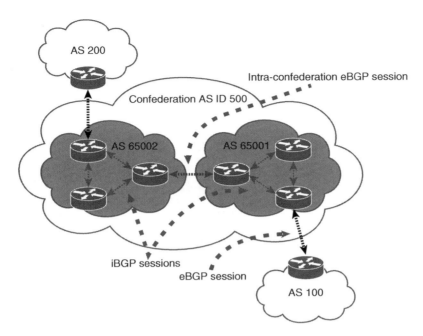

Figure 2-58   *BGP Confederation*

> **Note**   The intra-confederation eBGP session has a mixture of both iBGP and eBGP characteristics. For example, NEXT_HOP, MED, and LOCAL_PREFRENCE attributes are kept between sub-autonomous systems. However, the AS_PATH is changed with updates across the sub-autonomous systems.

> **Note**   The confederations appear as a single AS to external BGP autonomous systems. Because the sub-AS topology is invisible to external peering BGP autonomous systems, the sub-AS is also removed from the eBGP update sent to any external eBGP peer.

In large iBGP environments like a global enterprise (or Internet service provider [ISP] type of network), you can use both RR and confederation jointly to maximize the flexibility and scalability of the design. As illustrated in Figure 2-59, confederation can help to split the BGP AS into sub-autonomous systems, where each sub-AS can be managed and controlled by a different team or business unit. At the same time, within each AS, the RR concept is used to reduce iBGP full-mesh session complexity. In addition, network designers must make sure that IGP metrics within any given sub-AS are lower than those between sub-autonomous systems to avoid any possibility of suboptimal routing issues within the confederation AS.

Note To avoid BGP route oscillation, which is associated with RRs or confederations in some scenarios, network designers must consider deploying higher IGP metrics between sub-autonomous systems or RR clusters than those within the sub-AS or cluster.

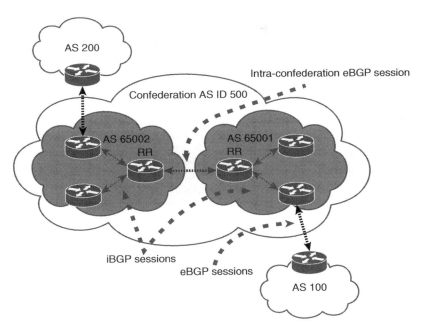

Figure 2-59 *BGP Confederation and RR*

Note Although BGP route reflection combined with confederation can maximize the overall BGP flexibility and scalability, it may add complexity to the design if the combination of both is not required. For instance, when merging two networks with a large number of iBGP peers in each domain, confederation with RR might be a feasible joint approach to optimize and migrate these two networks if it does not compromise any other requirements. However, with a large network with a large number of iBGP peers in one AS that cannot afford major outages and configuration changes within the network, it is more desirable to optimize using RR only rather than combined with confederation.

Confederation Versus Route Reflection

The most common dilemma is whether to use route reflection or confederation to optimize iBGP scalability. The typical solution to this dilemma, from a design point of view, is "it depends." Like any other design decision, deciding what technology or feature to use to enhance BGP design and scalability depends on different factors. Table 2-10 highlights the different factors that can help you narrow down the design decision with regard to BGP confederation versus route reflection.

Table 2-10 *Confederation Versus RR*

	Route Reflection (RR)	**Confederation (Conf)**	**Conf + RR**
IGP architecture	Ideally 1 IGP domain	Supports multiple IGP domains	Supports multiple IGP domains
Hierarchal topology	More flexible	Less flexible	Flexible within the sub-AS
Policy control	Less control	More control between domains	More control between domains
Control plane complexity	Moderate	The larger the sub-AS, the higher the control plane complexity	Low (optimized)
Optimal routing	May be effected	Maintained within and between sub-autonomous systems	May be effected
Integration with MPLS-TE	Simple	Simple within the same sub-AS, complex between sub-autonomous systems	Simple within the same sub-AS, complex between sub-autonomous systems

Again, there is no 100 percent definite answer. As a designer, you can decide which way to go based on the information and architecture you have and the goals that need to be achieved, taking the factors highlighted in Table 2-10 into consideration.

Further Reading

"BGP Case Studies": http://www.cisco.com/c/en/us/support/docs/ip/border-gateway-protocol-bgp/26634-bgp-toc.html

"Load Sharing with BGP in Single and Multihomed Environments: Sample Configurations": http://www.cisco.com

"Designing Scalable BGP Designs": http://www.ciscopress.com/articles/article.asp?p=1763921&seqNum=7

BGP Route Reflection - An Alternative to Full Mesh IBGP, RFC 2796: http://www.ietf.org

BGP Route Reflection: An Alternative to Full Mesh Internal BGP (IBGP), RFC 4456: http://www.ietf.org

BGP MULTI_EXIT_DISC (MED) Considerations, RFC 4451: http://www.ietf.org

Route Redistribution Design Considerations

Route redistribution refers to the process of exchanging or injecting routing information (typically routing prefixes) between two different routing domains or protocols. However, route redistribution between routing domains does not always refer to the route redistribution between two different routing protocols. For example, redistribution between two OSPF routing domains where the border router runs two different OSPF instances (process) represents the redistribution between two routing domains using the same routing protocol. Route redistribution is one of the most advanced routing design mechanisms commonly relied on by network designers to achieve certain design requirements, such as the following:

■ Merger and acquisition scenarios. Route redistribution can sometimes facilitate routing integration between different organizations.

■ In large-scale networks, such as global organizations, where BGP might be used across the WAN core and different IGP islands connect to the BGP core, full or selective route redistribution can facilitate route injection between these protocols and routing domains in some scenarios.

■ Route redistributions can also be used as an interim solution during the migration from one routing protocol to another.

Note   None of the preceding points can be considered as an absolute use case for route redistribution, because the use of route redistribution has no fixed rule or standard design. Therefore, network designers need to rely on experience when evaluating whether route redistribution needs to be used to meet the desired goal or whether other routing design mechanisms can be used instead, such as static routes.

Route redistribution can sometimes be as simple as adding a one-line command. However, the impact of it sometimes leads to major network outages because of routing loops or the black-holing of traffic, which can be introduced to the network if the redistribution was not planned and designed properly. That is why network designers must have a good understanding of the characteristics of the participating routing protocols and the exact aim of route redistribution. In general, route redistribution can be classified into two primary models, based on the number of redistribution boundary points.

■ Single redistribution boundary point

■ Multiple redistribution boundary points

Single Redistribution Boundary Point

This design model is the simplest and most basic route redistribution design model; it has minimal complexities, if any. Typically, the edge router between the routing domains can perform either one- or two-way route redistribution based on the desired goal without any concern, as depicted in Figure 2-60. This is based on the assumption that there is no other redistribution point between the same routing domains anywhere else across the entire network.

Figure 2-60   *Single Redistribution Boundary Point*

However, if the redistributing border router belongs to three routing domains, the route that is sourced from another routing protocol cannot be redistributed into a third routing protocol on the same router. For instance, in Figure 2-61, the route redistributed from EIGRP into OSPF cannot be redistributed again from OSFP into RIP. (This behavior is described as a *nontransitive attribute.*)

Figure 2-61   *Nontransitive Attribute of Route Redistribution*

Multiple Redistribution Boundary Points

Networks with two or more redistribution boundary points between routing domains require careful planning and design prior to applying the redistribution into the production network, because it can lead to a complete or partial network outage. The primary issues that can be introduced by this design are as follows:

- Routing loop
- Suboptimal routing
- Slower network convergence time

To optimize a network design that has two or more redistribution boundary points, network designers must consider the following aspects and how each may impact the network, along with the possible methods to address it based on the network architecture and the design requirements (for example optimal versus suboptimal routing):

- Metric transformation
- Administrative distance

Metric Transformation

Typically, each routing protocol has its own characteristic and algorithm to calculate network paths to determine the best path to use based on certain variables known as *metrics*. Because of the different metrics (measures) used by each protocol, the exchange of routing information between different routing protocols will lead to metric conversion so that the receiving routing protocol can understand this route, as well as be able to propagate this route throughout its routed domain. Therefore, specifying the metric at the redistribution point is important, so that the injected route can be understood and considered.

For instance, a common simple example is the redistribution from RIP into OSPF. RIP relies on hop counts to determine the best path, whereas OSPF considers link cost that is driven by the link bandwidth. Therefore, redistributing RIP into OSPF with a metric of 5 (five RIP hops) has no meaning to OSPF. Hence, OSPF assigns a default metric value to the redistributed external route. Furthermore, metric transformation can lead to routing loops if not planned and designed correctly when there are multiple redistribution points. For example, Figure 2-62 illustrates a scenario of mutual redistribution between RIP and OSPF over two border routers. Router A receives the RIP route from the RIP domain with a metric of 5, which means five hops. Router B will redistribute this route into the OSPF domain with the default redistribution metrics or any manually assigned metric. The issue in this scenario is that when the same route is redistributed back into the RIP domain with a lower metric (for example, 2), router A will see the same route with a better metric from the second border router. As a result, a routing loop will be formed based on this design (because of metric transformation).

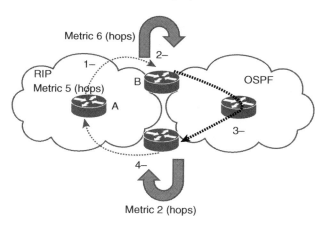

Figure 2-62 *Multipoint Routing Redistribution*

Hypothetically, this metric issue can be fixed by redistributing the same route back into the RIP domain with a higher metric value (for example, 7). However, this will not guarantee the prevention of routing loops because there is another influencing factor in this scenario, which is administrative distance (see the following section, "Administrative Distance," for more detail). Therefore, by using route filtering or a combination of route filtering and tagging to prevent the route from being re-injected back into the same domain, network designers can avoid route looping issues in this type of scenario.

Administrative Distance

Some routing protocols assign a different administrative distance (AD) value to the redistributed route by default (typically higher than the locally learned route) to give it preference over the external (redistributed route). However, this value can be changed, which enables network designers and engineers to alter the default behavior with regard to route and path section. From the route redistribution design point of view, AD can be a concern that requires special design considerations, especially when there are multiple points of redistribution with mutual route redistribution.

To resolve this issue, either route filtering or route tagging jointly with route filtering can be used to avoid re-injecting the redistributed (external) route back into the same originating routing domain. You can tune AD value to control the preferred route. However, this solution does not always provide the optimal path when there are multiple redistribution border routers performing mutual redistribution. If for any reason AD tuning is used, the network designer must be careful when considering this option, to ensure that routing protocols prefer internally learned prefixes over external ones (to avoid unexpected loops or suboptimal routing behavior).

Route Filtering Versus Route Tagging with Filtering

Routing filtering and route tagging combined with route filtering are common and powerful routing policy mechanisms that you can use in many routing scenarios to control route propagation and advertisement and to prevent routing loops in situations where multiple redistribution boundary points are exits with mutual route redistribution between routing domains. However, these mechanisms have some differences that network designers must be aware of, as summarized in Table 2-11.

Table 2-11   *Route Filtering Techniques Comparison*

Design Consideration	Route Filtering	Route Tagging with Filtering
Scalability	Low	High
Manageability	Complex	Simple
Multipoint redistribution loop prevention	Yes (complex)	Yes (simple)
Multipoint redistribution optimal routing	Yes (complex)	Yes (simple)
Flexibility	Limited	Flexible

Based on the simple comparison in Table 2-11, it is obvious that route filtering is more suitable for small and simple filtering and loop-prevention tasks. In contrast, route filtering associated with route tagging can support large-scale and dynamic networks to achieve more scalable and flexible routing policies across routing domains.

For example, in the scenario illustrated in Figure 2-63, there are two boundary redistribution points with mutual redistribution between EIGRP and IS-IS in both directions deployed at R1 and 2. In addition, R10 is injecting external EIGRP route for an organization to communicate with their business partner; this route will typically have by default an AD value of 170.

After this external route is injected into the EIGRP domain, internal users connected to the IS-IS domain started complaining that they could not reach any of the intended destinations located at their business partner network.

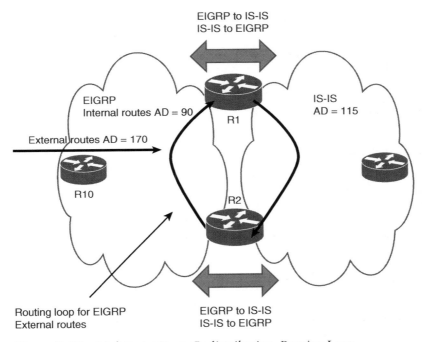

Figure 2-63 *Multipoint Route Redistribution: Routing Loop*

This design has the following technical concerns:

- Two redistribution boundary points

- Mutual redistribution at each boundary point from a high AD domain (external EIGRP in this case) to a lower AD domain

- Possibility of metric transformation (applicable to the external EIGRP route when redistributed back from IS-IS with better metrics)

As a result, a route looping will be formed with regard to the external EIGRP (between R1 and R2). With route filtering combined with tagging, as illustrated in Figure 2-64, both R1 and R2 can stop the re-injection of the redistributed external EIGRP route from IS-IS back into EIGRP again.

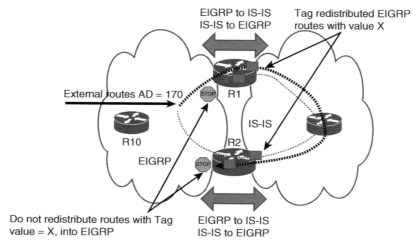

Figure 2-64 *Route Filtering with Route Tagging*

This is achieved by assigning a tag value to the EIGRP route when it is redistributed into IS-IS (at both R1 and R2). At the other redistribution boundary point (again R1 and R2) routes can be stopped from being redistributed into EIGRP again based on the assigned tag value. After you apply this filtering, the loop will be avoided, and path selection can be something like that depicted in Figure 2-65. With route tagging as in this example, network operators do not need to worry about managing and updating complicated access control lists (ACLs) to filter prefixes, because they can match the route tag at any node in the network and take action against it. Therefore, this offers simplified manageability and more flexible control.

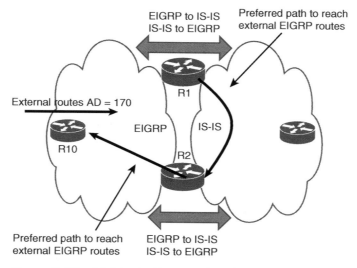

Figure 2-65 *Multipoint Route Redistribution: Routing Path After Filtering*

The optimal path, however, will not be guaranteed in this case unless another local filtering is applied to deny the EIGRP route from being installed in the local IS-IS routing table of the boundary routers. However, this must be performed only if optimal path is a priority requirement, to avoid impacting any potential loss of path redundancy. For instance, if R1. In Figure 2-65 filter the redistributed EIGRP external routes by "R2" from being installed into IS-IS local routing table (based on the assigned route tag by R2) optimal path can be achieved here. However if there is a LAN or hosts connected directly to R1, and R1 loses its connection to the EIGRP domain. In this case any device or network uses R1 as its gateway, will not be able to reach the EIGRP external routes (unless there is a default route, or a floating static route with higher AD, points to R2 within the IS-IS domain), in other words, to achieve optimal path, a second filtering layer is required at the ASBRs (R1 and R2 in this example) to filter the "redistributed" external EIGRP routes by the other IS-IS ASBR from being re-injected into IS-IS local routing table of the ASBR based on the route tag (refer to this sample example for more technical details,[5]). Also each ASBRs should use a default route (ideally static route, point to the other ASBR) to maintain redundancy to external prefixes in case of an ASBR link failure toward the EIGRP domain, as illustrated in Figure 2-66.

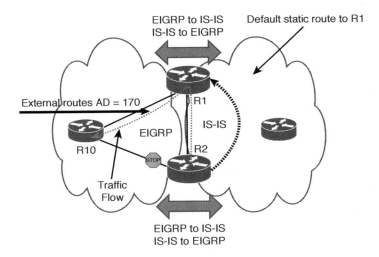

Figure 2-66 *Mutual Route Redistribution with Optimal Path—Failure Scenario*

From design point of view, achieving optimal network design does not mean optimal path must always be considered. For example, as a network designer you must look at the bigger picture using the "holistic approach" highlighted previously in chapter 1, in order to evaluate and decide, what are the possible options to achieve the design requirements optimally?, and what can be the implications of each design option?.

5. "Preventing route looping by using route tagging", https://supportforums.cisco.com/document/32191/preventing-route-looping-using-route-tagging

For instance in the scenario discussed above, if the IS-IS domain is receiving a default route from an internal node such as an Internet edge router. In this case, injecting a default route from the ASBRs (R1 and R2) most probably will break the Internet reachability for the IS-IS domain or any network directly connected to R1 and R2. Therefore, if both paths (over R1 and R2, with or without asymmetrical routing) technically satisfy the requirements for the communication between this organization and its partner network, in this case from network design perspective "optimal path" is not a requirement to achieve "optimal design". Because, optimal path can introduce design and operational complexity as well as it may break the internet reachability in this particular scenario.

Note Route tagging in some platforms require the IS-IS "wide metric" feature to be enabled in order for the route tagging to work properly, where migrating IS-IS routed domain from "narrow metrics to wide metrics" must be considered in this case[6].

Note If asymmetrical routing has a bad impact on the communications in the scenario above, between EIGRP and IS-IS domains, it can be avoided by tuning EIGRP metrics such as delay, when the IS-IS route redistributed into EIGRP to control path selection from EIGRP domain point of view and align it with the selected path from IS-IS side (to align both ingress and egress traffic flows).

Enterprise Routing Design Recommendations

This chapter discussed several concepts and approaches pertaining to Layer 3 control plane routing design. Table 2-12 summarizes the main Layer 3 routing design considerations and recommendations in a simplified way that you can use as a foundation to optimize the overall routing design.

Table 2-12 *IGP Design Considerations Summary*

Design Considerations	Design Recommendations
Scalability	Modular routing design (contain and optimize fault domains design). Reduce the number of prefixes (for example, suppress the advertisement of transport link IPs, routes summarization).
Resiliency and fast convergence	Reduce the number of prefixes (for example, suppress the advertisement of transport link IPs, routes summarization). Modular routing design. Fast detection, processing, and reaction to the failure. LFA can be used with link state in some scenarios. When possible, design in triangles rather than squares between the routed layers.

6. IETF RFC 3787, *Recommendations for Interoperable IP Networks using Intermediate System to Intermediate System IS-IS*

Table 2-12 *continued*

Design Considerations	Design Recommendations
Control and security	Enable routing authentication. Suppress peering with end-host VLANs (passive interface). Route filtering and tagging between routing domains.

Determining Which Routing Protocol to Use

In large-scale enterprise networks with different modules and many remote sites, selecting a routing protocol can be a real challenge. Therefore, network designers need to consider the answers to the following questions as a foundation for routing protocol selection:

- What is the underlying topology, and which protocol can scale to a larger number of prefixes and peers?

- Which routing protocol can be more flexible, taking into account the topology and future plans (for example, integrating with other routing domains)?

- Is fast convergence a requirement? If yes, which protocol can converge faster and at the same time offer stability enhancement mechanisms?

- Which protocol can utilize fewer hardware resources?

- Is the routing internal or external (different routing domains)?

- Which protocol can provide less operational complexity (for instance, easy to configure and troubleshoot)?

Although these questions are not the only ones, they cover the most important functional requirements that can be delivered by a routing protocol. Furthermore, there are some factors that you need to consider when selecting an IGP:

- Size of the network (for example, the number of L3 hops and expected future growth)

- Security requirements and the supported authentication type

- IT staff knowledge and experience

- Protocol's flexibility in modular network such as support of flexible route summarization techniques

Generally speaking, EIGRP tends to be more simple and scalable in hub-and-spoke topology and over networks with three or more hierarchical layers, whereas link-state routing protocols can perform better over flat networks when flooding domains and other factors discussed earlier in this book are tuned properly. In contrast, BGP is the preferred protocol to communicate between different routing domains (external), as summarized in Figure 2-67.

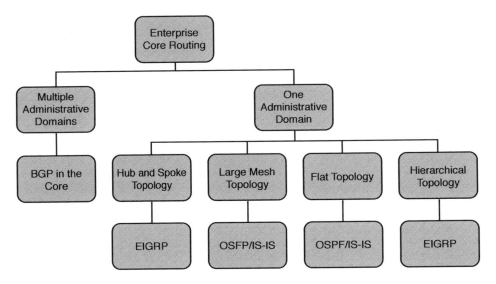

Figure 2-67   *Routing Protocol Selection Decision Tree*

Moreover, the decision tree depicted in Figure 2-68 highlights the routing protocol selection decision to migrate from one routing protocol to another based on the topology used. This tree is based on the assumption that you have the choice to select the preferred protocol.

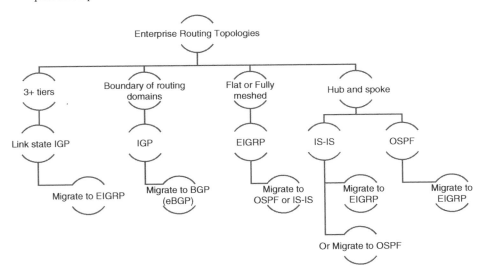

Figure 2-68   *Routing Protocol Migration Decision Tree*

Summary

For network designers and architects to provide a valid and feasible network design (including both Layer 2 and Layer 3), they must understand the characteristics of the nominated or used control protocols and how each behaves over the targeted physical network topology. This understanding will enable them to align the chosen protocol behavior with the business, functional, and application requirements, to achieve a successful business-driven network design. Also, considering any Layer 2 or Layer 3 design optimization technique such as route summarization may introduce new design concerns (during normal or failure scenarios) such as suboptimal routing. Therefore, the impact of any design optimization must be taken into consideration and analyzed, to ensure the selected optimization technique will not induce new issues or complexities to the network that could impact its primary business functions. Ideally the requirements of the business critical-applications and business priorities should drive design decisions.

Chapter 3

Enterprise Campus Architecture Design

A campus network is generally the portion of the enterprise network infrastructure that provides access to network communication services and resources to end users and devices that are spread over a single geographic location. It may be a single building or a group of buildings spread over an extended geographic area. Normally, the enterprise that owns the campus network usually owns the physical wires deployed in the campus. Therefore, network designers typically tend to design the campus portion of the enterprise network to be optimized for the fastest functional architecture that runs on high-speed physical infrastructure (1/10/40/100 Gbps). Moreover, enterprises can also have more than one campus block within the same geographic location, depending on the number of users within the location, business goals, and business nature. When possible, the design of modern converged enterprise campus networks should leverage the following common set of engineering and architectural principles [10]:

- Hierarchy

- Modularity

- Resiliency

Enterprise Campus: Hierarchical Design Models

The hierarchical network design model breaks the complex flat network into multiple smaller and more manageable networks. Each level or tier in the hierarchy is focused on a specific set of roles. This design approach offers network designers a high degree of flexibility to optimize and select the right network hardware, software, and features to perform specific roles for the different network layers.

A typical hierarchical enterprise campus network design includes the following three layers:

- **Core layer:** Provides optimal transport between sites and high-performance routing. Due the criticality of the core layer, the design principles of the core should provide an appropriate level of resilience that offers the ability to recover quickly and smoothly after any network failure event with the core block.

- **Distribution layer:** Provides policy-based connectivity and boundary control between the access and core layers.

- **Access layer:** Provides workgroup/user access to the network.

The two primary and common hierarchical design architectures of enterprise campus networks are the three-tier and two-tier layers models.

Three-Tier Model

This design model, illustrated in Figure 3-1, is typically used in large enterprise campus networks, which are constructed of multiple functional distribution layer blocks.

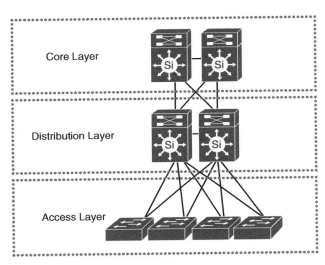

Figure 3-1   *Three-Tier Network Design Model*

Two-Tier Model

This design model, illustrated in Figure 3-2, is more suitable for small to medium-size campus networks (ideally not more than three functional disruption blocks to be inter-connected), where the core and distribution functions can be combined into one layer, also known as *collapsed core-distribution architecture.*

Note   The term *functional distribution block* refers to any block in the campus network that has its own distribution layer such as user access block, WAN block, or data center block.

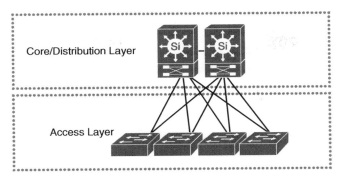

Figure 3-2 *Two-Tier Network Design Model*

Enterprise Campus: Modularity

By applying the hierarchical design model across the multiple functional blocks of the enterprise campus network, a more scalable and modular campus architecture (commonly referred to as *building blocks*) can be achieved. This modular enterprise campus architecture offers a high level of design flexibility that makes it more responsive to evolving business needs. As highlighted earlier in this book, modular design makes the network more scalable and manageable by promoting fault domain isolation and more deterministic traffic patterns. As a result, network changes and upgrades can be performed in a controlled and staged manner, allowing greater stability and flexibility in the maintenance and operation of the campus network. Figure 3-3 depicts a typical campus network along with the different functional modules as part of the modular enterprise architecture design.

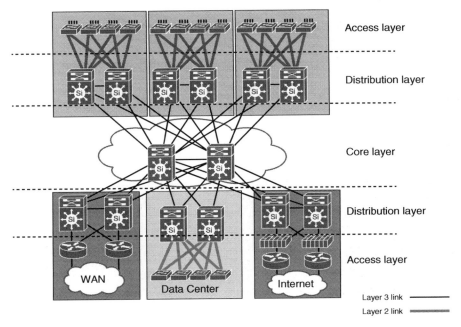

Figure 3-3 *Typical Modular Enterprise Campus Architecture*

> **Note**   Within each functional block of the modular enterprise architecture, to achieve the optimal structured design, you should apply the same hierarchal network design principle.

When Is the Core Block Required?

A separate core provides the capability to scale the size of the enterprise campus network in a structured fashion that minimizes overall complexity when the size of the network grows (multiple campus distribution blocks) and the number of interconnections tying the multiple enterprise campus functional blocks increases significantly (typically leads to physical and control plane complexities), as exemplified in Figure 3-4. In other words, not every design requires a separate core.

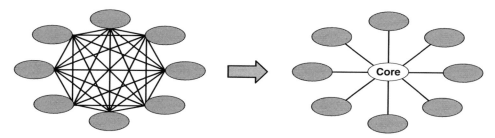

Figure 3-4   *Network Connectivity Without Core Versus With Core*

Besides the previously mentioned technical considerations, as a network designer you should always aim to provide a business-driven network design with a future vision based on the principle "build today with tomorrow in mind." Taking this principle into account, one of the primary influencing factors with regard to selecting two-tier versus three-tier network architecture is the type of site or network (remote branch, regional HQ, secondary or main campus), which will help you, to a certain extent, identify the nature of the site and its potential future scale (from a network design point of view). For instance, it is rare that a typical (small to medium-size) remote site requires a three-tier architecture even when future growth is considered. In contrast, a regional HQ site or a secondary campus network of an enterprise can have a high potential to grow significantly in size (number of users and number of distribution blocks). Therefore, a core layer or three-tier architecture can be a feasible option here. This is from a hypothetical design point of view; the actual answer must always align with the business goals and plans (for example if the enterprise is planning to merge or acquire any new business); it can also derive from the projected percentage of the yearly organic business growth. Again, as a network designer, you can decide based on the current size and the projected growth, taking into account the type of the targeted site, business nature, priorities, and design constraints such as cost. For example, if the business priority is to expand without spending extra on buying additional network hardware platforms (reduce capital expenditure [capex]), in this case the cost savings is going to be a design constraint and a business priority, and the network designer in this type of scenario must find an alternative design solution such as the collapsed architecture (two-tier model) even though technically it might not be the optimal solution.

That being said, sometimes (when possible) you need to gain the support from the business first, to drive the design in the right direction. By highlighting and explaining to the IT leaders of the organization the extra cost and challenges of operating a network that was either not designed optimally with regard to their projected business expansion plans, or the network was designed for yesterday's requirements and it will not be capable enough to handle today's requirements. Consequently, this may help to influence the business decision as the additional cost needed to consider three-tier architecture will be justified to the business in this case (long-term operating expenditure [opex] versus short-term capex). In other words, sometimes businesses focus only on the solution capex without considering that opex can probably cost them more on the long run if the solution was not architected and designed properly to meet their current and future requirements

Access-Distribution Design Model

Chapter 2, "Enterprise Layer 2 and Layer 3 Design," discussed different Layer 2 design models that are applicable to the campus LAN design, in particular to the access-distribution layer. Technically, each design model has different design attributes. Therefore, network designers must understand the characteristics of each design model to be able to choose and apply the most feasible model based on the design requirements.

The list that follows describes the three primary and common design models for the access layer to distribution layer connectivity. The main difference between these design models is where the Layer 2 and Layer 3 boundary is placed and how and where Layer 3 gateway services are handled:

- **Classical multitier STP based:** This model is the classical or traditional way of connecting access to the distribution layer in the campus network. In this model, the access layer switches usually operate in Layer 2 mode only, and the distribution layer switches operate in Layer 2 and Layer 3 modes. As discussed earlier in this book, the primary limitation of this design model is the reliance on Spanning Tree Protocol (STP) and First Hop Redundancy Protocol (FHRP). For more information, see Chapter 2.

- **Routed access:** In this design model, access layer switches act as Layer 3 routing nodes, providing both Layer 2 and Layer 3 forwarding. In other words, the demarcation point between Layer 2 and Layer 3 is moved from the distribution layer to the access layer. Based on that, the Layer 2 trunk links from access to distribution are replaced with Layer 3 point-to-point routed links, as illustrated in Figure 3-5.

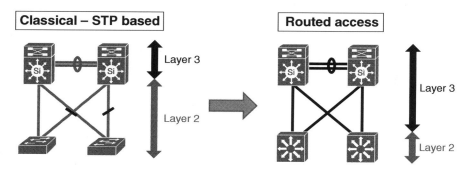

Figure 3-5 *Routed Access Layer*

The routed access design model has several advantages compared to the multitier classical STP-based access-distribution design model, including the following:

■ Simpler and easier to troubleshoot, you can use a standard routing troubleshooting techniques, and you will have fewer protocols to manage and troubleshoot across the network

■ Eliminate the reliance on STP and FHRP and rely on the equal-cost multipath (EMCP) of the used routing protocol to utilize all the available uplinks, which can increase the overall network performance

■ Minimize convergence time during a link or node failure

Note The routed access design model does not support spanning Layer 2 VLANs across multiple access switches, and this might not be a good choice for some networks. Although expanding Layer 2 over routed infrastructure is achievable using other different overlay technologies, this might add complexity to the design, or the required features may not be supported with the existing platforms for the access or distribution layer switches.

■ **Switch clustering:** As discussed in Chapter 2, this design model provides the simplest and most flexible design compared to the other models discussed already. As illustrated in Figure 3-6, by introducing the switch clustering concept across the different functional modules of the enterprise campus architecture, network designers can simplify and enhance the design to a large degree. This offers a higher level of node and path resiliency, along with significantly optimized network convergence time.

The left side of Figure 3-6 represents the physical connectivity, and the right side shows the logical view of this architecture, which is based on the switch clustering design model across the entire modular campus network.

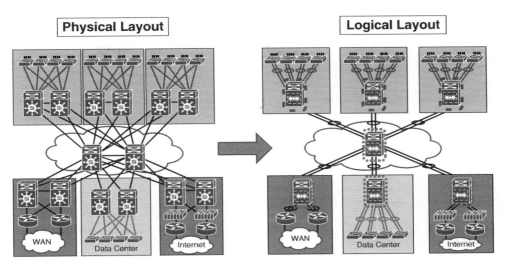

Figure 3-6 *Switch Clustering Concept*

Table 3-1 compares the different access-distribution connectivity design models from different design angles.

Table 3-1 *Comparing Access-Distribution Connectivity Models*

	Multitier STP Based	**Routed Access**	**Switch Clustering**
Design flexibility	Limited (topology dependent)	Limited (For example, spanning Layer 2 over different access switches requires an overlay technology)	Flexible
Scalability	Supports scale up and limited scale out (topology dependent)	Supports both scale up and scale out	Scale up and limited scale out (typically limited to 2 distribution switches per cluster)
Layer 3 gateway services	Distribution layer (FHRP based)	Access layer (Layer 3 routing based)	Distribution layer (may or may not require FHRP*)
Multichassis link aggregation (mLAG)	Not supported	Not supported (instead relies on Layer 3 ECMP)	Supported

Table 3-1 *continued*

	Multitier STP Based	Routed Access	Switch Clustering
Access-to-distribution convergence time	Dependent on STP and FHRP timers (relatively slow)	Interior Gateway Protocol (IGP) dependent, commonly fast	Fast
Operational complexity	Complex (multiple control protocols to deal with [for example, STP, FHRP])	Moderate (Advanced routing design expertise may be required)	Simple

* Some switch clustering technologies, such as Cisco Nexus vPC, use FHRP (Hot Standby Router Protocol [HSRP]). However, from a forwarding plane point of view, both upstream switches (vPC peers) do forward traffic, unlike the classical behavior, which is based on active-standby.

Note   All the design models discussed in this section are valid design options. However, the design choice must be driven by the requirements and design constraints, such as cost, which can influence which option you can select. For example, an access switch with Layer 3 capabilities is more expensive than a switch with Layer 2 capabilities only. This factor will be a valid tiebreaker if cost is a concern from the perspective of business requirements.

Enterprise Campus: Layer 3 Routing Design Considerations

The hierarchal enterprise campus architecture can facilitate achieving more structured hierarchal Layer 3 routing design, which is the key to achieving routing scalability in large networks. This reduces, to a large extent, the number of Layer 3 nodes and adjacencies in any given routing domain within each tier of the hierarchal enterprise campus network [27].

In a typical hierarchal enterprise campus network, the distribution block (layer) is considered the demarcation point between Layer 2 and Layer 3 domains. This is where Layer 3 uplinks participate in the campus core routing, using either an interior routing protocol (IGP) or Border Gateway Protocol (BGP), which can help to interconnect multiple campus distribution blocks together for end-to-end IP connectivity.

By contrast, with the routed access design model, Layer 3 routing is extended to the access layer switches. Consequently, the selection of the routing protocol is important for a redundant and reliable IP/routing reachability within the campus, considering scalability and the ability of the network to grow with minimal changes and impact to the network and routing design. All the Layer 3 routing design considerations discussed in previous chapters must be considered when applying any routing protocol to a campus LAN. Figure 3-7 illustrates a typical ideal routing design that aligns the IGP design (Open Shortest Path First [OSPF]) with the enterprise campus hierarchal architecture, along with the different functional modules.

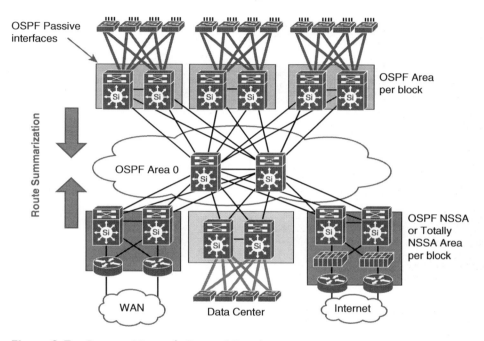

Figure 3-7   *Campus Network: Layer 3 Routing*

> **Note**   In the preceding example, the data center and other modules coexist within the enterprise campus to illustrate a generic IGP design over multiple modules interconnected over one core infrastructure (typical large campus design). However, in some designs, the data center is interconnected over a WAN or dedicated fiber links with the campus network. Also, the other blocks, such as Internet and WAN blocks, might be coresident at the data center's physical location as well. In this case, you can use the same IGP design concept, and you can treat the WAN interconnect as an external link, as illustrated in Figure 3-8. Also, the enterprise core routing (that is, OSPF backbone area) can be extended over the WAN. In other words, all the concepts of IGP and BGP design discussed earlier in this book have to be considered to make the right design decision. (There is no single standard design that you can use in different scenarios.)

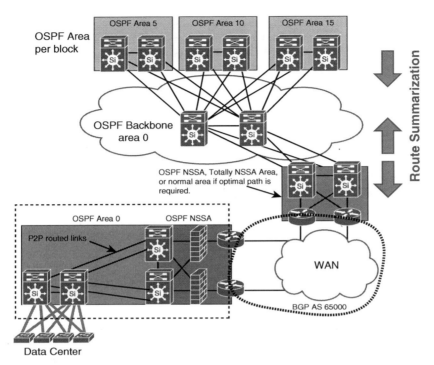

Figure 3-8   *Campus Network: Layer 3 Design with WAN Core*

EIGRP Versus Link State as a Campus IGP

As discussed in Chapter 2, each protocol has its own characteristics, especially when applied to different network topologies. For example, Enhanced Interior Gateway Routing Protocol (EIGRP) offers a more flexible, scalable, and easier-to-control design over "hub-and-spoke" topology compared to link state. In addition, although EIGRP is considered more flexible on multitiered network topologies such as three-tier campus architecture, link-state routing protocols have still proven to be powerful, scalable, and reliable protocols in this type of network, especially OSPF, which is one of the most commonly implemented protocols used in campus networks. Furthermore, in large-scale campus networks, if EIGRP is not designed properly with regard to information hiding and EIGRP query scope containment (discussed in Chapter 2), any topology change may lead to a large floods of EIGRP queries. In addition, the network will be more prone to EIGRP stuck-in-active (SIA) impacts, such as a longer time to converge following a failure event and as a SIA timer puts an upper boundary on convergence times.

Consequently, each design has its own requirements, priorities, and constraints; and network designers must evaluate the design scenario and balance between the technical (protocol characteristics) and nontechnical (business priorities, future plans, staff knowledge, and so on) aspects when making design decisions.

Table 3-2 provides a summarized comparison between the two common and primary IGPs (algorithms) used in large-scale hierarchal enterprise campus networks.

Table 3-2   *Link State Versus EIGRP in the Campus*

Design Consideration	EIGRP (DUAL)	Link State (Dijkstra)
Architecture flexibility	High (natively supports multitier architectures with routes summarization)	High, with limitations (The more tiers the network has, the less flexible the design can be.)
Scalability	High	High
Convergence time (protocol level)*	Fast (ideally with route summarization)	Fast (ideally with topology hiding, route summarization, and timers tuning)
MPLS-TE support	No	Yes

* This design aspect is covered in more detail in Chapter 9, "Network High-Availability Design."

Enterprise Campus Network Virtualization

Virtualization in IT generally refers to the concept of having two or more instances of a system component or function such as operating system, network services, control plane, or applications. Typically, these instances are represented in a logical virtualized manner instead of being physical.

Virtualization can generally be classified into two primary models:

- **Many to one:** In this model, multiple physical resources appear as a single logical unit. The classical example of many-to-one virtualization is the switch clustering concept discussed earlier. Also, firewall clustering, and FHRP with a single virtual IP (VIP) that front ends a pair of physical upstream network nodes (switches or routers) can be considered as other examples of the many-to-one virtualization model.

- **One to many:** In this model, a single physical resource can appear as many logical units, such as virtualizing an x86 server, where the software (hypervisor) hosts multiple virtual machines (VMs) to run on the same physical server. The concept of network function virtualization (NFV) can also be considered as a one-to-many system virtualization model.

Drivers to Consider Network Virtualization

To meet the current expectations of business and IT leaders, a more responsive IT infrastructure is required. Therefore, network infrastructures need to move from the classical architecture (that is, based on providing basic interconnectivity between different siloed departments within the enterprise network) into a more flexible, resilient, and adaptive architecture that can support and accelerate business initiatives and remove inefficiencies. The IT and the network infrastructure will become like a service delivery business unit that can quickly adopt and deliver services. In other words, it will become a "business enabler." This is why network virtualization is considered one of the primary principles that enables IT infrastructures to become more dynamic and responsive to the new and the rapidly changing requirements of today's enterprises.

The following are the primary drivers of modern enterprise networks, which can motivate enterprise businesses to adopt the concept of network virtualization:

- **Cost efficiency and design flexibility:** Network virtualization provides a level of abstraction from the physical network infrastructure that can offer cost-effective network designs along with a higher degree of design flexibility, where multiple logical networks can be provisioned over one common physical infrastructure. This ultimately will lead to lower capex because of the reduction in device complexity and number of devices. Similarly, it will open lower because the operations team will have fewer devices to manage.

- **Support a simplified and flexible integrated security:** Network virtualization also promotes flexible security designs by allowing the use of separate security policies per logical or vitalized entity, where users' groups and services can be logically separated.

- **Design and operational simplicity:** Network virtualization simplifies the design and provision of path and traffic isolation per application, group, service, and various other logical instances that require end-to-end path isolation.

Note   It is important that network designers understand the drivers toward adopting network virtualization from a business point of view, along with the strengths and weaknesses of each design model. This ensures that when a network virtualization concept is considered on a given area within the network or across the entire network, it will deliver the promised value (and not to be used only because it is easy to implement or it is an innovative approach). As discussed earlier in this book, the design that does not address the business's functional requirements is considered a poor design; consider the design principle "no gold plating" discussed in Chapter 1, "Network Design Requirements: Analysis and Design Principles."

Note   One of the main concerns about network virtualization is the concept of fate sharing, because any failure in the physical network can lead to a failure of multiple virtual networks running over the same physical infrastructure. Therefore, when the network virtualization concept is used, ideally a reliable and highly available network design should be considered as well. Besides the concerns about virtual network availability, there is always a concern about network virtualization (multitenant environment) where multiple virtual networks (VNs) operate over a single physical network infrastructure and each VN probably has different traffic requirements (different applications and utilization patterns). Therefore, there is a higher potential of having traffic congestion and degraded application quality and user experience if there is no efficient planning with regard to the available bandwidth, number of VNs, traffic volume per VN, applications in use, and the characteristics of the applications. In other words, if there is no adequate bandwidth available and quality of service (QoS) policies to optimize and control traffic behaviors, one VN may overutilize the available bandwidth of the underlying physical network infrastructure. This will usually lead to traffic congestion because other VNs are using the same underlying physical network infrastructure, resulting in what is known as *fate sharing*.

This section covers the primary network virtualization technologies and techniques that you can use to serve different requirements by highlighting the pros and cons of each technology and design approach. This can help network designers (CCDE candidates) to select the best suitable design after identifying and evaluating the different design requirements (business and functional requirements). This section primarily focuses on network virtualization over the enterprise campus network. Chapter 4, "Enterprise Edge Architecture Design," expands on this topic to cover network virtualization design options and considerations over the WAN.

Network Virtualization Design Elements

As illustrated in Figure 3-9, the main elements in an end-to end network virtualization design are as follows:

- **Edge control:** This element represents the network access point. Typically, it is a host or end-user access (wired, wireless, or virtual private network [VPN]) to the network where the identification (authentication) for physical to logical network mapping can occur. For example, a contracting employee might be assigned to VLAN X, whereas internal staff is assigned to VLAN Y.

- **Transport virtualization:** This element represents the transport path that will carry different virtualized networks over one common physical infrastructure, such as an overlay technology like a generic routing encapsulation (GRE) tunnel. The terms *path isolation* and *path separation* are commonly used to refer to transport virtualization. Therefore, these terms are used interchangeably throughout this book.

- **Services virtualization:** This element represents the extension of the network virtualization concept to the services edge, which can be shared services among different logically isolated groups, such as an Internet link or a file server located in the data center that must be accessed by only one logical group (business unit).

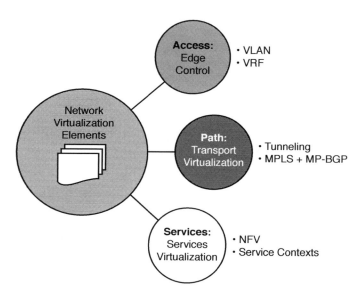

Figure 3-9 *Network Virtualization Elements*

Enterprise Network Virtualization Deployment Models

Now that you know the different elements that, individually or collectively, can be considered as the foundational elements to create network virtualization within the enterprise network architecture, this section covers how you can use these elements with different design techniques and approaches to deploy network virtualization across the enterprise campus. This section also compares these different design techniques and approaches.

Network virtualization can be categorized into the following three primary models, each of which has different techniques that can serve different requirements:

■ Device virtualization

■ Path isolation

■ Services virtualization

Moreover, you can use the techniques of the different models individually to serve certain requirements or combined together to achieve one cohesive end-to-end network virtualization solution. Therefore, network designers must have a good understanding of the different techniques and approaches, along with their attributes, to select the most suitable virtualization technologies and design approach for delivering value to the business.

Device Virtualization

Also known as *device partitioning*, device virtualization represents the ability to virtualize the data plane, control plane, or both, in a certain network node, such as a switch or a router. Using device level virtualization by itself will help to achieve separation at Layer 2, Layer 3, or both, on a local device level. The following are the primary techniques used to achieve device level network virtualization:

■ **Virtual LAN (VLAN):** VLAN is the most common Layer 2 network virtualization technique. It is used in every network where one single switch can be divided into multiple logical Layer 2 broadcast domains that are virtually separated from other VLANs. You can use VLANs at the network edge to place an endpoint into a certain virtual network. Each VLAN has its own MAC forwarding table and spanning-tree instance (Per-VLAN Spanning Tree [PVST]).

■ **Virtual routing and forwarding (VRF):** VRFs are conceptually similar to VLANs, but from a control plane and forwarding perspective on a Layer 3 device. VRFs can be combined with VLANs to provide a virtualized Layer 3 gateway service per VLAN. As illustrated in Figure 3-10, each VLAN over a 802.1Q trunk can be mapped to a different subinterface that is assigned to a unique VRF, where each VRF maintains its own forwarding and routing instance and potentially leverages different VRF-aware routing protocols (for example, OSPF or EIGRP instance per VRF).

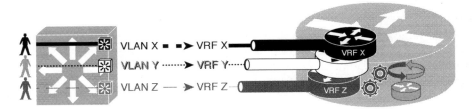

Figure 3-10 *Virtual Routing and Forwarding*

Path Isolation

Path isolation refers to the concept of maintaining end-to-end logical path transport separation across the network. The end-to-end path separation can be achieved using the following main design approaches:

■ **Hop by hop:** This design approach, as illustrated in Figure 3-11, is based on deploying end-to-end (VLANs + 802.1Q trunk links + VRFs) per device in the traffic path. This design approach offers a simple and reliable path separation solution. However, for large-scale dynamic networks (large number of virtualized networks), it will be a complicated solution to manage. This complexity is associated with design scalability limitation.

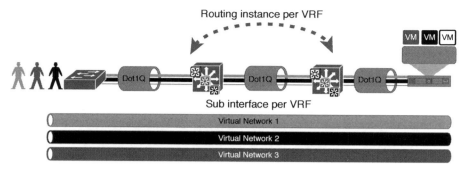

Figure 3-11   *Hop-by-Hop Path Virtualization*

- **Multihop:** This approach is based on using tunneling and other overlay technologies to provide end-to-end path isolation and carry the virtualized traffic across the network. The most common proven methods include the following:

  - **Tunneling:** Tunneling, such as GRE or multipoint GRE (mGRE) (dynamic multipoint VPN [DMVPN]), will eliminate the reliance on deploying end-to-end VRFs and 802.1Q trunks across the enterprise network, because the vitalized traffic will be carried over the tunnel. This method offers a higher level of scalability as compared to the previous option and with simpler operation to some extent. This design is ideally suitable for scenarios where only a part of the network needs to have path isolation across the network.

    However, for large-scale networks with multiple logical groups or business units to be separated across the enterprise, the tunneling approach can add complexity to the design and operations. For example, if the design requires path isolation for a group of users across two "distribution blocks," tunneling can be a good fit, combined with VRFs. However, mGRE can provide the same transport and path isolation goal for larger networks with lower design and operational complexities. (See the section "WAN Virtualization," in Chapter 4 for a detailed comparison between the different path separation approaches over different types of tunneling mechanisms.)

  - **MPLS VPN:** By converting the enterprise to be like a service provider type of network, where the core is Multiprotocol Label Switching (MPLS) enabled and the distribution layer switches to act as provider edge (PE) devices. As in service provider networks, each PE (distribution block) will exchange VPN routing over MP-BGP sessions, as shown in Figure 3-12. (The route reflector [RR] concept can be introduced, as well, to reduce the complexity of full-mesh MP-BGP peering sessions.)

    Furthermore, L2VPN capabilities can be introduced in this architecture, such as Ethernet over MPLS (EoMPLS), to provide extended Layer 2 communications across different distribution blocks if required. With this design approach, the end-to-end virtualization and traffic separation can be simplified to a very large extent with a high degree of scalability. (All the MPLS design considerations and concepts covered in the Service Provider part—Chapter 5, "Service Provider Network Architecture Design," and Chapter 6, "Service Provider MPLS VPN Services Design," —in this book are applicable if this design model is adopted by the enterprise.)

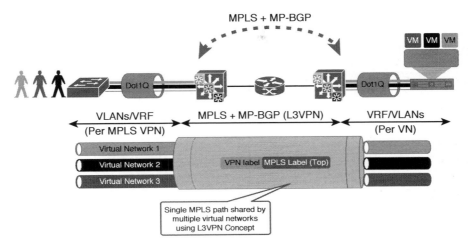

Figure 3-12 *MPLS VPN-Based Path Virtualization*

Figure 3-13 illustrates a summary of the different enterprise campus network's virtualization design techniques.

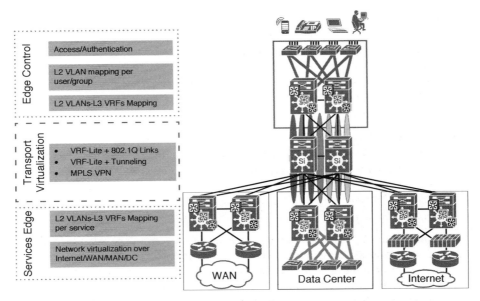

Figure 3-13 *Enterprise Campus Network Virtualization Techniques*

As mentioned earlier in this section, it is important for network designers to understand the differences between the various network virtualization techniques. Table 3-3 compares these different techniques in a summarized way from different design angles.

Table 3-3   *Network Virtualization Techniques Comparison*

	End to End (VLAN + 802.1Q + VRF)	VLANs + VRFs + GRE Tunnels	VLANs + VRFs + mGRE Tunnels	MPLS Core with MP-BGP
Scalability	Low	Low	Moderate	High
Operational complexity	High	Moderate	Moderate	Moderate to high
Design flexibility	Low	Moderate	Moderate	High
Architecture	Per hop end-to-end virtualization	P2P (multihop end-to-end virtualization)	P2MP (multihop end-to-end virtualization)	MPLS-L3VPN-based virtualization
Operation staff routing expertise	Basic	Medium	Medium	Advanced
Ideal for	Limited NV scope in terms of size and complexity	Interconnecting specific blocks with NV or as an interim solution	Medium to large overlaid NV design	Large to very large (global scale) end-to-end NV design

Service Virtualization

One of the main goals of virtualization is to separate services access into different logical groups, such as user groups or departments. However, in some scenarios, there may be a mix of these services in term of service access, in which some of these services must only be accessed by a certain group and others are to be shared among different groups, such as a file server in the data center or Internet access, as shown in Figure 3-14.

Therefore, in scenarios like this where service access has to be separated per virtual network or group, the concept of network virtualization must be extended to the services access edge, such as a server with multiple VMs or an Internet edge router with single or multiple Internet links.

Note   The virtualization of a network can be extended to other network service appliances, such as firewalls. For instance, you can have a separate virtual firewall per virtual network, to facilitate access control between the virtualized user network and the virtualized services and workload, as shown in Figure 3-15. The virtualization of network services appliance can be considered as a "one-to-many" network device level virtualization.

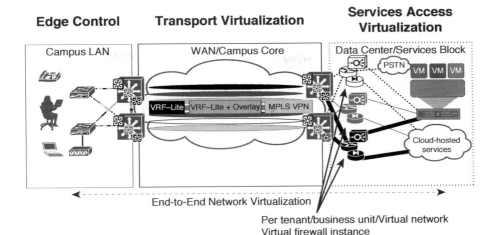

Figure 3-14   *End-to-end Path and Services Virtualization*

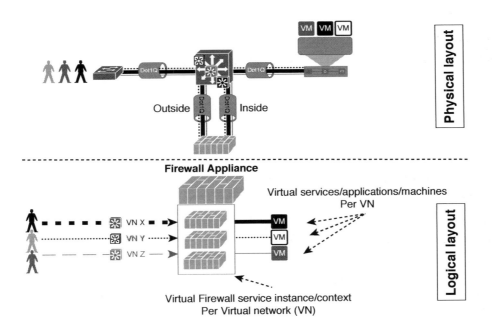

Figure 3-15   *Firewall Virtual Instances*

Furthermore, in multitenant network environments, multiple security contexts offer a flexible and cost-effective solution for enterprises (and for service providers). This approach enables network operators to partition a single pair of redundant firewalls or a single firewall cluster into multiple virtual firewall instances per business unit or tenant. Each tenant can then deploy and manage its own security polices and service access, which are virtually separated. This approach also allows controlled intertenant communication. For example, in a typical multitenant enterprise campus network environment with MPLS VPN (L3VPN) enabled at the core, traffic between different tenants (VPNs) is normally routed via a firewalling service for security and control (who can access what), as illustrated in Figure 3-16.

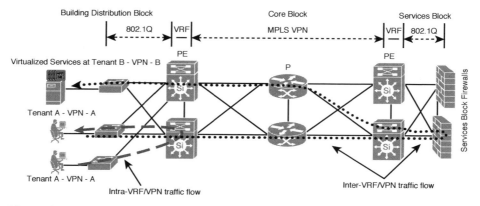

Figure 3-16   *Intertenant Services Access Traffic Flow*

Figure 3-17 zooms in on the firewall services contexts to show a more detailed view (logical/virtualized view) of the traffic flow between the different tenants/VPNs (A and B), where each tenant has its own virtual firewall service instance located at the services block (or at the data center) of the enterprise campus network.

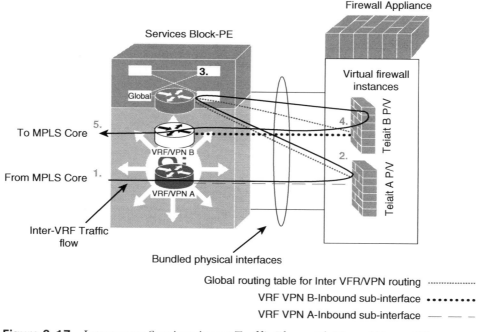

Figure 3-17   *Intertenant Services Access Traffic Flow with Virtual Firewall Instances*

In addition, the following are the common techniques that facilitate accessing shared applications and network services in multitenant environments:

- **VRF-Aware Network Address Translation (NAT):** One of the common requirements in today's multitenant environments with network and service' virtualization enabled, is to provide each virtual (tenant) network the ability to access certain services (shared services) either hosted on premise (such as at the emperies data center or services block) or hosted externally (in a public cloud). Also, providing Internet access to the different tenants (virtual) networks, is a common example of today's multitenant network requirements. To maintain traffic separation between the different tenants (virtual networks) where private IP address overlapping is a common attribute in this type of environment, NAT is considered one of the common and cost-effective solutions to provide NAT per tenant without compromising path separation requirements between the different tenants' networks (virtual networks). When NAT is combined with different virtual network instances (VRFs), it is commonly referred to as *VRF-Aware NAT*, as shown in Figure 3-18.

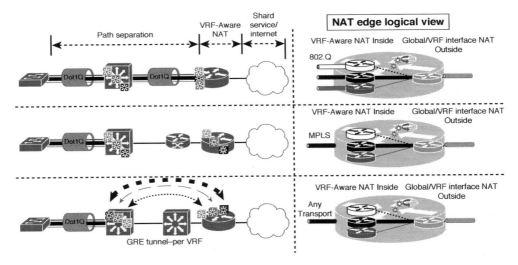

Figure 3-18 *VRF-Aware NAT*

Note   *VRF-aware service infrastructure* (VASI) refers to the ability of an infrastructure or a network node, such as a router, to facilitate the application of features and management services (such as encryption and NAT) between VRFs internally within the same node, using virtual interfaces. For two VRFs to communicate internally within a network node (router), a VASI virtual interface pair can be configured. Each interface in this pair must be associated with a different VRF so that those two virtual interfaces can be logically wired,[1] as illustrated in Figure 3-19. This capability is available in some high-end Cisco routers.

---

1. "Configuring VRF-Aware Service Infrastructure," http://www.cisco.com/c/en/us/td/docs/ios_xr_sw/iosxr_r3-8/vfw/ configuration/guide/vfc38/vfc38vas.pdf

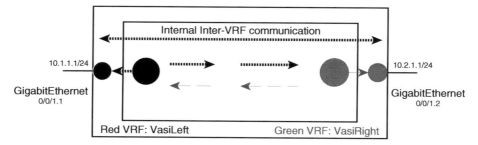

Figure 3-19   *VRF-aware Services Infrastructure*

- **Network function virtualization (NFV):** The concept of NFV is based on virtualizing network functions that typically require a dedicated physical node, appliances, or interfaces. In other words, NFV can potentially take any network function typically residing in purpose-built hardware and abstract it from that hardware. As depicted in Figure 3-20, this concept offers businesses several benefits, including the following:

  - Reduce the total cost of ownership (TCO) by reducing the required number and diversity of specialized appliances

  - Reduce operational cost (for example, less power and space)

  - Offer a cost-effective capital investment

  - Reduce the level of complexity of integration and network operations

  - Reduce time to market for the business by offering the ability to enable specialized network services (Especially in multitenant where a separate network function/service per tenant can be provisioned faster)

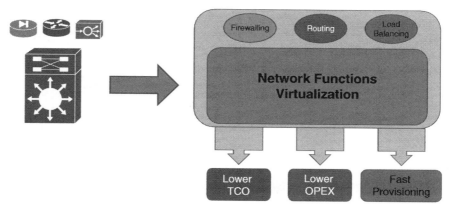

Figure 3-20   *NFV Benefits*

This concept helps businesses to adopt and deploy new services quickly (faster time to market), and is consequently considered a business innovation enabler. This is simply because purpose-built hardware functionalities have now been virtualized, and it is a matter of service enablement rather than relying on new hardware (along with infrastructure integration complexities).

Note The concept of NFV is commonly adopted by service provider networks nowadays. Nonetheless, this concept is applicable and usable in enterprise networks and enterprise data center networks that want to gains its benefits and flexibility.

Note In large-scale networks with a very high volume of traffic (typically carrier grade), hardware resource utilization and limits must be considered.

Summary

The enterprise campus is one of the vital parts of the modular enterprise network. It is the medium that connects the end users and the different types of endpoints such as printers, video endpoints, and wireless access points to the enterprise network. Therefore, having the right structure and design layout that meets current and future requirements is critical, including the physical infrastructure layout, Layer 2, and Layer 3 designs. To achieve a scalable and flexible campus design, you should ideally base it on hierarchal and modular design principles that optimize the overall design architecture in terms of fault isolation, simplicity, and network convergence time. It should also offer a desirable level of flexibility to integrate other networks and new services and to grow in size.

However, the concept of network virtualization helps enterprises to utilize the same underlying physical infrastructure while maintaining access, and path and services access isolation, to meet certain business goals or functional security requirements. As a result, enterprises can lower capex and opex and reduce the time and effort required to provision a new service or a new logical network. However, the network designer must consider the different network virtualization design options, along with the strengths and weaknesses of each, to deploy the suitable network virtualization technique that meets current and future needs. These needs must take into account the different variables and constraints, such as staff knowledge and the hardware platform supported features and capabilities.

Further Reading

"Borderless Campus 1.0 Design Guide," http://www.cisco.com

"Enterprise Campus 3.0 Architecture: Overview and Framework," http://www.cisco.com

"Cisco Wired LAN, Cisco Validated Design," http://www.cisco.com

"Network Virtualization Solutions, Design Guides," http://www.cisco.com

"Network Services Virtualization," http://www.cisco.com

Chapter 4

Enterprise Edge Architecture Design

Enterprise edge refers to the various enterprise network modules and components that facilitate efficient and secure communication between the different enterprise locations, including campuses, data centers, third-party external connections, remote sites, business partners, mobile users, and the Internet. Typically, enterprise edge can be divided into two primary modules as part of the modular enterprise architecture:

- WAN module
- Internet module

This chapter covers different design options and considerations for the WAN and Internet modules.

Note The WAN and Internet enterprise modules may vary from design to design in terms of naming, size, and functionality. For instance, some designers combine the functions of these two modules into one module. In spite of this, the overall design principles and goals are similar to a large extent.

Enterprise WAN Module

The WAN module is the gateway of the enterprise network to the other remote sites (typical remote branches) and regional sites. As part of the modular enterprise network architecture, this module aggregates and houses all the WAN or MAN edge devices that extend the enterprise network to the remote sites using different transport media types and technologies. Enterprises require a WAN design that offers a common resource access experience to the remote sites, along with sufficient performance and reliability.

As organizations move into multinational or global business markets, they require a flexible network design that reduces the time needed to add new remote sites. They also require the deployment of new technologies that support emerging business applications and communications. In addition, it is becoming a common business requirement for users to have a consistent experience when connecting to the enterprise's online resources (such as applications and files), whether they are at the company headquarters or at a remote site; therefore, the WAN design should be flexible enough to accommodate different business application requirements. It should also offer the ability to scale bandwidth or to add new sites or resilient links without any major change to the overall design architecture.

From an enterprise architectural point of view, the primary WAN module can be either coresident physically within the data center block of the enterprise or at the primary enterprise campus. In both cases, there is "no difference" for the WAN module architecture itself, because the aggregation layer of the WAN module will be connected to the core layer of either the enterprise campus or data center.

This chapter covers and compares the different design options that you can use to provide the most suitable WAN design to meet various business, functional, and technical requirements.

WAN Transports: Overview

One of the primary concerns of enterprise IT leaders is to manage costs and maintain reliable WAN infrastructures to meet their business goals. Furthermore, businesses are realizing that avoiding the complexities around the WAN transport between the different enterprise locations is becoming key to success in today's high-tech competitive market where technology solutions became the primary business enabler and facilitator. Most commonly, enterprise IT leaders are always concerned about adopting a WAN solution that is capable and agile enough to address the following considerations:

- Interconnect the different enterprise locations and remote sites that are geographically dispersed

- Meet enterprise security policy requirements by protecting enterprise traffic over the WAN (secure transport), to offer the desired end-to-end level of protection and privacy across the enterprise network

- Cost-effective and reliable WAN by providing flexible and reliable transport that meets the primary business objectives and critical enterprise application requirements and that supports the convergence of voice, data, and video to satisfy the minimum requirements of today's converged enterprise networks

- Support business evolution, change, and growth by offering the desired level of agility and scalability to meet the current and projected growth of remote sites with flexible bandwidth rates

Note   The preceding factors are not necessarily the standard or minimum requirements for every enterprise network. Even so, these factors are the generic and common concerns that most IT enterprises have. These concerns can vary from business to business. For instance, many businesses have no concern about having unsecured IP communications over their private WAN.

Furthermore, today's Internet service providers (ISPs) can offer a dramatically enhanced Internet bandwidth and price performance with significantly improved service reliability. From a business perspective, this can be seen as high-bandwidth capacity at a cheaper cost; however, the level of end-to-end service efficiency and the level of reliability of the Internet might not be suitable for many businesses. The main point is that nowadays the Internet with secure virtual private network (VPN) overlay is by many businesses as either their primary WAN transport or as a redundant WAN transport. The subsequent sections in this chapter cover it in more detail.

Consequently, there are multiple WAN topologies and transport models an enterprise can choose from, such as point to point, hub and spoke, and any to any. In addition, traffic over each of these topologies can be carried over Layer 2 or Layer 3 WAN transports either over a private WAN network such as a Multiprotocol Label Switching (MPLS) provider or overlaid over the Internet. Typically, each model has its strengths and weaknesses in some areas. Therefore, enterprise network designers must understand all the different aspects of each WAN transport and the supported topologies, to select the right solution that is the best fit for the enterprise business, application, and functional requirements.

Modern WAN Transports (Layer 2 Versus Layer 3)

The decision to select L2 or L3 for the enterprise WAN transport is completely a design decision, and ideally it has to be a business-driven decision. Therefore, it is hard to make a general recommendation that an L3 WAN is be better than an L2 WAN for an enterprise. However, some factors can drive the decision in the right direction based on business, functional, and application requirements, along with the enterprise WAN layout and design constraints. This section highlights the advantages and disadvantages of both modern WAN transports (L2 and L3 based), and then compares them from different design angles. Once the differences between these two WAN transport options are identified, the job of selecting the right WAN technology or transport will be easier. It will simply be a matter of identifying the requirements and mapping them to the most suitable WAN transport model.

Layer 3 MPLS VPN as a WAN transport enables true any-to-any connectivity between any number of sites without the need for a full mesh of circuits or routing adjacencies. This can offer significant scalability improvements for enterprises with a large number of remote locations. With L3VPN, the provider typically exchanges routing information with enterprise WAN edge routers and forwards packets based on Layer 3 information (IP). In addition, L3VPN service providers (SPs) offer a complete control plane and forwarding plane separation per enterprise (customer), with each enterprise IP service assigned to its own virtual IP network (VPN) within the SP MPLS network. With regard to Layer 2 VPN services, however, the providers typically have no participation in the enterprise Layer 3 WAN control plane. This is because the provider forwards the traffic of any given enterprise based on its Layer 2 information, such as Ethernet MAC addresses.

> **Note**   For the purpose of the CCDE exam, the scenario and the requirements always determine the right choice. There might be situations where both WAN options seem to be equally valid, but typically one of them should be more suitable than the other because of a constraint or a requirement given to you on the exam. However, in some cases, there might be more than one right answer or optimal and suboptimal answers. Therefore, you need to have the right justification to support your design decision (using the logic of *why*).

Layer 2 MPLS-Based WAN

Metro Ethernet (ME) services offered by ME SPs (Carrier Ethernet) are one of the most common Layer 2 WANs used by today's large enterprises. Layer 2 WAN (ME-based) offers two primary connectivity models for enterprises:

- E-Line, also known as *Ethernet Virtual Private Line* (EVPL), which provides a point-to-point service. With EVPL, the typical physical link is Ethernet (Fast Ethernet or Gigabit Ethernet), and the multiple circuits under one physical link are wired virtually over the ME provider cloud using VLANs as a service identifier.

- E-LAN provides multipoint or any-to-any connectivity, also known as *Virtual Private LAN Services* (VPLS), and offers any-to-any connectivity with high flexibility for the enterprise WAN.

From an enterprise perspective, the Layer 2 (ME) services provided by today's SPs over their MPLS core infrastructure appear either like a LAN switch for multipoint L2VPN services or like a simple passthrough link for the point-to-point L2VPN sites, as depicted in Figure 4-1.

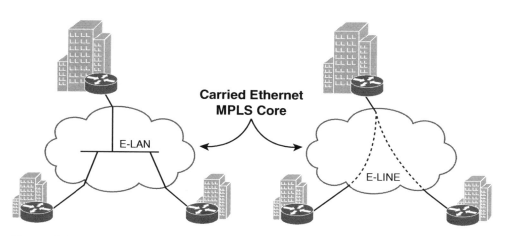

Figure 4-1   *Layer 2 WAN MPLS Based*

Note   Although E-Tree is another type of ME connectivity model, it is a variation from E-LAN to provide hub-and-spoke connectivity model.

Note   This section discusses these technologies from the enterprise point of view, as an L2 or L3 WAN solution. Chapter 6, "Service Provider MPLS VPN Services Design," discusses it from an SP point of view.

Note   L2VPN SPs can preserve the access media using the legacy access media type (such as ATM and Frame Relay) if this is required by the business or if there is a lack of ME coverage by the SP in certain remote areas. In addition, this type of connectivity (mixed) is a common scenario during the migration phase from legacy to modern L2 WAN services.

Layer 2 MPLS-Based WAN Advantages and Limitations

Table 4-1 highlights the primary advantages and limitations of a Layer 2 MPLS-based WAN.

Table 4-1   *Layer 2 MPLS-Based WAN Advantages and Limitations*

Advantages	Limitations
Bandwidth scalability: At the time of this writing, L2 WAN services can scale from 1 Mbps to 10 Gbp, which makes this transport highly scalable in terms of bandwidth requirements.	There might be limited service access coverage of the L2VPN (ME) in some locations.
Performance and quality of service (QoS): By increasing bandwidth on a WAN circuit with L2WAN technologies, enterprises can have a low-latency and low-jitter WAN transport, which can be a good fit for converged networks (video, voice, and data). Furthermore, it can support end-to-end QoS classes as part of the service level agreement (SLA) offered by the SP (class of service [CoS] or differentiated services code point [DSCP] based).	For large-scale networks with many remote sites connected over a common E-LAN service, there will be design limitations and issues on higher levels (control plane), such as a large number of routing adjacencies.

Table 4-1   *continued*

Advantages	Limitations
Routing control: With an L2 WAN, the enterprise will have full control over the design, implementation, and operations of routing across the WAN. This can also be considered added flexibility. For instance, with this model, enterprises have the freedom to choose the desired WAN routing protocol and can deploy enterprise controlled WAN network virtualization.	Routing protocol limitations on certain topologies can introduce limitations here, as well, because not every enterprise can afford to change its WAN routing protocol (for example, a full-mesh VPLS-based WAN with Open Shortest Path First [OSPF], where special care has to be taken for OSPF).
Service offering availability: SPs globally are moving toward adapting networks to provide ME services; therefore, it is available in a large number of places.	Enterprise staff knowledge and expertise can be considered a limiting factor as well. For instance, the staff might not be able to design, deploy, or operate large-scale WAN routing (for example, using Enhanced Interior Gateway Routing Protocol [EIGRP] or Border Gateway Protocol [BGP]).
Topology flexibility: With an L2 WAN, enterprises can have different topology layouts as required, such as point to point, point to multipoint, and multipoint to multipoint.	
Services flexibility: With an L2 WAN, the enterprise can run any advanced IP/non-IP services without any reliance on the SP's support, such as IPv6 or multicast.	
Cost-effective: An L2 WAN, such as ME, replicates the cost model of Ethernet to the WAN.	

Note   There are other variations of ME services, such as Ethernet private line (EPL), that support Ethernet over xWDM (dense wavelength-division multiplexing [DWDM], coarse wavelength-division multiplexing [CWDM]), SONET, or dedicated Ethernet interconnects over fiber. However, this type of service is more expensive than the other ones that are offered by MPLS SPs, such as VPLS or EVPL (Ethernet virtual circuit [EVC]) as an L2VPN ME service.

Layer 3 MPLS-Based WAN

MPLS L3VPN enables enterprise customers to route traffic across the SP cloud as a transit L3 WAN network, with a simplified "one-hop" single routing session per link between the enterprise WAN edge router and provider edge routers. This means that the SP will typically offload all the enterprise WAN control plane complexities in terms of design and operations of the core WAN routing. As a result, enterprises will gain a significant savings in terms of operational expenses and speed up the time to add new remote sites, especially if there hundreds or thousands of remote sites that need to be interconnected. In addition, this model will help to simplify and optimize end-to-end WAN QoS design and bandwidth volume planning of the enterprise WAN connectivity. Figure 4-2 illustrates a Layer 3 MPLS-based WAN. (The MPLS L3VPN cloud appears as single router [peer] from the remote site's point of view.)

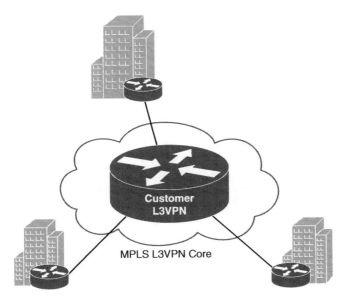

Figure 4-2   *Layer 3 MPLS-Based WAN*

Layer 3 MPLS-Based WAN Advantages and Limitations

Table 4-2 highlights the primary advantages and limitations of a Layer 3 MPLS-based WAN.

Table 4-2   *Layer 3 MPLS-Based WAN Advantages and Limitations*

Advantages	Limitations
Bandwidth scalability: An MPLS L3VPN WAN can provide flexible bandwidth capacity and smooth upgrades as compared to other WAN transports.	**Cost of bandwidth:** Although L3WAN (L3VPN) offers a scalable and high speed of bandwidth, L2VPN (such as ME services) offers a higher bandwidth scale (for example, 10G wire rates) with a lower cost.

Table 4-2   *continued*

Advantages	Limitations
Performance and QoS: MPLS L3VPN can support consistent end-to-end QoS (DSCP driven) that enterprises can take advantage of, especially for real-time delay-sensitive traffic such as Voice over IP (VoIP).	**IP addressing:** When enterprises move from legacy L2 WAN technologies such as Frame Relay, re-addressing of the WAN interfaces is required.
Cost-effective: L3VPN can reduce the operational cost because there will be no need to operate and maintain a large and complex routed WAN core infrastructure.	**SP dependencies:** With L3VPN, there is always dependency on SP support to deploy new network services, such as using IPv6 or multicast.
Service offering availability: Most of the SPs globally offer MPLS L3VPN. Therefore, it is available in a large number of places.	**Flexible topology:** For nonstandard layouts, such as hub and spoke, there might be an additional cost involved for the additional VPNs to be provisioned by the SP.
Topology flexibility: L3 WAN supports different topology layouts as required, such as point to point, point to multipoint, and any to any.	**LAN extension:** L3 WAN is typically a Layer 3 transit network, which by nature does not allow Layer 2 extensions. Therefore, if a LAN extension is required, it must be achieved using additional technologies. This will typically be an overlay technology, such as self-deployed L2VPN over MPLS over generic routing encapsulation (GRE) over L3VPN WAN, which can add an additional layer of complexity to the network with regard to operations and troubleshooting. It also might not be a desirable solution for the requirements of some applications, due to the increased packets' header that may lead to fragmentation or serialization delay along the WAN path.
Access flexibility: With L3 WAN, the enterprise can be provisioned with any type of access media depending on the access availability of that location (for example, Ethernet, WiMAx, and VPN, over the Internet or 3G/4G).	
Routing simplicity: With L3VPN, enterprises will typically offload the core routing to the SP. From the enterprise point of view, only one routing peer/session per link needs to be maintained.	

Internet as WAN Transport

Despite the fact that the nature of the Internet is a "best effort transport" that lacks end-to-end QoS support, the modern Internet can offer relatively high reliability and high-speed connectivity between various locations at a low cost. In addition, in today's modern businesses, many enterprises are increasingly hosting their services in the cloud and embracing many cloud-based services and applications offered as *software as a service* (SaaS) such as Cisco WebEx and Microsoft Office365, which is changing the traffic pattern to be more toward the Internet.

Furthermore, the Internet can be a reasonable and cost-effective choice for remote sites as a primary transport when it is not feasible to connect over other WAN transport options or when there is a lack of WAN access coverage in certain remote areas. This design primarily relies on using VPN tunneling (overlay) techniques to connect remote sites to the hub site (enterprise WAN module located at the enterprise campus or data center) over the Internet. Ideally, this design is based on a hub-and-spoke connectivity using dynamic multipoint VPN (DMVPN) as the VPN overlay technology for the "Internet as WAN transport" design model, which offers the flexibility to provide any-to-any connectivity as well (direct spoke to spoke). However, point-to-point tunneling mechanisms such as the classical IPsec and GRE are still viable overlay options to be considered (considering typical scalability limitations with peer-to-peer (P2P) tunnels [see Table 4-4 for a detailed comparison of the different VPN mechanisms]). Figure 4-3 depicts the different typical connectivity options available with the Internet as a WAN transport.

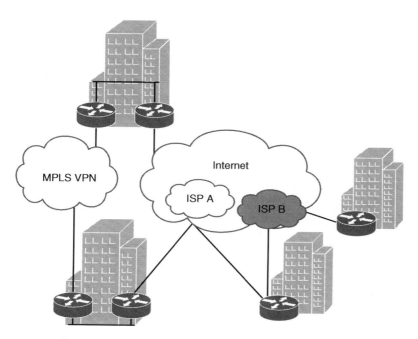

Figure 4-3 *Internet as a WAN Transport*

Note   The decision of when to use the Internet as a WAN transport and how to use it in terms of level of redundancy and whether to use it as a primary versus backup path depends on the different design requirements, design constraints, and business priorities (see Table 4-4).

Furthermore, Gartner Inc. report "Hybrid Will Be the New Normal for Next Generation Enterprise WAN" analyzes and demonstrates the importance of the integration of the Internet and MPLS WAN to deliver a cohesive hybrid WAN model to meet today's modern businesses and applications' trends and requirements such as Cloud-based services. "Network planners must establish a unified WAN with strong integration between these two networks to avoid application performance problems."[1]

Note   Cisco's implementation of this (hybrid WAN) concept is called *intelligent WAN* (IWAN), and combined with Cisco's intelligent routing is also known as *performance routing* (PfR), which offers more intelligent path control to protect critical applications and load balance traffic over multiple paths (for example MPLS + Internet) based on predefined criteria to optimize application performance and user experience.

Note   The connectivity to the Internet can be either directly via the enterprise WAN module or through the Internet model (edge). This decision is usually driven by the enterprise security policy, to determine where the actual tunnel termination must happen. For instance, there might be a dedicated demilitarized zone (DMZ) for VPN tunnel termination at the enterprise Internet edge that has a backdoor link to the WAN distribution block to route the decapsulated DMVPN traffic.

Internet as WAN Transport Advantages and Limitations

Table 4-3 highlights the primary advantages and limitations of the Internet as a WAN transport model.

---

1.   Document ID:G00266397, www.gartner.com

Table 4-3 *Internet as a WAN Transport Model Advantages and Limitations*

Advantages	Limitations
Offers low-cost WAN connectivity with relatively high bandwidth.	**Reliability:** Although today's ISP can offer a relatively high level of Internet service reliability, it still cannot satisfy the strict level of service reliability required by some businesses.
Offload traffic from traversing any private WAN path that is destined to the Internet, such as accessing services hosted in a public cloud provider via the direct Internet access (split tunneling).	**Consistent QoS:** Because the Internet by nature is best effort IP transport, enterprises cannot maintain true end-to-end service differentiation and consistent QoS.
Flexible access because the Internet connectivity can be provisioned over various media types such as wireless, Long-Term Evolution (LTE), 3G, digital subscriber line (DSL), or Ethernet.	**Operations complexity:** Typically, using the Internet as a WAN transport requires an overlay mechanism such as GRE and DMVPN combined with protection (IPsec). These multiple technologies may add a layer of complexity when there an issue to troubleshoot or a new site to be added, especially if other advanced IP services are enabled such as IP multicast.
Provisioning an Internet service is usually relatively quicker than provisioning other WAN services. This enables large enterprises that have many small remote sites they want to add quickly with flexible media access types and wide geographic coverage to accelerate their time to market; this is a common scenario in retail businesses.	

WAN Transport Models Comparison

Table 4-4 summarizes the selection criteria of different WAN transports discussed earlier in this chapter (from an enterprise point of view), considering various design aspects.

Table 4-4 *Comparison of WAN Transport Models*

	MPLS L2VPN WAN	MPLS L3VPN WAN	Internet as WAN
Topology	Flexible	Limited and very dependent on the SP	Limited (overlay technology dependent P2P or hub and spoke (DMVPN supports spoke to spoke)
Bandwidth	Very flexible (can vary between 1 Mbps to 10 Gbps)	Flexible (less than L2 MPLS-based WAN [ME])	Flexible with limitations, depending on the site location and connectivity provisioning type (DSL versus 3G versus 4G)
WAN core routing control	Enterprise managed and controlled	SP managed and controlled	Enterprise managed and controlled
Cost	Moderate	Usually more expensive than L2, especially when high bandwidth is required	Cheap
CoS	Depending on the SP, but can support CoS based on L2 marking and DSCP	End-to-end Layer 3 CoS (DSCP based)	End-to-end QoS guarantee not supported (only at the network edge)
Staff experience	Requires experienced staff to design and manage the core WAN routing	High level of routing expertise not required for the WAN	Requires experienced staff to design and manage the WAN routing and the overlay VPN setup
Remote site scalability	Introduce some routing/adjacency issues and limitations with a large number of sites	Can support very large scale of remote sites	Scalable to some extent (limited to the WAN router hardware capability [for example, supported number of VPN sessions])
Site physical connectivity	Limited options (for example, legacy Frame Relay, ME)	Very flexible, can be any type of access (legacy, Ethernet, VPN over Internet to SP MPLS)	Flexible (DSL, Ethernet, 3G/4G)

By understanding the differences between each WAN transport and the capabilities and limitations of each transport, network designers should be able to make a more business-driven design decision by mapping the suitable WAN transport to the different design requirements (for example, business, functional, and application). In addition, network designers ideally must consider the answers to the following questions during the planning phase of the WAN transport selection:

- Who is responsible for the core WAN routing management?

- Who manages the customer edge (CE) WAN devices?

- How critical is the WAN connectivity to the business? What is the impact of an outage on the WAN connectivity to the business in terms of cost and functions?

- What is the number of remote sites and what is the percentage of the projected growth, if any?

- Are there any budget constraints?

- What are the required WAN capabilities to transport business applications over the WAN with the desired experience (such as QoS, IP multicast, or IPv6)?

WAN Module Design Options and Considerations

This section highlights the design considerations and the different WAN connectivity design options that pertain to the enterprise WAN module and remote site WAN connectivity as well [31].

Design Hierarchy of the Enterprise WAN Module

The main goal of the WAN module is to aggregate the connectivity and traffic of the enterprise WAN that connects the enterprise with various types of remote locations. Therefore, this module provides the traffic and connectivity aggregation of the extended remote sites. Applying the hierarchical design principle can maximize the flexibility and scalability of this enterprise module. In addition, this structured approach will simplify adding, removing, and integrating different network nodes and services such as WAN routers, firewalls, and WAN acceleration appliances. As illustrated in Figure 4-4, applying hierarchy will enable each layer to perform certain functions using different features and tools in a more structured manner. Furthermore, the level of flexibility and adaptability offered by the hierarchal structure makes the WAN module design highly scalable and resilient.

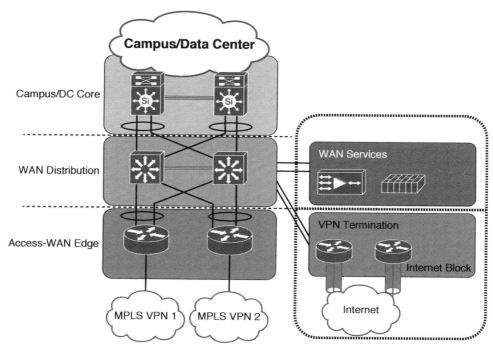

Figure 4-4   *WAN Module Hierarchal Design*

WAN Module Access to Aggregation Layer Design Options

The aggregation layer of the WAN module aggregates traffic and connectivity of access layer nodes, which is typically the WAN edge routers and other WAN services, such as firewalls and WAN acceleration appliances.

There are three common design options to interconnect WAN edge routers to the aggregation layer switches of the WAN module, illustrated in Figure 4-5.

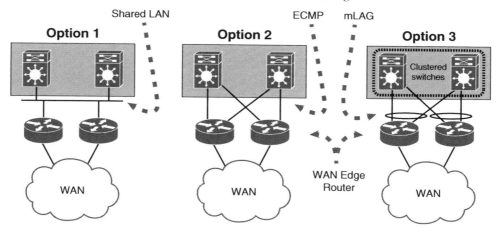

Figure 4-5   *WAN Access-Distribution Connectivity Options*

Both design options, 2 (equal-cost multipath [ECMP]) and 3 (multichassis link aggregation [mLAG]), offer a more flexible design compared to Option 1; however, there are some technical differences between these two design options. Table 4-5 summarizes these differences. Although both design options (2 and 3) can achieve the same goal to a large extent, network designers should select the most suitable option based on the environment and required capabilities and features (optimal versus suboptimal).

Table 4-5 *ECMP Versus mLAG*

Option 2	Option 3
ECMP based.	mLAG based.
Link redundancy based on redundant L3 links (more routing peers).	Link redundancy based on redundant L2 mLAG links (fewer routing peers).
Route reconvergence is required when one uplink fails.	No routing reconvergence is required if one mLAG member link fails.
Convergence time by default relies on routing protocol design and timers.	With mLAG, each flow typically utilizes one member link and will be limited to the capacity of that link (unless "flowlet" concept is used[2]).
Support both scale-out and scale-up. You can use more than two aggregation layer nodes.	Support scale-up (limited scale-out as a maximum of 2 aggregation layer nodes per mLAG can be used).
The more links to be added the larger routing database.	The more member of links to be added, the larger the number of Address Resolution Protocol (ARP) entries.
ECMP flow-based load balancing.	Supports L3/L4 load-balancing hashing (load distribution) across the mLAG member links.

Option 1, however, has several design limitations. For instance, without a careful interior gateway protocol (IGP) tuning, this design option can lead to a slow network convergence at the WAN edge, which can result (from a business point of view) in undesirable outcomes after a failure event. In addition, this design option has a potential of instability and scalability when the network grows in terms of nodes connectivity and routing adjacencies (over a single shared LAN segment). In other words, this design option is the least resilient and scalable option among the other design options. Despite that, design option 1 can still meet some design requirements that do not need a tight convergence

---

[2] "Dynamic Load Balancing Without Packet Reordering," IETF Draft, chen-nvo3-load-banlancing, http://www.ietf.org

time or any scalability considerations, such as regional HQ WAN model with only a pair of WAN edge nodes and no future plan to increase the number of nodes or links. Therefore, the requirements always govern which design option is the best, factoring in whether any design constraint may influence the design choice.

WAN Edge Connectivity Design Options

Enterprises can consider several WAN edge connectivity design options, such as single-homed or dual-homed, and using single or dual edge routers. The most important consideration here is to identify the business drivers and requirements that influence the selection of one option over others. Many variables will influence a business-driven design decision to select a specific WAN edge connectivity design option. The most common factors that drive this decision are as follows:

- Site type (for example, small branch versus data center versus regional office)

- Level of criticality (How much can the downtime cost? How critical is this site to the business if it goes offline for x amount of time?)

- Traffic load (For example, the load on the HQ data center is more than that of the regional data center.)

- Cost (Is cost-saving a top priority?)

Table 4-6 summarizes the various types of WAN edge connectivity design options depicted in Figure 4-6, along with the different considerations from network design perspective.

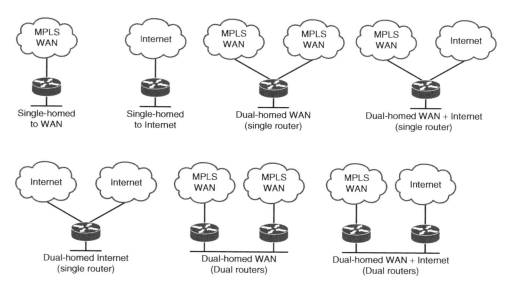

Figure 4-6 *WAN Edge Connectivity Options*

Table 4-6 *WAN Edge Connectivity Design Options*

Connectivity Model	Redundancy	Reliability	Cost	Supported QoS model	Suitability
Single-homed to WAN	None	Moderate	Moderate	Consistent end to end	Small to medium-size branch sites with high traffic volume
Single-homed to Internet	None	Low	Low	Internet edge only	Small branch sites with low fault-tolerance requirements
Dual-homed WAN (single router)	Link redundancy only	Moderate	High	Consistent End to end	Medium-size to large, critical, or regional remote sites
Dual-homed WAN + Internet (single router)	Link redundancy only	Moderate (lower than MPLS)	Moderate	Consistent End to end over the MPLS path	Medium-size to large or regional remote sites
Dual-homed Internet (single router)	Link redundancy only	Moderate (lower than MPLS + Internet)	Moderate	Internet edge only	Small to medium-size remote site
Dual-homed WAN (dual routers)	Link and device redundancy	Very high (single provider versus dual providers)	Very high	Consistent End to end	Hub, HQ, DC, or large regional site
Dual-homed WAN + Internet (dual routers)	Link and device redundancy	High	Moderate to high	Consistent End to end over the MPLS path	Hub, large remote or regional sites

Single WAN Provider Versus Dual Providers

The previous section discussed the various WAN edge design options and the characteristics of each option from a design point of view. This section focuses on the dual WAN edge connectivity, and takes it a step further to compare the impact of connecting a multihomed site to a single SP versus two different SPs, as summarized in Table 4-7.

Table 4-7 *Single Provider Versus Dual Provider*

	Single Service Provider	Dual (Different) Service Providers
Design simplicity (consistency, features)	Simple, consistent (for example, SLA, QoS design)	Can be inconsistent and more complex (for example, different SLAs, different QoS models, different routing protocols)
Cost	Fixed	May lead to a better competitive pricing
Availability	SP outage can lead to a WAN blackout	Offers a higher degree of WAN reliability and availability
Operational complexity	Simpler (consistent)	More complex (for example, dealing with different SLAs and maybe routing protocols)

Note Large enterprises with large geographic distribution can mix between the connectivity options (single versus dual WAN) by using single and dual providers, based on the criticality of the site and business needs. For instance, regional hub sites and data centers can be dual homed to two providers. In addition, this mixed connectivity design approach, where some remote sites are single-homed to a single provider while others are multihomed to dual providers (typically larger sites such data centers or regional HQs), can offer a transit path during a link failure, as depicted in the scenario in Figure 4-7. Ideally the transit site should be located within the same geographic area or country (in the case of global organizations) to mitigate any latency or cost-related issues, when applicable, by reducing the number of international paths traffic has to traverse. In addition, the second provider in Figure 4-7 can be an Internet-based transport such as DMVPN over Internet.

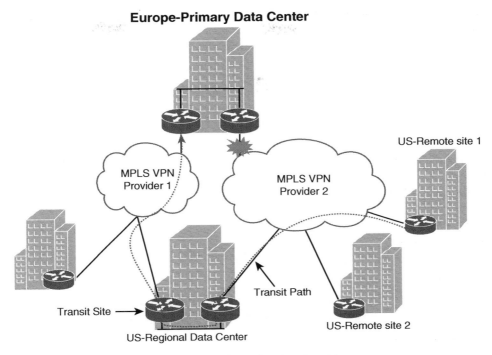

Figure 4-7   *Transit Path Scenario with Dual WAN Providers*

Remote Site (Branch) WAN Design Considerations

The WAN edge design options of a remote site can be based on any of the design options described in the previous section (see Table 4-6), where single or dual WAN edge routers can be used based on the requirements of each particular site. Most commonly, in large enterprises, remote sites are categorized based on different criteria such as size, criticality, location, and typically all the sites under the same categorization follow same design standards.

> **Note**   The edge node is usually either a CE node (for MPLS L3 or Layer 2 WAN) or a VPN spoke node. In some cases, a single WAN edge router can perform the role of both a CE router and VPN spoke router.

However, the level of availability is something that can be determined based on different variables, as discussed in the previous section, such as the level of criticality of the remote site. The rule of thumb for remote site availability is that "the network ideally should tolerate single failure conditions," either the failure of any single

WAN link or any single network device at the hub/HQ WAN side (by considering control plane or overlay failover techniques). However, as discussed earlier in his book, the different business drivers, constraints, and the level of site criticality can drive the level of availability of any given remote site. In other words, remote site availability is not always a requirement or a component that must be considered in the design. In general, remote sites with single-router, dual links must be able tolerate the loss of either of the WAN links. Remote sites with dual router, dual links can tolerate the loss of either a WAN edge router or a WAN link (multiple-failure scenarios).

In addition, from a design perspective, the selected WAN connectivity option has a significant influence on the LAN design of a remote site, as does the size of the site (in terms of the number of users and endpoints connected to the network). In general, the design models of a remote site fit into two primary models, as depicted in Figure 4-8 and Figure 4-9 (a and b) and compared in Table 4-8:

- Single-tier design model

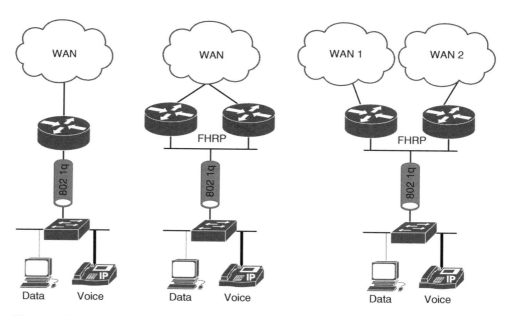

Figure 4-8   *Single-Tier Remote Site Design Model*

■ Multitier design model

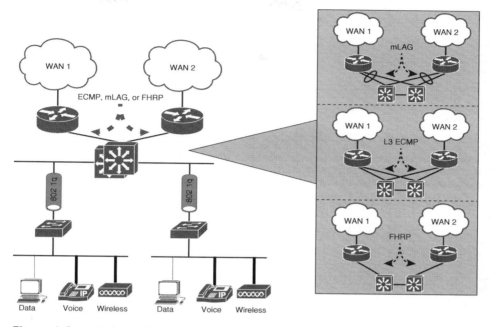

Figure 4-9a   *Multitier Remote Site: Dual WAN Router Design Model*

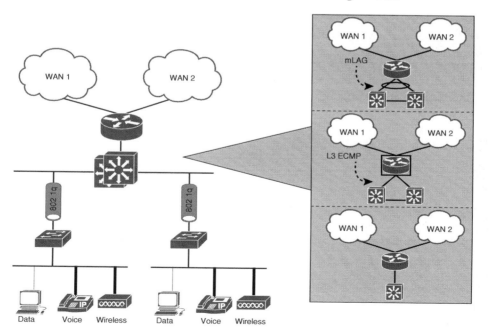

Figure 4-9b   *Multitier Remote Site: Single WAN Router Design Model*

Table 4-8   *Remote Site Design Models*

	Single-Tier Design Model	Multitier Design Model
LAN scalability	Very limited	More scalable
First-hop Layer 3 service	WAN edge router	Distribution layer switches
LAN flexibility	Very limited	More flexible
LAN to WAN edge Layer 3 connectivity options	FHRP (First Hop Redundancy Protocol), in dual edge routers scenario	IGP over ECMP FHRP mLAG with FHRP mLAG with IGP
Supported number of endpoints	Small	Small to medium-sized
Supported WAN connectivity options	Single WAN, single router Dual WAN, single router Dual WAN, dual routers	Single WAN, single router Dual WAN, single router Dual WAN, dual routers

Note   The WAN connectivity options in Table 4-8 apply for both private enterprise WAN or overlaid WAN over the Internet transport.

Internet as WAN Transport (DMVPN Based)

As discussed earlier in this section, using the Internet as a WAN transport in conjunction with DMVPN as the overlay transport offers several benefits to the business and enterprise WAN design, in particular for the remote site WAN connectivity, including the following:

- Offers a cost-effective and reliable (to a large extent) WAN connectivity over the Internet

- Reduces the time to add new remote sites over various media access types such as DMVPN over Internet over LTE, 3G, or DSL, combined with the support of zero-touch configuration of hub routers when introducing new spokes to the network

- Provides automatic full-mesh connectivity with simple configuration of hub and spoke

- Supports (any-to-any) spoke-to-spoke direct connectivity fashion

- Supports dynamically addressed spokes

- Supports provisioning behind devices performing Network Address Translation (NAT)

- Features such as automatic IPsec triggering for building an IPsec tunnel

- Supports multiple flexible hub-and-spoke design options that serve different design goals, scales, and requirements, as illustrated in Figure 4-10

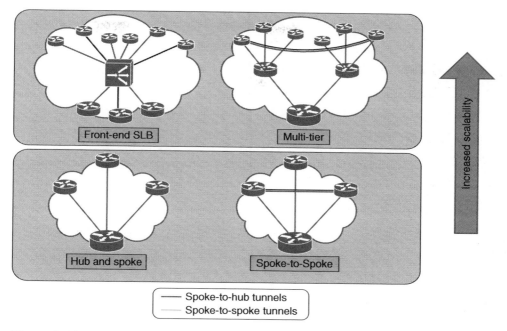

Figure 4-10 *DMVPN Connectivity Models*

> **Note**   Routing over GRE tunnels with large routing tables may require adjustments (normally lowering) to the maximum transmission unit (MTU) value of the tunnel interface.

As illustrated in Figure 4-11, Three primary connectivity options comprise this design model (remote sites DMVPN-based WAN).

- Single router, single link

- Single router, dual links

- Dual routers, dual links

These connectivity options are primarily driven by the desired level of redundancy over the Internet. For instance, the *dual routers, dual links* connectivity option eliminates any single point of failure at the WAN/Internet edge, and with the *single router, dual links*, the edge router is posing single point of failure to the design even though there are two redundant Internet links. Therefore, based on the different design requirements and constraints, the best "relevant" option can be selected. For example, if a retailer has a small remote site with a very small number of users that can perform transactions and save them locally in case of any WAN outage, adding redundancy may be considered overengineering in this particular scenario because it will not add significant value to the business, and it may be seen as additional unnecessary cost from the business point of view.

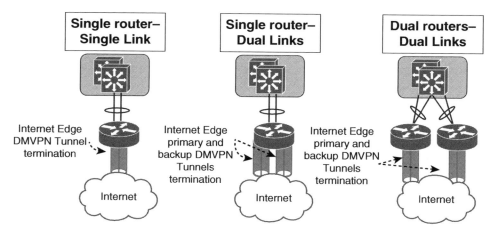

Figure 4-11   *Remote Site DMVPN-Based WAN Connectivity Options*

Enterprise WAN Module Design Options

Previous sections in this chapter discussed the design elements and components of the enterprise WAN module. This section highlights the common proven design models you can use as a foundational reference for the enterprise WAN module design, based on the scale of the remote sites [32].

> **Note**   As stated, you can use these design models as foundational reference architecture and scale them based on the requirements. For instance, the design Option 1 model can easily be migrated to design Option 2 when the number of remote sites increases and requires a higher level of redundancy. Similarly, the number of edge access nodes (WAN/ Internet edge routers) can be scaled out depending on the design requirements. For instance, an enterprise may consider design Option 1 with an additional redundant edge route to a second MPLS WAN, while the Internet edge router is to be used only as a third level of redundancy with a tunneling mechanism.

> **Note**   The number of remote sites in the following categorization is a rough estimation only (based on the current Cisco Validated Design [CVD] at the time of this writing). Typically, this number varies based on several variables discussed earlier in this book, such as hardware limitations and routing design in terms of number of routes.

Option 1: Small to Medium

This design option illustrated in Figure 4-12 has the following characteristic:

- Dual redundant edge routers.

- Single WAN connectivity (primary path).

- Single Internet connectivity (backup path over VPN tunnel).

- Ideally, each of the WAN and Internet routers are dual-homed to the WAN module aggregation clustered switches using Layer 3 over mLAG (or Layer 3 ECMP in case of no switch clustering).

- This design model ideally can support a small to medium number of remote sites (ideally for a few hundred, as a max, taking into account hardware limitations as well).

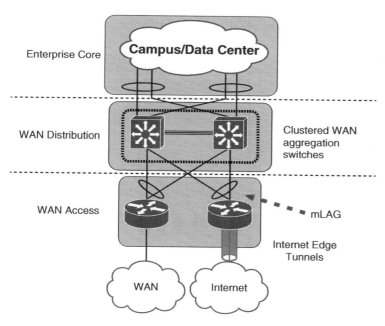

Figure 4-12 *Enterprise WAN Module Design Option 1*

Option 2: Medium to Large

This design option, illustrated in Figure 4-13, has the following characteristics:

- Dual WAN connectivity and dual WAN routers.

- Dual Internet connectivity and dual Internet routers (typically backup path over VPN tunnel as well as primary for VPN-only remote sites).

- Each of the WAN and Internet routers is dual-homed to the WAN module aggregation clustered switches using Layer 3 over mLAG mLAG (or Layer 3 ECMP in case of no switch clustering).

- This design model supports a medium to large number of remote sites (can support up to few thousand remote sites depending on the hardware capabilities of WAN routers and VPN termination routers).

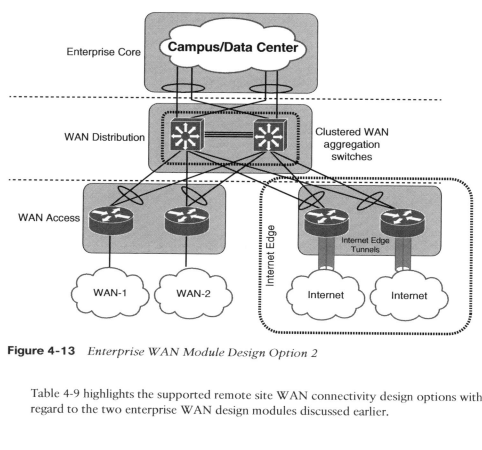

Figure 4-13   *Enterprise WAN Module Design Option 2*

Table 4-9 highlights the supported remote site WAN connectivity design options with regard to the two enterprise WAN design modules discussed earlier.

Table 4-9   *Supported Remote Site WAN Connectivity Design Options*

	WAN Module Design Option 1	WAN Module Design Option 2
Scalability with regard to the number of remote sites*	Small to medium	High
Support remote sites with single WAN link (MPLS only)	Yes	Yes
Support remote sites with single WAN link (over Internet)	Yes (single hub, single point of failure)	Yes
Support remote sites with dual WAN links (MPLS only)	No	Yes
Support remote sites with dual WAN link (MPLS + Internet)	Yes	Yes

Table 4-9 *continued*

	WAN Module Design Option 1	WAN Module Design Option 2
Support remote sites with dual WAN links (over Internet only)	Yes (single hub, single point of failure, which eliminates the benefit of the redundant Internet links of the remote site)	Yes

* Available hardware resources such as memory and CPU, as well as routing design in terms of prefix aggregation and timers tuning, are primary influencing factors to the solution scalability.

Option 3: Large to Very Large

This architecture, illustrated in Figure 4-14, targets very large-scale routed WAN deployments. This architecture encompasses branch, metro connectivity, and global core backbones.

This architecture consists of five primary modules:

- **Regional WAN:** Connects branch offices and aggregates remote locations

- **Regional MAN:** Connects remote offices and data centers across metro area transports

- **WAN core:** Interconnects regional networks and data centers within a country or theater or globally (provides connectivity between regional enterprises, interconnects within a theater and globally between theaters)

- **Enterprise edge:** Connects the enterprise network to other external networks and services (Internet service, mobile service)

- **Enterprise interconnect:** Used as an interconnection and aggregation point for all modules (provides connectivity between the regional WANs, MANs, data centers, enterprise edge, and campus networks)

This hierarchical structure offers flexibility for the design to be separated into different element tiers that are suitable to different environments. When a global footprint is required, all the elements of this architecture will likely apply. Whereas with a footprint that is solely within a single theater (region or country), it will not require the global core. However, it can be added when there is a requirement to expand into other regions [28]. The design of each element, such as the regional WAN and remote sites, should follow the design options discussed earlier in this chapter. For example, the regional "enterprise WAN module" can be based on any of the WAN design options discussed earlier in this chapter.

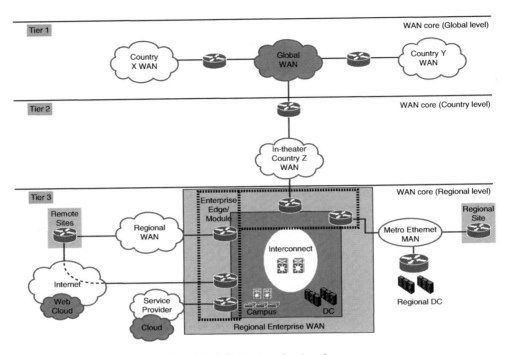

Figure 4-14 *Enterprise WAN Module Design Option 3*

WAN Virtualization and Overlays Design Considerations and Techniques

Chapter 3, "Enterprise Campus Architecture Design," covered drivers and advantages of considering network virtualization techniques within the enterprise, in particular the enterprise campus network. This section focuses on how the enterprise can extend network virtualization across the WAN to maintain end-to-end path isolation for the different logical networks and groups. Network virtualization over the WAN (WAN virtualization) can be achieved using various approaches and techniques. This section highlights these various design options and the characteristics of each, and suggests uses that can fit different business requirements. One of the primary and common foundational technologies used by enterprises to facilitate achieving WAN virtualization is overlay technologies. In fact, overlay (also referred to as *self-deployed VPN*) technologies are adopted by businesses to serve different purposes, from enterprise an network design perspective, such as the following:

- Build a cost-effective WAN model also known as *Internet as WAN transport model* (virtual private WAN). You can use this model either as a primary or backup WAN transport.

- Provide a mechanism to maintain end-to-end path isolation for logical groups or entities across the enterprise WAN.

- Secure IP communications over the private enterprise WAN or Internet.

- Provide a controlled remote-access method for mobile users or third-party entities that might require access to certain internal resources.

- Provide overlaid transport for services and applications that are not supported by the underlay transport infrastructure, such as multicast-based applications and IPv6 applications over "unicast-only" IPv4 IP network.

Therefore, it is critical that network designers have a very good understanding of the different overlay (VPN) options in terms of supported design models, strengths, limitations, and suitable use cases.

Table 4-10 compares the different overlay (VPN) technologies that commonly used to extend enterprise connectivity and facilitate network virtualization over IP transport networks.

Table 4-10 *Network Overlay Technologies Comparison*

	Remote Access VPN (Client-based)	DMVPN	IPsec	GRE
Targeted transport network	Public Internet transport	Private WAN and public Internet	Private WAN and public Internet	Private WAN and public Internet
Supported network topology	Hub-spoke (client to server)	Hub-spoke, spoke to spoke	Point to point	Point to point
Routing technique	Reverse-route injection	Static and dynamic routing	Reverse-route injection	Static and dynamic routing
Encryption style	Peer-to-peer protection	Peer-to-peer protection (with IPsec)	Peer-to-peer protection	Peer-to-peer protection (with IPsec)
IP multicast	Multicast replication at hub (if multicast is supported by the VPN client or may requires GRE with IPSec)	Multicast replication at hub	Point-to-point (with GRE)	Point to point
Scalability	Moderate	High	Low	Low
Design flexibility	Limited to client/server communication style	High	Low	Moderate

Table 4-10   *continued*

	Remote Access VPN (Client-based)	DMVPN	IPsec	GRE
Operational complexity	Moderate (only for remote-access users)	Moderate	High	High
Network virtualization techniques	Limited (VRF-aware remote access)	Flexible (end to end)	Limited (VRF-aware IPsec)	Flexible (end to end)

Note   The primary scalability limiting factor of any VPN solution is the support number of sessions by the used hardware platform.

Note   GET VPN is an encryption mechanism that enables you to preserve IP header information that supports true "any-to-any" encrypted IP connectivity model. Therefore, it is commonly used over private transport networks such a private WAN instead of the other IP tunneling mechanisms. Having said that, GETVPN is not always the ideal or optimal overlay and encryption solution over the private WAN. For example, if the existing WAN platforms of an organization do not support GETVPN (and the business has no intention or plan to upgrade any network hardware/software), then you need to deal with the design constraints and consider other options here, such as IPSec with GRE or mGRE.

These different VPN technologies highlighted in Table 4-10 are the foundation of achieving WAN virtualization. However, modern large-scale enterprises can use other approaches to maintain end-to-end path separation, such as "self-deployed" MPLS L3VPN. The following section classifies, discusses, and compares all the different primary technologies and design options that can help you achieve WAN virtualization to suit different design requirements.

WAN Virtualization

Introducing virtualization and path isolation over the WAN transport is commonly driven by the adoption of the network virtualization concept by the enterprise within the campus LAN, branches, or data center network. Therefore, to maintain end-to-end path isolation, network virtualization must be extended over the WAN transport in a manner that does not compromise path-isolation requirements. From a WAN design point of view, two primary WAN connectivity models drive the overall WAN virtualization design choices:

■ **Customer- or enterprise-controlled WAN:** Also known as *self-deployed*, this model provides full control for the enterprise to use the desired core routing design and the type of virtualization techniques that meet their requirements, such as MPLS in the core or tunneling with multiple VRFs. Furthermore, all the techniques discussed in the campus enterprise virtualizations section are applicable. Typically, this model is based on the fact that the enterprise controls the WAN core infrastructure or transport, as depicted in Figure 4-15.

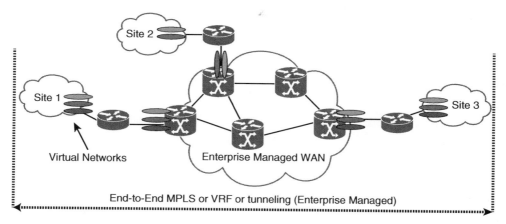

Figure 4-15 *Enterprise-Managed WAN*

Note   If the WAN SP in the middle provides L2 WAN transport, it can be categorized under the enterprise-controlled WAN model, because the enterprise will have the control and freedom, to a large extent, to deploy the desired end-to-end WAN virtualization techniques based on the business and technical requirements, such as MPLS-enabled virtualization or subinterfaces with VRFs, as illustrated in Figure 4-16.

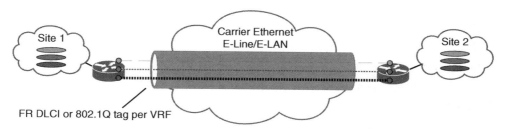

Figure 4-16 *Enterprise-Managed WAN over L2VPN Cloud*

- **SP-controlled WAN:** This model, compared to the previous model, provides the least control for the enterprise when it comes to routing an end-to-end network virtualization over an SP-controlled WAN transport, such as MPLS L3VPN, as depicted in Figure 4-17. Therefore, enterprises need to either extend the virtualization to the SP (to the PE node) or build an overlay over the SP managed network between their CE nodes to facilitate the formation of the required end-to-end network virtualization. This approach is commonly referred to as *over the top*.

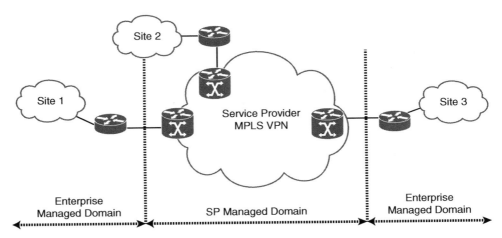

Figure 4-17   *Unmanaged Enterprise WAN*

Over-the-Top WAN Virtualization Design Options (Service Provider Coordinated/Dependent)

The following design options require coordination with the SP to support extending the enterprise network virtualization over the MPLS L3VPN provider network. The two common and proven approaches used to extend network virtualization of an enterprise over unmanaged L3VPN SP network are as follows:

■ **Back-to-back VRFs to provider PE:** This approach is based on using the concept of Multi-VRF CE. This approach provides L3 path virtualization extension without exchanging labels over IP tunnels or physical interfaces (subinterfaces) with the provider PE, as illustrated in Figure 4-18. Typically, a routing instance (process) per VRF is required at each CE and PE node to exchange routing information per virtual network.

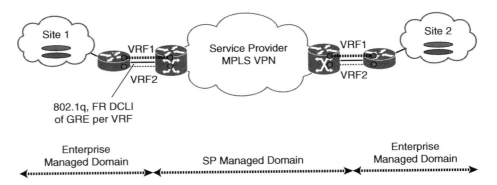

Figure 4-18   *Multi-VRF CE*

■ **Enable MPLS (Label Distribution Protocol [LDP]) with provider PE:** This approach is based on the Carrier Supporting Carrier design model (CSC, RFC 3107), where the CE node can send packets along with MPLS label to the provider PE, which ultimately can facilitate for enterprises the formation of their own multiprotocol BGP (MP-BGP) peering across the SP MPLS L3VPN backbone, as illustrated in Figure 4-19.

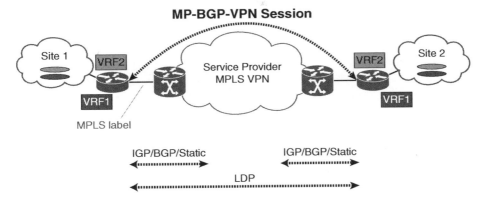

Figure 4-19 *CSC model*

Table 4-11 compares these two design approaches from different design angles.

Table 4-11 *Multi-VRF CE Versus CSC Model for Enterprise WAN Virtualization*

	CSC Model	Back-to-Back VRFs Model
Scalability	High	Low
Coordination with the SP	*Moderate*	*High*
Design complexity	Moderate	The larger, the more complex
Dependencies on SP (for example, multicast support)	High	High
Extra cost	No	Yes (SP might charge per additional VRF.)
Adding new virtual network/VRF requires coordination with SP	No	Yes
Requires label exchange with provider PE	Yes	No
Requires PE-CE routing instance per VRF	No	Yes
Control plane complexity	Moderate	High
Operational complexity	Moderate	High
Security and edge policy control	Moderate	High
QoS granularity	Moderate	High

Over-the-Top WAN Virtualization Design Options (Service Provider Independent)

This section discusses the different design options that use various overlay approaches, which can facilitate the extension of an enterprise network virtualization over an unmanaged L3 SP WAN. Unlike the approaches discussed in the previous section, the design options discussed in this section are end-to-end controlled and deployed by the customer or enterprise side without any coordination/dependencies with the WAN SP (simply because all the methods are based on the concept of using different tunneling [overlay] mechanisms that typically encapsulate and hide all the traffic and virtualization setup from the underlying SP transport network):

- **Point-to-point GRE tunnel per VRF:** This design option offers a simple private virtual network extension over GRE tunnels, where each GRE tunnel is assigned to a specific VRF per virtual network, without any need to coordinate with the WAN provider. However, this option can introduce operations and setup complexities in large deployments because of the large number of manual configurations of the point-point tunnels, each with its own control plane. In addition, this design option has the least scalability, because the number of tunnels can increase significantly when the number of sites and VRFs increases. For example, 60 sites with 3 VRFs each will require (N – 1) tunnel per VRF, (59 * 3) = 177 tunnels to create. Nevertheless, this design option can be a good choice for traffic isolation between a very small number of sites (ideally two or three sites only) with a very limited number of VRFs (ideally two or three) VRFs, as illustrated in Figure 4-20.

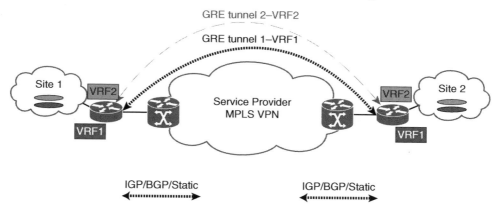

Figure 4-20   *Point-to-Point GRE Tunnel per VRF*

Note   For this design option and the subsequent ones, it is hard to generalize and provide a specific recommended number of remote sites or VRFs, because the decision has to be made based on these two variables when measuring the scalability of the design option. For example, evaluating this design option for a network that requires path isolation between 3 sites, where each site has 10 different virtual networks to transport, is different from when there are 3 sites with 2 virtual networks in each. In both cases, the number of sites is small; however, the number of VRFs (virtual networks) here becomes the tiebreaker:

■ **Dynamic multipoint GRE (DMVPN) per VRF:** This design option is typically based on using multipoint GRE tunnels (DMVPN) per virtual network, as illustrated in Figure 4-21, which helps to overcome some of the scalability issues of the previous option to some extent. This design option also supports direct spoke-to-spoke traffic forwarding (bypassing the hub) per VRF. Furthermore, it supports deployments of a larger scale than those of the point-to-point GRE tunnels. However, it still has scalability and operational limitations and complexities when the network grows, because there will be a DMVPN cloud per VRF. This means that the greater the number of VRFs required, the greater the number of DMVPN clouds that need to be created and operated with a separate control plane for each. This design option ideally supports the following design combinations:

■ Large number of remote sites with very small number of VRFs (ideally two)

■ Small number of remote sites with small number of VRFs (ideally not more than three)

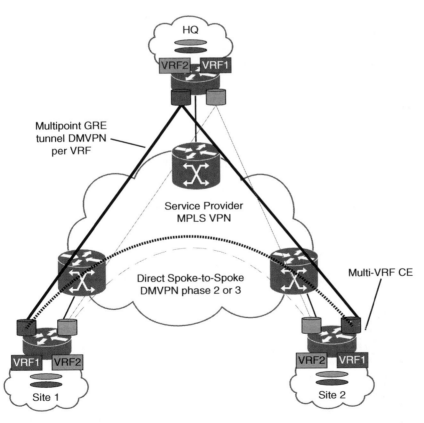

Figure 4-21 *DMVPN per VRF*

- **MPLS over point-to-point GRE tunnel:** This design option is based on the concept of encapsulating MPLS labels in a GRE tunnel, as described in RFC 4023, which helps to overcome some of the limitations of the point-to-point GRE tunnel per VRF design option, by using MPLS with an MP-BGP VPNv4/6 session over one GRE tunnel (RFC 2547 MP-BGP control plane style), as depicted in Figure 4-22. Consequently, there will be only one GRE tunnel required to carry LDP, IGP, and MP-BGP (VPNv4/6). Typically, there is no need to create a separate GRE tunnel per VRF with this design option. However, the number of remote sites is still a limiting factor in the scalability of this design option in the case where many remote sites need to be connected, either in a fully meshed manner or using hub-and-spoke overlay topology.

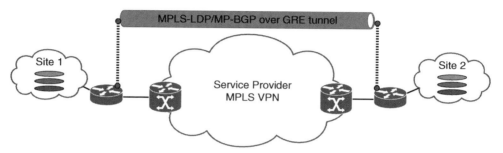

Figure 4-22   *MPLS over Point-to-Point GRE Tunnel*

Furthermore, this design option can help simplify the interconnection of disjoint MPLS-enabled infrastructures over a native IP backbone. As illustrated in Figure 4-23, MPLS over GRE is used to extend the reachability between two MPLS-enabled islands over a non-MPLS backbone (native IP).

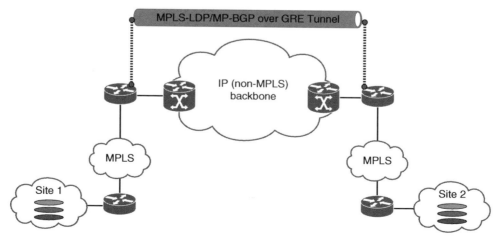

Figure 4-23   *Interconnecting MPLS-Enabled Islands over GRE*

■ **MPLS over dynamic multipoint GRE (DMVPN):** This design option, also known as *2547oDMVPN*, is based on using MPLS over DMVPN tunnels (standard RFC 2547 MP-BGP control plane), which allows MPLS VPN to leverage the DMVPN framework (Next Hop Resolution Protocol [NHRP] for dynamic endpoint discovery). Compared to the (DMVPN per VRF) design option, using MPLS over the DMVPN will help to avoid having a DMVPN cloud per VRF. In other words, there will be one DMVPN cloud (carrying LDP, IGP, MP-BGP VPNv4) to transport all the VRFs between the different locations (sites) in a hub-and spoke-topology, as illustrated in Figure 4-23. This makes it a very scalable solution for large hub-and-spoke deployments with multiple distributed virtual networks. Also, this option supports direct spoke-to-spoke communication. (At the time of this writing, DMVPN phase 2 for direct dynamic spoke-to-spoke communication is achievable.[3]). Multicast traffic, however, must traverse the hub site if enabled.

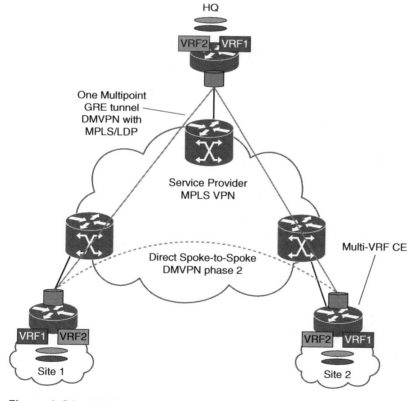

Figure 4-24   *MPLS over DMVPN*

---

3. Advanced DMVPN & Routing Fun in the Lab: Part 2 – The Forwarding Plane, http://www.networkingwithfish.com

■ **MPLS over multipoint GRE (using BGP for endpoint discovery):** MPLS over mGRE simplifies the design and implementation of overlaid (self-deployed) MPLS VPN using the standard RFC 2547 MP-BGP control plane, which offers dynamic tunnel endpoint discovery using BGP as the control plane. This solution requires only one IP address (typically a loopback address) of each of the enterprise CE routers to be advertised to the interconnecting SP cloud network, as depicted in Figure 4-25. In addition, there is no requirement to manually configure any GRE tunnel or enable LDP/RSVP (Resource Reservation Protocol) on any interface. Instead, mGRE encapsulation is automatically generated with the dynamic endpoint discovery capability. The VPNv4 label and VPN payload are carried over the mGRE tunnel encapsulation. This solution offers a simplified and scalable any-to-any unicast (IPv4, IPv6 6VPE based) and multicast (MDT based) MPLS VPN communication model.

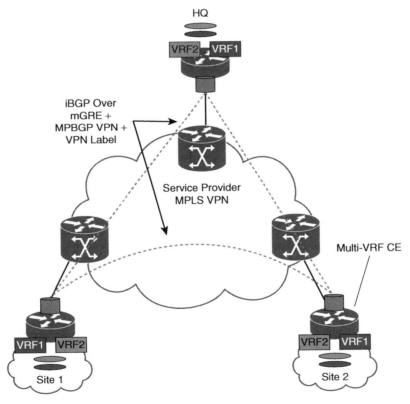

Figure 4-25   *MPLS over mGRE BGP Autodiscovery Based*

■ **EIGRP Over the Top (OTP):** As the name implies, EIGRP OTP offers enterprise customers the opportunity to form EIGRP adjacencies across unmanaged WAN transport (typically over an L3VPN MPLS provider cloud) using unicast packets for peering and exchanging route prefixes without being injected into the provider's

MP-BGP VPNv4/v6 routing table. With this approach, EIGRP OTP offers simplified dynamic multipoint encapsulation using Locator/ID Separation Protocol (LISP) to encapsulate its data traffic. EIGRP OTP relies on EIGRP routing tables rather than on the LISP mapping system to populate IP routing information. Furthermore, multiple instances of EIGRP can be deployed, along with other network virtualization techniques, to offer multiple routing instances.

This design approach offers significant design flexibility for enterprise WAN connectivity because WAN networks will be seen as a virtual extension of the network and enterprise customers can simply and transparently extend their infrastructure reachability over the provider's network using one unified control plane protocol, as shown in Figure 4-26.

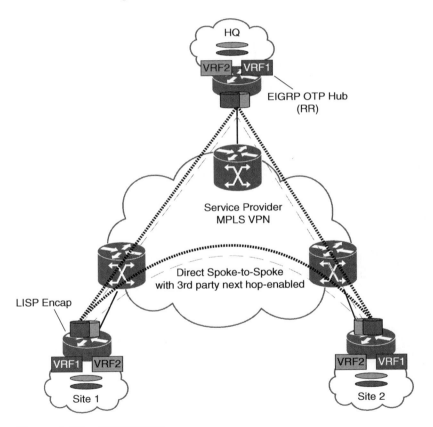

Figure 4-26   *EIGRP OTP*

Comparison of Enterprise WAN Transport Virtualization Techniques

Table 4-12 provides a summarized comparison, from different design aspects, between the different WAN virtualization techniques discussed in this chapter.

Table 4-12 *WAN Transport Virtualization Techniques Comparison*

	SP Dependent	Control Plane	Number of VNs Scalability	Number of Remote Sites Scalability	Direct CE-to-CE Forwarding	Multicast	IPv6	Encryption
VRF Lite	Yes	IGP/BGP	Limited	Very limited	Yes	SP dependent	SP dependent	GET VPN
CSC model	Yes	IGP + BGP/ MP-BGP	Scalable	Scalable	Yes	SP dependent	Yes	GETVPN
P2P GRE per VRf	No	IGP/BGP	Limited	Very limited	Yes (full-mesh P2P tunnels)	Yes	Yes	IPsec
P2P GRE + MPLS	No	IGP + MPMBGP	Scalable	Very limited	Yes (full-mesh P2P tunnels)	Yes	Yes	IPsec
DMVPN per VRF	No	IGP/BGP	Limited	Scalable	Yes	Yes (hub-and-spoke data path only)	Yes	IPsec
DMVPN + MPLS	No	IGP/BGP + MP-BGP	Scalable	Scalable	Yes (DMVPN phase 2)	Yes (hub-and-spoke data path only)	Yes	IPsec
BGP mGRE + MPLS	No	MP-BGP	Scalable	Scalable	Yes	Yes	Yes	GETVPN
EIGRP OTP	No	EIGRP	Limited	Scalable	Yes (with third-party next hop enabled)	No	Yes	GETVPN

Note   Operational complexity always increases when the network size increases and the WAN virtualization techniques used have limited scalability support and vice versa.

WAN Virtualization Design Options Decision Tree

Figure 4-27 is a summarized decision tree of the different design options for enterprise WAN virtualization.

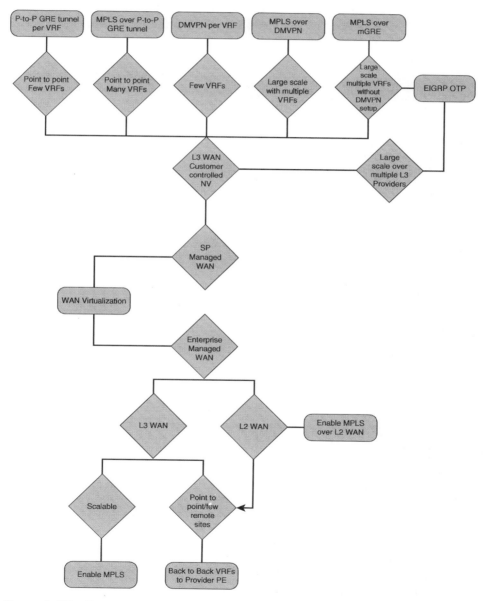

Figure 4-27   *Enterprise WAN Virtualization Decision Tree*

Enterprise WAN Migration to MPLS VPN Considerations

Network migration is one of the most challenging and critical projects of network design. Network designers sometimes spend a large amount of time focusing on the "end state" of their network designs. However, a good and successful design must consider a migration strategy to move the network from its current state to the new state. Similarly, a good migration plan should address how network control plane protocols and applications will interact when the network is partially migrated.

It is impossible to provide general definite guidance for network migration because many variables drive and influence the migration plan and its strategy, such as business and application requirements, network size, and the technologies used. However, the following are some approaches and rules of thumb based on proven WAN migration experiences that should be considered when generating strategic or tactical migration plans:

- The phased migration approach is always recommended for large-scale networks with a large number of remote sites where multiple links or external exit points might exist.

- Logical and physical site architecture must be analyzed and taken into consideration during the planning phase, such as backdoor links, OSPF areas if the PE-CE protocol is OSPF, and BGP autonomous system (AS) numbering if BGP is used across the remote sites.

- In L3VPN, review the selected PE-CE routing protocol and consider how it can integrate with the existing routing setup and design without introducing any service interruption after moving to the new MPLS cloud.

- It is important to identify where the default route is generated and whether the remote sites will use a locally generated default route or over the MPLS cloud.

- Review the routing and identify the places that have summarization because, in some situations, this may lead to suboptimal routing or route summarization black holes.

- In L2VPN, there might be different topologies that can be provisioned by the provider (hub and spoke, full mesh, or partial mesh). A careful review of the topology and the effect of the path that traffic will take after the migration is very important, especially if you are moving from one topology to another. For example, you may be migrating the WAN from a hub-and-spoke topology over Frame Relay to a full-mesh L2 WAN (for example, VPLS).

Migrating from Legacy WAN to MPLS L3VPN WAN Scenario

This section provides an example of a phased migration approach based on a migration scenario of an international media company that is currently using two separate Layer 2 (Frame Relay) clouds over hub-and-spoke topology across two different geographic regions (the United States and Europe). In addition, the hub sites of both the U.S. and Europe regions are interconnected over a Layer 2 virtual leased line (VLL) provisioned by an international Carrier Ethernet, as illustrated in Figure 4-28. After this media company finished a recent migration project of their video and broadcasting systems from a legacy time-division multiplexing (TDM)-based solution to an IP-based solution, they started facing degraded video quality because of the increased number of packets lost and delayed across the WAN. The obvious cause of this issue is the large number of video streams across the low-capacity Frame Relay WAN links and because of the long trip each video stream has to take to reach its intended destination. For instance, traffic between two sites located within the same region has to traverse the hub site first. In addition, traffic between sites across different regions has to traverse the local and remote hub sites over the VLL link, as shown in Figure 4-28. Therefore, to overcome these limitations, a decision has been made to migrate the current hub-and-spoke Frame Relay WAN to an any-to-any topology over a single global MPLS L3VPN provider, to meet current traffic flow requirements with regard to the available bandwidth and delay and to achieve more consistent end-to-end QoS.

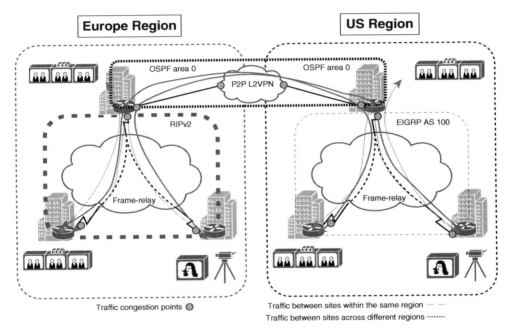

Figure 4-28 *Current Network Architecture and Traffic Flow*

Current state

- WAN is based on hub-and-spoke topology over Frame Relay.

- EIGRP is the routing protocol used over the U.S. region WAN.

- RIPv2 is the routing protocol used over the Europe region WAN.

- OSPF is the routing protocol used by each hub site and between the hub sites over the VLL.

- OSPF area 0 is used over the VLL and each hub LAN network.

- External BGP (eBGP) is the proposed protocol to be used over the new MPLS L3VPN WAN.

Assumption: WAN IP addressing and the desired amount of bandwidth per site is organized with the MPLS VPN provider before the migration starts.

Migration steps

Step 1.   (Illustrated in Figure 4-29):

> **a.** Select the hub site to act as the transit site during this migration process (per region).
>
> **b.** Establish physical connectivity between the hub site (per region) and the new MPLS L3VPN SP.
>
> **c.** Establish an eBGP session between the hub (CE) and the SP (PE).
>
> **d.** Configure redistribution between OSPF and BGP at each hub site.

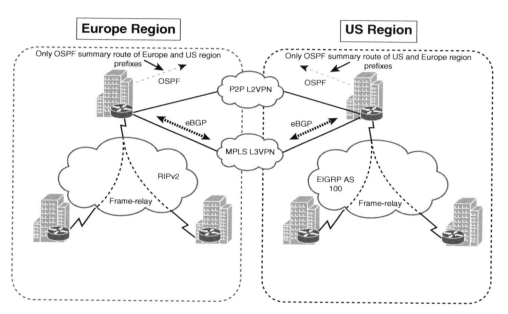

Figure 4-29   *WAN Migration Step 1*

Note   After the migration to the MPLS VPN, there will be two points of route redistribution with a backdoor link (over the L2VPN link between the hub sites). This scenario may introduce some route looping or suboptimal routing. Therefore, it is advised that over this L2VPN link each hub site (ASBR) advertises only the summary routes and not the specific to ensure that the MPLS WAN path is always preferred (more specific) without potential routing information looping. Alternatively, route filtering, as discussed in Chapter 2, "Enterprise Layer 2 and Layer 3 Design" (in the "Route Redistribution" section) must be considered.

Traffic between the LAN networks of each hub site will use the VLL (L2VPN) path as the primary path. Because the HQ LAN networks, along with the VLL link, are all part of the same area (area 0), the summarization at the hub (Autonomous System Border Router [ASBR]) routers will not be applicable here (same area). By reducing OSPF cost over the VLL link, you can ensure that traffic between the HQ LANs will always use this path as the primary path.

Step 2.   (Illustrated in Figure 4-30):

    a. Connect one of the spoke routers intended to be migrated to the MPLS VPN.

    b. Establish an eBGP session with MPLS VPN SP and advertise the local subnet (LAN) using the BGP network statement (ideally without route retribution).

    c. Once the traffic starts flowing via the MPLS VPN (eBGP has a lower AD 20), disconnect the Frame Relay link.

    d. At this stage, traffic between migrated spokes and nonmigrated spokes will flow via the transit hub site.

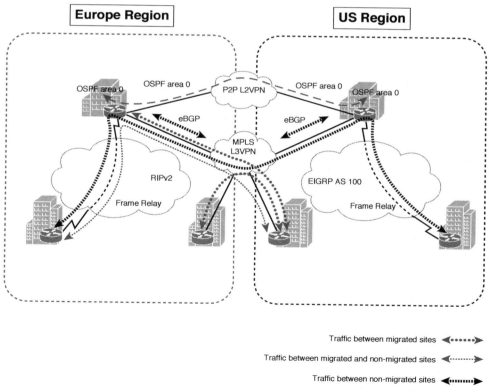

Figure 4-30   *WAN Migration Step 2*

Step 3.   Migrate the remaining spokes using the same phased approach.

Note   With this approach, connectivity will be maintained between the migrated and nonmigrated sites without introducing any service interruption until the migration of the remaining remote sites is completed.

Enterprise Internet Edge Design Considerations

The Internet edge is another module or block of the modular enterprise architecture and part of the enterprise edge module, which provides external connectivity to the other places in the network (PINs) across the enterprise. The Internet block in particular acts as a gateway to the Internet for the enterprise network. From a design point of view, the Internet edge design may significantly vary between organizations, because it is typically driven by the security policy of the business. In addition, large enterprises typically put the Internet edge or module either collocated within the campus network or within its data center network. Nevertheless, in both cases, the location will not impact the module design itself; it will only change the overall enterprise architecture and traffic flow. Therefore, the design concepts discussed in this section apply to both scenarios (location neutral, whether the Internet block is located within the campus or within the data center).

Internet Edge Architecture Overview

To a large extent, the Internet edge design will vary between different networks based on the security policy of the organization and industry type. For instance, financial services organizations tend to have sophisticated multilayer Internet edge design. In contrast, retail businesses usually have a less-complicated Internet edge design. Consequently, this can lead to a significant difference in the design, which makes it impractical to provide specific design recommendations for this block. However, Figure 4-31 illustrates a typical (most common) Internet block foundational architecture. It highlights the main layers and network components that form this module as part of the overall modular enterprise architecture.

This block should ideally follow the same principle of the hierarchical design model as part of the modular enterprise building block architecture. This hierarchical model offers a high level of flexibility to this block by having different layers, each focused on different functions. The distribution layer in this block aggregates all the communications within the block, and between the enterprise core and the Internet block, by providing a more structured design and deterministic traffic flow. This flexible design can be considered foundational architecture. It can then be changed or expanded as needed. For example, the demilitarized zone (DMZ) in Figure4-29 can be replicated into multiple DMZs to host different services that require different security policies and physical separation. Some designs also place the VPN termination point in a separate DMZ for an additional layer of security and control.

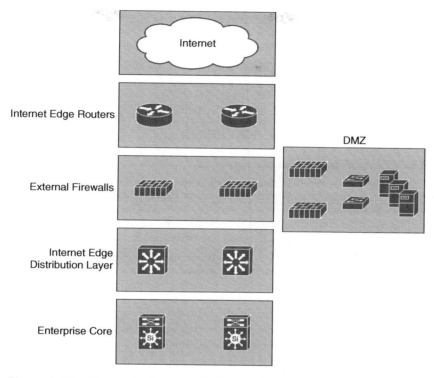

Figure 4-31 *Enterprise Internet Block Foundational Architecture*

Figure 4-32 highlights the typical primary functions and features at each layer of the Internet block architecture.

Note These functions can vary from design to design to some extent. Moreover, all of them are not necessarily required to be applied. For example, NAT can be applied at only one layer only instead of doing double NATing.

Consider, for instance, a scenario where the security requirements specify that all traffic passing through the external Internet block firewalls must be inspected, not tunneled. This slightly influences the design. Technically, it can be achieved in different ways, depending on the available options and platform capabilities. (For example, some next-generation firewalls can perform deep packet inspection, even for tunneled traffic.) Alternatively, the VPN tunnels can be terminated at the Internet edge router or a separate DMZ can be created for the VPN, where VPN tunnels can terminate (using VPN concentrator or dedicated firewalls/routes). The decapsulated VPN traffic will then be sent back to the Internet edge firewalls for traffic inspection before reaching the internal network.

- Packet filtering infrastructure ACL
- Internet routing (Static or BGP)
- VPN Termination
- NAT

Internet Edge Routers

- Packet filtering and traffic inspection
- VPN Termination
- NAT
- Routing (Static or IGP)

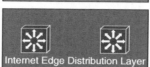

External Firewalls

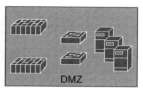

DMZ

- Layer 2 separation using (VLANs)
- Layer 3 separation using VRF-Lite
- Routing (Static, IGP, or BGP)

Internet Edge Distribution Layer

- Layer 2 separation using (VLANs)
- Firewalling and other services only for DMZ (NAT, Load balancing)
- Routing (Static, IGP)
- Switches only Layer 2

Figure 4-32   *Internet Block per Layer Functions and Features*

Enterprise Multihomed Internet Design Considerations

As discussed earlier in this section, the design of the Internet edge will vary to a large extent based on different variables and requirements. The major influencing factor is the organization's security policy. Similarly, the multihoming to the Internet follows the same concept, because it is part of this block. Because of this high degree of variability, this section covers the most common scenarios with multihoming to the Internet.

Multihoming Design Concept and Drivers

Multihoming refers to the concept of having two or more links to external networks, using either one or more edge nodes. This concept or connectivity model is common in large enterprises; however, the actual drivers toward adopting this connectivity model vary, and ideally the decision to do so should be driven by the business and functional requirements. In general, the most common drivers for enterprises include the following:

- Higher level of path and link redundancy

- Increased service reliability

- Offer the ability for the business to optimize the return on investment (ROI) of the external links through traffic load-balancing and load-sharing techniques

- Cost control, where expensive links can be dedicated for certain type of traffic only

- Flexibility and efficiency:

    - This design approach increases the overall bandwidth capacity to and from the Internet (by using load-balancing or load-sharing techniques).

    - Provides the ability to support end-to-end network and path separation with service differentiation by having different Internet links and diverse paths end to end from the ISP to the end users (for example, to serve different entities within the enterprise using different Internet links based on business demand or a security policy).

From a design point of view, network designers need to consider several questions to produce a more business-driven multihoming Internet design. These questions can be divided into two main categories:

- **Path requirements**

    - Is the business goal high availability only?

    - Is the business goal to optimize ROI of the existing external links?

    - Should available bandwidth be increased?

    - Should there be path and traffic isolation?

- **Traffic flow characteristics**

    - Is the business goal to host services within the enterprise and to be accessible from the Internet?

    - Is the business goal to host some of their services in the cloud or to access external services over the Internet?

    - Or both (hybrid)?

The reason behind considering these questions is to generate a design (typically BGP policies) that aligns with the business and functional requirements. In other words, designing in isolation without a good understanding of the different requirements and drivers (for example, business goals and functional and application requirements) will make it impossible to produce an effective business-driven multihoming design.

Note This information can be obtained in different ways, based on the gathered requirements. For example, it may be shown as functional requirements through utilization reports that show 75 percent of the traffic is outbound and 25 percent is inbound, in which it is clear that the traffic pattern is inclined toward accessing content over the Internet.

Note BGP is the most flexible protocol that handles routing policies and the only protocol that has powerful capabilities that can reliably handle multiple peering with multiple autonomous systems (interdomain routing). Therefore, this section only considers BGP as the protocol of choice for Internet multihoming design; however, some designs may use IGP or static routing with multihoming. Typically, these designs eliminate all the flexibilities that you can gain from BGP multihoming scenarios.

BGP over Multihomed Internet Edge Planning Recommendations

Designing a reliable business-driven multihoming connectivity model is one of the most complex design projects because of the various variables that influence the design direction. Therefore, good planning and an understanding of the multiple angles of the design are prerequisites to generating a successful multihoming design.

The following are the primary considerations that network designers must take into account when planning a multihomed Internet edge design with BGP as the interdomain routing protocol:

- A public BGP autonomous system number (ASN) versus private ASN. Typically, public ASNs offer more flexibility to the design, especially with multihoming to different ISPs.

- Provider-independent (PI) public IP addresses offer more flexibility and availability options to the design compared to provider-assigned (PA) IP addresses.

- A PI address combined with a public ASN obtained from the Regional Internet Registry (RIR), for example, provides the most flexible choice with Internet multihoming, especially for enterprises that host services to be accessed from the Internet across different ISPs.

- Receiving a full Internet route can help to achieve more detailed traffic engineering policies. (For example, you can specify outbound traffic to use a certain link on a per geographical region basis, based on the IP prefixes along with its assigned BGP community values.)

Note   BGP community values can provide flexible traffic engineering control within the enterprise and across the ISP. Internet providers can match community values and predefined application policies per community value. For example, you can influence the path local_preference value of your advertised route within the ISP cloud by assigning an x BGP community value to the route. Refer to RFC 1998.

BGP Policy Control Attributes for Multihoming

As discussed earlier in this book, several BGP attributes influence BGP path selection. However, Table 4-13 lists the most common simple and powerful BGP attributes that you can use to control route advertisements and influence the path selection in BGP multihoming design.

Table 4-13 *Common BGP Attributes for Internet Multihoming*

Attribute	Usage Description
Local preference (LP)	Influence outbound traffic flows
AS-PATH prepend	Influence inbound and outbound traffic flows
Community values + (LP, AS-PATH, or weight)	Influence inbound and outbound traffic flows within the customer AS and across the ISPs autonyms systems
BGP weight	Influence local router decision for outbound traffic flows (Cisco proprietary attribute)

Note   BGP community values technically can be seen like a "route tag," which can be contained within the one AS or be propagated across multiple autonyms systems to be used as a "matching value" to influence BGP path selection. For instance, one of the common scenarios with global ISPs is that each ISP can share the standard BGP community values used with its customers to distinguish IP prefixes based on its geographic location (for example, by region or continent). This offers enterprises the flexibility to match the relevant community value that represents a certain geographic location and associate it with a BGP policy such as AS-PATH prepending to achieve a certain goal. For example, an enterprise may want all traffic going to IP prefixes within Europe (outbound) to use Internet link 1, while all other traffic should use the second link. As illustrated in Figure 4-33, BGP community values can simplify achieving this goal to a large extent in a more dynamic manner.

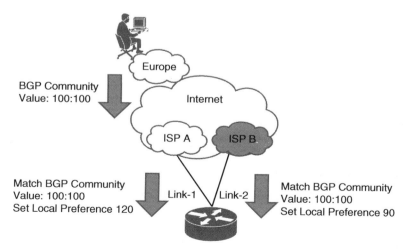

Figure 4-33 *BGP Community Value Usage Example*

Common Internet Multihoming Traffic Engineering Techniques over BGP

This section covers the primary traffic engineering models and techniques that you can use with multihomed Internet connectivity over BGP.

> **Note**   Throughout this section, *ingress* always refers to the inbound direction toward the enterprise, and *egress* refers to the outbound direction toward the SP cloud.

Scenario 1: Active-Standby

This design scenario (any of the connectivity models depicted in Figure 4-34) is typically based on using one active link for both inbound and outbound traffic, with a second link used as a backup. This design scenario is the simplest design option and is commonly used in situations where the backup link is a low-speed link and is only required to survive during any outage of the primary link.

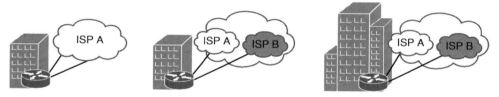

Figure 4-34   *Internet Multihoming Active-Standby Connectivity Models*

Figure 4-35 shows an active-standby scenario where ISP A must be used as the primary and active path for both ingress and egress traffic flows.

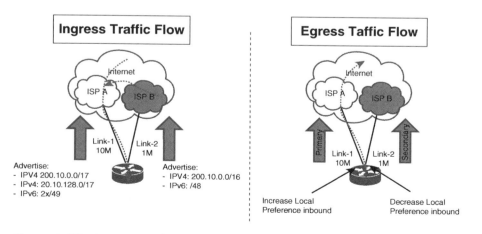

Figure 4-35   *Internet Multi-homing Active-Standby traffic flow*

Table 4-14 outlines a possible solution for this scenario.

Table 4-14   *Internet Multihoming Active-Standby*

Traffic Direction	BGP Policy
Ingress	Longest match over the preferred path, by dividing the prefix into 2 halves (For instance, advertise /16 as 2x /17 over the preferred ingress path toward ISP A in the scenario in Figure 4-35.)
Egress	Use local_preference (Set the preferred route/ path with higher value.)

Although AS-PATH prepending is one of the most common and obvious techniques that you can use here in this scenario to influence ingress traffic, ISPs usually allocate a higher local_preference value to prefixes learned by their customers than the ones learned through other peering ISPs. In other words, even though the prefix 200.10.0./16 is advertised to both ISP A and B with AS-PATH prepending applied toward ISP B, ISP B's customers will always use the path over ISP B because it will be assigned higher local_preference (within ISP B cloud) than the one learned via ISP A, when traffic is passing through ISP B. This means that the targeted goal will not be achieve optimally in this case because any traffic flow coming from any of ISP B's customers will use the low-bandwidth link (link 2 in this case) to reach 200.10.0.0/16. Therefore, by dividing the /16 network into two /17s and advertising it over ISP A, if there is a customer of ISP B that wants to reach your prefix (one of the 2 x /17s advertised by ISP A), ISP B will never get to the /16 sent over ISP B link because the longer match over ISP A will always win in this case, as illustrated in Figure 4-35.

Note   This behavior (where ISPs allocate a higher local_preference value to prefixes advertised within their cloud) is altered sometimes when the ISP enables their customers to control what BGP attribute and value they need to assign their prefixes when injected into the ISP cloud. This is normally achieved by using standard BGP community values to influence traffic routing within the ISP cloud (most commonly to change AS-PATH or local_preference values within the ISP cloud). For example, in the scenario illustrated in Figure 4-36, if you assign a BGP community value 300:110 to prefix 200.10.0.0/16 toward ISP A (AS 300), its BGP local_preference value within the SP cloud will be set to 110, which will be given preference across this SP cloud and its directly connected customers. Similarly, if you assign a BGP community value 500:70 to prefix 200.10.0.0/16 toward ISP B (AS 500), along with BGP AS-PATH prepending 3 x ASN, (100 100 100), this will make this prefix carry a low local_preference value within AS 500 (assuming, 70 is less than the common default BGP local_preference "100"). In addition, it will be seen (by AS 500) as a longer AS path (100 100 100) compared to the prefix learned via ISP A (AS 300). Technically, the prefix 200.10.0.0/16 within AS 500 will be seen as follows:

Via AS 100: Local_preference = 70, AS-PATH = (100 100 100)

Via AS 300: Local_preference = 100, AS-PATH= (300 100) (preferred path)

With this approach, network designers can achieve a true and optimal active-standby Internet connectivity model. However, two limitations apply to this approach. First, not every ISP provides this flexibility to their clients. Second, when customers are multihoming to different ISPs, the advertised prefixes must be PI to avoid having the upstream ISP aggregate the advertised prefix and break the entire design. For instance, if ISP A advertises the prefix 200.10.0/16 toward ISP B as 200.0.0.0/8, the path via R2 over ISP B will be always preferred by ISP B customers (longest match) regardless of which BGP attribute has been used.

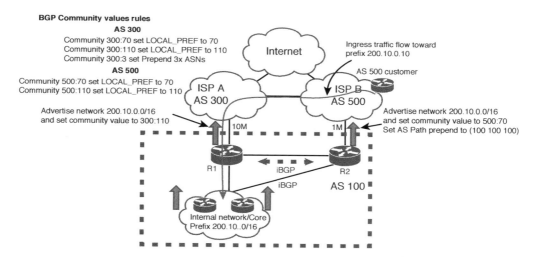

Figure 4-36 *Altering BGP Attributes Within the ISP Cloud*

Scenario 2: Equal and Unequal Load Sharing

These types of design scenarios are commonly used either when there are two Internet links with the same bandwidth value and traffic needs to be distributed evenly across the two links to increase the overall bandwidth and reduce traffic congestion (equal load sharing) or when the Internet links have a different amount of bandwidth where traffic can be distributed in a weighted manner. Ideally, the link with higher bandwidth should handle more traffic than the link with lower bandwidth, as summarized in Figure 4-37.

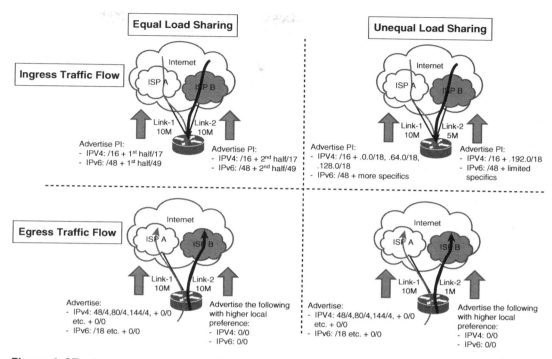

Figure 4-37 *Internet Multihoming Equal and Unequal Load Sharing*

Table 4-15 shows a typical solution.

Table 4-15 *Internet Multihoming Equal/Unequal Load Sharing*

Traffic direction	BGP Policy
Ingress	The typical mechanism to be used here is to divide the PI address into 2 halves. For example, an IPv4 subnet /16 can be divided into 2 subnets /17, similarly for IPv6 /48 to 2 /49. Then advertise each half over a different link along with the aggregate (IPv4 /16 or IPv6 /48 in this example) over both links to be used in case of link failure. For unequal load sharing, you can use the same concept with more small subnets to be advertised over the path with higher capacity.
Egress	For the outbound traffic direction, you need to receive the full Internet route from one of the ISPs along with the default route from both. Accept with filtering only every other /4 for IPv4 (for example, 0/4, 32/4). IPv6 can use same concept (IPv6 either selectively or the same concept). From the other link, increase the local_preference for the default route. In this case, the more specific route (permitted in the filtering) will be used over one link. Every other route that was filtered out will go over the second link using the default route. For unequal load sharing, more subnets can be accepted/allowed from the link with higher capacity.

Note   ISPs usually deploy route filtering policies with their customers and with other peering ISPs, where only certain subnet lengths are accepted, to avoid propagating a large number of small network such as v4/24 or v6/ 64. However, the subnets presented in this section are hypothetical to simplify the explanation of the discussed points.[4]

Although the typical mechanisms used to influence path selection equally (to certain extent) are the ones described in Table 4-15, this cannot guarantee fair or equal load distribution across both links (because traffic load cannot be measured based only on its network or subnet size). For instance, if a /24 subnet divided into two halves (.0/25 and .128/25), advertising each half (/25) over two separate Internet links will (in theory) provide equal load distribution across both Internet links in the inbound direction. In fact, what is hypothetically correct is not always practically achievable; the reason why is because if there are a few hosts such as an FTP or web server as part of the subnet (0/25), with high traffic volume destined to these servers, the link advertising (0/25) will be used more than the second Internet link. This same concept applies to the outbound traffic direction. In other words, achieving true equal load distribution must not be derived only by IP subletting (dividing and advertising the available IP range equally across the available links). Instead, it must be based on actual service utilization reports. Alternatively, you can use a specialized load-balancing appliance that that can distribute traffic flow equally based on real-time link utilization.

Similarly, if unequal load sharing is required (for example, 70/30 load distribution, which means 70 percent of traffic should use the link with higher bandwidth and 30 percent should use the other link with lower bandwidth), the same principle and concerns discussed earlier with regard to equal load sharing apply here. In other words, proper planning and a study of utilization reports must be performed before designing and applying BGP policies to influence which network or host should be reachable over which link. Also, the same applies to outbound traffic. (What are the most targeted services in terms of traffic volume and number of traffic flows, such as cloud-hosted applications like Cisco Webex?) After these facts are identified, network designers can provide a more practical multihoming with the desired proportional load distribution model (whether it is equal or unequal load distribution).

Note   Cisco Performance Routing (PfRv3) technology can achieve an advanced level of traffic load distribution based on different criteria and real-time link utilization.[5]

4. http://www.space.net/~gert/RIPE/ipv6-filters.html

5. http://docwiki.cisco.com/wiki/PfR:Technology_Overview

Scenario 3: Equal and Unequal Load Sharing Using Two Edge Routers

The design techniques described in the preceding scenarios all apply to this scenario for the ingress traffic flow direction. However, the egress traffic flow direction depends on the LAN side design behind the routers:

- **Using a firewall with a Layer 2 switch between the firewall and routers:** Use multiple groups of Hot Standby Routing Protocol (HSRP) or Virtual Router Redundancy Protocol (VRRP) for load sharing on the routers' side.

- **Using Layer 3 network node, such as a switch connecting directly to the edge routers:** You can use IGP with ECMP in this case.

> **Note** In both cases, you need to make sure that there is a link between the two Internet edge routers (physical or tunnel) with internal BGP (iBGP) peering over this link, to avoid traffic black-holing in some failure scenarios.

Asymmetrical Routing with Multihoming (Issue and Solution)

The scenario depicted in Figure 4-38 demonstrates a typical design scenario with a potential for asymmetrical routing. This scenario is applicable to two sites or data centers with a direct (backdoor) link, along with a layer of firewalling behind the Internet edge routers. In addition, these firewalls are site specific, where no state information is exchanged between the firewalls of each site. In addition, both sites are advertising the same address range toward the Internet (PI or PA) range. Therefore, a possibility exists that return traffic (of outbound traffic) originated from site 1 going to the Internet using the local Internet link will come back over the site 2 Internet link. The major issue here is that the firewall of site 2 has no "state information" about this session. Therefore, the firewall will simply block this traffic. This can be a serious issue if the design did not consider how the network design will handle situations like this, especially during failure scenarios.

To optimize this design to overcome this undesirable behavior, network designers need to consider the following:

- **Control plane peering between edge routers in each site:** The first important point here is to make sure that both Internet edge routers are connected directly and use iBGP peering between them. This link can be physical or over a tunnel interface, such as a GRE tunnel. A network designer can optimize this design and mitigate its impact by adding this link along with associated BGP policies (make site 1 internal prefixes more preferred over the site 1 Internet link), which will help to avoid the blocking by the site 2 firewall.

- **Organized IP addressing advertisement:** To make the preceding point work smoothly, we need to make sure that each site is advertising its own route prefixes as more specific (longest match principle), in addition to the aggregate of the entire PI subnet, as discussed earlier. For example, /16 might be divided to two /17s per site. (You can use the same concept with IPv6.).

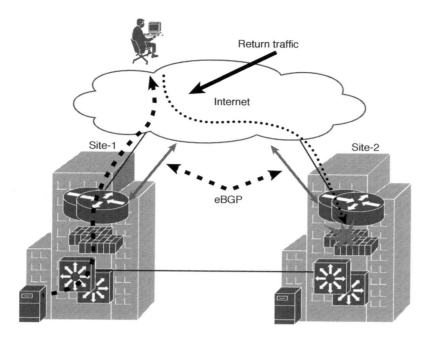

Figure 4-38 *Asymmetrical Routing*

- **NAT consideration:** The other point to be noted here is that if these prefixes are NATed by the edge firewalls, one of the common and proven ways to deal with this type of scenario is by forming direct route peering between the distribution/core layer nodes and the Internet edge routers. Consequently, the edge firewalls can perform NAT for traffic passing through them (as long as the two earlier considerations mentioned in this list are in place).

For instance, in Figure 4-39 the Internet edge distribution is peering with the Internet edge router using multihop eBGP with private AS and advertising the PI prefixes over BGP (using static routes with a BGP network statement to advertise the routes). The firewall is using a default route toward the Internet edge router, along with NAT.

By incorporating the design recommendations to optimize the preceding scenario, a network designer can make the design more agile in its response to failures. For example, in the topology in Figure 4-39, if the link between site 1 and the Internet were to go down for some reason, traffic destined for site 1 prefixes (part of 1st half of the /17) would typically go to the site 2 Internet link (because we advertise the full /16 from both sites). Then traffic would traverse the intersites link to reach site 1. As a result, this design will eliminate the firewall blocking issue, even after an Internet link failure event, as illustrated in Figure 4-40.

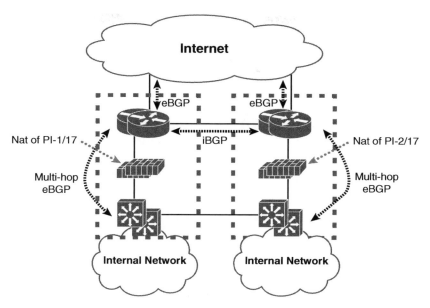

Figure 4-39 *Optimized Multihoming Design with Firewalls*

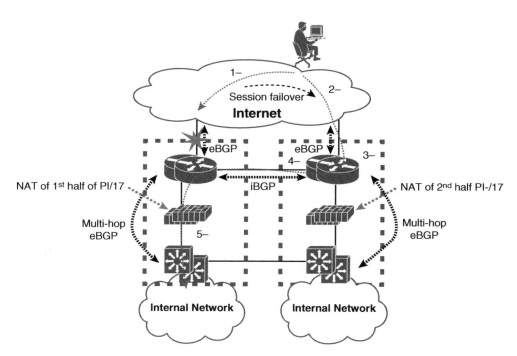

Figure 4-40 *Optimized Multihoming Design: Failure Scenario*

Summary

Today's enterprise businesses, in particular multinational and global organizations, primarily rely on technology services and applications to achieve their business goals. Therefore, the enterprise edge module (both WAN and Internet) is one of the most vital and critical modules within the modern modular enterprise architecture. It represents the gateway of the enterprise network to the other remote sites, locations, business partners, and the Internet. Therefore, network designers must consider designs that can provide a common resource access experience to the remote sites and users, whether over the WAN or the Internet, without compromising any of the enterprise security requirements, such as end-to-end path separation between certain user groups. In addition, optimizing Internet edge design with business-driven multihoming designs can play a vital role in enhancing the overall Internet edge performance and design flexibility and can maximize the total ROI of the available links. Last but not least, overlay integration at the enterprise edge in today's networks can offer enterprises flexible and cost-effective WAN and remote-access connectivity, even considering the additional layer of control plane and design complexity that may be introduced into the overall enterprise architecture.

Part III

Service Provider Networks Design and Architectures

Chapter 5

Service Provider Network Architecture Design

One of the common design questions is this: What is the difference between designing an enterprise network versus service provide network? Technically, both types of networks are entitled to use the same Layer 2 and Layer 3 technologies and protocols. The design principles with regard to each type of these networks can vary to some extent; however, due the fact that the goal of service provider (SP) business almost always is to provide transit connectivity services such as interconnecting the dispersed sites of their customers across the SP core infrastructure (providing WAN services) or providing transit path to reach the Internet and to reach services in the cloud, either hosted by the same provider or by other providers. Moreover, with enterprise networks, the boundary points with external networks are usually very limited due to the typical nature of enterprise communication that is either between internal employees or "to and from" services and applications that either hosted internally within the enterprise or externally in the cloud. In contrast, an SP is a transit network by nature for external customers, consisting of multiple (normally large number) boundary points "ingress and egress" (with each customer or peering SP interconnect an ingress and egress point). Therefore, the primary principle with regard to SP network design is to provide a scalable and reliable infrastructure that can transmit customer traffic fast and reliably enough from its ingress point to the intended egress point across the SP network "transit network."

Furthermore, SP networks (as transit transport networks) are commonly based on a two-tier hierarchy, as depicted in Figure 5-1. Typical SP networks are constructed of multiple points of presence (POPs), with the provider edge (PE) nodes normally linked to each other over the SP backbone. The core is often structured of a meshed network, partially meshed network, or a set of rings, and each POP is usually made up of a ring or a multilayer hierarchy network. In addition, in an SP environment, routing information is normally carried via internal Border Gateway Protocol (iBGP) or multiprotocol iBGP (MP-iBGP). The interior gateway protocol (IGP) within the SP network is used only to carry next-hop information for BGP peers. As a result, the optimal path to the BGP next hop is decided by the SP's IGP by default. Nonetheless, several techniques enable you to alter this default behavior within the SP network, such as Multiprotocol Label Switching Traffic Engineering (MPLS-TE).

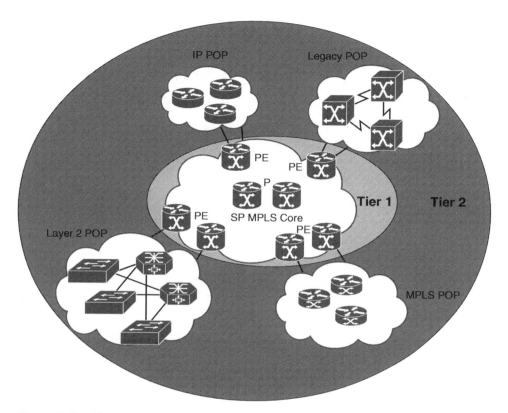

Figure 5-1   *Classic Service Provider Network Architecture*

Note: There are some enterprises that provide transit services to their customers; therefore, what should define the design principles is the nature of the business functions and offered services, even if its categorized as an enterprise business.

However, it is still debatable whether, by using overlays and virtualization techniques like MP-BGP VPN with MPLS, a "layer in layer" hierarchy can be achieved, in which these technologies can provide a sort of abstraction layer of the underlying physical infrastructure where customer routes are carried over the MP-BGP in its own virtual private network (VPN) (which can be considered another logical layer). This is a completely valid point. Other examples where more layers can be added to the SP architecture either physically or virtually (overlaid) include the following:

- Hierarchal MPLS architecture
- Hierarchal VPLS

- MPLS VPNv6 over an IPv4 SP core
- SP network with multilevel POPs (to cover wide geographic areas)

Note   The simplicity of SP network architecture compared to large enterprise networks architecture is relative and not absolute. For instance, a large SP network with thousands of nodes deployed under a single BGP autonomous system (AS) with one IGP flooding domain, such as single Intermediate System-to-Intermediate System (IS-IS) level, is simpler than a global enterprise network with BGP in the core and multiple IGP islands across different geographic regions combined with IPsec tunnels over the Internet as a backup path.

In contrast, an SP network with a few hundred routers only, distributed across different BGP autonomous systems with MP-BGP inter-AS, along with MPLS VPN, MPLS-TE, and MPLS-TE fast reroute (FRR) across both autonomous systems that each has its own IGP domain and protocols, will be to a large extent a complex type of SP architecture. In other words, as highlighted in Chapter 1, "Network Design Requirements: Analysis and Design Principles," network complexity is not only measured by size or number of nodes. However, multiple additional factors can drive the level of complexity, such as control plane design and structure, number of network protocols used, and how the routing domain design may affect other protocols. For example, the design and deployment of MPLS-TE in conjunction with MPLS-TE FRR over different routing domains is more complicated than over a single routing domain from both design and operational point of views.

Service Provider Network Architecture Building Blocks

The next-generation networks (NGNs) of SPs offers a converged infrastructure for video, mobile, and cloud services interconnected over different technologies and services over one converged MPLS-enabled core that provides various Layer 3 and Layer 2 interworking functions (IWFs), commonly referred to as *IP NGN SP networks*.

In a typical SP network (classic and NGN), each architecture has two main components: the core and POP. This section covers these two components from a network architecture point of view. Generally, as mentioned earlier, an SP network architecture consists of two tiers of hierarchies: SP core and the distributed POPs connected to it. POPs, however, can be divided into multiple tiers depending on the size, coverage of the geographic area, and type of service access provided by the POP, such as residential services, mobile backhaul aggregation, or MPLS L2/L3 VPN. Figure 5-2 illustrates a typical SP network with a POP that consists of multiple tiers.

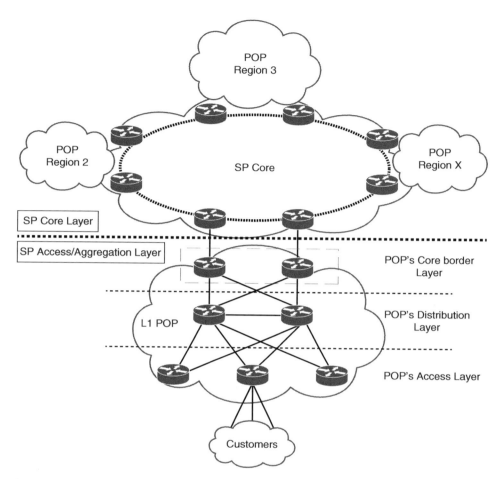

Figure 5-2   *Multitier POP Architecture*

Point of Presence

In SP networks, a POP represents the network edge module in certain geographic areas where customer connectivity terminates. In general, the network design of a POP, which can sometimes be seen from a high-level architectural point of view, is like a small to medium-size LAN design. In this LAN-like design, there can be multiple interconnected Layer 3 nodes over point-to-point links or aggregated through Layer 2 or 3 switches in a hierarchal manner. However, a POP network might span multiple areas in a city over an optical network to cover a metropolitan-area network (MAN). In fact, there is no standard POP design because several factors drive its design and components, such as the following:

- **The services a POP is providing:** For instance, Internet access only, and Layer 3 or Layer 2 service terminations. Layer 2 termination itself can vary, as well. For example, it can be legacy connectivity such as Frame Relay or modern such as Metro Ethernet.

- **The geographic area a given POP is covering:** For example, if it is covering a large city with a large number of customers, the POP might need to be designed in multiple levels to optimally provide the required area coverage and access capacity.

Consequently, the topology of POPs vary and take different forms, such as the following:

- Ring topology (fiber/xWDM [x wavelength-division multiplexing] rings)

- Hierarchal topology (two tier or three tier)

- Mix of hierarchal and ring topologies

In general, a typical POP consists of some or all of the following architectural components/layers:

- **Core border:** High-speed and -capacity devices interconnect the POP with SP core. In addition, there are some POPs designed in multiple levels to cover larger geographic areas, with the core border layer aggregating the connections and traffic of smaller POPs within the same geographic area (level 1 and level 2 POPs), as illustrated in Figure 5-3.

- **Distribution:** The POP distribution layer is required in multitier POP architectures when the number of access layer nodes is large. For example, in the Metro Ethernet POPs in large cities, there might be a high density of access nodes within the POP, and the distribution nodes can optimize the design to aggregate those links, such as with a Hierarchical Virtual Private LAN Services (H-VPLS) architecture.

- **Access:** The access layer represents the termination point and aggregation of the customer's access links and connections. Normally, the access node can take different forms; it could be a PE router in an MPLS VPN environment or a Layer 2 switch in an H-VPLS architecture or a digital subscriber line access multiplexers / broadband remote-access server (DSLAM/BRAS) for DSL services.

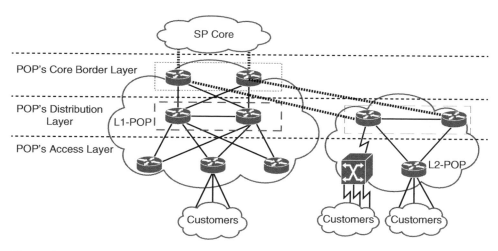

Figure 5-3   *Multilevel POP*

Note   As highlighted earlier, there is no one standard connectivity model for the POP network. For instance, sometimes only two tiers per POP is required, where the distribution and core border functions are combined in one tier, This is common in MPLS L3VPN POPs with several PEs in which the distribution/core border layer performs links aggregation, MP-BGP session aggregation (distribution nodes deployed as BGP route reflectors [RRs]), and traffic aggregation, as illustrated in Figure 5-4.

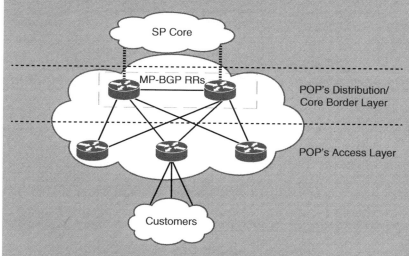

Figure 5-4   *MPLS L3VPN Multitier POP*

In addition, besides the multitier POP connectivity model illustrated in Figure 5-3, Figure 5-5 illustrates another two connectivity models of multiservice POPs that provide different services access such as enterprise Layer 2 Metro Ethernet, L3VPN, as well as residential services access such as IPTV. (Hypothetically, the POP architecture shown in Figure 5-3 should be more able to support large-scale POPs in terms of number of nodes, traffic volume, and geographic coverage.)

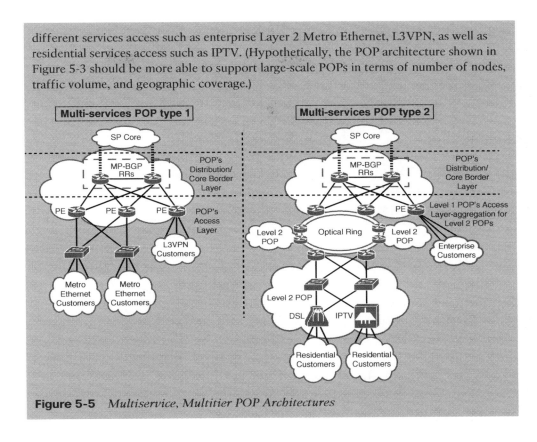

Figure 5-5   *Multiservice, Multitier POP Architectures*

Service Provider Network Core

The concept of the core in SP networks is not different from enterprise networks discussed earlier in this book; however, the core in SP networks from a topological point of view provides the interconnection between the different POPs and regions. Therefore, the underlying physical topology of an SP core may vary depending on the size of the SP, number of customers, geographic locations (national or international), and the services offered (Internet service provider [ISP], MPLS VPN, data center [DC] hosting SP). Even so, the most typical core topologies used in SP-grade networks are either ring or partial-mesh topologies, and commonly the core topology selection is driven by the following factors.

■ Geographic area coverage.

■ Available physical connectivity in certain areas.

■ Cost.

■ Primary business services and application requirements. For instance, content providers may invest in long-distance high-capacity optical links, whereas ISPs may use other intermediate providers to offload the cost of extending the core across certain areas.

Service Provider Control Plane Logical Architectures

In today's SP network architectures, several technologies and control protocols independently or collectively transform the network into a "carrier grade" type of network. This section covers the main control plane and forwarding protocols used by modern SPs from a high-level network architecture point of view. The subsequent sections cover the possible design options and considerations in greater detail. This section covers the following SP architecture elements that can all collectively construct the logical overlay and the core transport (forwarding and control plane) of a typical SP network:

- IGP

- BGP

- MPLS

- MP-BGP

Chapter 6, "Service Provider MPLS VPN Services Design," focuses on the following two primary services enabled by the protocols in the preceding list and offered by today's SPs:

- MPLS L3VPN

- MPLS L2VPN

IGP in Service Provider Networks

The principles of IGP routing designs covered earlier in this book, such as topology and reachability information hiding techniques, are all applicable with regard to the physical and logical layouts. However, there are some differences between designing IGP for enterprise networks compared to SP networks, as summarized in the list that follows. Therefore, network designers must identify the nature of the targeted environment when evaluating, planning, and designing the IGP:

- The goal of IGP in SP networks is not to carry customer routes but to carry infrastructure addresses and provide next-hop reachability to BGP. (BGP is the de facto protocol of SP networks, regardless of whether MPLS enabled or non-MPLS.)

- The IGP protocol for the SP core networks is typically either Open Shortest Path First (OSFP) or IS-IS for several known reasons, such as supporting MPLS-TE.

- In SP networks, IGP routes must be contained within the SP network only and are not to be exchanged or leaked with any customer network.

- In addition to external BGP (eBGP) and static routing, IGP is also used by some SPs as a PE-CE (customer edge) routing protocol. This IGP is intended to extend customer Layer 3 domain toward to the SP network (virtually separated per customer at the directly connected PE), and it is not an extension of the SP core IGP. (Chapter 6 discusses MPLS VPN designs in more detail.)

Despite the simplified IGP design of SP networks compared to enterprise networks, several factors may influence the logical design of the IGP in an SP network. For instance, breaking IGP flooding domains may optimize the IGP design and facilities, enhancing the scalability of the network. However, at the same it may add complexity to the design of other protocols, such as MPLS-TE. More details are covered later in Chapter 6. (See the section "Service Provider Control Plane Scalability Design Options and Considerations" in that chapter.)

BGP in Service Provider Networks

In SP networks—such as ISPs that have either no MPLS enabled across the network and traffic forwarding is based mainly on native IP or MPLS enabled across the network— BGP (iBGP) is the de facto protocol that carries all the routes that do not contribute to the internal SP IGP routing, such as the Internet routing table and customer-assigned addresses. This concept applies to both IPv4 and IPv6.

The main difference between BGP design in ISP networks and large enterprises is the number of the prefixes and the scale of the network size that BGP needs to handle. Accordingly, scalability within a manageable size is one of the primary goals of SP networks. However, BGP scalability design considerations, discussed earlier in "Chapter 2", using BGP RR and confederations are still all applicable to the BGP design in ISP-grade networks. Furthermore, later in Chapter 6, in the section "Service Provider Control Plane Scalability Design Options and Considerations," you will learn about additional scaling techniques that are more SP related, which can be considered to scale BGP design, such as multitier RR architecture.

In fact, the SP business by nature is a revenue-driven business. Therefore, SPs always aim to satisfy service-level agreement (SLA) requirements with their customers. In addition, network designers must keep in mind that any design decision that may lead to negatively impacting customer satisfaction must always be avoided, even if the proposed design option might (technically) offer significant benefits. BGP, as the primary control plane protocol in SP networks, can be a significant influencer. For instance, some BGP design decisions, such as route aggregation, hot-potato routing, and cold-potato routing, can have a direct impact on the SP business in terms of losing or generating revenue. The subsequent sections highlight how these technical design decisions may impact the SP's business.

BGP Route Aggregation (ISP Perspective)

One of the primary revenue-generating services of today's SPs is Internet access provision. Normally, Internet SPs peer with other peering or transit providers to build their Internet reachability. In ISP networks, it might seem easy to handle routes within and between peering ISPs. However, sometimes simple design decisions, such as aggregation, can make a significant difference in the overall network performance and may impact the ISP business. For instance, from the ISP perspective, it is sometimes advised to advertise the aggregate of the prefixes that are owned by the ISP and allocated to its customers. However, the question to be asked here is this: Will this make a tangible difference? And how will this decision impact the ISP business? Consider the scenario depicted in Figure 5-6.

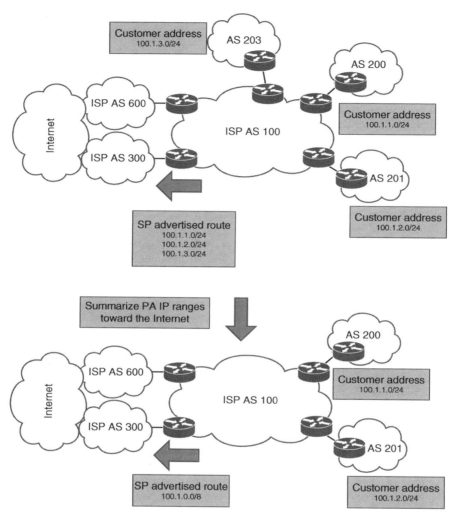

Figure 5-6   *The Impact of BGP Aggregation Between Peering ISPs*

Note   The subnet length advertised between the peering ISPs presented in this section (such as /24) is only to simplify the illustration of the advantages or implications of the decision to enable BGP aggregation or not, at the peering boundary points. However, some ISPs may not accept a subnet like /24 due to "net policing" they use with their peering ISPs. This filtering is commonly based on the Regional Internet Registry (RIR) minimum IP subnets allocation (/20). Consequently, several ISPs that enable net police filtering at their peering boundaries with other ISPs will drop or filter any advertised provider-assigned IP prefix larger than /20.

The scenarios illustrated in Figure 5-6 are common in ISP peering types of networks. The bottom scenario in this figure represents an optimized route's advertisement between AS 100 and its peering ISPs (AS 300 and 600), where the ISP (AS 100) summarizes the provider-assigned/aggregatable (PA) IPs allocated to its customers toward the Internet (typically toward the other peering ISPs). With this approach, any link failure or flapping with any of its customer links will not propagate this failure event information to other peering ISPs (fault isolation based on reachability information hiding principle). As a result, BGP aggregation in this scenario can optimize the overall performance of the network and over the Internet, and can provide a better quality of experience for their customers. It can also meet a tight SLA in terms of Internet reachability following a recovery from a failure event. In other words, the BGP design decision in this scenario (summarization) can be seen as a "business enabler."

Note   BGP PA IP range summarization by this ISP can specifically optimize customer experience following a PE-CE link failure event, because this ISP advertises only the summary. When the customer link recovers from the failure, there is no need for BGP to converge across the Internet (across the multiple peering ISPs) for this customer to be reachable over the Internet. This will also help to avoid BGP "path hunting" behavior in which a prefix withdrawal may create a major flap event over multiple AS hops away in the Internet.

However, in this particular scenario, if the customer is connected to a second ISP (multi-homed) using its same PA IP range allocated by the first ISP (AS 100) and the customer aims to use the second ISP as a backup path only (for example by using AS-PATH prepending over the backup path), this will result in an undesirable outcome, regardless of what BGP attribute they use to influence BGP path selection. This is simply because the second ISP does not own this PA IP range; therefore, it cannot aggregate this range. This will usually lead to a situation where the Internet (other peering ISPs) will see a more specific route (longest match) via the second ISP, which will be the preferred path regardless of what BGP attribute has been used, as illustrated in Figure 5-7.

To avoid situations like this, customers commonly use a provider-independent (PI) IP range, which the ISP does not summarize; alternatively, address summarization can be negotiated with the ISP to send more specific prefixes, as illustrated in Figure 5-8.

Note   Sending more-specific customer routes (PA IPs) to peering ISPs is not always achievable, because of the net police route filtering used between ISPs (discussed earlier).

Note   Traffic originating from customers of the second AS in this example may still prefer the path via the local AS if this AS assigned higher BGP local preferences for routes learned from its customers, as discussed in the section "Enterprise Multihomed Internet Design Considerations" in Chapter 4.

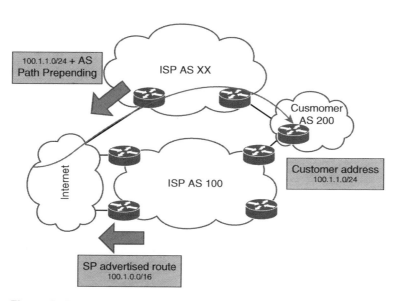

Figure 5-7   *ISP Summarization and Suboptimal Routing*

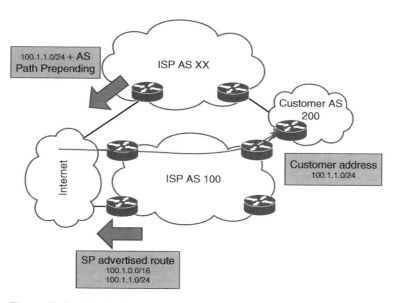

Figure 5-8   *Optimal Routing over Peering ISPs*

However, sending more-specific prefixes may lead to a longer recovery time (BGP convergence across the Internet also will be impacted by BGP path hunting behavior) following a failure event. This will be a concern from the ISP if there is a strict SLA they have to meet with regard to service recovery time, considering that what is a priority for the business has to always be given preference and the technology must serve as a facilitator.

This was an example of how BGP design decision can directly impact the ISP business in terms of performance and customer satisfaction.

Hot- and Cold-Potato Routing (SP Perspective)

One of the common methods to forward transit traffic in SP networks (commonly ISPs) is by sending the traffic to the closest exit point considering IGP metrics/cost to achieve traffic fast forwarding. This approach is commonly known as *hot-potato routing*. The name of this approach exemplifies the situation where a hot potato is held by someone in the hands, and he/she quickly passes it to the next person. Anyone holding the hot potato will attempt to pass it to the next person as quickly as possible. Hot-potato routing is the typical behavior on the Internet.

In Figure 5-9, the direct path via the western region represents typical hot-potato routing. One of the main benefits of this traffic routing approach is the fast forwarding of transit traffic from the point of entry to the closest exit point. This can be cost-effective to those SPs that have an agreement to use other providers' physical networks between cities to forward transit traffic in scenarios where adding more bandwidth involves paying extra cost. However, when there is a BGP RR in the path, this behavior may be broken. Typically, an RR in a BGP environment will advertise the best path from its point of view of the topology, which might not be the closest exit point from a given PE/border router point of view. This BGP RR path hiding behavior can prevent efficient use of BGP multipath, lead to multi-exit discriminator (MED) oscillations and suboptimal hot-potato routing, as illustrated in Figure 5-9 (the path via the northern region) [34].

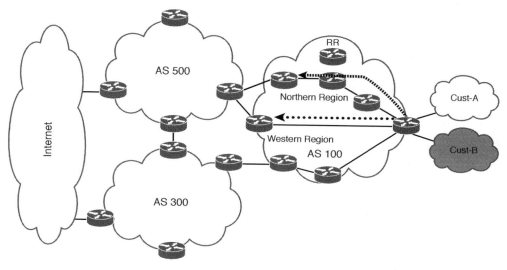

Figure 5-9 *BGP RR and Hot-Potato Routing*

Multiple options can be considered to overcome this behavior (this behavior might be undesirable for some requirements and not always), such as the following:

■ BGP ADD-PATH capability

■ BGP diverse paths (RFC 6774)

■ BGP partial mesh of iBGP sessions in addition to existing sessions to the RR, to add the optimal path for those edge routers that need to be used for hot-potato routing

BGP ADD-PATH

ADD-PATH is a BGP feature that allows BGP speakers to advertise more than one path over a single neighbor session. This capability can prove useful when there is an RR in the BGP architecture to send multiple paths to the RR clients (overcomes RR issues when hot-potato routing in a transit network is required), as illustrated in Figure 5-10. However, some considerations must be taken into account when considering this feature as a design option:

■ All routers may require software upgrade to support this feature.

■ Network designers need to identify how many paths and what paths to announce.

■ There will be additional memory overhead on the receiving PE because of the additional paths and the increases in CPU utilization (updates processing and other internal processing such as next-hop trigger).

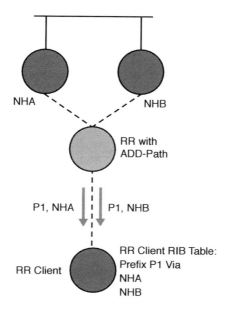

Figure 5-10 *BGP ADD-PATH*

BGP Diverse Paths

With this approach, BGP can achieve the same goal of what ADD-PATH does; however, it does not require an upgrade of the entire network or any protocol changes. Diverse paths can be announced using two deployment models, as illustrated in Figure 5-11:

- Single RR with a second iBGP session to the PE's "shadow session" that announce only diverse paths (advertises next best path)

- Adding a second RR to the cluster, where the second RR "shadow RR" calculates and advertises the diverse paths (next best path to the same prefix with a different next hop)

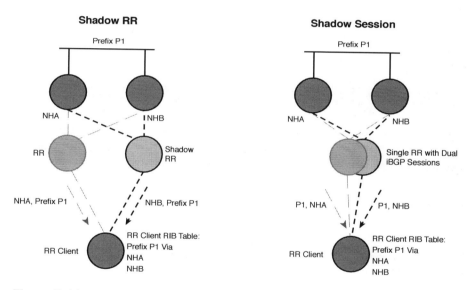

Figure 5-11   *BGP Diverse Path*

In addition, this model can easily integrate in a large-scale "multitier BGP RR" network, as illustrated in Figure 5-12.

However, some design aspects need to be considered with regard to this design approach:

- The required additional sessions to enable diverse paths

- The required additional memory to store diverse paths

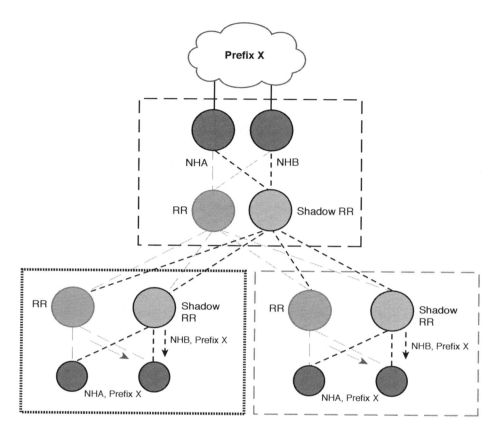

Figure 5-12 *BGP Diverse Path with in Multitier BGP Design*

Note In general, the goal of the preceding two options is to send more than one best path known by the RR to the iBGP speaker. The iBGP speaker would then have these paths and can install them in the Routing Information Base (RIB) table if the multipath option is enabled. Routes could also be programmed into the Forwarding Information Base (FIB) as an alternate backup path if BGP prefix-independent convergence (PIC) is enabled. Nevertheless, these two options are not analogous. For instance, with the "diverse path," the RR iBGP client receives only two paths per prefix (best and the next best path). In cases of hot-potato routing, where an ISP's network has multiple exit points for the same prefix, let's say five equal-cost multi-path routing (ECMP) routes, and you want to use all of them, the ADD-PATH option with *N* paths is more feasible in this case compared to the diverse path option.

BGP Partial Mesh

As illustrated in Figure 5-13, in some scenarios a partial mesh can be considered an option as well to achieve optimal hot-potato routing when there is BGP RR in the BGP topology; however, this approach may lead to scalability limitations if many border routers need a direct iBGP session.

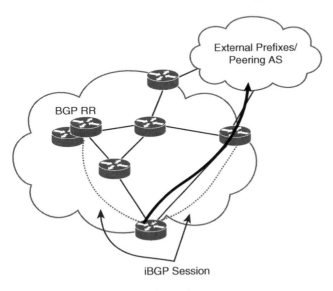

Figure 5-13 *BGP Partial-Mesh Sessions*

Although all these options are valid approaches, the decision of selecting the optimal option depends on the environment and some other design aspects such as the network scale and performance impact. Table 5-1 compares these options from different design perspectives.

Table 5-1 *Hot-Potato with BGP RR Optimization Options*

Design Consideration	BGP ADD-PATH	BGP Diverse Paths	BGP Partial Mesh + RR
Software/code upgrade to enable the capability	Yes (network-wide)	Yes, partially (BGP RR only)	No
Required BGP sessions to receive multiple paths	1	Two	Depends on the network
Number of paths	2 or more (configurable)	2 paths *	Depends on the iBGP sessions + the RR BGP session

Table 5-1 *continued*

Design Consideration	BGP ADD-PATH	BGP Diverse Paths	BGP Partial Mesh + RR
Scalability	Moderate	High	Moderate
Manageability	Simple	Simple	The more sessions, the more complex the network
Hardware resources utilization (memory, CPU)	Moderate to high (depends on the number of paths and prefixes)	Moderate	Moderate to high (depending on the number of iBGP session besides the BGP session to the BGP RR)

* Assuming two upstream BGP RRs used per BGP RR client to provide the diverse path functionality.

Note You can use the unique RD approach for similar situations in MPLS VPN environments (see Chapter 6 for more details). Furthermore, placing the RR physically close to eBGP speakers (at the AS boundary) along the edge of the network would allow traffic to more accurately follow the IGP metrics when destined toward external prefixes. Although technically this can be a valid option, practically it will not scale in large SP environments, especially when there are multiple boundary points (such as peering with multiple external networks/SPs).

Hot-potato routing is seen as a good approach for transit providers to route transit traffic as quickly as possible over the closest exit point; however, this behavior may lead to undesirable customer experiences in some situations, which can affect the SLA between the provider and its customers. For example, the customer with AS 500 in Figure 5-14 has an SLA with ISP AS 100 to offer a certain level of Internet bandwidth; however, forwarding the traffic over to AS 300 to reach the Internet using the hot-potato approach will lead to sending AS 500 customer traffic over the low-bandwidth link of AS 300. This will result in an undesirable experience for this customer. Therefore, in this situation, cold-potato routing can be a more efficient solution.

Cold-potato routing, however, tends to keep traffic within the same AS until reaching the closest exit point to the destination. In other words, cold-potato routing aims to hold a packet within the AS from its entry point to the AS. This approach offers more granule "end-to-end" control of packet forwarding because they will have visibility and control over the end-to-end path. In addition, this approach can be beneficial to data center hosting and content SPs because they can control and offer better quality, which will lead to a better SLA and more satisfied customers. SPs normally use BGP attributes such as local_preference to keep the path within the same AS as the preferred one, in addition to BGP MED and the accumulated IGP metric attribute for BGP AIGP. However, cold-potato routing can be an expensive approach because SPs might be required to use their own intercity or international links more often for transit traffic. Sending transit traffic over other providers' infrastructures (interprovider) might offer a cheaper rate (cost versus quality).

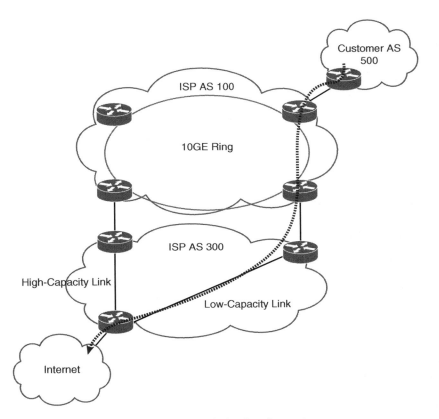

Figure 5-14 *Hot-Potato Routing Limitation Scenario*

Therefore, the decision to adopt a hot-potato or cold-potato routing approach with the SP network has to be aligned with the business priorities, constraints, and requirements. This alignment will achieve a successful business-driven design decision, which is not solely based on technical best practices recommendations.

Multiprotocol Label Switching

MPLS is a standard IETF technology, defined in a multiple RFCs, and can be described literally as a Layer 2.5 networking protocol. Typically in the OSI model, Layer 2 refers to protocols like Ethernet, which normally carries IP packets over a LAN or WAN network, while Layer 3 on the higher layer of the Open System Interconnect (OSI) controls the routing of packets over Internet Protocol (IP routing control plane). In contrast, MPLS is provisioned between these two layers, offering additional capabilities for the transport of data across the network. MPLS offers a less-hardware-intensive mechanism to forward traffic based on label switching.

In today's SP networks, MPLS is driving the network overlay concepts that enable it to support multiple technologies and protocols over one common physical infrastructure. Consequently, MPLS-based SP networks can offer various services and are more responsive to market trends and changes by relying on the high degree of flexibility and simplicity provided by MPLS to the network to introduce new services.

The following are the primary drivers for SPs (also large-scale enterprises) to adopt and invest in MPLS-enabled core infrastructure:

- Accelerate time to the market. MPLS offers the ability to enable the delivery of different transport services across the same packet-switched network infrastructure (for example, L2VPN, L3VPN, and interworking between legacy and modern Layer 2 services [ATM to Ethernet]). This can enable SPs to introduce new services that meet market trends and customer needs in a timely manner using the same underlying core infrastructure.

- Offer differentiated services and meet tight SLAs. MPLS offers the ability to enable a source-based routing mechanism (MPLS-TE) that can control where and how traffic is routed across the network to manage capacity and congestion, and prioritize different services and path protections that can meet various strict SLAs requirements.

- Enhance network resiliency with MPLS FF (MPLS-TE, RLFA).

- Reduce operational complexity because the different control plane protocols that serve different services will be transported over one core infrastructure (multiservice infrastructure) such as L3VPN and L2VPN. This means that there will be fewer technologies and protocols to support, which translates into a lesser amount of expertise required.

Consequently, by adapting a service convergence strategy, SPs can decrease the time to the market to introduce new services and capabilities to their customers. Furthermore, it helps to significantly reduce operational expenditures (OPEX) by managing one multiservice-aware IP MPLS core rather than multiple separate networks that require different expertise and increase troubleshooting complexity (for instance, the combination of legacy services like ATM, Frame Relay, time-division multiplexing [TDM], and IP). However, the MPLS core can still support legacy services at the edge to maintain and protect current customer investments and to provide access diversity, which can offer a high degree of service access flexibility to enterprise customers with the least capital expenditure (CAPEX) by using same existing infrastructure in scenarios where minimizing cost is one of the highest business priorities.

MPLS Label-Switched Path

Label-switched path (LSP) is a fundamental requirement for any MPLS forwarding to occur. Typically, LSP is routed across an MPLS network via forming a unidirectional tunnel between any two routers,. The ingress node or router that first encapsulates a packet inside an MPLS LSP in MPLS terms is called the *label edge router* (LER), and the node that performs only MPLS switching in the middle of an LSP is called the *label-switching router* (LSR). Finally, the LSP termination node is the egress node where the MPLS label is removed (popped).

In an MPLS network, an MPLS signaling protocol performs the mapping of LSPs to specific label values. Two primary MPLS signaling protocols are in use today:

- **Label Distribution Protocol (LDP):** A simple nonconstrained protocol

- **Resource Reservation Protocol (RSVP) with Traffic Engineering (RSVP-TE):** A complex protocol compared to LDP, with more overhead, and most commonly used for MPL-TE setup

In today's SP networks, both protocols are actually used. The LDP is typically used for MPLS VPN and other services, and RSVP-TE is used for traffic engineering services.

MPLS Deployment Modes

The typical and most common deployment mode of MPLS is the frame mode. In the frame mode, the MPLS label is assigned between Layer 2 and Layer 3 headers (Layer 2.5), where Layer 2 can be a standard Ethernet or a legacy Frame Relay. As illustrated in Figure 5-15, this mode provides flexibility to SPs to maintain the legacy access media type if required. This connectivity model is most commonly used between the PE-CE links or between a level 2 POP/PE and level 1 POP (a regional POP), whether as a permanent or as a temporary solution (during the migration from FR to IP).

MPLS cell mode, however, is specifically developed and used in MPLS over ATM environments where ATM switches are used (typically to forward data based on virtual circuits [VCs]). In this mode, the MPLS label value is driven from the ATM virtual path or channel identifiers. This mode is commonly used when the core ATM network cannot be upgraded for some reason, such as limited budget. From the design point of view, this can be considered a design constraint for network designers that must be dealt with.

Accordingly, MPLS cell mode offers network designers the flexibility to deliver MPLS over ATM infrastructure. This can provide the business with the various benefits of MPLS-enabled infrastructure highlighted earlier in this chapter without any additional CAPEX to upgrade the underlying hardware infrastructure, taking into consideration its scalability limitations and slower overall convergence time, along with the increased operational complexity (this is commonly known as *multiple operations support systems*, which can lead to operational inefficiency associated with increased OPEX). As a result, some businesses, over the long term, may end up spending more on OPEX in an attempt to save on CAPEX. In other words, a network architect with good strategic planning can justify the suggested solution (for instance, to migrate to pure end-to-end

MPLS and IP only) if the proposed or intended solution is for the long term, as illustrated in Figure 5-15.

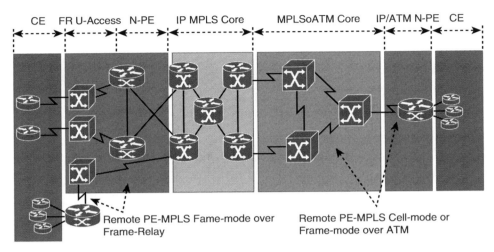

Figure 5-15 *MPLS Modes*

Note Scenarios where the core (transit) ATM switches either do not support MPLS (cell mode) or are in a transition period to complete IP-based infrastructure MPLS frame mode over ATM can be a viable choice.

Multiprotocol BGP

BGP is extended to provide multiprotocol support (MP-BGP) that enables BGP to carry routing information for different network layers and address families. In modern SPs, MP-BGP, along with MPLS, is mainly used to facilitate the control and forwarding of MPLS VPNs. This is commonly where private Layer 2 and Layer 3 for both unicast and multicast network services can be delivered over a common MPLS- and MP-BGP-enabled infrastructure, which can significantly optimize control plane design and operational complexity. Logically, MPLS in SP-grade networks represents the underlay control protocol across the SP transport network, and MP-BGP is the overlay control protocol that hosts and controls customer prefixes. Furthermore, in modern SP-grade networks, MP-BGP is used not only for Layer 3 IP routing information exchange; it is also used for Layer 2 VPN service as an autodiscovery mechanism and Layer 2 MAC routing information (as described in IEFTF draft "draft-ietf-l2vpn-evpn-11"), where the MAC learning between PEs happens at the control plane level. Therefore, MP-BGP plays a vital role as its the primary control protocol for the main services offered by today's SPs (such as Layer 3 and Layer 2 VPN services). Chapter 6 covers these MPLS VPN services in more detail. Figure 5-16 illustrates the building blocks of the various services and protocols that are enabled by MPLS and controlled on a higher level by MP-BGP.

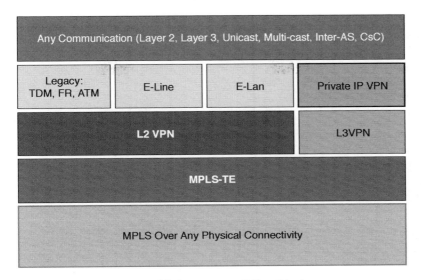

Figure 5-16 *MPLS-Enabled Service Building Blocks*

MPLS Traffic Engineering

Multiprotocol Label Switching (MPLS) Traffic Engineering is a constrained source-based routing mechanism that helps network operators to optimize traffic routing across MPLS-enabled networks based on multiple advanced path attributes that is impossible to achieve with the classic IP routing only. This section covers the drivers toward adopting MPLS-TE to act as a business enabler, along with the different MPLS-TE design considerations, advantages, and the associated implications.

Business and Technical Drivers

One of the common questions that network architects and designers face is this: Do we need MPLS Traffic Engineering and why? Typically, a good network design must accommodate traffic requirements in terms of traffic volume and traffic pattern, considering its characteristics as well, such as the delay of sensitive traffic. However, in reality, traffic requirements in many situations change over time (normally after years of the initial network deployment). This change results from several variables, such as business organic growth, merger and acquisition, or the business's adoption of new services and applications. This is typical in SP networks; after all, the number of customers may significantly grow within a few years. Consequently, a network designed for yesterday's traffic requirements may not optimally deliver today's traffic requirements.

Furthermore, many businesses cannot afford to upgrade their core infrastructure within a short period of time. (This might be cost related, or the business cannot afford upgrade outages and so on.) Consequently, network designers need to incorporate a solution that can offer the business the flexibility to overcome these limitations with minimal infrastructure changes or upgrades. For instance, in the scenario depicted in Figure 5-17, an SP based in Australia has five primary POPs (Sydney, Brisbane, Melbourne, Adelaide, and Perth) with different intercity optical link capacities.

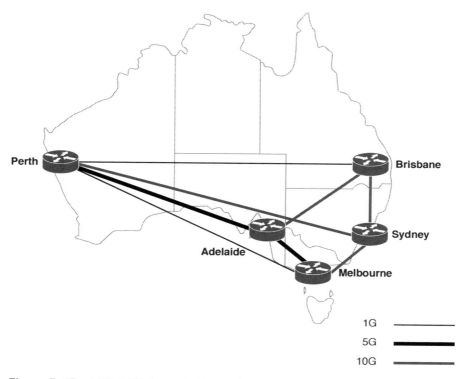

Figure 5-17   *MPLS-TE Scenario Network Layout*

This SP has a new demand to provide point-to-point virtual leased line (VLL) over Layer 2 MPLS VPN service for two of its customers (between Perth and Brisbane POPs) with bandwidth requirements of 1 Gbps each. In addition, path protection for this VLL service is part of the SLA in case of any link failure in the path.

However, with the current infrastructure using typical routing traffic engineering techniques (which is typically hop-by-hop destination-based routing), this SP will not be able to accomplish this requirement optimally. Moreover, although policy-based routing (PBR) may be used (technically) to achieve this goal, PBR often introduces several limitations to the design and the overall network performance. These limitations include operational complexities, instability, potential routing loops, and high hardware resource utilization.

With MPLS-TE, network designers can achieve a more scalable and constrained sourced-based routing solution. By applying MPLS-TE, this SP can selectively route the VLL L2 VPN traffic over the higher-capacity path (Brisbane to Sydney, then Perth), as illustrated in Figure 5-18. In addition, MPLS-TE fast reroute (FRR) can offer path protection to reroute traffic over an alternate path that meets minimum bandwidth capacity requirements to align with the offered SLA. In this example, the alternate path will be Brisbane to Adelaide, then Perth, as illustrated in Figure 5-18.

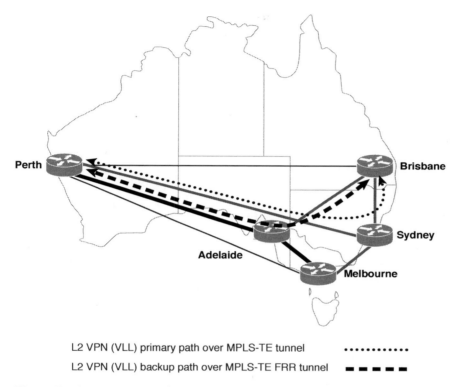

L2 VPN (VLL) primary path over MPLS-TE tunnel   •••••••••••

L2 VPN (VLL) backup path over MPLS-TE FRR tunnel   ■ ■ ■ ■ ■

Figure 5-18   *MPLS-TE Solution 1*

Furthermore, this SP needs to accommodate new requirements for two of its key customers who have main offices in Melbourne and Perth. The first customer needs a VLL point-to-point service between Melbourne and Perth with 1 Gbps of bandwidth, and the second customer requires all their voice traffic between their main offices in Melbourne and Perth to be treated differently (routed over a lower-congested path with the least latency, along with path protection in case of a link failure).

MPLS-TE can help this SP to optimize traffic utilization over its intercity optical links with regard to the available bandwidth and customer requirements. For example, VLL traffic between Melbourne and Perth for the first customer can be redirected over the Sydney POP when its link between Sydney and Perth is underutilized. This offloads some of the traffic between Melbourne and Perth using MPLS-TE constrained routing.

At the same time, the voice traffic of the second customer can be sent over a TE tunnel that has better bandwidth and with minimal latency. In this example, the path will be Melbourne to Adelaide, then Perth, while the direct path between Melbourne and Perth can be used as a backup (alternate path) for voice traffic in case of any failure in the primary path, as illustrated in Figure 5-19. In addition, this SP is planning to enable unequal load sharing for data traffic with low priority (such as marked-down traffic with an EXP value of 0) between Melbourne and Brisbane POPs via both Adelaide and Sydney POPs, thereby taking advantage of the MPLS-TE capability to provide equal and unequal load balancing over multiple paths.

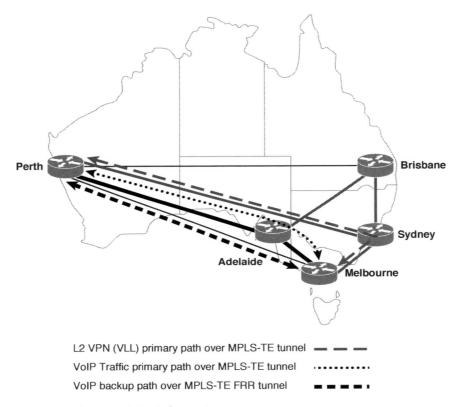

L2 VPN (VLL) primary path over MPLS-TE tunnel   — — —
VoIP Traffic primary path over MPLS-TE tunnel   ‧‧‧‧‧‧‧‧‧‧‧
VoIP backup path over MPLS-TE FRR tunnel   ▬ ▬ ▬ ▬ ▪

Figure 5-19   *MPLS-TE Solution 2*

From this example, we can conclude that several benefits may drive businesses and network designers to consider traffic engineering, including the following:

- Offer businesses a cost-effective solution to optimize the utilization of infrastructure links (optimized bandwidth management).

- Opens new markets for SPs by enabling them to offer more reliable services with very strict SLAs (for example, end-to-end high-bandwidth capacity, highly reliable service with MPLS-TE FRR, end-to-end low latency, and low packet loss services).

- Constrained source-based routing with MPLS-TE provides network designers a flexible and proven mechanism to have a more granular control over traffic passing through the transport network supported by various powerful MPLS-TE features, such as FRR and DS-MPLS-TE.

■ Offer network designers multiple design options to enhance the overall network design in terms of path utilization and path protection by using MPLS-TE unequal-cost load balancing and MPLS-TE FRR, respectively.

However, MPLS-TE is not a feature or mechanism that must be used with MPLS-enabled networks. For example, networks overprovisioned with links and bandwidth normally do not need MPLS-TE to optimize and balance the utilization of links. Enabling MPLS-TE in networks such as this can sometimes be seen as added complexity without a real business value.

Therefore, network designers must understand the goals and requirements during the planning phase to suggest the suitable solution and the optimal MPLS-TE design approach. Otherwise, lack of good planning and a structured approach in designing MPLS-TE can significantly increase operational complexities.

This section covers the common planning approaches of MPLS-TE to generate a business-driven solution, along with the different design considerations that influence MPLS-TE design.

Note In some situations, the network does not require MPLS-TE to optimize link utilization. However, MPLS-TE is mainly used to provide path protection with MPLS-TE (FRR). MPLS-TR FRR and MPLS with quality of service (QoS) are covered later in this book. Therefore, good planning with a good understanding of the targeted goal is crucial with MPLS-TE.

MPLS-TE Planning

In Chapter 1, planning was divided into two main approaches: strategic and tactical. These two approaches can be adopted to plan a business-driven MPLS-TE design to help network designers make the most suitable design choices based on the selected approach, which is typically driven by the business's needs and strategy.

MPLS-TE Strategic Planning Approach

In this approach, network designers must accommodate a long-term business and design objective to be reflected on the MPLS-TE design. For instance, an SP may decide to offer differentiated services to its clients to generate more revenue. One of these services may be to provide guaranteed end-to-end voice delivery with minimal to zero service disruption in the event of any network component failure within the SP network.

In the aforementioned scenario, network designers must make sure that customer Voice over IP (VoIP) traffic is routed over the least-congested paths without introducing any unnecessary latency to the traffic. In addition, a path-protection mechanism should be incorporated to meet the promised SLA by this SP after any failure event. Based on that, network designers can plan MPLS-TE combined with differentiated service (DS)

MPLS-TE and FRR to meet this new long-term business strategy or direction. Similarly, Figure 5-20 represents a network where both R1 and R2 can send traffic peaking up to 5G, which can lead to potential congestion on the link between R3 and R5. Therefore, a long-term solution is required here.

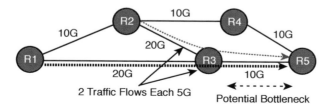

Figure 5-20   *Traffic Flow Before Applying MPLS-TE*

By introducing MPSL-TE, this network can permanently overcome this limitation (during normal, not failure, situations) by shifting the traffic flow of R2 to go over R4, then R5, assuming that the goal in this design is to provide optimization based on bandwidth only, as shown in Figure 5-21.

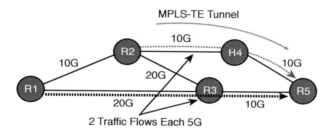

Figure 5-21   *Traffic Flow After Applying MPLS-TE*

MPLS-TE Tactical Planning Approach

In this approach, however, network designers typically are required to incorporate certain requirements that are normally temporary as a quick fix to an issue or a short-term solution that is to be changed later. For example, the scenario depicted in Figure 5-22 shows a global SP that currently has two interconnections between the North American and European regions. Currently, the first link (link 1) is facing high traffic utilization. The business decided to upgrade this link to accommodate the increased traffic volume. However, this upgrade may take several months to complete. Therefore, this SP needs to temporarily offload some of the traffic from link 1 and send it over link 2, which is currently underutilized.

In this scenario, network designers can temporarily set up MPLS-TE to force certain traffic selectively (for example, traffic from customers without strict VoIP SLA) to traverse the second path. Even though the second path is longer from a classic routing point of view (more hops) and has a lower bandwidth, the reality is this path is underutilized, which can reduce packet drop possibility, because the first path is overutilized.

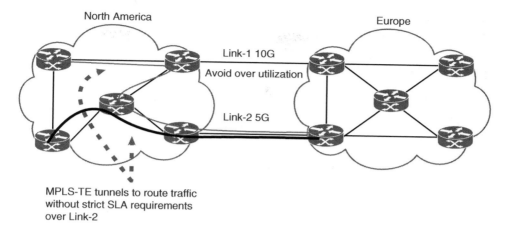

Figure 5-22 *MPLS-TE Technical Planning Scenario*

During the planning phase, it is important that network designers understand the goal to be achieved and whether MPLS-TE is the right solution. From a design point of view, the more protocols and features in the network, the more complex the design and operation will be. Answers to the following questions can help network designers, to a large extent, drive the MPLS-TE design in the right direction:

- Is the solution intended to be an interim solution or a long-term solution?

- What is the ultimate goal that needs to be achieved?

    - Provide more balanced and efficient bandwidth utilization across the network

    - Provide path protection (fast failover in milliseconds)

    - Protect certain traffic from paths with a high degree of fate sharing (shared link risk group SLRG)

    - Provide service differentiation to meet tight SLA requirements

    - Combination of the above

- Is the targeted environment under single or multiple IGP or BGP domains?

- What is the scope of the solution (within a POP, between certain regional POPs, or across the entire network)?

MPLS-TE Design Considerations

Technically, there are two primary functions to set up MPLS-TE:

- Path computation that is driven by a set of predefined constraints to satisfy the desired design goals

- How to place and forward the desired traffic through the established MPLT-TE tunnel path

Therefore, it is important that network designers understand the mechanisms that MPLS-TE uses and supports to calculate the path in a constrained manner. Network designers must also be able to identify and understand the different options that can be used to forward the traffic along the path. In addition, the design architecture of the underlying Layer 3 routing (single versus multiple flooding domains) and the placement of the MPLS-TE tunnels (outer mesh versus inner mesh) are critical influencing factors to the MPLS-TE design and operation in large-scale networks. This section highlights and compares these aspects and discusses the advantages and the associated implications.

Constrained Path Calculation

The constrained shortest path calculation (CSPF) leverages the classic IGP shortest path first (SPF) algorithm to take into account different constraint variables. For instance, let's consider the same scenario of the previous section and assume that this SP has added a new POP in Tasmania with two interconnections, one to the Melbourne POP over an optical link and another to Perth's POP over a satellite link, as illustrated in Figure 5-23. With the typical SPF calculation, which is normally (directly or indirectly) calculated based the link bandwidth, the path via the satellite link will always be preferred over others. However, satellite links typically can offer high bandwidth with high latency. Based on that, if this SP wants to provide a tight SLA for real-time "delay-sensitive" traffic (VoIP) to its customers with sites connected in Tasmania and Perth, the satellite path must be avoided for this type of traffic, even though it has high bandwidth.

With CSPF, network designers can influence the CSPF calculation to include additional attributes, also known as *link coloring* or *affinity attributes*, where each path can be assigned a value or attribute to its physical link. If this value does not match the one configured at the TE tunnel, this link or path will be excluded from the CSPF calculation. This attribute can reflect different design criteria such as fate-sharing or high-latency paths. These attributes are carried by the link-state IGP-specific TE extensions (RFC 3630, 2784). Based on that, each node within the MPLS-TE-enabled domain (typically a single IGP domain) will have all the relevant information (bandwidth required for LSP setup and link attributes) stored in the MPLS Traffic Engineering Database (TED).

Consequently, the SP in the example depicted in Figure 5-23 can take advantage of the CSPF and send voice traffic over the path with less bandwidth and low latency while data traffic can still travel over the high-bandwidth, high-latency satellite path, as long as the appropriate mechanism to place traffic into the TE tunnel is selected to send voice and data each into its respective TE tunnel, as illustrated in Figure 5-24.

Furthermore, after the TE LSP setup is completed over the selected path that meets the CSPF criteria, the TED needs to be updated about the path state. For instance, the path selected for voice traffic in Figure 5-24 (Tasmania to Melbourne, then Perth) may become congested after a while because the link-state advertisement that is typically sent periodically, and also after any state change (for example, bandwidth or link attribute changes). In a process commonly known as *path reoptimization*, MPLS-TE will initiate CSPF to recalculate a new LSP that satisfies the minimum predefined requirements. In addition, MPLS-TE provides the ability to assign priorities to TE LSPs. This means that LSPs with a higher priority will have the ability to tear down lower-priority LSPs during the setup and during the recalculation of the LSP over a new path.

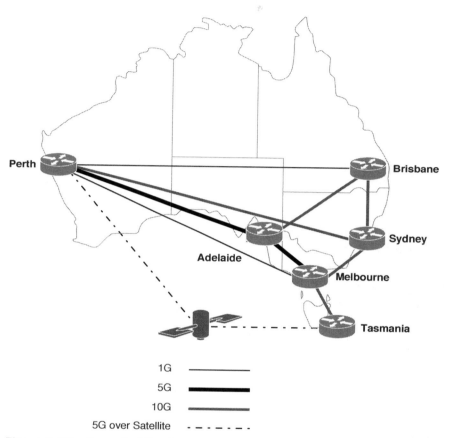

Figure 5-23   *Scenario 2 Pre-MPLS-TE*

Path reoptimization with MPLS-TE can offer a more dynamic and updated traffic pattern from the TED point of view, which may provide better bandwidth optimization. However, in networks with a high degree of traffic pattern changes across them or in the scenario when high MPLS-TE physical paths have a flapping issue, it will lead to significant network instability. This instability is especially pronounced if there are multiple MPLS-TE LSP priorities defined (flapping). Therefore, if network designers need to consider this capability, proper preemption delay timers need to be considered, as well, to avoid network instability situations. In addition, MPLS-TE relies on the "make-before-break" mechanism when building a new LSP in a path optimization situation to avoid tearing down an active LSP before building a new one. However, this approach can lead to double booking of bandwidth during the setup of the new LSP and before tearing down the original LSP.

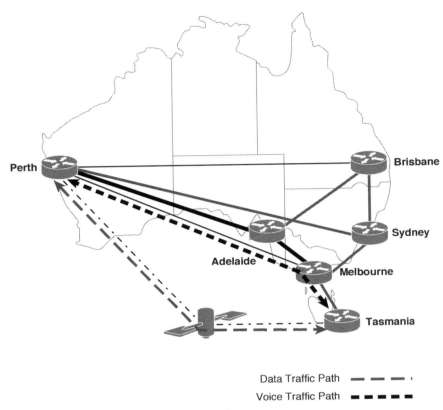

Figure 5-24   *Scenario 2 MPLS-TE Solution*

It is obvious from this example that the CSPF can offer more flexibility when it comes to path computation and selection criteria. However, if the considered CSPF approach does not align with the actual design goal, it will most probably be considered an added complexity to the design. For instance, if the design goal is only to provide better bandwidth utilization across the links, while the design considered an advanced CSPF criteria to select paths based on different attributes such as latency and shared risk link groups (SRLGs), this design typically falls under the principle discussed in Chapter 1, called *gold plating*. Gold plating occurs when the design adds more than what is required. Typically, this will be seen as an added complexity from both the design and operational perspectives. Therefore, it is critical to identify the actual intended goal of the solution during the planning phase before selecting any approach, because each component of the MPLS-TE can achieve different design goals in different ways.

Note   Link coloring or affinity attributes with regard to SRLG is only used to identify and mark SRLG points/links to be used in scenarios where the calculated path has to be free of any SRLG fate sharing.

Most MPLS-TE deployments are based on one of the mechanisms to calculate available bandwidth for the MPLS-TE LSP setup:

- **Offline calculation:** As the name implies, the offline calculation is typically performed outside the network using third-party specialized tools that can build and create sophisticated LSP setup. In particular, with the offline tools, SPs can overcome LSP packing issues because the tool has awareness of the entire LSP that needs to be set up. However, LSPs with the offline tools are sometimes built based on a stable traffic situation, which may lead to congestion during traffic spikes due to the lack of online visibility and reaction to traffic changes.

- **Online calculation:** With the online calculation, the router (headend) is responsible for the LSP setup. This may be seen by some providers as a way to simplify operational complexity because it can dynamically react to network/traffic pattern changes without the need to rely on another tool, which typically requires additional expertise and offline work. However, with the online approach, the LSP packing issue must be taken into account.

MPS-TE Tunnel Placement

As discussed earlier in this chapter, typical SP networks are structured of two tiers (POPs and core). On top of these two primary tiers, there are multiple overlays and control protocols running, including MPLS-TE. The misconception of MPLS-TE deployment over this type of architecture is that it should be run between PEs (PE to PE MPLS; TE tunnels). However, as explained earlier in this section, the successful MPLS-TE design must be driven by the intended goal or facilitated by MPLS-TE. Therefore, the two primary potential places to create and terminate MPLS-TE (headend and tail end) are either PE-to-PE or P(core)-to-P(core). Table 5-2 compares the implications of using either approach with regard to different design aspects.

Table 5-2 *MPLS-TE PE Mesh Versus P Mesh Tunnels*

	PE-to-PE MPLS-TE (Outer Mesh)	P-to-P MPLS-TE (Inner Mesh)
Number of LSPs	Large	Moderate
End-to-end traffic differentiation	Supported with high control	Partially supported (not end to end) with limited control (over the core)
Path protection	End-to-end LSP	Across the core only
Design simplicity	The larger the number of PEs, the more complex the design	Almost always simpler than PE to PE
Operational complexity	The larger the number of PEs, the more complex to manage the network	Almost always simpler than PE to PE

Table 5-2   *continued*

	PE-to-PE MPLS-TE (Outer Mesh)	P-to-P MPLS-TE (Inner Mesh)
Design scalability	Relatively scalable (the more PEs/LSPs, the more memory and CPU required)	Almost always more scalable than PE to PE because number core nodes usually fewer than PEs (ideally)
LSP stacking (LDP over TE tunnel with MPLS VPN)	Not required	Required

As highlighted in Chapter 1, for a design to be successful and reliable with regard to scalability, it has to be within a manageable scale. Otherwise, the added operational complexities may outweigh the advantage of scaling by size only. The following are primary factors that influence the scale of a MPLS-TE:

- LSP information state

- RSVP-TE information state

- Manageability level

- Processing overhead

In fact, in large environments with a mesh of TE tunnels, the placement of MPLS-TE headend and tail end (whether it is PE to PE or P to P) has significant impact on the factors in the preceding list, as shown in Figure 5-25.

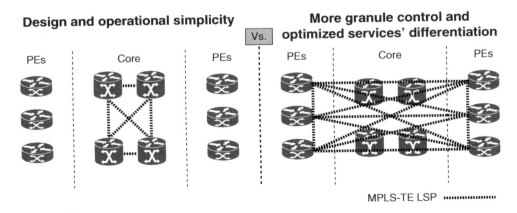

Figure 5-25   *MPLS-TE Tunnels: PE to PE Versus P to P*

Consequently, network designers and architects can decide suitable placement of the TE tunnels by aligning the design's goals, constraints (such as hardware limitations), and the design implications highlighted in Table 5-2. In addition, you can use a hybrid approach in some situations to satisfy different requirements. An example of a hybrid approach may be to provision a full mesh of TE tunnels across the core network to provide bandwidth optimization and path protection while using PE-to-PE TE tunnels to optimize end-to-end path selection and control between certain PEs only. Table 5-3 provides some examples of design requirements and possible MPLS-TE solutions with regard to TE tunnel placement.

Table 5-3 *MPLS-TE Solution with Regard to TE Tunnel Placement*

Design Requirements	Possible Solution
Path/bandwidth optimization for congestion points across the network	MPLS-TE on only the edge nodes (PEs) that face congestion such as regional Internet edge services PE (partial PE to PE)
Bandwidth optimization across the core network	MPLS-TE with a full logical mesh over a partial physical mesh or ring core, ideally with the help of an offline capacity planning tool service (ideally P to P)
Meet tight SLA requirements for providing L2VPN for a VLL service	MPLS-TE combined with tunnel priories using DS-TE and associated with MPLS-TE FRR (typically PE to PE)
Path protection to minimize convergence time to milliseconds across an overprovisioned bandwidth in the core	MPLS-TE FRR, ideally over one-hop primary TE tunnels and backup tunnel for each primary tunnel (ideally P to P) combined with automesh
Provide service differentiation for MPLS L3VPN customers such as voice and data over different paths	MPLS TE combined with tunnel priories using DiffServ-aware DS-TE and/or link affinity attributes along with a path/TE selection (QoS DiffServ based) to forward traffic based on QoS marking (You can use MPLS-TE FRR to protect critical TE tunnels only, ideally PE to PE.)

Routing Domains

One of the primary and critical MPLS-TE design factors is the Layer 3 routing design for both IGP and external gateway protocol (EGP) domains. As discussed earlier in this section, CSPF typically relies on the information flooded by the link state with the relevant TE extension that carries specific information for the MPLS-TE commutation. In addition, earlier in this book, the term *interdomain routing* described the concept of routing between two independent routing domains via an EGP protocol. However, in this section, interdomain routing *for the purpose of MPLS-TE design* refers to the routing between either two BGP domains (autonomous systems) or different IGP flooding domains.

Typically, in both cases, the MPLS-TE ingress node "headend node" does not have the required information in its TED to build an LSP to the destination (tail-end) node that resides in another routing domain. Therefore, the headend node cannot calculate the path to the tail end by itself with this limited vision. Therefore, the border routers (Area Border Routers [ABRs] or Autonomous System Border Routers [ASBRs]) along the path can complement the computation of the path segment relevant to the "downstream" flooding domain, because only the ABR knows the TE topology of the area to which it belongs. Based on that, the headend node will find the path to the next ABR, then this ABR will perform the RSVP-TE explicit route object (ERO) to specify the path of an MPLS LSP via a sequenced list of label-switching routers (LSRs) and will be expanded by the next ABR or LSR, also known as *ERO expand*. As illustrated in Figure 5-26, with the ERO expanded, when an LSR node receives an RSVP Path message, if the next hop in the ERO is specified as a "loose subobject," it should compute a path segment to that loose hop (typically an ABR).

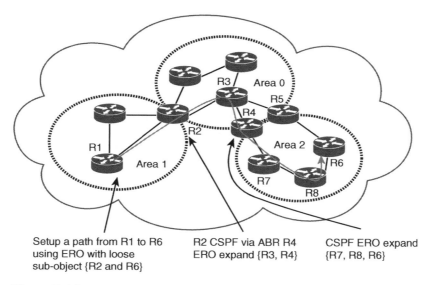

Setup a path from R1 to R6 using ERO with loose sub-object {R2 and R6}

R2 CSPF via ABR R4 ERO expand {R3, R4}

CSPF ERO expand {R7, R8, R6}

Figure 5-26   *MPLS-TE Interdomain*

One of the main limitations of this approach is it cannot guarantee optimal end-to-end shortest path selection (CSPF based). This is because each node will calculate the path up to the next loose subobject in the ERO path list (headend to the next ABR and ABR to the next ABR), which may not always lead to a desirable outcome.

For instance, in Figure 5-26, the end-to-end shortest path optimally should go via R5 to reach R6 (assuming the path to R5 meets other CSPF requirements such as minimum available bandwidth). However, because the calculation of the path is performed up to the ABR, suboptimal routing in situations like this is expected.

Alternatively, you can use a network component with the ability to calculate routes based on network graph known as *path computation element* (PCE) and described in RFC 4655. In PCE architecture, the MPLS-TE headend is technically considered a path computation client (PCC) and communicates over PCEP (Path Computation Element

Protocol) with the PCE. The PCE component can be any node sitting somewhere in the network (in a router or as a software running on a server), ideally providing full visibility of the network topology. This approach can offer a more optimal end-to-end path computation, because the PCE typically has a better view of the network topology; however, network nodes must support this protocol for the PCE architecture to function properly because it requires additional control system integration (PCC to PCE). This might not be achievable in some situations (for example, the business cannot afford any additional cost to upgrade any hardware or software to support PCE), or it might be seen as an added complexity to the design (additional components and additional control protocol).

Furthermore, BGP link state (BGP-LS, described in IETF draft idr-ls-distribution-impl-xx) introduces another mechanism in which BGP can be used to collect link-state (link-state database [LSDB]) information and traffic engineering (TED) information from different routing domains and share it with external components such as external BGP speaker (different IGP domains or multi-AS BGP scenario) using a new BGP network layer reachability information (NLRI) encoding. As a result, multiple paths and links attributes stored in any given routing domain LSDB such as link metric, link bandwidth, preemption, and SRLG can now be shared with other domains over specific BGP NLRI. With this approach, the IGP collected information per IGP domain such as link metrics and TED-related information can be exported to the BGP control plane. BGP, however, will be able to reliably and selectively share their information with other external BGP speakers such as a peering SP, and more efficiently than typical LSDB information sharing (support information aggregation of multiples IGP flooding domains and autonomous systems). However, due to the fact that with this approach BGP will be carrying information from links-state IGP, which may lead to more frequent NLRI updates, it is better to avoid using an existing BGP RR for this purpose (peering directly to BGP RR), to avoid any impact on the existing BGP stability in large networks.

It is obvious that MPLS-TE design and deployment is more complicated over multiple routing domains. In addition, path reoptimization (TE LSP reoptimization) in interdomain types of scenarios can prove challenging. This may introduce confusion when designing a large network as to whether to optimize routing design with more modular (multiple logical flooding domains) or to keep it under one single flooding domain. The solution to this dilemma depends completely on the design requirements, goals, and priorities (more scalable module routing design versus simplified MPLS-TE design, with flatter routing design under a single flooding domain).

Forwarding Traffic via the TE Tunnel

The other vital element of MPLS-TE design is how to place or forward traffic through the TE tunnel. Although this element might seem like an implementation decision; in fact, the method used to steer traffic through the TE tunnel can impact not only the MPLS-TE design, but it can also impact other routing and forwarding behavior if it is not aligned well (considering the holistic principle discussed in Chapter 1). Table 5-4 summarizes and compares the common and primary mechanisms that you can use for this purpose.

Table 5-4   *Primary Traffic Forwarding Mechanisms into MPLS-TE Tunnels*

Mechanism	Characteristic	Design and Operational Considerations	Possible Use Scenario
Static route	Manually and selectively point traffic flows through TE tunnel	Configuration and design complexity Operational complexity with large-scale networks	Small number of flows or a temporary redirection of traffic over a TE tunnel such as P2P L2VPN PW
Policy-based routing (PBR)	Manually and selectively select flows (sourced based)	Configuration and design complexity Operational complexity with large-scale networks May introduce some routing loops Can significantly increase hardware utilization in large deployments	Small number of flows or to temporarily redirect traffic over a TE tunnel
Autoroute	Automatic injection of the TE-tunnel tail end and the downstream destinations behind the tail end	Simple and dynamic Easier to deploy Lower operational complexity Less control of what traffic to use which TE when not combined with other capabilities like CBTS	Can support various scenario that need automatic injection of next hop reachability information via TE tunnel
Class-based tunnel selection (CBTS)	TE selection QoS DiffServ based (typically based on EXP marking value)	Simple and dynamic Provides high degree of service Differentiation by routing traffic based EXP marking Offers more granule bandwidth control when combined with MPLS DS-TE	Ideal for QoS-enabled solutions that need service differentiation such as voice, video, and data

Table 5-4 *continued*

Mechanism	Characteristic	Design and Operational Considerations	Possible Use Scenario
Forwarding adjacency (FA)	Replicate the typical IGP behavior in term of reachability to remote prefixes (The TE tunnel will be seen as a direct link that will be considered in the IGP's path calculation.)	Can impact the entries' IGP routing domain of a network, which may lead to suboptimal routing across the network Introduces scalability limitation to the IGP because it significantly increases the IGP (typically LSDB) size Facilitates load sharing across physical and TE tunnel paths in some scenarios	Limited scenarios such as load sharing over physical and TE tunnel paths

Based on the information highlighted in Table 5-4, each mechanism of routing or placing traffic into the TE tunnel has different characteristics and will logically impose different design considerations that network designers must be aware of, because it may impact other protocols such as IGP stability and lead to a more complex network to operate.

Summary

SP network architectures may look more flat than enterprise network architectures in terms of the depth of tiers. However, the number of control planes, virtualization, and overlays integrated across SP networks can result in a complicated "layer in layer" multi-tier architecture. In addition, the large scale of SP networks, from both the infrastructure and number of prefixes perspectives, makes the operational complexity a critical aspect to be considered by the network designer when adding and integrating any new feature or protocol.

This chapter also covered the common physical architectural components of SP networks, along with the primary control plane protocols that all can construct a modern converged SP-grade network. In addition, this chapter highlighted how a technical design decision can directly impact the SP business if it is driven only from a technical point of view. Last but not least, this chapter explained how MPLS-based SP networks can take advantage of MPLS-TE and add several benefits and optimization to the overall network design and performance if it is planned well using the top-down approach, taking into account the different design considerations of MPLS-TE covered in this chapter.

Further Reading

RFC 4105, *Requirements for Inter-Area MPLS Traffic Engineering*, http://www. ietf.org

"PCE-Initiated Traffic Engineering Path Setup in Segment Routed Networks," http:// tools.ietf.org/html/draft-sivabalan-pce-segment-routing-00

RFC 3031, *Multiprotocol Label Switching Architecture*, http://www.ietf.org

"PCEP Extensions for MPLS-TE LSP Automatic Bandwidth Adjustment with Stateful PCE," https://tools.ietf.org/html/draft-dhody-pce-stateful-pce-auto-bandwidth-00

RFC 1771, *A Border Gateway Protocol 4 (BGP-4)*, http://www.ietf.org

RFC 7149, *Software-Defined Networking: A Perspective from Within a Service Provider Environment*, http://www.ietf.org

Service Provider MPLS VPN Services Design

Chapter 4, "Enterprise Edge Architecture Design," discussed the various design considerations, advantages, and limitations of the modern Multiprotocol Label Switching (MPLS) virtual private networking (VPN) solutions as a wide-area network (WAN) transport from the enterprise network design perspective. This chapter covers the different design options and considerations of MPLS VPN (both Layer 2 and Layer 3) from the service provider perspective.

MPLS VPN (L3VPN)

MPLS L3VPN is the most popular and proven service offered by the majority of today's service providers. This is because of several benefits (covered in Chapter 4) that enterprises can leverage to meet their business and technology requirements, specifically for the modern converged enterprise customer networks. Typically, the aim of any service provider is to meet the varied requirements of their customers, which will ultimately lead to maximizing their profit. Generally, service provider businesses aim to offer services that can

- Support a large number of customers and large number of sites per customer (scalable).

- Provide customers with value-added services that can create new revenue-generation sources such as service differentiation capable transport with end-to-end quality of service (QoS) (flexible and reliable).

- Support various services for all of their customers over one unified infrastructure. Having a single consolidated network reduces capital expenditure (capex) and can offer a significant return on investment (ROI) to the service provider on their hardware equipment (with the virtualized or overlaid architectures).

- Provide flexible service provisioning over various media access methods.

In addition, the MPLS L3VPN peer model has proven its flexibility and reliability in fulfilling these goals for service providers and many enterprise customers by offering

■ Single infrastructure that can serve all VPN customers (as shown in Figure 6-1)

■ The optimization of OPEX. For instance, adding a new customer or a new site for an existing customer will require simple changes to the relevant edge nodes (provider edge [PE] nodes) only as the core control plane intelligence is pushed to the provider rather cloud, as shown in Figure 6-1.

■ The opening of new revenue-generation sources to the business by offering differentiated services for their customers such as prioritization and expedited forwarding for voice.

■ The optimization of time to market to introduce new services to their L3VPN customers, such as IPv6 and multicast support.

■ A high degree of flexibility to service providers in offering various media access methods for their customers, such as legacy equipment, Ethernet over copper or fiber, and Long Term Evolution (LTE) or 3G.

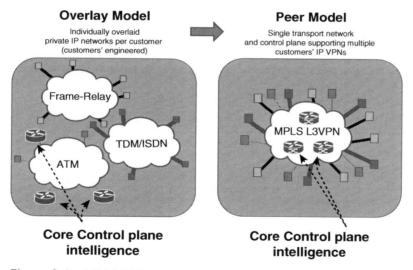

Figure 6-1   *MPLS L3VPN Peer Model*

MPLS L3VPN Architecture Components

In a typical MPLS L3VPN environment, the architecture is constructed of the following components:

■ Customer edge (CE)

■ Provider edge (PE)

■ Provider nodes (P)

In the typical MPLS L3VPN architecture, the provider edge nodes (PEs) carry customer routing information to inject customer routes from the directly connected customer edge nodes (CEs), each to the relevant Multiprotocol Border Gateway Protocol (MP-BGP) VPNv4/v6, along with the relevant VPN and transport MPLS labels (label edge router [LER]). This achieves the optimal routing of traffic that pertains to each customer within each VPN routing domain. However, provider routers (Ps) at the core of the network are mainly responsible for switching MPLS labeled packets. Therefore, they are also known as *label switching routers* (LSRs). Figure 6-2 illustrates the primary component of an MPLS L3VPN architecture:

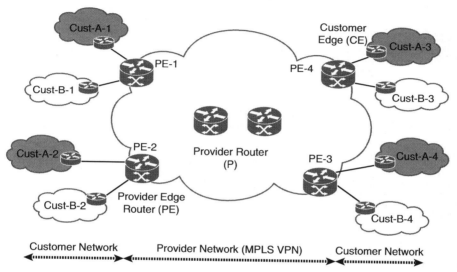

Figure 6-2 *Primary Elements of an MPLS L3VPN Architecture*

On top of the architectural components shown in Figure 6-2, the different control plane protocols discussed in Chapter 5, "Service Provider Network Architecture Design," are overlaid on top of this architecture to construct the control and forwarding planes for each VPN network (per customer). Figure 6-3 shows the relationship between the different control and forwarding plane components in an MPLS L3VPN architecture.

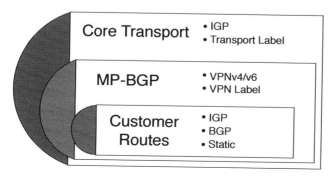

Figure 6-3 *MPLS L3VPN Control Plane Components*

The actual communication in a typical MPLS L3VPN environment is driven by following three primary elements:

- Routing information isolation between different VPNs (for example, virtual routing forwarders [VRFs])

- Controlled sharing of routing information to sites within a VPN or between different VPNs (for example, Route distinguisher [RD] + Route target [RT] + MP-BGP)

- MPLS L3VPN traffic forwarding of packets across the service provider core (for example, VPN and transport labels)

L3VPN Control Plane Components

This section covers the primary control plane elements of an MPLS L3VPN environment.

Virtual Routing and Forwarding

As discussed in Chapter 3, "Enterprise Campus Architecture Design," VRFs are one of the primary mechanisms used in today's modern networks to maintain routing isolation on a Layer 3 device level. In MPLS L3VPN architecture, each PE holds a separate routing and forwarding instance per VRF per customer, as shown in Figure 6-4. Typically, each customer's VPN is associated with at least one VRF. Maintaining multiple VRFs on the same PE is similar to maintaining multiple dedicated routers for customers connecting into the provider network. In addition, maintaining multiple forwarding tables at the PE is essential to support overlapping address spaces. Normally, the routing information of each customer (VPN) is installed at the relevant VRF routing tables of a PE, either from directly connected CEs (using a VRF-aware interior gateway protocol [IGP], BGP or static route) or routes of other CEs learned via remote PEs over MP-BGP VPNv4/v6.

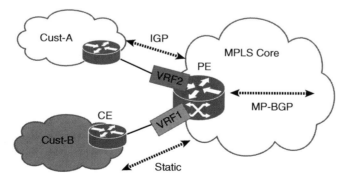

Figure 6-4   *MPLS L3VPN: Virtual Routing and Forwarding*

Route Distinguisher

For an MPLS L3VPN to support having multiple customer VPNs with overlapping addresses and to maintain the control plane separation, the PE router must be capable of using processes that enable overlapping address spaces of multiple customer VPNs. In addition, the PE router must also learn these routes from directly connected customer networks and propagate this information using the shared provider backbone. This is accomplished by using a route distinguisher (RD) per VPN or per VRF. As a result, service providers can seamlessly transport customers route (overlapped and nonoverlapped) over one common infrastructure and control plane protocol to take advantage of the RD prepended per MP-BGP VPNv4/v6 prefix. Normally, the RD value can be allocated using different approaches. Each approach has its strengths and weaknesses, as covered Table 6-1.

Table 6-1 *MPLS L3VPN RD Allocation Models*

RD Model	Strength	Weakness	Suitable Scenario
Unique RD per VPN	Simple to design and manage Lower hardware resource consumption compared to other models	Lacks the ability to support load-balancing capability when VPN route reflection (RR) is used in the MPLS VPN network and there are customers that have multihomed CE routes	Very large-scale MPLS VPN without load-balancing or load-sharing requirements toward multihomed sites
Unique RD per VPN per PE*	Offers the ability to load balance traffic toward multihomed sites that are part of the same VPN but connected to different PEs	Requires more hardware resources such as memory to store the additional VPN routes Higher design and operational complexity than the unique RD per VPN model	Large-scale MPLS VPN with load-balancing or load-sharing requirements toward multihomed sites**

Table 6-1   *continued*

RD Model	Strength	Weakness	Suitable Scenario
Unique RD per VPN per interface of each PE	Simplifies identifying sites within a VPN	Highest hardware resources utilization (a separate VRF per CE) High design and operational complexity	MPLS VPN of an enterprise with small number of VPNs with requirements to have a simplified mechanism for the operation team to identify the origin of any route (from which site per VPN) through its RD value***

* Load balancing or load sharing for multihomed sites using unique RD per VPN per PE is covered in more detail later in this chapter.

** In large-scale networks with a large number of PEs and VPNs, unique RD per VPN RD allocation should be used. The unique RD per VPN per PE RD allocation model can be used only for multihomed sites if the customer needs to load balance/share traffic toward these sites.

*** BGP site of origin (SoO) can be used as an alternative to serve the same purpose without the need of a unique RD per interface/VRF.

Figure 6-5 illustrates these different RD allocation models discussed in Table 6-1.

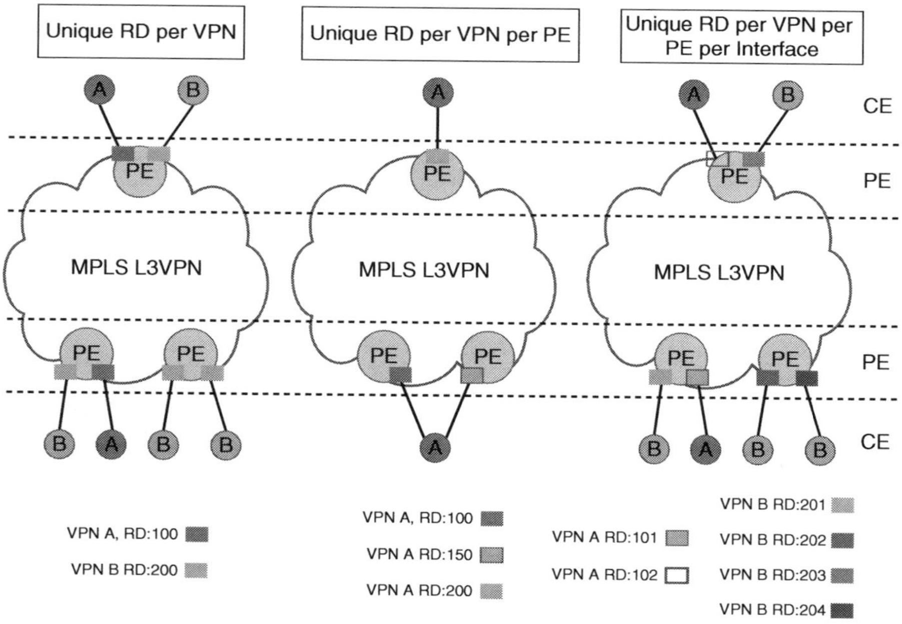

Figure 6-5   *MPLS L3VPN RD Allocation Models*

Note   Based on the RD allocation models covered in Table 6-1, a single VPN may include multiple RDs with different VRFs. However, the attributes of the VPN (per customer) will not change and is still considered an intra-VPN because technically the route propagation is controlled based on the import/export of the RT values.

Route Targets

Route targets (RTs) are an additional identifier and considered part of the primary control plane elements of a typical MPLS L3VPN architecture because they facilitate the identification of which VRF can install which VPN routes. In fact, RTs represent the policies that govern the connectivity between customer sites. This is achieved via controlling the import and export RTs. Technically, in an MPLS VPN environment, the export RT is to identify a VPN membership with regard to the existing VRFs on other PEs, whereas the import RT is associated with each PE local VRF. The import RT recognizes and maps the VPN routes (received from remote PEs or leaked on the local PE from other VRFs) to be imported into the relevant VRF of any given customer. In other words, RTs can offer networks designers a powerful full capability to control what MP-BGP VPN route is to be installed, in any given VRF/customer routing instance. In addition, it provides flexibility to create various logical L3VPN (WAN) topologies for the enterprise customer, such as any to any, hub and spoke, and partially meshed, to meet different connectivity requirements.

L3VPN Forwarding Plane

In addition to the control plane discussed earlier, the data or forwarding plane forms the other major component of typical MPLS L3VPN building blocks. In MPLS VPN environments, the data plane is based on forwarding packets based on labels (transport labels, VPN labels, MPLS Traffic Engineering [MPLS-TE] labels, and so on). This section focuses on the VPN label.

VPN Label

Typically, VPN traffic is assigned to a VPN label at the egress PE (LER) that can be used by the remote ingress PEs (LER), where the egress PE demultiplexes the traffic to the correct VPN customer egress interface based on the assigned VPN label. In other words, the VPN label is generated and assigned to every VPN route by the egress PE router, then advertised to the ingress PE routers over an MP-BGP update. Therefore, it is only understood by the egress PE node that performs demultiplexing to forward traffic to the respective VPN customer egress interface/CE based on its VPN label.

The VPN labels in MPLS VPN architectures can be allocated by the PE nodes using different models for MP-BGP L3VPN routes, based on the scenario and the design requirements. It also offers network designers the flexibility to achieve a level of trade-offs between network performance and scalability when possible. The following are the common MPLS VPN label-allocation models.

- **Per prefix:** In this model, a VPN label is assigned for each VPN prefix. Although this model can generate a large number of labels, it is required in scenarios when the VPN packets sent between the PE and CE are label switched.

- **Per VRF:** In this model, a single label is allocated to all local VPN routes of any given PE in a given VRF. This model offers an efficient label space and BGP advertisements, and the lookup does not result in any performance degradation. In addition, some vendor platforms support the same per-VRF label for both IPv4 and IPv6 prefixes.

- **Per CE:** The PE router allocates one label for every immediate next hop; in most cases, this would be a CE router. This label is directly mapped to the next hop, so there is no VRF route lookup performed during data forwarding. However, the number of labels allocated is one for each CE rather than one for each VRF. Because BGP knows all the next hops, it assigns a label for each next hop (not for each PE-CE interface). When the outgoing interface is a multiaccess interface and the media access control (MAC) address of the neighbor is not known, Address Resolution Protocol (ARP) is triggered during packet forwarding [37].

Network designers must be careful if they plan to change the default label allocation, behavior because any inconsistency or simple error can lead to a broken forwarding plane that can easily bring down the entire network or a portion of the network. In a service provider, a PE that goes down this way may result in several customer sites (usually single homed ones) being out of service, which can impact the business signifi-cantly, especially if there is a strict service level agreement (SLA) with its customers.

Figure 6-6 shows a summary of end-to-end forwarding and control planes of an MPLS L3VPN architecture.

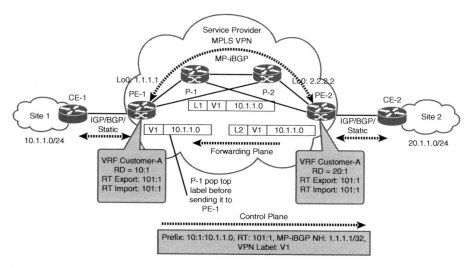

Figure 6-6   *Forwarding and Control Planes of MPLS L3VPN Architecture*

L3VPN Design Considerations

This section discusses the primary design considerations common in an MPLS L3VPN environment, along with the possible design options of each.

Load Sharing for Multihomed L3VPN CE

One of the common connectivity models of enterprise customers to the MPLS L3VPN-based WAN is multihoming. Enterprise customers with this connectivity model often need to load balance traffic across both WAN links (this model includes both, one CE with two links or one site with two CEs and links), as shown in Figure 6-7.

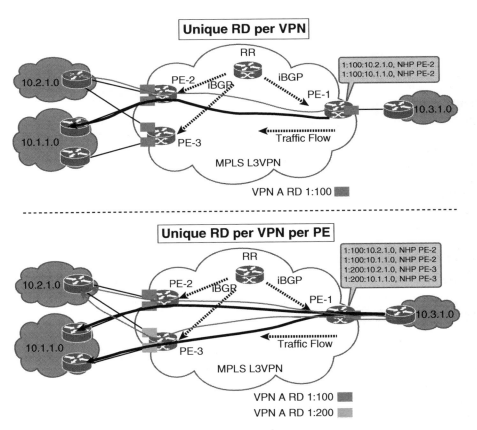

Figure 6-7 *Mutihoming in MPLS L3VPN Environment*

As shown in Figure 6-7, there is an MP-BGP route reflector (RR) part of the MP-BGP control plane architecture. Normally, the RR will advertise only the best route to its clients (other PEs) from the RR point of view to the topology, which will usually break the requirement of load balancing or sharing for those multihomed enterprise customers. One simple solution is to remove the RR and use a full mesh of M-iBGP sessions.

However, this might not be an ideal solution for many carrier networks because it may introduce MP-BGP scalability limitations on the provider network. The other common and simple solution to this requirement is to configure the multihomed VPNs/VRFs of the multihomed sites with different RDs, where each route will appear as a unique VPN route to the RR. Consequently, the RR will send these VPN routes to the other remote PEs (PE-1 in Figure 6-7, with PE-2 and PE-3 as the MP-BGP next hops).

Note   The BGP multipathing feature must be enabled within the relevant BGP VRF address family at the remote PE routers (for example, PE-1 in the preceding example). Similarly, enabling BGP multipathing is required in a single CE dual-attached use case to enable the load balancing/sharing from the CE end as well.

MPLS L3VPN Topologies

As covered earlier in this section, RT values enable you to control the import and export of VRF routes, which can control VPN membership per customer. This facilitates the creation of different L3VPN overlaid topologies based on customer requirements. The following are the most common L3VPN WAN topologies, which are controlled by RTs.

Full Mesh

The full-mesh topology shown in Figure 6-8 is the simplest and most common topology that represents the typical MPLS L3VPN layout. Simply, the any-to-any communications model between different customer sites that normally belong to the same customer (under a single VPN or multiple VPNs) must carry the same RT values of the import and export among them (among the relevant PEs).

This design model logically can be shown as one large router with all other locations connected directly to it, as shown in Figure 6-9, where the big router in the middle is the MPLS L3VPN cloud and all other sites are directly attached to it in a start topology.

Hub-and-Spoke L3VPN Service

In some situations, MPLS L3VPN customers require, for different reasons, that the communication between remote sites has to go through the main or hub site (for example, to align with the enterprise security policy requirements). From the L3VPN service provider point of view, a hub-and-spoke topology can be provisioned for this type of requirement by controlling MP-BGP VPN route propagation (using RT import and export), as shown in Figure 6-10.

The most common and proven way to achieve a hub-and-spoke topology over L3VPN network is to deploy two links with one VRF per link between the PE and the directly connected CE hub, as shown in Figure 6-11.

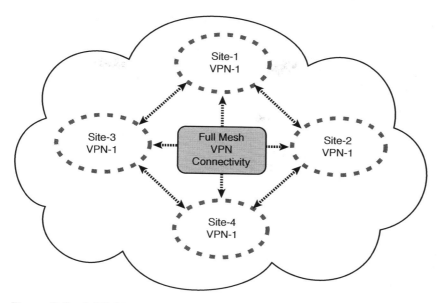

Figure 6-8   *MPLS L3VPN Full-Mesh Topology*

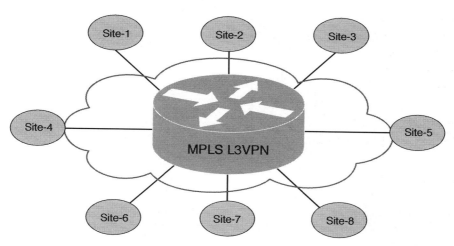

Figure 6-9   *MPLS L3VPN Conceptual View*

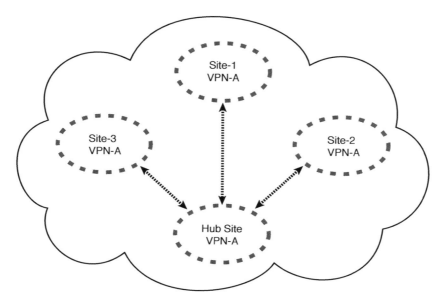

Figure 6-10   *MPLS L3VPN Hub-and-Spoke Topology*

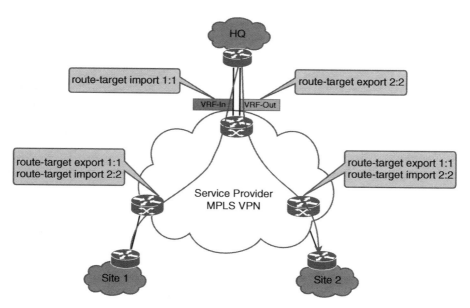

Figure 6-11   *MPLS L3VPN Design*

Achieving a hub-and-spoke topology in an MPLS L3VPN environment is as simple as controlling the import and export of RT values. However, network designers must be aware of the following design features to avoid breaking the communications across the overlaid hub-and-spoke topology:

- If the BGP used as the PE-CE routing protocol across the hub-and-spoke topology over L3VPN and each site uses the same BGP autonomous system number (ASN), BGP AS-override should be used by the PE connected to the hub-and-spoke sites. This avoids blocking communication among the sites as a result of BGP loop-prevention behavior. Although BGP allows the AS-in feature to be used for the same purpose from the CE side, it must be planned carefully to avoid any unexpected BGP AS_PATH looping.

- If more than one spoke is connected to the same PE half duplex, VRF is required to avoid traffic bypassing the hub site.

- If the hub site has two edge CE routers connected to the MPLS L3VPN cloud, in this case each CE must (ideally) be assigned the role of handling route/traffic in one direction; one hub CE is connected to the receiving link, and the other hub CE is connected to the sending link.

Multilevel Hub and Spoke

In this model, large enterprise customers (usually with distributed sites in multiple geographic areas) can take advantage of multitiered hub-and-spoke topology, as shown in the logical layout in Figure 6-11. For instance, remote sites distributed across different regions can be aggregated into level 1 hub sites per region, while the level 1 hub sites connect to each other in a hub-and-spoke topology and to a second level hub site, such as a centralized data center.

In Figure 6-12, each group of hub and spoke is allocated its own MPLS VPN, which can represent the grouping of sites based on geographic location. With an architecture like this, global enterprises can achieve a more structured network design and traffic flow between different sites and geographic regions. At the same time, service providers can easily provision this type of architecture by controlling routing information propagation among the different VPNs by controlling the import and export of RT values between the VPNs.

Extranet and Shared Services

In this particular design model, communication between one or more different VPN networks and a centralized VPN network is required. This is achieved in the same manner as the previous models: by controlling the import and export RT values. In this particular model, the central VPN must have import RT values matching the different export RT values of the VPNs that require access, as shown in Figure 6-13.

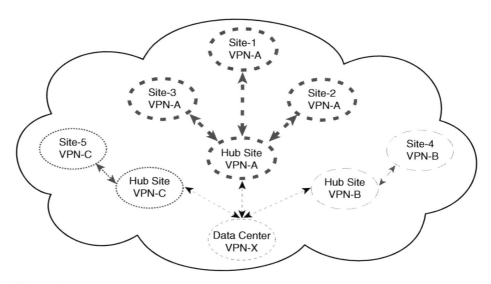

Figure 6-12   *MPLS Multilevel Hub and Spoke*

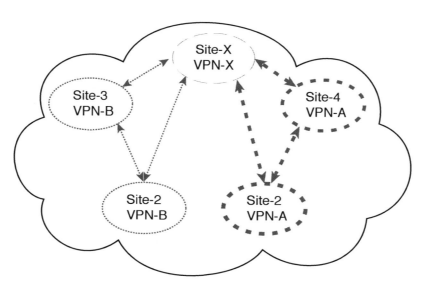

Figure 6-13   *MPLS L3VPN Extranet Topology*

Figure 6-14 illustrates a detailed view of how the import and export routes happen in a shared services VPN architecture.

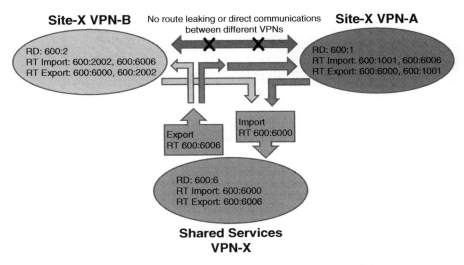

Figure 6-14 *MPLS L3VPN Shared Services Connectivity Model*

With this design, the shared services VPN will be accessed by the both VPN A and VPN B without compromising routing and reachability separation requirements between these VPNs (no communication between VPN A and VPN B). However, because the shared services VPN will have visibility on both VPNs routes in this example, the IP prefixes of VPN A and B must be unique; otherwise, VRF-aware Network Address Translation (NAT) should be deployed.

The following are the most common scenarios used with this design model:

■ **Management:** Network operations center (NOC) management access. For example, the service provider can offer managed CE services to its clients. Accordingly, the NOC or management VPN of the service provider requires access to the relevant customer's VPN, to manage or monitor its CE routers.

■ **Shared services:** In general, shared service access refers to several services that have to be accessible from different MPLS L3VPN networks, such as file services, Voice over IP (VoIP) gateways, and hosted applications (software as a service [SaaS]) or Internet connection.

■ **Extranet or business-to-business (B2B) communication:** This scenario is common in modern enterprises where vendors and partners, for example, can share limited reachability between their networks to facilitate different types of communications, such as business-to-business telepresence.

■ **Community communication:** In this model, a centralized entity provides central services access via a common MPLS VPN cloud. An example of this is an educational system, where commonly a centralized entity provides shared services access to the different schools across different locations while maintaining traffic separation between the schools.

Note   Depending on the network environment, the number of prefixes to be exported and imported can be limited in a controlled manner. For example, in the case of managed services, only the loopback IP of each CE is exported from the customer VPN to the NOC/management VPN for monitoring and remote-access purposes. At the same time, controlling the number of exported and imported prefixes prevents the leaking of extra prefixes, which can lead to other issues such as exposing customer internal routes and unnecessary extra overhead on the PE nodes.

MPLS VPN Internet Access Design Options

The flexibility provided by MPLS-based infrastructures, specifically MPLS VPN, allows operators to offer more than basic private IP WAN connectivity to their customers. One of the primary services that today's MPLS VPN service providers offer to their customers is Internet access as a value-added service, taking advantage of the flexible MPLS VPN architecture that uses the same service provider infrastructure to provide various connectivity models and services. In addition, it is an additional source of revenue, from the operator's business perspective.

However, from a network design perspective, Internet access for MPLS VPN customers can be provided using multiple design options. Typically, each option has its strengths and weaknesses. This section discusses and compares the most common design options used to provide Internet service from the MPLS VPN service provider's perspective. The design models are categorized as follows:

■ Non-MP-BGP VPN Internet routing

■ MP-BGP VPN-based Internet routing

Note   Although this section targets service provider networks with these design models, all the concept and design options still apply to any enterprise network that has MPLS VPN enabled (commonly across the campus or WAN core "service provider style").

Non-MP-BGP VPN Internet Routing

The primarily concept of this design model is that Internet routes are carried across the carrier network using the global routing table. The following are the two common design options of the model:

■ **Option 1:** VRF specific default route. This design option is based on using the static default route to redirect traffic from a customer VRF to the Internet gateway (Autonomous System Boundary Router [ASBR]) using the PE's global routing table, as shown in Figure 6-15. For the traffic in the other direction (Internet to VPN customers), the same concept is used (static route to move Internet traffic from the global routing table to the corresponding VRF/VPN per customer).

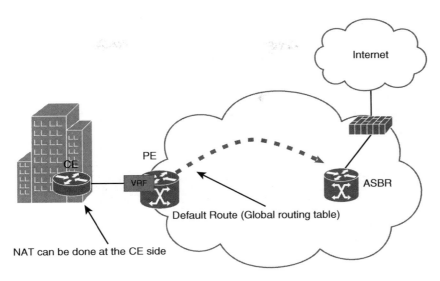

Figure 6-15 *MPLS L3VPN Internet Access Option 1*

- **Option 2:** Separate PE-CE subinterface. This design option uses the conceptual model of Option 1, but with the ability to separate Internet traffic and IP VPN traffic over two physical links or subinterfaces (such as 802.1Q based, or interface or data link connection identifier [DLCI] based in case of FR CE-PE physical connectivity). For the operators to propagate Internet routes (or default only) between a PE and the directly attached CE, either a static route or BGP is used over the Internet link (the non-VRF interface), as shown in Figure 6-16.

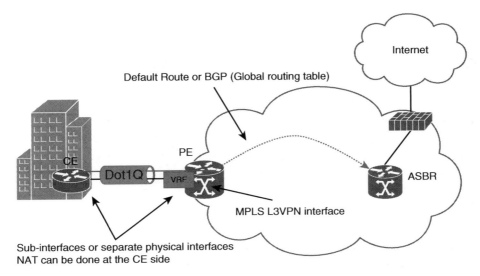

Figure 6-16 *MPLS L3VPN Internet Access Option 2*

MP-BGP VPN Internet Routing

This design model relies primarily on MP-BGP VPN to carry Internet routes across the carrier network. The following are the two common design options of the model:

Note The sequence of numbers of the following design options continues from the two other design options previously discussed, to facilitate the reference of each model in Table 6-2.

- **Option 3:** Extranet with Internet-VRF. This design option is based on the principle discussed earlier in this chapter, which is the extranet or shared VPN where the Internet gateway (ASBR) installs Internet routes in its own VPN. This VPN has bidirectional communication with the customer's VPN, a customer that requires Internet access over the same link/VPN (operators control the propagation of the Internet routes or default route into a customer's VRF routing table via the import and export RT values), as shown in Figure 6-17. In addition, if the full Internet routes are injected into the customer VPN, it is highly recommended to change MPLS VPN label allocation mode to either per CE or per VRF. This prevents the default behavior per-prefix allocation mode, which will usually allocate a label per prefix. Based on the size of the Internet routes, there can be noticeable performance inefficiencies in the case of the per-prefix label allocation model.

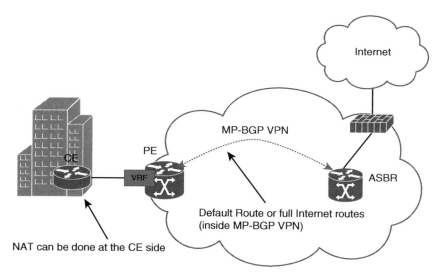

Figure 6-17 *MPLS L3VPN Internet Access Option 3*

- **Option 4:** VRF-aware NAT. This design option relies on MP-BGP VPN to customer Internet traffic, like Option 3. However, in this design option, the Internet gateway (ASBR) is not placed in a shared VPN. Instead, each VRF/VPN is created at the

ASRB and each VRF is injected with a default route to be propagated to the corresponding VPN across the MPLS VPN network (toward the ASBR inside interface), while performing VRF-aware NATing on the outside interface (Internet facing) for both ingress and egress Internet traffic. As result, with this design option, customers may retain their private IP addressing even if there is overlap with other customer IP addressing ranges, as shown in Figure 6-18.

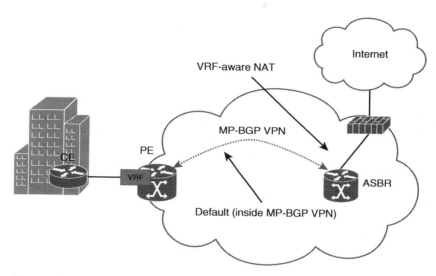

Figure 6-18   *MPLS L3VPN Internet Access Option 4*

Table 6-2 compares these design options from different design aspects.

Table 6-2   *MPLS L3VPN Internet Access Design Options Comparison*

Design Consideration	Option 1	Option 2	Option 3	Option 4
PE manageability	Moderate.	Simple.	Simple.	Simple.
ASBR manageability	Simple.	Simple.	Moderate.	Complex.
CE simplicity	Simple.	Simple.	Moderate.	Moderate.
Scalability	High.	High.	Moderate.*	High.**
Supports overlapped customer' IPs	No (should be direct public provider independent / provider assigned [PI/PA]).	No (should be direct public PI/PA).	Yes.	No.

Table 6-2   *continued*

Design Consideration	Option 1	Option 2	Option 3	Option 4
Full Internet routes at the PE	Yes.	May.	May.	No.
Design concerns	Static routing may lead to configuration errors and operational complexity.	May add routing/BGP configurations to the CE side.	Several VRFs on the same PE, each with full Internet routes, can add significant load on the PE.	VPN customers do not receive full Internet route.

* If the full Internet route is installed per VRF, there can be scalability limitations at the PE level.

** There might be limitations at the ASBR level (VRF routes or NATing entries/sessions).

The comparison in Table 6-2 might make it seem like one option is better than others for certain design requirements, but usually the network environment and the situation drive the design choices (for instance, if an Internet service provider [ISP] wants to start providing MPLS VPN to their customers, but at the same time, they cannot afford any service interruption to their existing Internet customers). In this situation, keeping the Internet routing at the BGP global routing table can be a viable solution. Similarly, if an MPLS L3VPN provider wants to offer Internet as a value-added service for their customers, it may be less interruptive to add the Internet as a new VPN (extranet VPN connectivity model). Therefore, always consider the other factors such as business priorities, design constraints, and the targeted environment, in addition to the technical aspects, before making any design decision.

PE-CE L3VPN Routing Design

Designing routing between PE and CE in an MPLS L3VPN environment can sometimes be challenging. This is applicable for any MPLS L3VPN environment, whether it is a service provider or an enterprise with MPLS L3VPN core. Although the CE and PE sides are most commonly managed and deployed by different teams (usually the CE controlled by the enterprise and the PE controlled by the service provider side), the routing design of the CE to PE should (ideally) *not* be performed in isolation. It should be coordinated and aligned to achieve a successful design, because of dependencies in some scenarios that can impact the overall design and end-to-end communication. This section discusses the design considerations from both the CE side (usually the enterprise) and MPLS L3VPN side (either a service provider or self-deployed enterprise MPLS L3VPN).

PE-CE Routing Design Considerations

For network designers to achieve a successful PE-CE routing design, they must follow the top-down approach in a structured manner to identify the goals and direction of the design during the planning phase. To achieve that, network designers must have a good understanding of the business, functional, and business-critical application requirements. The following questions can be considered the foundation, during the information-gathering and planning phases, for making a suitable design choice that can deliver value to the business:

- **Business requirements:**

  - Is it to reduce the cost of existing expensive links (for example, as an alternative connectivity to dark-fiber)?

  - Is it to reduce the time to expand the business (for example, to add new remote sites and integrate them into the network very quickly)?

  - Is it to increase the reliability of business applications and services with minimal cost (to be used as backup path)?

  - Is it to optimize the ROI of the links by using multiple links in a load-balancing/sharing manner?

- **PE-CE functional and application requirements:**

  - Provide primary WAN connectivity?

  - Provide backup WAN connectivity?

  - Provide WAN and Internet access?

  - Provide a primary path for applications that need high bandwidth or strict end-to-end quality of service (QoS) requirements?

  - Provide efficient bandwidth utilization over multiple paths (multihoming)?

  - Provide connectivity to remote areas with limited optical coverage (for example, remote sites connect over 3G)?

- **Technical requirements (connectivity characteristics):**

  - Is the CE single-homed or multihomed to the MPLS L3VPN network (PE) ?

  - Is there any backdoor link from the CE side?

  - Is there any limitation to run any specific routing protocol (such as lack of staff knowledge, software limitations, or is it not supported by the SP side)?

After identifying the different requirements, network designers can have a good understanding of the design goal and direction, so as to achieve a successful design. For example, it is always common for the MPLS L3VPN to be used as the primary path;

however, in some scenarios, the backdoor link between any given sites might have a high-bandwidth capacity and offer lower latency and more control from the enterprise point of view. Therefore, in this case, the enterprise may prefer to use the MPLS L3VPN as a backup path only, which has to be reflected in the routing design.

PE-CE Routing Protocol Selection

One of the critical parts in designing PE-CE is the routing protocol selection, because normally each protocol has its strengths and weaknesses. In particular, in the PE-CE type of scenarios, the alignment of routing design between the service provider and the enterprise (CE side and PE side) is important. Otherwise, the lack of coordination and alignment between these two networks can lead to serious issues, such as suboptimal routing and routing loops. As shown in Figure 6-19, in the PE-CE type of scenario, what normally happens is a route is received from one CE via a routing protocol. Next, this route is converted into a MP-BGP route, along with some protocol related information that is normally transformed into BGP extended community values. These values can be used at the remote egress PE when the route is reconverted back into the original routing protocol, such as Open Shortest Path First (OSPF) or Enhanced Interior Gateway Routing Protocol (EIGRP) (assuming both CEs are using the same routing protocol with the PEs; otherwise, this specific routing protocol information most probably will be invaluable). Nonetheless, each routing protocol behaves differently in these types of scenarios.

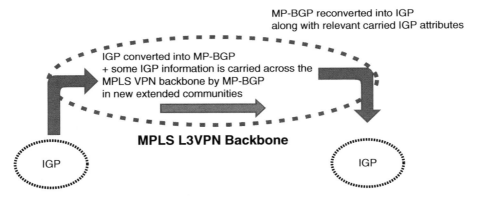

Figure 6-19 *PE-CE Routing Principle*

Therefore, understanding the business and functional requirements and the targeted topology (single-homed versus multihomed versus sites with backdoor link) can help you select the right routing protocol to a large extent, taking into consideration the specific protocol attributes and behaviors with regard to the underlying network topology, WAN connectivity, and path selection requirements.

PE-CE Design Options and Recommendations

As already mentioned, each routing protocol has its own strengths and weaknesses with regard to PE-CE routing design. This section discusses the technical design considerations and recommendations per routing protocol. Figure 6-20 shows the reference network architecture exemplifying various PE-CE connectivity models that will form the foundation of the design considerations and recommendations in this section.

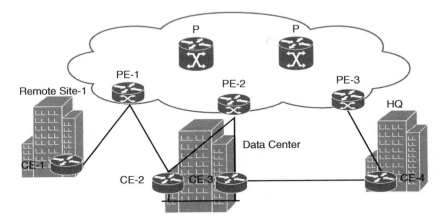

Figure 6-20   *Reference Architecture*

Note   This section covers the primary and most commonly used PE-CE routing protocols (static, OSPF, EIGRP, and BGP).

Static Route PE-CE

Applying a static route to the reference architecture network shown in Figure 6-20 can lead to some design limitations and operational complexities. For example, CE-2, CE-3, and CE-4 have multiple links (direct PE-CE and backdoor links) using a static route, which can lead to limited design scalability and flexibility. In addition, managing these multiple edge devices with multiple links can be complicated and is associated with the high possibility of human (configuration) errors. However, the static route between CE-1 and PE-1 is a feasible design option because it is a single-homed site; even a single default route in CE-1 can be used, assuming the Internet is through the same link.

Link State: OSPF as a PE-CE Routing Protocol

OSPF is not commonly used for PE-CE routing by service providers. As stated earlier in this section, however, this design concept is not only applicable to typical enterprise to service provider MPLS WAN connectivity, it is also applicable to self-deployed MPLS L3VPN by enterprises (and OSPF is one of the most common routing protocols used by enterprises). The reason why OSPF is not commonly used as the PE-CE routing protocol is because the design can be tricky and complicated with OSPF, especially when there are sites with backdoor links or multihomed. As shown in Figure 6-21, by using the same reference architecture network in Figure 6-20 and applying different OSPF area designs, the implications of each differs significantly.

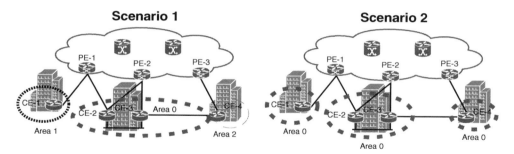

Figure 6-21   *PE-CE: OSPF*

Note   If you are unfamiliar with the OSPF terms used in this section such as OSPF DN bit, OSPF domain identifier and OSPF sham link, it is recommended that you refer to IETF RFC 4577 to build a foundational knowledge about these terms before reading this section.

Scenario 1 in Figure 6-21 represents a multi-area OSPF design, where each site or branch is deployed with its own OSPF area. The service provider side is usually part of the super backbone area (area 0). Although this design scenario may look simple and straightforward, any lack of coordination between the service provider side and the enterprise (CE) side can break the functional requirements. For instance, if the CE side is configured with a different OSPF process ID than the PE side, traffic between the data center and the HQ will always prefer the backdoor link, as shown in Figure 6-22. If the functional requirements dictate that the traffic should always prefer the MPLS cloud as the primary path, this will lead to a design failure.

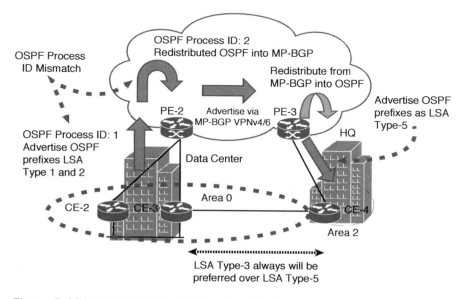

Figure 6-22   *PE-CE: OSPF with Backdoor Link*

This issue can be avoided by considering a single (matching) OSPF process ID between the CEs and the PEs. Nevertheless, practically speaking, this option can add operational complexity from the service provider point of view. Alternatively, service providers (PE side) can overcome this issue by deploying the same OSPF identifier on both ingress and egress PEs, along with OSPF tuning and the OSPF cost metric (to ensure that the WAN link has a lower OSPF cost metric).

In fact, OSPF incorporates multiple attributes, such as DN bit and route tag (for loop prevention) and the OSPF domain identifier. The technical reason behind these attributes is to help BGP carry this route across the MP-BGP backbone and convert the route back to OSPF appropriately, in a transparent way to the OSPF peers at the edge of the network (CEs). For instance, in Figure 6-23, when PE-1 sets the DN bit to prefixes of remote site 1 (CE-1), when advertising it to CE-2 it will help PE-2 to stop re-advertising the same prefix back to the MPLS VPN super backbone when it is sourced from CE-2 or CE-3. In other words, when any of the PEs receives a type 3, 5, or 7 LSA from any CE with the DN bit set, the routing information from this LSA will not be considered in the OSPF route computation. As a result, this LSA will not be converted into a BGP route. This will ultimately help to avoid the potential loop in this scenario.

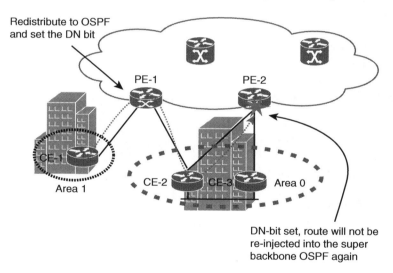

Figure 6-23 *OSPF PE-CE Loop Prevention*

Note In some scenarios, such as a the multi-VRF CE (covered in Chapter 4) and the hub-&-spoke topology over MPLS L3VPN covered earlier in this chapter (see Figure 6-12), when OSPF is used as the PE-CE routing protocol with the hub-and-spoke over MPLS L3VPN topology, there will usually be multiple PE nodes communicating with a central/hub PE router that connects to the hub CE router over dual interfaces/subinterfaces (each in a separate VRF). Technically in this scenario, when two remote sites (spokes) need to communicate, the OSPF link state advertisements (LSAs) from each remote site will reach the central/hub PE, then the hub CE router, where the traffic flow loops and comes back into a different VRF (typical hub-and-spoke model). The issue here is that when these LSAs are type 3, 5, or 7, the LSAs will not be considered by the central/hub PE because OSPF will not consider them because they have the DN bit set. Therefore, the "DN bit ignore" feature is required in this scenario to "disable DN bit checking" at the hub PE node, in order to meet traffic flow and routing information distribution requirements (in which the route/LSA must be considered when it loops and comes back into a different VRF on the hub/central PE in order to reach other spokes). This OSPF feature is also known as capability VRF-lite. Ideally, before considering this feature a careful analysis is required to avoid introducing any potential routing information loop.

However, these attributes (DN bit or route tag) will be stripped from the prefixes if the route is redistributed into another routing domain (such as EIGRP) and then redistributed back into OSPF and then to MPLS L3VPN from another PE. As discussed earlier in this book, in discussions about route redistribution, route redistribution can cause metric transformation. This is a good example of how multiple redistribution may lead to a routing loop, as shown in Figure 6-24.

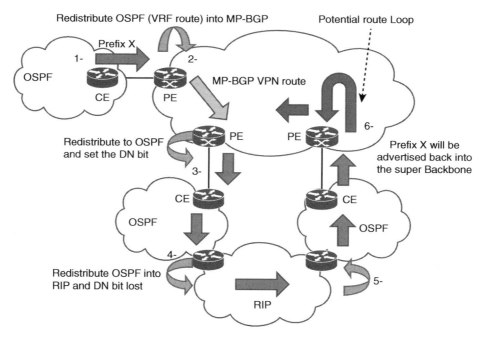

Figure 6-24 *PE-CE OSPF with Multiple Redistributions*

Consequently, the network designer must be careful when there is a possibility of multiple redistribution points across multiple routing domains, because it can break down the communication between OSPF islands across the MPLS L3VPN backbone.

In contrast, in Scenario 2 in Figure 6-25, all the sites are deployed in OSPF area 0. Although in high level this design might look simpler, the most significant issue here is that all the routes between the data center and HQ site will be seen as OSPF intra-area routes. In other words, no matter what the WAN link cost metric is, the backdoor will always be the preferred path between the data center and the HQ (because the route from the MPLS L3VPN will be seen as either an interarea route or external route). This might not always be a desirable design. To resolve this issue, based on the OSPF area design, network designers must make sure that the route coming from the MPLS L3VPN backbone is received as an intra-area route as well. To achieve this, the service provider must coordinate and set up the OSPF sham link between the relevant PEs (in this scenario, PE-2 and PE-3) to create a logical intra-area link between the ingress and egress PEs (area 0 in this example).

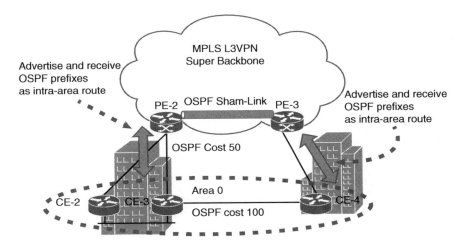

Figure 6-25 *OSPF Sham Link*

After the OSPF sham link is set up and the OSPF adjacency is established over this logical link, the network can manipulate the OSPF cost metric on the relevant interface to make the MPLS L3VPN link the preferred path.

Note For the enterprise (CE side) to avoid the reliance on the SP side to set up a sham link, OSPF areas design can be migrated to use a unique OSPF area per site (for the sites connected with a backdoor link), if this option is available.

Consequently, using OSPF as the PE-CE routing protocol can be challenging if there is any lack of coordination between the PE side (super backbone) and the CE side. Furthermore, even if the design is performed with good coordination, OSPF can still impose some design limitations in certain scenarios, including the following:

■ If any CE needs to send a summary route to other CEs or any given CE, this has to be deployed by the provider or PE side.

- In scenarios like the one discussed in this chapter, the data center has multiple paths (links and routes) to the MPLS L3VPN. OSPF can offer network designers very limited control to achieve a detailed load sharing over these paths. In addition, there is no such mechanism to influence the service provider's route selection from the CE, like BGP AS-PATH prepending.

Therefore, the protocol selection has to be aligned with all the different design requirements (business, functional, and application) to achieve a successful design.

Note Intermediate System-to-Intermediate System (IS-IS) acts similarly to OSPF when there is a backdoor link, as the redistributed prefixes within the MPLS cloud (from MP-BGP into IS-IS) will be seen as an external route by the receiving CE while the same route over the backdoor will be received as internal route. This usually leads to always preferring the backdoor link. To overcome this issue, BGP support carries some of the critical IS-IS information as part of BGP extended communities, which can be converted back into IS-IS link-state packet (LSP). For example, if the original route was received as level 1, it will be reconverted into an IS-IS level 1 route at the other end (PE). (For more detail, refer to this IETF draft draft-sheng-isis-bgp-mpls-vpn.)

EIGRP as a PE-CE Routing Protocol

Using EIGRP as a PE-CE routing protocol may offer a simpler design compared to OSFP if it is designed properly. This is because there are certain scenarios, especially when there is a backdoor link between the CE sites, where any design mistake can lead to serious connectivity issues. Therefore, network designers must be aware of EIGRP behavior and the possible techniques and mechanisms to optimize the design.

As discussed earlier in this section, the typical routing behavior in PE-CE scenarios is that the CE routing protocols (IGP) are converted at the ingress PE router to MP-BGP route, to be carried across the MPLS VPN backbone to the egress PE router, and to be reconverted back to the relevant PE-CE routing protocol on that VRF. As with link-state protocols, MP-BGP carries specific EIGRP information in new BGP extended communities set by the PEs (usually the ingress PE), which carries EIGRP ASNs and multiple EIGRP attributes across the MPLS L3VPN backbone, such as delay, bandwidth, hop count, and reliability. This can help the receiving PE EIGRP instance to have usable information.

However, as mentioned earlier, PE-CE EIGRP design requires special considerations from network designers in some scenarios to avoid undesirable behaviors. Figure 6-26 illustrates different EIGRP application scenarios using the same reference network architecture of this section.

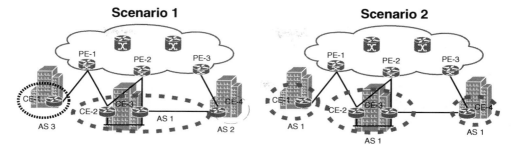

Figure 6-26   *PE-CE EIGRP*

In Scenario 1 in Figure 6-26, EIGRP is applied with different ASNs per site. Each site will receive the EIGRP route of the other site as an external route. This is because the ASN is the carrier in the new BGP extended community. When it is redistributed from MP-BGP into EIGRP at the egress PE with ASN mismatch, EIGRP will install the route as an external route. However, the concern is always with where the backdoor link exists between different sites, because the EIGRP does not have a built-in mechanism like OSPF does to detect a loop. Therefore, there is potential that the EIGRP information will circulate in this looped topology. It is also possible as well that the EIGRP will introduce unpredictable behavior because of what is known as *race condition*, where the route is accepted based on the timing of the EIGRP and BGP updates with the local router decision.

Route racing in Scenario 1 can be mitigated to some extent by limiting the maximum number of EIGRP hop counts. However, with this approach, the network will continue to experience the undesirable (looping) behavior because of the route racing condition until the EIGRP reaches its maximum configured hop counts. In addition, it is difficult to determine the right number of hops to be configured (and there is a high degree of human configuration errors and added operational complexities). Alternatively, you can use a route tagging-based solution to offer a more deterministic and simplified solution known as *EIGRP site of origin (SoO)*, which is technically an extended BGP community associated with the route. When redistributed from EIGRP into MP-BGP, any route assigned an SoO value will not be advertised over links (interfaces) deployed with the same SoO value, which helps to avoid or mitigate the impact of routing loops in complex topologies, such as sites with EIGRP used as a PE-CE routing protocol that contain both MPLS VPN and backdoor links, as shown in Figure 6-27.

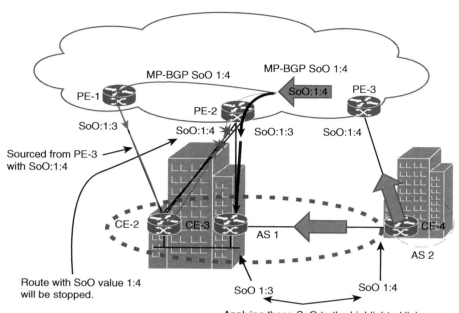

Figure 6-27 *PE-CE EIGRP SoO*

Table 6-3 summarizes the behavior of EIGRP SoO in different situations.

Table 6-3 *EIGRP SoO Actions*

Received Route SoO Details	Action
SoO value matches the SoO value on the sending or receiving interface.	Route is will be filtered out.
CE deployed with SoO value that does not match.	Route is added to the EIGRP topology table so that it can be redistributed into BGP and the SoO value preserved.
Does not contain an SoO value.	Route is accepted into the EIGRP topology table, and the SoO value from the interface that is used to reach the next-hop CE router is appended to the route before it is redistributed into BGP.

In Figure 6-27, SoO helps to optimize the EIGRP looping (race condition) by preventing the route from being re-injected back to the network based on the attached SoO value to the route and the deployed SoO value on the interface. For instance, traffic sourced from the HQ LAN (CE-4) passing through PE-3 will have an SoO value of 1:4 assigned to it. Then, any interface in the scenario shown in Figure 6-27 that has an SoO value of 1:4 will not pass this route information through.

Although in this type of scenario SoO can help to mitigate route looping and racing issues to a certain extent, it might sometimes be necessary to introduce other limitations, such as reduced redundancy. For example, if the SoO values are applied on the backdoor link (as covered in Figure 6-27), and the PE-3-CE-4 link goes down, any traffic with SoO value of 1:3 or 1:4 destined for the HQ (behind CE-4) will be isolated (because of the SoO filtering at backdoor link), even though the backdoor link is available. Therefore, as a network designer, you must understand the design goals and priorities and what the impact is of applying SoO on the different interfaces/path (for example, redundancy + suboptimal routing versus stability + optimal routing). In other words, if the time required for the EIGRP to stabilize following a failure event is acceptable, a simple SoO design should be sufficient, like the one shown in Figure 6-28, in which SoO stops the information feedback looping faster than relying on the hop count for EIGRP to stabilize after CE-2 failure.

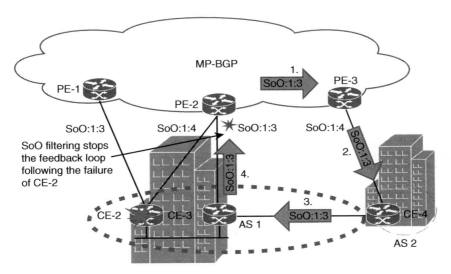

Figure 6-28 *EIGRP PE-CE Loop Prevention with SoO: Failure Scenario*

However, Scenario 2 shown in Figure 6-26 is designed with the same EIGRP ASN on all sites, which is typical in that all the routes learned over MPLS L3VPN and the backdoor links will be an internal EIGRP route.

One of the common design concerns with this setup is when the backdoor link is intended to be used only as a backup path (because with this design there is a possibility that some remote sites will use the backdoor link to reach either the DC LAN or the HQ LAN). For instance, in Figure 6-29, the HQ LAN prefix is advertised in EIGRP to the MPLS VPN PE-3 and to CE-2 and CE-3 over the backdoor link. Likewise, CE-2 and CE-3 advertise this route to PE-1 and PE-2, respectively. Therefore, PE-1 in this case has two BGP paths available for the HQ LAN: iBGP path via PE-2 and PE-3, and the locally redistributed BGP route from EIGRP advertisement via CE-2 EIGRP.

Consequently, from the PE-1 point of view, the locally originated route will be preferred based on the BGP best path selection. As a result, traffic from CE-1 destined for the HQ site (CE-4) will use the backdoor link as a primary path, as shown in Figure 6-29.

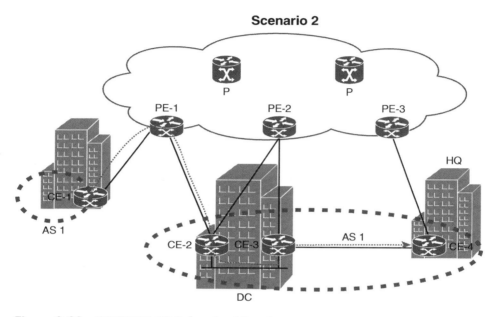

Figure 6-29 *EIGRP PE-CE Suboptimal Routing*

There must be an attribute to influence PE-1 path selection in which the internal BGP (iBGP) learned routes is to be preferred over other routes. One possible and common solution that can be used in this scenario is "BGP cost community" to influence BGP path selection.

EIGRP routes injected into MP-BGP with a point of insertion (POI) value of 128, along with the cost set to the EIGRP composite metric (in this case, the community's value), must be considered before the typical BGP path selection algorithm (such as local_ preference and AS-PAT H). Consequently, when the PEs redistribute the EIGRP routes into BGP, the BGP cost community attribute will be populated along with the accumulated EIGRP metrics. This means that each PE will have a level of visibility of the EIGRP path cost. As a result, PE-1 will prefer the HQ LAN route advertised by PE-3, because the associated EIGRP metric of this LAN route advertised by either CE-2 or CE-3 contains the accumulated path cost, including the backdoor link, while the BGP cost community of the iBGP (from PE-3) has a lower cost. Therefore, it will be the preferred path, as shown in Figure 6-30.

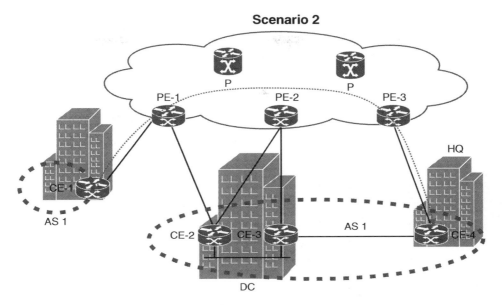

Figure 6-30 *EIGRP PE-CE Optimal Routing*

Furthermore, BGP cost community helps to optimize optimal routing in scenarios like this (and scenarios like Scenario 1 shown in Figure 6-27). For example, if the route from site 1 (CE-1) is assigned a BGP cost community value at the ingress PE (PE-1), it will always be preferred by PE-2 and PE-3 over any other BGP advertisement that has no cost community attached to it, regardless of what BGP attributes it has. As a result, the site 1 route will always be preferred via PE-1 (directly connected PE to site 1), as shown in Figure 6-31.

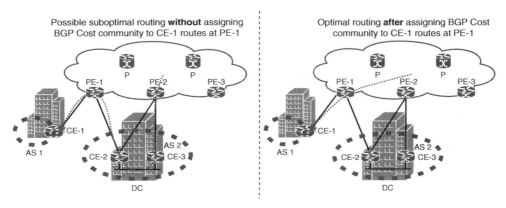

Figure 6-31 *EIGRP Suboptimal Routing-2*

> **Note** This cost community may transform BGP to act in way it is not designed for (like IGP), which may lead to undesirable behaviors in some scenarios.

Consider, however, what happens when a new remote site is added (for example, in a new country where the current service provider does not have presence and requires inter-AS communication to extend the MPLS-L3VPN reachability). In this scenario, the BGP cost community will not be a valid solution because it does not support propagation over external BGP (eBGP) sessions, as shown in Figure 6-32.

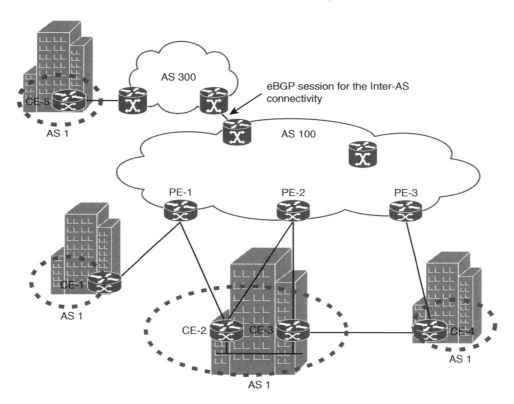

Figure 6-32 *PE-CE EIGRP: BGP Cost Community Limitation Scenario*

Consequently, using EIGRP as PE-CE routing protocol may add simplicity to the enterprises that already use EIGRP as the enterprise routing protocol. However, when there are multihomed sites to the MPLS provider or sites with backdoor links, the design may prove too complicated, and overall flexibility and stability may be reduced. EIGRP Over the Top (OTP), however, can offer more flexible PE-CE design and is independent of the service provider routing control (as covered in Chapter 4).

BGP as a PE-CE Routing Protocol

BGP, however, as a PE-CE routing protocol can achieve the optimal routing and traffic control over the most complex connectivity layouts because it has multiple powerful attributes that can influence inbound and outbound path selection. All the design considerations and options discussed earlier in this book (especially in the "Enterprise Multihoming" section in Chapter 4) are applicable to the design of BGP as a PE-CE routing protocol. In addition, the BGP SoO attribute uses the same concept of the EIGRP SoO to control route propagation when there is a backdoor link between the customer sites.

In other words, when possible, it is always desirable to consider BGP as the PE-CE routing protocol for multihomed sites to single- or multiple-provider networks. For network designers, this can facilitate the achievement of a very advanced level of traffic engineering with flexible BGP policies. This, in turn, offers the business adequate flexibility to use the available paths in a way that aligns with the business, functional, and application requirements in a more dynamic manner regardless of the extent of the physical connectivity's complexity. The flexibility of BGP can obviously provide an optimized ROI of the available paths and lower operational complexities when there is complicated connectivity with multiple links.

Normally, MPLS VPN providers consider two BGP ASN allocation models when BGP is used as a PE-CE routing protocol as following (see Figure 6-33):

- **Same ASN (ASN) per site:** With this model, the MPLS provider allocates the same ASN to all the customer sites. One of the main advantages of this model is reduced BGP ASN collisions.

- **Single ASN per site:** With this model, the MPLS provider allocates each of the customer sites a separate BGP ASN. This model offers network designers and operators the ability to identify the source of prefixes (from which site) in simple way (based on BGP ASN in the AS PATH attribute of each prefix). However, it may introduce scalability limitation with regard to the available ASNs.

Although allocating the same BGP ASN offers better scalability with regard to the number of ASNs/sites and reduced ASN collisions, this model introduces some design concerns for multihomed sites. For example, in Figure 6-34, the service provider must rewrite the customer ASN (AS override) to overcome the default BGP loop-prevention mechanism and allow all the sites with the same ASN to communicate. However, the primary issue with the rewriting of the BGP AS_PATH is that the CE routers will not be able to detect BGP looping. As shown in Figure 6-34, after Prefix X is received by the provider PE from CE-2, AS override applied to this prefix and AS_PATH rewriting converted the original AS_PATH to become (300 300). Technically, when this prefix is received by CE-1, it will be accepted because the AS-PATH has been altered and the original AS was removed from the AS_PATH. As a result, a route loop will be formed in this case. To overcome this loop, the SoO concept discussed earlier with EIGRP can be used, and a BGP extended community attribute can be attached to BGP prefixes; network operators and PEs can use that to identify the actual prefix source, and based on the deployed SoO value, the route can be permitted or denied. As with EIGRP, if the SoO value of a prefix is equal to the deployed SoO for a BGP peer, the prefix will be stopped from being advertised. By applying this concept to the scenario shown in Figure 6-34, both PEs facing CE-1 and CE-2 configure the same SoO to its direct BGP peering (CE-1 and CE-2, respectively). The route looping will be stopped without impacting the communication with any other remote site belonging to the same customer (AS).

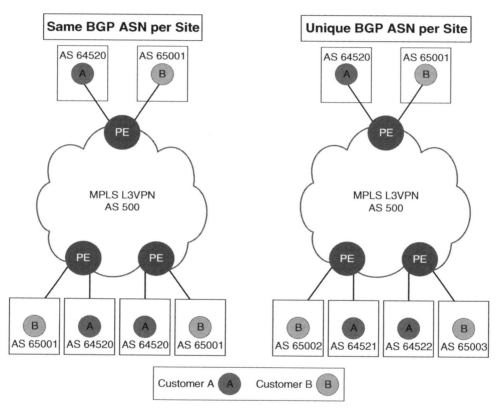

Figure 6-33 *BGP ASN Allocation Models as an MPLS VPN PE-CE Routing Protocol*

From a design perspective, rewriting ASN along with SoO considerations can be seen as an added complexity to the design and operation of this model (same ASN per site).

Nevertheless, BGP cannot always practically be considered. Design constraints that may prevent network designers from considering BGP include BGP not being supported as PE-CE by the service provider or BGP not being supported by the software of the CE nodes. A lack of BGP knowledge among the enterprise's IT staff may also be a constraint. In these cases, the network designer has to find an alternative supported routing protocol that can achieve the intended goal.

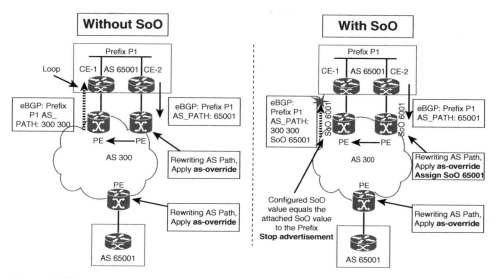

Figure 6-34 *BGP PE-CE Routing Protocol Loop Prevention*

Table 6-4 summarizes the characteristics (cons and pros) of each routing protocol with regard to the PE-CE routing design.

Table 6-4 *Comparison of PE-CE Routing Protocols*

Routing Protocol	Strengths	Weaknesses
Static	Simple and reliable "when combined with IP SLA". Low operational complexity in small environments with a small number of prefixes.	Nonscalable. High operational complexity in large environments. Limited flexibility in multihomed scenarios with automatic failover limitation.
Link state*	Reliable to certain extent (for example, supports built-in loop prevention). Supports multiple connectivity and flooding domain design scenarios.	High design and operational complexity. Limited flexibility in large environments with backdoor links and multihoming scenarios.

Table 6-4   *continued*

Routing Protocol	Strengths	Weaknesses
EIGRP*	Reliable to a certain extent (topology dependent) EIGRP OTP can simplify and optimize CE-PE design to a large extent.	High design and operational complexity and limited flexibility in large environments with multihoming scenarios. EIGRP SoO may lead to inefficient use of available paths or lack of redundancy in multihoming scenarios with backdoor links.
BGP	Most powerful and flexible protocol that can support all types of connectivity.	For multihomed sites with complex policies, it requires advanced operational staff expertise. May not be supported by some low-end routers (for very small remote sites).

* Not commonly used as a PE-CE routing protocol

Layer 2 MPLS VPN (L2VPN)

Operators understand the importance and the real need for an infrastructure that offers flexible and responsive network architecture, which supports current and future requirements without requiring any major change or upgrade to the network in the future. Therefore, in today's market, almost all service providers have either partially or fully migrated their core infrastructure to be MPLS enabled. This enables them to take advantage of the MPLS infrastructure and offer the same services to their customers (Layer 2 over legacy and modern WAN protocols) over one unified MPLS core infrastructure. This is a big incentive for those service providers that already offer MPLS L3VPN, because it will significantly reduce capital expenditures and operational expenses where the same core infrastructure and control plane can be used to transport both L2 and L3 services. Commonly, modern service providers that offer Layer 2 Ethernet services (for example, Metro Ethernet) are referred to as *Carrier Ethernet providers*. Based on that, the following are the primary business drivers for service providers to adopt and invest in modern Layer 2 services (L2VPN for example, Metro Ethernet):

■ **Flexible offerings:** Customized solutions with a flexible mix of services, data rates, and revenue (Ethernet private line [EPL], Ethernet virtual private line [EVPL], Ethernet LAN [E-LAN]).

■ **Flexible bandwidth:** For example, service providers can provision 1G or 10G Ethernet physical links and offer fractional line access rates based on the agreed

SLA. This provides operators and customers seamless roadmap upgrades in the future without changing any link or device (as compared to legacy services, such as a time-division multiplexing (TDM)-based WAN). Also, with today's flexible Ethernet nodes, an access port upgrade from 1G to 10G can be as simple as port shortest path first [SFP] replacement.

- **Flexible media access:** A variety of access networks that leverage Ethernet, such as WiMAX, IP digital subscriber line access multiplexers (DSLAMs), Ethernet over Fiber, Ethernet over Copper, and so on. Also supports interworking between legacy access media, such as ATM and Frame Relay, which might need to be retained for some remote areas where Metro Ethernet access coverage is not available.

- **Cost savings:** Moving to Ethernet infrastructure offers lower capex compared to legacy hardware such as ATM switches. In addition, bandwidth flexibility, discussed earlier in this list, offers an optimized capex and investment protection for both service providers and customers.

- **Scalable services that can increase revenue:** Support a large number of customers over one common infrastructure.

Note This covers the technologies and designs from a service provider point of view. Nevertheless, these technologies and designs can be applicable to enterprises that deploy any of these services across their networks, such as self-deployed L2VPN to interconnect enterprise data centers over a Layer 3 WAN core network.

Figure 6-35 illustrates the different Layer 2 media access methods and topologies that can be transported over an MPLS-enabled backbone (L2VPN).

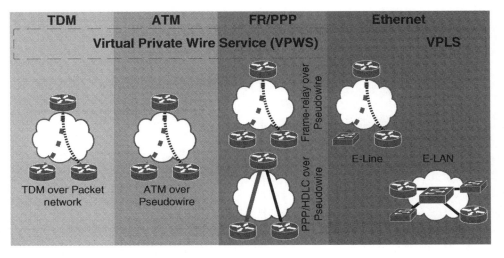

Figure 6-35 *MPLS L2VPN Connectivity Models*

This section focuses on the L2VPN MPLS (Ethernet-based) models of modern service provider networks, as covered in Figure 6-36.

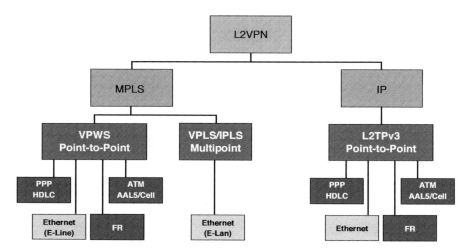

Figure 6-36   *L2VPN Models*

IP NGN Carrier Ethernet

The IP NGN Carrier Ethernet refers to the modern service provider architectures that offer a cost-effective converged network infrastructure capable of delivering new and future services by providing scalable and flexible designs and technologies that can meet the different bandwidth and network requirements. As a result, IP NGN Carrier Ethernet offers a wide range of modern services, including the following:

- Business services such as Metro Ethernet enterprise connectivity services (E-Line, E-LAN)

- Consumer and residential services (VoD, IPTV)

- Business services over DOCSIS

- Broadband mobility services

- Wholesale services

Figure 6-37 shows a high level view of the IP NGN Carrier Ethernet architecture.

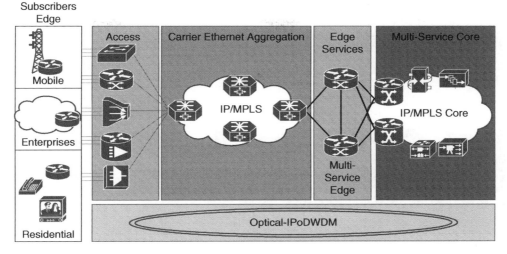

Figure 6-37 *IP NGN Carrier Ethernet Architecture*

The following components are as primary elements that comprise the architecture shown in Figure 6-37:

■ **Access:** Provides access to residential and business customers over digital subscriber line (DSL), fiber, cable, or wireless.

■ **Carrier Ethernet aggregation:** Aggregates the access network across a Carrier Ethernet network and provides interconnectivity to the IP/MPLS edge and IP/MPLS core.

■ **IPoDWDM optical network:** Enables optical aggregation services with intelligent Ethernet multiplexing using MPLS/IP over dense wavelength-division multiplexing (IPoDWDM).

■ **Multiservice edge:** Interface services with the IP/MPLS core; this is the provider edge for both residential and business subscriber services.

■ **IP/MPLS core:** Provides scalable IP/MPLS routing in the core network.

Metro Ethernet (ME) services can be classified into the following two general categories:

■ **Point to Point (P2P):** In which a P2P Ethernet circuit can be provisioned between two user network interfaces (UNIs).

■ **Multipoint to Multipoint (MP2MP):** In which a multipoint-to-multipoint Ethernet circuit can be provisioned between two or more UNIs. If there are only two UNIs in the circuit, more UNIs can be provisioned to the same Ethernet virtual connection if required, which distinguishes this from the point-to-point type.

Metro Ethernet Forum (MEF), however, defines the two categories just discussed as two main types of Layer 2 Ethernet services:

- **Ethernet line service (E-Line):** Point to point, such as Virtual Private Wire Service (VPWS)

- **Ethernet LAN service (E-LAN):** Multipoint to multipoint such as Virtual Private LAN Services (VPLS)

> **Note**   There is also a P2P Metro Ethernet service known as E-Tree, as an abstraction E-LAN, in which the spoke "leaves" can communicate with the hub or "root" location but not with each other, as shown in Figure 6-38. The typical application for E-Tree is in franchise operations [43].

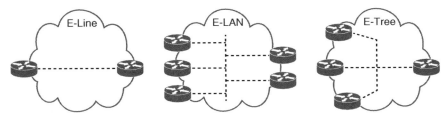

Figure 6-38   *ME models*

Metro Ethernet services can be created by assigning values to a set of attributes grouped according to the following [44]:

- **User network interface (UNI):** Represents a physical demarcation point between the connection and the subscriber. Also known as *port based*.

- **Ethernet virtual connection (EVC):** Represents the association of two or more UNIs, which limits the exchange of service frames to UNIs within the EVC in Ethernet. When multiple EVCs could exist per single UNI and each EVC is distinguished by 802.1Q VLAN tag identification, this is known as *VLAN based* (ERS or EVPL).

Table 6-5 summarizes the relationship between the transport model and the MEF Ethernet service definitions.

Table 6-5   *MEF Transport Models*

Service Type	Port Based	VLAN Based
E-Line	Ethernet private line (EPL)	Ethernet virtual private line (EVPL)
E-LAN	Ethernet private LAN (EPLAN)	Ethernet virtual private LAN (EVPLAN)

In addition to E-Line and E-LAN services, additional services are available for Layer 2 that are mainly to facilitate carrying legacy WAN transport over MPLS networks, such as the following:

■ Frame Relay over MPLS (FRoMLS)

■ ATM over MPLS (ATMoMPLS)

> **Note**   Cisco's implementation of VPWS is known as *Any Transport over MPLS* (AToM) and delivers what is known as *Ethernet over MPLS* (EoMPLS). L2TPv3, however, can be used as an analogous service to AToM over any IP transport.

Virtual Private Wire Service Design Considerations

VPWS is based on the concept of pseudo wire (PW) described in (RFC 3916), which can be defined as a connection between two edge nodes connecting two attachment circuits (ACs) to emulate a direct AC connection of a packet-switched network (PSN), as shown in Figure 6-39 [45]. The typical implementations of PWs are carried either over a native IP, such as L2TP, or over an MPLS network, such as EoMPLS. Within an MPLS-enabled network, the core visibility is limited to the transport MPLS labels (LSP) that each PW uses to communicate with the remote end, while the remote PE relies on the virtual circuit (VC) label to identify the intended AC per pseudo wire (PW-to-AC mapping), as shown in Figure 6-39 [46].

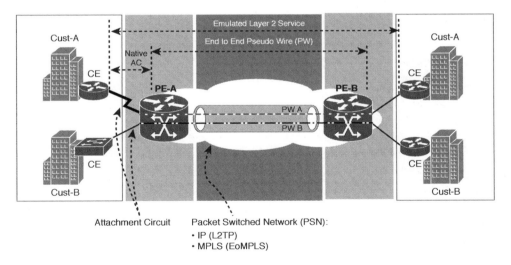

Figure 6-39   *Virtual Private Wire Service*

Transport Models

As covered earlier in this chapter, the primary goal of service providers is to offer services that can satisfy their customer requirements; therefore, their core public services network (PSN) is the main business enabler. Pseudo wire over PSN gives the service provider flexibility to handle customer connectivity using primary connectivity models, each of which can serve different set of requirements:

■ **VLAN-based model:** As its name implies, it is a VLAN-based transport model. VLANs defined on the physical port can be switched to different remote PEs (for example, the scenario in Figure 6-40 where enterprise customers are seeking a service from the service provider to be analogous to their current WAN service [traditional Frame Relay or ATM], in which no routing and IP addressing changes are required).

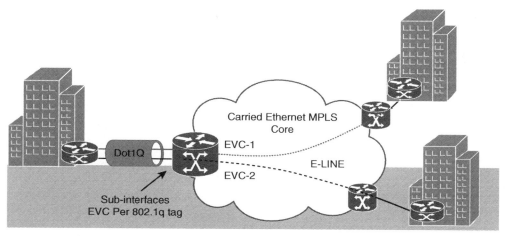

Figure 6-40 *PW VLAN-Based Model*

■ **Port-based model:** This transport model tunnels all traffic entering the AC physical port and transports it to the targeted remote PE without any change. This model can be applicable in scenarios where the Layer 3 customer network is traditional WAN serial links and needs to be replaced with higher-speed P2P links. Another possible usage of this model is the case of a customer that needs to interconnect two LAN islands over the service provider's Layer 2 P2P PW (whether it is native IP core or MPLS enabled). Furthermore, this model is commonly used to provide Layer 2 data center interconnection to support the extending of multiple Layer 2 VLANs over the same link, as shown in Figure 6-41.

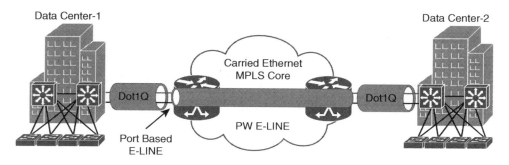

Figure 6-41 *PW Port-Based Model*

Furthermore, in some situations, the user access side may not always be provisioned as Ethernet. Instead, customers with legacy WAN media access such as ATM and Frame Relay might to be provisioned with L2VPN services. With the VPWS (L2VPN MPLS based), carriers still can maintain customer access as it is and offer the same service capability. In addition, service providers can even maintain the connectivity between sites that have different media access methods, such as Frame Relay, ATM, and standard Ethernet [45,46]. Table 6-6 compares and summarizes the primary L2 WAN media access technologies (AC) along with its transport models over PWs.

Table 6-6   *PWs L2 Media Access*

L2 Technology	Transport Mode over PW
Frame Relay	Port based Per DLCI
ATM	AAL5 protocol data units (PDUs) over PW Cell relay over PW
Ethernet	Protocol based VLAN based

VPWS Control Plane

In general, the control plane in L2VPN is responsible for two primary functions:

- Identify the remote end (PE) with which the PW session needs to be established

- Negotiate the setup of the PW session with the relevant remote node (PE)

For the PEs to set up PWs for the VPWS, a control plane mechanism should exist to establish the session. The following are the two primary control plane models used for this purpose:

- LDP based (RFC 4447)

- BGP based (RFC 6624)

In fact, LDP based and BGP based have different attributes with regard to L2VPN signaling. However, both mechanisms have the same operational duties in L2VPN environments. For instance, with both signaling models, each PE needs to know the VPN label of the remote PE where the remote CE is attached, in addition to the consistency check via the exchange of PW attributes such as the PW maximum transmission unit (MTU) value. In addition, both signaling models support the ability to inform local and remote PEs during connectivity failure scenarios, such as PE-CE link failure. Table 6-7 compares the characteristics of each control protocol [46, 47, 48].

Table 6-7   *L2VPN PW Control Plane*

	LDP Based	**BGP Based**
Control plane sessions	Fully meshed	Can use route reflectors or confederations to avoid full mesh
Autodiscovery	No	Yes
Complexity of full mesh	Complex	Simple
Inter-AS support	Supported but can be complex with a large number of PWs	Supported, using analogous concept to L3VPN Inter-AS
Scalability	Not scalable	Scalable
P2P deployments (EPL) between 2 sites (virtual leased line)	Recommended	Not required if BGP is not used as a control plane anywhere in the network

Note   Typically, as part of the control plane signaling, PEs exchange PW payload MTUs and must agree to use the same MTU value. The PW MTU is usually derived from the directly attached circuit (AC) MTU. Therefore, the MTU within the SP core must be large enough to carry PW payload and MPLS stack to avoid any failure because of payload fragmentation. In contrast, L2TPv3 does support MTU path fragmentation.

From a design perspective, the nature of the L2VPN solution and the environment in general influence to a large extent the selection of the L2VPN control plane (LDP versus BGP). For example, the typical use of VPWS is as a P2P L2VPN solution, and mostly used to connect either two sites or a very small number of remote sites, in which control plane scalability is less of a concern, whereas the number of PWs supported by any PE is more of a concern here. Therefore, LDP is still a feasible choice as a control plane in this case. Nonetheless, if the same L2VPN carrier offers L3VPN to its customers over the same infrastructure, then having BGP as the control plane for L2VPN (VPWS) will help to simplify the overall solution manageability because there will be a unified control plane for both L2VPN and L3VPN (and so the same operation folks with the same expertise can manage both MPLS VPN services). This translates into lower operational complexity and cost from the business point of view. If VPWS is used to interconnect many remote sites with increased LDP-based control plane complexity, however this complexity here is as a result of selecting the inappropriate L2VPN solution. Consequently, the network designer may consider introducing VPLS in this case to provide a more scalable L2VPN solution for those customers with several dispersed remote sites.

Virtual Private LAN Service Design Considerations

The preceding section discussed how today's service providers can take the advantage of their MPLS-based infrastructure and provide a P2P MPLS L2VPN network, also known as a *virtual leased line* (VLL). The VLL can support sites with different WAN media access methods, which offers increased flexible and reliable solutions in terms of bandwidth and satisfying tight SLAs.

However, in today's market, where technology has become the primary key driver and facilitator for many businesses to achieve their goals, there is a significantly increasing demand for interconnected multiple sites over one common Layer 2 network. Along with that, there is an increasing demand to extend multiple modern data centers over Layer 2 transport. This supports the requirements of the next generation of data centers and the mobility of applications, such as virtual machine mobility and distributed workload (geoclustering), which supports the overall business continuity plan of the customer's business. Taking the aforementioned into consideration, this section covers how service providers can leverage the P2P PWs L2VPN architecture to offer any-to-any LAN service to their customers (usually enterprise customers). This architecture is known as *Virtual Private LAN Service* (VPLS), or in Metro Ethernet Forum (MEF) terms, *E-LAN*.

With the VPLS architecture, end users see their network nodes are interconnected directly over a shared Ethernet LAN segment; this shared segment is an emulated LAN created by the VPLS domain (emulated switched network), as shown in Figure 6-42. In addition, it does support legacy media access methods that support Ethernet encapsulation, such as Frame Relay.

As with L3VPN, in a typical VPLS architecture service providers are normally required to update the PE or PEs, to which the customer needs to be connected to the same VPLS domain of a certain customer (equivalent to the concept of adding a new L3VPN customer to an existing VPN customer). In contrast, with the P2P Layer 2 VPN solutions, the service provider must reconfigure each of the peering PEs every time a change is required (typical scalability limitation of a P2P architecture). This optimized Layer 2 VPN architecture, along with its simplified operation compared to legacy Layer 2 WAN services, is a key business driver that attracts many Carrier Ethernet providers to adopt it and offer it to their customers quickly. As a result, VPLS in today's market is one of the most common reliable and mature Layer 2 WAN services.

Note   Although this section always refers to the network as a service provider network, in fact all the concepts are applicable, to certain extent, to large-scale enterprise networks that have self-deployed Layer 2 VPN services, such as VPLS.

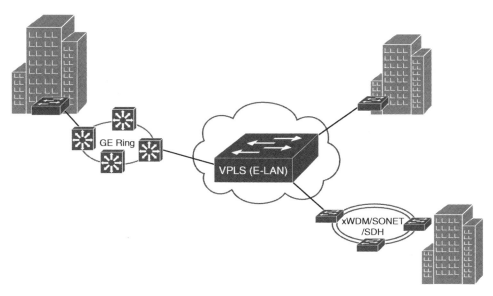

Figure 6-42   *VPLS Conceptual View*

VPLS Architecture Building Blocks

In general, VPLS brings the standard IEEE 802.1 MAC address learning, flooding, and forwarding concept over the MPLS-based packet-switched network extended by the pseudo wires (PWs), which commonly interconnect different customer LANs. In other words, VPLS is like the glue that interconnects the multiple LANs across one common packet-switched network over MPLS. Like any system architecture, multiple components construct the overall VPLS architecture. Each component performs specific functions to achieve the desired end-to-end result. In addition, as VPLS becomes a more mature architecture, there are multiple design models of the VPLS-induced architecture, with the components and their functions differing slightly based on the architecture used. This section discusses these different design models.

VPLS Functional Components

Figure 6-43 illustrates the common functional components that construct a typical VPLS architecture. However, these components may vary slightly based on the used VPLS model, as covered in the following section:

- **N-PE:** Provides VPLS termination/L3 services
- **U-PE:** Provides customer UNI
- **CE:** The customer device

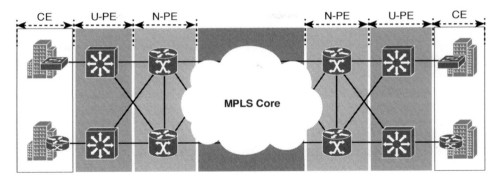

Figure 6-43 *VPLS Architecture Functional Component*

Virtual Switching Instance

The virtual switching instance (VSI) performs standard LAN (that is, Ethernet) bridging functions, including the participation in the learning and forwarding process based on MAC addresses and VLAN tags. Each VSI defined at each provider edge node usually handles the forwarding decisions of a single VPLS instance.

VPLS Control Plane

To a large extent, the concept of the VPLS control plane is the same as VPWS (covered earlier in this chapter). However, the primary difference with VPLS is the need of full-mesh PWs among all the participating PEs in any given VPLS instance. With VPWS, in contrast, the typical scenario is P2P PWs between two sites or a few sites in a full-mesh or hub-and-spoke connectivity model. Consequently, with VPLS, the automation of the PE discovery and the PWs set up among the relevant PEs are important factors to consider. Otherwise, the design will encounter increased operational complexity when the network grows with a large number of customers (VPLS instances) and remote sites (PEs per VPLS instance).

Nonetheless, as covered earlier, VPLS can be deployed by enterprises across their backbone to form an overlaid L2VPN connectivity (self-deployed VPLS). In such an environment, the number of PEs and VPLS instances can be limited compared to service provider networks. Therefore, using a manual mechanism to set up the PWs, such as LDP, can be a viable solution in this type of scenario. Furthermore, LDP is accustomed to more people and is a widely deployed control plane for L2VPN, even though it may not be the optimal scalable choice. However, upgrading this control plane may not be an option for those operators because of certain constraints and concerns, such as the operator cannot afford any service interruption to their existing VPLS customers or the existing PE nodes do not support BGP as L2VPN control plane protocol. In these scenarios, network designers are forced to comply or accommodate their design suggestion with regard to these design constraints.

In general, designing a typical VPLS with automated PE discovery and signaling can offer a more scalable and simple operational solution. This is can be achieved by BGP as an L2VPN control plane for signaling and autodiscovery (RFC 4761), or by a suboptimal solution that offers an optimized version of the only LDP control plane that retains the signaling to be based on LDP while automating the discovery of the participating PEs in each VPLS instance using BGP (as specified in RFC 6074).

VPLS Design Models

One of the main drivers in the selection of one VPLS design model over others is the level of scalability possible. The primary factors that influence VPLS solution scalability are the supported number of VLANs (customers) and the number of PWs established between the PE nodes. Therefore, network designers should consider the answers to the following questions, which can help to build the foundation of the design decision during the planning phase:

- What is the goal of the solution (enterprise grade to interconnect multiple data centers of an enterprise; offer E-LAN services by a carrier Ethernet service provider grade)?

- Number of customers?

- Number of participating PEs?

- Scale of the interconnected sites in terms of the amount of MAC addresses? (For instance, hosting cloud providers usually requires support for an extremely huge number of MACs.)

- PW termination between N-PEs versus between U-PEs along with the VSI?

- Any platform limitation, such as supporting VPLS VSI configuration or hardware resource capacity?

- Is traffic load-balancing/sharing for the multihomed sites required not (active-active versus active-standby)?

- What is the targeted resiliency level? And how can be archived (for example, MPLS-TE FRR, redundant PWs)?

Flat VPLS Design Model

The flat VPLS design model is the classic VPLS design model. It is the simplest design model among other VPLS models, with the least functional components, as shown in Figure 6-44.

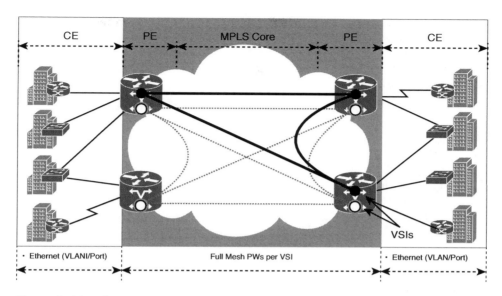

Figure 6-44 *Flat VPLS*

With this design model, each PE usually hosts the VSIs of VPLS domains, along with a full mesh of PWs among the participating PEs per VPLS domain. Based on this, each PE will maintain a P2MP perspective of all other PEs per VPLS domain, and each PE will be seen as the root bridge of the PW's mesh to other PEs, as shown in Figure 6-45.

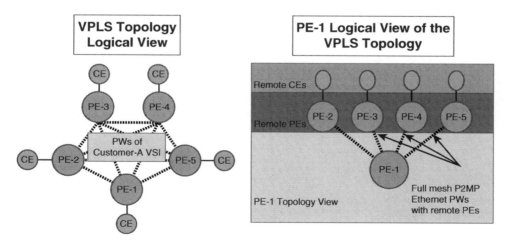

Figure 6-45 *PE PW Topology View*

When PEs maintain a full mesh of PW connectivity, it eliminates the need to rely on or enable Spanning Tree Protocol (STP) across the PSN MPLS network. However, from the customer point of view, their STP (bridge protocol data units [BPDUs]) can be transparently carried over the emulated VPLS LAN between the different sites without impacting the service provider network. The split-horizon concept, however, is used with the model to block any potential loop of traffic received over one core/PE PW into another core/PE PW. Based on that, the following summarizes the characteristics of this VPLS design model:

- Limited scalability. The more PEs and VSIs there are, the more network hardware resources are consumed per PE associated with operational complexity:

  - A large number of PWs because of the nature of this model, where a full mesh of directed LDP sessions is required (N * (N - 1) / 2 PWs required)

  - Potential signaling and packet replication overhead, when the number of PWs increases across multiple PEs to cover multiple remote sites (CEs) per customer VSI using LDP as the control plane protocol

  - Large amount of multicast replication, which may result in inefficient network bandwidth utilization (unless some mechanisms is used to mitigate it such as Interior Gateway Management Protocol [IGMP] snooping with VPLS)

  - CPU overhead for replication

  - MAC distribution across the network limitations

  - Support limited number of customers/VLANs (maximum 4096)

- VLAN and port-level support (no QinQ)

- Support multihomed CEs in active-standby manner

- Suitable for simple and small deployments, such as a self-deployed enterprise VPLS solution

Hierarchical VPLS Design Model

The hierarchical VPLS (H-VPLS) design model aims to optimize the high complexity of PW mesh complexity and the limited scalability of the flat VPLS design model by introducing a hierarchical structure to the VPLS design. This hierarchical structure consists of hub-and-spoke and full-mesh networks, as shown in Figure 6-46.

As shown in Figure 6-46, this design model provides a more structured multistage PW connectivity model, where the hub or core of fully meshed PWs in each PE node form a multipoint-to-multipoint forwarding relationship with all other PE nodes at the same level within the VPLS domain. At the hub-and-spoke level, each PE node needs a single PW to the hub PE node and can operate in a non-split-horizon mode. This allows inter-VC connectivity between PEs at the same level connected to the same hub PE node. In other words, the hub PE nodes perform PW aggregation of the edge node PWs.

Consequently, this hierarchical VPLS model offers significant reductions to the number of mesh PWs, as shown in Figure 6-47. The model also overcomes the scalability and performance efficiency limitations of the flat VPLS model to a great extent.

As shown in Figure 6-47, H-VPLS has some additional terms for its functional components:

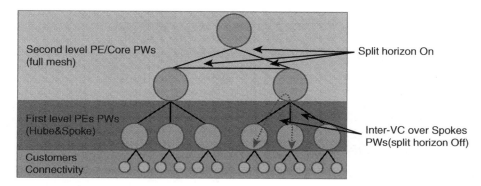

Figure 6-46 *H-VPLS Structure*

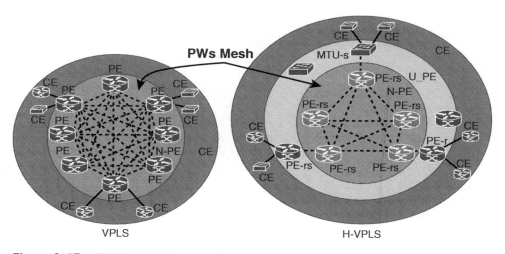

Figure 6-47 *H-VPLS PW Aggregation*

- **MTU-s:** Multitenant unit switch capable of bridging (U-PE)

- **PE-r:** Nonbridging PE router

- **PE-rs:** Bridging and routing capable PE

Moreover, H-VPLS supports two primary access models (the access tier):

- Ethernet access model

- MPLS access model

Ethernet Access Model

This model is primarily based on Ethernet and 802.1ad (QinQ), as shown in Figure 6-48. With this model, service providers (Carrier Ethernet) can extend their access to different geographic areas to offer flexible Ethernet WAN/MAN access. However, this model can be limited to up to 4094 service instances per bridged access network.

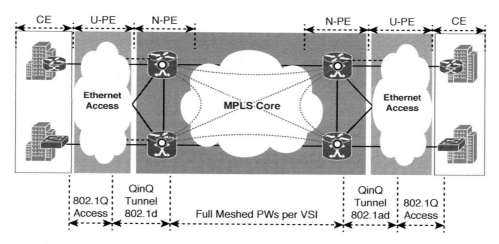

Figure 6-48 *H-VPLS: Ethernet Access Model*

Furthermore, with this access model, local edge traffic between ACs (within the same VLAN/VPLS domain) does not have to traverse across the N-PE. Instead the MTU-s can switch traffic locally; this can offload some of the traffic load from the core and PEs, which ultimately will lead to optimized bandwidth efficiency on circuits to the N-PE, as shown in Figure 6-49.

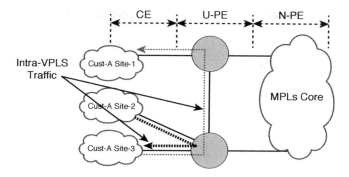

Figure 6-49 *H-VPLS: U-PE Local Forwarding*

MPLS Access Model

It is obvious, given the name of this model, that it is based on extended MPLS to the access model. This can offer flexibility to service providers to take advantage of certain points of presence (POPs), which indeed provide multiservice access, such as L3VPN and L2VPN (VPLS) access termination. With this model, the PWs from the U-PE to the N-PE usually connect in a hub-and-spoke fashion, and the N-PEs connect in a full mesh, as discussed earlier in this section. This can offer an optimized version of E-LAN service as compared to the flat VPLS model, as shown in Figure 6-50. In addition, with regard to the optimization of the scalability and efficiency levels of this model, in a large-scale network with a large number of PWs/VSIs, the N-PE will encounter performance and scalability limitations because it will aggregate all the PWs of U-PEs connected to it.

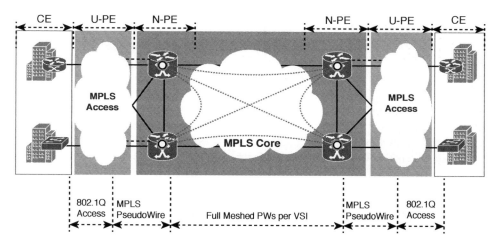

Figure 6-50 *H-VPLS: Ethernet Access Model*

Note   Each access model of the H-VPLS offers a slightly different level of scalability.
Network designers must consider the following points, and should always ask why before
selecting any given approach or design model. This ensures the selected design approach
is driven by factors that collectively align with the business goals and priorities. For
instance, if a POP (access network) is required to provide Ethernet access in a specific city
(for example, E-LAN) and the existing infrastructure does not support MPLS, is it feasible
to enable MPLS in this POP network? Yes! Why? No! Why?

- **Ethernet access:** Limited to 4096 service instances (per access network); also STP in
  the Ethernet access network might slow down network convergence time
- **MPLS access:** Increased complexity when the number of PWs between the U-PE
  and N-PE increases significantly

The MPLS access model can offer more flexibility if other services are required to be
terminated at the same access POP/node, such as L3VPN.

With these two variant access models of the hierarchical VPLS, service providers can
take advantage of the multiple access model options. For example, in one region/city,
MAN access can be based on Ethernet access (QinQ), where only Metro Ethernet
services are required, whereas in other regions, the access can be based on MPLS, where
multiaccess services nodes are required to provide L2VPN and L3VPN client access
termination, as shown in Figure 6-51. In this approach, the SP core appears like the hub
that connects the different access networks (spokes).

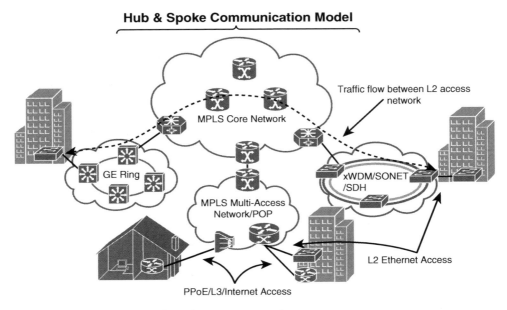

Figure 6-51   *H-VPLS with Multiaccess Network*

This architecture has the following characteristics:

- Offers a more structured design, where the full PW mesh is required among core nodes only, in addition to the partitions node discovery process

- Minimizes signaling overhead

- Full PW mesh among core devices only

- Packet replication done on the core only

- Provider H-VPLS flavors: H-VPLS with Ethernet access and H-VPLS with MPLS access

- Suitable for larger-scale deployment

> **Note**   There is another variation of VPLS solution called *Advanced-VPLS* (A-VPLS), which is the Cisco enhanced version of the standard VPLS and offers the following:[1]
>
> - Capability to load balance using equal-cost multipathing concept (ECMP)
>
> - Simplified operations though the command-line interface (CLI) enhancements to facilitate configuration of the L2VPN A-VPLS feature
>
> - Optimized DCI redundancy as its support for redundant DCI and PE switches (in active-active and active-standby modes)
>
> - Optimized overall convergence time for a solution with multiple edge nodes and operating in active-active manner

H-VPLS with Provider Backbone Bridging

The H-VPLS model offers an optimized version of the flat VPLS in terms of scalability and performance efficiency. However, there are still scalability and performance limitations with this design model for Carrier Ethernet, which offers services to a large number of customers with large-scale networks; in particular, large-scale modern data centers (virtualized and cloud-based data centers) with layer interconnect between them, where the service provider may need to carry millions of MAC addresses across their backbone. With H-VPLS, the following limitations are most probably going to constrain the service provider from achieving this goal:

- In both flat and hierarchical VPLS models, each PE that performs MAC switching has to learn customer MAC addresses, which often leads to performance and scalability deficiencies.

- With the H-VPLS Ethernet access model, each access network is limited to about 4094 customer instances. With the MPLS access model, the larger the number of customers, the larger the number of PWs and VSIs to be handled by the N-PE (limited performance and scalability).

---

1. "Advanced Virtual Private LAN Service," http://www.cisco.com/c/en/us/solutions/collateral/data-center-virtualization/data-center-interconnect/design_guide_c07-647422.html

Therefore, the IEEE standard was developed to provide an optimized approach that can scale to a very large number of customer instances and MAC addresses (millions) without compromising network performance efficiency. This standard is called *provider backbone edge* (PBB). This section covers the high-level architecture of the PBB and how it can be integrated with VPLS/H-VPLS to enable service providers to meet the requirements of today's large-scale enterprise customers and cloud-based data center interconnect requirements.

Provider Backbone Bridging Overview

PBB is an IEEE (802.1ah-2008) technology that defines an architecture based on a MAC tunneling mechanism, which enables service providers to build a large-scale Ethernet bridged network. The primary concept behind PBB is the hierarchical MAC address learning and forwarding in a similar manner to the MPLS label staking concept, where the typical top label used for the transport within the SP core network and the bottom labels are relevant to the customer VPN or VCID in L2VPN. Instead, PBB uses multitier MAC address learning and forwarding in which the core PEs, also known as *backbone core bridges* (BCBs), communicate based on backbone MAC addresses of the core components. Customer MAC frames (C-MAC), however, are encapsulated (tunneled) at the edge of the bridged network into the backbone MAC, which enables Carrier Ethernet to scale a large number of C-MACs without impacting core components, because the communication (including broadcast, unicast, and multicast flooding BUM [broadcast, unknown destination address, multicast]) will based only on the backbone MACs. Figure 6-52 shows the high-level architecture of the PBB.

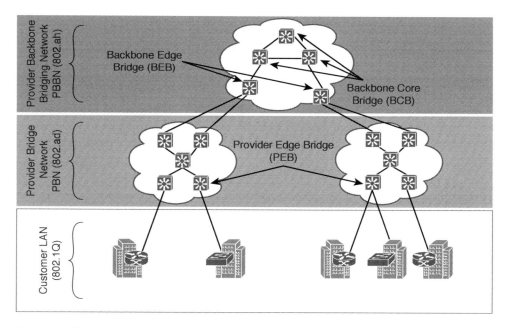

Figure 6-52 *PBB Architecture*

With PBB architecture, besides MAC tunneling, the network provides VLAN tunneling as well, at two stages. First, at the edge of the bridged network, where customer VLANs (C-VLAN) are tunneling using 802.1ad IEEE standard (QinQ), in this architecture referred to as *service provider tag* or *S-VLAN*. The second stage is where the S-VLANs are mapped into the PBB backbone VLAN (B-tag or B-VLAN).

Note This concept can be applied to flat VPLS model, as well, where the BEB in Figure 6-52 will be facing the CEs directly and performing forwarding based on both the backbone and customer MAC address (mapping between C-MAC and B-MAC).

Across the PBB bridged network, the end-to-end mapping and identification of each customer instance is based on the service instance ID (I-SID), which has to be unique across the entire bridged network and is usually performed at the edge of the network and not within the backbone. Based on that, PBB architecture is broken down into two primary components.

The forwarding database (FDB) within the SP backbone is selected based on B-VLAN, not the customer MAC/VLAN. PBB has two main components (as shown in Figure 6-52):

- I-Component
  - Face the 802.1Q or 802.1ad network (customer side)
  - Learns and forwards using C-MACs
  - Maintains a mapping table of C-MACs to B-MACs
  - Performs PBB encapsulation/decapsulation facing the PBB component (adding PBB header for ingress traffic)
- B-Component
  - Learns and forwards using PBB encapsulated frames (B-MAC, B-VLAN)
  - Pushes/pops B-VLAN on CBP

Figure 6-53 illustrates the conceptual architecture of PBB encapsulation and forwarding.

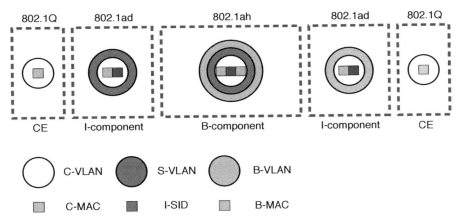

Figure 6-53 *Conceptual Architecture of PBB Encapsulation*

Note In the case of broadcast of unknown unicast and multicast (BUM) traffic, the ingress BEB sets the B-MAC destination address (DA) to a B-MAC multicast group address, where one or multiple egress BEB can listen to this group address.

Furthermore, the flexibility of the PBB architecture offers multiple options to network designers to map between customer VLANs and the service interface, which is more flexible compared to the typical L2VPN VLAN- and port-based forwarding modes discussed earlier in this chapter.

PBB with this hierarchal architecture can offer the following:

- Up to 2^{24} service instances per bridge domain by defining a 24-bit service identification field (I-SID). In other words, 224 service instances per B-VLAN, also known as MAC-in-MAC.

- PBB provides the MAC address hiding (tunneling) technique from the SP core, which can significantly increase the solution scalability by confining customer MAC address learning to the edge and mapping customer MAC addresses to the backbone MAC addresses on BEBs. (In this architecture, all the intelligence is on the BEBs, because they are responsible for translating frames to/from the new PBB format.)

H-VPLS Optimization with PBB

As covered earlier in this section, PBB provides VPLS deployment a significant scalability optimization for both the flat and hierarchical models. Typically, customer MACs and VLANs will be tunneled inside the backbone MAC and VLANs along with the unique I-SID assigned to each customer instance at the network edge. B-VLAN, however, has a 1:1 mapping to VPLS VSI instance, where each B-VLAN associates with a VSI instance along with a B-MAC range.

In a backbone network, the architecture of the typical VPLS (control plane and forwarding) remains the same. However, inside each B-VLAN, there can be multiple customer VLANs, each with its I-SID encapsulated, as shown in the Figure 6-54 and Figure 6-55 in the next sections. In other words, each VPLS VSI in the core can carry multiple customer instances (also known as *service multiplexing*) without adding any performance inefficiencies, with the ability to scale to a large number of customer MAC addresses, because the core only learns and forwards based on the B-MAC and B-VLAN instances. The sections that follow describe the different VPLS design models combined with PBB.

Flat VPLS

For the flat VPLS model, the primary optimization here is the reduction of the number of meshes of VPLS VSIs per customer. With PBB, a single VPLS (VSI) instance can multiplex multiple customer service instances, as discussed earlier and shown in Figure 6-54.

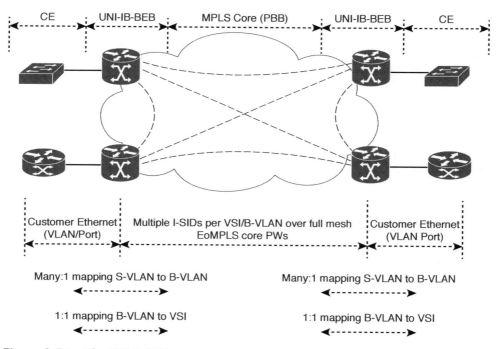

Figure 6-54   *Flat VPLS: PBB*

Hierarchical VPLS

PBB supports both access models of the hierarchical VPLS (Ethernet based and MPLS based). With the Ethernet model, PBB transforms the access network from being based on 802.1ad (QinQ) to being based on PBB. Therefore, it is referred to as *Ethernet access*

B-tagged. This approach will significantly optimize the overall scalability limitation of this model (which is limited to about 4094 customer), in addition to the multiplexing of multiple customer service instances into one VPLS instance across the core, as shown in Figure 6-55.

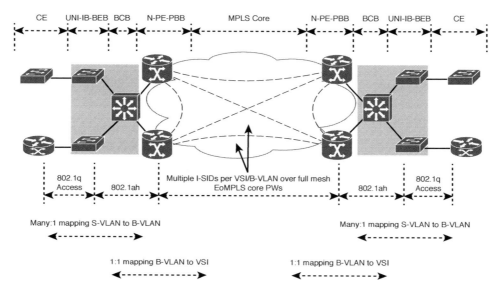

Figure 6-55   *H-VPLS (B-Tagged) Ethernet Access: PBB*

Note   This model can also support access network with 802.1ad (QinQ), where the C-VLAN is usually encapsulated with the access network by the S-VLAN per customer; at the N-PE-PBB, one or multiple customer VLANs can be mapped to a single B-VLAN and VSI toward the core.

When PBB is combined with VPLS with the MPLS access network, the U-PE will perform the functions of encapsulation/decapsulation of the PBB header (IB-BEB) and provide the 802.1Q or 802.1ad service interface toward the CEs, as shown in Figure 6-56. As with the other models, PBB provides the ability to multiplex multiple customers' service instances (I-SIDs) under a single VPLS instance (B-VLAN/VFI), which will significantly reduce the number of PWs within the access and core network, along with providing more scalable MAC address learning.

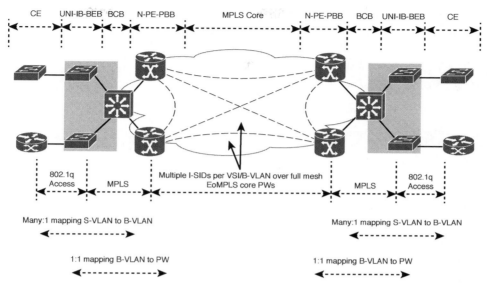

Figure 6-56 *H-VPLS MPLS Access: PBB*

It is obvious that PBB is not changing the actual concept of VPLS in terms of address learning, forwarding, and building the PW mesh. However, its incorporates the concept of MAC and VLAN tunneling on different stages in the bridged network, depending on the design model used, which can offer significant improvement to overall performance and scalability.

EVPN Design Model (Next-Generation MPLS L2VPN)

Ethernet VPN (EVPN) technology is a next-generation Ethernet L2VPN (defined in RFC 7432), which uses the same principle of MPLS L3VPN, in which the BGP control plane for Ethernet segment and MAC address signaling and learning over the service provider MPLS core, in addition to for access topology and VPN endpoint discovery, will eliminate the need to use PWs (thereby avoiding its operational complexities and scalability limitations). In fact, the introduction of EVPN marks a significant milestone for the industry, because it aligns the well-understood technical and operational principles of IP VPNs to Ethernet services. Operators can now leverage their experience and the scalability characteristics inherent in IP VPNs to their Ethernet offerings. In addition, EVPN supports various L2VPN Ethernet over MPLS topologies, including Ethernet multipoint (E-LAN), Ethernet P2P (E-Line), and Ethernet rooted-multipoint (E-Tree) [49].

Businesses Drivers

One of the main drivers toward EVPN is the increased demand on distributed virtualized and cloud-based data centers, which commonly require a scalable and reliable stretched layer concavity among them. Recently, DCI has become a leading application for

Ethernet multipoint L2VPNs. Virtual machine (VM) mobility, storage clustering, and other data center services require nodes and servers in the same Layer 2 network to be extended across data centers over the WAN. Consequently, these trends and customer needs add new requirements for L2VPN operators to meet, such as the following:

- Flow-based load balancing (PE based and multipathing) across the PSN.

- Fast convergence (avoid C-MAC flushing).

- Support large-scale, virtualized data centers.

In addition, with the increased demand and expectations from enterprise customers or cloud hosting providers, operators also need to consider a solution that offers the following:

- Flexible forwarding policies and topologies

- A scalable solution that supports a very large number of customers and MAC addresses

- Operational simplicity

EVPN Business Strengths

Based on the market trends and new requirements and expectations of modern enterprise customers, EVPN can offer the following advantages for L2VPN service providers (carrier Ethernet):

- Ability to meet very strict customer SLA requirements for business continuity by offering the ability of all-active (per-flow) access load balancing and fast convergence (at different levels: link, node, and MAC moves), in addition to optimizing the customer ROI of their multiple links (multihomed).

- Scalable design that avoids any PW limitations and supports extremely large numbers of customers and MAC addresses.

- Simplified operations, such as EVPN. Uses the same L3VPN address learning and forwarding principle where no additional staff is required to manage or maintain the network because the same control plane (MP-BGP) is used for both. Furthermore, with the autodiscovery of PEs adding new nodes, it becomes very simplified and eliminates all the complexities of PWs that network operators need to deal with.

- Topology flexibility because EVPN supports the primary Ethernet services topologies (E-LAN, E-Line, E-Tree, and VLAN-aware bundling).

- Seamless interworking between TRILL, 802.1Qaq, and 802.1Qbp (draft-ietf-l2vpn-trill-evpn-01).

- EVPN offers investment protection to service providers because it is open standard technology and supported by multiple vendors (RFC 7432).

From the enterprise (customer) point of view, the greatest advantage of EVPN is that they can have a flexible and reliable L2 WAN/MAN service that meets their new requirements, such as large-scale next-generation data center interconnects (virtualized and cloud based).

Provider Backbone Bridging with Ethernet VPN (PBB-EVPN)

By combining the principle of MAC tunneling and hiding of PBB (802.1ah) with the principle of MP-BGP-based MAC learning and PE discovery of the EVPN, network designers can achieve the optimal L2VPN architecture, which supports an extremely large number of customers and MACs. At the same time, it can reduce control plane overhead and scale to a larger extent than EVPN alone. In addition, it will help operators to offer L2VPN with faster convergence time. As a result, combining PBB with EVPN can achieve a superior solution for modern DCIs (virtualized and cloud based) and next-generation E-LAN offerings.

In other words, both LDP and BGP are valid and proven choices. The selection of one over the other should be based on the target environment (VPWS versus VPLS) and the scale of the network (SP versus enterprise), considering design constraints.

For instance, if the SP is offering both MPLS L2 and L3VPN services and there are many clients who have full mesh or several sites to be connected using either VPLS or VPWS, the use of the BGP for L2VPN signaling with autodiscovery can be considered a scalable solution (especially if the same PEs are involved in the Layer 3 VPN service and Layer 2VPN service). Consequently, the same BGP sessions can be used for both the L3VPN network layer reachability information (NLRI) and the L2VPN NLRI, and the same BGP architecture can be used (for example, BGP RRs). This solution also simplifies the design and operations of the network because there is no need to maintain multiple separate protocols (BGP and LDP) for the control plane of L2VPN and L3VPN services.

EVPN Architecture Components

The architecture of EVPN has three primary foundational building blocks, as described in more detail in the sections that follow:

- EVPN instance (EVI)

- Ethernet segment (ES)

- EVPN BGP routes and extended communities

EVPN Instance

An EVI represents an L2VPN instance on a PE node. Similar to the VRF in MPLS L3VPN, import and export RTs are allocated to each EVI. In addition, a bridge domain (BD) is associated with each EVI. Mapping traffic to the bridge domain, however, is dependent on the multiplexing behavior of the user to network interface (UNI). Typically, any given EVI can include one or more BDs based on the PE's service interface deployment type, as summarized in Figure 6-57.

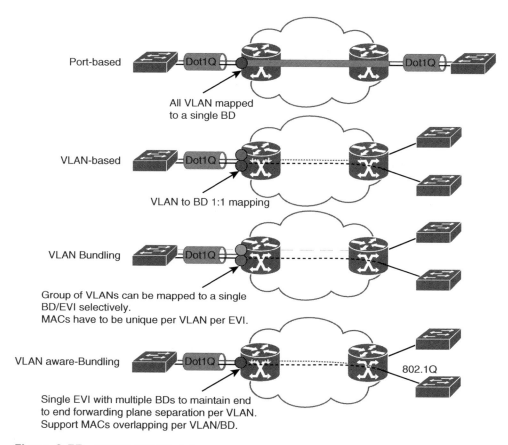

Port-based

All VLAN mapped
to a single BD

VLAN-based

VLAN to BD 1:1 mapping

VLAN Bundling

Group of VLANs can be mapped to a single
BD/EVI selectively.
MACs have to be unique per VLAN per EVI.

VLAN aware-Bundling

802.1Q

Single EVI with multiple BDs to maintain end
to end forwarding plane separation per VLAN.
Support MACs overlapping per VLAN/BD.

Figure 6-57   *EVPN EVI Models*

For instance, you can use the VLAN bundling model in environments that require
multiple VLANs to be carried transparently across the EVPN cloud between two or
more sites. In contrast, the VLAN-aware bundling is more feasible for multitenant data
center environments where multiple VLANs have to be carried over the DCI over a
single EVI with multiple DBs (VLAN to BD 1:1 mapping), because the overlapping of
tenant MAC addresses across different VLANs is supported.

Ethernet Segment

Ethernet segment (ES) refers to a site that is connected to one or more PEs. (ES can be
either a single CE or an entire network.) Typically, each network segment is assigned to
a single unique identifier, commonly referred to as *Ethernet segment identifier* (ESI),
which can eliminate any STP type of protocol used for loop prevention and normally
will add limitations to the design, especially for the multihomed CE scenarios. Based
on this identifier, EVPN can provide access redundancy that offers georedundancy and

multihoming, where a site (CE or entire network with multiple CEs) can be attached to one or multiple PEs that connect to the same provider core using multiple combinations of the CE-PE connectivity. Figure 6-58 illustrates the various EVPN supported access connectivity models:

- Single-homed device (SHD)

- Multihomed device (MHD) with mLAG

- Single-homed network (SHN)

- Multihomed network (MHN)

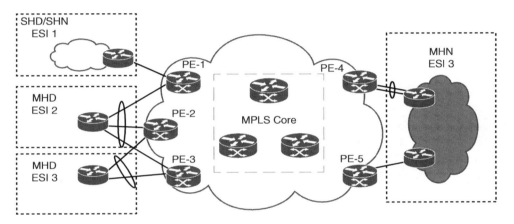

Figure 6-58 *EVPN Access Connectivity Models*

Note In EVPN, the PE advertises in BGP a split-horizon label (ESI MPLS label) associated with each multihomed ES to prevent flooded traffic from echoing back to a multihomed Ethernet segment.

EVPN BGP Routes and Extended Communities

Because both EVPN and PBB-EVPN PEs signal and learn MAC addresses over the core via BGP, a new MP-BGP address family and BGP extended communities were created to allow PE routers to advertise and learn prefixes that identify MAC addresses and Ethernet segments over the network. Therefore, this control plane learning significantly enhanced E-LAN capability over EVPN architecture to address the VPLS (data plane learning) short-comings discussed earlier, such as supporting multihoming with per-flow load balancing. In addition, the sequence number BGP extended community attribute offers optimized MAC mobility control plane learning and forwarding to the EVPN solution, because it facilitates and enhances the triggering of the advertising PE to withdraw its MAC advertisement in case of a MAC move (mobility) to a new network with a different ESI. This can offer a reliable solution for customers of a DCI with a stretched Ethernet segment.

Furthermore, by using BGP as a common VPN control plane, providers can now leverage their operational experience and the scalability characteristics inherent to IP VPNs for their Ethernet offerings.

EVPN Load-Balancing Models for Multihomed Devices

EVPN and PBB-EVPN support two primary load-balancing models for multihomed devices (CEs):

- **All-active load balancing (per-flow LB):** This connectivity model, shown in Figure 6-59, supports multihomed devices with per-flow load balancing. Access devices are connected over a single Ethernet link aggregation bundle (mLAG) to multiple PEs, and traffic of the same VLAN can be sent and received from all the PEs by the same Ethernet segment.

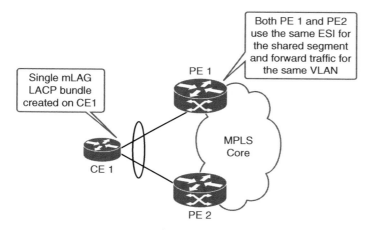

Figure 6-59   *All-Active Load-Balancing EVPN*

- **Single-active load balancing (per-service LB):** This connectivity model, shown in Figure 6-60, supports multihomed devices with a per-VLAN load-balancing model. The access devices in this model connect over separate Ethernet bundles to multiple PEs. PE routers, in turn, automatically perform service carving to divide VLAN forwarding responsibilities across the PEs in the Ethernet segment. The access device learns, via the data plane, which Ethernet bundle to use for a given VLAN. This is unlike the traditional VPLS model, where manual administration is required to compensate for the lack of access, autodiscovery, and automatic service carving mechanisms.

> **Note**   RFC 6391 describes a mechanism that introduces a flow label that allows P routers to distribute flows within a PW.

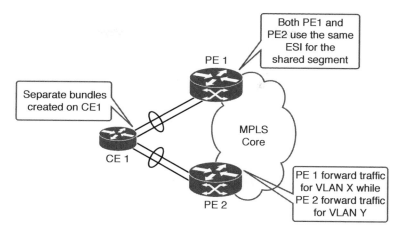

Figure 6-60 *Per VLAN Load-Balancing EVPN*

Table 6-8 provides a summarized comparison of the different VPLS design models discussed in this chapter.

Table 6-8 *VPLS Solution Comparison*

	VPLS	**H-VPLS**	**PBB-VPLS**	**EVPN**	**PBB-EVP**
Scalability	Very limited	Limited	Highly scalable	Scalable	Highly scalable
Control plane protocol	BGP/LDP	BGP/LDP	BGP/LDP	BGP	BGP
Network core control plane complexity	Very High	High	Moderate	High	Low
Flow-based load balancing (CE-PE)	No	No	No	Yes	Yes
Flow-based load balancing (CE-PE)	No	No	No	Yes	Yes
Flow-based multipathing in the core	Yes	Yes	Yes	Yes	Yes
Operational complexity	High*	High*	High	Low	Moderate

Table 6-8   *continued*

	VPLS	H-VPLS	PBB-VPLS	EVPN	PBB-EVP
Service interface VLAN-aware bundling	No	No	No	Yes	Yes
Loop prevention with multihomed CEs	STP	STP	STP	Split-horizon label (ESI MPLS Label)	Split-horizon label (ESI MPLS Label)
Fast convergence with local repairer	No	No	No	Yes	Yes
MAC mobility	Yes	Yes	Yes	Yes	Yes
Optimized control plane learning of MAC mobility	No	No	No	Yes, by the sequence number attribute	Yes, by the sequence number attribute
Targeted DCI solution**	Small (for example, enterprise controlled)	Medium	Very large	Large	Very large

*If BGP used as the control plane for VPLS, operational complexity will be reduced.

**What determines small, meduim and large DCI solutions is the number of interconnected sites per customer, scale of the VMs/MACs, and the number of customers; therefore, the suggestion here can be considered as a generic and not absolute.

Final Thoughts: L2VPN Business Value and Direction

This chapter covered the various L2VPN design models, protocols, and approaches, along with the characteristics of each. In addition, Table 6-8 compared the different VPLS flavors available (at the time of this writing) from different design aspects. From a design perspective, all these design options and protocols are technically valid and proven solutions and still in use by many operators today. However, as a network designer, you must evaluate the scenario that you are dealing with, ideally using the top-down design approach, where business goals and requirements are at the top, followed by the application requirements that should collectively drive the functional and technical requirements.

For instance, if an enterprise needs a basic self-deployed Layer 2 DCI solution between three distributed data centers with a future plan to add a fourth data center within two years, a flat VPLS solution can be cost-effective and simple to deploy and manage, in addition to scalable enough for this particular scenario. By contrast, if a service provider is already running flat VPLS and experiencing high operational complexity and scalability challenges and they are interested in a solution that supports their future expansion plans with regard to the number of L2VPN customers while minimizing the current operational complexity then H-VPLS with BGP signaling, H-VPLS with PBB, EVPN, or EVPN PBB are possible solutions here. More detail gathering would be required to narrow down the selection. For example, is this operator offering MPLS L3VPN? Is it part of the plan to offer multihoming to the L2VPN customers with active-active forwarding? If the answer to any of these questions is yes, EVPN (with or without PBB) can be an optimal solution. Because if they are offering L3VPN, that means the same control plane (BGP) can be used for both MPLS VPN services (simplifies operational complexity and offers a more scalable solution). Adding PBB to this solution will optimize its scalability to a large extent, especially if this operator provides L2VPN connectivity to cloud-based data centers where a large number of virtual machine MAC addresses is expected to be carried over the L2VPN cloud. If multihoming with active-active forwarding is required, EVPN here will be a business enabler, along with optimized scalability and simplified operation as compared to the existing flat VPLS. However, there might be some design constraints here (for example, if the current network nodes do not support EVPN and the business is not allocating any budget to perform any hardware or software upgrade; or if this provider has existing an interprovider L2VPN link with a global Carrier Ethernet, to extend its L2VPN connectivity for some large enterprise customers with international sites, and this global Carrier Ethernet does not support EVPN).

In both situations, the network designer is forced to look into other suitable design alternatives such as H-VPLS. Again, the design requirements and constraints must drive the decision for which solution is the suitable or optimal one by looking at the bigger picture and not focusing only on the technical characteristics of the design option or protocol.

Service Provider Control Plane Scalability

This section discusses the different design considerations that, individually or collectively, enhance the scalability of service provider type of networks.

Note   All the recommendations and design considerations covered in the enterprise architecture section about scalability of both IGP and BGP are all valid and applicable and must be taken into account. This section is only adding more design options and considerations that are more relevant to service provider grade networks.

As discussed earlier in this chapter, today's service provider networks rely mainly on different control planes and overlay protocols to offer various transport services that meet the different connectivity attributes and requirements of modern enterprises. Regardless of the services offered by the operators to their customers, the primary control protocols used for the learning and forwarding of customer prefixes while maintaining end-to-end path isolation are as follows:

- MPLS

- IGP

- BGP/MP-BGP

Therefore, for a service provider to scale its network, it must consider how to scale these control protocols in terms of number of sessions, number of nodes/routers, and utilization of router resources (memory and CPU) to a manageable and reliable scale. The following subsections cover the primary design techniques that can enhance the scalability of these protocols in large-scale networks. This, in turn, can support a more responsive and scalable service provider-grade network.

IGP Scalability Considerations

As discussed earlier, IGP in service provider types of networks is primarily used to carry reachability information for BGP next hop and is not intended to carry any customer route. Therefore, to enhance the scalability of a service provider network, the underlying control plane (IGP) must be designed to provide a reliable, scalable control plane transport that can respond to any network change within an acceptable period.

Note   The ability of any routing protocol to react to any network change (usually after a failure event) is critical and governed by multiple factors. The acceptable time for the control plane protocol to react and converge will vary from network to network and from business to business.

Ideally, a successful IGP design in service provider-grade networks should provide the following:

■ Reliable and stable control plane transport

■ Flexible design that takes into consideration interaction with any other control protocol across the network, such as MPLS-TE

■ A scalable design that supports the growth of the network by size without compromising its acceptable levels of stability and manageability

The concept of modular IGP design in SP-grade networks is similar to the design of modular enterprise networks, where each module can be placed in a separate routing domain, such as OSPF area or IS-IS level, to provide optimized control plane scalability and stability (fault isolation). With this approach, the SP core ideally should be the backbone of the IGP (such as OSPF area 0 or IS-IS L2) that glues all the different POP networks each into its own flooding domain, as shown in Figure 6-61.

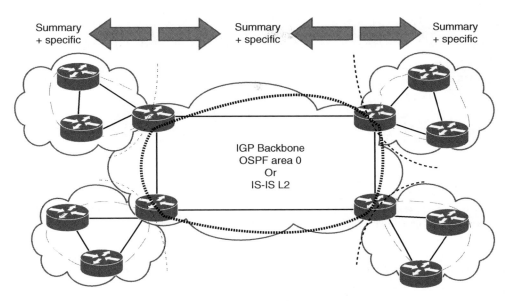

Figure 6-61 *Modular IGP Design in SP Network*

The nature of any service provider is a transport network, and it usually provides
a transit path for other networks' traffic (customers). Therefore, the scalability and
stability factors of its control plane are a primary factor for the P business to succeed.
The following summarizes the design considerations and advantages of the modular IGP
design in the SP type of networks:

- Placing the backbone in the middle and each POP in its own IGP flooding domain
  helps to make the overall logical architecture more modular.

- This module logical architecture is used to reduce the number of advertised routes
  from each POP to the core and from the core to each POP.

- Specific routes are requested in some situations. For example, if this is an MPLS SP
  /32 loopback address, it is required to be injected as /32. The Fast EtherChannel
  (FEC) element should exactly match an entry in the IP Routing Information Base (RIB)
  according to LDP specification RFC 3036. Therefore, in this case, a combination
  of summary and specific routes can be sent. Alternatively, you can use the concept
  known as longest-match label mapping when that choice is available (RFC 5283).

- In OSPF, you can use stub areas or not-so-stubby areas (NSSAs) in the POP; with
  IS-IS, the POP can be placed in L1.

- You can use IS-IS route leaking to help with injecting the /32 loopback address into
  the L2 POPs for MPLS VPN SPs.

- This structured design can help optimize the design and convergence time and
  provide fault-isolation domains. For example, if a link is flapping in one POP, it will
  not affect other POPs' stability in this case.

> **Note** Some service providers prefer simplicity over any other aspect. Therefore, a single IGP domain is sometimes used to offer a simple network, which provides better flexibility to support other services without adding any complexity to the design. Although breaking the IGP domain can add several benefits, it might introduce added complexity to other services. For instance, having multiple OSPF areas or IS-IS levels can complicate MPLS-TE design. Therefore, network designers must prioritize based on the primary goals to produce a proper design.

Route Reflection Design Options in SP Networks

Providing a scalable design of IGP is only half the job of achieving an optimal scalable, stable, and manageable control plane in service provider networks. BGP is the primary routing protocol used in service provider networks that carry customer prefixes, which is where the actual load happens. Therefore, to achieve the optimal control plane design, each IGP and BGP has to be designed in a way that can function at the desired level and support the business's future plans and current investments. For example, as discussed earlier, IGP design must provide a stable and scalable design to reliably carry next-hop reachability for BGP. At the same time, it must not add complexity to the design of other control protocols in the network. Similarly, BGP design must provide a reliable transport for the customer prefixes, considering the priority factors of the design, such as optimal path or provision of a highly scalable design, without compromising the desired level of reliability along with simplified operation.

Chapter 2, "Enterprise Layer 2 and Layer 3 Design," discussed multiple proven mechanisms that provide a more scalable and reliable BPG design. They are all applicable to BGP design in service provider types of networks. This section covers some advancements to these mechanisms, in particular to the BGP RR design, to fit very large-scale BGP networks with multiple services provided by BGP at the same time, such as Internet routing and MPLS L3VPN.

RR design in service provider networks can vary depending on the service provider architecture (for example, whether it is an MPLS-based network or native IP [non-MPLS]). Also as covered in Chapter 2, if BGP confederation is used, the design choices of BGP RR will be impacted, because BGP RR design must align with the BGP confederation sub-autonomous systems.

The design consideration of BGP route reflection in MPLS-based VPN networks varies slightly from the IP only (non-MPLS) based network, as summarized here:

- RR in an MPLS-based VPN network provides the destination PE IP of the desired L3VPN customer IP address.

- Because the forwarding is based on MPLS labels, the MPLS VPN RRs are not required to be in the forwarding path, because they will only provide the destination PE IP and the PE will use IGP to reach the other PE IP along with MPLS transport label.

This section covers the following BGP RR design options:

■ Provider routers as RRs for MPLS-VPN

■ Separate RR for MPLS-VPN and IPv4/v6

■ Separate RR per service (MPLS-VPN and IPv4/v6)

■ MPLS VPN partitioned RR

■ Hierarchical RR

Provider Routers as RRs for MPLS-VPN

This design is can offer cost-effective, dedicated BGP RR for MP-BGP VPN peers.
However, this means that the (P) routers need to have MP-BGP VPN enabled and
MPLS-VPN routes installed, along with MP-BGP VPN VPN peering reflections, as
shown in Figure 6-62. This design option is feasible in the service provider grade of
network with a limited number prefixes (PEs and MP-BGP VPN instances), ideally in
self-deployed MPLS-VPN by enterprise networks. For the typical service provider
networks, the P routers should always be left for fast MPLS switching functions only.

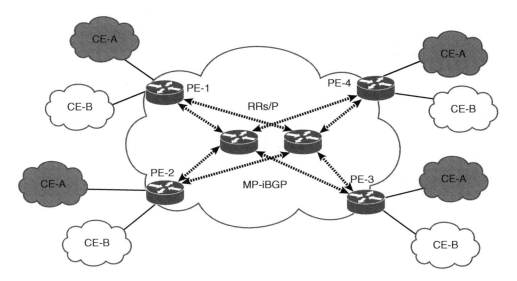

Figure 6-62   *P Nodes as BGP RR*

Separate RR for MPLS-VPN and IPv4/v6

This option offers a simple and cost-effective solution for service providers that provide
both Internet (non-MPLS IP service) and MPLS VPN-based services where a dedicated
RR will be used to serve both IP and MPLS VPN route reflection, as shown in the
Figure 6-63. However, this option still lacks the scalability for the increased load on those
RRs if this service provider is expanding rapidly and if a number of PEs (BGP peers) are

increasing dramatically along with a very large number of prefixes. Therefore, this design option is suitable to regional or medium-sized service provider networks and for large-scale enterprise networks with self-deployed MPLS VPN and native IP.

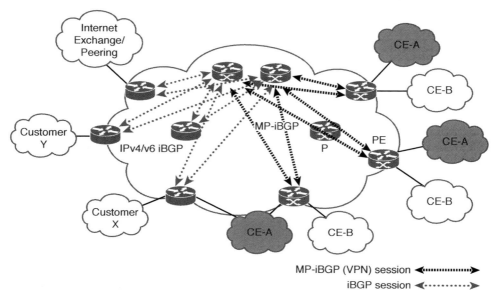

Figure 6-63   *Dedicated BGP RR for VPN and IP*

Separate RR per Service (MPLS-VPN and IPv4/v6)

In large-scale service provider networks, where there may be tens of hundreds of routers and different services offered (such as MPLS- and non-MPLS-based services), along with hundreds of thousands of prefixes, it is more feasible to have separate RRs per function (for example, RRs for MPLS-VPNv4, RRs for MPLS-VPNv6, and RRs for IPv4/v6 iBGP), as shown in Figure 6-64.

In contrast, in smaller-scale networks, the same RRs can service multiple functions such as MPLS-VPNv4/VPNv6. In fact, it is a design decision where network designers must have a good understanding of the current state of the organization and its future plans to select the most suitable design option. For instance, if there is a limited number of MPLS-VPNv6 customers yet the plan is to increase IPv6 offerings, it makes more sense to separate the RR functions of MPLS-VPNv4 and MPLS-VPNv6, for the following reasons:

- Optimizes performance and scalability

- Eliminates any single point of failure of dependencies between the two worlds (V4 and V6)

- Offers more structured, flexible, and simplified management and policy control

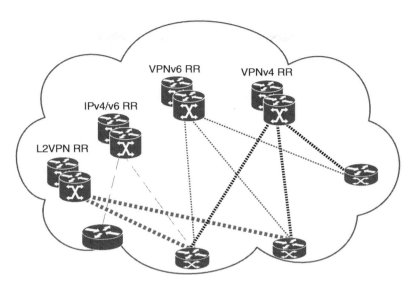

Figure 6-64 *Dedicated BGP RR per Service*

Hierarchical RR

As discussed earlier in Chapter 1, "Network Design Requirements: Analysis and Design Principles," the optimal scalable design should be reliable and manageable at the same time. One of the key factors to achieve this is by reducing the number of prefixes to be processed and stored by the nodes. The concept of BGP RR can significantly optimize BGP design (MPLS based and native IP) because by default it usually performs implicit route aggregation by advertising the single best route only. However, in large BGP environments (usually service provider-grade network), multiple layers of BGP speakers are distributed across multiple regions (such as POPs). For example, in Figure 6-65, the iBGP sessions of the edge nodes are terminated within the same region (POP) at the POP/core border nodes (RR aggregation nodes per POP) to provide a more modular BGP design that scales and adapts easily without adding significant operational complexity to the overall design. However, in this particular scenario, the mesh among the RRs across the core can introduce increased sessions and prefix states to the border nodes of each POP. For instance, the network shown in Figure 6-65 has two RRs per POP. Based on this design, if a new prefix is advertised (like Prefix X in POP 3), each RR will usually reflect this update to all its clients and normal e/iBGP peers. As a result, each RR (such as the PE_A in POP 1) will receive several routes for a single prefix (the more POPs in the network, the more prefixes received). This design can become even worse when there is a large number of BGP prefixes and a large number of POPs, which can impact the overall network performance and limit the design scalability and manageability in very large-scale networks with multiple tiers and regions.

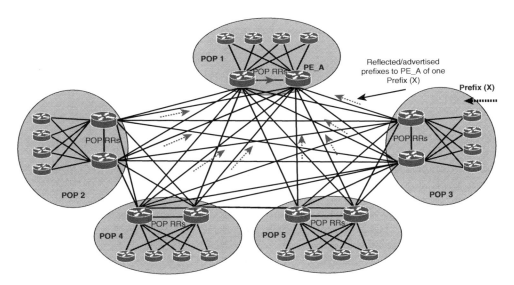

Figure 6-65   *Single-Tier RR in a Large BGP Environment*

Therefore, by introducing another tier of RRs, the design can be optimized to scale better by aggregating the full-mesh sessions between the RRs of the POPs, relaxing the full mesh of the level 2 RRs, as shown in Figure 6-66.

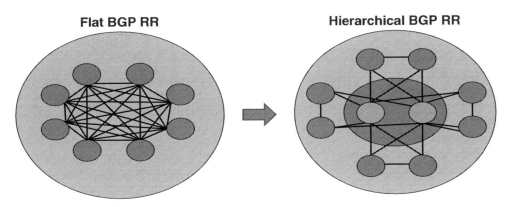

Figure 6-66   *Multitiered BGP RR*

This will usually result in a more refined number of iBGP sessions at multiple layers and a significant reduction in the number of routes each level 2 RR at the (POP border) will receive. As shown in Figure 6-67, regardless of the number of POPs, each POP border (RR) will receive two routes per remote prefix (one from each level 1 RR, assuming the level 1 RRs deployed with different CLUSTER_IDs). In other words with this design, level 1 RRS will reduce the number of prefixes being carried to the BGP speaker at the lower tiers.

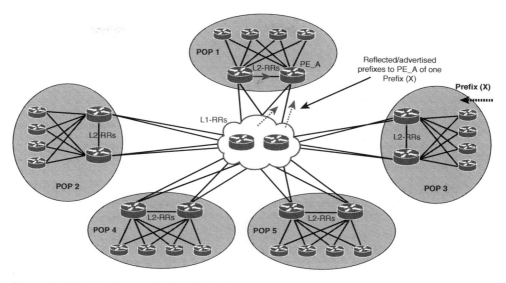

Figure 6-67 *Multitiered BGP RR Optimization*

Although this hierarchical BGP RR design approach offers a more structured and optimized design to handle very large-scale BGP environments, having multiple layers of RRs can break hot-potato routing requirements (if it is a requirement). Also multiple tiers of RRs may introduce route oscillation and a noticeable increased network convergence time following any failure event. Therefore, network designers must evaluate the environment and prioritize based on the more critical (priority) goals. In addition, Chapter 5 covered the design options that help to overcome RR suboptimal routing and low convergence time issues that can be incorporated with BGP RR design.

> **Note**   In IP (non-MPLS) environments, it is recommended to have the RR in the forwarding path (no peering over nonclients for example) to avoid possibilities of suboptimal routing or routing information loops.

Partitioned MPLS-VPN RR

With this design model, network designers can optimize the performance efficiency of the BGP RR for MPLS-VPN by distributing a range of VPNv4/v6 to each RR or pair of RRs (usually by carving up a range of RTs per RR cluster). This model can offer large-scale MPLS-VPN operators control to distribute the peering of the VPN based on certain criteria; for example, global service providers can allocate a pair of RRs to serve each local VPN customer per region. Although this design option offers more structured RR design than a typical flat MPLS-VPN RR design, it requires more iBGP peering sessions per PE, which means that RRs will send all the VPNv4v/6 routes to the PEs and that the PEs will usually drop the routes that have no importing VRF (extra unnecessary processing), as shown in Figure 6-68.

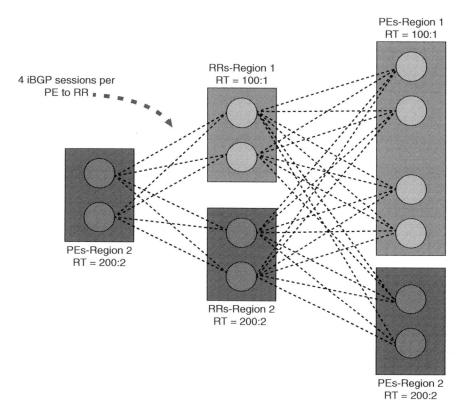

Figure 6-68   *Partitioned BGP RR (RT Based)*

Furthermore, this design can be enhanced with the RT constraint feature (RTC). With the RTC, each PE will receive VPNv4/v6 prefixes that have important matching VRF RT values per VRF per PE, which helps to avoid unnecessarily sending of VPNv4/v6 prefixes to the PE routers by the RRs (RFC 4684).

Table 6-9 compares the different BGP RR design options covered in this chapter.

Table 6-9   *BGP RR Design Options*

	P as BGP RR	BGP RR for MPLS VPN and BGP RR for IP	BGP RR per Service	MPLS VPN Partitioned RR	Hierarchical BGP RR
Scalability	Limited	Moderate	High	High	Very high
Targeted environment	Native IP and MPLS VPN	Native IP and MPLS VPN	Native IP and MPLS VPN	MPLS VPN	Native IP and MPLS VPN
Operational complexity	Moderate	Moderate	High	High	High

Table 6-9 *continued*

	P as BGP RR	BGP RR for MPLS VPN and BGP RR for IP	BGP RR per Service	MPLS VPN Partitioned RR	Hierarchical BGP RR
Flexibility	Limited	Moderate	High	Moderate	High
Physical and logical topology should be kept congruent	For native IP only	For native IP only	For native IP only	No	For native IP only
Potential suboptimal routing*	Yes, mainly for native IP	Yes, mainly for native IP	Yes, mainly for native IP	Yes, low	Yes, mainly for native IP
Optimize RR routing table size	No	Yes, moderate	Yes, high	Yes, moderate	Yes, high

* Typically in MPLS L3VPN environments there is very low possibility of suboptimal routing because each CE/prefix of a given VPN is advertised by the directly connected PE only, unless there is a dual-homed CE of the same VPN customer connected to two different PEs and advertised with the same RD value.

Hierarchical LSP (Unified MPLS)

This concept, also known as the *seamless MPLS* (or *unified MPLS*), is primarily based on a divide-and-conquer strategy where the core, aggregation, and access networks are partitioned in different MPLS LDP/IGP domains. Typically, by partitioning a single large routed domain into independent and isolated IGP/LDP domains, it helps optimize the size of the routing and forwarding tables of the routers in each domain, which in turn will significantly enhance overall network stability and result in faster convergence time. As a result, each domain can host a larger number of nodes without impacting network stability or performance.

In this design model, the reachability is achieved among the network nodes within each routing domain via intradomain LDP LSPs, while the reachability across the routed domains is achieved using RFC 3107. In RFC 3107, BGP allocates labels to routes between BGP peers to build hierarchical LSPs across the routed domains. In other words, for end-to-end reachability between two PEs on different access networks, there will be a transport LSP with label stacking that carries the inner label driven by BGP and the outer label driven by LDP per routed domain, as shown in Figure 6-69.

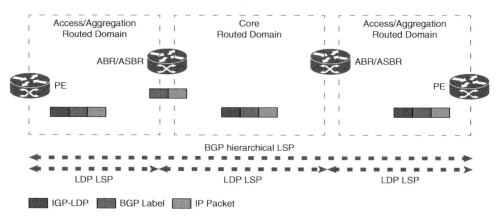

Figure 6-69   *Hierarchical LSP*

This design offers operators (like mobile operators with next-generation mobile backhaul for data transport 3G/LTE) that have a large number of external nodes and prefixes to be carried across the network. It usually maintains the routing and forwarding tables of the small IGP in each domain (such as link-state database). This is because only PE loopbacks are required to be leaked between the routed domains; all external reachability information is carried via BGP, which is designed to scale to the order of millions of routes. In addition, this architecture supports an easy provisioning of services such as L3VPN and L2VPN without the reliance on complex mechanisms such as PW stitching, as shown in Figure 6-70. From a business point of view, in addition to the previously mentioned benefits, it offers simplified operation of such huge networks with the flexibility to support various access networks.

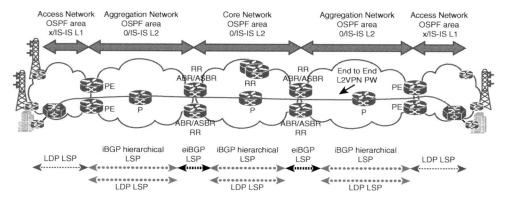

Figure 6-70   *End-to-End Seamless MPLS Architecture*

Note   The design shown in Figure 6-70 supports both single BGP AS and multi-BGP AS design models between the routed domains.

Note For the node in the access domains, if IGP is not supported (such as on legacy or low-end devices), you can use static routing instead, considering IP information requirements for the LDP setup covered earlier in the "IGP Scalability" section in this chapter.

Summary

This chapter covered how MPLS VPN services have become primary business enablers for service providers by meeting enterprise customer connectivity requirements, whether it is a Layer 3 or Layer 2 type of connectivity. In addition, the different design models and considerations of each have been discussed from the service provider point of view. These design models can directly or indirectly impact the service provider design efficiency and the ability to meet certain customer requirements, such as the load-balancing requirement for customers with multihomed sites to the MPLS L3VPN cloud.

In addition to the design models and considerations, this chapter covered the different design approaches that offer a scalable design to support large-scale service provider networks with a very large number of nodes and prefixes. In multiple sections in this chapter, comparison tables were included to simplify the design decision for network designers from various design angles, where each fits different design and business requirements. Last but not least, the design decision of selecting a certain design approach or protocol has to be based on the holistic approach, to avoid designing in isolation of other parts of the network, regardless of whether it is for a physical, virtual, underlay, or overlay entity.

Further Reading

RFC 4364, *BGP/MPLS IP Virtual Private Networks (VPNs)*, http://www.ietf.org

RFC 4762, *Virtual Private LAN Service (VPLS) Using Label Distribution Protocol (LDP) Signaling*, http://www.ietf.org

RFC 7432, *BGP MPLS-Based Ethernet VPN*, http://www.ietf.org

RFC 4761, *Virtual Private LAN Service (VPLS) Using BGP for Auto-Discovery and Signaling*, http://www.ietf.org

GP MPLS Based Ethernet VPN IETF draft, https://tools.ietf.org/html/draft-ietf-l2vpn-evpn-11

RFC 6368, *Internal BGP as the Provider/Customer Edge Protocol for BGP/MPLS IP Virtual Private Networks (VPNs)*, http://www.ietf.org

RFC 4577, *OSPF as the Provider/Customer Edge Protocol for BGP/MPLS IP Virtual Private Networks (VPNs)*, IETF http://www.ietf.org

ISI-S as the PE/CE Protocol in BGP/MPLS VPNs, IETF draft, https://tools.ietf.org/html/draft-sheng-isis-bgp-mpls-vpn-00

RFC 5654, *Requirements of an MPLS Transport Profile*, http://www.ietf.org

Chapter 7

Multi-AS Service Provider Network Design

The previous chapters of this book focused on Multiprotocol Label Switching virtual private network (MPLS VPN) services within one domain where all VPN customers are connected to one autonomous system (AS). This chapter, in contrast, covers the design options and considerations of service providers that need to interconnect different autonomous systems and offer end-to-end services for multiple VPN and non-VPN customers (including native IP, L2VPN, and L3VPN). Typically, in multi-AS scenarios, two or more carriers need to work jointly to facilitate end-to end-connectivity for their VPN customers who need connectivity across geographically dispersed networks. However, the varied connectivity needs can have different design models. For example, for clients who have VPN sites that need to interconnect over different MPLS VPN backbones belonging to different service providers, an inter-AS solution is required to maintain end-to-end connectivity. The same concept is applicable in scenarios where the same provider network owns multiple autonomous systems, similarly when two provider networks merge while each retains its Border Gateway Protocol (BGP) AS and possibly its administrative control. However, sometimes the service provider itself needs to interconnect two of its network islands located in different regions or countries over a transitional (backbone) provider, also known as *carrier supporting carrier* (CSC), to maintain its end-to-end connectivity, as illustrated in Figure 7-1.

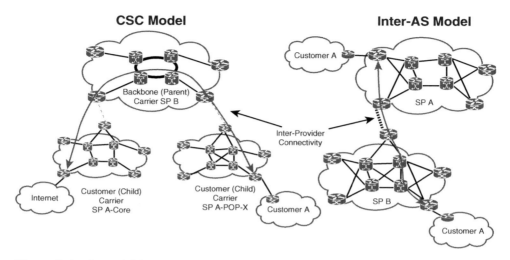

Figure 7-1   *Inter-AS Versus CSC*

This chapter covers the different design and connectivity options of both models (inter-AS and CSC).

Inter-AS Design Options and Considerations

According to RFC 4364, there are three design options for the inter-AS scenarios. These design options are commonly referred to by their respective subsection number in RFC 4364 as Option A, B, and C.

Inter-AS Option A: Back-to-Back VRF (VRF-to-VRF)

In this inter-AS design option, the provider border routers located at the boundary of the different autonomous systems (Autonomous System Boundary Routers [ASBRs]) interconnect directly over either a single physical link with logical interfaces (subinterfaces) or multiple physical links. Each ASBR associates one VPN/virtual routing and forwarding (VRF) to one of the logical or physical interfaces (1:1 mapping) for those VPNs that require inter-AS communication, as illustrated in Figure 7-2. This inter-AS option is considered the simplest and most secure among the other options to exchange VPN routes across different autonomous system boundaries where per-VPN filtering, accounting, and policing can be applied in a more controlled manner.

Each VRF can run external Border Gateway Protocol (eBGP), an interior gateway protocol (IGP), or static routing to exchange the respective VPN routes with its adjacent peer. Simply, each ASBR treats the facing ASBR link/VRF as a customer edge (CE) peer, where they exchange IP routes per VRF (exactly the same concept as the PE (provider edge)-CE routing concept); typically, native IP forwarding between the two autonomous systems is used (without MPLS) over this link. However, eBGP is commonly used in scenarios like this (and it is recommended) because eBGP can provide optimized scalability and policy control mechanisms. One of the major issues with this design option is the limited scalability when there is a large number of VPNs to be exchanged between the peering providers, which typically leads to an increased operational complexity.

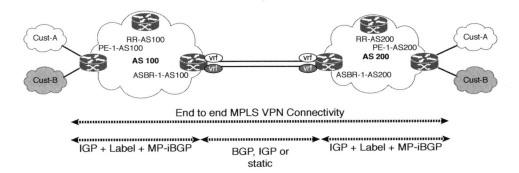

Figure 7-2 *Inter-AS Option A*

Inter-AS Option B: ASBR to ASBR with MP-eBGP Approach

This inter-AS design option is based on the concept of having a single direct multiprotocol eBGP (MP-eBGP) session between the ASBRs of the two adjacent autonomous systems that need to be interconnected. Therefore, inter-AS Option B eliminates the need to have per-VPN configuration on the ASBRs. Moreover, in L3VPN deployments, only VPN customer prefixes need to be installed and not the local VRF Routing Information Base (RIB) at the ASBR, as compared to inter-AS Option A, which typically will allow MPLS VPN prefixes to be exchanged across multiple providers.

To allow the transport of VPN prefixes, the interconnect link between the ASBRs of the two autonomous systems should normally support Label Distribution Protocol (LDP). However, there are three primary approaches to deploy this interconnect link, where it is not always the case that the LDP must be enabled on the interprovider link. Therefore, network designers must be aware of the design variations of the inter-AS Option B to be able to consider the desired approach that meets the design requirements and constraints. For instance, in some situations, the peering provider might not allow MPLS/LDP to be enabled on the physical interconnecting link, which will compel the designer to consider an approach that can accommodate this design constraint. The following sections highlight the different approaches that you can use to achieve inter-AS Option B.

Option B-1: Next-Hop-Self Approach

With Option B-1, each AS ASBR is seen as the next-hop for the MP-eBGP routes received from the adjacent AS/ASBR. Normally with this approach, the next hop and the VPN labels are rewritten when propagated over the Inter-AS MP-eBGP session. Typically, almost always there is no transport LDP distribution over the inter-AS

Option B link. Therefore, the receiving ASBR will receive only the VPN label over the MP-eBGP session, and because this label was not assigned by this ASBR, it will either not be able to forward the packet or might conflict with a label already assigned by the ASBR for something else. The same concept is applicable when the receiving PE of the local AS receives a VPN label assigned by the remote ASBR (of the peering AS); it will not be able to forward the packet properly to the respective VPN/CE destination. That is why, with MPLS and MP-BGP when the next-hop is modified a new label has to be generated for the BGP prefixes. Accordingly, when you use the *next-hop-self approach* with inter-AS Option B, the MP-BGP next hop will technically be changed twice in this case: when the route is advertised from the local AS (ASBR) to the adjacent AS (remote ASBR) over the MP-eBGP, and when the route is propagated by the local AS ASBR (with next-hop-self) to the internal BGP peers such as PEs or BGP route reflectors (RRs). Consequently, a new VPN label will be generated by each border ASBR when the route is propagated to the local AS MP-iBGP (internal BGP) peers (PEs or RRs) and to the adjacent ASBR of the neighbor AS, as illustrated in Figure 7-3. (For simplicity, in this figure the topmost IGP transport label is not shown.)

Note   eBGP label exchange is used in this approach. Therefore, there is no need to enable LDP on the physical link.

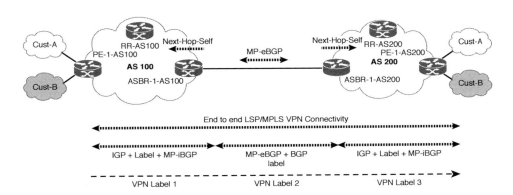

Figure 7-3   *Inter-AS Option-B: Next-Hop-Self Approach*

Option B-2: Redistribute Connected Approach

In Option B-2, the receiving ASBR accepts the route without modifying the next-hop attribute (the peering ASBR IP as MP-eBGP next hop will be advertised "redistribute connected" into the local AS), and the VPN label information will stay intact. With this approach, the MPLS VPN label is changed only when the ASBR advertises the VPN routes to the neighbor ASBR of the other AS. This is where the next hop is changed (once only along the path). In other words, the VPN label will be changed once with this approach, as illustrated in Figure 7-4.

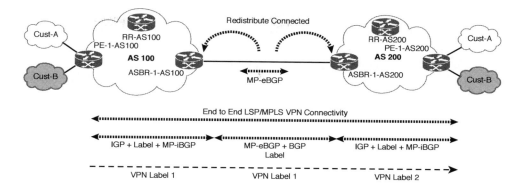

Figure 7-4   *Inter-AS Option-B: Redistribute Connected Approach*

However, this design option may break some load-balancing requirements. For instance, if ASBR-1-100 is interconnected to two ASBRs of AS 200, and AS 100 needs to load balance traffic from its PEs toward AS 200 over these two links, this approach can break this design requirement because technically it will announce the peering ASBRs' next-hop IPs to the PEs of AS 100. Therefore, traffic will be tied directly to one of these remote ASBRs' IP as a MP-BGP next hop from AS 100 PE's point of view. As illustrated in Figure 7-5, in the next-hop-self approach, ASBR-1-AS100 will be the next hop to reach all AS 200 prefixes. In this case, ASBR-1-AS100 can perform the load balancing/sharing (assuming BGP attributes are equal and BGP multipathing is enabled at this ASBR).

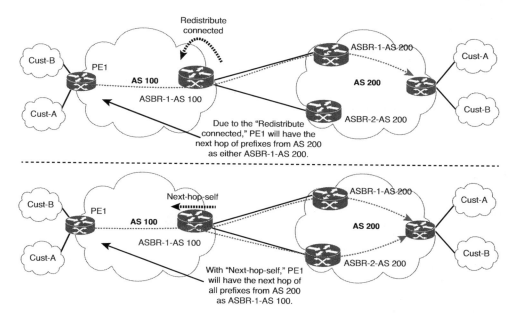

Figure 7-5   *Inter-AS Option B: Load-Balancing Consideration*

Option B-3: Multihop MP-eBGP Approach

In Option B-3, the MP-eBGP session is established using the ASBRs' loopback address of the two adjacent autonomous systems. One of the main incentives to using this approach is when there are multiple links between the two ASBRs and load balancing across these multiple links is required to increase bandwidth capacity and optimize the links' return on investment (ROI). In this scenario, to maintain an end-to-end LSP path, MPLS is enabled between the ASBRs, as illustrated in Figure 7-6.

> **Note**   For security purposes, sometimes the service provider (SP) does not enable LDP on the inter-AS link unless both autonomous systems belong to the same company. In this case, you might consider using a combination of static label binding, static route, and eBGP label exchange.

In addition, this approach is considered as a variation of options B-1 and B-2 previously discussed; therefore, we can use both approaches to propagate the next-hop IP (next-hop-self or redistribute static).

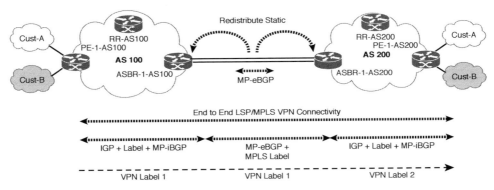

Figure 7-6   *Inter-AS Option B: Multihop MP-eBGP Approach*

> **Note**   The default behavior of a PE router or ASBR is to keep only the routes that carry a route target (RT) for which the receiving router has a VRF defined with the corresponding **import** statement configured within that VRF. This functionality is called *automatic route filtering* (ARF). Therefore, ARF must be disabled with Inter-AS Option B to avoid defining all the VRFs on the ASBR manually to install the VPN's prefixes.

> **Note**   All three approaches of achieving inter-AS Option B are viable solutions. The difference between them is minimal from a design point of view, because all of them are driven from the same inter-AS design model, which is Option B. However, each approach is achieved by a different technical method. Therefore, network designers must take these technical differences into consideration, particularly their impact on the design requirements and on operational complexity, along with any technical or design constraint.

Inter-AS Option C: Multihop MP-eBGP Between RR

Option B, discussed in previous section, still requires that all VPN routes be maintained and advertised by the ASBR, which makes the solution not very scalable in situations where there is a significantly large number of VPN prefixes. Inter-AS design Option C, however, overcomes this issue. The principle of this approach is based on establishing the inter-AS MP-eBGP session directly between the RR of each AS. In other words, the ASBRs in this option only exchange BGP next-hop address using IPv4 labels, and the RRs form an MP-eBGP session to transport VPNv4 information. As a result, the ASBRs do not need to carry any of the VPN routes, which makes this option the most scalable compared to the other options discussed earlier in this section, as illustrated in Figure 7-7.

Note This design option requires that the BGP next hop of the VPN-IPv4 routes exchanged across the multihop MP-eBGP session not be changed.

Note Because Option C requires sharing internal IPs (at least loopback IPs of the PEs) of the both interconnected autonomous systems, it is most commonly used by providers who own multiple autonomous systems in different regions (for example, a global SP) or in the same region and operate under the same administrative authority. Because each AS will have visibility of the other autonomous systems to a great extent, this design option is typically not a common practice between different SPs / autonomous systems that are under different administrative authorities and owned by different stakeholders. This is due to several reasons, the foremost of which is network security.

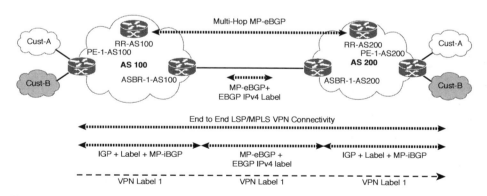

Figure 7-7 *Inter-AS Option C*

Inter-AS Option D

The MPLS VPN inter-AS Option D, also known as AB, combines the best functionalities of both inter-AS Option A and Option B (defined in RFC 4364) to allow MPLS VPN providers to facilitate the interconnection of different autonomous systems with end-to-end VPN services.

From the control plane perspective, inter-AS Option (AB) addresses the scalability limitations of inter-AS Option A by using a single MP-BGP session between the peering ASBRs. VRF routes are exchanged between the two adjacent ASBRs using a unique MP-BGP session referred to as an *Option AB peer*. Similarly, the VRFs are defined in a special way in each ASBR, called *Option AB VRFs*.

From the forwarding plane perspective, each VRF will have a next-hop IP configured under the VRF configurations specifying the next-hop IP (the VRF interface/subinterface) between the ASBRs. In other words, the route will be received per VRF/VPN over one MP-BGP session, while the forwarding will use the respective VRF interface/subinterface, as illustrated in Figure 7-8. This design option requires two types of interfaces between the adjacent ASBRs: one type allocated per VRF basis (main or subinterfaces), and the other interface has to be in global routing to be used for the MP-eBGP peering session.

Isolating the forwarding plane traffic on a per-VRF basis offers an optimized security control and reasonable quality of service (QoS) granularity between ASBRs to maintain customer service level agreements (SLAs).

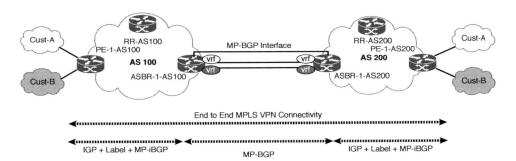

Figure 7-8   *Inter-AS option-D*

Inter-AS IPv6 VPN

The design options discussed earlier in this section support transporting IPv6 routes between two MPLS VPN providers in the same manner for MP-BGP VPNv6 routes (6VPE), where IPv4 peering can be preserved for PE to ASBR or RR, and for ASBR to ASBR. For example, in Figure 7-9, the inter-AS Option B is formed between AS 100 and AS 200. In this particular scenario, the IPv6 VPN prefix will be seen by each ASBR associated with the neighbor ASBR IPv4 as the BGP next hop (NH).

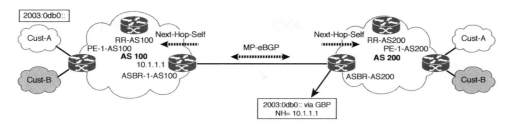

Figure 7-9 *Inter-AS IPv6 VPN*

Similarly, if inter-AS Option C is used, the BGP NH will be the actual remote PE's IPv4/32 loopback addresses. This offer operators the flexibility to retain their current MPLS and IPv4 infrastructure and enables IPv6 transport for their VPN customers.

Inter-AS MPLS-TE

Large and global service providers do not always have the infrastructure to cover the geographic distances across countries or sometimes within the same country. Therefore, they partner with other service providers, either local or international providers, to extend their presence. In this type of scenario, there are usually separate routing islands per AS or provider. Normally, for security purposes, not many providers are willing to expose their internal network topology or internal IP addressing. Similarly, when two providers merge, each with different routing domains (AS), a mechanism is required here to facilitate the setup of the end-to-end Multiprotocol Label Switching Traffic Engineering (MPLS-TE) label switched-paths (LSPs) and to provide the capability to enforce policy control at the provide edge (ASBR), such as bandwidth policing, message types, and authentication.

As discussed Chapter 5, "Service Provider Network Architecture Design," the interdomain MPLS-TE (whether its IGP interarea or BGP inter-AS) both share the same attributes in terms of the limited information in the TE database to set up end-to-end MPLS-TE LSPs by relying only on the headend node. Therefore, a different approach has to be adopted in scenarios like this (commonly by either considering Explicit Route Object [ERO] loose object expansion or the Path Computation Element [PCE]). As illustrated in Figure 7-10, the MPLS-TE headend R1 defines ASBR3 and ASBR4 as a loose explicit route object (ERO) of the MPLS-TE path messages along with the tail-end node (R10). Based on this setup, the Constrained Shortest Path First (CSPF) will be completed along with the creation of TE LSP setup.

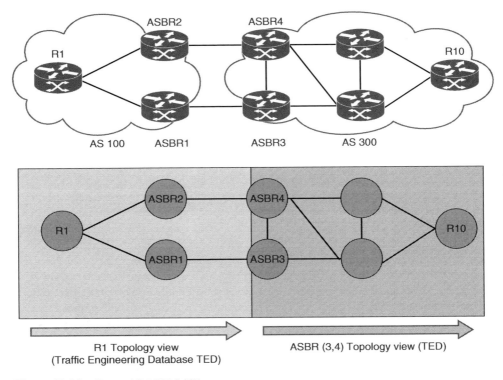

Figure 7-10   *Inter-AS MPLS-TE*

> **Note**   As highlighted in Chapter 5, PCE and BGP Link State (BGP-LS) are both valid
> mechanisms to be considered in MPLS-TE inter-AS scenarios, because both offer the
> ability to share TE information between different routing domains; however, these
> options when used between different service provider businesses must cater for
> constraining the type and amount of the shared information between the different
> provider networks.

Inter-AS L2VPN

Provisioning L2VPN over inter-AS links is one of the common and primary connectivity
requirements in today's modern service provider networks. This is applicable to any of
the following scenarios:

■ Inter-AS or provider integration scenario (between two separate service providers)

■ Inter-AS scenario across different autonomous systems that belong to a single
administrative authority

■ Service provider merger and acquisition scenarios

Technically, the main inter-AS connectivity options (A, B and C) discussed earlier in this chapter are applicable and commonly used to provide L2VPN inter-AS connectivity for both point-to-point pseudo wires (PWs) (E-Line) and multipoint VPLS (E-LAN). Like L3VPN, each inter-AS option has different attributes when used to provision inter-AS L2VPN connectivity, as summarized here:

■ **Inter-AS Option A:** In this model, each of the L2VPN PWs terminates at the local AS ASBR, and the inter-AS connectivity is based on the used native attachment circuit technology. (At the time of this writing, it has to be Ethernet with Virtual Private LAN Services [VPLS].) The ASBR at the remote AS (peering AS) must create a separate (new) PW to link it to the relevant attachment circuit to maintain end-to-end connectivity, as illustrated in Figure 7-11. In other words, there will be two separate PWs segments, across each AS, while over the inter-AS link the transport will be native based on the technology used, such as Ethernet, time-division multiplexing (TDM), or Frame Relay. Although this option offers a more controlled and secure connectivity model, the high level of operational complexity, along with scalability limitations, makes it least preferred in large environments where a large number of PWs and customers need to be extended over the inter-AS link. As with the IP/VPN, where a large number of prefixes add more load on the ASBRs, with the L2VPN the number of VLANs needs to be maintained, and the number of MAC addresses in the case of VPLS can introduce hardware resource constraints in this option.

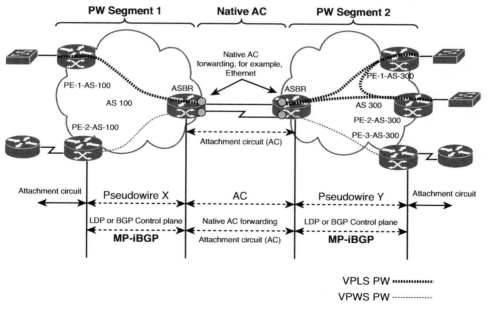

Figure 7-11 *L2VPN Inter-AS Option A*

■ **Inter-AS Option B:** In this model, each of the L2VPN PWs terminates at the local ASRB. In turn, this ASBR will create another PW (performing what is known as *PW stitching* or *PW switching*) that terminates at the remote AS ASBR over the inter-AS link (inter-AS link does not have to be Ethernet). The remote AS ASBR again will create a PW that terminates at the egress PE node where the CE attachment circuit is connected, as illustrated in Figure 7-12. It is obvious that this option with the multisegment PW (as specified in RFC 5659) provides the ability to pass the PWs over single inter-AS link with targeted LDP (T-LDP), which offers more granular and strict security policies for control plane traffic going across the autonomous systems. However, this multisegment PW approach makes it a more complicated option to manage, and its scalability is limited in large network with a large number of PWs because the PWs' control plane will be constrained to the hardware/software limits of the ASBR.

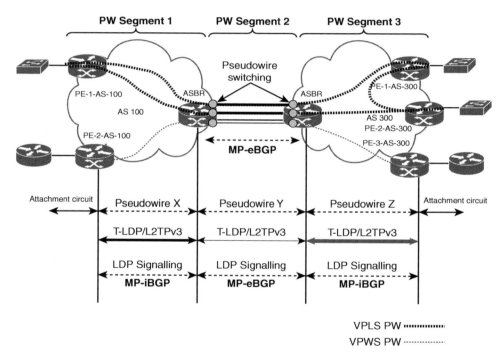

Figure 7-12   *Multisegment PW L2VPN: Inter-AS Option B + LDP Signaling + LDP/BGP Autodiscovery*

Note   The introduction of VPLS BGP signaling for L2VPN inter-AS Option B, that supports RFC 4761, offers a more simplified PE nodes discovery (autodiscovery) as well as signaling of all participating PE devices per VPLS instance by using BGP for both functions. However, before the introduction of the combined BGP autodiscovery and signaling over inter-AS Option B, some L2VPN inter-AS deployments used LDP for the signaling and BGP for autodiscovery, as specified in RFC 6074. Technically, RFC 6074 and RFC 4761 use a different network layer reachability information (NLRI) encoding format for the autodiscovery protocol. Therefore, network designers must avoid mixing the implementation of these RFCs together, because they are incompatible with each other (at the time of this writing). In addition, it can be a design concern when interconnecting two autonomous systems and each uses one of these RFCs for BGP autodiscovery. In this case, inter-AS Option A can be considered as one solution if it's not possible to migrate any of the autonomous systems to be compatible with the other one with regard to the deployed BGP autodiscovery RFC.

Note   For interprovider VPLS Option B, there are two common possible deployment flavors. The first one (described above) allows direct PWs (LDP signaled) among all PEs in both autonomous systems per VPLS instance, and the ASBRs in this case hold all the control plane for each VPLS instance (performing PW switching). The second flavor is based on BGP signaling over the inter-AS link, in which the number of PWs can be reduced to a single ASRB to ASBR BGP signaled PW session, which helps to significantly optimize the scalability and reduce the overhead of the control plane of this inter-AS solution in general, as illustrated in Figure 7-13. With this model, the ASBR might participate in the data plane (MAC learning) when interconnecting different domains with different signaling protocols (LDP and BGP).

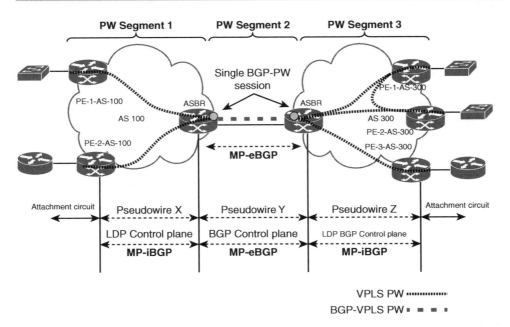

Figure 7-13   *Multisegment PW L2VPN: Inter-AS Option B with BGP for Signaling and Autodiscovery*

■ **Inter-AS Option C:** This connectivity model is the most scalable option compared
to the other inter-AS options with regard to L2VPN, because the ingress and egress
PEs can establish the L2VPN PWs directly over a targeted LDP (T-LDP) session
or a direct PE-to-PE L2TPv3 PW, without any termination point along the path,
as illustrated in Figure 7-14. This option is most commonly used in environments
where both autonomous systems belong to the same administrative authority, such
as a global server provider with multiple autonomous systems. Because this inter-AS
option technically requires some of the IP addressing of the internal IP infrastructure (typically loopback IPs) to be shared (reachable directly) between the interconnected autonomous systems, it is not common and may not even applicable to the
L2VPN "interprovider" scenario, where each provider belongs to completely a separate business/stakeholders. In addition, there might be many LDP or L2TPv3 PW
sessions traversing the inter-AS link. Technically, these PWs may "connect to many
devices within an AS. In the case where the ASes belong to different providers, one
might imagine that providers would like to have fewer signaling sessions crossing the
AS boundary and that the entities that terminate the sessions could be restricted to
a smaller set of devices."[1] A merger and acquisition scenario, in contrast, is another
example where the L2VPN inter-AS Option C is commonly used.

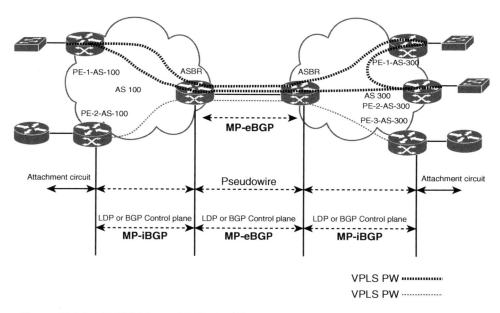

Figure 7-14 *L2VPN Inter-AS Option C*

---

1. IETF RFC 6074, http://www.ietf.org

Furthermore, with VPLS another layer of constraints must be taken into account: MAC learning. In other words, in addition to the number and setup of the PWs considerations, network designers must take into account the scalability and manageability with regard to MAC address learning and flooding per VPLS virtual switching interface (VSI). For instance, VPLS along with provider backbone bridging (PBB) and with inter-AS Option B can offer an optimized and scalable solution. As with PBB, MAC learning and forwarding within the core will be based on the backbone MACs only (B-MAC) using the PBB MAC-in-MAC encapsulation concept. Similarly, the VPLS with PBB over inter-AS Option C will offer the most scalable and seamless connectivity model. However, as highlighted earlier, this model is the least secure among the other options when used between different service provider businesses, due to the fact that each provider (AS) will have visibility on the other AS network (leaking IP information between the two provider networks to create end-to-end LSPs for transport, T-LDP, and MP-BGP for PW, and so on).

Ethernet VPN (EVPN), in contrast, as highlighted earlier in Chapter 6, is based on the BGP control plane using a separate NLRI for MAC address learning and forwarding. This means that all the design considerations discussed in this chapter with regard to Layer 3 inter-AS options apply to EVPN. The only difference here is the addresses learned and shared by this BGP NRLI are MACs and not IPs.

Inter-AS QoS

Quality of service (QoS) is one of the primary influencing factors with regard to selecting the interprovider (inter-AS) connectivity model because it directly impacts the end-to-end differentiated services offered as part of the SLA between each provider and its customers. Table 7-1 summarizes the characteristics of the inter-AS connectivity models discussed in this chapter that pertains to end-to-end QoS provisioning and consistency.

Table 7-1   *Comparison of QoS Considerations per Inter-AS Option*

	Option A	Option B	Option C	Option D
Traffic control and QoS policy granularity per VPN	High	Low	Low	High
QoS policy scalability with regard to the number of VPN/ VRFs	Limited*	High	High	Limited*
Operational complexity to set up and maintain QoS policies	High	Low	Low	High

Table 7-1   *continued*

	Option A	**Option B**	**Option C**	**Option D**
Supports mapping between different providers' class of service (CoS) models	Yes (re-marking over the interprovider link based on the original IP differentiated services code point [DSCP] per VPN customer) (Original customer's DSCP marking must be left intact.)	Yes (re-marking over the interprovider link based on MPLS EXP) (Mapping normally happens at EXP tag, while the original customer's DSCP marking is left intact.)	Yes (re-marking over the interprovider link based on MPLS EXP) (Mapping normally happens at EXP tag, while the original customer's DSCP marking is left intact.)	Yes (re-marking over the interprovider link based on the original IP DSCP marking per VPN customer) (Original customer's DSCP marking must be left intact.)

* This is hardware/software dependent.

Note   The selection of the MPLS DiffServ tunneling mode, such as uniform or pipe mode, can influence to a large extent the preservation and consistency of the original customer's IP DSCP marking across a single or different autonomous systems. DiffServ tunneling modes are covered in more detail in Chapter 10, "Design of Other Network Technologies and Services."

Comparison of Inter-AS Connectivity Options

Technically, all the inter-AS options discussed in this chapter are all valid and proven design options; however, each has its own characteristic that fit certain design requirements.

Table 7-2 briefly compares the four MPLS L3VPN inter-AS design options discussed in this section from different design aspects.

Table 7-2   *Inter-AS Connectivity Options Comparison*

	Option A	**Option B**	**Option C**	**Option D**
Scalability	Low	Moderate	High	Moderate
L2/L3VPN Security/Control	High	Moderate (e.g. Label spoofing concerns)	Low (For example, the PE's IPs are visible to the remote AS.)	High

Table 7-2 *continued*

	Option A	Option B	Option C	Option D
Requires leaking some internal IP information between the interconnected autonomous systems	No	No	Yes	No
Flexibility (IPv6, L2VPN, Multicast)	Moderate	Moderate	High	Moderate
State/prefixes at ASBR	High (per VRF state)	Moderate- VPN routes states maintained	Minimal (Only remote AS PE's IP are maintained.)	High (per VRF state)
VRF configuration at the ASBR	Yes	No	No	Yes
Label at the AS boundary (interconnect)	No	Yes (LDP/BGP)	Yes	Not required for data plane
ASBR control plane peering sessions	Multiple (per VRF state)	Single MP-eBGP session per peering ASBR	Single multihop MP-eBGP session per RR	Single MP-eBGP session per peering ASBR
QoS granularity per VPN at the ASBR	High	Low	Low	High
End-to-end seamless QoS marking	Yes (Complex-mapping between DSCP and MPLS EXP may be required at each ASBR.)	Yes (simple; end-to-end MPLS EXP based)	Yes (simple; end-to-end MPLS EXP based)	Yes (complex; mapping between DSCP and MPLS EXP may be required at each ASBR.)
End-to-end L2VPN simplicity and scalability	Low	Moderate	High	Low (not common)
MPLS-TE end-to-end simplicity (seamless)	Low	Moderate	High	Low
ASBR operational complexity	High	Moderate	Low	Moderate

Carrier Supporting Carrier

As described earlier in this chapter, the CSC model aims to facilitate the connectivity between two or more dispersed points of presence (POPs) or backbones (customer carriers) over a middle carrier (backbone carrier). For the backbone carrier to facilitate end-to-end route propagation for the customers' carriers, an LSP path is required (label stacking). Hence, the link between the customer carrier CE and the backbone carrier PE must be MPLS enabled. There are two primary ways to achieve this:

■ **Label exchange over IGP:** This is used when the PE-CE routing is IGP and MPLS needs to be enabled on the interface level.

■ **Label exchange over BGP:** This method relies on using BGP for label exchange (the same concept used with inter-AS).

In some scenarios, however, this backbone network runs native IP, in which case other mechanisms are required here, such an overlay to facilitate the CSC connectivity model. This section covers the following CSC connectivity scenarios:

■ Non-MPLS customer over MPLS VPN carrier

■ MPLS customer over MPLS VPN carrier

■ MPLS VPN customer over MPLS VPN carrier

■ MPLS VPN customer over MPLS carrier

■ MPLS VPN customer over IP-only carrier

Note   The customer provider in this section can be an enterprise that needs to interconnect multiple large sites that has either a large number of routes or MPLS-VPN enabled, application service providers, MPLS VPN service providers, or ISPs. In addition, some backbone service providers do not offer CSC as a connectivity option to enterprise customers and this connectivity model is only offered to service provide businesses (customers). Therefore, the network designer should make it clear whether this is a supported connectivity model by asking the SP before producing the design for the customer.

Non-MPLS Customer over MPLS VPN Carrier

In this design model, the customer carrier runs native IP (not MPLS enabled) across its internal network. For example, this can be an ISP that needs to interconnect different IP backbone islands of the same provider, or a global enterprise with a very large number of prefixes to be shared across the different locations. To maintain the end-to-end LSP connectivity of the CSC backbone carrier, you can enable IGP with MPLS on the

interface level over the PE-CE link, as illustrated in Figure 7-15. From the carrier backbone point of view, each CSC customer will be seen as a typical MPLS VPN customer,
where no route overlapping can occur, nor does the backbone carrier need to participate
and process the routes, except at the PE edge (VRF level). In addition, this minimizes
the number of prefixes that need to be installed and processed by the backbone carrier
(the parent carrier in the middle) because the only prefixes to be processed in this case
are the internal routes, such as BGP next-hop IPs of the different customer BGP islands.
Other external prefixes will be MPLS encapsulated (for instance, if an ISP needs to
propagate full Internet routes to a remote POP over the CSC backbone). In this particular scenario, the CSC backbone carrier does not need to install all the Internet routes for
this ISP customer. Instead, it will provide only next-hop reachability for the customer
BGP speakers (ASBRs), along with end-to-end LSP over the backbone carrier network.

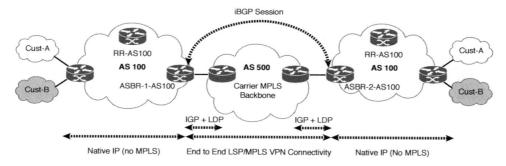

Figure 7-15 *Non-MPLS over MPLS VPN Backbone*

Note If BGP is used as the PE-CE routing protocol, it can also be used for label
exchange without the need to manually enable MPLS/LDP on the interface level.

MPLS Customer over MPLS VPN Carrier

In this design model, the customer carrier is running MPLS but not MPLS VPN. This
design model is similar to the one described earlier. The main difference is that MPLS is
enabled across the customer carrier backbone/POPs, and hence forwarding is based on
label switching (LSP) end to end. At the edge of the customer carrier, the label must be
exchanged with the carrier backbone to maintain end-to-end LSP inside the transit AS.
As described earlier, label exchange can be done using either BGP label or IGP with LDP
manually enabled on the link level. As illustrated in Figure 7-16, the iBGP peering can
be formed directly between the ASBRs of AS 100 over the backbone carrier. Also, this
iBGP session can be established directly between the BGP RRs in each network island of
AS 100. However, terminating the iBGP session at the ASBR offers more "control plane"
security control at the network boundary.

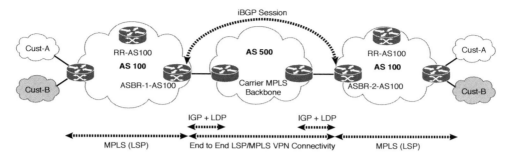

Figure 7-16   *MPLS Customer over MPLS VPN Carrier*

MPLS VPN Customer over MPLS VPN Carrier

In this model, the customer carrier performs MP-BGP VPN peering between the dispersed sites (for example, between the BGP RRs in each location) to exchange MPLS VPN routes over the carrier backbone, where only the loopback IPs required for the MP-BGP session are propagated across the backbone carrier. From the backbone carrier point of view, each customer carrier is an MPLS VPN customer. In other words, the MPLS VPN router will be the carrier over the MPLS VPN of the CSC backbone carrier. Accordingly, this design model is also known as *hierarchal VPN* and is illustrated in Figure 7-17.

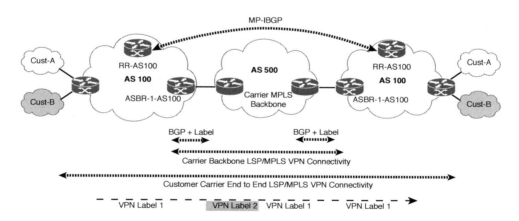

Figure 7-17   *MPLS VPN over MPLS VPN Backbone*

MPLS VPN Customer over MPLS Carrier

Like the previous CSC design model, in this model the customer carrier performs MP-BGP VPN peering between the dispersed sites (for example, RRs each location) to exchange MPLS VPN routes over the carrier backbone, where only the loopback IPs required for the MP-BGP session are propagated across the backbone carrier. The backbone carrier, however, performs only label switching (Non-MPLS VPN); it is usually LDP or hierarchical MPLS (such as the seamless MPLS model), where both LDP and BGP labels are used across the backbone carrier network to carry loopback IP addresses of the customer carriers or at least the loopback IPs of the MPLS VPN RRs at the dispersed domains, as illustrated in Figure 7-18.

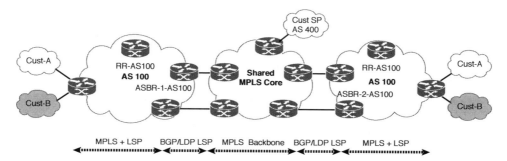

Figure 7-18 *MPLS VPN over MPLS Non-VPN Backbone*

One of the primary concerns about this model is the "none separated" control plane per customer across the backbone carrier network, because each customer PE may have visibility or reachability to other customer's IPs. Therefore, this design model is more feasible for environments where the same network operator owns both the backbone MPLS network and the MPLS VPN islands.

MPLS VPN Customer over IP-Only Carrier

In some scenarios, dispersed MPLS-enabled networks have to interconnect over a native IP network. The following are common scenarios of interconnecting MPLS islands over native IP non-MPLS infrastructure:

- Enabling MPLS applications among multiple remote MPLS networks interconnected over a native IP core carrier infrastructure (where MPLS is enabled at the edge networks only)

- During migration and acquisition scenarios

Therefore, MPLS must be tunneled across the native IP core to extend and connect these MPLS islands. A common and simple method is to use MPLS over a manual tunneling/encapsulation mechanism. As shown in Figure 7-19, the edge PEs/ASBRs can set up a manual MPLS over Layer 2 Tunneling Protocol (L2TP), generic routing encapsulation (GRE) tunnel, or MPLS over IP. In all cases, the source and destination addresses are set to the addresses of the encapsulating and decapsulating label switching routers (LSRs) over the native IP core. The main difference between these options is that with GRE and L2TPv3, there will be additional encapsulation overhead for the packet header. In contrast, MPLS over IP is considered the easiest to spoof among other options; therefore, IPsec can be added as an optional protection mechanism if required (RFC 4023).

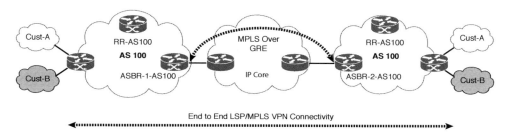

Figure 7-19 *MPLS-VPN over Native IP over Manual Overlay Tunneling*

However, in some scenarios, there might be multiple edge PEs/ASBRs that need to be interconnected over the native IP core, where the manual setup of the tunnels can add operational complexity. Therefore, instead of manually configuring tunnels, the tunnel reachability information can be sent via a BGP next-hop tunnel subsequent address family identifier (SAFI; described in draft-nalawade-kapoor-tunnel-safi-01.txt and RFC 5512). This option offers the capability of advertising which tunnel method is best to reach a given PE, such as GRE, L2TPv3, IP in IP, or IPsec. In addition, a full-mesh overlaid topology can be created among the PE routers over native IP network, such as MPLS VPN over mGRE (0 tunnels to be deployed by the network operator), which allows network operators to provision MPLS VPN services without using LSP or LDP over the IP core. Technically, IPv4-based mGRE tunnels are used to encapsulate VPN-labeled IPv4 and IPv6 packets between dispersed PEs. Similarly, the L2TPv3 multipoint tunnel is another common mechanism that offers similar transport capability for MPLS VPN over native IP core in which only one tunnel per PE is required to be deployed, as shown in Figure 7-20.

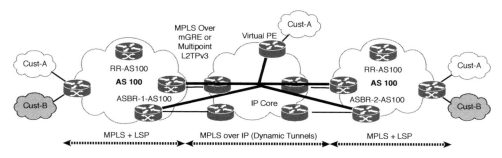

Figure 7-20 *MPLS-VPN over Native IP over Dynamic Tunneling*

Note Considering staff knowledge/experience, hardware/software support, security considerations (such as encryption) and the number of nodes to be interconnected, can help to a large extent to select one option over others.

Note IP-only backbone carriers can consider enabling BGP/MPLS IP-VPN, (specified in RFC 4364), also known as *virtual private routed network* (VPRN), which enables IP backbone carriers to retain their native IP backbone and provide IP VPN-like services for their transit customers. With this method, each individual customer's VPN is routed to the respective PE of each VPN instance, while maintaining its own routing table space isolated, so that customers with overlapping prefixes can be transported over the same shared infrastructure. Technically, VPRN uses MPLS labels to identify paths between ingress and egress PEs, in addition the multiprotocol extensions is incorporated into BGP to facilitate carrying a route distinguisher (RD) along with each prefix when sending updates to ensure that you can use a single protocol instance to carry different routes for different VPNs even if there is overlapping addressing between VPNs.

Note The technologies and design options discussed in this section are similar to the ones discussed in the enterprise WAN virtualization section in Chapter 4, "Enterprise Edge Architecture Design." However, the enterprise WAN virtualization was focused on how to connect the main or hub site with the remote sites. In this subsection, though, the selection of the suitable option is from the service provider point of view (transit network). In other words, the technologies and principles are all the same; however, the selection criteria might differ from a design principles point of view.

Table 7-3 summarizes the characteristics of each CSC model discussed in this chapter by highlighting the main advantages and design considerations of each.

Table 7-3 *CSC Connectivity Options Comparison*

CSC model	Advantages	Design Considerations
Non-MPLS customer over MPLS VPN carrier	Flexible and scalable B-Carrier option. C-Carrier will have more flexibility to exchange large number of prefixes B-Carrier does not need to install and process external customer prefixes. Offers transport separation (VRF/VPN) per C-Carrier across the B-Carrier network.	Requires MPLS between the C-Carrier and B-Carrier. May requires mapping between MPLS EXP and DSCP QoS marking at the C-Carrier edge to the B-Carrier. To extend IPv6 between C-Carrier Islands, you can use 6PE.
MPLS customer over MPLS VPN carrier	Same as the above (only difference is the customer is MPLS enabled).	Requires MPLS between the C-Carrier and B-Carrier. Supports seamless QoS design (MPLS EXP based). To extend IPv6 between C-Carrier Islands, you can use 6PE.

Table 7-3 *continued*

CSC model	Advantages	Design Considerations
MPLS VPN customer over MPLS VPN carrier	Flexible, scalable B-Carrier option, supports expanding MPLS VPN services. B-Carrier does not need to install and process external prefixes of the C-Carrier. Offers transport separation (VRF/VPN) per C-Carrier across the B-Carrier network.	Requires MPLS between the C-Carrier and B-Carrier. Supports seamless QoS design (MPLS EXP based). To extend IPv6 between C-Carrier Islands, you can use 6VPE.
MPLS VPN customer over MPLS carrier	Simple, scalable B-Carrier option, supports expanding MPLS VPN services. With MPLS in the core, the B-Carrier does not need to install or process external customer prefixes.	Requires MPLS between the C-Carrier and B-Carrier. Supports seamless QoS design (MPLS EXP based). To extend IPv6 between C-Carrier islands, you can use 6VPE. Does not provide isolation between the different customers/tenants across the backbone.*
MPLS VPN Customer over IP-only carrier	Simple and basic native IP routing across the B-Carrier.	Has the least scalability and flexibility among other options. May requires each customer to build their own overlay to extend their routing or MPLS VPN services. May requires mapping between MPLS EXP and DSCP QoS marking at the C-Carrier edge to the B-Carrier. Does not provide isolation between the different customers/tenants across the backbone.**

C-Carrier = customer carrier, B-Carrier = backbone carrier

* Apart from networks migration and merger scenarios, it is not practically feasible to have MPLS core only without enabling L2/L3VPN and taking advantage of its benefits.

** If BGP/MPLS IP-VPN defined in RFC 4364 is deployed by the B-Carrier, in this case the (non-MPLS) IP backbone will offer a scalable solution that can support the MPLS IP L3VPN connectivity model.

Acquisition of an MPLS-L3VPN Service Provider Design Scenario

This design scenario focuses on the common L3VPN interconnection design options used to provide interprovider connectivity. Carrier Supporting Carrier (CSC) presented in this scenario is one of the common connectivity models offered by today's global MPLS providers. In addition, the inter-AS connectivity model is incorporated into this scenario to provide the desired connectivity solution based on the different design requirements.

Background Information

ABC Corp. is an MPLS L3VPN service provider located in the United States. ABC Corp. is currently facing several scalability and integration issues with other global MPLS VPN providers, due to the increased number of customers who require extending their L3VPN connectivity to the UK and across Europe. Consequently, ABC Corp. decided to acquire XYZ Corp., an MPLS L3VPN service provider located in the UK with several POPs distributed across Europe. This will help ABC Corp. to overcome their current issues and expand their business.

Design Requirements

- ABC Corp. requires the network merger project with XYZ Corp. to be completed as quickly as possible.

- Both ABC Corp. and XYZ Corp. must maintain their current BGP AS numbers.

- The security team within ABC Corp. dictated that this network integration should use a connectivity model that does not share internal infrastructure IP addressing of both SP networks.

- The same SLAs must be offered across the two SP networks for those customers who are located within the United Sates and have remote sites located in the UK or Europe that require end-to-end reliability and service consistency.

- Because of the increased number of customers who need to extend their L3VPN service, the proposed solution must be scalable enough to satisfy this increased demand.

- A secondary path is required to provide load sharing and fault tolerance.

- Cost should be considered as a tiebreaker only if there are two connectivity options that both meet the primary requirements.

- Customers who have an SLA with expedited forwarding for their delay-sensitive applications, such as VoIP, should have their traffic forwarded over the low-latency path as the primary path.

Figure 7-21 summarizes the requirements on a high level.

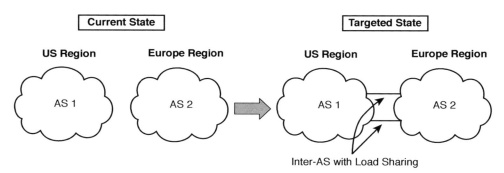

Figure 7-21   *Network Merger Connectivity Requirements*

Available Interconnection Options

The following are the available (offered) connectivity options for ABC Corp. for their interprovider integration project:

- **Option 1, direct point-to-point Layer 2 link provided by an international carrier Ethernet provider (L2VPN):** This high-speed (10-Gbps) link can be provisioned quickly with high service reliability and is cost-effective.

- **Option 2, carrier supporting carrier:** This high-speed (5-Gbps) option is provided by a global MPLS VPN provider and its cost is higher than Option 1. In addition, this option has good level or service reliability; however, this link has higher latency compared to Option 1 and may require a longer time for the service and link provisioning.

- **Option 3, carrier supporting carrier:** This option is offered by a European MPLS VPN provider that has few POPs in the United States. The offered connectivity is over high speed, 5 Gbps, but because this provider does not offer any QoS model, it has higher latency compared to Option 1 and 2. The pricing in euro is considered a bit higher for this link than other options.

- **Option 4, overlay tunneling over the Internet:** This option offers 100 Mbps of bandwidth and is considered the cheapest and quickest in terms of provisioning and implementation. However, there might be some concerns about service reliability, security, and end-to-end latency (lack of end-to-end QoS).

Note   Both Option 1 and 2 support end-to-end six-class CoS (QoS model).

Inter-AS Connectivity Model Selection

In scenarios like this where there are multiple options with several design requirements, you should create a decision matrix, using the business-driven selection criteria depicted in Figure 7-22, to simplify the optimal design decision.

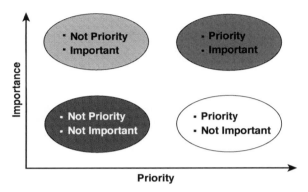

Figure 7-22 *Business-Driven Selection Criteria*

Table 7-3 maps each of the technical requirements to the relevant selection criteria shown in Figure 7-16 in a decision matrix style.

Table 7-3 *Interprovider Connectivity Model Selection Decision Matrix*

	Priority: Important	Priority: Not Important	Not Priority: Important	Not Priority: Not important
Reliability	X			
Scalability	X			
Security			X	
Encryption				X
Cost			X	
Service provisioning time*		X		
Consistent QoS	X			
Variety of access media				X
High capacity	X			

* Based on the design requirements, the service provisioning time is a priority (to complete the project as soon as possible), but it is not important to the business, nor will the business pay a penalty or lose customers if some delay occurs in the service provisioning.

Based on ABC Corp. requirements and the decision matrix listed in the Table 7-3, the two possible solutions that you should consider are Option 1 and 2. Option 3 cannot be considered because its lack of QoS support and the fact that it is not cheap. Options 4 has several design limitations and concerns; therefore, it will not be considered even though it is the quickest in terms of service provisioning.

Proposed Solution

Based on the selected interconnect options and the security requirements. inter-AS Option B with next-hop-self will be used in this design to establish the provider inter-connect between the two SP networks over a 10-Gbps point-to-point Layer 2 Ethernet link (over L2VPN).

Note   Inter-AS Option A was not selected because scalability is a "priority and important" requirement.

In addition, the secondary link will be established over a global MPLS VPN provider using the CSC connectivity model (using inter-AS Option B as well) to establish the second inter-AS path between AS 1 and AS 2 with maximum bandwidth capacity of 5 Gbps. For the purpose of the traffic load sharing and service differentiation requirement, customers will be divided across those two paths based on the offered SLA. For example, customers with strict SLA requirements (such as need low-latency connectivity for VoIP or video traffic) will be connected over the direct L2VPN interconnect as a primary path, while other customers will be using the interconnection over the CSC provider as the primary path. Thus, if any of these links fails, the remaining path will be used to carry traffic for all customers. So, traffic load and link capacity planning for situations like this have been considered. Technically, the distribution of customer traffic across these two paths will be achieved by altering BGP attributes (for simplicity, BGP community and local preference attributes will be considered), as illustrated in Figure 7-23.

Note   For simplicity, in this scenario customer A (Cust-A) represents customers with strict SLA, and customer B (Cust-B) represent customers that have no special requirements in their SLA such as VoIP traffic.

Figure 7-23 illustrates a logical view of the MP-BGP policies to control path selection over the interprovider links.

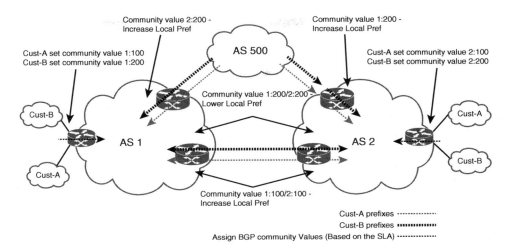

Figure 7-23 *Influencing MP-BGP Path Selection over the Interprovider Links*

Furthermore, to provide a more scalable and manageable solution, BGP community values is considered in the scenario to tag traffic at each customer-facing PE with the relevant BGP community value, which can be used by the different ASBRs across both AS 1 and AS 2 to assign the routes with the desired local preference value based on its BGP community value (tag). This way, network operators do not need to maintain a large number of prefix lists at the ASBRs that contain all the customers' prefixes (because this may results in a high potential for operational complexity and errors that ultimately will result in customer dissatisfaction).

The end result of these BGP policies must provide traffic load distribution as illustrated in Figure 7-24.

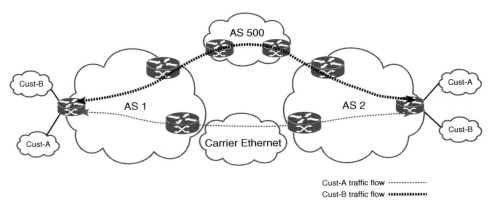

Figure 7-24 *Traffic Flow Distribution Across Different Interprovider Paths*

Network Merger implementation Plan

Figure 7-25 lists the required steps to move ABC Corp. from the current state to the targeted state discussed earlier.

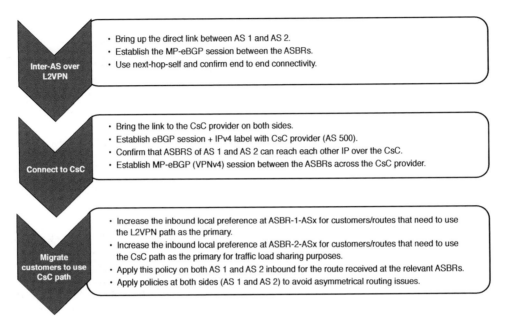

Inter-AS over L2VPN
- Bring up the direct link between AS 1 and AS 2.
- Establish the MP-eBGP session between the ASBRs.
- Use next-hop-self and confirm end to end connectivity.

Connect to CsC
- Bring the link to the CsC provider on both sides.
- Establish eBGP session + IPv4 label with CsC provider (AS 500).
- Confirm that ASBRS of AS 1 and AS 2 can reach each other IP over the CsC.
- Establish MP-eBGP (VPNv4) session between the ASBRs across the CsC provider.

Migrate customers to use CsC path
- Increase the inbound local preference at ASBR-1-ASx for customers/routes that need to use the L2VPN path as the primary.
- Increase the inbound local preference at ASBR-2-ASx for customers/routes that need to use the CsC path as the primary for traffic load sharing purposes.
- Apply this policy on both AS 1 and AS 2 inbound for the route received at the relevant ASBRs.
- Apply policies at both sides (AS 1 and AS 2) to avoid asymmetrical routing issues.

Figure 7-25 *Implementation Plan to Activate the Interprovider Integrations*

Summary

Interconnecting multiple autonomous systems is a common design practice used between service providers and by large global enterprise networks. As discussed in this chapter, there are various connectivity options and models. Therefore, selecting the right design connectivity model is critical, because all the following communications between the interconnected autonomous systems will flow over this interconnect. For example, interconnecting two autonomous systems that belong to the same service provider is different from connecting two autonomous systems that belong to two different service providers. Technically, both examples can use the exact same connectivity option; however, other aspects drive the design choice, such as security considerations. Besides, although inter-AS and CSC work on the same logic, each model has different characteristics and targets different design goals, as summarized in Table 7-4.

Table 7-4 *Inter-AS Versus CSC*

	CSC	Inter-AS
Topology model	Hub and spoke.	Point to point.
Typical SP POP connectivity	POPs of the backbone carrier (the carrier in the middle) can be interconnected over MPLS VPN, MPLS only, or Native IP.	Typically POPs of a given SP are not available in the geographic area required by their customers.
Typical customers	ISPs, MPLS VPN providers, and large-scale enterprises.	Any two autonomous systems need to interconnect, commonly with MPLS VPN services.
MPLS L3VPN support	Customer (child) provider network may or may not have MPLS enabled. Backbone carrier (parent) network can be based on MPLS VPN, MPLS only, or native IP.	Participating providers must support MPLS VPNs (either L2VPN or L3VPN).
MPLS L2VPN support	With this connectivity model, the backbone carrier that provides L2VPN transport will not participate in any label distribution or Layer 3 routing with the customer provider network (see the "L2VPN" section in Chapter 6).	L2VPN is one of the common extended services between the interconnected providers' networks using same L3VPN inter-AS connectivity options
Route distribution	Internal routes and BGP next-hop reachability information can be shared with the backbone carrier, but external routes are not shared with the backbone carrier.	Depending on the inter-AS model used (for example, A, B, C, or D).

Part IV

Data Center Networks Design

Chapter 8   Data Center Network Design

Chapter 8

Data Center Networks Design

The data center network (DCN) is the primary element interconnecting the various components that all collectively comprise a data center. These components include the following computing, application, storage, and security nodes and services, where scalability, resiliency, security, and performance are the most common fundamental considerations of a successful DCN design.

This brief definition of a DCN emphasizes the important role of the data center's network infrastructure. In fact, all the communications between applications and services into and out of the data center are steered and carried by the network. As a result, any network availability or capacity issue within the underlying network infrastructure will impact the overall data center responsiveness, even if you have the best network overlay, servers, and application designs in the world. It is exactly like a building with a weak foundation; it cannot scale and be developed reliably, even if it has very promising architecture. For this reason, the data center's design and architecture must be business driven. All the business's requirements (its vision, continuity, and service priorities) should be taken into account when architecting a data center network, regardless of whether it is an enterprise data center or a service provider data center.

From a business point of view, the data center is the place where the business stores its data and applications; the data center houses the most critical assets of today's businesses. Sometimes, the data center even represents the core revenue source of the business, such as hosting data center providers (like software as a service [SaaS] and infrastructure as a service [IaaS] providers). Therefore, the design of a data center ideally should always offer a flexible and reliable design capable of accommodating the evolutions of business requirements and market trends. In addition, one unique and challenging design aspect of DCNs is that to produce a successful business-driven DCN design, you must connect with multiple players within the organization. These players usually belong to different teams, such as the server team, the storage team, the applications team, and the security team. Ideally, the input from these teams should drive the overall data center design, including the network.

This section starts by covering the traditional way of designing DCNs. It then covers the drivers and design considerations of the next generation of data centers, and how yesterday's data centers are not architected to meet today's modern data center requirements. This chapter also discusses the design options and challenges of modern data center interconnect solutions.

Note This chapter, like other chapters in this book, covers the various architectures, protocols, and technologies used by traditional and today's data centers regardless of whether they are not recommended or whether they are commonly used and highly recommended. After all, the reality is that organizations may have considered some of these technologies or design architectures during a time when their business and application requirements differed from today's requirements. In addition, technologies are always in evolving state; this implies that what was considered a best practice or fit for any given design yesterday will probably not be the case for today's data center design. Consequently, network designers must be aware of the various design options and technologies and have a good understanding of the strengths and weaknesses of each to be able to evaluate current designs and to suggest design optimization or a complete redesign (always taking into account, of course, the different design requirements, starting from business and application requirements all the way up to the technical traffic flow and routing).

Traditional Data Center Network Architecture

During the past decade, the classic three-tier network architecture has been the predominant network architecture for mid- and large-scale data centers, because this multitier siloed approach offered the desired level of design flexibility, availability, and performance for the various application and server requirements at that time. The overall architecture of a DCN, at a high level, is built on the same concept as the hierarchal network architecture discussed earlier in the enterprise campus section in this book, which usually consists of the core, distribution, and access layers. A common question with regard to the classic three-tier design is this: How does a three-tier DCN design differ from a typical three-tier campus LAN design? Although these two designs follow similar concepts and architecture (for example, they both employ the concept of hierarchal network architecture), they are not identical in their detailed design requirements. This is summarized in Figure 8-1.

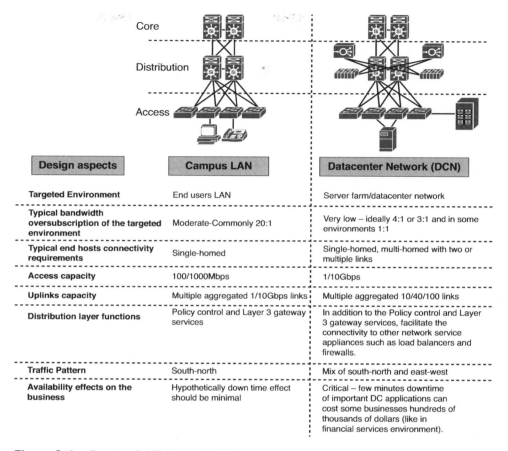

Design aspects	Campus LAN	Datacenter Network (DCN)
Targeted Environment	End users LAN	Server farm/datacenter network
Typical bandwidth oversubscription of the targeted environment	Moderate-Commonly 20:1	Very low – ideally 4:1 or 3:1 and in some environments 1:1
Typical end hosts connectivity requirements	Single-homed	Single-homed, multi-homed with two or multiple links
Access capacity	100/1000Mbps	1/10Gbps
Uplinks capacity	Multiple aggregated 1/10Gbps links	Multiple aggregated 10/40/100 links
Distribution layer functions	Policy control and Layer 3 gateway services	In addition to the Policy control and Layer 3 gateway services, facilitate the connectivity to other network service appliances such as load balancers and firewalls.
Traffic Pattern	South-north	Mix of south-north and east-west
Availability effects on the business	Hypothetically down time effect should be minimal	Critical – few minutes downtime of important DC applications can cost some businesses hundreds of thousands of dollars (like in financial services environment).

Figure 8-1 *Campus LAN Versus DCN*

STP-Based Data Center Network Architecture

As discussed earlier, there is not a significant difference between the overall architecture of a classic three-tier DCN and the campus design (at a high level). Therefore, all the Spanning Tree Protocol (STP) and Layer 2 considerations discussed in Chapter 2, "Enterprise Layer 2 and Layer 3 Design," apply here. The only crucial difference is that in a DCN you need to consider the deployment model and failure scenarios for the services provisioned at the data center distribution layer. This is because, in most cases, these services (either service module or appliance based) work in active-standby or active-active modes. In these modes, Layer 2 communication is almost always required between these services across the upstream distribution layer nodes.

If the network, and Layer 2 in particular, was not designed to properly take the connected services to the distribution layer nodes into consideration, the network will most likely face a dual-active or split-brain situation during some failure scenarios. This usually occurs when two service appliances (such as firewalls), operating in active-standby mode, lose communication with each other. As a result, each device thinks that it is the only active device. (The active firewall will continue in active mode, and the standby firewall will move from standby to active mode as well.) Both firewalls handling traffic independently (operating in dual-active mode) is highly undesirable and dangerous because the risk of asymmetrical connection failure is extremely high, as shown in Figure 8-2.

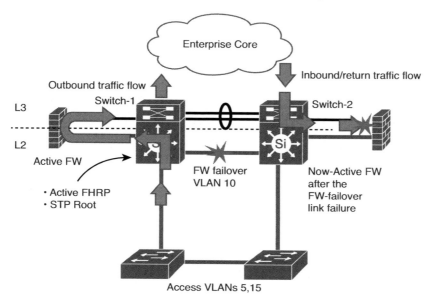

Figure 8-2   *Asymmetrical Connection Failure Scenario*

In Figure 8-2, a loop-free *U* topology is used. In case of L2 link failure between the two distribution switches that carry the data center firewall failover VLANs, both firewalls will be in active mode (split-brain). First Hop Redundancy Protocol (FHRP) active will continue to be on switch 1 because the heartbeat messages flow through the access switch, which means outbound traffic flows through distribution switch 1. If inbound traffic from the core arrives at the distribution switch 2 during this failure scenario, it attempts to flow through the now-active firewall. Traffic will be dropped because of this failure because the now-active firewall has no state information of this session. This issue can be temporarily fixed by enforcing all the inbound traffic to flow via the active FHRP switch. Nonetheless, the main reason behind this example is to highlight the different considerations when designing Layer 2 for a data center compared to a typical campus LAN. Even though the overall topologies and features are similar to some extent, the functions and traffic flow are normally more complicated in DCNs.

As a general rule, to achieve the highest capacity in DCNs, always select the technologies and techniques that provide you with the maximum possible number of forwarding paths (taking into account that too much redundancy might not always be a good idea). Therefore, multichassis link aggregation architecture (mLAG)and Clos fabric architectures, from an L2 design point of view, are always preferred over traditional STP.

Note The influence of introducing network service security appliances, such as firewalls and load balancers, into the data center aggregation layer is critical. It must be seriously considered, along with all the possible failure scenarios, when contemplating an STP-based access-distribution Layer 2 topology. This is applicable for both services, which are either module or appliance based.

mLAG-Based Data Center Network Architecture

As discussed earlier in this book, the mLAG architecture keeps STP in place but overcomes its shortcomings by using mLAG functions with switch clustering enabled at the aggregation layer. Compared to an STP-based design, this architecture offers a more flexible and resilient DCN with significant performance and bandwidth capacity optimization. However, scalability (scale-out) is one of the main concerns with this architecture for large-scale data centers that are based on virtualized workloads. Typically, only two aggregation switches can be clustered to serve as one logical device for the downstream switches (access switches). Consequently, access switches connecting to different clustered upstream aggregation switches have to communicate via the Layer 3 core, which may break the requirements of seamless end-to-end Layer 2 VM mobility or distributed workloads across different points of delivery (PODs), as shown in Figure 8-3.

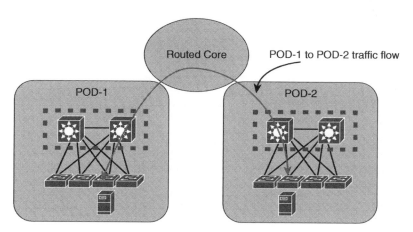

Figure 8-3 *mLAG-Based DCN*

Next-Generation Data Center Network Design

This section discusses the different design options and protocols used in today's modern DCNs and the drivers toward adopting these new architectures.

Data Center Virtualization and Cloud-Based Services Overview

In the world of servers, the term *virtualization* refers to the ability to run multiple operating systems and application instances on a single physical server. The abstraction layer of virtualization is usually provided by software (OS) known as a *virtual machine manager* (VMM), also commonly known as a *hypervisor*. The VMMs/hypervisors provide the capability to control and manage multiple operating systems and emulate a dedicated environment to each server over one shared physical system using its hardware resources. As shown in Figure 8-4, the shared resources include CPU, memory, and network cards, which separate computing environments from the actual physical infrastructure. This approach has proven to reduce costs (capital expenditure [capex] and operating expenditure [opex]), and it enables IT and businesses to gain increased efficiency and flexibility from the existing computing hardware.

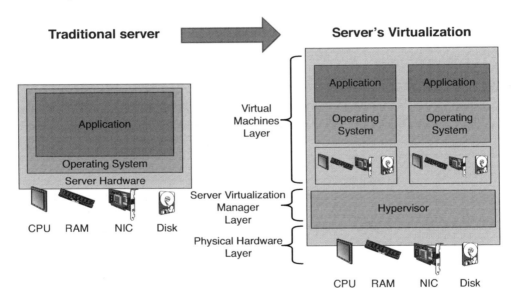

Figure 8-4 *Server Virtualization*

It is important for network architects and designers to understand the logical difference between the terms *change* and *transformation*. Change always takes the past as a foundation, and modifies it in a manner to make it more optimized; more scalable or more reliable. However, transformation refers to something new, such as designing a future goal or target, and then achieving it. Unlike change, transformation does not mainly rely on something that already exists, and then modifying it so as to make it more secure or reliable; instead, it's more about creating a concept that does not exist already (new)[1].

Based on that, the concept of cloud or cloud computing in the world of data centers is a transformation in how data centers are designed and operated. In fact, it is a completely new era in the world of data centers. Technically, cloud computing further leverages the

1.   http://theprimes.com/change-vs-transformation/

concept of server virtualization by adding an additional layer of virtualization and service abstraction. This offers on-demand network and service access to a shared pool of resources. These resources usually include network, storage, and computing resources, which ultimately enable multitenancy capabilities in the data center. Also *cloud services* incorporate self-service portals, automation, and orchestration to more effectively leverage these shared pools of resources.

Cloud computing also provides an *X*-as-a-S offering, such as IaaS and ITaaS. This is when scalable IT-related capabilities are provided "as a service," which allows more elastic and on-demand service provisioning and access. Furthermore, cloud services can help to transform IT from being a capex model to an opex model, which will help organizations to better control costs. In sum, virtualization is fundamental to enabling cloud services in a data center. Virtualization generally takes the following forms:

- Server virtualization

- Network virtualization

- Storage virtualization

- Management virtualization and cloud orchestration

This chapter focuses on network virtualization and the new trends and architectures of next-generation data centers, which are propelling the change in DCN designs, approaches, and technologies.

That said, this does not mean that each and every single data center design needs to be transformed to a cloud-based DC model. Doing so depends entirely on the business goals, model, vision, cost (capex versus opex), and various other requirements (such as elastic business-continuity requirements), which in turn will help you to identify the current and anticipated future size of the organization and its DC network and understand mission-critical applications, the services provisioning model, traffic pattern, and so on. These collectively can help you to decide whether it is more feasible to "change" the existing DC design and architecture to a more optimized one or to "transform" it to a completely new DC model/architecture.

Drivers Toward New Fabric-Based Data Center Network Architectures

It is commonly known that the DCN sits at the core of the IT infrastructure. Therefore, it is crucial to understand how IT can deliver services and value back to the business. The new business demands and technology trends are changing the role of IT and introducing new challenges to the availability of applications; yesterday's data centers were not designed to address these challenges, which include mobile and virtualized workloads, cloud applications, big data analytics, and dynamic policy provisioning. In this new environment, it is obvious that bandwidth demand is much higher and that the traffic pattern is unpredictable as compared to traditional data centers. Traditionally, the DCN is based on the classic three-tier hierarchy, as shown earlier in Figure 8-1.

Typically, the classic three-tier architecture introduces significant oversubscription and blocking architecture, which is unsuitable for the requirements of today's workloads and application requirements. This is simply because the higher the traffic moving in the network hierarchy (bottom-top) of the multitiered network, the more bandwidth sharing there will be among the nodes in the lower tiers (bandwidth aggregation), as shown in Figure 8-5.

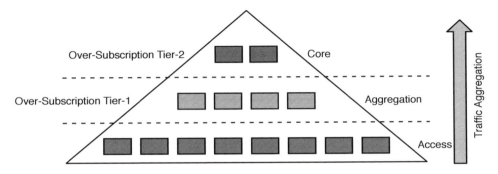

Figure 8-5 *Traffic Aggregation*

Note   Oversubscription and blocking in traditional architectures can be described as follows:

Oversubscription is when the ingress capacity exceeds the egress capacity. For example, for 48x 10G attached servers, the access switch needs at least 480 Gbps of port capacity toward the upstream or distribution layer to provide 1:1 oversubscription (1:1 here meaning zero or no subscription). However, if the access switch has only 2x 10G uplinks, in this case the oversubscription is 24:1. Although not every network is required to provide 1:1 performance, oversubscription needs to be minimized in modern large-scale DCNs (for example, ideally 4:1 or 3:1) [55]. *Blocking* is a situation, at a device level, caused by oversubscription, which can lead to network queuing. As a result, the overwhelmed node, such as a distribution switch handling inter-POD or rack traffic, will start blocking the new traffic flows. Ideally, during the planning phase, the network architect or designer should obtain enough information (such as baseline conditions and application traffic patterns) before attempting to define any oversubscription standard or deciding whether a nonblocking DCN architecture is required.

Note   As a network designer, always ask for information that helps you to derive the DCN design decision based on the requirements of the systems and mission/business-critical applications hosted in the data center.

Note The term *POD* (point of delivery) represents a standardized structured block constructed primarily of network, computing, and storage resources. In virtualized data centers, this concept serves the foundation of achieving standardized design modularity that can support high scale-out and scale-up heterogeneous workload requirements; this will ultimately help in minimizing the overall design and operational complexity.

A move from the traditional architecture to a more flexible, high-speed (nonblocking), low-latency, and agile network architecture was required to accommodate these evolutions and the transformation of modern data center requirements using fabric based infrastructure.

Fabric is defined by Gartner, Inc. as *"a set of compute, storage, memory and I/O components joined through a fabric interconnect and the software to configure and manage them."*[2]

The new switch fabric concepts and architectures came into the picture to meet today's data centers trends and requirements, which primarily derived from the following factors:

■ **Traffic pattern:** Server virtualization and cloud-based services are a game changer in data center design concepts and architectures, in particular the traffic flow within a data center and between interconnected data centers. Traditionally, traffic flow was mainly north-south, sourced from internal or external users to the application hosted in the data center. In contrast, modern data centers are moving toward a more distributed workload and workload mobility, taking advantage of the vitalization concepts and distributed virtual machines (VMs) across one or multiple data centers between hosts, as shown in Figure 8-6. Therefore, the traffic pattern is becoming more of a combination of east-west (server-to-server) and north-south (client-server), which makes it unpredictable. As a result, the traditional three-tier DCN design is becoming more of a limiting factor for the new server and application traffic requirements (increased east-west traffic flow).

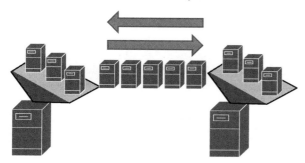

- East – West Traffic Flow
- Workload Mobility

Figure 8-6 *Workload Mobility*

2. http://www.gartner.com/it-glossary/fabric-computing

- **Cost:** Because of the limitations of the classic multitier architecture, it will be necessary to have a larger number of switches with a larger number of ports (scale up) to handle the increase in the data center size. This will lead to extra cost (capex) and a more complicated design, which will increase the operational cost (opex) as well.

- **Reliable scalability:** Server virtualization and VM mobility increase demand on the network infrastructure to support the ability to scale-out, considering the extremely increased number of virtual hosts compared to traditional data centers. Take, for example, an access switch that has 16 physical hosts connected to it. Traditionally, there will be 16 servers to handle; with the server virtualization concept, if these hosts have 10 VMs each, this access switch needs to handle 160 servers. Typically, these 16 physical hosts, if they used to be connected over a 1G port, now must each be connected over a 10G access port. In other words, this tremendous increase in the number of hosts (virtual) and traffic volume needs a new architecture that is built to scale without compromising bandwidth efficiency.

- **High flexibility:** The emergence of virtualized and cloud-based data centers requires networks with architecture that supports simple and flexible automated provisioning, such as application programming interface (API) integration with cloud orchestration systems.

- **Ultra-low-latency network:** Today, some environments require high-frequency trading, such as in financial services (where thousands of trading transactions are expected to be performed in a few seconds), which can be a big challenge when traditional data center platforms and design are used. Consequently, to meet the requirements of this type of environment, you need a network architecture that can support ultra-low-latency forwarding and a nonblocking switch fabric architecture that can forward packets in full size within microseconds. These are required to satisfy the needs of this type of environment, in which the extremely low-latency, high-performance, high-bandwidth and reliable transport form the foundation of today's high-frequency trading DCN

Modern data center architectures are moving from the classic three-tier architecture toward flatter fabric-based architectures, which are specifically built and architected for the new requirements of the next-generation data centers and to overcome all the limitations discussed earlier. Moreover, the any-to-any, nonblocking fabric architecture enables IT to align with the business needs and priorities by delivering tangible outcomes. These outcomes include a reduction in the number of full server I/O adapters (support of server virtualization and unified I/O), significant enhancement of the reliable scalability of the network, and the simplification of cabling. Furthermore, power and cooling costs are lowered by the elimination of unnecessary switching infrastructure used by the traditional data center architecture, and overall operational cost is also reduced.

Modern Data Center Network Architectures and Overlays

As discussed earlier, the traditional three-tier DCN design has many limitations when used in a virtualized or cloud-based data center with workload mobility, high-bandwidth capacity, and fast forwarding requirements, simply because at each tier in the network, the uplink bandwidth is distributed across the next-higher tier. Consequently, the more tiers traversed by traffic between servers (east-west), the greater the potential for bandwidth shortage (traffic aggregation) associated with increased latency and limited scale-out capabilities. Therefore, a new and more scalable network architecture, combined with a switch fabric architecture capable of providing any-to-any nonblocking connectivity, is required to overcome these limitations. Figure 8-7 shows the evolution of DCN architectures.

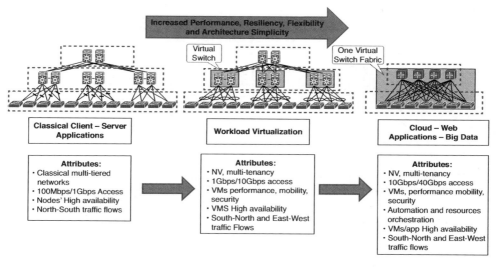

Figure 8-7   *Evolution of Data Center Network Architectures*

Consequently, modern data center fabrics should accelerate the deployment of applications and meet development and operations (DevOps) needs by

- Eliminating any dependencies on traditional protocols, such as STP

- Offering fast forwarding underlay for multidimensional traffic (high bisectional bandwidth)

- Providing optimized scalable forwarding (scaling forwarding tables and segments)

- Providing cloud integration and automated provisioning (such as API integration with cloud orchestrator systems)

- Providing virtualized networking to support mobility and virtual devices across the DCN

- Providing a reliable scale-out capability

At the time of this writing, there were a few modern data center fabric architectures, such as single virtual fabric and Clos architecture. This section focuses on the most common and proven architecture in today's data centers, which is the Clos architecture.

Different design considerations and options are discussed, as are the drivers of each that help network designers select the right architecture to offer modern DCNs a higher degree of flexibility, reliability, scalability, and performance.

Clos Architecture

Clos architecture offers a nonblocking architecture based on multistage topology, which can maximize the overall network performance by increasing the available bandwidth to higher than what a single node can provide. The mathematical theory of this architecture was initially created by Charles Clos in 1953, hence the reason it is called Clos. In a nutshell, this architecture is based on associating each output with an input point. In other words, the number of outputs equals the number of inputs, or there is precisely one connection between nodes of one stage with those of another stage [55]. Figure 8-8 illustrates this architecture that offers zero oversubscription (1:1) where a 3-stage Clos topology is used to connect 18 host (edge ports) using 3x of 6 port switches in each stage.

Note   Although the Clos architecture can offer scalable 1:1 (zero) oversubscription, this level of oversubscription is rarely required. Typically, 4:1 or 3:1 offers an efficient level of oversubscription with modern data centers that are built on 10/40/100G Ethernet. In fact, application and service requirements should drive the required level of oversubscription during the planning phase, taking into account the anticipated traffic load.

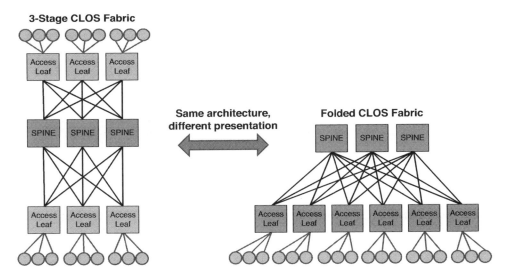

Figure 8-8   *Clos Architecture*

This architecture can be considered a two-tier hierarchy, in which the access layer switches are called leafs and the aggregation layers are called spines. With this two-tier leafs and spines architecture, each leaf switch is connected to every spine switch on the aggregation layer, which makes the DCN architecture flatten and eliminate bandwidth aggregation/oversubscription, because of bandwidth being the same at every tier. As a result, this architecture offers a high degree of network redundancy and a simplified design, and supports a large volume of bisectional traffic (east-west), as shown in Figure 8-9. Moreover, it can support multipathing, which can efficiently use network resources to support more leaf switches. Network designers can either consider scaling up, scaling out spine switches, or moving to a five-stage Clos topology for significantly larger scale DC networks.

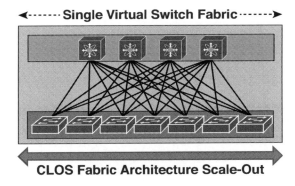

Figure 8-9 *Clos Architecture Scale-Out*

Unlike traditional data center architecture where Layer 3 gateway services and other network and security services are provided by the aggregation layer, in Clos (spines and leafs) architecture, the role of the spine is only to forward traffic between the leafs in the same manner that P routers work in a Multiprotocol Label Switching (MPLS) network. Furthermore, DC services and Layer 2 and Layer 3 demarcation points are moved in the architecture down to the leaf (also known as the *border leaf*), taking advantage of the high capacity and performance of the bisectional bandwidth of this architecture, as shown in Figure 8-10. As a result, additional spine switches can be introduced to the network to increase its scalability and reliability without any changes required to network and security services. In other words, unlike the traditional design, Clos is not tied to a pair of aggregation switches only. Therefore, Clos offers the optimal architecture for today's multitenant virtualized and cloud-based data centers.

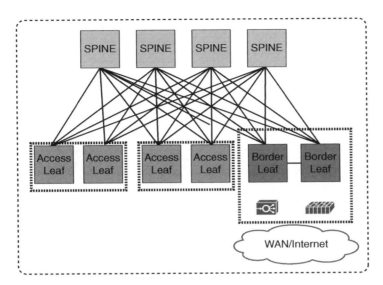

Figure 8-10   *Clos: Border Leafs*

Note   The definition of a *tenant* varies based on the targeted business and the data center environment. For example, in an enterprise environment, the tenants can be the different departments or business units (like in ITaaS environment), whereas in a cloud-hosting service provider, the most typical tenants are the external customers.

Clos Transport Protocols

To provide any-to-any nonblocking seamless connectivity and eliminate the reliance on STP, Clos fabric architectures rely on transport protocols that offer the ability to use all the available links between any two leaf switches over the intermediate spine nodes (equal-cost multipath routing [ECMP]).

Overlay Transport

In fact, network overlays are the representations of virtual networks of interconnected nodes that share an underlying physical network, allowing deployment of applications that require specific network topologies without the need to modify the underlying network. Ultimately, this can offer to the Clos fabric design the optimal level of flexibility, scalability, and performance required by today's modern data centers.

At the time of this writing, the following are the primary protocols considered by the majority of modern data centers to offer scalable and flexible ECMP forwarding over the Clos fabric architecture:

- MAC-in-MAC

- MAC-in-IP

- MPLS based

MAC-in-MAC

As mentioned earlier in this chapter, a primary goal of the Clos architecture is to eliminate any reliance on Layer 2 STP and optimize traffic distribution in multiple directions. To achieve this and facilitate the MAC-in-MAC encapsulation to work over all available paths, Intermediate System-to-Intermediate System (IS-IS) is used instead of traditional STP, because it is actually a Layer 2 routing protocol that does not rely on IP for carry frames. Therefore, IS-IS routing is used to distribute link-state information and to calculate the shortest paths through the Clos network (usually between the multiple leaf stages via the spine nodes) to form the underlay of the Clos fabric network.

MAC-in-MAC, however, can be achieved using different protocols, such as IETF TRILL (Transparent Interconnection of Lots of Links), IEEE 802.1aq SPB (shortest path bridging), or Cisco FabricPath. Furthermore, TRILL/FabricPath brings the stability and performance of Layer 3 routing to Layer 2 switched networks, which offer a highly agile and reliable Layer 2 fabric that supports high scale-out DCN design requirements,[3] as shown in Figure 8-11.

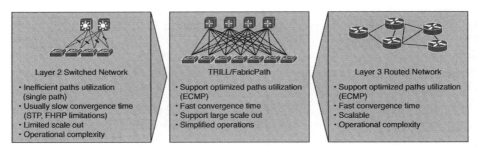

Figure 8-11 *The Evolution of the TRILL/FabricPath Concept*

Although TRILL and FabricPath are similar conceptually, FabricPath offers a more flexible and scalable design than TRILL when applied to the DCN. For example, the conversational MAC address learning of FabricPath offers a higher degree of MAC learning and forwarding efficiency to large-scale networks with a large number of MACs (such

---

3. "Scale Data centers with Cisco FabricPath," http://www.cisco.com

as a virtualized DC environment). In addition, FabricPath allows network designers and data center operators to optimize DCN efficiency and manageability by considering the FabricPath multitopology design, as shown in Figure 8-12.

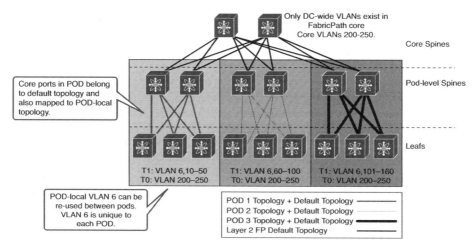

Figure 8-12   *FabricPath Multitopology*

As shown in Figure 8-12, the core is not required to hold all the VLANs from different downstream PODs if they are not used for inter-POD communication (local to the POD only). It can also be feasible in scenarios such as migration designs, VLAN localization, VLAN reuse, traffic engineering, and security. Network designers can take advantage of this multitopology architecture to optimize not only unicast but multidestination as well. This optimization is achieved by isolating and containing BUM (broadcast, unknown unicast, and multicast) traffic of the POD's local VLANs with the POD boundary without flooding this traffic unnecessarily to the core and other PODs, because each FabricPath topology can have its own multidestination tree (MDT), as shown in Figure 8-13.

Furthermore, FabricPath enhances FHRP gateway services by offering the ability to provide four active HSRP peers in active-active mode (also known as *anycast HSRP*), whereas TRILL forwards traffic based on the traditional active-standby mode, as shown in Figure 8-14. Traffic forwarding based on the traditional active-standby mode usually offers lower forwarding efficiency and higher convergence time in the event of an FHRP gateway failure.

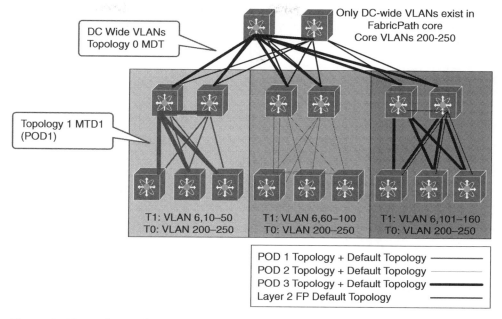

Figure 8-13 *FabricPath MDT Tree*

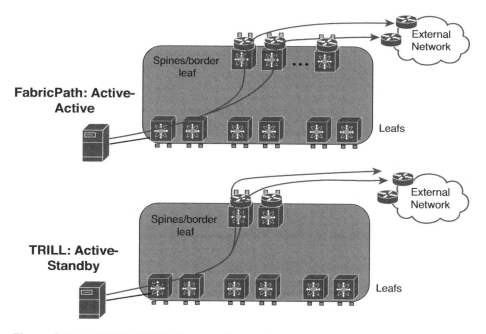

Figure 8-14 *FHRP: TRILL Versus FabricPath*

Note   With TRILL/FabricPath design, the Layer 3 gateway services can be deployed either at the spine nodes or can be moved to the border leaf nodes. Therefore, in Figure 8-14 the spine nodes are labeled as spines/border leaf.

Table 8-1 highlights the primary differences between FP, TRILL, and SPB.

Table 8-1   *FP Versus TRILL Versus SPB*

	TRILL	**FabricPath**	**SPB**
Standard	IEEE	Cisco propriety	IETF
Frame routing: ECMP	Yes	Yes	Yes
Frame routing: TTL	Yes	Yes	No
Active-active FHRP	No	Yes, anycast HSRP	Yes
End-Host reachability and distribution	Flood and learn	Flood and learn with conversational MAC learning	Flood and learn with Provider Backbone Bridging (PBB) (802.1ah) (Shortest-Path Bridging-MAC Address [SPBM])
Service instances	~4K	~16M (by extending 12-bit VLAN ID to a 24-bit segment ID)	~16M with MAC in MAC
C-MACs learned only at the edge	Yes	Yes	Yes (SPBM)
Applicability	Enterprise & SP grade DC	Enterprise & SP grade DC	Enterprise DC and service provider (SP)-grade network

Note   The Shortest Path Bridging VLAN ID (SPBV) version of SPB is Q-in-Q rather than MAC-in-MAC.

MAC-in-IP

With MAC-in-IP, it is obvious that the transport will be IP based from the network underlay point of view. Typically (not always), designing a Clos with MAC-in-IP overlay will rely on IS-IS to form the underlay of the Clos fabric network (ECMP). However, unlike MAC-in-MAC, the concept of MAC-in-IP overlay transport is based on the formation of virtual Layer 2 topologies on top of a physical Layer 3 network (IP encapsulation) combined with the concept of virtual network identifier, which is primarily used to forward frames to the required virtualized network context. Furthermore, MAC-in-IP overlay provides network based overlay, and it is also considered to be a host-based overlay solution offering multitenancy at scale with more simplified and automated workload provisioning capabilities. Figure 8-15 illustrates this concept with VxLAN applied as the MAC-in-IP overlay and the VxLAN tunnel endpoints (VTEPs) created at different levels.

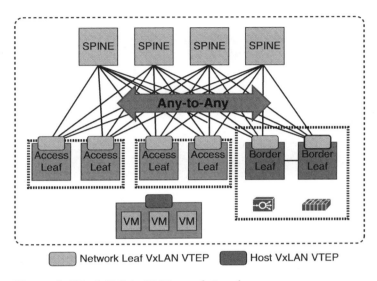

Figure 8-15   *MAC-in-IP Network Overlay*

At the time of this writing, the following are the primary protocols used for this purpose:

- Network Virtualization Using Generic Routing Encapsulation (NVGRE)
- Virtual Extensible LAN (VxLAN)
- Stateless Transport Tunneling (STT)

Table 8-2 compares the characteristics of these protocols.

Table 8-2   *MAC-in-IP Protocol Comparison*

	NVGRE	**VxLAN**	**STT**
Standards	IETF draft, sridharan-virtualization-nvgre.	IETF RFC 7348.	IETF draft, davie-stt
Encapsulation	Generic routing encapsulation (GRE)-based encapsulation.	UDP-based encapsulation.	TCP-based encapsulation

Table 8-2   *continued*

	NVGRE	VxLAN	STT
Widely supported/ considered by vendors	Moderate: Microsoft, Arista, Emulex, Huawei, and HP.	Highly: Cisco, VMware, Arista, Brocade, Citrix, Red Hat, and Broadcom.	Least: VMware and Broadcom
Overlay identification	24-bit virtual subnet identifier (VSID).	24-bit virtual network ID (VNI).	64-bit context ID
Layer 2 forwarding of BUM traffic	Each VSID is mapped to a multicast group; multiple VSIDs can share the same multicast group.	Each VNI is mapped to a multicast group; multiple VNIs can share the same multicast group.	Either ingress replication or encapsulate IP multicast as destination IP
Overly ECMP	32 bits of VSID plus the flow ID for ECMP purposes.	UDP based (derived from a hash of the inner headers).	TCP based (derived from a hash of the inner headers)
Underlay ECMP hashing	Hashing based on GRE header is not common (not support by most if not all switches).	UDP 5-tuple-based hashing.	TCP 5-tuple-based hashing

Although host-based overlay may offer capabilities that optimize the overall architecture and its flexibility with regard to workload mobility and automated provisioning, a robust and reliable underlay transport still forms the foundation of this overlay. If there is any inefficiency within the underlay design or performance, it will be reflected directly on the overlay efficiency as well. Therefore, a successful overlay DCN design must be architected over a reliable networked infrastructure that supports the desired level of resiliency and performance.

Note   The Cisco Application Centric Infrastructure (ACI) provides optimized traffic forwarding over a Clos architecture associated with flexible network-based VxLAN forwarding where each leaf performs encapsulation-normalization, which offers the freedom for DC operators and server administrators to consider any type of host-level tagging, such as 802.1Q, network virtualization using GRE (NVGRE), VxLAN, or untagged.

Note   Today's modern and cloud-based data centers are moving rapidly toward the concept of a centralized control plane that offers an abstracted centralized view of the network and can manage traffic and deploy services centrally (manually and automatically provision services) to meet today's data centers needs, which are mainly built around simplicity, high-speed forwarding, and fast services provisioning with automation without having to touch each individual network node in the forwarding plane across the DCN. This concept is known as *software-defined networking* (SDN). Although SDN is beyond the scope of this book, it is highly recommended that network designers (regardless preparing for the CCDE or not) have a good understanding of this concept and how it can simplify and optimize virtualized and cloud-based data center designs.

MPLS Based

Although other protocols discussed earlier in this chapter provide end-to-end path separation optimally by using different mechanisms, with MPLS the design can be feasible for scenarios requiring integration with other MPLS domains (for instance, data centers that belong to MPLS L3VPN providers that offer hosting services to their customers as well). Therefore, enabling MPLS L3VPN across the DCN can facilitate end-to-end MPLS L3VPN integration and offer seamless access with a scalable architecture.

That said, using MPLS across the leaf and spine architecture is becoming less common in today's DCNs as other protocols and overlay technologies such as VxLAN offer more simplified and flexible provisioning and integration with cloud orchestration (host based and network based) at a high scale. Therefore, data center operators can consider any hybrid approach, where you can use one of the protocols discussed earlier across the DC Clos fabric, such as TRILL or VxLAN, while MPLS L3VPN can be extended from the Clos (border leafs) at the DC edge, as shown in Figure 8-16. In addition, the flexibility and efficiency of this design offers a simplified migration approach for data center operators to move from a pure MPLS-based DC to FabricPath or VxLAN based while retaining MPLS VPN enabled at the data center Clos fabric border leafs. In addition, this approach offers a seamless integration with other MPLS domains such as MPLS L3VPN, as shown in Figure 8-16.

Note   If the leaf switches do not support MPLS, virtual routing and forwarding (VRF), or Multiprotocol Border Gateway Protocol (MP-BGP), MPLS can enabled at the DC edge nodes only to interconnect with other MPLS L3VPN domains. This approach requires extending the relevant DC VLANs to the DC edge nodes that will operate like an SP provider edge (PE) nodes, which in turn will increases its operational complexity.

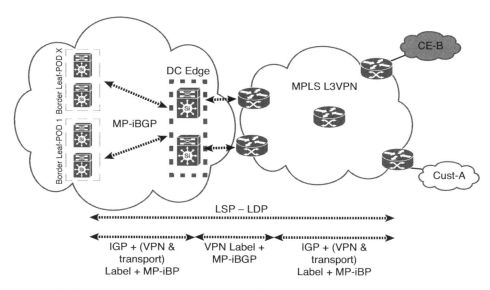

Figure 8-16 *MPLS at the Border Leafs of the DCN*

> **Note** MPLS over Clos is still a valid and doable design option; however it depends on the requirements and situation whether to consider it; see Table 8-3 for more detail.

> **Note** In this design, Layer 2 communications between different PODs can be facilitated by considering inter-POD L2VPN.

> **Note** In general, overlays can lead to increased operational complexity, because normally these overlays will require network operators to investigate the mapping of the virtual topology on top of the physical topology.

Layer 3-Based Transport (Nonoverlay)

This design model is based on the concept of using Layer 3 routing only to handle the packet forwarding across the Clos fabric network by extending Layer 3 routing across the leaf and spine nodes, as shown in Figure 8-17. Therefore, this model is not actually overlaid. Instead, it is based on an end-to-end routed network from leaf to leaf (top-of-rack [ToR] switches) over the spines. This design model offers an increased level of network scalability and stability by limiting Layer 2 flooding domains to the minimum (usually up to the ToR/leaf switches).

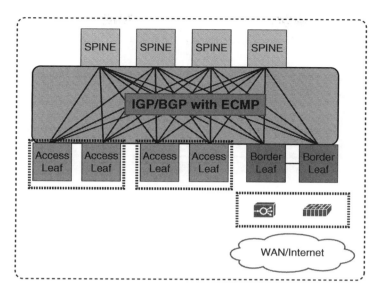

Figure 8-17 *Layer 3-Based Clos*

Furthermore, this design model facilitates to a high degree Clos architecture scale-out in large-scale DCNs. In addition, using one unified control plane protocol can significantly simplify overall network manageability and troubleshooting. Therefore, this routed Clos fabric architecture can support large-scale data centers that host tens of thousands of systems (physical or virtual). However, this design approach is more suitable for large-scale data centers where the highest priority is a stable and scalable network that can host extremely large number of servers (instead of using large Layer 2 adjacencies across the network) [61]. However, the degree of the network scalability and stability with this architecture is still dependent on the characteristic of the used Layer 3 control plane protocol and its design.

Typically, you can use either an interior gateway protocol (IGP) (such as link-state routing protocols) or BGP as the control plane protocol to provide the control plane routing and forwarding. However, link state requires some fine-tuning to the protocol to optimize its performance and reduce the amount of link-state flooding and processing overhead over such a topology (Clos). In addition, the shortest path first (SPF) algorithm limitations on Clos topology can add some design and operational complexities, because each leaf might appear as a transit path to reach a spine or another leaf switch.

In contrast, using BGP as the control plane protocol within the data center over the Clos fabric architecture, in particular external BGP (eBGP), can offer a more controlled, simplified, and scalable routed Clos fabric design as compared to IGP. However, this approach may introduce some limitations around network convergence time. As highlighted earlier, this design model is more suited for environments that do not require extending Layer 2 across different leaf nodes or PODs; therefore, if VM mobility is required in this architecture, you can use a MAC-in-IP overlay, which means another protocol to manage, and this translates into higher design and operational complexity in this case.

Table 8-3 compares the different transport options that you can use with the Clos DCN architecture covered in this section.

Table 8-3   *DCN Transport Protocol Options Comparison*

	MAC-in-MAC	Layer 3 Based	MAC-in-IP	MPLS
Fault domain	Large	Minimal	Moderate, depending on the tunnel (VTEP) termination point	Minimal with L3VPN, larger with L2VPN
Scalability	Large	Extremely Large when used with eBGP as the control plane	Very large when used with BGP as a control plane	Large
Encapsulation	Frame encapsulation	N/A	IP encapsulation	MPLS label
Support extended Layer 2 within a DC and multiple DCs	Yes	Requires an overly such as VxLAN or multitier Overlay Transport Virtualization (OTV)	Yes	Yes (L2VPN)
Underlay control-plane (static, IGP, BGP)	IS-IS	IGP/BGP	Any unicast routing	Any unicast routing
ECMP	Yes	Yes	Yes	Yes
Support host-based overlay	No	No (requires other protocols)	Yes	No (unless the end host can do MPLS encapsulation)
Requires staff routing knowledge	Not required	Advanced	Minimal	Advanced
Operational complexity	Low	Generally high, depending on the size and routing design	Moderate	Moderate to high, depending on the size and design (for example, L3VPN with L2VPN)

Note Dynamic fabric automation is a variation of the Clos architecture that offers automation and API northbound integration with the cloud orchestrator. For instance, with Cisco Dynamic Fabric Automation (DFA), when a VM is provisioned, the DFA leaf node autodetects the VM, and pulls and applies the policies associated with the VM on the connected port. The fabric tracks a VM and moves these port profiles within the fabric automatically [38]. The Cisco DFA fabric can apply this automation workflow to a similar physical server.

Comparison of Data Center Network Architectures

Table 8-4 compares the primary characteristics of each of the most common design models of DCNs available today and discussed earlier in this chapter.

Table 8-4 *DCN Architectures Comparison*

	Three-Tier Classic STP Based	Three-Tier mLAG Based	Clos Fabric Architected
Scalability	Limited. Usually each access node is limited to only 2x upstream nodes.	Limited. Each access node is limited to only 2x upstream nodes.	Can scale out up to the limit of the HW/SW of the underlay and overlay protocols, such as up to 32 upstream nodes (spines) (web scale).
Operational complexity	High (manage STP, FHRP LAG configuration, and so on)	Moderate. The larger the network, the more mLAG port channels to be created and managed.	Simple. No LAG or mLAG is required.*
Seamless Layer 2 communication	With this design model in large networks, access switches in different PODs can end up communicating via the L3 core.	With this design model in large networks, access switches in different PODs can end up communicating via the L3 core.	The nature of two-tier switch fabric Clos architecture supports large scale-out and end-to-end L2 communications between the leafs without L3 core in the path. (seamless end-to-end Layer 2)

Table 8-4   *continued*

	Three-Tier Classic STP Based	Three-Tier mLAG Based	Clos Fabric Architected
Performance and bandwidth efficiency	This design model offers the least because of STP limitations and the limited upstream switches and bandwidth aggregation toward the core.	This design model offers enhanced network performance and bandwidth capacity compared to STP based, but still has limited upstream switches (2x) and bandwidth aggregation toward the core.	This design model (two-tier leaf and spine) offers the optimal design model with regard to performance and increased bandwidth capacity (leaf to leaf).
Availability	In the event of aggregation switch failure, there will be usually 50 percent loss of the available bandwidth for each of the affected access switches.	In the event of aggregation switch failure, there will be usually 50 percent loss of the available bandwidth for each of the affected access switches.	If the design is based on 4x upstream switches (spines), the failure of a spine switch reduces the available bandwidth at the leaf switch by only 25 percent.
Convergence	Depends on the STP design, but in general this design model is lowest in terms of convergence time.	Fast. Failure of one mLAG member link or upstream switch will technically have minimal to zero impact.	Fast. Failure of leaf uplink or a spine switch will technically have minimal to zero impact
Layer 2 - VM mobility and distributed workload	Supported with limited scale (when access to access switch communicate via a Layer 3 node/ core switch).	Supported with limited scale (when access to access switch communicate via a Layer 3 node/core switch).	Seamless support end to end at a web scale.
Suitability	Small to medium DCs. Limited bandwidth requirements. Limited hosts connectivity. Flexibility requirements. Nonvirtualized and very limited scale of virtualized workload.	Small to medium DCs. More scalable bandwidth requirements. Flexible hosts connectivity. Nonvirtualized and limited scale of virtualized workload.	Large to very large scale (web scale). Highly scalable bandwidth. Flexible hosts connectivity. Nonvirtualized and virtualized workload.

* If pure Layer 3 routing is used as the Clos control plane, there will be added operational complexity in configuring and managing a large-scale routed network.

Note Network designers might sometimes need to integrate one of the modern DC designs discussed here, such as TRILL or VxLAN, with a DC environment that is based on a traditional design (STP based), which is common in migration scenarios. Therefore, in this type of scenario, one of the primary design principles that must be considered is that flooding domains (failure domains) have to be minimalized and contained. For instance, the classic Layer 2 VLANs of an existing DC LAN can terminate at the VxLAN gateway node that performs bridging and routing between the different DCN domains.

Data Center Interconnect

The concept of distributing business applications and services across geographically dispersed data centers has existed for years; it is not a new concept or a design approach. Primarily, it is driven by the need to maintain business resilience and provide reliable disaster recovery (DR) capabilities for the data center IT infrastructure and resources. The emergence of cloud computing has further covered the need for extremely robust network resilience strategies, addressing security, availability, and virtual machine (VM) mobility while maintaining the flexibility and agility of a cloud model. Cloud computing promises to offer services that can have dynamic resource allocation and are accessible from anywhere (over the Internet) in a completely virtualized on-demand environment. Accordingly, the availability of the cloud data center and its elements (network, computing, and storage) are critical to supporting business continuity.

The nature of a cloud data center built on a fully virtualized environment introduces some challenges to maintaining business continuity, in comparison to traditional data centers. For example, the physical components of the cloud data center (computing, network, and storage) may not all be located within the same physical location. Instead, they may be distributed across more than one physical location and interconnected over a transport mechanism that maintains an end-to-end path isolation. To achieve the desired level of data center business continuity, there must be a reliable DR plan and procedures in place.

Businesses and stakeholders are realizing the importance of business continuity. For instance, the loss of connectivity to a data center in a financial services business, for a few minutes, may cost the business hundreds of thousands of dollars. This makes considerations of a DR plan a common business requirement to achieve the desired level of business continuity during and after failure situations. Typically, disasters can be classified based on the degree and geographic coverage of the impact (local, metro, regional, or global) and can result from

- **Natural catastrophe:** Such as fire, flood, or earthquake

- **System outage:** Such as power outage at the Main Distribution Frame (MDF) that provides the external connection to the DC

- **Human error:** Such as misconfiguration, which may lead to bringing one or all interconnected data centers into a blackout situation

Based on the business's targeted level of continuity and data protection, you can use a different remote DR site model along with the appropriate DR solution. A remote DR site refers to the site to where some or all of the vital business operations and applications can be moved in the event of any outage (whether a planned or unplanned outage). Typically, a DR site is one that is dedicated to the data center's failover purposes, such as a secondary data center. Nonetheless, sometimes it is expensive for businesses to maintain a dedicated DR site. Therefore, these businesses consider other sites, such as a regional data center, with its primary function being to serve regional remote sites as the primary DC. At the same time, it operates as a DR data center for the centralized or primary data center.

In addition, some public cloud providers offer DR as service (DR-as-a-S). This service is for customers who do not need to build or dedicate a data center. These customers can benefit from this cost-effective approach, because the data center operator does not need to build and maintain cooling, power, cabling, and internal and external network connectivity. Moreover, data center operators that already have their own private cloud can consider what is known as a *hybrid cloud*. A hybrid cloud is where the DR site can be hosted by one of the public cloud providers as well, for the same purpose, while maintaining connectivity between the two cloud DCs using an intercloud solution.

Besides the remote DR site consideration, the DR solution should be selected based on how long the organization can wait for services to be restarted (in particular, the extent to which the business can afford to lose data after the failover happens). Should the business restart in a degraded mode, or must all services be fully available immediately after the switchover? Financial services normally require a recovery time objective (RTO) of less than one hour with a recovery point objective (RPO) equal to zero without a degraded mode [39]. This is a fairly widespread practice so that no transactions are lost. The data center interconnect (DCI) plays a primary role in reaching and delivering these requirements. Table 8-5 compares the typical DR models in terms of the levels of RTO and RPO each model can support; this relationship also shown in Figure 8-18.

Table 8-5 *DR Models*

DR Model	RTO	RPO	Operational Mode
Cold standby	High	High	Active-standby
Warm standby	Moderate	Moderate	Active-standby/active-active
Hot standby	Low	Low	Active-active

Note Business continuity (BC) is not analogous to DR. Typically, BC should answer the questions of "How can you keep the business running at the recovery site?" and "How can you eventually transfer business functions back to the primary site?" DR answers the question, "How can you recover/move services on the recovery site during and after a disaster or data center failure?" In other words, a DR plan is one component to achieving BC.

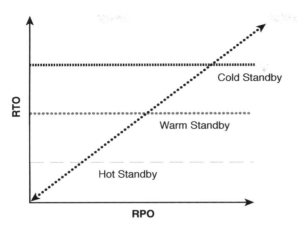

Figure 8-18 *DR Models and RTO-RPO Relationship*

Note Even though the cold standby has high RPO and RTO, it might not be suitable for a business that has systems capable of operating offline and storing data locally then replicating it later to the data center. In other words, network design decisions always depend on the business goals and needs and on the characteristics of the systems and applications used.

Note Although the focus of this section is on modern data centers based on virtualization and cloud services with VM mobility, all the design options and considerations discussed in this section apply to traditional data centers. In fact, with traditional data centers where little or no virtualization has taken place, the job is much easier because there is no VM mobility. Instead, the main focus is on selecting which DR approach to use, and how L3 routing is designed to address inbound and outbound traffic flow when the interconnected data centers are designed to work in either an active-standby or active-active manner.

Note BC aims to continue business activities (business as usual) after a disaster or failure. From the network point of view, this goal is to be achieved across two or more data centers where a redundant external network path (communication with the external users WAN, MAN, or Internet) is in place. The subsequent sections assume the external connection to the WAN or Internet is already in place (locally per DC) and focus on the design consideration of the DCI part and how to optimize traffic flows to the different DCs to meet BC goals.

DCI Building Blocks

The following elements are the primary functional components that comprise the DCI building block architecture to provide transport elasticity, flexibility, transparency, and resiliency between two or more sites:

- **DCI Connectivity**

  - **Extended LAN:** Provides transparent transport for application and operating system mobility that requires Layer 2 adjacency, such as geoclustering.

  - **Layer 3 based:** Provides the typical routed connectivity between the interconnected data centers and provides a reliable transport for workload mobility for the systems that support it over Layer 3.

  - **Hybrid:** This connectivity option is usually based on having a mixture of both Layer 3 and Layer 2 DCI, where the only LAN extension across the DCI is provisioned used for certain VLANs that require Layer 2 extension, while all other subnets will communicate over the DCI using the Layer 3 based DCI model.

- **Intra and inter-DC routing:** Provides remote site and end-user access to the DC resources, such as applications and cloud services, in addition to facilitating the communications between the segmented networks across the interconnected data centers. (Usually each DC should have its own WAN or Internet connectivity to external networks.)

- **Path optimization:** Enhances (ideally localizes) ingress and egress (south-north) traffic flows and server-to-server (east-west) workflows.

- **SAN extension:** Provides data access for applications (either locally or remotely) along with the desired data replication type (such as synchronous and asynchronous replication).

Figure 8-19 shows the conceptual view of the DCI building blocks.

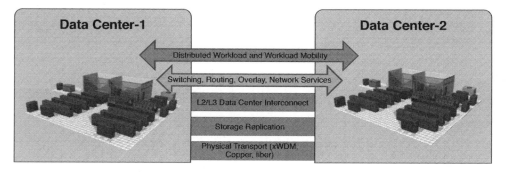

Figure 8-19 *DCI Building Blocks*

The design options, considerations, and drivers of each of the DCI functional components in the preceding list are covered in the subsequent sections.

DCI Connectivity Options

Workload mobility and distributed workload of the virtualized applications among data centers across dispersed geographic locations offer businesses and IT teams flexible efficiency to meet various operational requirements, such as data capacity expansion, workload allocation flexibility, seamless application and system migrations, disaster avoidance, and so on. The design of the DCI solution forms the foundation of today's interconnected data centers. Failure to meet the desired requirements or to understand how the different services and applications behave before, during, and after any failure event can take the entirety of the data centers out of service, as would be the case in a dual-active scenario when the applications are not designed to perform in this manner (active-active).

Simple VM mobility from one DC to another can introduce a blackout situation to the data centers or the DCI. Similarly, a lack of good understanding about how the various systems and applications are integrated and communicate with each other can also introduce a blackout situation. Therefore, the design of a DCI solution must address the DR and BC goals, in addition to workload functions (mobile or distrusted) between geographically diverse data centers, to ensure nonstop access to business-critical applications and information and to prevent complicating the design and operations of the data center.

From the DCI design point of view, the main drivers toward considering a Layer 2 or a routed DCI solution are the requirements supporting the elasticity of applications and storage access. Commonly, stretched Layer 2 (LAN) DCI is required to enable the transparent movement of VMs and the transparent access of stored data. However, this is not always the case. Therefore, the decision whether to go with a routed or with a Layer 2-based DCI solution is primarily derived from the requirements of the applications and systems at the higher layers to meet the overall BC goals. For example, it is important that network architects distinguish between workload mobility and distributed workload design requirements. Typically, with workload mobility, the moved VMs from one DC to another should maintain their IP information. This can be achieved by either extending the Layer 2 LAN segment over the DCI or by considering an IP mobility solution over a routed DCI, such as Locator/ID Separation Protocol (LISP).

The distributed workload, however, refers to the concept of geoclustering (the clustering of servers over DCI), which might not always be deployed as virtualized systems. Typical geoclustering systems require a nonroutable connectivity between the distributed systems for the heartbeat sessions, whereas the front-end virtual IP (VIP) of the cluster can follow the same concept of IP mobility or extend the LAN DCI to fail over after any failure event. In other words, besides understanding the business goals in terms of DR and BC, identifying systems and applications architectures to achieve these goals is a key point to achieve a successful DCI design [39, 40]. This section covers the various DCI connectivity options and highlights the strength and weaknesses of each.

Note   Although many modern data center architectures offering seamless workload mobility over long-distance DCI tend to support a robust DR level, mobility itself is not the DR solution. The DR plan can take advantage of VM mobility to optimize the overall desired BC goal, but there are many components other than VM mobility (for example, data replication, external connection failover, and geoclustering).

Note   This section does not intend to recommend one design or connectivity option over another. Nevertheless, it will analyze potential design and connectivity options and highlight the strengths and weaknesses of each. The best choice is always the one that meets business goals, DR/BC requirements, and the service and application requirements, which collectivity drive the design choice. Therefore, a good understanding of each design option and its components is essential.

Routed DCI

This design model is based on Layer 3 routed interconnection between the different data centers. In fact, this design model follows the same design concepts discussed in Chapter 4, "Enterprise Edge Architecture Design," in the "Enterprise Multihomed Internet Design Considerations" section.

Although extended Layer 2 (LAN) as a DCI solution is more common, this does not mean that it is the optimal or more reliable DCI design. In general, the routed DCI design model offers a simpler and more predictable design compared to the extended LAN model. However, as covered earlier, the design choice must always be derived from the upper-layer requirements (applications, workload, and virtualized and nonvirtualized) that align with the business DR and BC goals. Therefore, if the Layer 2 extension is technically not required to achieve the desired goals, the routed DCI can be considered in this case. The routed DCI can help to avoid several design and operational complexities (as discussed later in this chapter, along with the possible solutions). Furthermore, with the routed DCI model, fault domains will be contained within each site (fault-isolation principle). This offers a more stable and reliable DCI solution, as shown in Figure 8-20.

The DCI solution shown in Figure 8-20 reflects typical interconnected data centers over a routed DCI, where each site has its own IP range (either full range or a divided range). At the same time, each site advertises the other site's IP range (such as summary of the both site's IP range if its summarizable) for failover purposes. However, in some scenarios, the functional requirements of the interconnected DCs require each DC to provide connectivity to its local resources only in alignment with the architectures of the organization's applications.

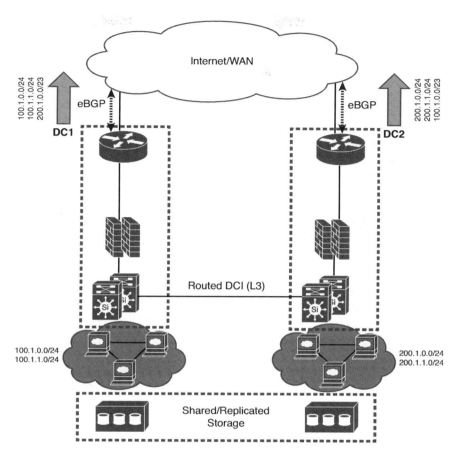

Figure 8-20 *Routed DCI*

From the networking design point of view, this means that the DCI must not be used for failover of traffic coming from the external networks (WAN/Internet) and that the load distribution for external connections should be controlled via higher layers, such as global load balancers (also known as *global site selector* [GSS]). Consequently, in this design approach, each DC location will advertise only its own local IP range. This ensures that each DC will provide connectivity only to the local resources and will not provide connectivity to the other DC during some failure scenarios. Data replication between the DCs is handled by the storage design and hypothetically should ensure that both data centers can have valid and updated replicas of the data that aligns with the BC goals by achieving the desired level of RTO and RPO. This example demonstrates how the entire typical routed DCI design can change based on business, functional, or application requirements. Another example is that some data center operators advertise the same IP ranges from multiple data centers to offer an "anycast" style of load distribution; traffic will usually always prefer the closest data center in scenarios where multiple data centers exist across different geographic areas and advertise the exact same IP subnets.

As with any design solution, network designers must understand the different aspects of the routed DCI design to be able to identify when and why to position it as a reliable DCI solution for a given DCN design (ideally based on the top-down approach). Table 8-6 summarizes the main strengths and design concerns of the routed DCI.

Table 8-6   *Routed DCI Strengths and Design Concerns*

Strengths	Design Concerns
Offers more stable DCI solution	Workload mobility with IP mobility can add design and operational complexity.
Provides a scalable solution that can support multiple interconnected DCNs	Not all geoclustering supports routed DCI.
Offers more deterministic control of ingress and egress traffic flows to avoid and minimize asymmetrical routing issues	May lead to DCI congestion in the event of one DC external link failure (WAN/Internet).
Supports VM mobility with an IP mobility solution	Active-active can be a challenging design to achieve if it is not aligned well with other services and components at higher layers such as global site load balancers.
Supports active-active and active-standby interconnected DCs design model	

Layer 3 DCI Connectivity Options

The provisioning of a routed DCI connectivity between data centers can be achieved with different types of layers 3 transport mechanisms, including the following:

- MPLS L3VPN WAN

- Tunneling over the Internet

- Dedicated link such as dark fiber configured as a routed link

- L3 over MPLS L2VPN (E-line, E-LAN)

Although all these connectivity types will deliver a routed DCI, each one has its strengths and weaknesses with regard to a routed DCI solution. Table 8-7 compares the primary design aspects of each of the connectivity types listed here.

Table 8-7 *Routed DCI Connectivity Options Comparison*

Connectivity	Strengths	Weaknesses/Concerns
MPLS L3VPN	Scalable. Seamless end-to-end QoS support Simplifies routing over the WAN with reduced operational complexity.	Achieving path visualization (isolation) over the DCI can be a challenging task because it is controlled by the WAN provider. Using dual providers for high availability (HA) can increase operational complexity. Quality of service (QoS) differentiation or high bandwidth can add additional cost to the DC operators.
Tunneling over the Internet	Offers a low-cost connectivity. Simple, quick to set up. Fully controlled by the DC operator. Can be secured to some extent with IPsec.	Low end-to-end service reliability. Higher latency. Security and compliance concerns. Bandwidth limitation for any DCI that needs gigabits of bandwidth.
Dedicated link (for example, dark fiber)	High bandwidth. Full control of routing, virtualization, QoS and security setup Highly reliable (ideally with protected/redundant links).	High capex. Limited geographic coverage. Higher opex to operate both physical and control plane.
L3 over MPLS L2VPN	High bandwidth with lower cost compared to other options. Full control of routing, virtualization, and security setup. Supports end-to-end seamless QoS. Global Carrier Ethernet can support global DCI between countries.	Weaknesses depend on the deployed L2VPN technologies (Virtual Private LAN Services [VPLS], Hierarchical VPLS [H-VPLS], or Ethernet VPN [EVPN]).* Apart from EVPN, there is active-active multihoming limitation with VPLS. VPLS with link state such Open Shortest Path First (OSPF) can introduce operational complexities.

*The limitations from the L2VPN itself, such as MAC scalability, are not an issue with this design model because the edge nodes are deployed in Layer 3 mode (routed connectivity).

Layer 2 DCI

As discussed earlier, data center applications and services must always drive the design decisions of the DCI solution in terms of distance (latency), capacity, and network communication required (L2 versus L3). In today's data centers, there are several systems, especially around the clustering of servers (geoclustering) and system virtualization, that mandate stretching Layer 2 LANs between the interconnected data centers. This stretching enables the resiliency and clustering mechanisms offered by the different applications at the web, application, and database layers to achieve specific design goals, such as application resiliency and workload allocation flexibility via workload mobility and distributed workload across multiple data centers. In today's data centers, many system virtualization vendors require nonroutable (Layer 2) adjacency between the distributed workloads as well to achieve VM mobility, as shown in Figure 8-21.

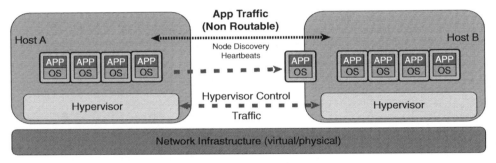

Figure 8-21 *LAN extension for distrusted workload and VM mobility*

Therefore, LAN extension between data centers became one of the most popular DCI solutions even though it is one of the most complex designs for several reasons, which are covered in this section (as are with the recommended solutions and optimization techniques later in this chapter). Table 8-8 summarizes the main strengths and design concerns of the Layer 2-based DCI.

Table 8-8 *Layer 2-Based DCI Strengths and Design Concerns*

Strengths	Design Concerns
Supports distributed workload over the WAN/Internet.	Deign complexity, because special design considerations are required to overcome asymmetrical routing and what is also known as *traffic trombone* or *ping-pong traffic*.
Supports live VM migration (VM nobility) that disassociates IP/VM from a physical location.	*Dual-active* situations for the distributed workloads and network security services such as firewall after can lead to a serious outage of interconnected data centers.

Table 8-8 *continued*

Strengths	Design Concerns
Any IP (physical or virtual) entity can retain its IP address when moved between DCs.	Operational complexity, due the increased scope of the failure domain (large Layer 2 domain), and therefore special consideration is required with regard to Layer 2 flooding.
Supports active-standby and active-active DR models.	Active-active is a challenging design to achieve because it has to align well with other services and components at higher layers such as local FHRP, global site load balancers.
Supports stretched network services and security appliances such as load balancers and firewalls between interconnected data centers.	
Facilitates data center migration projects to maintain minimal to zero downtime of resource availability.	

Layer 2 DCI Connectivity Options

Today's DCI solutions, which are capable of providing LAN extension to meet modern data center requirements, can be classified into three primary connectivity models:

- **Dark-fiber based:** Typically, this DCI model is applicable to DC operators that own the physical layer (interconnect), which offers them the freedom to enable any of the desired solutions appropriate for their requirements.

- **SP controlled:** This type of DCI connectivity is based on the fact the DCI (WAN/MAN) provider deploys and controls the service for the DC customers (LAN extension), such as E-Line and E-LAN services.

- **DC operator controlled (overlay):** This type of DCI is usually based on an overlaid LAN extension solution, where the DC operator deploys and controls the emulated Layer 2 service over an IP transport such as VxLAN, OTV, and L2VPN, over GRE.

Note Technically, any of the listed Layer 2 technologies and protocols can be enabled over a dark fiber; all are valid and proven solutions. However, this section focuses on enabling classic 802.1Q over a dark fiber. The other technologies, like VxLAN and OTV, are discussed as a transport agnostic where any IP transport is applicable, including dark fiber configured as routed link. An L2VPN deployed by the DC operator, however, follows the same concept with only one fundamental difference: The underlay transport must be MPLS enabled. You can either use GRE for this purpose or you can enable MPLS at the link level in case of dark fiber.

Layer 2 DCI solutions (SP controlled versus DC operator controlled) can be divided into two primary layers:

■ The service layer is the actual extended Layer 2 services; it is almost always between the customer edges (CEs) facing the PEs.

■ The network layer represents the service emulation across the IP/MPLS network (overlay), as shown in Figure 8-22. This layer varies based on who is deploying and controlling the service (SP controlled versus DC operator controlled)

Note The services offered by SPs are almost always L2VPN based, whereas the ones that are deployed and controlled by the DC operator (CE side) can be any DCI overlaid solution.

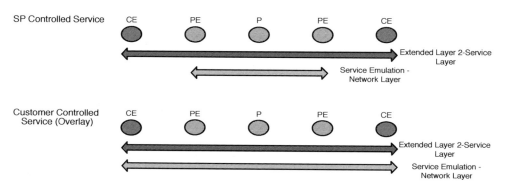

Figure 8-22 *Layer 2 DCI Service Provisioning Models*

For the purpose of simplicity, this section covers the characteristics of these Layer 2 DCI solutions on a per-technology basis, as listed here:

■ Dark fiber based

■ Layer 2 over Metro Ethernet (ME) transport such as E-line and E-LAN, including the following:

  ■ SP provisioned and controlled ME

  ■ DC operator provisioned and controlled ME over any IP transport

■ TRILL/FabricPath-based DCI

■ EoMPLSoGRE (OTV) over any IP transport

■ VxLAN over any IP transport

Dark Fiber-Based DCI

This DCI solution is based on a direct physical dark fiber link controlled by the data center operator. With this solution, the DC operator has the freedom to run any of the protocols listed earlier to establish the DCI connectivity. However, this section focuses on the usually extended LAN over 802.1Q link (dark fiber) along with mLAG, as shown in Figure 8-23. Although the following design enables data center operators to use all the mLAG member links to carry the traffic passing between the two data centers, several design optimizations must be considered, such as FHRP localization and Layer 2 flooding control (DCI path optimization, covered in greater detail later in this chapter). In addition, as covered earlier in this book, every traffic flow normally uses a single LAG/mLAG member link; this means that each traffic flow will be limited to a single member link capacity (unless the *flowlet* concept is used).[4]

Note   The dynamic load-balancing capability available today in Cisco Application Centric Infrastructure (ACI) "adjusts the traffic allocations according to congestion levels. It measures the congestion across the available paths and places the flows on the least congested paths, which results in an optimal or near optimal placement of the data, DLB can be configured to place traffic on the available uplinks using the granularity of flows or of flowlets." [84]

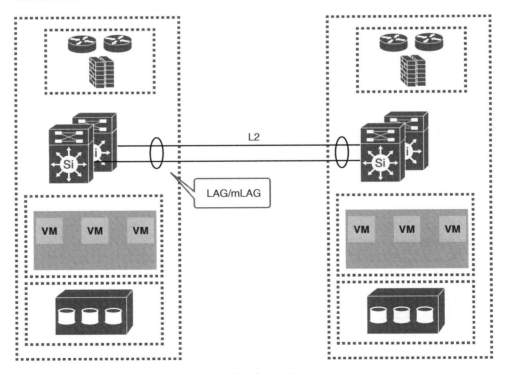

Figure 8-23   *802.1Q Layer 2 over Dark Fiber DCI*

4.   "Dynamic Load Balancing Without Packet Reordering," IETF draft, chen-nvo3-load-banlancing, http://www.ietf.org

Besides the design challenges and the operational complexity that can be introduced to the DCN by the extended LAN across multiple locations, interconnecting more than two data centers over 802.1Q dark fiber links in a triangle or square topology can lead to serious design complexity and operational inefficiencies because STP is the Layer 2 control protocol in this particular design model. This means that there will be inefficient utilization of the links associated with suboptimal routing, which can be very sensitive in data center environments that require low-latency communications across the DCI. As shown in Figure 8-24, if the hosts belonging to VLAN X distributed across DC1 and DC2 need to communicate, traffic has to traverse DC3 because of STP blocking.

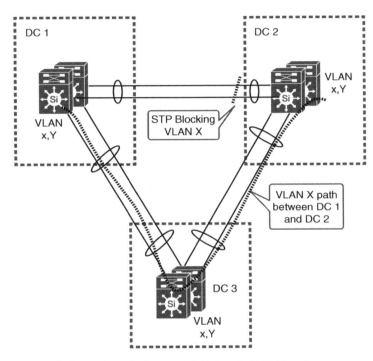

Figure 8-24 *STP Blocking with Triangle DCI Topology*

Although this can be fixed with STP traffic engineering (where network operators can control which link can be blocked for which VLAN from the STP point of view), this will introduce a high degree of operational complexity and limit optimal communications across to data centers only. This issue can be resolved by either considering a protocol that does not rely on STP such as TRILL, VPLS, or VxLAN (which is beyond the scope of this subsection) or by introducing the concept of *core DCI* to transform the design model into one that is more flexible and scalable to interconnect multiple data centers, as shown in Figure 8-25.

Core DCI is based on introducing two core switches deployed in switch clustering mode, ideally distributed across two different data centers to avoid introducing any single point of failure to the design. The physical connectivity of the underlying fiber, however, should be provisioned over an x wavelength-division multiplexing (xWDM) ring, where the logical point-to-point links from each DC to the core DC are created via xWDM transport lambda or wavelength over the optical ring. Ultimately, this will create a logical start topology that will eliminate STP limitations and offer a flexible and reliable DCI solution, as shown in Figure 8-25.

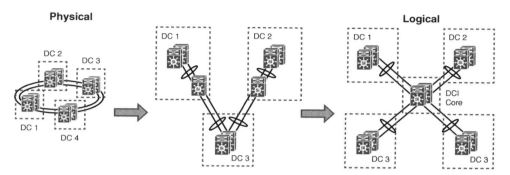

Figure 8-25   *Dark Fiber DCI over xWDM: Logical Star Topology*

However, in addition to the fact that this design can be an expensive option in terms of capex and opex, not every location (geographic area) has xWDM available. Therefore, these design constraints have to be considered during the planning and design optimization stage to avoid providing impractical design recommendations. (An *impractical* design is one that is technically valid but practically cannot be deployed because of certain design constraints.)

Layer 2 DCI over ME Transport

This design option is primarily based on emulating a Layer 2 LAN over an IP MPLS-enabled infrastructure, as discussed earlier in this chapter. The most common connectivity models for the data center DCI solution are either the E-Line or E-LAN connectivity models.

This DCI connectivity design option can be provisioned either by the SP or by the DC operator, as described here:

- **SP controlled:** In this scenario, the SP owns the MPLS infrastructure and emulates the Layer 2 transport transparently to the DC side for the DCI (E-line, E-LAN).

- **DC operator controlled:** In this scenario, the DC operators (enterprise or SP DC) design and set up their own overlaid ME solution, such as E-Line or E-LAN, over any IP transport with the aid of a tunneling mechanism to enable MPLS for the pseudo wires (PWs) of the emulated LAN, such as VPLS-over-GRE-over-IP. Similarly, if the DC operator has a dark fiber-based DCI MPLS, it can be enabled across this DCI. Run either Ethernet over MPLS (EoMPLS) or VPLS based on the physical layout.

Furthermore, as discussed earlier in Chapter 6, "Service Provider MPLS VPN Services Design," EVPN and Advanced VPLS (A-VPLS) can provide DCI capabilities similar to dark fiber with mLAG but on a larger scale over an emulated L2 LAN and with a cheaper price, as shown in Figure 8-26. In addition, EVPN with PBB can meet very large-scale public cloud-grade DCI requirements (scales to millions of MACs) with a simplified and optimized control plane (BGP based) combined with the PBB MAC hiding principle.

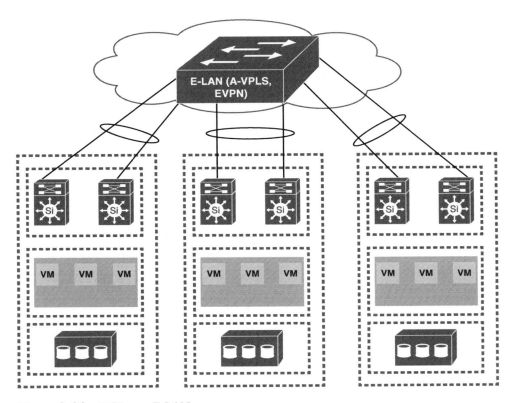

Figure 8-26 *DCI over E-LAN*

TRILL-FabricPath-Based DCI

As discussed earlier, the MDT in FabricPath (FP) controls the forwarding of multidestination traffic. Normally, a root for each MDT is assigned per FP topology in a multitopology environment. From the perspective of design performance and efficiency within a single LAN/DCN environment, this is not a concern because the traffic is still within the boundary of the same high-speed LAN/DCN.

In contrast, when FP is extended over the DCI, this behavior can impact the entire DCI solution simply because the multidestination traffic (BUM traffic) will traverse the DCI link all the way to the MDT root that might be residing at the remote DC. This will result in high utilization (most probably congestion) to the DCI link, especially if there are applications using multicast. In other words, the placement of the MDT root with FabricPath enabled over DCI is critical. The scenario in Figure 8-27 shows how multidestination traffic from host B's access switch (for example, multicast or unknown unicast) is sent back to DC1 to the MDT root then back to DC2, even though both host A and host B are located within the same physical data center.

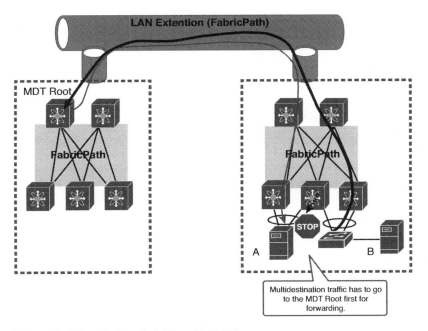

Figure 8-27 *FP-Based DCI and MDT Issue*

However, TRILL/FP can be considered a valid and feasible DCI solution in scenarios where the distance between the interconnected DCs is short, with connectivity over high-capacity links, such as 10/40/100-Gbps interconnections (ideally overprovisioned). In this case, traffic trombone may not be an issue, and TRILL/FabricPath can offer a scalable design of multiple interconnected data centers in terms of number of sites and MAC address table scaling, along with failure domain containment, as shown in Figure 8-28.

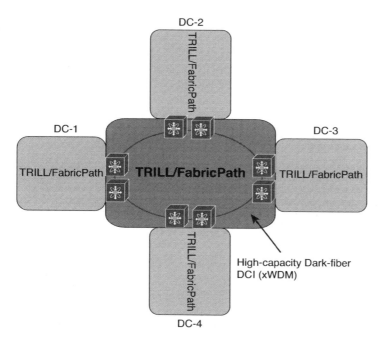

Figure 8-28   *TRILL/FP Multiple Data Center DCI*

Overlay Transport Virtualization

Overlay Transport Virtualization (OTV) is an IP-based functionality designed by Cisco Systems specifically to offer simplified and scalable Layer 2 extension capabilities over any transport infrastructure, such as Layer 2, Layer 3, or label switched. OTV introduced the concept of *MAC routing*, where IS-IS, as a control plane protocol, exchanges MAC reachability information between OTV edge nodes, providing seamless LAN extension functionality. Furthermore, OTV provides a native built-in multihoming capability, increasing the HA of the overall solution.

As a result, OTV provides the capability to extend Layer 2 segments over multiple DCI edges of multiple data centers without introducing any loop or unicast flooding that can impact the effectiveness of the DCI solution and the overall stability of the interconnected data centers. Concurrently, STP is kept contained within each data center domain, as shown in Figure 8-29. Therefore, using OTV (when applicable and the choice is available) over any transport, including dark fiber, to provide LAN extension can simplify and improve designing, implementing, and maintaining the DCI solution, especially when multiple data centers need to be interconnected.

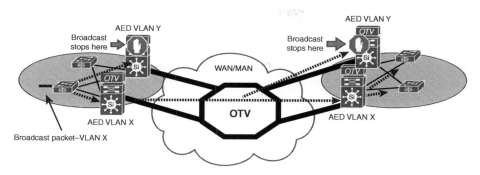

Figure 8-29 *OTV-Based DCI*

OTV selects an authoritative edge device (AED) for each group of the extended VLANs to control the MAC address advertisement for these VLANs and the ingress and egress traffic forwarding for these VLANs per site. As shown in Figure 8-29, only the AED of VLAN X will forward broadcast traffic sourced from the local site across the OTV DCI. Similarly, only the AED of VLAN X at the remote site will forward the broadcast traffic internal to VLAN. This capability offers an optimized behavior for an extended LAN over a DCI (mitigate the impact of broadcast storms across the DCI).

There are some scenarios involving large data centers with several PODs interconnected over Layer 3 links (such as Layer 3-based Clos fabric) per DC. In these types of scenarios, if the DC operator needs to extend Layer 2 VLANs across multiple PODs within the same DC and across multiple DCs in different regions, an overlay solution is required to achieve this, as shown in Figure 8-30. With the typical flat OTV design, this can be a challenging design, especially if many DC sites need to be interconnected. The OTV has limits in terms of maximum supported sites to be interconnected; this number varies based on the platform/software release.

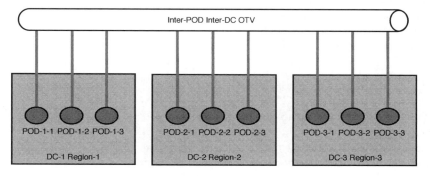

Figure 8-30 *Single-Tier OTV Limitation*

By introducing the multitier OTV design approach, network designers can accommodate the requirements of extending Layer 2 within each DC (across the different PODs) and at a global level (across different data centers in different regions) [60]. This design can overcome scaling limitations with regard to the supported number of interconnected sites with OTV and achieve a more structured Layer 2 extension, where VLANs can be extended selectively between the different tiers/regions, as shown in Figure 8-31. In spite of these advantages, this design approach requires careful path optimization considerations, which may lead to increased design and operational complexity. (The more data centers to be interconnected, the more complex to design and manage.)

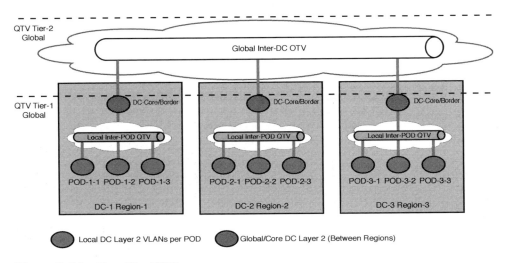

Figure 8-31   *Two-Tier OTV*

VxLAN-Based DCI

The IETF standard VxLAN was created and commonly used as a data center fabric overlay protocol to facilitate and optimize modern data center performance and agility in response to virtualized and cloud-based data center requirements. In VxLAN, VMs can be moved anywhere within the DC, because of abstraction between the location of the VM/application within the DC and the physical access/leaf switch and port VM mobility. VxLAN adds simplicity, transparency to applications, and flexibility to modern Clos fabric architectures; in addition, it enhances its ability to scale an extremely large number of VMs/MACs, especially when an MP-BGP EVPN control plane is used for VxLAN.

BGP as a control plane, together with VxLAN headend replication, can optimize VxLAN behavior with regard to multidestination traffic for MAC learning (broadcast and unknown unicast), especially as the behavior has become like Layer 3 routing (MAC learning is based on MAC address advertisement). Flooding will be eliminated unless there is a host that has not advertised or learned MAC, and only in this case will the typical Layer 2 flooding be used. At the time of this writing, VxLAN began to be considered a DCI solution, especially the unicast mode of VxLAN, because it can be more controllable at the DCI edge (can be policed more deterministically than multicast mode). This is applicable to any of the VxLAN design models (host based or network based), as shown in Figure 8-32.

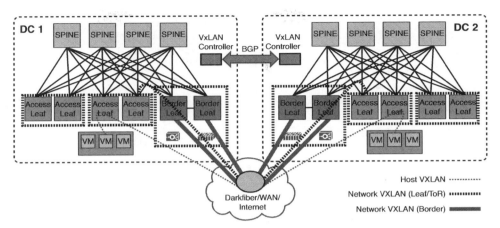

Figure 8-32 *VxLAN-Based DCI*

Note The placement of the functionality of a VxLAN controller with BGP (EVPN) as a control plane (where all the hosts' MAC addresses are hosted and updated) can vary from vendor to vendor and from solution to solution. For example, it can be placed at the spine nodes of the Clos architecture, as well as cloud be placed at the virtualized (software-based) controller, such as the Cisco nexus 1000v virtual supervisor module VSM. It also can be used as a route reflector to exchange VTEP list between multiple VSMs.

Note Technically, you can use all the VxLAN models discussed earlier (host and network based) at the same time. However, from a design point of view, this can add design complexity and increase operational complexity. Therefore, it is always recommended to keep it simple and start with one model that can achieve the desired goal.

Currently, one of the challenges of using VxLAN as a DCI solution is the behavior of the distributed controller across the two DCs following a DCI failure event (split-brain) and after DCI link recovery. In addition, considerations about the VxLAN gateway location (localized versus at a remote location) can impact the design. However, at the time of this writing, advancements in VxLAN are increasing rapidly. Therefore, it is quite possible that new features and capabilities will be available in the near future to make VxLAN a more robust DCI solution.

Note The scope of each DC VxLAN can be contained within each DC locally, while the terminated VxLAN VTEPs at the DC/SP border nodes can be extended across the SP network that has EVPN enabled. Each VxLAN VNI is mapped to a unique EVPN instance (VNI-to-EVI 1:1 mapping) to maintain end-to-end path separation per VxLAN. This design offers a scalable, integrated DCI solution that takes advantage of both solutions in scenarios where EVPN is already in place as a DCI and the DC operator is deploying VxLAN within each DC,[5] as shown in Figure 8-33.

5. IETF draft, boutros-l2vpn-vxlan-evpn-xx, http://www.ietf.org.

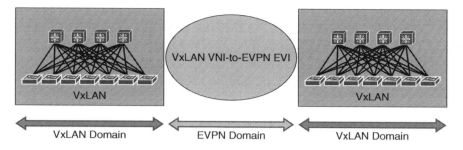

Figure 8-33   *VxLAN over EVPN*

Each of the preceding DCI solutions has different characteristics and strengths and weaknesses. Table 8-9 compares the DCI solutions from different design aspects.

Table 8-9   *DCI Connectivity Options Comparison*

Design Considerations	802.1Q over Dark Fiber	E-Line	E-LAN	EoGREoMPLS (OTV)	VxLAN
Scalability (number of sites)	Limited (expensive)	Limited	High	Moderate	Limited
Transport independence	No	No (requires MPLS)	No (requires MPLS)	Yes	Yes
Multihoming and end-to-end loop prevention	Yes (limited between 2 sites with mLAG)	Yes (limited to 2 sites with mLAG)	Yes	Yes	Depends on the underlay DCI (for example, over mLAG)
Flow-based multipathing and load balancing	Yes (limited between 2 sites with mLAG)	Yes (PW EVPN based)	Yes (EVPN based)	No (load balancing VLAN based)	Yes - Depends on the underlay DCI (for example, over mLAG)
End-host detection	Flood and learn	Flood and learn (EVPN based will be localized flood and learn with Address Resolution Protocol [ARP] suppression.)	Flood and learn (EVPN based will be localized flood and learn with ARP suppression.)	Flood and learn locally and MAC routing across the DCI	Flood and learn (EVPN based will be localized flood and learn with ARP suppression.)

Table 8-9 *continued*

Design Considerations	802.1Q over Dark Fiber	E-Line	E-LAN	EoGREoMPLS (OTV)	VxLAN
End-host reachability and distribution	Flood and learn	Flood and learn (EVPN based will be MP-BGP EVPN.)	Flood and learn (EVPN based will be MP-BGP EVPN.)	MAC routing (IS-IS based) over the DCI	Flood and learn (EVPN based will be MP-BGP EVPN.)
Localized L3 GW	No (requires manual filtering)	No (requires manual filtering)	No (requires manual filtering)	Yes (feature to turn on)	No - requires manual filtering
Location identifier	Port ID	VCID	VCID + VSI/ EVI	OTV edge node IP	VTEP IP
Host identifier	C-MAC	C-MAC	C-MAC	C-MAC	C-MAC
Site independence (STP, flood domain)	No	No	No	Yes	No
Multivendor support	Yes	Yes	Yes	Cisco proprietary	Yes
Operation complexity	High	High*	Moderate*	moderate	Moderate to high**
Commonly deployed***	Yes	Yes	Yes	Yes	No

* Operational complexity here has different layers. The first layer relates to the emulated solution itself, which depends on who is deploying and managing the solution. For example, if the VPLS solution is an enterprise self-deployed solution, the complexity is relevant to the enterprise and vice versa. The second layer is related to managing an extended LAN across two or more locations (large fault domain), which can add many complexities. Because of these complexities, the second layer requires careful planning and design for path optimization, as covered in the following section.

** The larger a VxLAN fault domain scope, the more complex to operate.

*** This point can be relevant to staff knowledge and expertise availability.

DCI Design Considerations

The complexity of designing data center interconnect solutions does not only pertain to the selection of the right DCI connectivity option (for example, Layer 2 or Layer 3). Several other components and considerations must be taken into account to achieve an optimal and reliable design. It is obvious from the design options discussed in the previous section that Layer 2 DCI has a wider range of connectivity options. At the same time, its design is the most challenging one. Therefore, it requires a careful and structured planning and design approach.

To achieve an optimal DCI design that is business driven and supports current and future requirements, network architects and designers must have a good understanding of the business goals and drivers with regard to BC. This is to be followed by a good understanding of the applications and services within the data center and its architecture in terms of communications and network requirements (for example, multitier applications, data replication in use, and bandwidth and latency requirements).

For instance, if you are designing a data center that hosts public services, such as Internet banking services and applications, traffic spikes can increase rapidly because of an extremely large number of sessions, which are unpredictable to some extent. In contrast, designing a data center to host HR applications for a large-scale organization is more predictable in terms of the number of sessions. This relates to the expected design scale and bandwidth requirements to understand what these applications require (bandwidth, latency) and how they will behave during and after any DC failure scenario. In other words, the top-down design approach must be followed during the planning and design stages to achieve a successful DCI solution, as summarized in Figure 8-34.

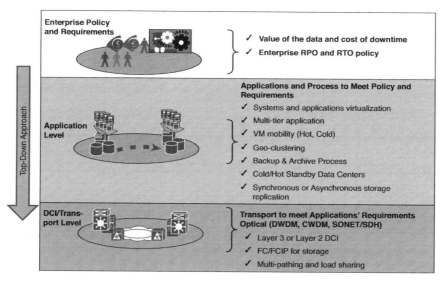

Figure 8-34 *DCI Design: Top-Down Approach*

The previous section focused more on DCI connectivity options and their characteristics (the focus was individually per DCI option). This section, however, focuses on the important design aspects of a DCI as a solution by highlighting the limitations and challenges and the recommended solutions that you can use to optimize the design. In general, an ideal data center interconnect design must consider the design aspects in Table 8-10 to achieve a scalable, stable, reliable, and flexible business-driven DCI solution.

Table 8-10 *DCI Design Considerations*

Design Aspects	Design Considerations
Control plane hierarchy and federation within and across domains	Avoid merging large networks' DCN control planes for both Layer 2 and Layer 3 by clearly delineated fault domain boundaries. (For instance, STP must be constrained within the local DC, also IGP flooding domains should be contained within each DC boundary)
Storage/data protection	Storage-area network (SAN) extension method to facilitate data replication between the interconnected sites to maintain the desired RTO and RPO levels.
Reliable DCI solution*	Ideally to increase the DCI solution reliability and efficiency between two or more data centers, there should be loop-free redundant paths connected to redundant edge nodes/
Resiliency	Ability of the DCI to fail over to a redundant component following any failure event.
Path optimization (to support workload mobility and geoclustering)	Elimination or reduction of traffic trombone to the minimal, ideally by considering the following: Outbound: FHRP localization per DC for localized default gateway services Inbound: An intelligent path redirection such as LISP or GSS to localize ingress traffic
Flexible	Ability to adapt to business and technology changes such as support virtualization, multitenancy, and SDN.
Scalable**	Ability to support growth in terms of traffic volume, hosts, and the number of interconnect DCs through the selected DCI connectivity option and fault-isolation techniques

* The level of the DCI reliability and fault tolerance can vary from business to business based on different factors such as service availability, service level agreement (SLA), and the impact of application downtime on the core business functions.

** This also varies and depends on the targeted organization, goals, and scale; in other words, scalable DCI is not a must for each solution.

This section covers the following design considerations with regard to DCI solution design:

- SAN extension
- Path optimization techniques with DCI
- Network and Security Services Placement

SAN Extension

The protection of the data via replication, caching, or backup is foundational to achieving the desired level of DR, BC, and business resilience (BR), and must take into account the RTO and PRO levels required by the business. Figure 8-35 describes the relationship between DR, BC, BR and the level of data protection.

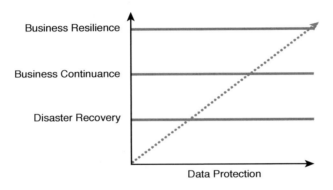

- Business Resilience: Continued operation of business during a failure.
- Business Coninuance Restoration of business after a failure.
- Disaster Recovery Protecting data through off site data replication and backup.

Figure 8-35   *DR, BC, BR and Data Protection*

Consequently, understanding the required or in-use data protection mechanism (for example, replication, caching) and how the application uses the storage is key to planning and designing a DCI solution. For example, some virtualization solutions are designed in a way that when a VM moves from one data center to another, the VM will continue use the storage located at the source/home data center.

In addition, moving application members across data center locations should not break the application. For instance, applications residing on top of the moved VMs need storage access (for example, database), as shown in Figure 8-36. Therefore, the storage design and replication can significantly impact the performance of the DCI. The dashed line in Figure 8-36 illustrates the scenario in which a moved VM continues to access data via the remote storage over the DCI link. The (nondotted) line shows the optimized solution in which the moved VM uses local storage when possible.

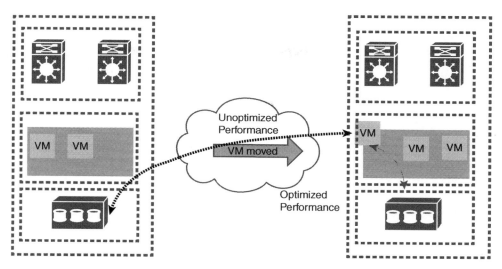

Figure 8-36 *The Impact of Storage Access on DCI Design*

Understanding this behavior can impact the DCI connectivity option selection in terms of distance (latency) and capacity.

Synchronous Versus Asynchronous Data Replication

Synchronous and asynchronous are the primary methods of data replications used in a majority of today's data centers; each has its own characteristic and influence to the overall DCI design:

- **Synchronous data replication:** With this method, an application receives the acknowledgment of I/O completion when both the main and secondary sites are updated. This method offers almost zero data loss and very fast recovery time from failures that can occur at the main site. Appropriately, it is also known as the *zero data loss replication method* (zero RPO). A potential downside of this method is cost, because it can be an expensive choice with distance limitations because of its high-bandwidth and low-latency requirements.

- **Asynchronous data replication:** Based on this method, an application receives the acknowledgment of I/O completion once the main disk is updated, while the copy continues to the remote disk array. Because the data is replicated to the remote array after the I/O is acknowledged as completed to the host, the remote disk array can be located anywhere, virtually or physically, at any distance. However, this method has a higher risk of data loss if the DC goes down before the data is completely replicated.

Furthermore, the distance between the interconnected data centers can influence to a large extent the selection of the data replication method that you can use on the disk arrays of the connected data centers, because the distance almost always impacts the response time (latency), which in turn will impact the maximum I/O per second (IOPS) performance across the interconnected data centers. However, if the application is designed to tolerate some IOPS, the distance impact may be reduced.

From the network and DCI design point of view, regardless of which method applications are operating with (synchronous or asynchronous), the design must identify the used method or methods [41,72]. Concurrently, it must take into account how the methods can impact the DCI design, especially with regard to factors such as bandwidth, latency, and distance. These factors must all collectively act as a solution to meet the DR and BC goals, from a business point of view.

Figure 8-37 summarizes the most common SAN extension options.

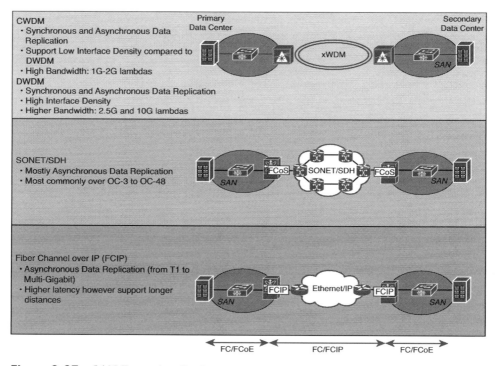

Figure 8-37 *SAN Extension Options*

Note The highlighted data replication methods and each SAN extension option in Figure 8-37 are based on very generic link or application characteristics. However, these are not absolute, because as discussed earlier in this section, it can change based on various factors such as distance, latency, bandwidth, application attributes, and so on.

DCI Path Optimization Techniques

As covered earlier in this chapter, designing a DCI solution is one of the most challenging design tasks. For instance, selecting a DCI connectivity option, such as E-LAN, does not mean the network engineers can deploy it and everything will work fine to achieve the desired goals. In fact, selecting the DCI connectivity option is only the foundation of the DCI solution design. In other words, network designers should consider the behavior of the other components in the higher layers of the data center (storage, workload, applications, security services) when this DCI is enabled and when workload is moved from one location to another.

Throughout this process, several other considerations must be kept in mind. These include the targeted design goal of the DC (such as active-active versus active-standby) and the method through which external users should access the data center resources (ingress and egress traffic flow considerations). Therefore, the network designer needs to perform what is commonly known as *DCI path optimization*.

This section covers the different design considerations and techniques that must be taken into account when designing a DCI solution to optimize the traffic flow. In general, the traffic flow of DCNs can be categorized into three main categories:

- **User to host:** This traffic flow usually refers to ingress traffic sourced from external or internal users to the local data center resources. The entry point of this traffic flow is normally controlled by the routes advertised by the DC network edge node.

- **Host to user:** This traffic flow represents the return traffic or sessions from the server to the external users. The first exit point is controlled by the server's Layer 3 gateways, usually the FHRP VIP.

- **Host to host:** This traffic flow represents the traffic flowing between hosts within the same physical DC or between interconnected DCs over a DCI link, such as a multitier application. (With workload mobility, this is also known as *east-west traffic flow*.)

In data center types of networks, packets often have to traverse multiple network services and security nodes in both ingress and egress directions (depending on the detailed design) before any given packet reaches its targeted destination (whether an internal host or an external user). These nodes are most commonly load balancers, firewalls, web application firewalls, intrusion prevention/detection systems (IPS/IDS), and DC edge routers. If you fail to take these nodes along the path into consideration, the entire data center design can be broken.

To a large extent, a good understanding and analysis of the three primary traffic flow types mentioned earlier can enhance the design by optimizing the path any traffic flow should take to avoid overloading the DCI link and breaking some application requirements. For example, asymmetrical routing can either lead to black-holing the traffic because of some security nodes in the path, or it may increase its latency. The subsequent sections discuss some of the impacts and possible solutions of these different traffic flows with regard to DCI path optimizations.

Understanding Multitiered Application Architecture

A thorough understanding of how multitiered applications and services within a data center work and communicate is vital for network designers during the planning of positioning or optimizing of a DCI solution. This is because with system virtualization and workload mobility, the physical host and IP localization is not associated anymore with a fixed physical location (data center).

For instance, several business applications, such as customer relationship management (CRM) and enterprise resource planning (ERP), consist of multiple elements interconnected in a sophisticated manner that construct the overall service or application. In addition, some of these elements may need to have a level of protection. For example, a web server might need to be placed behind a web application firewall, and the database behind a network firewall. As result, what is seen as a cohesive service or application is, in fact, a combination of multiple services and applications that communicate in the back end to provide the unified interface to the end user.

So to reiterate, a thorough understanding of how these services and applications communicate between each other can help the network designer make better decisions and provide a better DCI solution. What is meant by *decisions* here is not only related to the DCI connectivity type and routing design. It also refers to when an alignment needs to be done with other teams, such as server and application teams. With certain applications (multitiered), it is better to migrate them together rather than move only one element of the multitiered application. For example, in Figure 8-38, a web server (VM) that is part of a multitiered application consisting of a web server, application server, and database server was moved to the secondary DC.

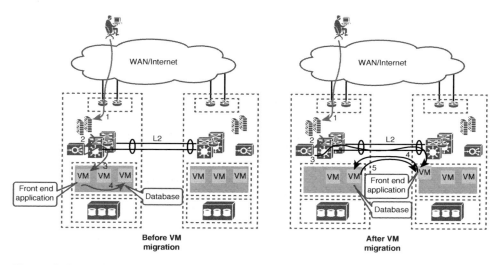

Figure 8-38 *The Impact of Migrating Multitiered Applications on DCI*

As shown in Figure 8-38 (the scenario on the left), before the front-end application is moved, VM traffic is routed and switched within the same physical DC (the traffic flow between different network and security components, also known as *ping-pong traffic*). In the scenario on the left, the effect of the ping-pong traffic has no impact on the latency because it is contained with the same DC. However, after moving the front-end VM traffic between the two data centers over the DCI, it can be increased. The ping-pong traffic, in this situation, can significantly impact the latency and efficiency of the DCI link. For example, traffic between each application tier will have to return to the primary DC where the active Layer 3 gateway and firewall are located. If additional network services are integrated between the different application tiers (which is the case in most of the deployments) such as load balancer, Secure Sockets Layer (SSL) offload, or web application firewall enabled, there might be about ten round trips (ping-pong traffic) for a simple web/DB query crossing the DCI. Consequently, by understanding how the multitiered application works, and to avoid the impact of this critical issue, it may be more feasible to move the entire multitiered application rather than only a single VM or application.

Note To simplify the illustration, Figure 8-38 shows only one direction of the traffic flow.

Optimize Routed DCI with Stateful Security Services

As discussed in Chapter 4, this design must consider a direct interconnection between the edge routers connected to the external connections (physical or tunneled interface) to avoid any traffic black-holing in the event of WAN/Internet link failure of the active DC by the stateful nodes in the path such as the firewalls (usually each DC maintains its own independent pair of firewalls), which potentially leads to resetting the existing active sessions. This solution assumes that the time for the failover process to complete is less than the timeout duration of the active sessions. For a more detailed analysis, along with design considerations, see Chapter 4, the section titled "Asymmetrical Routing with Multihoming (Issue and Solution)."

Egress Traffic Flow Optimization Using FHRP Localization

One of the primary path optimization principles with regard to an extended LAN over a DCI is the localization of the Layer 3 gateway services (FHRP) of the outbound traffic flow by the moved workload between the different data center locations. With LAN extension, FHRP such as Hot Standby Routing Protocol (HSRP) will usually be active on the primary DC only, which will result in suboptimal (nonlocalized) egress traffic flow. This might be acceptable in some scenarios where the interconnected DCs are located in the same building or campus and interconnected over high speed links, such as 10G or 40G dark fiber links. However, for large DCs with a high workload and interconnected over a private MAN, WAN, or over an SP-provisioned DCI, this can be unacceptable behavior. One simple and common solution is to use a VLAN access control list (VACL) or port ACL (PACL) to filter out FHRP over the DCI to maintain an active FHRP node per DC to process egress traffic flows locally, as shown in Figure 8-39.

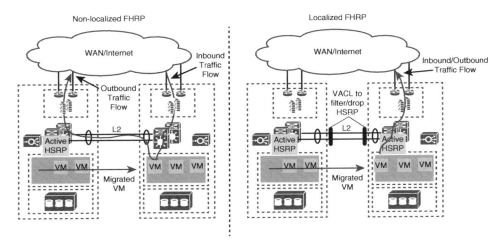

Figure 8-39   *FHRP Localization*

Ingress Traffic Flow Optimization

Optimizing egress traffic flow is only half the job in achieving acceptable and reliable path optimization for interconnected data centers. This section covers the most common techniques that you can use to optimize (localize) ingress traffic flow when the resources are moved or migrated between data center locations across a Layer 2 or Layer 3 DCI. Furthermore, these techniques can help achieve an active-active data center DR model:

- Domain Name System (DSN) based

- Route injection

- IP mobility (for example, LISP)

Figure 8-40 summarizes how ingress traffic flow optimization with interconnected DCs can decouple IP from its physical location.

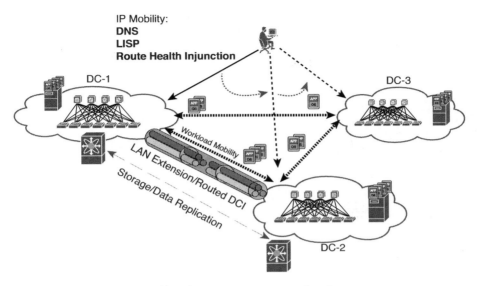

Figure 8-40 *Ingress Traffic Flow Optimization with DCI*

DNS Based

This design approach is one of the most common and proven approaches (but *most common* does not always mean the best). This solution relies on DNS (name to IP) redirection, most commonly deployed by using a global load balancer that acts as a DNS forwarder to resolve DNS queries to local (site-specific) load balancers per DC.

Normally, the global load balancer (also known as the *global site selector* [GSS]) performs keepalive checking with each DC load balancer while the local load balancers probe the real local servers. Hence, the global load balancer can populate the DNS entries with the appropriate IPs based on the keepalive response. In fact, the GSS can consider various criteria, such as response time and percentage of network utilization, in addition to weighting capabilities that can distribute traffic across different sites (active-active).

Therefore, this approach can achieve intelligent ingress traffic control and distribution across multiple DC locations facilitated by the GSS for the new ingress sessions. Existing sessions, however, cannot be redirected (even if the VM was moved) as long as the session is active, as shown in Figure 8-41. Although this behavior is most common with regard to GSS, load-balancing vendors may introduce new capabilities to overcome this limitation. Therefore, detailed traffic handling can vary while the overall design concept stays the same.

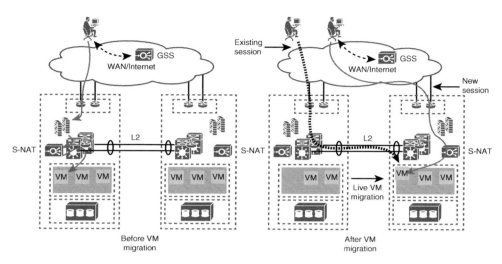

Figure 8-41   *DN-Based Ingress Traffic Flow Control*

Although DNS-based ingress traffic control is an easy and reliable solution, this design has the following limitations:

■ Supports traffic/session that use DNS (name) only.

■ Proxy cache of DNS entries can lead to traffic black holing until it is refreshed with a new DNS entry.

> **Note** The GSS concept described here is a generic concept that is available by leading load-balancing vendors.

With the DNS-based solution, Layer 2 extension over the DCI is not a prerequisite (unless it required by the applications or the distributed workloads). In addition, if a routed DCI in each DCI can maintain its own IP rang, this in turn will simplify the design by avoiding the egress traffic flow optimization considerations and other challenges related to the extended Layer 2 over DCI.

Route Health Injection

The route health injection (RHI) approach is also facilitated by load balancing (LB) nodes located across the interconnected data centers. With this approach, LBs are used in each DC to probe the local subnet/VLAN per host for an availability check with probe filtering over the DCI, as shown in Figure 8-42.

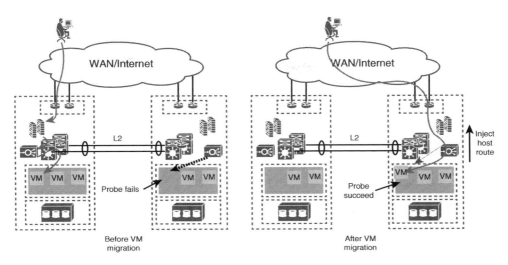

Figure 8-42   *RHI*

The scenario on the left in Figure 8-42 illustrates the DCs in a normal situation, in which the VM/server is located in the primary DC (DC-1) and the load balancer in DC-2 is monitoring the VM/host IP. At this stage, the probe should fail because the IP of the intended host is not located at the secondary DC. Once the VM has migrated to the secondary DC, the probe will succeed. This will trigger the load balancer to inject the host IP to the upstream edge routers (/32), which will redirect ingress traffic destined for this IP at the secondary DC (longest match principle).

Locator/ID Separation Protocol

LISP is developed to work in multihoming environments and facilitate communication in the IP mobility scenario in between LISP and non-LISP sites by separating IP addresses into two new numbering spaces: endpoint identifiers (EIDs) and routing locators (RLOCs), along with a dynamic endpoint tunneling encapsulation. Figure 8-43 summarizes the LISP architectural components.

Note   Each DC edge node in Figure 8-43 of the LISP sites ideally should have both xTR roles (ITR and ETR) to correctly process both inbound and outbound traffic flows with regard to IP mobility to the internal EIDs. However, remote branches usually have only end users needing to access DC resources. Therefore, it is possible for the LISP edge nodes of the remote sites (benches) for only the ITR role to be deployed, in which return traffic or any traffic sourced from the DC LISP site will reach remote site subnets using the typical native routing. The LISP Mapping DB server role can also be deployed internally within the DC either by using dedicated nodes (in large-scale DC environments) or to be co-located at the DC aggregation nodes in smaller scale ones.

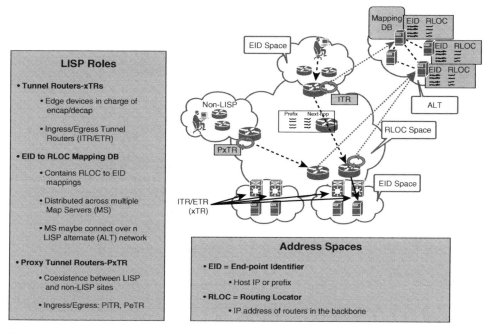

Figure 8-43 *LISP Architectural Components*

As an IP mobility routing mechanism, LISP offers data center operators the flexibility to either enable the transport over Layer 2 or routed DCI. In both scenarios, moved or migrated workloads (VMs) can maintain their original IP address. However, for LISP to deliver its promised value, remote sites must be LISP enabled, as much the nodes mapping between the non-LISP and LISP domain (PxTR), as shown in Figure 8-43.

Furthermore, although LISP offers data center operators the flexibility to use either the Layer 2 or routed DCI connectivity model between the different data centers, they do not operate exactly in the same manner with regard to workload mobility. That is why when migrating or moving VMs over routed DCI it is recommended (at the time of this writing) to target cold VM migration and not live migration. This avoids some ARP issues that can break the communications between the moved workload and other nodes (end users or hosts) after the migration. In addition, LISP supports multitenant environments that require path separation between networks within LISP sites and between non-LISP sites, as shown in Figure 8-44.

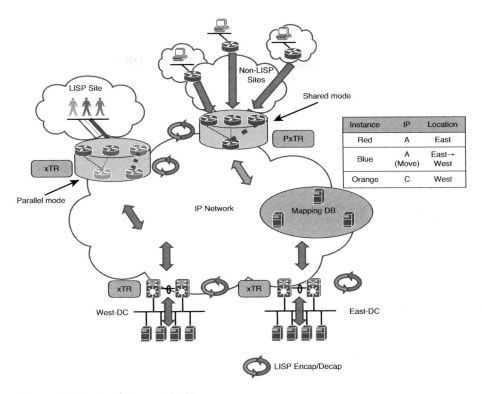

Figure 8-44 *Multitenant: LISP*

As shown in Figure 8-44, there are two modes in which the xTRs can be deployed with regard to LISP and network virtualization. With the shared mode, usually there will be a shared (single) IP range of the RLOC nodes in the backbones (multiple VRFs/EIDs mapping to a single RLOC). In contrast, the parallel mode offers the ability to maintain a separate IP range (may be separate virtual or physical nodes or interfaces) of the RLOC IPs (multiple RLOC VRFs can run in parallel).

Table 8-11 compares the design options discussed in this section with regard to IP mobility over interconnected data centers.

Table 8-11   *Comparison of Ingress Traffic Flow Optimization and IP Mobility Techniques*

	Strengths	**Design Concerns**
DNS based	Supports multiple data centers No core networking design changes Proven and commonly used by many DC operators (staff knowledge) Provides flexible load balancing based on the traffic sources (for example, geographic load distribution) Reasonable operational complexity Supports multitenancy	The already established sessions to the "live moved" workload will traverse the DCI link. Failover time (DNS failover/flush) may not be desirable for some data centers with fast failover time requirements. Does not support DC applications and services that are reachable by IP only. Requires other network components to function (load balancers, global load balancers).
RHI	Simple to design and implement Offers an automated mechanism to detect workload move No or minimal core networking design changes Supports multitenancy	Because this solution is based on injecting the host route, it will probably impact Layer 3 node routing tables considerably and may introduce significant amount of churn in the routing protocol in large virtualized or cloud-based DC environments. Because of this, it can lead to instability or increased latency. Increased operational complexity, Requires other network components to function (load balancers). Limited scalability.
Mobile IPv4	IPv4-based solution Supports multitenancy	Increased design and operational complexity because there will always be a triangular traffic pattern combined with IP tunneling as one mobile IP moves between home and the foreign agent. Endpoints need an IPv4 mobility agent. Core network changes. Can lead to suboptimal traffic routing. Multicast is an issue with IPv4 mobility. Because of this described limitation, this solution offers limited flexibility; scalability will be associated with increased design and operational complexity. Limited to IPv4.

Table 8-11   *continued*

	Strengths	Design Concerns
Mobile IPv6	IPv6-based solution Provides optimal data paths between server and client compared to mobile IPv4 Supports multitenancy	Supported IPv6 only (for both endpoint and the end-to-end data path). Core network changes. Endpoints must have IPv6 mobility agents installed on them. Increases design and operational complexity in large deployments.
LISP	No core network changes. Supports IPv4, IPv6, and hybrid mode as well (IPv4-IPv6 communication) Supports live and cold VM migration. Supports both Layer 2- and Layer 3-based DCI Supports communication with non-LISP sites Offers a scalable and flexible solution that can interconnect multiple sites Supports multitenancy	For this solution to work properly, the remote site should be LISP enabled (edge node to be xTR). Requires additional network components such as a mapping server. Network nodes need to support LISP (at least the participating nodes such as the edge xTRs). Increases the design complexity. Adds operational complexity to configure and troubleshoot. With L3 DCI, cold migration is supported. (Live is technically doable, but it will be associated with operational limitations.)

Network and Security Services Placement

The main concern with these devices in the data center traffic flow is that these devices normally operate in a stateful manner by maintaining information about the *state* of each specific traffic flow that passes through them. Therefore, to achieve smooth integration between data centers over a DCI without adding additional complexity, it is recommended to avoid stretching network service and security devices such as load balancers and firewalls, for the following reasons:

- Redundancy is usually controlled by two devices, whether they operate in active-standby or active-active modes. Stretching these devices across two different locations limits the maximum number of data centers to two.

- Maintaining a reliable connectivity for the failover link between the redundant devices (the physical interconnect between devices used for health check and session state synchronization) is difficult because of its sensitivity to latency. Any failure in this link can lead to a split-brain situation, which can bring both data centers down.

- Stretching the redundant devices can increase traffic trombone over the DCI.

- In addition, when considering LISP to steer flows between data center locations, special attention needs to be paid to the following concerns:

  - Because the LISP xTR nodes performs the User Datagram Protocol (UDP) encapsulation for the original IP packets, firewalls must be deployed *south* to the LISP xTR nodes to permit the application of security policies on the original IP packets.

  - If a firewall needs to be placed between the host default gateway and the xTR, LISP multihop host mobility functionality is required.

Summary

It is obvious that data center design combined with data center interconnect is one of the most challenging network design tasks. It requires the involvement of several teams and has to consider the different components collectively forming a data center environment. This chapter also covered how the workload and applications of today's data centers are driving the change of modern DCN architectures. In addition, various approaches to designing modern data centers were discussed and compared, with regard to the underlay and overlay protocols. Furthermore, this chapter stressed the importance of BC and DR models on the overall DCI design, while considering the different application requirements and how they can influence design decisions about DCI connectivity and traffic path optimization.

Further Reading

"Software-Defined Networking: A Perspective from Within a Service Provider Environment," https://tools.ietf.org/html/rfc7149

"VxLAN DCI Using EVPN," http://tools.ietf.org/id/draft-boutros-l2vpn-vxlan-evpn-04.txt

IETF draft, "Extending TRILL over WAN," https://tools.ietf.org/html/draft-xl-trill-over-wan-01

"VMDC 3.0.1 Design Guide," http://www.cisco.com/c/en/us/td/docs/solutions/Enterprise/Data_Center/VMDC/3-0-1/DG/VMDC_3-0-1_DG.html

"Data Center Access Layer Design," http://www.cisco.com/c/en/us/td/docs/solutions/Enterprise/Data_Center/DC_Infra2_5/DCInfra_6.html

"Cisco Application Policy Infrastructure Controller Data Center Policy Model," http://www.cisco.com/c/en/us/solutions/collateral/data-center-virtualization/application-centric-infrastructure/white-paper-c11-731310.html

"Routing Bridges (RBridges): Base Protocol Specification," https://tools.ietf.org/html/rfc6325

"IS-IS Extensions Supporting IEEE 802.1aq Shortest Path Bridging," https://tools.ietf.org/html/rfc6329

IETF draft, "An Architecture for Overlay Networks," draft-ietf-nvo3-arch-03, http://www.ietf.org

High Availability

Chapter 9

Network High-Availability Design

Business application and service availability considerations in today's modern converged networks have become a vital design element, especially now that many businesses understand the IT network's availability impact and cost to the organization, whether it is an enterprise or service provider network. Practically, the cost of a service downtime due to a network outage can take different forms: tangible, intangible, or a combination of both. Some of the common losses that can be caused by network downtime (which normally impact the business either directly or indirectly) are as follows:

- Tangible such as data loss, revenue loss, and reduced user productivity

- Intangible such as degraded reputation, customer dissatisfaction, and employees dissatisfaction

Consequently, the availability of the different IT infrastructure and services becomes one of the common primary requirements of today's modern businesses that rely to a large extent on technology services to facilities achieving their business goals, such as mobility, cloud-hosted services, e-government services, Internet of Things (IoT), and smart connected cities. Therefore, many of these businesses with converged next-generation networks are aiming to achieve the *five nines* of network and IT services availability when developing their network designs.

Note The term *five nines* usually refers to the degree of service availability. Literally, it refers to 99.999 percent of the functional time of a system, which can be translated to time of downtime per month/year as listed in Table 9-1.

Table 9-1   *Service Availability and Downtime*

9's Designation	Downtime per Year	Downtime per Month
9.99 percent (three nines)	~ 8.76 hours	43.8 minutes
9.999 percent (four nines)	~ 52.56 minutes	4.38 minutes
9.9999 percent (five nines)	~ 5.26 minutes	25.9 seconds

Although it is hard to achieve the absolute five nines, it is becoming common nowadays for it to be targeted as an availability requirement in network service level agreements (SLAs). Achieving a true end-to-end five nines level of availability for a given service or application is not an easy goal to achieve because there are multiple influencing factors. For example, multiple factors impact the overall level of availability of any given application in a data center, such as network infrastructure availability, server component availability, storage availability, and all other components that are part of this application architecture on higher layers such as database, front-end application, and so on. Therefore, this chapter focuses only on the network infrastructure part and the design aspects and considerations that pertain to the network elements only (elements that helps to optimize the overall availability of the other elements carried over the network such as critical business applications).

Note   As discussed earlier in this book, the need for network availability is increasing with the increased adoption of converged types of network and service consolidation. However, several variables dictate the level of network availability. It is not always the case that every part of the network requires the same level of network availability. In other words, the high level of availability is not always a common requirement.

Although network availability is not always a common requirement, it must be evaluated based on different criteria such as level of criticality and business priorities, which can specify the level of impact of the downtime on the business. In addition, sometimes it is too difficult to define when the network is down. For instance, is network downtime based on a specific application's downtime, or is it based on specific part of the network, such as the data center? In fact, business requirements, goals, and the level of impact caused by the downtime with regard to these business priorities and goals can determine the standards of how network downtime is defined.

In general, the term *network availability* is an operations parameter reflected by the ratio of the time a network can be considered functional and performing as expected. Moreover, a system is seen as reliable when functioning without failure over a certain period of time. In fact, a system's reliability can be measured either by the level of its operational quality within a given time slot (when the system was up and running) until the system went to a down state, which is also known as *mean time between failures* (MTBF = Total operational time / Number of failures), or by calculating a system's failure rate (Number of failures / Total operational time).

The term *operational quality* here refers to some scenarios where a system might be technically up, yet is not performing its functions at the minimum required level. This means that the system not delivering the intended service or performing a function reliably even if is technically up. It is important to note that system reliability is one of the primary contributing elements to achieving the ultimate level of system or network availability.

The importance of system reliability is illustrated in the following case, where there is a network designed with a high level of availability (including redundant components). However, the interconnections between the core components of this network have low reliability. Examples of low reliability include the following:

- Unreliable line cards used at the core node.

- The transport medium is unreliable, and the links keep flapping.

Despite the fact that this network was designed with high-availability considerations, the low level of reliability of the core components in this network will impact the overall service availability.

However, the mean time to repair (MTTR) reflects the actual time required to repair a system from a failure condition. The following standard formula shows the correlation between availability, MTBF, and MTTR to calculate a system's availability:

Availability = MTBF / (MTBF + MTTR)

Based on this formula, it is obvious that increasing the MTBF and decreasing MTTR can offer an improved overall level of availability. Thus, you can improve the availability of a network by optimizing the capability of its elements, such as the interconnecting transport links, to function without failures. A reliable network must be designed to tolerate at least a single component failure. Some designs may require the network to cater for multiple failures to meet certain design requirements. This usually translates into more redundant components, higher cost, and probably higher operational complexity.

Hypothetically, the more redundant paths we add to the network design, the higher the MTBF we can achieve. However, increasing MTBF is only half of the job. Therefore, network designers must consider how to reduce the repair time as well. Technically, adding more redundancy, which means increasing the parallelism here (redundant paths/links) leads to a higher MTTR at the network control plane layer. This will result in an increased control plane complexity and probably slower convergence time. In sum, for network designers to achieve the desired level of network availability, there must either be very highly reliable components end to end that reduce the probability of failure to a minimum or there must be redundant components that can take over in the event of a failure (reducing the possibility of failures versus reducing complete network outages).

Many recent industry studies and reports show that the majority of system downtime occurs because of either a deficiency in design analysis, testing (proof of concept [POC]), or operational mistakes. The minority of system downtime results from hardware or software failures. Therefore, decreasing the possibility of service or network outages can be more efficient and achievable than focusing only on eliminating any system or network component failure possibility. Consequently, this chapter always focuses on how to balance between having a reliable and fault-tolerant design to achieve the intended goal in a resilient and effective manner.

Fault Tolerance

In general, network *fault tolerance* can be defined as the capability of a network to continue its service (no downtime) in the event of any component failure, with minimal service interruption using a redundant component that can take over in transparent fashion. Ideally, this should be unnoticeable by the end users or applications. However, the operating quality may decrease, depending on the considerations for the post-failure situation, with regard to whether the redundant component can fully handle the load or partially handle it.

In addition, some businesses deem it acceptable for their networks to stay operational with degraded quality, rather than facing a complete network failure. In other words, a network can be considered fault tolerant when it offers the capability to function (fully or partially) for the duration of any network component failure, usually over a redundant component. Commonly, the more network nodes and components that are added, the more likely it is for network high availability to be undermined. Therefore, network designers need to consider how to optimize these types of designs and reduce single points of failure to achieve the desired level of the network uptime. To achieve the desired level of network availability and a high level of resiliency to cater for different types of failure conditions, the following fault-tolerance design aspects must be considered:

■ **Network level redundancy:** It is also referred to as *network path redundancy*, and is essential to catering to link failures, such as fiber cuts, incorrect cabling, and so on. It is uncommon in LAN environments that end hosts connect with dual links at the access layer. Even though this will reduce the end-to-end reliability level, it is almost always acceptable as long as path redundancy is from the access layer onward (excluding data center high-availability [HA] considerations, because redundant connections are critical at the server access layer), as illustrated in Figure 9-1.

■ **Device and component redundancy:** Typically, redundant nodes provide redundancy during a node failure triggered by hardware or software. There are two types of node-level redundancies: redundant nodes and redundant components within a single device. You can use one or both types, based on the level of availability required and the targeted network environment (criticality). Considerations regarding passing traffic through the failure (for example, using redundant supervisors) versus passing traffic around the failure (using redundant devices) are primary influencing factors to the choice here as well. In addition, remember that redundant components (for example, redundant line cards for the uplinks) help to increase the overall level of system reliability. In general, redundant devices with diverse network paths offer better resiliency compared to a single device with redundant components. That said, a device with redundant components is more feasible for nodes that represent a single point of failure, such as a provider edge (PE) node in service provider networks.

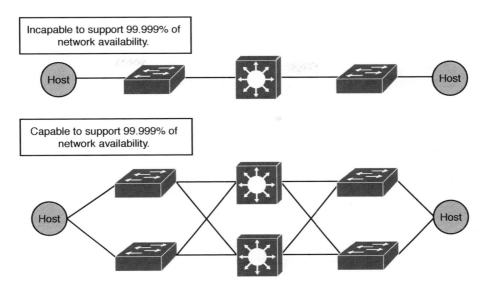

Figure 9-1   *Network Path Redundancy*

- **Operational redundancy:** Although the focus is almost always on how to optimize network redundancy and availability during unplanned failure scenarios, it is also important to consider how to provide redundancy during planned network outages, such as using in-service software upgrade (ISSU) or software maintenance update (SMU) capabilities.

- **Network architecture:** The network architecture itself can facilitate, to a large degree, achieving an optimized level of availability. For instance, a hierarchical network design stresses redundancy at multiple layers to overcome any possible single point of failure. The other good example is "how" Clos architecture (TRILL or VxLAN based) helps to achieve large scale-out expansion in data center networks with several redundant components at the spines level without introducing complexity to the overall architecture. Furthermore, design redundancy at site or module level can help achieve optimized business and service availability for critical sites. A typical example of this is a disaster recovery (DR) data center with data center interconnect (DCI), as illustrated in Figure 9-2.

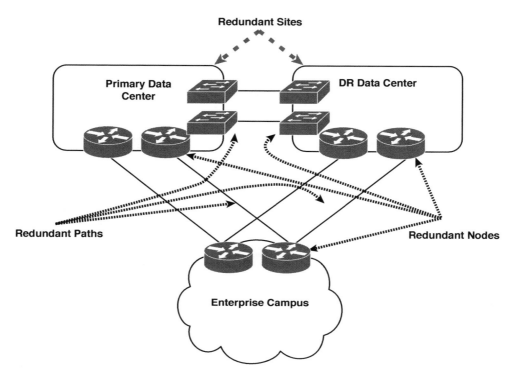

Figure 9-2 *Redundancy at the Network Architecture Level*

> **Note** In Figure 9-2, the network can operate in an active-standby or active-active manner using the available redundant paths/components.

> **Note** In any network, fault tolerance relies on different process and mechanisms to achieve the desired level of switchover to the backup component, as discussed in subsequent sections.

Fate Sharing and Fault Domains

It is important that network architects and designers understand the difference and relation between fate sharing and fault domains. *Fate sharing* refers to the philosophy of system design in which a single system is constructed of multiple subsystems or components, with a failure of one subcomponent leading to a complete system failure (sharing the same fate). For instance, a failure of the CPU of a smartphone will normally lead to a complete device failure as a result of a single subcomponent failure. Moreover, in the networking world, fate sharing also refers to the scenarios where multiple virtual networks share a single network infrastructure (more specifically, single network element such as a physical link with multiple subinterfaces where each subinterface carries a different virtual network).

However, *fault domain*, as highlighted earlier in this book, refers to a domain where multiple systems reside under a single domain (physical or logical) and a failure in one component can impact all other components within the same domain, such as flooding of updates or error messages. Let's consider the following example to demonstrate the impact and relationship between these concepts.

The scenario illustrated in Figure 9-3 shows two data center networks interconnected over a Layer 2 DCI. In addition, some virtualized networks are interconnected over the same DCI over a generic routing encapsulation (GRE) tunnel (with Multiprotocol Label Switching [MPLS] Layer 3 virtual private networking [L3VPN] enabled over the GRE tunnel). In this scenario, if any failure happens to the MPLS labels inside this tunnel, all the virtual networks passing through this tunnel will be impacted (sharing the same fate) as a result of a subcomponent failure of the entire MPLS L3VPN over GRE solution.

Similarly, the failure of the DCI in this particular scenario will lead to the failure of the multiple virtual networks carried over the GRE tunnel and of the extended VLAN over the Layer 2 DCI, resulting in a fate sharing situation as well. Another common terminology applicable here is the shared risk link group (SRLG), which is commonly used in traffic engineering designs where multiple links share a single point of failure, in which all the links pass through one network node (for example, all the cables are going into a single device on the same line card). A failure of this node or any subcomponent (such as the line card where the links terminate) will usually lead to complete failure for all the networks that have their links passing through this node (the SRLG point).

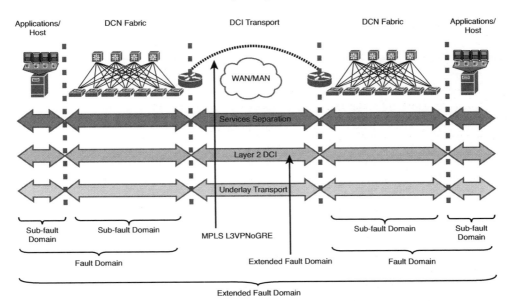

Figure 9-3 *Fate Sharing and Fault Domains*

Moreover, as shown in Figure 9-3, each Layer 2 segment in each data center (DC) represents a fault domain. Extending the LAN over the DCI, however, will in turn lead to extending the fault domain of each DC to the other one. For instance, any host MAC flooding in an extended VLAN in one DC will be propagated across the DCI to the other DC. Layer 2 flooding may lead to DCI congestion, which will usually impact all other traffic passing over this path, including the GRE tunnel. For instance, if a host or node fails in one of the DCs, in some situations this may lead to a significant amount of flooding within a single failure domain (in this scenario, the failure domain extended across the DCI), which most probably will lead to congestion of the DCI link. As a result, all the virtual networks passing over the MPLS L3VPN over GRE will be impacted as well. In other words, the impact of a failure in a fault domain can affect all the systems in that domain, unlike fate sharing, which is normally limited to a given system or subcomponent of the entire network such as the GRE tunnel (described in the example), or it can be a group of MPLS Traffic Engineering (MPLS-TE) tunnels passing through an SRLG point.

One of the common design principles used to generate a design that is reliable and resilient enough and that caters for different failure scenarios (like the one described in this section) is called *design for failure*. This principle is discussed in the following section.

Network Resiliency Design Considerations

Today's converged networks that carry voice and other real-time applications must recover in the event of network component failure in a few seconds (and sometimes within milliseconds) to effectively transmit traffic without affecting the end-user experience. Convergence times of less than one second could be highly desirable or a requirement for some networks, such as MPLS VPN service providers that offer virtual leased line (VLL) services. Therefore, network designers who aim to achieve the desired level of HA of network services must eliminate any single point of failure throughout the network. The network must recover during a component failure, such as link or node failure, to a redundant component that can continue the service operation. In other words, a redundant component that takes over in the event of a node or link failure must offer a fast network recovery (self-healing), also known as *fast convergence*, to maintain the desired level of network and service availability.

Furthermore, the redundant component should ideally take over within an acceptable period (for example, before mission-critical business application sessions restart) and handle the required functions reliably during the failure event. For example, you may have link- and device-level redundancy in your network that eliminates any single point of failure along the network path. However, in the event of any component failure, the network could take up to five minutes to recover from a simple failure to start using the redundant component. This may not be an acceptable resiliency level by the business, and this downtime in a next-generation converged network will impact many other services, such as mission-critical business applications and IP telephony services. Therefore, in this case, the availability goal from the business point of view is not optimally achieved, and so this does not justify the cost of buying and deploying redundant components.

The other factor that needs to be considered is how reliably the redundant component can function following a network failure event to provide a truly resilient network design. For example, one common scenario where the increased parallelism (redundancy) may not lead to optimized service availability is with an enterprise Internet edge designed with multiple paths (links) with the intention to maximize the overall performance and provide a reliable solution.

However, the concern in this type of design is when the business requires maximizing the utilization of the available Internet links to increase the return on investment (ROI) of these links and to improve application and Internet service performance, as illustrated in Figure 9-4. If one of the Internet links goes down, the second link, with a maximum of 10 Mbps of bandwidth, will start handling 20 Mbps during the link 1 failure, which will lead to an almost 50 percent degraded performance (assuming both links are fully utilized). Therefore, unplanned redundancy probably leads to an undesirable outcome following a failure event.

For this enterprise to resolve this issue, it should add a third link to offload some of the traffic during any link failure. However, this solution will increase control plane and operational complexity and will add additional cost from the business point of view (capital expenditure [capex]). Alternatively, this enterprise needs to consider accurate link capacity planning, where each link utilization should not reach more than ~45 percent in a normal situation to cater to both links' bandwidth requirements during a link failure scenario. Although this solution will incur additional cost, it adds no operational and control plane complexity to the existing design.

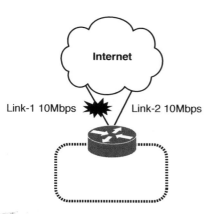

Figure 9-4   *Unplanned Failover Design*

Note   Both solutions are valid, and the goal of this scenario is to highlight the importance of the planning and the analysis of the different failure scenarios and its impact on achieving a true resilient network design.

Network designers must aim to create a network design that offers resistance to failures (reliable) and that can recover quickly and reliably in the event of a failure (resilient). In this regard, network designers should always consider the analytical principle used today by public cloud providers such as Amazon AWS Cloud, commonly known as *design for failure*, in which network designers ensure that the possible failure scenarios (including root causes and the failure scenario's impact on the business) have been analyzed and addressed within the design. Applying this design for failure principle facilitates the desired level of availability. It also helps network architects and designers identify and understand the impact and risk of different failure events on the business, such as the estimated outage period and to what degree this failure can disrupt business operations.

Consequently, when you design a network for failure with the objective of offering a highly fault-tolerant, reliable, and resilient network design, consider the following as you construct the foundation of the design architecture:

- Perform analysis of different downtime failure scenarios and their impact on the business's critical functions and data to be aligned with the business's expectations, such as recovery time objective (RTO) and recovery point objective (RPO) levels.

- Optimize network services availability on higher layers to the desired level that meets business and user expectations, such as web-application firewalls, Domain Name System (DNS), and load balancers.

- Every network component should be redundant (when possible) to eliminate any single point of failure across the network path.

- The network should be adequately capable of recovering in the event of a node or link failure with minimal or no service interruption during the recovery process, and without any operator intervention (resilient).

- The redundant component can continue to function at the desired level during a failure scenario (reliable resiliency).

- Classify and set recovery priorities from both business and technical points of view. (Critical functions and prerequisite services for other functions must always recover first.)

Note   The desired level of a network's availability or convergence time will vary from business to business. Therefore, for the purpose of the CCDE exam, only consider fast network recovery time if it is explicitly required or implied through other requirements.

When designing a highly available and resilient network that can converge fast enough without impacting any business-critical activities or applications, network designers need to consider a number of things. In other words, it is not limited to the scope of tuning control plane timers; in fact, it is an end-to-end process. Network designers need to consider all the network layers involved in this convergence process to achieve a true and effective convergence.

As a network designer, start by asking the following questions to understand whether the network is performing at the desired level, and to meet application requirements and business expectations:

■ **The characteristics of business-critical applications:** How much time does each business-critical application or service running on the network require before it loses its state or session? For instance, the CEO's voice call might be dropped because of minor packet loss (over 3 percent of packet loss) during network convergence time.

■ **Network reaction:** How long does the network take to converge following a component failure? You should consider end-to-end recovery time because the network might reconverge in some parts quicker than other parts and introduce microloops.

■ **Network security components:** Are there network security devices in the path, such as firewalls? If yes, are they redundant? How quick is its failover process? Is it a stateful or stateless failover?

> **Note** It is important to note that the target here is not only routing convergence, but the overall network convergence. As a network designer, always ask the question, "What can be done apart from the typical control plane timers to minimize loss in the event of a failure?"

This section discusses various mechanisms that network designers can consider to optimize network availability and convergence time to achieve the optimal targeted level of resiliency at different levels:

■ Device-level resiliency

■ Protocol-level resiliency

> **Note** As mentioned earlier, this chapter focuses only on network availability. In reality, the overall service and application availability must be measured end to end (at all layers; instance, if a voice control system [such as Cisco CallManager] is running on a cluster distributed across two data centers). In the event of the primary (active) data center failure, the network may reconverge in a few seconds, whereas Session Initiation Protocol (SIP)-based IP phones may take up to three minutes to register with the new active call control system because of a DNS failover delay (timeout duration).

Device-Level Resiliency

Device-level resiliency (also referred to as *component resiliency*) aims to maintain or keep traffic forwarding intact during a component failure at the network node level, such as routing processor failure. Therefore, it is critical for network designers to not get this concept confused with protocol-level resiliency, which usually aims to route traffic around the failed component. If routing protocols are tuned to converge quickly (subseconds), this will demolish the value of deploying device-level redundancy. Therefore, a balance between the device-level resiliency and the protocol-level must be considered when the device-level resiliency is a requirement.

Different protocols and mechanisms aim to offer a network design that can continue to forward traffic through a network node with a failure (such as a primary routing processor failure), with the assumption that a redundant routing processor is available on the same device. The following are the primary mechanisms used to achieve device-level resiliency:

- **Stateful switchover (SSO):** Allows the standby route processor to take immediate control and maintain connectivity protocols

- **Nonstop forwarding (NSF):** Continues to forward packets until route convergence is complete

- **Graceful restart (GR):** Reestablishes the routing information bases without churning the network

- **Nonstop Routing (NSR):** Continues to forward packets and maintains routing state

GR and NSR suppress routing changes on peers to SSO-enabled devices during processor switchover events (SSO), reducing network instability and downtime. In addition, the following protocol-specific considerations must be taken into account with regard to device-level resiliency design:

- NSR is desirable in cases where the routing protocol peer does not support the RFCs necessary to support GR. However, it comes at a cost of using more system resources than would be used if the same session used GR.

- For MPLS-enabled networks, you can use the following features to enhance network resiliency during a component failure:

  - Label Distribution Protocol (LDP) GR (RFC 3478)

  - LDP-IGP synchronization (RFC 5443)

  - LDP session protection (based on the LDP targeted hello functionality defined in RFC 5036)

- Because NSR is a self-contained solution, it is more feasible for when the peer routing node is not under the same administrative authority, as is the case with PE-CE (customer edge) routers. In addition, NSR improves the overall system's reliability.

Network edge nodes such as PE devices in a service provider (SP) environment represent a single point of failure; therefore, features such as NSF and SSO, along with redundant components (redundant supervisors), are more common with these devices to provide redundant intra-chassis route processors and network resilience. Backbone network nodes, however, are more commonly deployed with protocol-level resiliency, in which network convergence depends on protocol convergence to an alternate primary path such as using tuned interior gateway protocol (IGP) for fast convergence or MPLS-TE fast reroute (FRR).

Note Operationally, a major consequence and benefit of SSO is that adjacent devices do not see a link failure when the route processor switches from the primary to the hot standby route processor. This applies to route processor switchovers only. If the entire chassis were to lose power or fail, or a line card failure were to occur, the links would fail, and the peer would detect such an event. Of course, this assumes point-to-point Gigabit Ethernet interfaces, Packet over SONET (POS) interfaces, and so on, where link failure is detectable. Even with NSF enabled, physical link failures are still detectable by a peer and override NSF awareness.[1]

Protocol-Level Resiliency

As highlighted earlier in this chapter, a resilient network is a network that can recover following any network failure event. Network recovery, however, refers to the overall required time for all network nodes participating in path calculation, and traffic routing and forwarding, to complete restructuring or updating network reachability information following a network component failure (for example, a link or node failure). This is usually performed at the control plane "protocol" level. The faster the convergence time, the quicker a network can react to any change in the topology. There are two primary network recovery approaches:

- **Network restoration approach:** A reactive approach that computes an alternate primary path to reroute traffic over it after detection of a network component failure. Normal Open Shortest Path First (OSPF) behavior after failure of the primary path is a good example of this approach.

- **Network protection approach:** This approach is a proactive concept that precomputes (or signals) a backup loop-free alternate path in advance before any failure event. In the event any failure is detected, the protected traffic is moved over to the backup path transparently (commonly within 100 ms or less).

In general, at any given layer in the network, network protection approach offers faster convergence than restoration. However, in some scenarios, it can be an expensive option, such as with optical layer protection. It may also introduce an added layer of complexity to the design, control plane, and the manageability of the network, such as using a full mesh of MPLS-TE tunnels among a large number of nodes.

That said, there is no single best approach; it always depends on the business goals and functional and application requirements to be satisfied. For instance, a five-minute recovery time might not be an issue for a retail business, whereas in a financial services environment, this duration may cost the business hundreds of thousands of dollars. Therefore, the cost of a failure here can justify the expensive but fast and reliable network recovery solution. The subsequent sections cover the two primary approaches of protocol-level resiliency in more detail.

---

1. http://www.cisco.com/en/US/technologies/tk869/tk769/technologies_white_paper0900aecd801dc5e2.html

Network Restoration

As described earlier, the concept of network restoration or convergence refers to the time required for network nodes to recompute their routing and forwarding tables and calculate a new primary path reactively following a network component failure. Convergence time is an essential measurement of "how long" routers within a routing domain can take to reach the state of convergence. In addition, network and protocol convergence can be seen as a primary performance indicator. However, achieving the desired level of convergence time is not as simple as tuning a few protocol timers. In fact, multiple elements determine how quickly and reliably a network or routing protocol convergence can occur at different network layers. Hence, any design that aims to optimize a routing protocol convergence time has to take all of these elements into consideration. These elements are categorized as follows:

■ Event detection

■ Event propagation

■ Event processing

■ Update routing and forwarding tables

As depicted in Figure 9-5, each of these elements contributes to the overall convergence time. Therefore, the optimization of these elements collectively reduces the time a network needs to recover following a failure event.

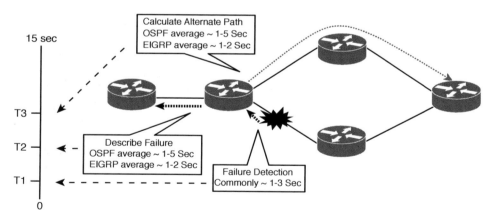

Figure 9-5 *Network Convergence Influencing Factors*

To achieve the desired convergence time, all these elements must be considered. In other words, the optimization of one or a subset of these elements only does not necessarily lead to an optimized convergence time at the desired level. The following subsections, considering the different characteristic of each routing protocol, discuss how each of these elements influence the overall convergence time.

Event Detection Considerations

The declaration or detection of a peer failure is a primary element in optimizing network convergence, simply because it is the trigger to starting the network recovery process. The detection of a failure in networking can happen at different layers, such as the physical layer (IP over dense wavelength-division multiplexing [IPoDWDM]), data link layer (Point-to-Point Protocol / High-level Data Link Control [PPP/HDLC] keepalive messages), network layer (routing protocols), and up to the application layer. This section focuses on the network convergence at the network layer and below.

The most commonly used mechanism to detect a link failure and to check a control plane neighbor's reachability is a "poll-driven" mechanism that relies on the Layer 3 control plane hello messages and hold timers, also commonly referred to as *fast hellos*. Due to the deployment simplicity of fast hellos, it is one of the most common mechanisms used in many networks today. However, in large-scale networks and networks with strict convergence time requirements, this mechanism introduces several limitations that may inhibit achieving the desired level of network convergence, such as the following:

- **Scalability limitations:** Typically occur in a network with a large number of Layer 3 control plane peers

- **Hardware resource consumption overhead:** Normally, when the number of Layer 3 control plane peers increases, there will be potential CPU spikes that may introduce what are called *false positives*, where links might be incorrectly declared to be broken

To overcome the limitations of this poll-based failure detection mechanism, you can use an event-driven mechanism instead to add more reliable and faster detection capabilities with low overhead. The most common and proven protocol used for this purpose is the bidirectional forwarding detection (BFD). BFD operates independently of the Layer 3 control plane protocols based on the concept of hello or heartbeat type protocols. Moreover, BFD supports several control protocols such as Hot Standby Routing Protocol (HSRP), link-state, Border Gateway Protocol (BGP), and Enhanced Interior Gateway Routing Protocol (EIGRP), where each protocol can register with BFD to be notified when BFD detects a neighbor loss. As a result, these routing protocols can overcome the delay and limitations of the poll-based failure detection mechanism that is mainly based on protocol hello and hold timers. BFD offers a more simplified, reliable, and faster failure detection mechanism (within tens of milliseconds).

Note   Typically, routers connected over direct point-to-point links can be notified by the physical layer when a link fails, which accelerates failure detection by the Layer 3 nodes. BFD, however, enables network operators to achieve fast failure detection in scenarios where two or more Layer 3 nodes are interconnected over a Layer 2 switched network. In this scenario, these Layer 3 nodes do not need to rely on control plane fast hellos and hold timers to detect a Layer 3 peer link or node failure.

Note   Besides the BFD-supported control protocols highlighted earlier, BFD is also supported with static routing, and based on the status of the associated BFD session, the static route is either added to or withdrawn from the Routing Information Base (RIB) table, which makes static routing more reliable.

In BGP environments, however, the IGP fast failure detection and subsecond convergence time may lead to temporary traffic black-holing because of the typical significant convergence time difference between IGP and BGP by default. For instance, in a typical enterprise network with BGP in the core or an MPLS VPN SP network, such as a Carrier Ethernet (MPLS L2VPN Ethernet VPN [EVPN] based), the operator may deploy its backbone IGP to detect a link's failure and recover within one second to achieve fast-converging next-generation L2VPN transport. As a result, in this scenario after a link or node failure, IGP will converge in one second, whereas Multiprotocol BGP (MP-BGP) continues to use the same next hop to reach a MAC addresses advertised in BGP by a remote PE for a given EVPN-EVI (EPVN instance) that is no longer a valid next hop after the last failure event. This is because MP-BGP, in this situation, is still relying on the poll mechanism to deal with the changes in the RIB, where "every 60 seconds, the BGP scanner recalculates best path for all prefixes." In other words, MP-BGP in this case may take up to 60 seconds to realize that the next hop is not anymore useable, and during this 60 second time period between scan cycles, IGP instability, invalid BGP next-hop, or other network failures can cause black holes and routing loops to temporarily form[2].

However, with BGP next-hop tracking (NHT) and the address tracking filter (ATF), if the next-hop IP of MGP-BGP routes changes because of link failure followed by fast failure detection and IGP convergence, BGP now can respond faster (by lowering the response time to next-hop changes for prefixes installed in the RIB) without the need to wait for the initial 60 seconds of the "scanner." Therefore, it is always important to understand what other protocols are running over the network besides IGP, and to understand how fast failure detection and IGP fast convergence (for example, subsecond convergence time) will impact the performance and behavior of these protocols or applications.

In spite of the benefits of deploying fast failure detection (subsecond), the following are the main design concerns that must be considered when designing a fast convergence network with subsecond failure detection:

■ **Instability:** In many situations, very fast failure detection can lead to flapping and can add high overhead on the network hardware and routing protocols because of unnecessary processing and calculation.

■ **Break device-level resiliency:** Very fast failure detection breaks the concept of device-level resiliency described earlier (SSO, NSF, NSR). Therefore, the design cannot mix these two approaches (passing traffic through the failure versus passing

2.   "BGP Support for Next-Hop Address Tracking", http://www.cisco.com

traffic around the failure). This is because it may take about one to two seconds for the secondary route processor (supervisor) to start the failover process. Therefore, detecting a failure too fast (such as using BFD or too-low-tuned fast hellos) will usually override the entire failover process.

- **Traffic black-holing:** If the fast failure detection was not aligned properly with the other protocols and overlay technologies running over IGP, such as MP-BGP or IP tunneling keepalives, the network could possibly face temporary traffic black-holing after a failure.

Event Propagation and Processing Considerations

The propagation of a network failure event and the computation process after detecting the failure refers to the reaction of the control plane to describe the failure event to other peers and finding an alternate primary path, respectively. With regard to route convergence design considerations, what is important is how long each of these processes takes and how they can be optimized. In general, there are two primary influencing factors to optimize these processes:

- **Protocol characteristic and its timers:** This varies based on the control plane protocol in use.

- **Network design:** This is common for all protocols, to a large extent.

As discussed earlier, each protocol has different characteristics and its own philosophy for propagating and processing routing changes and updates, whether its link state, distance vector, or path vector. Typically, when a failure is detected by a Layer 3 node running a link-state routing protocol, this node and any other node connected to the failed component will start propagating this event by flooding OSPF link-state advertisements (LSAs) or Intermediate System-to-Intermediate System link-state packets (IS-IS LSPs) to every node within the link-state flooding domain. The overall event propagation duration of each LSA/LSP is normally governed by three primary timers: generation delay, reception delay, and processing delay.

Both IS-IS and OSPF, however, can use the incremental shortest path first SPF (iSPF) algorithm to optimize SPF computations and converge faster in response to network events and topology changes, simply because iSFP is more efficient than the full SPF algorithm. In contrast, EIGRP uses a completely different logic and sequence. EIGRP finds an alternate path (usually precalculated using EIGRP feasible successor, thus avoiding the entire EIGRP query process, which significantly improves EIGRP convergence following failure event detection). Then, EIGRP propagates the failure to the peers. Table 9-2 highlights the fundamental differences between link state and EIGRP with regard to each protocol's convergence characteristic.

Table 9-2   *Protocol Convergence Characteristics: EIGRP Versus Link State*

	Within a Flooding Domain	Between Flooding Domains
Link State	By default, can converge within ~3 to 10 seconds With tuned times, such as fast hellos, can converge within milliseconds	Depends on the flooding domain design with regard to reachability information hiding and topology information hiding (acts like a typical distance-vector protocol)
	With Feasible Successor	**Without Feasible Successor**
EIGRP	Usually within tens of milliseconds	Primarily depends on the network design (for example, number of nodes to handle queries, EIGRP query scope, EIGRP stuck-in active [SIA] delay)

In contrast, with BGP as a path-vector protocol, its propagation philosophy of a failure event is based on the propagation of withdrawal update messages that normally can be tuned to reduce the overall duration. In addition, the tuning of the following elements that technically influence BGP transport offer an optimized BGP performance to handle a large number of prefixes during the propagation and processing following a failure in the BGP path:

- TCP maximum segment size (MSS)

- TCP window size

- Path maximum transmission unit (MTU) discovery (RFC 1191)

- BGP minimum route advertisement interval (MRAI)

- Router queues (for example, input queue hold)

Note   BGP prefix-independent convergence (PIC), described later in this chapter, helps to significantly enhance BGP convergence time.

From a network design perspective, the following common design considerations can help to optimize the convergence time and improve network stability:

- **Fault isolation:** As discussed earlier, fault isolation has a significant influence on enhancing the operation of routing protocols and reducing the amount of information that needs to be propagated. It also enhances the scope of the topology information shared between logical routing domains, which ultimately reduces hardware overhead utilization and the time required for the Layer 3 nodes to complete the propagation, processing, and finding an alternate primary path.

- **Number of routes:** One of the primary influencers on the overall time required for propagating, processing, and updating routing and forwarding tables is the number of the effected prefixes with a network change. Therefore, the information reachability hiding techniques discussed earlier in this book will help considerably in optimizing network convergence time and at the same time reduce the impact on its stability. For instance, with EIGRP, in addition to route summarization, stub routers help to reduce the processing of the DUAL algorithm and the scope of query messages. This will enhance the overall EIGRP convergence time while keeping the network as stable as possible (minimal to zero impact on the remote stub networks). Similarly, with link-state protocols, such as IS-IS (L1) or OSPF, in stub areas or totally stubby areas, the router's LSA database size can be reduced, which will enhance the overall convergence time as well.

■ **Multiple available paths:** The availability of a second path can significantly enhance convergence time. Therefore, with EIGRP, it is essential that the design supports the precomputation of EIGRP feasible successor. In addition, apart from EIGRP feasible successor, if a BGP speaker has two available paths to a given destination network, the time required to process and find an alternate path can be eliminated because there is already an alternate path. However, unlike IGP, achieving this with BGP is sometimes challenging, especially in large networks where there is an route reflector (RR) in the path. The features and techniques covered in Chapter 5, "Service Provider Network Architecture Design," are designed specifically to overcome these limitations in some BGP topologies. Similarly, availability of a second route in link state will offer an almost immediate failover with minimal to zero service interruption.

Let's consider the scenario illustrated in Figure 9-6 to demonstrate the impact of link-state design on convergence time and the overall network stability following a network failure event. In this scenario, if PE1 needs to calculate the possible paths to reach PE3 loopback IP, there is a high number of possible paths to be considered part of the path computation process. It is obvious that this design has an increased MTTR because of the high degree of parallelism (redundant paths). Therefore, when network designers evaluate a design like the one depicted in Figure 9-6, they should consider the following fundamental questions when there is a link or node failure:

■ How many possible paths must PE1 calculate and process?

■ How many routers will be notified about a single link failure?

■ How many routers will not be effected by this failure, but yet will unnecessarily receive and process the update messages?

Note   Even if EIGRP were used in this design, the question is, "How big should the EIGRP query scope be?"

In conclusion, the design presented in this scenario will slow down the convergence time, stability, and the performance of the network, as well, because of the flat routing design, especially if there is a large number of prefixes carried by the control plane.

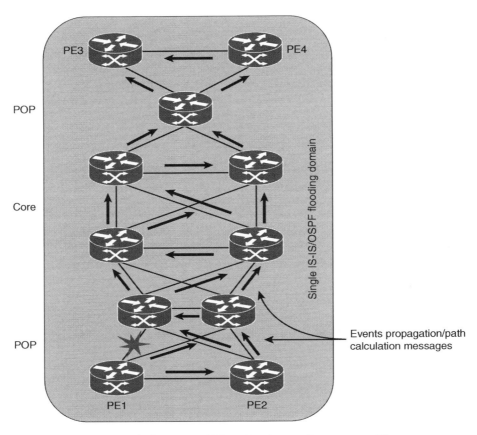

Figure 9-6 *Impact of Flat Control Plane Design on Convergence Time*

If you introduce the principle of fault isolation with IGP logical flooding domains (using IS-IS levels, OSPF areas, or EIGRP summarization) depending on the used control plane protocol, PE1 will have a significantly optimized topology because it will have a fewer number of paths to calculate to reach PE3 (the calculation and updates flooding will usually be up to the border of the flooding domain), as illustrated in Figure 9-7. As a result, the design offers faster network convergence time with a higher level of stability (fault isolation).

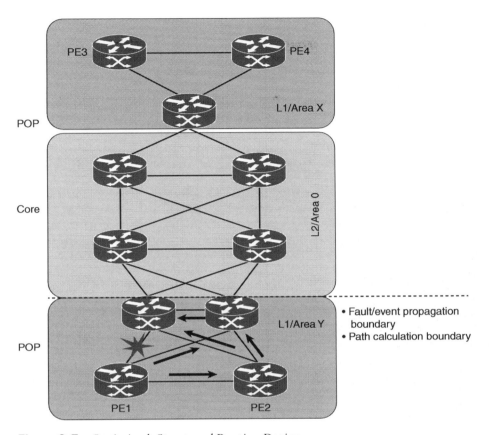

Figure 9-7 *Optimized, Structured Routing Design*

Note It is important, from a design point of view, to understand the location and role of the node that needs to be optimized for network convergence (for instance, if it is a core router or edge [PE] router) because the impact of applying some optimizations techniques can differ. Typically, PE devices handle more customer routes; consequently, tuning IGP timers aggressively down may introduce noticeable stability and performance issues.

Updating the RIB and FIB

Updating the Routing Information Base (RIB) and Forwarding Information Base (FIB) are other influencing factors within the network convergence process. Typically, after the control plane updates the Layer 3 node RIB table, the updates are propagated and reflected to the FIB table (either centrally or distributed depending on the hardware platform architecture). Normally, any process containing prefix installation will first be impacted by the number of prefixes to be installed (the larger the number of prefixes, the longer the duration of installation). Therefore, for networks with a significantly large number of prefixes (thousands or hundreds of thousands of prefixes), this process will be impacted at both levels:

- Updating the RIB table

- Populating the updates to the FIB table or tables

One common mechanism to optimize the prefix installation process is prefix prioritization, in which network operators can assign a higher priority for certain prefixes, such as loopback IPs, to establish an LDP session quickly (in MPLS networks) before other prefixes, such as BGP prefixes. Similarly, the BGP event-based VPN import helps to accelerate route installation, where (PE) nodes in an MPLS L3VPN environment can propagate VPN routes to the CE nodes without relying on the scan time delay. Furthermore, Link-state offers the flexibility to network operators to avoid packets loss (instability) when a network node reloads or recovers from a failure. In this particular scenario, IGP most probably will converge (build its routing table) before BGP, and some routers may start forward traffic through the just reloaded node, which may lead to packs' loss. Because at this point of time, BGP is still rebuilding its routing tables (not fully populated with all IP prefixes). Link-state overcomes this issue by advertising routes with higher metrics "for a fixed period of time" after a node reload or a recovery from a failure. This ultimately will help to avoid impacting transit traffic that is currently using other alternate routes and gives BGP more time to rebuild its routing table. Technically to achieve this, OSPF uses the "wait-for-bgp" feature to send route-LSAs with infinity metric after a reload until BGP is converged or the predefined timer is expired, in the same way, IS-IS uses "set-overload-bit" to wait until BGP converged or the predefined timer is expired[3].

Network Fast Restoration Versus Network Stability

Today's converged networks carry sensitive real-time traffic (such as Voice over IP [VoIP] and business video) and should offer a relatively fast restoration time following any network failure event (usually by tuning routing protocol timers aggressively low). However, the very fast reaction may sensitize the network, causing it to potentially take an action and converge and reconverge again because of the very fast failure detection and protocol reaction for any simple link flap or packet loss. As a result, this will impact the overall stability of the network and probably will outweigh any benefit of the fast convergence.

Therefore, network designers must compromise between both (fast convergence and stability) to achieve a stable fast converging design. There are multiple ways at different layers to optimize the overall network stability when the network is tuned to converge quickly. For instance, a dampening mechanism can relatively mitigate the effect of network instability. Dampening mechanisms are applicable at the protocol and link level, such as link-state exponential backoff and IP interface dampening, respectively. In addition, link-state protocol "throttling" of SPF and LSA/LSP generation mitigates the impact of network instability, such as link flapping, to some extent.

3.   "Uses of the Overload Bit with IS-IS", "Using OSPF Stub Router Advertisement Feature", http://www.cisco.com

Furthermore, the design considerations discussed earlier in this chapter and previous chapters in this book, such as fault isolation, can play a primary role in optimizing the overall network stability. This is because the flooding and bad behavior caused by an unstable component in one domain will be contained and will not be propagated across the entire network (multiple flooding domains concept). As a general rule of thumb, tuning control plane timers aggressively low should be done with very careful planning, considering the different design aspects and influencing factors, along with a thorough testing of multiple failure scenarios.

Microloops

Microloops, also known as *transient loops*, occur when different nodes in the network calculate new alternate paths following a failure event independently of each other and at different times. This behavior is typical in a ring full- or partial-meshed topology running the link-state control plane. For instance, in Figure 9-8, if host A is communicating with host B and the link between R3 and R5 fails, R5 will reconverge and send the traffic to R4. Assuming R4 is converged as well, it will usually then forward the traffic toward R1. If R1 has not converged yet, traffic will loop between these two nodes (R4 and R1). If the duration of this microloop is small, where the network can converge quickly, packets will usually loop for a short duration before their time to live (TTL) expires. Eventually, the packets from host A will reach host B in this scenario. However, if the application is very sensitive, such as voice traffic, this might lead to a call dropped or low voice quality. In other words, application characteristics and their level of tolerance must be considered here as well.

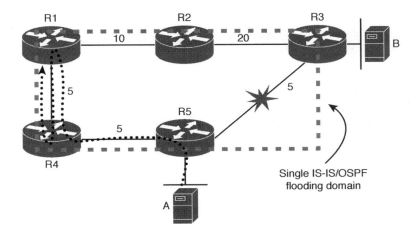

Figure 9-8 *Link-State Microloop*

In contrast, if the duration of the microloop is long, in this scenario it may be because of the slow R1 convergence time. In this case, a packet's TTL will normally expire, or the packet's rate may exceed the available bandwidth. In both cases, it will result in packet drop. Practically, this type of microloop is not always an issue and is acceptable by many businesses. However, it might not be an acceptable behavior for other businesses. In these cases, where this type of microloop is unacceptable, network designers need to either use a triangle topology or a different approach to control network convergence in fully meshed, partially meshed, square, or ring topologies following a network component failure. This limitation can be resolved with the network protection approach, which is covered in the following section.

Note   R1 prefers the path via R4-R5 to reach R3 before the failure event in the scenario described earlier, because of the lower path cost.

Note   Network designers may use the microloop prevention feature described in IETF draft "litkowski-rtgwg-uloop-delay-xx" to mitigate the impact of link-state routing protocol transient loops during topology changes when possible.

Network Protection Approach

Although the network restoration approach is the most commonly used approach to optimize network recovery duration, this approach has the following limitations, which may impact the requirements of some networks:

■ With the restoration approach, large-scale networks may face microloops (as discussed earlier) for a few seconds until the entire core and network has converged properly, which will usually lead to some packet loss within this duration.

■ Tuning routing protocol timers to react and converge very quickly is required to achieve subsecond network convergence time. However, this will result in reduced network stability, which increases the likelihood that the network may react to any simple packet loss. It will also add operational complexity in large networks with a large number of nodes.

In contrast, the network protection approach may be more suitable for satisfying the requirements of large-scale networks that need very fast convergence time (subsecond) without sacrificing network stability. Typically, with the network protection approach, the alternate path is always preestablished and does not need to wait for a protocol calculation across several devices throughout the network following network component failure detection. However, regardless of how fast the switchover method is, if the failure detection mechanism is slow it will overweigh the benefits of the FRR. Therefore, the issues and mechanisms discussed earlier in this chapter regarding failure detection must be considered to achieve a true fast convergence.

This section discusses the primary and most common technologies used to achieve the network protection approach. Each of these technologies can be deployed solely or in combination with other protocols, based on the goal to be achieved, supported features, targeted topology, and network environment.

MPLS-TE Fast Reroute

MPLS-TE fast reroute (MPLS-TE FRR) is commonly used by service provider networks and large-scale enterprise networks where fast recovery after failure detection is a fundamental requirement. It is normally driven by application requirements, such as real-time applications (VoIP), where a network has to reconverge following a network component failure in a relatively undetectable time from the application perspective. However, designing an MPLS-TE with FRR can be a complex task, especially when the network is large and has a large number of paths and nodes. Therefore, to select the right design approach, you must identify the goal to be achieved There are two primary MPLS-TE FRR approaches:

- **Path protection (end to end):** With MPLS-TE FRR, there are usually two LSPs used. The first one is the primary, and the second one is the presignaled backup LSP. The end-to-end FRR approach has some limitations with this behavior that network designers must consider [115]:

  - **Resource overutilization:** When the secondary path is preestablished, it will lead to what is known as *double booking* for the network resources, in particular bandwidth booking, with Resource Reservation Protocol (RSVP) to maintain the same bandwidth constraints as the primary LSP (TE tunnel) to keep the same level of the offered service level agreement (SLA) (1:1 protection).

  - **Overprotection:** This can occur when other mechanisms are used to protect a given set of links within the path, because this approach cannot protect links selectively along the path.

  - **Longer restoration time:** The path protection approach is usually based on a headend-controlled switchover; therefore, this behavior may lead to unexpected delays because it relies on the propagation time of RSVP error message to the headend node to perform the switchover following a failure event.

  However, the path protection approach may offer lower operational complexity when a small number of LSPs need to be set up with a more controlled end-to-end LSP backup path.

- **Local protection:** Both local and path protection rely on the concept of a preestablished or signaled backup LSP. However, with the local protection MPLS-TE FRR, the protection is based on a segmented approach rather than end to end. In other words, the aim of MPLS-TE FRR is to locally repair the protected LSPs by rerouting them over a preestablished backup path (MPLS-TE tunnels) that bypasses either failed links or nodes. This offers an improved scalability (fewer network states) and recovery time compared to the path protection approach. The two primary MPLS-TE FRR local protection approaches are as follows (shown in Figure 9-9):

  - Link protection

  - Node protection

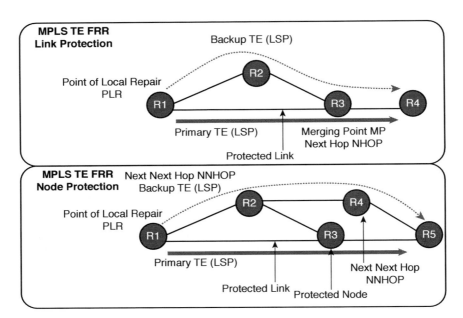

Figure 9-9   *MPLS TE FRR Link Versus Node Protection*

The decision of whether to use link protection or node protection, or both, is mainly based on the network architecture, physical topology layout, level of protection, and the ultimate goal to be achieved by the FRR. However, under general design principles, it is always recommended to keep it as simple as possible. For instance, consider protection for one failure rather than double failure scenarios to avoid situations where you design MPLS-TE FRR to cater for both link and node protection. In addition, if the network node has a reliability level of 99.999 percent, while the line cards or the interconnecting optical links have 99.5 percent of reliability, it is more reasonable to use link protection rather than node protection. Similarly, if a high level of end-to-end LSP availability is required and the next hop (NHOP) passes through an SRLG but the next-next hop (NNHOP) does not, it might be more feasible to use NNHOP to satisfy this design requirement. Again, these are only general design decision considerations. The actual decision has to be driven by the design requirements in terms of business requirements, functional requirements, and application requirements.

MPLS-TE FRR Design Considerations

In addition to the points highlighted with regard to the different approaches of MPLS-FRR, some technical considerations must be taken into account during the planning and design phases of any MPLS-TE FRR to achieve a successful and effective solution that can deliver its promised value. This section discusses the most common considerations with regard to MPLS-TE FRR design.

Multiple Backup Tunnels and Tunnel Selection   The only limiting factor for the maximum configurable number of backup tunnels to protect a given interface is memory limitations. However, the more tunnels and backup tunnels in the network, the more design and operational complexity is added to the network. Therefore, as a rule of thumb, it is always recommended to not overengineer the network with an extremely high number of MPLS-TE tunnels and backup tunnels (the same concept discussed earlier when having many redundant links will overweigh the benefits at higher layers, such as the network routing layer). Nonetheless, in some scenarios, having multiple TE back tunnels can be beneficial, such as the following:

- **Additional redundant paths:** It may be feasible to consider additional backup tunnels to protect the LSPs of critical traffic with a higher level of redundancy requirements, to cater for a double-failure scenario.

- **Link capacity purposes:** Sometimes the protected interface has a high bandwidth, whereas the alternate paths each individually cannot offer the same level of link capacity. Therefore, distributing the traffic over multiple backup tunnels can protect this high-capacity link over multiple paths (backup LSPs) to maintain adequate bandwidth protection following a failure event.

For instance, if the protected interface is a high-capacity link and no single backup path exists with an equal capacity, multiple backup tunnels can protect that one high-capacity link. The LSPs using this link will fail over to different backup tunnels, allowing all the LSPs to have adequate bandwidth protection during failure (rerouting). In other words, if bandwidth protection is not desired, the router spreads LSPs across all available backup tunnels (load balancing across backup tunnels).

However, technically, if multiple backup tunnels are deployed, the backup tunnel selection process will consider the following selection criteria when choosing the preferred one:

- Tunnel that terminates at the NNHOP over a tunnel that terminates at NHOP.

- Tunnel deployed with subpool reservation will be preferred over a tunnel deployed with any pool (same concept applies to tunnels delayed with global pool reservation, global pool over the one with any).

- Tunnel deployed with the lowest sufficient subpool reservation will be preferred over a tunnel deployed with a higher bandwidth subpool reservation.

- Tunnel deployed with limited backup bandwidth over a tunnel deployed with unlimited bandwidth.

For instance, in the scenario illustrated in Figure 9-10, if an LSP at R1 requires a backup tunnel with a 1-Mbp subpool bandwidth, the preferred tunnel will be selected based on the tunnel selection preferences previously listed, as follows:

1. TE2, TE3, and TE4 are first, because they all terminate at NNHOP.

2. TE2 will be eliminated because it protects only LSPs using global-pool bandwidth.

3. TE3 will be preferred over TE4 because it is deployed with a subpool that has the least sufficient backup bandwidth available as compared to TE4.

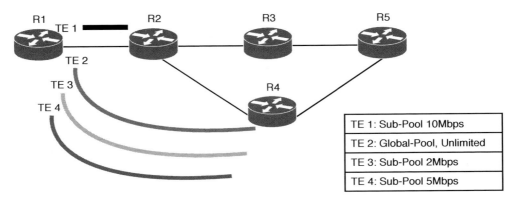

Figure 9-10 *MPLS-TE FRR tunnel selection*

Therefore, to ensure that the protected traffic flows can be distributed across multiple backup TE tunnels, the attributes of the backup TE tunnels with regard to the selection criteria highlighted above must be the same.

Path Reoptimization and MPLS-TE Tunnel Promotion   One of the most common requirements with MPLS-TE with FRR is that traffic must reuse the original LSP/ MPLS-TE tunnel after the failed link or node has recovered. Another common requirement is that MPLS-TE paths should be moved across links/paths that are less congested or optimal when they are available. From a high-level design point of view, both requirements are valid points and offer a value to the business (more optimized and dynamic paths and bandwidth utilization). However, two primary design concerns should be considered:

- **Network stability:** Moving traffic from one MPLS-TE tunnel to another in a matter of subseconds can impact network stability in some situations, such as when there is a link flap and traffic will keep moving between the primary and backup MPLS-TE tunnels.

- **RSVP double booking of bandwidth:** In each of the design requirements above, traffic has to be moved from one MPLS-TE tunnel to another. Ideally, traffic transition must be performed in a transparent manner in which no service interruption must occur (unnoticeable by applications). To achieve this MPLS-TE, use a principle called *make before break* (refer to IETF, RFC 3209).

In addition, the conditions of MPLS-TE backup tunnels may change for any given LSP, in which case it will cause reevaluation or what is commonly known as *promotion*. Such scenarios include the following:

■ A new backup tunnel comes up. For instance in Figure 9-11, the MPLS-TE tunnel 1 is protected by TE tunnel 20 (NHOP). When backup TE tunnel 30 (NNHOP) comes up on line, this may cause reevaluation of the current backup tunnel.

■ The actual available bandwidth (or required bandwidth) for the current active back-up tunnel may change.

■ The current active backup tunnel may go down.

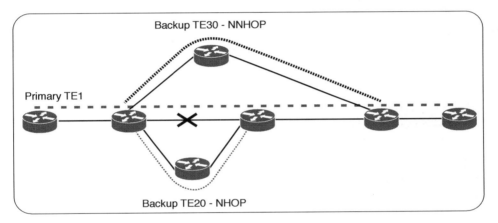

Figure 9-11   *MPLS-TE FRR Tunnel Promotion*

Note   Reevaluation of the current TE backup does not mean the protected LSP must switch over to a new path immediately. In other words, if an LSP is actively using a backup tunnel and a better backup tunnel becomes available, the active LSP is not switched to the better backup tunnel; instead, it might be considered during the next periodic promotion cycle [63].

Path Diversity and Fate Sharing   The main goal of FRR is to provide a precomputed backup path with an extremely fast switchover time from the primary (failed path) to the backup path. However, sometimes the backup path may traverse an SRLG point. This can introduce a risk for a certain type of traffic that must meet a tight SLA with a high degree of end-to-end path reliability and service availability. Therefore, network designers in scenarios like this should cater to a double-failure scenario and make sure that the backup TE tunnel takes a diverse path from the primary path. Network designers should also avoid any SRLG in the path (if possible) to avoid fate sharing during failure scenarios.

Scalability Considerations   One of the main concerns with MPLS-TE and FRR is the scalability limitations when the network grows to an extremely large number of nodes due to the mesh nature of MPLS-TE. Therefore, a combined approach of MPLS-TE FRR and other FRR mechanisms, such as loop-free alternate (LFA), is sometimes used to lessen the impact of having a very large number of primary and backup tunnels across the network.

In addition, the location of the TE headend and tail end and how the backup tunnels handle the backup LSPs are primary influences on the level of scalability of the TE and FRR design (as highlighted earlier in Chapter 5) (in other words, if the TE tunnels are set up between PEs versus across the core only [P] routers and whether one backup tunnel is designed to protect multiple interfaces, where one backup tunnel can protect hundreds or thousands of LSPs [also known as *N:1*]. For example, using MPLS-TE FRR directly between PEs in a service provider network with tens or hundreds of PEs can significantly complicate the design and increase operational cost and control plane complexity.

The aforementioned points are purely design decisions. Practically, it is impossible to generalize and advise that a certain design option is almost always better. Yet by understanding the impact of these points on the overall network and FRR solution scalability, network designers can make a better design decision, considering the goals that need to be achieved, business priorities, network size, and the supported technologies and capabilities. For example, some networks may have a software code that does not support LFA, and a software upgrade is not an option. In this case, LFA will be eliminated from the design options. Similarly, if a service provider wants to meet certain levels of an SLA for its VIP customers, where no single point of failure must exist along the primary and backup paths, it is more feasible to set up MPLS-TE along with FRR end to end (PE-to-PE), which excludes any SRLG in the path that meets bandwidth and other constrained SPF (CSPF) requirements. As highlighted in Chapter 5, the planning of the MPLS-TE is crucial to generate a viable and reliable design, including FRR considerations.

Bandwidth Protection Considerations   Bandwidth protection with regard to MPLS-TE FRR back tunnels is one of the main design considerations that must be accounted for during the planning phase of the solution. From a design point of view, an MPLS-TE FRR design strategy that includes bandwidth protection offers a more reliable FRR solution. With this approach, the backup tunnel selection takes into consideration bandwidth availability over any given path. As a result, operators can satisfy strict SLA requirements. For example, delay-sensitive traffic, such as VoIP traffic riding a TE tunnel, can be protected with MPLS-TE FRR, which can avoid placing the backup TE tunnel over congested paths following a link or node failure. Bandwidth protection with MPLS-TE FRR commonly uses the following approaches:

- **Limited bandwidth:** With this approach, the LSPs must have a predefined bandwidth to be protected with an MPLS-TE backup tunnel. However, the aggregate value of the LSP's bandwidth that needs to use the TE backup tunnel must not exceed the assigned bandwidth value of the TE backup tunnel. This approach is simple to deploy, but it may introduce limitations with regard to bandwidth sharing of MPLS-TE backup tunnels protecting different independent failures/LSPs.

■ **Unlimited bandwidth:** With this approach, the MPLS-TE backup tunnel does not provide any bandwidth protection, and the LSPs over this backup TE tunnel will share the same backup tunnel in a best effort fashion. However, only the MPLST-TE LSPs signaled with zero bandwidth can use the backup tunnels that have unlimited backup bandwidth. This approach offers a cost-effective (economical bandwidth usage) solution that supports oversubscription by sharing bandwidth protection used to cater for multiple independent failures. However, this approach does not offer differentiated treatment for different types of LSPs such as VoIP and data. Therefore, it is commonly used when MPLS-TE is intended to provide basic link protection only.

Moreover, it is important to identify the backup protection strategy used, whether the protection is N:1 (facility) or 1:1. For instance, let's assume that an N:1 MPLS-TE backup strategy is used (without DS-TE). This means a single backup tunnel is protecting multiple LSPs. If there is an LSP carrying VoIP (delay-sensitive traffic) while other LSPs carrying data, in this case, even though an explicit bandwidth is signaled for the backup tunnel, in the case of a failure all the LSPs crossing the link will be using the same backup TE tunnel, in which VoIP traffic will not get any priority over other tunnels for data traffic. This does not mean that VoIP will always suffer with this strategy because the backup path might be overprovisioned. However, it is more of a concern that the backup path may introduce congestion in a failure scenario.

Note   As mentioned earlier, when multiple TE backup tunnels are available with different bandwidth allocation models such as global pool, subpool, or no bandwidth limit, the TE backup tunnel selection will be impacted. Furthermore, the LSPs signaled with zero bandwidth might even be demoted. This "demotion" occurs when there are one or more LSPs (without the bandwidth protection bit set) to be removed from the current assigned TE backup tunnel to provide backup to an LSP that has its bandwidth protection bit set. This scenario happens when there is insufficient backup bandwidth.

Loop-Free Alternate Path (IP FRR)

The goal of IP FRR is to reduce failure reaction time to tens of milliseconds by applying the same concept of EIGRP feasible successor to link-state routing protocols. A precomputed loop-free alternate next hop is used if the currently selected primary next hop fails, as soon as the failure is detected. A network with this feature usually experiences less traffic loss and less microlooping of packets than a network without IP FRR [Loop-free Alternate IETF draft-ietf-rtgwg-ipfrr-spec-base-12], as illustrated in Figure 9-12.

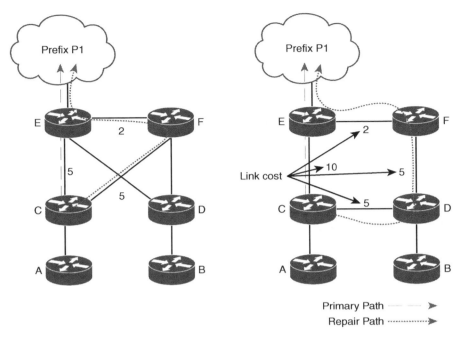

Figure 9-12   *LFA Applicability*

> **Note**   In Figure 9-12 (square topology), the node D primary path to reach prefix P1 is via node F (lower path cost). Therefore, LFA is applicable in this topology (because forwarding traffic immediately after a C to E link failure will not impose any potential looping).

LFA usually offers per-prefix protection (fast convergence) for simple triangular topologies. Ring topologies, however, require considerations of the other flavor of LFA, known as *remote LFA*. In remote LFA, the headend node uses a tunneling mechanism (typical LDP based) to configure an MPLS path. This alternate path is installed as an LFA in the Cisco Express Forwarding (CEF) table. As a result, the LFA can bring the overconvergence time in the supported topologies to less than 50 ms after the detection of the failure because the protocol does not need to wait for the failure propagation, processing, and SPF calculation. Instead, the node can switch over quickly to the precomputed alternate path within a few milliseconds.

Despite the fact the LFA offers simple and native IP FRR support with link-state routing protocols, the following limitations, in which LFA may not be an optimal solution for every design, must be considered:

■ LFA consumes hardware resources, which makes it less than ideal when there are many interconnections between the network nodes, such as with partially meshed and fully meshed topologies, in addition to the added complexity if LFA is in these types of topologies.

■ LFA is limited within a single IGP flooding domain.

■ Ring and some square topologies require packets tunneling such as MPLS to be enabled for the remote LFA to establish an LDP session, as illustrated in Figure 9-13.

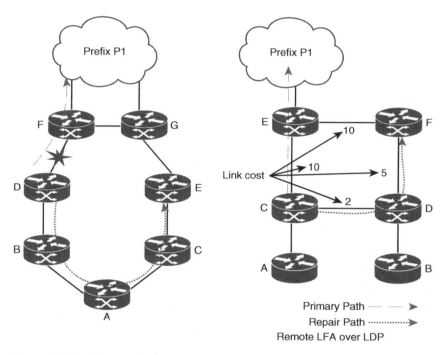

Figure 9-13   *Remote LFA*

Note   By comparing the square topology in Figure 9-13 to the one illustrated in Figure 9-12, it is obvious that in Figure 9-13 node D's preferred path to reach prefix P1 is via node C. Therefore, remote LFA R-LFA (with LDP encapsulation) is required to avoid any microlooping following C to E link failure.

The decision whether to use LFA needs to be made with input from network designers about the topology, to what extent the solution has to be deterministic, and the required FRR coverage; for example, in an SP environment across the edge networks only (points of presence [POP]), core, or both. Practically, LFA is more applicable to POP design, in particular to the ones designed in triangles. It can offer a fully protected LFA solution against both link and node failures compared to the square topology, where some prefixes may not offer a full LFA without considering the remote LFA concept.

The core of the network, however, might not be as simple and common as with the POPs. For instance, the underlying physical topology can influence the decision of whether LFA applies. Redesigning a POP network topology is almost always easier, cheaper, and less disruptive than redesigning a core network. Therefore, if the core topology is not fully supported by LFA or the network designer aims to achieve a more precise and deterministic path protection mechanism, MPLS-TE can be a better choice here. These issues will drive us to ask the question: LFA versus MPL-TE: Which one is better? Table 9-3 compares both solutions from different design aspects. Based on the scenario, requirements, and design constraints, network designs can select the most suitable approach.

Table 9-3 *MPLS-TE FRR Versus LFA*

Design Considerations	MPLS-TE FRR	LFA
Requires separate control protocol in addition to the IGP used	Yes.	No.
Adds control plane complexity	Yes. The level of complexity depends on several factors, such as the number of protected LDPs and nodes.	Yes. The level of control plane complexity depends on the topology (mesh versus triangle) and protected prefixes.
Topology dependent	No.	Yes (some topologies not supported).
MPLS required	Yes.	No. Supports native IP and MPLS, but LDP is required to support R-LFA.
Supports advanced path selection attributes	Yes, such as bandwidth, differentiated services (DiffServ) based, and SRLG exclusion.	Yes (very limited compared to MPLS-TE based).
Offers end-to-end deterministic path protection/selection	Yes, to a high degree (for example, PE to PE).	Yes, to a limited degree (for example, within a POP network).
Requires knowledge for the operations staff	Requires advanced knowledge/expertise in MPLS and MPLS-TE.	Same link-state IGP knowledge/expertise.
Scalability	Depends on several factors discussed in this chapter and Chapter 5, such as the number of LSPs, PE-to-PE versus P-to-P TE tunnel termination, and hardware resources.	Depends on the network size and topology (triangle versus partial mesh), available hardware resources, and number of protected prefixes.

Table 9-3 *continued*

Design Considerations	MPLS-TE FRR	LFA
Flexibility	Flexible (topology independent, supports various path/tunnel selection criteria, supports load balancing/sharing, and supports multiple routed domains.	Limited flexibility compared to MPLS-TE FRR (for instance, works within single link-state flooding domains and can be impacted by the underlying physical topology).

Like the MPLS-TE planning approaches discussed in Chapter 5, LFA is no different here. Network designers must

- Assess the goal of the solution (for example, only path protection or provide differentiated services with path protection)

- Assess the current environment in terms of

    - Routing protocol in use

    - Physical topology.

    - Native IP or MPLS based

    - Single or multiple routing (flooding) domains

- Level of flexibility (for example, how flexible and easy it is for this topology to be altered or redesigned [based on the situation])

After this foundational information has been identified, network designers can make the call whether to use LFA, MPLS-TE, or a combination of both, considering the design aspect listed in Table 9-3.

For instance, an MPLS VPN service provider with the network architecture depicted in Figure 9-14 requires very low network convergence time (path protection) across the entire network and highly flexible with advanced path protection capabilities across the core without any requirement of service differentiation. Also the suggested solution should cater for ease of deployment requirements of this operator.

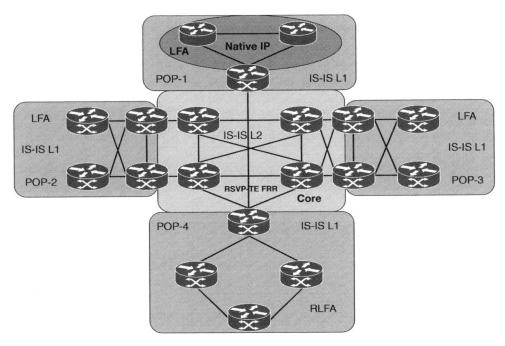

Figure 9-14   *FRR Mixed Approach (MPLS-TE FRR and LFA)*

Based on the requirements provided and the network architecture, it is feasible to use LFA at the edge of the network (single flooding domain, no additional protocol to design and manage and no physical connectivity change required at the POP or core levels), while one-hop MPLS-TE along with autotunnel backup MPLS-TE FRR can be applied at the core of the network, which provides path protection that offers advanced TE capabilities without being impacted by the underlying physical connectivity (full mesh in this scenario) and with minimal operational efforts. For more details, refer to the "Further Reading" list at the end of this chapter.

BGP FRR

BGP fast reroute (FRR) accelerates BGP convergence time significantly to minimize packet loss and to avoid traffic black-holing situations after a failure event when IGP is tuned to converge in a subsecond, without sacrificing network stability. The BGP FRR concept enables BGP to use alternate paths within a subsecond following a failure event of the current active path. BGP FRR is achieved through BGP prefix-independent convergence (PIC) concept, where BGP installs a backup path or paths in RIB/FIB tables that are ready for immediate use. Therefore, a more predictable and constant convergence time of BGP can be achieved no matter how large the number of BGP prefixes is.

For example, in the MPLS VPN scenario in Figure 9-15, PE1 always considers PE2 as the preferred MP-iBGP next-hop to reach AS 600 prefixes. However, with BGP PIC, PE1 also installs an alternate path in its RIB/FIB tables (P4 in this example). When PE2 fails,

PE1 will be aware of this event through the removal of the host prefix by IGPs in sub-second (assuming IGP is tuned to converge in subsecond) and will start to redirect traffic toward the alternate next-hop (via PE4). In the meantime the standard BGP convergence can take place while BGP PIC is forwarding the traffic through PE4 without introducing packet loss (or it will be very minimal, if there is any). As a result, BGP PIC offers more structured RIB/FIB tables (at the core or edge of the network) that helps network designers to align with the underlying IGP fast convergence as well as minimize packet loss and network instability following any network component failure.

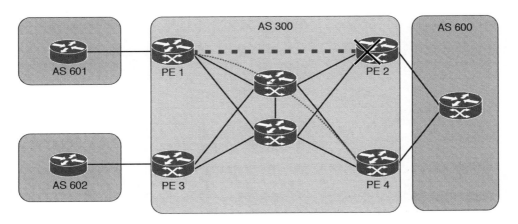

Primary BGP path ▪ ▪ ▪ ▪ ▪
Backup/alternate BGP path (PIC) ·····················

Figure 9-15 *BGP FRR (PIC)*

Similarly, BGP PIC offers more structured RIB/FIB tables that helps to achieve faster network convergence and minimize packets loss at the edge of the network, usually in an SP-style environment following a PE-CE link failure for multihomed CE sites. For instance, AS 600 in Figure 9-16 can be protected with BGP PIC to achieve BGP FRR using the same concept discussed earlier, where PE2 holds primary and backup paths (primary via the directly connected PE-CE link and the backup via PE4 best external). As soon as PE2 detects the link to AS 600 CE failure, traffic will be shunted to PE4 to reach the AD 600 CE to avoid packet loss, while BGP will continue its typical route withdrawal and update propagation to converge the network, as illustrated in Figure 9-16. However, because PE-CE communication is normally over an external BGP (eBGP) session (no IGP to react to the failure and updated RIB/FIB), bidirectional forwarding detection (BFD) is required to detect a failure of an eBGP one-hop peer in less than a second. This can be combined with the BGP failover feature to track the availability of the BGP neighbor (CE), not only based on link status.

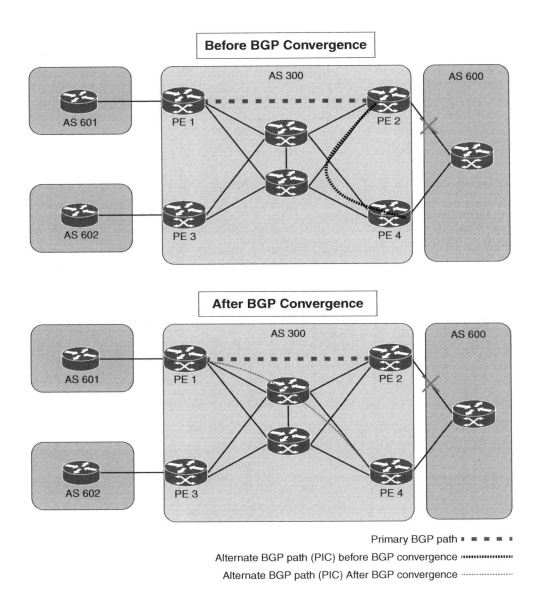

Figure 9-16 *BGP FRR (PIC Best External)*

Note Typically, at the FIB level, after a failure event where a next hop to a prefix fails, the FIB (Cisco CEF) will look for another path to reach the same prefix by searching through the FIB table to find the next longest matching path to the prefix. This proves beneficial when the next hop is several hops away and there are multiple paths to reaching that next hop, such as a router with a loopback interface IP address that is reachable via multiple physical interfaces/paths. However, this feature (recursion) may impact and conflict with the BGP PIC concept, because there is a precomputed alternate path already in place with BGP PIC. Moreover, the searching process through the FIB table almost always slows down convergence time in general. Therefore, ideally, the CEF recursion feature should be disabled at least for the learned host routes when BGP PIC is in use. In some Cisco platforms, "When the BGP PIC functionality is enabled, Cisco Express Forwarding recursion is disabled by default for next hops learned with /32 host routes and next hops that are directly connected."[4]

BGP Multiple Path Announcement Solutions

The natural behavior of BGP, as defined in RFC 4271, is to announce only a single path to its BGP neighbors, known as the *BGP best path*. However, in some scenarios, the announcement of multiple paths within BGP is becoming a requirement, especially when BGP fast convergence is required. Furthermore, BGP path hiding of BGP RRs may prevent the efficient use of BGP multipath or keep BGP PIC from working properly. BGP path hiding also inhibits fast and local recovery because the network has to wait for the standard BGP control plane convergence to restore traffic across the network [34]. Therefore, a solution that offers path diversity is required for networks that need to use the available path or need to maintain a fast network convergence at the control plane level (BGP). Multiple solutions are available to change this default behavior of BGP and facilitate the ability to advertise multiple paths with BGP, some of which were already discussed in Chapter 5 with regard to hot-potato routing with RR. In addition, these mechanisms serve to optimize BGP FRR in similar scenarios:

- BGP additional paths
- BGP best external
- BGP diverse paths
- Different route distinguisher (RD) approach with MP-BGP in MPLS VPN environments

Summary

This chapter covered high-availability network design and the primary elements and approaches to achieve it at multiple layers. This chapter also discussed how the concept of network convergence consists of multiple elements that all collectively work together to achieve the overall desired convergence time. In addition, two primary approaches at the protocol level (the network protection approach and the network recovery approach) to achieve the desired level of network resiliency were also examined, with each having advantages and limitations, as summarized in Table 9-4.

4. "BGP PIC Edge for IP and MPLS-VPN," http://www.cisco.com

Table 9-4 *Network Protection Approach Versus Network Recovery Approach*

	Network Protection Approach	Network Recovery Approach
Scalability	Moderate	High
Convergence	Very fast	IGP potentially fast with tuning
Hardware resource consumption (memory, CPU)	Moderate to high (depends on the number of protected routes/LSPs)	Moderate (depends on some factors such as number of routes and routing domains design)
Design and configuration complexity	Protocol dependent (for example, LFA simpler than MPLS-TE FRR)	Simple
Operational complexity	The larger, the higher	Moderate (however, more prone to human error [such as mismatching timers])
Network stability with subsecond convergence	Stable (taking into consideration the fail-over time and frequency between the protected and back paths)	High possibility of instability and microloops
Solution example	LFA, MPLS-TE FRR	Tuned IGP for fast convergence

Last but not least, this chapter explained, in multiple places, that the level of availability will vary from network to network and from part to part within the same network, based on multiple variables and mainly driven by the application criticality and business priorities. In other words, not every network or every part of the network needs HA considerations or fast network convergence. For network designers to identify when and where to consider it, a good understanding of the application, functional, and business requirements is required. (For instance, identify what is critical and high priority to the business, versus what is important but not high priority, versus what is not critical and not high priority.)

Further Reading

"High Availability Campus Recovery Analysis Design Guide," http://www.cisco.com

RFC 6571, *Loop-Free Alternate (LFA) Applicability in Service Provider (SP) Networks*, http://www.ietf.org

"Remote Loop-Free Alternate (LFA) Fast Re-Route (FRR)," draft-ietf-rtgwg-remote-lfa-11, http://www.ietf.org

RFC 6413, *Benchmarking Methodology for Link-State IGP Data-Plane Route Convergence*, http://www.ietf.org

RFC 4090, *Fast Reroute Extensions to RSVP-TE for LSP Tunnels*, http://www.ietf.org

"MPLS Traffic Engineering (TE) - Autotunnel Primary and Backup," http://www.cisco.com

"Redundancy Mechanisms for Carrier Ethernet Networks and Layer 2 VPN Services," http://www.ciscolive.com

RFC 6981, *A Framework for IP and MPLS Fast Reroute Using Not-Via Addresses*, http://www.ietf.org

Other Network Technologies and Services

Chapter 10

Design of Other Network Technologies and Services

This chapter covers multiple networking and IP service design concepts and considerations that are considered as noncore topics for the purpose of the CCDE practical exam at the time of this writing. Although these topics are not considered as core technologies for the CCDE exam, one or more of these technologies are expected to be part of each scenario. The different topics discussed in this chapter might be presented as an application or service to be used to achieve a business need. For example, a business-critical application might require multicast to be enabled across the network to work properly.

Note, as well, that this chapter focuses on the design drivers, considerations, and approaches that network designers can consider based on the different design requirements, without covering any deep technical details. This chapter covers the following:

- IPv6 design considerations

- IP multicast design considerations

- Quality of service (QoS) design considerations

- Network security design considerations

- Network management

IPv6 Design Considerations

IPv6 is a broad topic. Therefore, this section focuses on one of the most critical and important topics, which is the integration and coexistence of IPv4 and IPv6, by covering the different design and technical options and how to follow a business-driven lifecycle design approach.

IPv6 Business and Technical Drivers

Although the initial IPv6 draft "The Case for IPv6" was published as an IETF draft more than a decade ago (1999) (draft-ietf-iab-case-for-ipv6-06.txt), there was no serious move or adoption of IPv6 by enterprises and service providers. However, during the past few years, billions of smartphones and various mobile devices have been connecting to the public Internet and private networks. The overall Internet needs to evolve and grow to support this continuous growth, not to mention that the increased adoption of Internet-based services and public cloud hosting has added more demand on public IP addresses.

Furthermore, the new trends and technologies, such the as Internet of Things (IoT) and smart connected cities, are leading to a increasingly growing number of Internet-connected users, applications, sensors, and services that require a huge number of IPs. According to Gartner, Inc., "The Internet of Things (IoT), which excludes PCs, tablets, and smartphones, will grow to 26 billion units installed in 2020, representing an almost 30-fold increase from 0.9 billion in 2009" [92]. As the Internet transitions, organizations must start consider adopting IPv6 to support and facilitate achieving their business goals in terms of organic growth, merger and acquisition, and continuity in the market. With the exhaustion of IPv4 addresses and the increased demand on IPs, organizations face many challenges, such as the following:

■ The exhaustion and constraints of IPs (IPv4), which adds many challenges to managing and provisioning new services that require new addressing spaces

■ Added complexity to merger and acquisition scenarios, where Network Address Translation (NAT), with its limitations to overcoming the overlapping addressing issue, is considered a primary design option

■ New market and service trends, where mobility and numerous connected devices (smart cities, IoT, and so on) are key drivers for both enterprise and service providers that are trying to adopt innovation and the provision of new services, for which a large number of IPs are required to accommodate the various IP-enabled endpoints

Therefore, the adoption of IPv6 is becoming a necessity to overcome these challenges and to meet these new technology solution requirements and demands. Hypothetically, if an organization is encountering one or more of the following situations, it is time to migrate or at least start to consider enabling IPv6:

■ Unable to expand the business to other global regions because of the exhaustion of the public IPv4 addresses.

■ Deploying innovative network environments, applications, and devices such as IoT with a huge number of connected sensors required to support smart connected communities.

■ A service provider or an enterprise needs to maintain seamless connectivity across fixed and mobile users when using collaborative applications, and NAT is no longer an option.

■ Enabled IPv6-based 4G/LTE mobile networks or connecting workforces to these networks.

- Organizations that primarily work as a supplier or partner with public sector or government entities are required to comply with their standards. In these entities, IPv6 is fast becoming the standard.

- Encountering IPv6 need in the network driven by the deployments of end-user and host operating systems and applications such as Microsoft Windows 7, Windows 10, Windows Server 20xx, Apple OS X, system virtualization, and large scale multitenancy.

IPv6 Addressing Types (Review)

Before taking a look at the different types of IPv6, it is important that network architects and designers be aware of the high-level differences and similarities between the two IP versions. Table 10-1 summarizes some of the technical similarities and differences between IPv4 and IPv6.

Table 10-1 *Summary of IPv4 Versus IPv6*

	IPv4	IPv6
Address scope	32 bit	128 bit, multiple scopes
IP allocation	Manual, Dynamic Host Configuration Protocol (DHCP)	Manual, stateless address autoconfiguration (SLAAC), DHCP
Address types	Unicast, multicast, broadcast	Unicast and multicast
QoS	Differentiated services, integrated services	Differentiated services, integrated services, flow label
Multicast	Internet Group Management Protocol (IGMP), Protocol-Independent Multicast (PIM), Multiprotocol Border Gateway Protocol (MP-BGP)	Multicast Listener Discovery (MLD), PIM, MP-BGP
Security	No built-in- support	IPsec built in

Note Although IPv6 supports built-in IPsec, it is considered a myth and misconception that IPv6 is more secure than IPv4. This assertion stems from the original mandated use of IPsec in host-to-host communication, as specified in RFC 2401. Consequently, if IPsec is implemented, it will provide confidentiality and integrity between two hosts, but it still will not address any link operation vulnerabilities, attacks, and most of the denial-of-service (DoS) attacks.[1]

1. http://www.cisco.com/c/dam/en/us/products/collateral/ios-nx-os-software/enterprise-ipv6-solution/aag_c45-707354.pdf

With regard to IPV6 addressing, IPv6 has three types of unicast addresses:

■ **Link local:** This address is nonroutable and can exist only on a single Layer 2 domain (fe80::/64). As described in RFC 4291, even when one or more routable IPv6 addresses are assigned to a certain interface, an IPv6 link-local address is still required to be enabled on this interface.

■ **Unique local address (ULA):** This address, also known as a *site-local address*, is routable within the administrative domain of a given network (fc00::/7). This address, in concept, is similar to the IPv4 private address range (RFC 1918).

■ **Global:** This address is routable across the Internet (2000::/3). This address is similar in concept to the IPv4 public ranges.

Network designers can mix and match the different IPv6 addressing types when designing an enterprise network. However, there are some issues associated with each design model, as summarized in Table 10-2.

Table 10-2   *IPv6 Address Types*

IPv6 Addressing Model	Scope	Design Simplicity	Manageability	Scalability
ULA only	Internal	Moderate	Moderate	Low
ULA + global	Internal and external	Complex	Complex	Moderate
Global only*	Internal and external	Simple	Simple	High

* Because NAT is primarily used with IPv4 to overcome IP address shortages, it is always arguable that this is a less-secure model because it exposes internal device IPs to external networks (no address hiding using NAT). In addition, it is commonly claimed that NAT offers a layer of secure communication; however, that argument fails to cover the impact of NAT on many applications at higher layers. "This is amplified through the widespread sharing of vendor best practice documents and sample configurations that do not differentiate the translation function of address expansion from the state function of limiting connectivity."[2]

Migration and Integration of IPv4 and IPv6

Considerations related to transitioning to IPv6 and planning and designing the integration of both IP versions to coexist are critical aspects since the introduction of IPv6. However, the most common critical and challenging question for network architects and designers with regard to migrating and enabling IPv6 is where to start. For network architects or designers to achieve a successful IPv6 migration or integration, they must follow a structured approach based on the top-down design methodology, which consists of network discovery, assessment, planning, design, implementation, monitoring, and optimization, as shown in Figure 10-1.

2. *Local Network Protection for IPv6*, RFC 4864

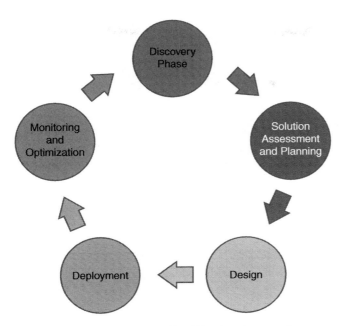

Figure 10-1 *Migration to IPv6 Design Approach*

The sections that follow explain the phases shown in Figure 10-1.

Discovery Phase

At this phase, network architects or designers usually focus on understanding and identifying the business goals and drivers toward the enablement of IPv6, in addition to other influencing factors such as project timeframe, government compliance, and the geographic distribution of the sites with regard to IP addressing availability. Information about other influencing factors from the network point of view at this stage also needs to be identified and gathered at a high level, such as whether the existing network infrastructures (LAN, WAN, security nodes, services, and applications) support IPv6 and whether the business is willing to invest and upgrade the nodes that do not support IPv6. Therefore, it is critical that the right and relevant information be gathered at this phase so that it can be analyzed and considered during the planning phase.

Solution Assessment and Planning

Migrating or integrating IPv4 and IPv6 networks might seem as simple as enabling IPv6 routing across certain network areas; however, the reality is that several other factors must be considered during the planning phase to ensure that the design will deliver its intended goal and be prepared for the challenges and constraints that may arise during the deployment phase. After the completion of the high-level business and network discovery, network designers need to analyze each of the identified influencing factors and generate a migration or integration plan based on the gathered information. In general, the following considerations help at this phase to influence and drive the detailed design of the transition strategy and approaches at later stages.

- **Goal:** Understanding the main purpose of the migration or integration (based on the information gathered during the previous phase) is important to driving the design in the most suitable direction. For instance, is the transition to IPv6 to access certain services in the data center? To comply with "regularity compliance"? Or to enable IPv6 at the Internet edge only (for example, lack of public IPv4 pools)?

- **Infrastructure support:** Furthermore, the answers with regard to the goal become vital during the planning phase, because it is important to understand whether the entire infrastructure supports IPv6 or only the network edges (for example, provider edges [PEs] in service provider [SP] network and access or distribution in campus networks) and whether the business is willing to upgrade the devices that do not support IPv6. Based on this, the migration or integration plan guides the next phase (design) as you consider a technology solution to overcome any constraint with regard to IPv6 support across the network.

- **Existing services and applications:** Although many applications already support IPv6, many still do not, especially those that are developed in house. Therefore, understanding and assessing application support is critical because the upgrade, if it fails to consider how the IPv6 networks will reach these IPv4-only applications, will break the communication with these applications. Such a break may seriously impact the business.

In other words, the planning phase takes the output information from the discovery phase and analyzes it and uses it as a foundation to drive the selection of the appropriate migration/integration approach. Consider, for example, that an enterprise needs to migrate its network to be IPv6 enabled (end to end), but at present the core network components do not support IPv6 and the business is not allocating any budget to upgrade these components. In addition, access to some new IPv6-enabled applications hosted at the data center is an urgent requirement. This information should be collected during the discovery phase, and the network designer at the assessment and planning phase is expect to select the right approach to meet the requirements for this enterprise, taking into consideration the relevant constraints. In this case, the network designer may suggest either an IPv6 over IPv4 tunneling mechanism (either sourced from the workstation or using access/distribution switches), Domain Name System (DNS)-based translation, or 64NATing to facilitate accessing the new IPv6-based applications over the existing IPv4 core infrastructure.

The following subsections cover the approaches possible during the planning phase with regard to IPv6 based on the targeted environment (enterprise versus service provider). The selected approach should ideally be complemented with one or more of the technical mechanisms listed later in Table 10-5 at the design phase. Therefore, each phase (ideally) must take the outcomes of the previous phase as a foundational input to achieve a cohesive end-to-end business-driven design that avoids any "design in isolation" throughout all the phases.

Transition Approaches to IPv6 (Enterprise Networks)

After identifying the objectives of the migration or integration of IPv4 and IPv6, network designers must decide which approach is the most suitable, taking into consideration the objectives, the different requirements, and design constraints, such as timeframe, available budget, and whether IPv6 is supported by the network nodes. Table 10-3 summarizes the most common approaches, based on different design goals and priorities, to transition an enterprise network to be IPv6 enabled.

Table 10-3 *Approaches to Enable/Transition to IPv6: Enterprise*

Design Goal	Priorities	Timeframe	Design Approach	Design Considerations
Migrate the enterprise network to be pure IPv6 or dual stack	No service interruption	Flexible	Migrating the core to be in dual-stack mode first, then other enterprise modules can be gradually migrated to IPv6. (Either only IPv6 or dual stack depends on the goals and requirements.)	Increased utilization of hardware resources. Increased control plane complexity in dual-stack mode. Core network component must support IPv6. Partially migrated blocks may require tunneling as an interim solution.
Migrate the enterprise network (fully or partially) to be pure IPv6 or dual stack	Certain enterprise modules have to be (quickly) migrated first, such as data center	Limited	Migrating certain modules of the enterprise network first. DNS translation or tunneling mechanism such as ISATAP is required to maintain the communications between IPv6 and IPv4 islands within the network.	This approach is suitable when the core device does not support IPv6 and requires either hardware or software upgrades. Increases design and control plane complexity. Increases operational complexity.

Table 10-3 *continued*

Design Goal	Priorities	Timeframe	Design Approach	Design Considerations
Migrate the data center network (fully or partially) to support communication with IPv6 hosts	Support virtualized and nonvirtualized IPv6 hosts	Flexible	Depends on the data center architecture different approach can be used. For example, a DC design can consider a typical dual stack, or an overlay can be considered using VxLAN to support IPv6 hosts; also MPLS enabled DC may consider 6PE/6VPE.	In all cases, dual stack increases hardware resource utilization, control plane complexity, and operational complexity. If the timeframe is limited, one quick and common solutions is host-based tunneling (ISATAP, RFC 5214), assuming endpoints and hosts support this tunneling mechanism.
Provide IPv6 access either inbound or outbound at the enterprise Internet edge	Support translation between IP4 and IPv6 at the Internet edge	Flexible	A translation mechanism is required that is either based on a load balancer, pure DNS, or classical "64" NATing based.	Increases operational complexity at the Internet edge. Requires additional security consideration with regard to IPv6 enablement. If the timeframe is limited, it is always quicker to consider the current infrastructure support. (For example using NAT at the existing Internet edge router is quicker than provisioning a new DNS server to do the translation.)

Transition Approaches to IPv6 (SP Networks)

In its overall approach and goal, enabling IPv6 in an SP network is slightly different from in enterprise networks. Typically, the SP networks enable IPv6 either to provide a transit path for other SPs (such as transit and peering Internet service providers) or to offer IPv6 connectivity to its customers. Which mechanism to use is mainly driven by the goal and the transport used by the SP, whether it is based on native IPv4 only or Multiprotocol Label Switching (MPLS) based (with or without MPLS VPN). Table 10-4 summarizes these approaches from the SP point of view.

Table 10-4 *Approaches to Enable/Transition to IPv6: SP*

Goal	Transport	Possible Approaches
Provide IPv6 Internet transit	Native IPv4	Dual stack, tunneling (manual RFC 2893, generic routing encapsulation [GRE], Layer 2 Tunneling Protocol Version 3 [L2TPv3])
Provide IPv6-based services and Internet access to residential clients	Native IPv4	Dual stack, 6rd, tunneling such as IPv6 over L2TP
Provide IPv6 Internet access/transit	MPLS	6PE, IPv6 over pseudowires
Provide IPv6 connectivity for MPLS L3VPN customers	MPLS	6VPE
Provide IPv6 Internet access for MPLS L3VPN customers over a separate virtual private network (VPN) or within the same customer VPN	MPLS	6VPE

Unlike with enterprise networks, enabling IPv6 in an SP network can be more flexible and less interruptive, as covered in Chapter 5, "Service Provider Network Architecture Design." SP networks by nature are transport networks where no endpoints or hosts are directly connected. This means that there is no need to consider any directly connected host with this transition, except host and services used by the SP to deliver specialized functions such as network management, DHCP, and authentication/authorization services. Besides, when MPLS is enabled (nowadays MPLS to a large extent is the de facto protocol for SP networks), the integration and enablement of IPv6 will be simpler with the MP-BGP overlay capability (MP-BGP-based 6PE, 6VPE). Furthermore, operators can consider the phased approach in which only the PE nodes that need to provide IPv6 transit connectivity need to be enabled with IPv6 first without introducing any change to the core (P) routers. However, the additional load and hardware resource limits must be calculated and taken into consideration.

Note   One of the primary considerations that must be taken into account when migrating or integrating with IPv6 is to secure IPv6 in the same manner that IPv4 is secured. Otherwise, the entire network will be vulnerable to network attackers and breaches. For instance, since the release of Microsoft Windows Server 2008, IPv6 has been native to the Windows OS, which supports transition technologies at the server/client level such as ISATAP. In this case, if one of these servers is compromised and the network security rules do not consider IPv6, malicious traffic can ride an IPv6 tunnel or packet without being blocked or contained by the security devices in the path.

As covered so far, the migration to IPv6 differs slightly in SP networks as compared to in enterprise networks, based on the fact that SPs mainly need to provide a transit path to their customers and other peering providers. However, today's SPs are not limited to just providing transit paths; they also offer many other services, such as hosted services and applications, software as a service (SaaS), cloud-based hosting data centers, and content services such as IPTV. Practically, service providers cannot simply migrate to native IPv6, because they normally have other services and customers who need IPv4. Therefore, the coexistence of IPv4 and IPv6 is inevitable nowadays for SPs. What is important to plan and design for is the strategy that can be used to incorporate IPv6 into the existing provider network in a way that is not interruptive and at the same time offers enough flexibility and reliability to optimize SPs' time to market with regard to IPv6-enabled services and transport while maintaining IPv4 support intact. One common approach that application and content provider use to support IPv6 is to enable IPv6 at the services level first. With this approach, providers that offer hosted services and applications, whether it is cloud offering (such as SaaS) or any other IP service such as VoIP and Internet, usually enable or migrate these services to be IPv6 enabled first, and so customers that need to use these services must be IPv6 enabled, using a form of translation at the customer side such as NAT v4 to v6 at the enterprise Internet edge, or the provider might offer the translation service at a different cost or as value-added service such as DNS-based translation. Also, the SP must ensure the underlay transport can carry IPv6 communications. In fact, this approach is similar (to a large extent) to enabling or rolling out IPv6 applications in an enterprise data center in which the enterprise needs to incorporate an interim solution to provide and maintain access to these applications to users with only IPv4 endpoints.

When the desired approach is decided on based on the design requirements and constraints, network design can move to the next phase to start connecting the dots and generate a solution driven by the outcomes of the previous phases.

Detailed Design

After selecting the suitable approach for the migration or integration between IPv4 and IPv6 networks, ideally based on the gathered and analyzed information during the planning phase, network designers at this stage can put together the details of the design, such as selecting the suitable integration mechanism, deployment details such as tunnels termination, IP addressing, routing design, network security details, and network virtualization considerations, if any are required. Typically, the outcome of the design phase will be used by the implementation engineers during the deployment phase to implement the designed solution. Therefore, if there is any point that is not doable or practically cannot be implemented, it will be reported back to this phase (to the network designer) to be revised and changed accordingly. There are various mechanisms and approaches with regard to integrating IPv6 and IPv4. For simplicity, these mechanisms can be classified as following:

- Dual stack

- Tunneling based

- Translation based

- MPLS environment solutions

Table 10-5 lists the various technical mechanisms that can be used to integrate and support the coexistence of both IPv4 and IPv6, taking into consideration some of the primary design aspects that influence the solution selection based on the design requirements.

Note Information in Table 10-5 is not a best practice or a must to be followed with regard to IPv6 integration and migration options. However, it is based on the most commonly considered technology solutions for certain scenarios. And network designers must always assess the different influencing factors before suggesting any approach or mechanism.

Table 10-5 *Mechanisms to Support Coexistence of IPv4 and IPv6*

Mechanism	Scenario	Targeted Environment	Design Concern
Dual stack	End-to-end IPv6 + IPv4.	Any environment that ultimately needs to move to end-to-end IPv6	IPv6 support in all L3 aware platforms is required. Increased control plane complexity. May introduce scalability weaknesses when both IP versions are running together (depends on the available hardware resources such as memory).

Table 10-5   *continued*

Mechanism	Scenario	Targeted Environment	Design Concern
Tunneling: point to point (P2P) (L2TPv3, GRE RFC 2473)	Transit IPv6 over IPv4-only network.	Small number of IPv6 islands that need to interconnect over IPv4 network	Scalability, encapsulation overhead. Increased control plane complexity.
Tunneling: ISATAMP (RFC 5214)	Host-sourced tunnels that terminate at IPv6-enabled modules or services.	For trial IPv6 services or in case of IPv6 enabled partially (for example, only at the DC) (mostly enterprise networks)	Affects the overall network architecture. QoS, multicast, and NAT issues. Adds control plane complexity. Increases operational complexity.
Tunneling: mGRE	Interconnect IPv6 over IPv4 in a hub-and-spoke topology.	Interconnects IPv6-enabled remote sites in hub-and-spoke topology over IPv4 WAN Interconnects private IPv6 islands across public IPv4 cloud	Multicast traffic has to go via the hub. Adds control plane complexity. Increases operational complexity.
Tunneling: 6rd (RFC 5969)	Used to extend IPv6 deployment to customer sites (usually residential gateway), with limited impact on existing IPv4 infrastructure.	SP networks that offer IPv6 services/ Internet access over IPv4 SP network to residential customers Simple, stateless, automatic IPv6-in-IPv4 encap/decap that offers fast IPv6 enablement	Whether the network equipment supports 6rd. Adds control plane complexity. Increases operational complexity.
Tunneling: IPv6 over L2TP software	To offer IPv6 access for residential gateway.	Digital subscriber line (DSL)/residential SPs With limited investment Stateful architecture on L2TP network server (LNS)	Dual-stack IPv4/IPv6 service on residential gateway LAN side. Increases operational complexity.

Table 10-5 *continued*

Mechanism	Scenario	Targeted Environment	Design Concern
Translation 64: NAT/SLB	Allow IPv6 handsets/endpoints to access IPv4 Internet over Long Term Evolution (LTE)/3G or IPv4 services.	Green-field IPv6 service providers or enterprise networks that need to be interconnected to legacy/existing IPv4 network/services	Does not support every application type or protocol today. Performance may not match dual-stack design, depending on traffic load.
Translation: DNS	DNS in this scenario offers the translation between the v4 and v6 based on the source and targeted host.	Access applications or services by name	Limited to services and applications that can be reach by name, not IP.
Translation: LISP	LISP encapsulation can facilitate the IPv6 communication only over IPv4 transport.	enterprise edge, DC or WAN with mix of IPv4 and IPv6 networks	High operational complexity. Increased control plane complexity. Network devices must support LISP.[3]
MPLS: 6PE	Facilitate enabling IPv6 over an existing MPLS and MP-BGP IPv4 network.	Large enterprises and SPs that want to provide IPv6 over their IPv4 infrastructure	Does not provide traffic separation between different customer networks (no MPLS VPN support). May introduce scalability limitation because a separate Routing Information Base (RIB) and Forwarding Information Base (FIB) is required per customer. Increased control plane complexity.

3. "Enterprise IPv6 Transition Strategy Using the Locator/ID Separation Protocol," http://www.cisco.com

Table 10-5 *continued*

Mechanism	Scenario	Targeted Environment	Design Concern
MPLS: 6VPE	Facilitate enabling IPv6 over an existing MPLS/MP-BGP IPv4 network for VPN customers.	MPLS VPN providers or enterprises with MPLS VPN networks	Increased control plane complexity.

Note Typically, adding any overlay or tunneling mechanism to the network will almost always increase the level of its operational complexity. However, this level varies based on several factors, such as network size, routing design, staff knowledge, and the nature of the selected technology itself.

Deployment, Monitoring, and Optimization

These steps usually are more relevant to the implementation of the design followed by continuous monitoring for the implemented solution to ensure that the network is delivering the promised value and meeting the expectations. Ideally, the implementation should follow an implantation plan that specifies what the services are, and the futures that need to be enabled before proceeding with any step. It should also cover any potential risk associated with any change (for example, whether it is going to be interruptive to the existing production network). For instance, enabling IPv6 at the routing protocol level may lead to resetting the existing IPv4 peering sessions; normally this depends on the routing protocol, hardware platform, and software in use.

Transition to IPv6: Scenario

ABC Corp. is an international real-estate company headquartered in Singapore, with 116 remote sites distributed across Asia, Australia, and Europe, as shown in Figure 10-2.

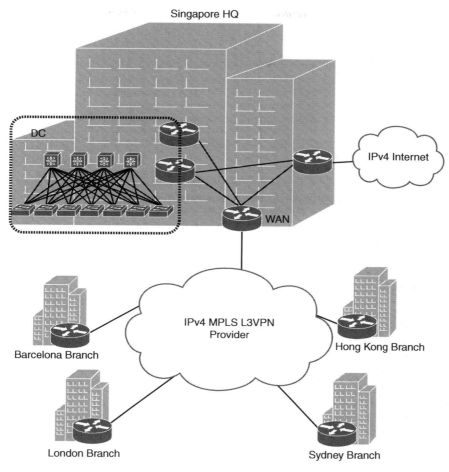

Figure 10-2 *ABC Corp. Network*

The CIO of ABC Corp. has decided to migrate their entire IP network infrastructure and applications to be primarily based on IPv6 to support some of the long-term business innovation and strategic plans. In addition, ABC Corp. wants to achieve the following with this transition project to maintain business continuity:

■ Retain the ability for their internal users to access some legacy applications that do not support IPv6 and to access the IPv4 Internet

■ Provide the ability for external users to access the ABC Corp. new IPv6 web-based services over the IPv4 Internet

Therefore, they decided to add another Internet link dedicated to accessing IPv6 Internet services. Moreover, the security team of ABC Corp. requires accessing some (pre-defined) IPv4 Internet websites, "web-based services," by the internal IPv6-enabled users to appear as if they are accessible over the IPv6 Internet. For example, when an IPv6-enalbed user accesses a website across the IPv4 Internet using a typical site, "URL/domain name, such as www.exmple.com", the resolved source IP of the website's domain name by the DNS should appear to the user as IPv6 instead of IPv4 source IP address.

One of the ABC Corp. primary requirements is that the go-live of the IPv6 network project be within 6 weeks. Therefore, they hired a network consultant to provide a strategic approach that can help them to achieve this goal within this limited timeframe.

Network Requirements Analysis

Based on the information provided, the following are the primary design constraints:

- ABC Corp. needs a quick (transition) solution to enable IPv6.
- ABC Corp. Internet and data center services are all located at the HQ/hub site (centralized model).
- The current MPLS VPN WAN provider does not support IPv6.

Design considerations include the following:

- The network must be end-to-end IPv6 enabled.
- Provide the ability to ABC Corp. end users to access the IPv4 Internet and IPv4-only legacy applications.
- Web services accessed over the IPv4 Internet by internal IPv6 clients must appear as if they are accessed over the IPv6 Internet.
- ABC Corp. IPv6 web services must be accessible over the IPv4 Internet.

The assumption is that network nodes across the network, end-user devices, applications, and hosts within the data center support IPv6

Design Approach

To meet the primary requirements of ABC Corp., taking into account the design considerations covered earlier, ABC Corp. can consider the following phased approach.

Phase 1

Provide fast IPv6 enablement across the network (see Figure 10-3):

- Enable IPv6 on all network nodes (dual stack), starting from the DC followed by other nodes such as WAN routers.
- Enable IPv6 routing on the network nodes (DC, WAN routes hub and spokes, and Internet edge).

- Enable Stateful NAT64 at the IPv4 Internet edge gateway toward the IPv4 Internet to provide Internet access for the internal IPv6 devices.[4]

- Introduce DNS64 functionality to satisfy the requirement of hiding Internet service IPv4 source addresses to appear as its sourced from an IPv6 address (by synthesizing DNS A record into AAAA record).[5]

- Enable Static NAT64 at the DC edge nodes, where the IPv4 to IPv6 static mapping can provide internal IPv6-Enabled users to access legacy IPv4-only applications.[6]

- Enable Static NAT64 at the IPv4 Internet gateway where the IPv6 to IPv4 static mapping can enable external users to access ABC Corp. IPv6 web-based services over the IPv4 Internet.

- Interconnect the IPv6 network islands (spokes/remote sites) with the HQ/hub site using an IP overlay tunneling mechanism (preferably IPv6 over mGRE IP tunneling dynamic multipoint VPN [DMVPN]) over the IPv4 MPLS VPN WAN.

Phase 2

Design optimization (see Figure 10-3):

- Migrate the WAN to a provider that supports IPv6 MPLS L3VPN to be used instead of the overlaid IPv6 DMVPN over the WAN.

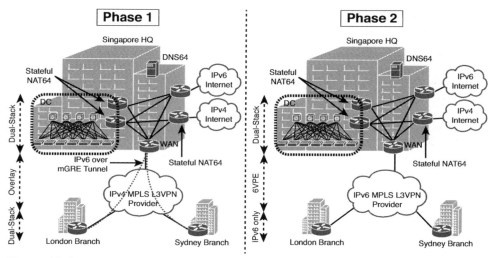

Figure 10-3 *ABC Corp. Transition Approach to IPv6: Phase 1 and 2*

4. *Framework for IPv4/IPv6 Translation*, RFC 6144
5. *DNS64: DNS Extensions for Network Address Translation from IPv6 Clients to IPv4 Servers*, RFC 6147
6. *Stateful NAT64: Network Address and Protocol Translation from IPv6 Clients to IPv4 Servers*, RFC 6146

- Disable IPv4 routing from the network areas where no IPv4 clients/hosts exist, such as remote sites, which helps to reduce the load from the remote site network nodes (holding separate RIB/FIB tables for each IP version).

> **Note**   For a sample WAN migration example, see Chapter 4, "Enterprise Edge Architecture."

Further Reading

RFC 4029, *Scenarios and Analysis for Introducing IPv6 into ISP Networks*, http://www.ietf.org/rfc/rfc4029.txt

"Deploying IPv6 in Broadband Access Networks," https://supportforums.cisco.com/docs/DOC-13985

"Deploying IPv6 in Campus Networks (CVD)," http://www.cisco.com

IP Multicast Design Considerations

The typical behavior of unicast traffic is to send a copy of each packet to each receiver in any given network segment, as shown in Figure 10-4. As a result, the more receivers in the network of any given application, such as streaming video, the more bandwidth consumed. The impact of this behavior in small networks is almost always acceptable because of the limited number of receivers (end users). In contrast, in large-scale enterprises and SP-grade networks, where there might be thousands or even more of receivers of certain applications such as IPTV streaming, this behavior wastes a large amount of bandwidth because of the unnecessary extra bandwidth required to transport unicast packets, which will ultimately lead to additional cost and overutilization of the available bandwidth.

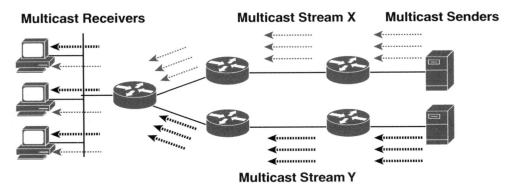

Figure 10-4   *Unicast Traffic Streams*

Broadcast transmissions, however, lead to even worse situations, because it will forward data packets to all portions of the network, which can consume a lot of bandwidth and hardware resources across the network when there are actually only a few intended recipients.

Therefore, in today's networks, there are many applications and services developed to operate over multicast-enabled transport to help network operators overcome the afore-mentioned limitations. In general, with multicast, organizations can gain several advantages, such as the following:

- **Efficient and cost-effective transport:** More efficient network and bandwidth utilization can help to reduce the cost of network resources.

- **Optimized bandwidth and efficiency:** Enhancing the overall utilization over the network can reduce congestion caused by existing applications that are inefficiently transmitting unicast to groups of recipients, thereby allowing the network to support a larger number of recipients with simultaneous access to the application in a more efficient way, as shown in Figure 10-5.

- **Provide the business access to new applications:** Many applications and services nowadays developed to operate over multicast-enabled networks that offer more efficient and scalable communication, specifically distributed multimedia business applications such as trading, market data, distance learning, and videoconferencing.

- **Open new business opportunities:** Opens new revenue-generating opportunities for both enterprises and SPs, by offering innovative services that were not possible over unicast transport, such as content SPs and IPTV.

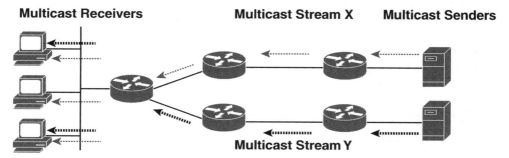

Figure 10-5 *Multicast Traffic Stream*

Note   Practically and ideally, the decision to enable multicast should be driven by business application requirements. However, as a network architect or designer, you can sometimes suggest that the business migrate certain applications from the unicast version to multicast version if the option exists and the transition is going to optimize the network and application performance. For instance, Moving Picture Experts Group (MPEG) high-bandwidth video applications usually consume a large amount of network bandwidth for each stream. Therefore, enabling IP multicast will enable you to send a single stream to multiple receivers simultaneously. This can be seen from the business point of view as a more cost-effective and bandwidth-efficient solution, especially if the increased bandwidth utilization translates to increased cost (such as WAN bandwidth).

Enterprise Multicast Design Options and Considerations

This section focuses on multicast design considerations on typical enterprise networks.

Application Characteristic

Designing IP multicast is just like all other IP network designs. To be a business-driven design and facilitate business goals, it has to follow the top-down approach by first focusing on the business goals and needs, taking into account the characteristics of the applications to be used. With regard to multicast applications, they can be categorized into three primary types, as listed in Table 10-6.

Table 10-6 *Multicast Applications Types*

Application Characteristic	Application Examples
One to many	Newsfeeds, push media, paging, announcements, some database updates
Many to many	Multimedia conferencing, multiplayer games, concurrent processing
Many to one	Data collection, polling, resource discovery

Therefore, understanding at a high level the characteristics of the multicast applications is essential to determine which multicast protocol and design might be appropriate.

Multicast IP Address Mapping into Ethernet MAC Address

Normally, in any IP multicast-enabled environment, hosts (receivers) are required to receive a single traffic stream that has a common destination MAC address that maps to a multicast channel or group. Therefore, a mapping of IP to MAC is required here per multicast destination group IP. The range from 0100.5e00.0000 through 0100.5e7f.ffff is the available range of Ethernet MAC addresses for IPv4 multicast, and only half of these MAC addresses are available for use by IP multicast, where the IP to MAC mapping will place the lower 23 bits of the IPv4 multicast group address into these available 23 bits in the MAC address. As a result, MAC addressing will not always be unique in Layer 2 switched networks, because the upper 5 bits of the IP multicast address are dropped as part of the IP to MAC mapping,[7] as shown in Figure 10-6.

In other words, as shown in Figure 10-6, the first 4 bits of the IP multicast 32 bits are always set to 1110 (Class D). Therefore, there will be only 28 unique bits left of the IP multicast addresses information. Furthermore, because the remaining 28 unique bits that belong to the Layer 3 IP multicast address information cannot be mapped in a 1:1 manner to the available 23 bits of Layer 2 MAC address space, this will lead to the loss of 5 bits of the address information in this mapping process. Consequently, it will result in what is known as *32:1 address mapping*, which means that each Layer 2 multicast MAC address can potentially map to 32 IP multicast addressees.

---

7. "IP Multicast Technology Overview," http://www.cisco.com

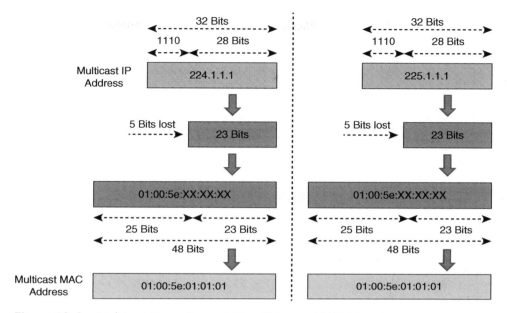

Figure 10-6 *Multicast Group Layer 3 IP-to-Ethernet MAC Mapping*

To illustrate this point, consider a scenario of two IPTV channels streaming over different IP multicast group IDs (per channel), such as 224.1.1.1 and 225.1.1.1. Based on the mapping mechanism described earlier, hosts connected to a common Layer 2 switch and interested in receiving different IPTV channels will end up receiving both streams because both multicast groups' IPs will map to the same multicast MAC address on the Layer 2 switch. In this particular example, this will usually result in reduced efficiency in a large network with a large number IPTV receivers connected to the same Layer 2 switched network.

Similarly with IPv6, the mapping will be from 128-bit Layer 3 IPv6 multicast addresses to the 48-bit MAC address, where only the lower 32 bits of the Layer 3 address are preserved, while 80 bits of information are lost during the mapping process. This means, like IPv4, there is a possibility that more than one IPv6 multicast address might map to the same 48 bit MAC address.

Therefore, even though this might not always be an issue in LAN environments, it is still a critical point to be considered by network designers with regard to IP multicast design over a switched network. This can be even more critical if the switched network is connecting two different multicast domains (interdomain multicast scenario).

Internet Gateway Management Protocol (IGMP) snooping offers a simple solution for Layer 2 switched networks by eliminating the flooding to every single port (avoiding broadcast forwarding style). With IGMP snooping, the switch intercepts IGMP packets as they are being flooded and uses the information in the IGMP packets to determine which host/port should receive packets directed to a multicast group address. Similarly, Multicast Listener Discovery (MLD) snooping must be considered in a Layer 2 switched network when IPv6 multicast is used.

Nevertheless, even when multicast optimization protocols in a Layer 2 network are used, such as IGMP snooping, Layer 2 switches may flood all multicast traffic that belongs to the MAC address range of 0x0100.5E00.00xx, which belongs to the respective Layer 3 addresses in the link-local block (reserved for the use of routing protocols and topology discovery protocols) to all the ports within the same Layer 2 segment on the Layer 2 switch. Therefore, when possible, IP multicast addresses that map to the MAC address range 0x0100.5E00.00xx should be avoided whenever possible.

Moreover, in scenarios such as the one shown in Figure 10-7, when there are multiple Layer 3 routers connected over a Layer 2 switch using one shared segment / VLAN, IGMP snooping cannot optimize multicast traffic flooding within the layer 2 switch. This is because these routers technically do not send IGMP membership reports for the desired multicast flows. Instead, the routers use routing protocol control messages among them, such as PIM. As a result, there will be no IGMP messages for IGMP snooping to intercept and use for multicast traffic forwarding optimization, and the multicast video stream will be forwarded to all the routers connected to this switch within the same VLAN.

To optimize this design and overcome this issue, routers that are not supposed to receive the multicast stream simply can be placed in a different VLAN in this switch, such as the router connected to the WAN in Figure 10-7. Alternatively, the IGMP mroute proxy feature may be used to convert PIM join messages back into IGMP membership reports.

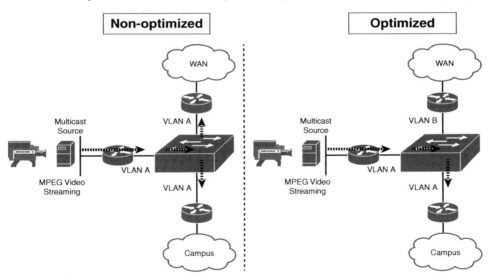

Figure 10-7 *Design Issue: IGMP Snooping*

Note Network designers must consider maintaining the existing Layer 3 unicast communication between the WAN router and other routers in this network after placing the WAN router in a different VLAN, such as adding Layer 3 VLAN interfaces or adding additional interfaces/subinterfaces from other routers within the same VLAN.

> **Note** IGMP snooping may maintain forwarding tables based on either Ethernet MAC addresses or IP addresses. Because of the MAC overlapping issues covered earlier with regard to mapping IP multicast group address to Ethernet addresses, the forwarding based on IP address is desirable if a switch supports both types of forwarding mechanisms.

Multicast Layer 3 Routing

This section starts by discussing the key consideration to achieve successful multicast pack forwarding, and then covers the most common protocols used to route multicast traffic within a single multicast domain (and also discusses multicast routing between different multicast domains).

Reverse Path Forwarding

It is critical to understand the concept of reverse path forwarding and how it can impact multicast traffic forwarding and design. Reverse path forwarding (RPF) is the mechanism used by Layer 3 nodes in the network to optimally forward multicast datagrams. The RPF algorithm uses the rules shown in the Figure 10-8 to decide whether to accept a multicast packet, forward it, or drop it.

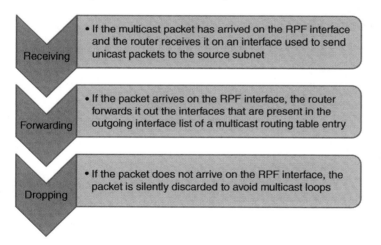

Figure 10-8 *Multicast RPF Check Rules*

Therefore, a successful RPF check is a fundamental requirement to establishing multicast forwarding trees and passing multicast content successfully from sources to receivers. For instance, in the scenario shown in Figure 10-9, multicast was enabled only on interface G0/1, while unicast routing prefers interface G0/0 to reach the multicast sender (host IP 192.168.1.10). Hence, multicast traffic will not be received in this case because of RPF check failure. This issue can be fixed in different ways, such as aligning multicast-enabled interfaces with the unicast routing table, using static multicast route (mroute) or MP-BGP to overcome the issue associated with the failure of RPF check. However, the primary goal here is first to be aware of the RPF impact. Then, as a network designer, you can decide which mechanism is more feasible to use to avoid the failure of RPF check. In other words, to achieve a successful IP multicast design, RPF check must be considered along with the possible mechanism that helps to avoid any forwarding failure while at the same time minimizing increased control plane complexity. For example, if BGP is used as the unicast control plane proto-col, MP-BGP will avoid adding extra control plane complexity, because one rout-ing protocol will be used to control both unicast and multicast routing in this case. Technically, MP-BGP here will only help to avoid RPF check failure over the desired interface to be used for multicast forwarding when the existing unicast routing pre-fers another path or interface.

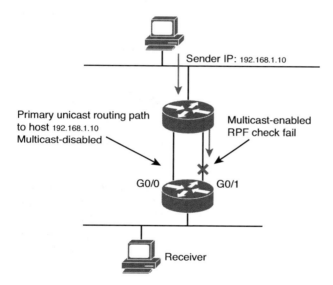

Figure 10-9 *RPF Check Failure Scenario*

Multicast Routing Protocols

Multicast traffic flows are IP traffic, which almost always traverses the network using the existing unicast routing. However, for the multicast receivers and senders to locate each other across the network and communicate using the underlay IP network, a multicast routing protocol must use this function, and usually each multicast routing protocol has its own characteristics in terms of the discovery and forwarding style (multicast trees) of IP multicast traffic streams. Table 10-7 compares the most common multicast routing protocols.

Table 10-7   *Comparison of Layer 3 Multicast Routing Protocols*

Multicast Protocol Type	IP Version	Supported Multicast Trees	Rendezvous Point (RP)	Suitable Applications	Supported IGMP/MLD Version	Scope
PIM-DM	4	Source tree only	Not required	Legacy	IGMP 1, 2 and 3	Intradomain
PIM-SM	4/6	Shared tree and source tree	Required	One to many	IGMP 1, 2, and 3 / MLD 1, 2	Intradomain and interdomain
PIM-SSM	4/6	Forwarding only use shortest path first (SPT)	Not required	One to many	IGMP 3 / MLDv2	Intradomain and interdomain
PIM-Bidir	4/6	Shared tree only	Required	Many to many Many to one	IGMP 1, 2, and 3 / MLD 1, 2	Intradomain
PIM-BSR (PIMv2)	4/6	Shared tree and source tree	Required	One to many	IGMP 1, 2, and 3 / MLD 1, 2	Intradomain and interdomain

Note   Although some of the PIM protocols covered in Table 10-7 technically support multicast interdomain routing, it is not common for it to be used to provide multicast interdomain routing without other protocols such as Multicast Source Discovery Protocol (MSDP).

Although having multiple flavors of PIM might be seen like an added complexity to the multicast network design, it can be seen as added flexibility for an environment with different types of multicast applications. For instance, PIM-SSM can be deployed for certain enterprise communication applications, PIM-Bidir for financial applications, and PIM-SM for other general IP multicast communications.

RP discovery, however, is one of the primary design aspects that must be considered during the planning and design phase of any IP multicast design task. Table 10-8 summarizes the common mechanisms used to locate or discover the intended multicast RP within a multicast domain.

Table 10-8   *Multicast RP Discovery Mechanisms*

	Manual/Static	Automatic (Auto-RP)	BSR	Embedded RP
Supported IP version	Support IPv4/v6.	IPv4	IPv4/IPv6	IPv6
Scalability	Scalable, with a potential of increased operational overhead.*	Scalable	Scalable	Scalable
Operational simplicity and flexibility	Inflexible with management overhead in large deployments. Changing RP's IP requires all the nodes to be updated.	Flexible with simplified operation.** Offers more protocol's filtering capabilities than BSR	Flexible with simplified operation. Offers less traffic overhead (as RP information is encapsulated in PIM packets)	Flexible with simplified operation, dynamic

*If static RP used with a redundant RP mechanism such as anycast-RP with MSDP or anycast-RP PIM (RFC 4610), static RP can offer a scalable solution without significant increase in the operational overhead.

** Taking into account traffic and processing overhead because of the specific multicast groups used to propagate RP information, also special consideration in hub-and-spoke topology "NBMA" is required.

Note   Auto-RP is a Cisco proprietary protocol. Bootstrap Router (BSR), in contrast, is the standards body method of electing an RP (RFC 5059). BSR operates completely based on PIMv2 and PIM-SM, which offer an optimized bandwidth during the flooding and discovery process as compared to Auto-RP. In contrast, Auto-RP can scope multiple RP address per domain and operate over either PIMv1 or PIMv2, with the ability to fall back to dense mode if required. As a general rule, network designers should avoid considering BSR and Auto-RP protocols within the same domain at the same time. That said, in some scenarios where a multicast PIMv2 domain that does not support Auto-RP (for example, non-Cisco network nodes) needs to interoperate with a multicast PIMv1 domain running Auto-RP, both Auto-RP and BSR functions are required. One simple solution to facilitate the interoperability between these two different multicast PIM domains is to deploy a network node at the multicast domain's boundary to perform the Auto-RP mapping agent and the BSR functions. Also, this approach is applicable to PIM migration scenarios between Version 1 and Version 2.[8]

8. http://www.cisco.com/c/en/us/td/docs/switches/lan/catalyst3750x_3560x/software/release/15-2_2_e/multicast/configuration_guide/b_mc_1522e_3750x_3560x_cg/b_mc_3750x_3560x_chapter_010.html

Note The RP is required to initiate new multicast sessions with sources and receivers. During these sessions, the RP and the first-hop router (FHR) may experience some periodic increased overhead from processing. However, this overhead will vary based on the multicast protocol in use. For instance, the RP with PIM-SM Version 2 requires less processing than in PIM-SM Version 1, because the sources only periodically register with the RP to create state. In contrast, the location of the RP is more critical in network designs that rely on a shared tree, where the RP must be in the forwarding path, such as PIM-Bidir. (The following section covers this point in more detail.)

RP Placement

Normally, the placement of the a multicast RP is influenced primarily by the following factors:

- The used multicast protocol

- The multicast tree model

- Application characteristics (for example, one to many versus many to many)

- Targeted network between the sources and receivers (LAN versus WAN)

As a rule of thumb, when the source tree along with shortest path tree (SPT) are considered, RP placement is not a big concern even though it is commonly recommended to be placed closer to the multicast sources, because in this case the RP is not necessarily required to be in the data forwarding path. However, some multicast applications, such as many-to-many type of multicast applications the recoveries, might operate as senders at the same time using different multicast groups for receiving and sending. Technically, even when SPT is enabled (where the last-hop router [LHR] cuts over to SPT source tree), the source tree is always created between the source and the RP, in which a (S,G) state is created on all the nodes between each source and its RP before the switch over to SPT takes place, as shown in Figure 10-10. This may lead the nodes in the path (between the many receivers/senders and the RP) to hold a large number of (S,G) states. (In trading environments, this number can reach up to a few thousands of source feedback streams sourced from the receivers that operate as multicast senders as well.)

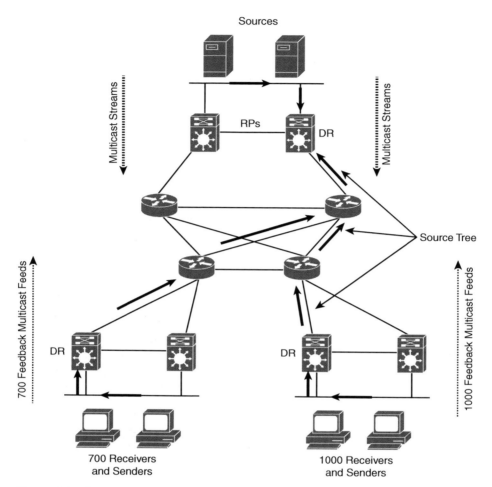

Figure 10-10   *Many-to-Many Multicast Applications Using PIM-SM RP*

Therefore, to reduce the number of (S,G) states on these nodes, you can add different RPs close to the receivers that require sending feeds to the feedback groups, as shown in Figure 10-11. Also, MSDP can be introduced in this design among the RPs to ensure that all RPs for any given group will be aware of other active sources. This design is suitable in a multicast environment that requires the receivers to be able to send feedback/streams using a separate group from the actual data source group. Alternatively, PIM-SM can be migrated to PIM-Bidir in this environment.

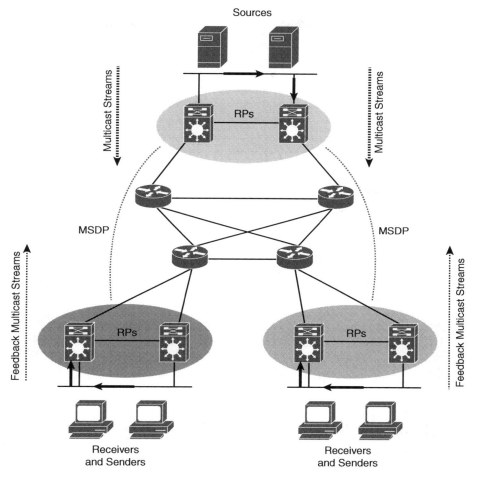

Figure 10-11 *Optimized - Many-to-Many Multicast Applications Using PIM-SM RPs*

However, when the shared tree is used as the forwarding multicast tree, such as using PIM-Bidir where the RP will be in the data path, network designers must carefully and wisely consider the placement of the RP within the network because all the traffic will flow through the RP. For example, if multiple multicast streams are sourced from different senders distrusted at different locations across the network, identifying which stream should be given priority is a key to place the RP in the most optimal path between the sources and receivers based on the following:

- Application's criticality to the business

- Bandwidth consumption of each application's stream

- Number of sources and receivers of each application

- The underlying transport and topology of the network between the sources and receivers (LAN versus WAN, hierarchical versus hub and spoke)

For example, in the scenario shown in Figure 10-12, there are two hub nodes each connected to a different data center with multicast applications streaming over a shared tree. Although hub 1 is connected directly to the business-critical multicast application that requires high bandwidth, multicast streams will reach each of the remote site's receivers via hub 2. This is because hub 2 is defined as the RP for the multicast shared tree (such as PIM-Bidir), where the RP must be in the data forwarding path, which can result in a congested data center interconnect (DCI) link and degraded application quality. Therefore, to optimize the path for the business-critical application with high-bandwidth requirements, the RP function must be moved to hub 1 to serve as an RP either for the entire multicast domain or at least for the multicast groups used by the applications located in DC-1. This can provide a more optimal path for multicast streams sourced from DC-1 toward the spokes/receivers.

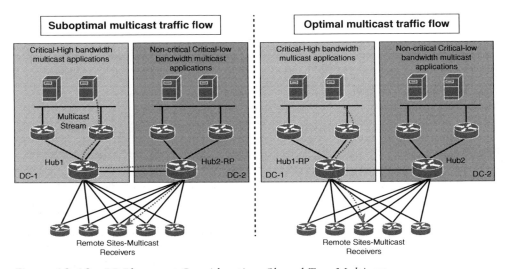

Figure 10-12 *RP Placement Consideration: Shared-Tree Multicast*

Note In both scenarios, the assumption is that the RPF check is considered based on the utilized path for multicast traffic.

Interconnecting Multicast Islands

One of the most common multicast design challenges occurs when two or more multicast-enabled networks need to communicate over a unicast-only network—for example, when a retail business is planning to roll out a digital media signage solution across all the remote sites, where the media server of this solution will stream the media contents centrally from the data center to the remote sites "acting as a multicast streaming source." This digital media signage solution requires multicast to be enabled end to end. However, the WAN provider in this scenario supports only unicast. In this case, this enterprise either needs to migrate to a new WAN provider or transport that supports multicast or consider a tunneling mechanism such as GRE in which IP multicast traffic can ride this tunnel and be transported over the IP unicast WAN network, as shown in Figure 10-13. Moreover, if the network in the middle is MPLS enabled, this may facilitate building a self-deployed L2VPN (such as point-to-point E-Line), then on top of it multicast routing can be enabled and transported.

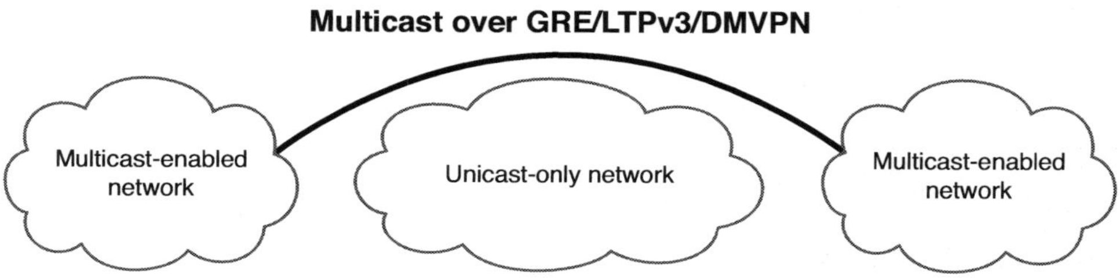

Multicast over GRE/LTPv3/DMVPN

Figure 10-13 *Connecting Multicast Islands*

Which decision is better depends entirely on the situation and the requirements, such as timeframe to deploy the solution, cost considerations, and equipment support to the overlay technology. (For example, do the WAN edge nodes support GRE?) Furthermore, the most important influencing factor here is the characteristics of the multicast application used. For instance, IP tunneling such as GRE or DMVPN may introduce some limitations, such as limited scalability if a many-to-many multicast application is used. Therefore, in this case, it might be more feasible for large-scale organizations to consider a core/WAN transport that supports multicast routing rather than considering a solution that may potentially introduce limitations to the business in the future.

The other common scenario here is when there is a network device in the network path that does not support multicast, such as a firewall. This device will usually break the multicast network into two networks, where a mechanism such as IP tunneling is required to pass multicast traffic through this device, as shown in Figure 10-14, assuming this approach (tunneling traffic through the firewall) will not breach the organization's security policy standards.

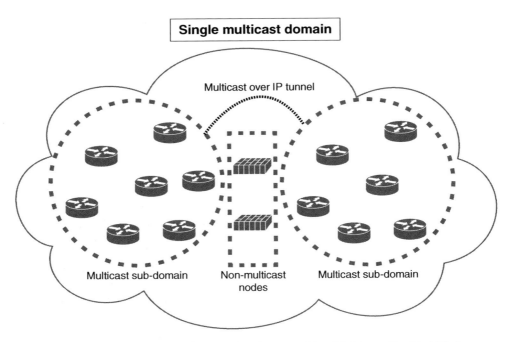

Figure 10-14   *Connecting Multicast Islands over a Non-Multicast-Enabled Node*

Interdomain Multicast

The multicast protocols discussed earlier focused mostly on handling multicast in one multicast domain. The term *multicast domain* can be defined as an interior gateway protocol (IGP) domain, one BGP autonomous system (AS) domain, or it can be based on the administrative domain of a given organization. For example, one organization might have multiple multicast domains, with each managed by a different department; for instance, one domain belongs to marketing, and another domain belongs to engineering. Other common scenarios of multiple multicast domains are between service providers and after merger or acquisitions between companies. Therefore, it is important sometimes to maintain the isolation between the different multicast domains by not sharing streams and RP feeds and at the same time offering the ability to share certain multicast feeds and RP information as required (in a controlled manner). This section covers the most common protocols that help to achieve this type of multicast connectivity.

Multicast BGP

As discussed earlier, a successful RPF check is a fundamental requirement to establish multicast forwarding trees and pass multicast content successfully from sources to receivers. However, in certain situations, unicast might be required to use one link and multicast to use another, for some reason, such as bandwidth constraints on certain links. This situation is common in interdomain multicast scenarios. Multicast Border Gateway

Protocol (MP-BGP and sometimes referred to as MBGP as well) is based on RFC 2283, "Multiprotocol Extensions for BGP-4". MP-BGP offers the ability to carry two sets of routes or network layer reachability information (NLRI) (sub-AFI) set for unicast routing and one set (NLRI) for multicast routing. BGP multicast routes are used by the multicast routing protocols to build data distribution trees and influence the RPF check. Consequently, service providers and enterprise networks can control which path multicast can use and which path unicast can use using one control plane protocol (BGP) with the same path selection attributes and rules (such as AS-PATH, local_preference, and so on).

Multicast Source Discovery Protocol

MSDP is most commonly used to provide a mechanism of RP redundancy along with Anycast-RP (covered later in this chapter). MSDP is the most common protocol used to interconnect multiple IPv4 PIM domains because of its controlled and simplified approach of interconnecting PIM domains, in which it allows PIM domains to use an interdomain source tree instead of a common shared tree. With PIM, each RP is usually aware of the multicast sources and receivers within its PIM boundary (domain). MSDP peers use TCP sessions and they send Source Active (SA) messages to inform other MSDP peers about an active source within the local multicast domain, as shown in Figure 10-15.

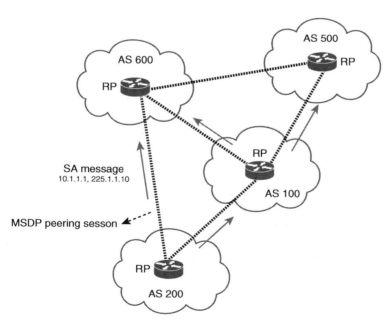

Figure 10-15   *Typical Interdomain Multicast Scenario with MSDP*

Consequently, all the MSDP peers (RPs) will be aware of all sources within the local domain and in other domains. RPF check is a fundamental consideration here, as well. However, with MSDP, some rules drive whether RPF check for SA messages is to be performed, as summarized in Table 10-9 [106].

Table 10-9   *MSDP RPF Check Rules*

RPF Check Performed	RPF Check Not Performed
The sending MSDP peer is also an interior (MP-)BGP peer.	The sending MSDP peer is the only MSDP peer (for example, if only a single MSDP peer or a default MSDP peer is configured).
The sending MSDP peer is also an exterior (MP-)BGP peer.	The sending MSDP peer is a member of a mesh group.
The sending MSDP peer is not an (MP-)BGP peer.	The sending MSDP peer address is the RP address contained in the SA message.

One common design issues with regard to multidomain multicast using MSDP and BGP that leads to RPF failure is that the IP address of the i(MP-)BGP peer is different from the MSDP IP (for example, BGP using physical IP, while MSDP using loopback IP), as shown in Figure 10-16.

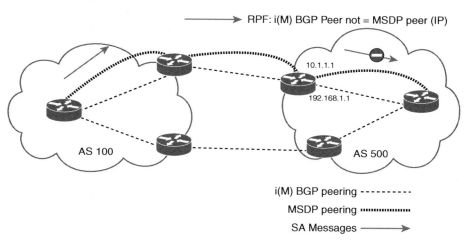

Figure 10-16   *Common RPF Check Failure with MSDP and BGP*

Therefore, it is important that the address used for both i(MP-)BGP and MSDP peer addresses is the same.

Interdomain Multicast Design Scenario   In the scenario shown in Figure 10-17, AS 500 is providing transit connectivity service to a content provider (AS 300) that offers IPTV streaming. End users need to connect to the streaming server IP 10.1.1.1 over AS 500. AS 500 has two inter-AS links, and they want to offer this transit service with AS 300 using the following traffic engineering requirements:

- Unicast traffic between AS 500 and AS 300 must use the link with 5G as the primary path and fail over to the 10G link in case of a failure.

- Multicast traffic must use the 10G link between AS 500 and AS 300. However, in case of a link or node failure, multicast traffic must not fail over to the other link (to avoid impacting the quality of other unicast traffic flowing over the 5G inter-AS link).

- Multicast group addresses that are in the range of 232/5 must not be shared between the two domains (AS 300 and AS 500).

- Currently, the IPTV system needs to use only the range of 225.1.1.0/24. Therefore, only sources in AS 300 with this range must be accepted by AS 500.

To achieve these requirements, the following design aspects must be considered:

- To ensure multicast traffic flow is over the 10G link only and without facing RPF check failure, MP-BGP will be used to advertise the multicast sources IPs (e.g. 10.1.1.1) and filter out these IPs from being advertised/received over the 5G link.

- MSDP peering must be established between multicast RPs of AS 300 and AS 500 to exchange SA messages about the active source within the local domain in each AS.

- PIM RP filtering and MSDP filtering[9] is required to ensure that the RPs will only send/accept sources within the multicast group IP range (225.1.1.0/24).

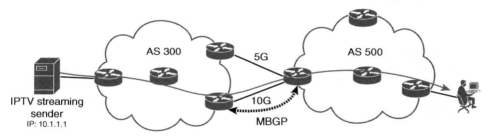

Figure 10-17 *Interdomain Multicast Design Scenario*

Embedded RP

Although PIM SSM offers the ability for IPv6 multicast to communicate over different multicast domains, PIM SSM still does not offer an efficient solution for some multicast deployments where few-to-many and many-to-many types of applications exist, such as videoconferencing and multi-user games applications. Also, in some scenarios, the multicast sources between domains may need to be discovered. Furthermore, MSDP cannot be used to facilitate interdomain multicast communication as with IPv4, because it has deliberately not been specified for IPv6. Therefore, the most common and proven solution (at the time of this writing) to facilitate interdomain IPv6 communication is the IPv6 Embedded-RP (described in RFC 3306) "in which the address of the RP is encoded in the IPv6 multicast group address, and specifies a PIM-SM group-to-RP mapping to use the encoding, leveraging, and extending unicast-prefix-based addressing."[10] The IPv6 Embedded-RP technique offers network designers a simple solution to facilitate interdomain and intradomain communication for IPv6 *Any-Source Multicas* ASM applications without MSDP.

---

9. "Multicast Source Discovery Protocol SA Filter Recommendations," http://www.cisco.com

10. RFC 3306, *Embedding the Rendezvous Point (RP) Address in an IPv6 Multicast Address*

However, network designers must consider that following an RP failure event, multicast state will be lost from the RP after the failover process because there is no means of synchronizing states between the RPs (unless it is synchronized via an out-of-band method, which is not common). In addition, with MSDP, network operators have more flexibility to filter based on multicast sources and groups between the domains. In contrast, with Embedded-RP, there is less flexibility with regard to protocol filtering capabilities, and if there is no other filtering mechanism, such as infrastructure access lists, to limit and control the use of the RP within the environment, a rogue RP can be introduced to host multicast groups, which may lead to a serious service outage or information security risk.

SP Multicast Design Options and Considerations

This section focuses on the design considerations and options that apply to SP-grade networks (whether it is an enterprise or an SP).

MVPN (Draft-Rosen Model)

Traditionally, a separate function was required to support IP multicast over an MPLS VPN network because MPLS had no native ability to support it. The most commonly deployed MPLS VPN multicast solution is the MVPN based on IETF Draft-Rosen, where multiple domain trees (MDTs) are created per VPN over GRE tunneling across the MPLS network. This architecture usually uses the following concepts and components:

- Default MDT (per virtual router and forwarder (VRF)/customer).

- VPNv4 or VPNv6 needed to build up unicast control plane (to ensure that the customer multicast source IPs will be reachable and to avoid RPF check failure).

- Optionally, the DATA MDT can be created for high rate sources and to offload the PEs that do not need to join the multicast stream, as shown in Figure 10-18.

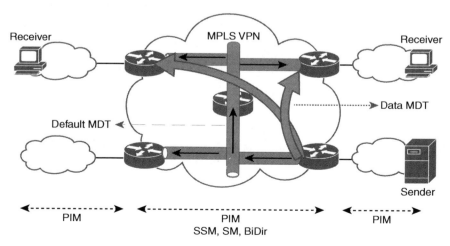

Figure 10-18 *MVPN Draft-Rosen Based*

In fact, this approach is the most widely deployed approach, not because it is the best approach, but because of the limited options. With this approach, for example, all PEs will receive multicast traffic on the default MDT that is attached to a given VPN, even if the PE has no interested receiver in that VRF for the (*,G) or (S,G). Therefore, the data MDT is used to overcome this issue. Furthermore, to work, this approach requires PIM to be enabled across the core. Therefore, it will increase control plane complexity of the SP core infrastructure to maintain multicast states and PIM adjacencies. In addition, each PE across the network requires PIM adjacency with each remote PE (per VPN/VRF). Therefore, new approaches were introduced to offer more scalable and flexible design options to meet next-generation (NGN) requirements. These options are discussed in the subsequent sections.

Note   This model is the most widely deployed MVPN model at the time of this writing. This means that it is a proven model with a larger number of people who have expertise to design, deploy, and operate it. Therefore, regardless of the limitations mentioned previously, many SPs and enterprises (with SP network style) still prefer to deploy the MVPN (Draft-Rosen) model because of staff expertise and knowledge.

MVPN - Label Switch Multicast

Label Switch Multicast (LSM), defined in RFC 5332, offers the next generation of IP multicast over MPLS networks, where packets are transported using MPLS encapsulation. With LSM, service providers now have the flexibility to run both unicast and multicast together while sharing the same label space. In addition, the two primary MPLS protocols, Resource Reservation Protocol Traffic Engineering (RSVP-TE) and Label Distribution Protocol (LDP), were modified to support point-to-multipoint (P2MP) and multipoint-to-multipoint (MP2MP) label-switched paths (LSPs), respectively. The MVPN LSM-based model brings several benefits, such as the following:

- LSM simplifies overall control plane design complexity through its ability to share the same control plane of the unicast routing.

- One unified forwarding plane for both unicast and multicast using MPLS encapsulation.

- Offers the ability to use advanced unicast MPLS features such as fast reroute (FRR) and bandwidth reservation.

Foundation Protocols to Build Multicast LSPs

MLDP and RSVP-TE P2MP are the primary protocols that can build multicast LSPs in MPLS networks. Although both protocols are used for the same general purpose with regard to LSM, each has its own characteristics, as listed in Table 10-10.

Table 10-10   *MLDP Versus MPLS-TE P2MP*

MLDP	RSVP-TE P2MP
LSPs are built from the leaf to the root.	LSPs are built from the headend to the tail end, which may require manual static joins on the tunnel.
Supports P2MP and MP2MP LSPs (trees).	Supports only P2MP LSPs (tree).
FRR requires setup of RSVP-TE unicast backup path.	Native support of traffic engineering (bandwidth reservation, FRR).
No periodic signaling because it is reliable over TCP (hard state).	Signaling is periodic (soft state)
Control plane signaling over either P2MP or MP2MP.	Control plane signaling is built over P2P (scalability limitations).
Forwarding plane is based on P2MP and MP2MP as well.	Forwarding plane is based on P2MP (packet replication in the core).
Can be suitable for all multicast applications, especially for many to many.	Can be suitable for video delivery. Best for one/few to many

Next-Generation MVPN

The next-generation MVPN solution introduces BGP as a control plane protocol for MVPN. After the success of unicast BGP in SP networks, SPs now have the flexibility to leverage the same unicast control plane used in their network to support multicast routing as well (BGP-based), along with the same MPLS switching using LSM to encapsulate multicast within the core in MPLS labels. BGP offers the ability to separate functions of the control plane and data plane by relying on BGP to perform PEs' automatic discovery and distributing customer multicast (C-multicast) routes between the PEs. By using one flexible control plane for both unicast and multicast (including IPv4 and IPv6), SPs can achieve the ultimate level of architecture flexibility and simplified manageability, because no new skills or expertise are required to manage two different protocols and overlaid architectures. The following are some of the primary drivers toward NG MVPN:

- Unified signaling protocol for unicast and multicast VPN that offers SPs simplified control plane architectures.

- Unified forwarding plane using MPLS labels (LSM)

- Automated learning of participating nodes (PEs) with unidirectional P-Tree

- Customers' PIM-SM carried per VRF without the need of a shared-tree creation over the SP core (PIM free core)

- Flexibility to support different trees, such as P2MP and MP2MP, which can meet different application requirements

- Supports MPLS VPN inter-AS models

- Inherits the well-known BGP stability and reliability

Figure 10-19, an MPLS L3VPN SP, is offering multicast service to its clients, in addition to content services (IPTV). By using MVPN, this provider will use the same BGP control plane architecture (for example, RR) to perform the PE discovery for interested multicast receivers and to propagate the IP C-multicast between the PEs. Typically, BGP carries the C-multicast from the receiver sites to the sender sites (among PEs), which will result in the dynamic discovery of the multicast receivers. In addition, the core is kept PIM free by using LSM across the MPLS network, where each PE can perform PIM to BGP to LSP mapping.

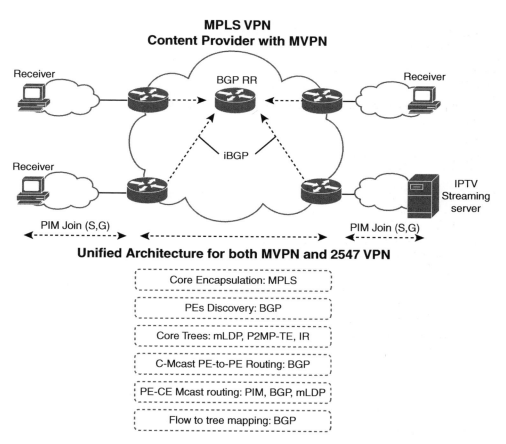

Figure 10-19 *NG-MVPN High-Level Architecture*

However, as covered earlier, because of the lack of expertise with this model (at the time of this writing), this model is not always the preferred option for enterprises and SPs. In addition, the support of mLDP capability is mostly available in high-end network products (SP grade). Therefore, it is not always a cheap option for enterprises to consider.

Multicast Resiliency Design Considerations

In today's modern and converged networks, it is common that several business-critical applications run over multicast, where packet or connectivity loss is a highly undesirable experience, especially if the application is serving some core business applications, such as in financial services and trading applications, where minutes of disconnectivity can translate to the loss of hundreds of thousands of dollars.

Similarly, for content providers such as the IPTV provider, the quality of the multimedia and its availability is critical to maintaining its reputation and meeting the service level agreement (SLA) requirements with the subscribers. Therefore, the design of IP multicast must incorporate the consideration of high availability and resiliency of the solution. However, with IP multicast, two levels can be considered to offer a reliable service. The first level is the underlying unicast IP infrastructure (covered in Chapter 9, "Network High-Availability Design"). The second level is the core component of the multicast network, such as RPs and other network-based solutions that are multicast specific, such as redundant sources, multicast with path diversity, and FRR. Specifically, the availability of RP in a PIM multicast domain is critical, especially for PIM-Bidir and PIM-SM. Therefore, a design for a reliable multicast-enabled infrastructure must consider the availability of the RP as well. This section covers the common mechanisms and approaches used to address multicast resiliency design requirements.

Anycast RP

The concept of Anycast RP is based on using two or more RPs configured with the same IP address on their loopback interfaces. Typically, the Anycast RP loopback address is configured as a host IP address (32-bit mask). From the downstream router's point of view, the Anycast IP will be reachable via the unicast IGP routing. Because it is the same IP, IGP normally will select the topologically closest RP (Anycast IP) for each source and receiver. MSDP peering and information exchange is also required between the Anycast RPs in this design, because it is common for some sources to register with one RP and receivers to join a different RP, as shown in Figure 10-20.

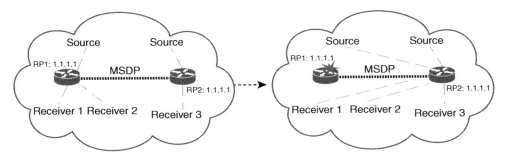

Figure 10-20   *Anycast-RP with MSDP*

In the event of any Anycast RP failure, IGP will converge, and one of the other Anycast RPs will become the active RP, and sources and receivers will fail over automatically to the new active RP, thereby maintaining connectivity.

> **Note** IPv6 does not support MSDP. Therefore, each RP has to define other RPs in the network as PIM RP-set to maintain a full list of sources and receivers in the network. Alternatively, Anycast-RP using PIM, described in IETF RFC 4610, can be used instead where the "Anycast-RP functionality can be retained without using MSDP."

Anycast-RP Using PIM

Anycast-RP with PIM (described in RFC 4610) enables both IPv4 an IPv6 to retain the same ultimate goal network designers aim to achieve using Anycast-RP with MSDP, and with fewer protocols. In other words, Anycast-RP can still be used without the need to establish MSDP peering sessions between the RPs. The primary difference is that each RP will send copies of the Register messages to the other (peering) RPs that usually received them from the registered sources or the designated router (DR) that is directly attached to the multicast source LAN. Consequently, each RP can maintain a list of the sources of each multicast group registered with different RPs (S,G). As a result, the multicast streams from the different sources distributed across the PIM multicast domain can reach all receivers even if they are associated with different RPs.

As shown in Figure 10-21

1. The closest RP (anycast loopback IP) for each source and receiver will be selected by the underlying unicast routing protocol (IGP).

2. When RP-B receives the PIM Register message from multicast source S-B via R-1(DR), it will decapsulate it and then forward it across the shared tree toward the interested (joined) receivers.

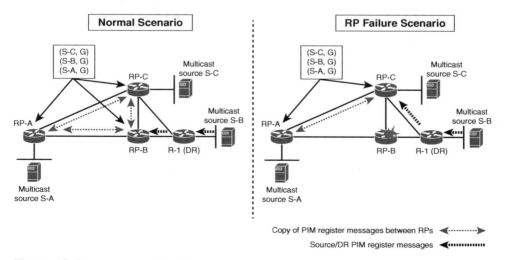

Figure 10-21   *Anycast-RP PIM*

3. Assuming all RPs (RP-A, RP-B, and RP-C) are deployed as Anycast-RP PIM among each other, in this case RP-B will send a copy of this Register message to RP-A and RP-C.

4. PR-A and RP-C will usually decapsulate the Register message sent from RP-B and in turn will forward it down to the shared tree (if there is any interested/joined receiver; otherwise, the RP can discard the packet).

5. If RP-B fails, IGP will route any multicast messages from the multicast source behind R-1 (S-B) toward the closest Anycast-RP (in this example, RP-C).

However, MSDP may still be required in IPv4 interdomain multicast scenarios (for example, if the internal sources need to be advertised to multicast RPs outside of the local PIM domain, and similarly if learning of external multicast sources is required). In addition, MSDP rides on top of TCP, so it also offers guaranteed delivery. Also, from an operations and troubleshooting point of view, MSDP compared to Anycast-RP RFC 4610 offers higher flexibility because it has an SA-cache and multiple **show** commands that help network operators to know in a simplified way where it learned stuff from and what is in the cache.

Phantom RP

With PIM-Bidir, all the packets technically flow over the shared tree. Therefore, redundancy considerations of the RP become a critical requirement. The concept of phantom RP is specifically used for PIM-Bidir, and is not necessarily to be a physical RP/router. However, an IP subnet that is routable in the network can serve the purpose as well, where the shared tree can be rooted as shown in Figure 10-22.

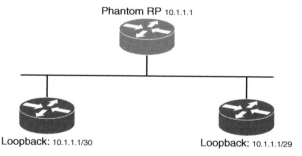

Figure 10-22 *Phantom RP*

As shown in Figure 10-22, if you configure two routers in a network with the same IP and different subnet mask, IGP can control the preferred path for the root (phantom RP) of a multicast shared tree based on the longest match (longest subnet mask) where multicast traffic can flow through. The other router with the shorter mask can be used in the same manner if the primary router fails. This means the failover to the secondary shared tree path toward the phantom RP will rely on the unicast IGP convergence. Furthermore, if Auto-RP is used as a dynamic RP discovery mechanism to reduce operational overhead, a mapping agent is required for Auto-RP to work properly.

Live-Live Streaming

The term *live-live* refers to the concept of using two live simultaneous multicast streams through the network using either a path separation technique or a dedicated infrastructure and RPs per stream. For instance, as shown in Figure 10-23 and Figure 10-24, the first stream (A) is sent to one set of multicast groups, and the second copy of the stream (B) is sent using a second set of multicast groups. Each of these groups will usually be delivered using separate infrastructure equipment to the end user with complete physical path separation, as shown in Figure 10-23. This design approach offers the ultimate level of resiliency that caters for any failure in a server or in network component along the path.

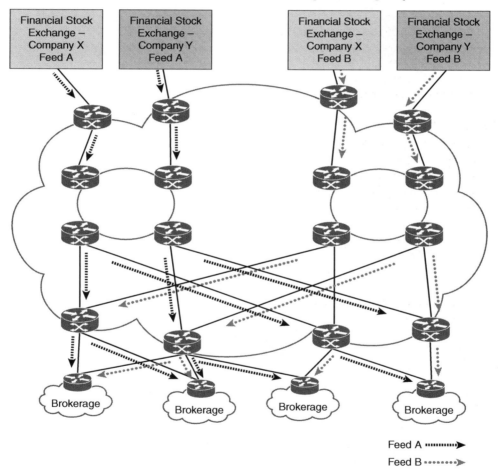

Figure 10-23 *Live-Live Stream over Separate Core Networks*

However, using single infrastructure such as MPLS-enabled core associated with MPLS-TE to steer the streams over different paths across the core infrastructure, as shown in Figure 10-24, offers resiliency for any failure on the server side; however, it may not offer full network resiliency (because both streams will use the same core infrastructure).

That said, if the MPLS provider catered for different failure scenarios (optical, node, link, and so on, along with switchover time that is fast enough to be performed without being noticed by the applications, such as using MPLS-TE FRR, and also avoids any shared risk link group [SRLG] along the path), in this case it can offer a reliable and cost-effective solution.

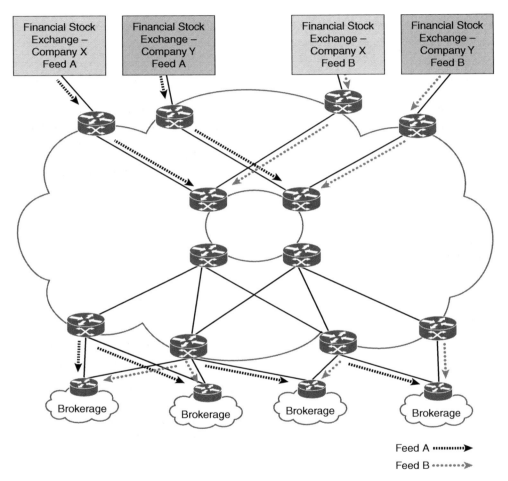

Figure 10-24 *Live-Live Stream over Single Core Network*

One of the primary drivers to adopt such an expensive design approach (live-live) is the strict requirement of some businesses (commonly in financial services industry because each millisecond is worth money) to aggressively minimize the loss of packets in the multicast data streams and a reliable and low-latency multicast solution that does not introduce retransmissions.[11]

11. "Market Data Network Architecture (MDNA) Overview," http://www.cisco.com

First Hop Redundancy Protocol-Aware PIM

In a shared LAN segment with a pair of Layer 3 gateways deployed with First Hop Redundancy Protocol (FHRP) such as Hot Standby Routing Protocol (HSRP) to provide first-hop redundancy, the PIM designated router (DR) election is unaware of the FHRP redundancy deployment. As a result, the HSRP active router (AR) and the PIM DR of the same LAN segment will probably not be the same router because PIM has no inherent redundancy capabilities and normally operates independently of HSRP.

HSRP-aware PIM helps network designers to ensure that multicast traffic is forwarded via the HSRP (AR) that will be acting as the PIM (DR) for the LAN segment as well. This will allow PIM to leverage HSRP redundancy and to offer failover capability derived from the HSRP states in the device. "With HSRP-Aware PIM enabled, PIM sends an additional PIM Hello message using the HSRP virtual IP addresses as the source address for each active HSRP group when a device becomes HSRP active."[12] Therefore, downstream devices such as a Layer 3 node or a multicast streaming server can use either a static route or a default gateway that points to the FHRP virtual IP (VIP), which offers a more reliable and simplified operation with simple configuration at the downstream node side, as shown in Figure 10-25.

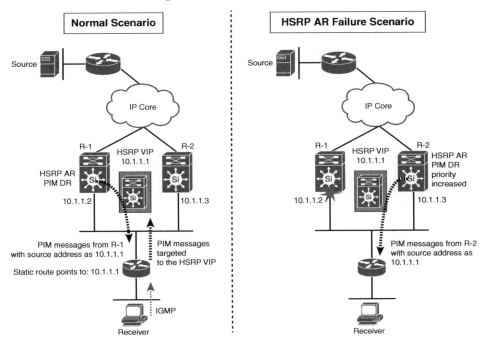

Figure 10-25 *HSRP-Aware PIM*

From a resiliency point of view, following an HSRP AR failover or recovery event, the newly elected HSRP AR will assume the responsibility for the routing and forwarding of all the traffic sent to the HSRP VIP. At the same time, PIM will tune the priority of the

12. "HSRP Aware PIM," "VRRP Aware PIM," http://www.cisco.com

DR based on HSRP state to maintain the alignment of the HSRP AR and the multicast DR functions on the same node.

Final Thoughts on IP Multicast Design

Based on the multicast design options, considerations, and constraints covered in this section, network designers should always answer the following questions before considering any design recommendation or strategy:

- What is the targeted business or environment (enterprise versus SP)?

- Why is multicast required? Is it to run a business-critical application, to provide a transport network for customers to run their applications, or to provide a service, such as IPTV?

- What are the characteristics of the multicast application? Many to many versus one to many, IPv4 or IPv6? This can help to decide the type of RP and where the RP should be positioned in the network.

- Is the targeted network under single or multiple administrative domains? If multiple, is there any requirement to provide multicast communications between the different domains (interdomain)?

- What is the Layer 3 routing protocol in use, and what does the logical design look like? This helps to determine RPF check failure considerations.

- Is there any constraint related to enabling multicast across the network path? (For example, the WAN provider may not support multicast.)

- Does any network device in the path not support multicast, such as firewalls?

- Are there any staff knowledge limitations with regard to certain IP multicast protocols, such as LSM?

- Are there any high-availability requirements, such as redundant RPs?

Further Reading

"General Information About IP Multicast," http://www.cisco.com/go/multicast

"Interdomain Multicast Solutions Using MSDP," http://www.cisco.com

RFC 2117, *Protocol Independent Multicast-Sparse Mode (PIM-SM): Protocol Specification*, http://www.ietf.org

"Bidirectional PIM Deployment Guide," http://www.cisco.com

RFC 6826, *Multipoint LDP In-Band Signaling for Point-to-Multipoint and Multipoint-to-Multipoint Label Switched Paths*, http://www.ietf.org

Multicast Only Fast Re-Route, draft-ietf-rtgwg-mofrr-06, http://www.ietf.org

QoS Design Considerations

In today's converged networks, there is an extremely high reliance on IT services and applications. In particular, there is increased demand on real-time multimedia applications and collaboration services (also known as *media applications*) over one unified IP network that carries various types of traffic streams such as voice, video, and data applications. For instance, voice streams can be found across the network in different flavors, such as standard IP telephony, high-definition audio, and Internet Voice over IP (VoIP). In addition, video communications also have various types, where each has different network requirements, such as video on-demand, low-definition interactive video (such as webcams), high-definition interactive video (such as telepresence), IP video surveillance, digital signage, and entertainment-oriented video applications [94]. However, there can be an unlimited number of data applications. (See Table 2-1, Chapter 2, "Enterprise Layer 2 and Layer 3 Design," for an example of the various applications of today's converged networks.)

Therefore, to deliver the desired quality of experience to the different end users (as discussed in Chapter 1, "Network Design Requirements: Analysis and Design Principles"), network designers and architects need to consider a mechanism that can offer the ability to prioritize traffic selectively (usually real-time and mission-critical applications) by providing dedicated bandwidth, controlled jitter and latency (based on the application requirements), and improved loss characteristics, and at the same time ensuring that providing priority for any traffic flow will not make other flows fail. This mechanism is referred to as *quality of service* (QoS). The following sections discuss the design approaches and considerations of QoS using a business-driven approach.

QoS High Level Design: Business-Driven Approach

To design and deploy QoS successfully across the network, in particular converged networks, network designers or architects need to consider the top-down design approach to initially understand the critical and important applications from the business point of view. Then, they can assess the optimal QoS design strategies to meet the business and application requirements.

As discussed earlier, the goal of the network is to become a business enabler. To achieve that, the network ideally should act as a service delivery mechanism that facilitates the achievement of the business's goals. Therefore, it is critical to align QoS design with business priorities, expectations, and requirements to deliver the desired level of quality of experience.

For instance, an organization may have a financial application that is sensitive to packet loss, and any loss of connectivity can cost the business a large amount of money. Accordingly, this application must be treated as a high-priority application. Similarly, if an SP needs to meet a very strict SLA with its customers to deliver their voice traffic with no more than 1 percent of end-to-end packet loss, this SP must consider a suitable QoS strategy and apply the right QoS design to meet these SLA requirements. Otherwise, it will lead to a business loss. This loss can be tangible, such as a penalty, intangible, such as reputation, or most probably both. Therefore, network designers must have the right QoS design approach and strategy to avoid the high volume of application complexities in today's networks and provide the desired level of quality of experience to the business and end users. Table 10-11 provides a summarized (top-down) QoS design approach and strategy (in order).

Table 10-11   *Top-Down QoS Design Approach Summary*

Strategic Goal	Approach	Design Considerations
Understand business requirements.	Understand business priorities and goals.	Identify primary business drivers. Highlight the constraints (for example, budget).
Identify the scope.	Understand the scope of the QoS design such as campus, WAN, VPN or SP edge or end to end across different blocks.	Is the application used within the campus, across the WAN, or over VPN? Is there any network in the path not directly controlled such as WAN?
Identify mission-critical applications.	Identify which application need to be treated differently (prioritized). Identify which application is a nonbusiness application (deprioritize).	What are the mission-critical applications or services (for example, SAP, FCoE, VoIP, TelePresence)
Understand application requirements.	Identify the characteristic of each application.	What sort of network delivery is required: TCP, UDP, unicast multicast, and so on? Application sensitivity to pack loss, jitter, delay.
Select a design strategy and identify the technical constraints.	Clarify the end-to-end design strategy in terms number of QoS classes, QoS toolset to be used, and so on.	What traffic classification strategy is to be used within the LAN (for example 8 or 12 classes)? What MPLS DiffServ tunneling mode is used? Is the core/WAN underlay native IP or MPLS based? What are the classes of service (CoS) supported over the WAN (for example, MPLS provider)? Can the targeted network node support the required number of queues? Or does it support any priority queuing (technical constraints)?

QoS Architecture

In general, there are two fundamental QoS architecture models:

- **Integrated services (IntServ):** This model, as specified in RFC 1633, offers an end-to-end QoS architecture based on application transport requirements (usually per flow) by explicitly controlling network resources and reserving the required amount of bandwidth (end to end along the path per network node) for each traffic flow. Resource reservation protocols, such as RSVP, and admission control mechanisms form the foundation of this process.

- **Differentiated services (DiffServ):** This model, specified in RFC 2475, offers a QoS architecture based on classifying traffic into multiple subclasses where packets flows are assigned different markings to receive different forwarding treatment (per-hop behavior, or PHB) per network node along the network path within each differentiated services domain (DS domain).

Note The aforementioned QoS architectural models are applicable for both IPv4 and IPv6, because both IP versions include the same 8-bit field in their headers, which can be used, for example, for DiffServ (IPv4: Type of Service [ToS]; IPv6: Traffic Class). Therefore, the concepts and methodologies discussed in this section are intended for both IPv4 and IPv6 unless otherwise specified, such as if an application supports and uses the added 20-bit Flow Label field of the IPv6 header (RFC 2460, 3697). However, the larger IPv6 packet's header needs to be considered when calculating the aggregate bandwidth of traffic flows.

QoS DiffServ Architecture and Toolset

A true and effective QoS design must cover traffic flows of applications and services end to end. This can sometimes be complicated because each single traffic flow traverses multiple networks and is architected with a different QoS philosophy. Therefore, for network architects and designers to create such a cohesive design model, the design must be divided into domains commonly called and as described in RFC 2475 as *differentiated services domains* (DS domains). Each DS domain usually consists of multiple interconnected network nodes (such as switches and routers) operating under a common service provisioning policy, along with set of PHB groups enabled on each node that offers network designers a framework to facilitate the design of scalable and flexible DS domains.

Note Per-hop behavior (PHB) defines a forwarding behavior with regard to the treatment characteristics for the traffic class, such as its dropping probabilities and queuing priorities, to offer different levels of forwarding for IP packets (described in RFC 2474). DS domains described in this section refer to any domain with QoS polices and differentiated treatments regardless if it is IP Precedence based (RFC 791), Assured Forwarding based (RFC 2597), or a mixture of both.

> **Note**   *Service provisioning policy* refers to the attributes of traffic conditioners (QoS policies) deployed at each DS—domain boundary and mapped across the DS domain.

Each single DS domain can be divided into two primary types of DS network nodes. The first type is internal, which usually refers to the nodes belonging to a single DS domain. As described earlier, these nodes should have the same QoS or DS provisioning policy. The second type of DS node is the DS boundary node, which faces other DS or non-DS-capable domains. Typically, these nodes are the ones that must be responsible for applying traffic polices (QoS policies) on traffic flows in both directions (ingress and egress) based on a predefined or agreed model between the DS domains that is ideally driven by traffic and application requirements, as shown in Figure 10-26.

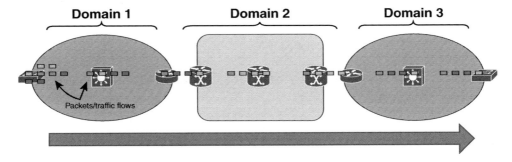

Figure 10-26   *QoS DS-Domains*

Practically, DS domains can take different forms, such as the following:

■ Enterprise domain with a SP domain in the middle (WAN transport).

■ Within an enterprise, there can be multiple DS domains: campus LAN, WAN, DC, and DMVPN over Internet.

The second scenario consists of multiple DS domains, which all belong to a single administrative authority and that can be combined under one global DS domain or region. Each DS domain in that region has the flexibility to have its own QoS provisioning standards to offer more structured and tiered QoS domains design for large-scale networks with a large number of distributed blocks, as shown in Figure 10-27.

Each domain is usually under a single administrative and control authority. Hypothetically, each authority defines cohesive end-to-end, measurable, and quantifiable attributes per DS subdomain and per global DS domain, which should be driven by the characteristics and requirements of the services or applications running across this domain (traffic flow aggregates). Typically, there can be multiple possible points across each QoS domain specifying where policies and traffic treatment can be enforced to influence the experience of packets as they enter, cross, and exit a DS domain. Traffic conditioning and QoS polices

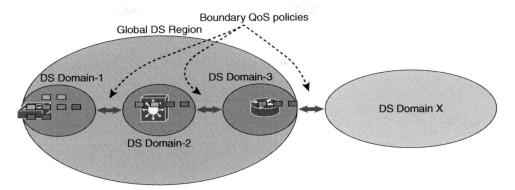

Figure 10-27 *Multitier DS Domains*

are the key QoS elements that serve this purpose within each domain and between the different domains using the following primary QoS toolset:

- Traffic classification and marking

- Traffic profiling and congestion management

- Congestion avoidance (active queue management)

- Admission control

The subsequent subsections cover these QoS toolset in more detail.

Traffic Classification and Marking

Classification refers to the process of selecting frames or packets in a traffic stream based on the content of some portion of the frame or packet header to which different policies can then be applied. Traffic marking, on the other hand, writes a value into the packet header to be identified by QoS policies and placed in the desired class with the desired treatment at different stages during the end-to-end packet trip from the source to the intended destination (within and across DS domains).

However, classification of traffic does not always require marking to be applied. For instance, in some scenarios, traffic only needs to be selected based on the value of a combination of one or more IP header fields, such as source address, destination address, source port, destination port numbers, or an incoming interface then to be associated with a QoS policy action, such as placing it in a predefined QoS queue. Classification of traffic almost always should be performed at the point of network access (as close to the traffic source as possible), and then to be associated with the appropriate marking value (usually ToS header bits) in which network designers can have the flexibility to select this traffic and apply the desired QoS policies at any node across the network (usually within a single DS domain or region).

In addition, marking can establish trust boundaries at the edge of the network. A *trust boundary* refers to the point within the network where markings such as

CoS or differentiated services code point (DSCP) begin to be accepted as its set by the connected node or endpoint, such as an IP phone that set its voice traffic with a DSCP-PHB value of EF. However, not every endpoint can mark its traffic. Therefore, trust boundaries are commonly classified into three primary models: trusted, untrusted, and conditional trust, as shown in Figure 10-28.

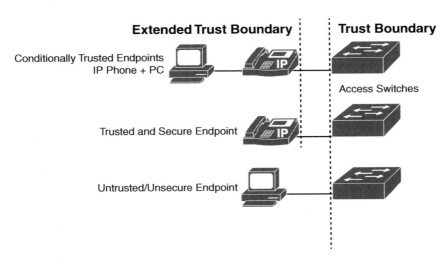

Figure 10-28 *QoS Trust Boundaries*

- **Trusted model:** This model can be used with endpoints that can mark their traffic. At the same time, these endpoints have to be approved and trusted from a security point of view, such as IP phone, voice gateways, wireless access points, videoconferencing, and video surveillance endpoints. In addition, "ideally" these trusted endpoints should not be mobile (instead fixed endpoints) to be reflected at the switch port level in a more controlled manner.

- **Untrusted model:** This model usually considers using a manual traffic classification and marking. The most common candidates of this model are PCs and servers, because these endpoints are subject to attack and infection by worms and viruses that can flood the network with a high volume of malicious traffic. Even worse, this traffic might be marked with a CoS or DSCP value that has priority across the network, which usually leads to a true denial-of-service (DoS) situation. However, PCs and servers normally run business-critical applications that need to be given certain service differentiation across the network, such as a PC running a software-based phone or server running business-critical applications such as SAP or CRM. With this model network, designers can selectively classify each of the desired application's traffic flows to be treated differently across the network and mark it with the desired CoS/DSCP value along with a policy that either limits each application class to a predefined maximum bandwidth or marks down the out-of-profile traffic to a

CoS/DSCP value that has lower priority across the network. Furthermore, as a simple rule of thumb, any endpoint that is not under control by the enterprise should be considered as untrusted, and the classification and marking of traffic flows can be controlled selectively and manually.

■ **Conditional trust model:** This model offers the ability to extend the trust boundary of the network edge to the device or endpoint connected to. This is based on an intelligent detection of a trusted endpoint, usually an IP phone. (In Cisco solutions, this is achieved by using Cisco Discovery Protocol [CDP].) However, the IP phone in this scenario has a PC connected to the back of the IP phone. Therefore, by extending the trust boundary to the IP phone, the IP phone can send its traffic in a trusted manner while overriding PC traffic to DSCP value of 0. This model offers a simple and easy method to roll out large IP telephony deployments with minimal operational and configuration complexity. However, if the PCs have some applications that need to be marked with a certain DSCP value, such as a softphone or a business video application, in this case manual traffic classification and marking is required at the edge port of the access switch to identify this traffic and mark it with the appropriate CoS/DSCP value and ideally associate it with a policer.

Furthermore, marking values can be changed (re-marked) based on the QoS design requirements at any location within a DS domain or between DS domains. The most common example is that between DS domains there might be a mismatch between the ToS values used to classify traffic. Therefore, at the egress or ingress, re-marking has to take place to maintain an end-to end unified QoS model. In contrast, in a single DS domain, re-marking is commonly used to move traffic that is out of profile (out of policy limit) into a QoS class with lower bandwidth or priority as a protective countermeasure by re-marking the out-of-profile traffic flows with a different ToS value at any location within a the DS domain. Table 10-12 summarizes the most common classification and marking options.

Table 10-12 *Summary of QoS Classification and Marking Options*

OSI Layer	Classification	Marking
Physical layer	Input interface	N/A
Layer 2	VLAN ID, MAC, IEEE 802.1Q/p CoS	IEEE 802.1Q/p CoS
Layer 2.5	MPLS label, MPLS EXP	MPLS EXP
Layer 3	IP DSCP, IP based (such as IP source/ destination)	IP (IPP, DSCP)
Layer 4	Port-based source/destination	IPP, DSCP, EXP
Higher layers up to 7	Application signature such as using a network-based application recognition (NBAR) framework	IPP, DSCP, EXP

> **Note**   DSCP marking is more commonly used than IP Precedence (IPP) because of
> its higher flexibility and scalability to support a wider range of classes. However, in
> some scenarios, a mix of both may be required to be maintained, such as migration or
> integration between different domains (such as in merger and acquisition scenarios and
> WAN MPLS VPN SPs that offer their CoS classes based on IPP) where seamless QoS
> interoperability has to be maintained. In this case, class selector PHB is normally used to
> provide backward compatibility with ToS-based IP Precedence (RFC 4594, 2474).

Logically, after traffic flows are classified and marked (whether manually at the edge of
the DS domain or automatically by being considered one of the trust boundary models
discussed earlier), traffic flows have to be grouped in DS classes. Usually, application
flows that share similar or the same traffic characteristics and network requirements such
as delay, jitter, and packet loss can be placed under the same DS class to achieve a structured traffic grouping that helps network operators to assign the desired treatment at
different locations across the DS domain (per class), such as assigning different queuing
models per class to control traffic flows during periods of traffic congestion.

Traffic Profiling and Congestion Management

During normal situations where traffic passing through the network is under or equal to
the actual maximum available bandwidth capacity of its links, packets are usually sent
out of the interface as soon as they arrive. In contrast, in traffic congestion situations,
packets normally arrive faster than the outgoing interface can handle them. This will lead
to undesirable outcomes to traffic flows that most probably will impact the business-
critical application's performance and users' quality of experience. In other words, technically, if the network is overprovisioned with bandwidth, there may be no need for QoS
considerations, because it will add minimal value. However, it is a common practice for
QoS to be enabled with a minimum number of classes to cater for critical applications
in case of unpredicted congestion that might occur, such as a failure of the upstream
network node, which may lead to overutilization of the secondary path if the capacity
planning did not consider different failure scenarios.

Therefore, to cater for network congestion situations, a network designer must plan
for an effective mechanism to be used to manage traffic during congestion periods.
This is commonly referred to as *congestion management*. When congestion management is used across the network, nodes can queue the accumulating packets at the
outbound interface until the interface (Tx-Ring) is free to send the queued packets.
The transmission of the queued packets, however, is scheduled based on the assigned
desired priority and queuing mechanism configured at the interface level per traffic
flow aggregate (predefined traffic profiling).

In fact, with congestion management, placing packets in a predefined transmission queue
is one half of the job. The other half of it is how the different queues are serviced with
respect to each other during a congestion period at the router/interface level. Table 10-13
summarizes the common queuing mechanisms that can be used for the purpose of congestion management, along with the characteristics of each.

Table 10-13 *Common QoS Queuing*

	Weighted Fair Queuing (WFQ)	Priority Queuing (PQ)	Class-Based Weighted Fair Queuing (CBWFQ)
Characteristic	The WFQ algorithm offers a dynamic fair distribution among all traffic flows based on weight.	Typically supports four queues with different priority levels, and the higher-priority queues are always serviced first	Provides class-based queuing (user-defined classes) with minimum bandwidth guarantee. Supports flow-based WFQ for nondefined classes, such as class- default. Supports low-latency queuing (LQQ)

Note There other queuing techniques not covered in this section because they are less commonly used or offer basic queuing capabilities. However, this does not mean that they are not used or cannot be considered as an option. These other techniques include weighted round-robin (WRR) and custom queuing. First-in, first-out (FIFO) queuing on is the default queuing when no other queuing is used. Although FIFO is considered suitable for large links that have low delay with very minimal congestion, it has no priority or classes of traffic.

Although WFQ offer a simplified, automated, and fair flow distribution, it can impact some applications. For instance, a telepresence endpoint may require end-to-end 5 Mbps for the video Rapid Transport Protocol (RTP) media stream over a 10-Mbps WAN link, and there may be multiple flows passing over the same link, let's say ten flows in total. Typically, with WFQ fairness, telepresence video streams will probably get one-tenth of the total available bandwidth of the 10 Mbps, which will lead to a degraded video quality. With CBWFQ, though, network designers can place the flows of the telepresence RTP media streams in their own class with a minimum bandwidth guarantee of 5 Mbps during congestion periods. In addition, interactive video traffic can be assigned to the LLQ to be prioritized and serviced first during an interface congestion situation, as shown in Figure 10-29.

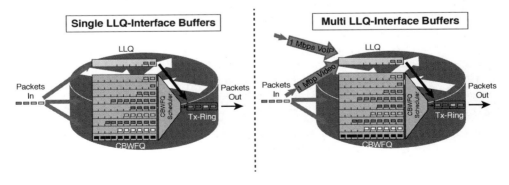

Figure 10-29 *CBWQ with LLQ*

As shown in Figure 10-29, CBWFQ supports two models of LLQ: single LLQ and the multi-LLQ. Typically, with the multi-LLQ model, there will be a single aggregate LLQ from the software point of view, and multiple sub-LLQs can be enabled inside this strict priority queue. With this model network, operators can assign multiple traffic flow types to the LLQ, such as VoIP and video. However, inside the LLQ itself, the service is based on the FIFO concept. Therefore, within each parent LLQ admission control, it is required to protect LLQ from another LLQ, such as protecting a voice LLQ from a video LLQ.

Note   The different Cisco software versions, such as IOS, include a built-in policer (implicit policer) with the LLQ, which limits the available bandwidth of the LLQ (such as real-time traffic flows) to match the bandwidth allocated to the strict-priority queue, thus preventing bandwidth starvation of the nonreal-time flows serviced by the CBWFQ scheduler. However, this behavior (implicit LLQ policing) is applicable only during periods of interface congestion (full Tx-Ring). A similar concept is applicable to the multi-LLQ model, where a state implicit policer is enabled per LLQ [83].

Hierarchical QoS

The most common scenario at the enterprise edge is that links are provisioned with sub-line rate. For instance, the WAN SP may provision the physical connectivity over a 1-Gbps Ethernet copper link, whereas the actual provisioned bandwidth can be 10 Mbps, 50 Mbps, or any sub-line rate. The problem with this setup, even if QoS policies are applied on this interface, such as CBWFQ, is that it will not provide any value or optimization because QoS policies normally kick in when the interface experiences congestion. In other words, because the physical link line-rate in this scenario is higher than the actual provisioned bandwidth, there will be no congestion detected even if the actual provisioned sub-line rate is experiencing congestion, which means that QoS has no impact here. Therefore, with hierarchical QoS (HQoS), the shaper at the parent policy (as shown in Figure 10-30) can simulate what is known as *back pressure* to inform the router that congestion has occurred in which QoS policies can take place.

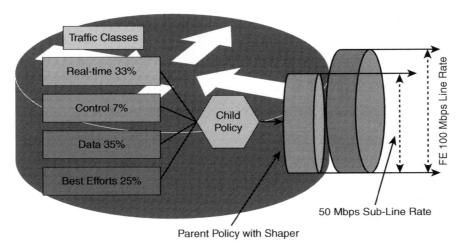

Figure 10-30   *HQoS*

Congestion Avoidance (Active Queue Management)

The congestion management techniques discussed in the previous section help network designers and operators to manage the front of the queue in terms of which packets should be sent out first. Congestion avoidance algorithms, in contrast, manage the tail of the queue in terms of which packets should be dropped first when queuing buffers are full. One of most commonly used and proven techniques here is the weighted random early detect (WRED), where packets are dropped based on their ToS markings, either IP Precedence based (where packets with lower IPP values are dropped more aggressively than higher IPP values) or DSCP based (where higher AF drop precedence values are dropped more aggressively). When the WRED algorithm starts selectively dropping packets, it will usually impact TCP windowing mechanisms to adjust the rate of flows to manageable rates. Therefore, WRED helps to optimize TCP-based applications [83].

Admission Control

Admission control is a common and essential mechanism used to keep traffic flows in compliance with the DS domain traffic conditioning standards, such as an SLA between a SP and its customers that specifies the maximum allowed traffic rate per class and in total per link, where excess packets will be discarded to keep traffic flows within the agreed traffic profile (SLA). There are two primary ways that admission control can be performed: traffic policing and shaping. With traffic policing, when traffic streams reach the predefined maximum contracted rate, excess traffic is either dropped or re-marked (marked-down), as shown in Figure 10-31.

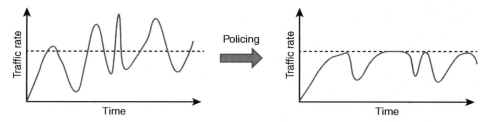

Figure 10-31   *Traffic Policing*

Traffic shaping, in contrast, keeps excess packets in a queue, buffered and delayed, and then schedules the excess for later transmission over increments of time. As a result, traffic shaping will smooth packet output rate and prevent unnecessary drops, as shown in Figure 10-32. However, the buffering of excess packets may introduce delay to traffic flows, especially with deep queues. Therefore, with real-time traffic it is sometimes preferred to police and drop excess packets rather than delay it and then transmit it, to avoid degraded quality of experience.

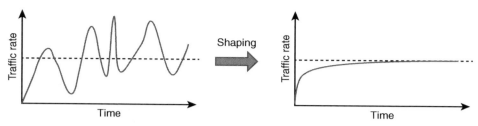

Figure 10-32   *Traffic Shaping*

QoS Design Strategy

Effective QoS design must be always be measured end to end with regard to the packet's trip or traffic flow aggregates across the network (from the source to the intended destination). Otherwise, QoS will not deliver its value back to the business and end users. Therefore, it is important that network designers consider a consistent and unified QoS design model based on the different requirements, taking into consideration the underlying network infrastructures in terms of available bandwidth, traffic characteristics, and scope of the network, such as campus only versus WAN only or end to end across the entire enterprise (which translates to single DS domain versus multiple DS domains).

One of critical element of QoS design is traffic classification, marking, and profiling using a unified end-to-end approach. In particular, the strategy of marking IP traffic with a ToS value and mapping each type of traffic to a predefined QoS class will vary based on different factors. However, Figure 10.33 provides a generic summarized recommendation of a QoS design model (strategy) that can serve as a baseline. This 12-class model is based on both Cisco's QoS Baseline and the informational RFC 4594. One of the main benefits of this model is that it provides a common and unified traffic marking and profiling characteristic across single and multiple DS domains, to a large extent.

Note   While the IETF DiffServ RFCs provide a consistent set of PHBs for applications marked to specific DSCP values, they do not specify which application should be marked with which DSCP value. Therefore, considerable industry disparity exists in application-to-DSCP associations, which led Cisco to put forward a standards-based application marking recommendation in their strategic architectural QoS Baseline document (in 2002). Eleven different application classes were examined and extensively profiled and then matched to their optimal RFC-defined PHBs. More than four years after Cisco put forward its QoS Baseline document, RFC 4594 was formally accepted as an informational RFC (in August 2006). RFC 4594 puts forward 12 application classes and matches these to RFC-defined PHBs [96], as summarized in Figure 10-33.

Application Class	Per-Hop Behavior	IETF RFC	Queuing & Dropping	Application Examples
VoIP Telephony	EF	3246	Priority Queue (PQ)	IP Telephony (IPT)
Broadcast Video	CS5	2474	(Optional) PQ	IP Video Surveillance/IPTV
Real-time Interactive VC	CS4	2474	(Optional) PQ	Telepresence
Multimedia Conferencing	AF4	2597	BW Queue + DSCP WRED	IPT Video
Multimedia Streaming	AF3	2597	BW Queue + DSCP WRED	Video on Demand (VoD), E-learning
Network Control	CS6	2474	BW Queue	EIGRP, OSPF, BGP, HSRP, IKE
Call-Signaling	CS3	2474	BW Queue	SCCP, SIP, H.323
Mgmt (OAM)	CS2	2474	BW Queue	SNMP, SSH, Syslog
Low-Latency Data	AF2	2597	BW Queue + DSCP WRED	ERP Apps, CRM Apps, Database Apps
High-Throughput Data	AF1	2474	BW Queue + DSCP WRED	E-mail, FTP, Backup Apps, Content Distribution
Best Effort	DF		Default Queue + RED	Default Class
Low-Priority Data	CS1	3662	Min BW Queue (Deferential)	YouTube, iTunes, BitTorent, Xbox Live

Figure 10-33 *Twelve-Class QoS Baseline Model Based on Cisco and RFC 4594 Baselines*

Note The most significant of the differences between Cisco's QoS Baseline and RFC 4594 is the RFC 4594 recommendation to mark call signaling to CS5. Cisco has completed a lengthy and expensive marking migration for call signaling from AF31 to CS3 (as per the original QoS Baseline of 2002). It is important to remember that RFC 4594 is an informational RFC; in other words, it is only an industry best practice and not a standard [96].

The twelve-class QoS model is a comprehensive and flexible model, which can be standardized and considered across the enterprise network. However, this model is not always viable or achievable for the following several reasons:

■ Not all enterprises or SPs are ready or need to deploy such a wide QoS design model.

■ This 12-class QoS design can introduce a level of end-to-end QoS design and operational complexity, because most WAN providers offer either 4- or 6-class QoS models across the WAN.

Note The biggest concern with regard to the operational complexity is the issues caused by human errors; this point is covered later in the "Network Management" section.

Ideally, what drives the number of classes (QoS model) is the applications used across the network that need special consideration and the level of service differentiation required for delivering the desired level of quality of experience. As shown in Figure 10-34, if the WAN provider is offering a 4-class QoS model, it is not an easy task to map from the 12-class model to the 4 classes (outbound), and from 4-class model to the 12-class model (inbound) at each WAN edge, especially if there is a large number of sites. In contrast, if the enterprise is using a 4-, 6-, or 8-class QoS model, the operation and design complexities will be minimized with regard to QoS polices and configurations.

However, both 4- and 6-class models include provisioning for only a single class for real time (usually for voice), and if video is added to the network, either a higher QoS class model (such as 8-class model) is required to be considered or both voice and video traffic have to be provisioned under a single class, which may not be a desirable option for large deployments with a large number of IP telephony and video endpoints across multiple sites. Therefore, considering the top-down approach to identifying the business and user expectations, needs, and priorities in terms of the services and applications used, in addition to their level of criticality to the business, will help, to a large extent, drive the strategy of QoS design in the right direction (business driven).

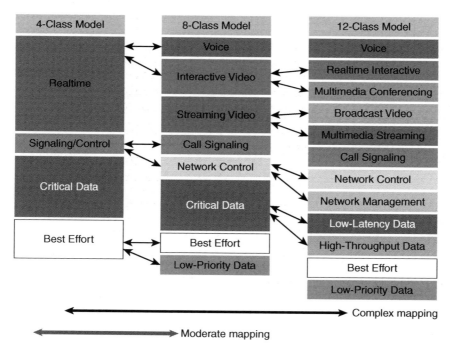

Figure 10-34 *Mapping Between QoS models with Different Classes*

Note Network orchestration and automation tools may help eliminate the operational complexity discussed earlier. However, this is something that depends on the configuration and change management and on the platforms and architecture used. For instance, the level of automation in software-defined networks (SDNs) is always high, but with simplified manageability compared to other models.

Network designers must aim to balance between application requirements and QoS design with regard to the added design and operational complexity. As a general rule, network designers should always consider using the phased approach when possible, by starting with a simple QoS model (such as the 4-class model) as a baseline. In the future, if the requirements mandate more classes, it will be easier to cater to the new requirements by adding and incorporating new classes to the existing setup. This is based on the assumption that starting with a 4- or 6-class QoS model will be sufficient at that point of time with regard to the existing services and applications to be classified and profiled.

Although there are some standard recommended percentages of bandwidth allocation per class in multiple best practices design guides and white papers, such as real-time traffic (LLQ) to be assigned 33 percent of the available or interface bandwidth and the best effort class to be allocated 25 percent of the interface bandwidth, it is important to understand that these values represent a generic recommended bandwidth allocation per class based on common proven best practices. However, it is not a rule to consider these values as the standard bandwidth allocation ratios; instead, they should be considered as a foundation or a proven, tested reference when there is not enough information to build an accurate figure about bandwidth allocation in which these values can serve as a good baseline to start with. For example, Figure 10-35 illustrates a classic three-tier campus network with a WAN edge. In this network, there are 20 access switches dual-homed over 1G uplinks to the distribution switches. Similarly, the distribution switches are dual-homed to the core switch over 10G links.

Each access switch has 30 IP phones connected to it, and VoIP calls are all based on G7.11 codec (with approximately 80 kbps required per VoIP call). Typically, with the LAN, there is no restriction on how many calls can be placed at the same time. However, over the WAN, the voice system is designed to allow a maximum of 20 simultaneous calls.

Take these requirements and map them to the standard allocation of the LLQ, which is 33 percent. Within the campus LAN, allocating 33 percent of the links across the LAN is not an issue, because the network is already overprovisioned. However, provisioning the real-time (VoIP) LLQ with 33 percent of the 10G uplinks means that there will be 3.3G of bandwidth reserved during a period of congestion. This can be seen as a security risk by the security team, because someone can flood the network with malicious traffic marked as DSCP EF, which will take precedence over other legitimate traffic and will consume the available 3.3G of bandwidth per uplink.

The WAN edge, however, has a 10-Mbps WAN link. Based on the voice system design, there will be only 20 simultaneous calls, meaning a maximum of (80 kbps * 20) 1.6 Mbps. Based on this, allocating 33 percent (= 3.3M) of the available WAN interface bandwidth to the LLQ (VoIP) means a waste of bandwidth in this case. Nevertheless, in this scenario, this organization still can allocate 25 percent of the links' available

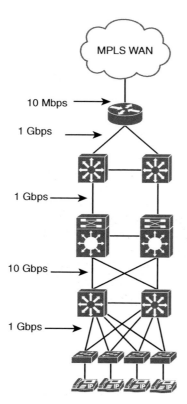

Figure 10-35   *QoS Bandwidth Allocation Example*

bandwidth to best effort (the default class) because there is no absolute requirements here on that part. Therefore, network designers need to consider the best practice recommended bandwidth or percentage allocation per class as a baseline and tweak the allocation based on the actual traffic flow requirements, taking into consideration security concerns, the available amount of bandwidth, and whether it is across the WAN, LAN, or a data center network.

Taking into consideration the different QoS design aspects, techniques, and strategies covered earlier in this section, network designers can consider the QoS design framework shown in Figure 10-36 as a foundational reference when approaching any QoS design task during the planning phase.

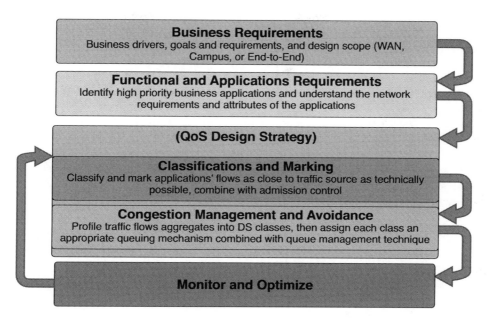

Figure 10-36 *QoS Design Framework*

Enterprise QoS Design Considerations

This section discusses QoS considerations that are applicable to enterprise-grade networks.

Enterprise Campus

Today's campus networks are almost all provisioned with Gigabit/10 Gigabit of bandwidth across the LAN, in which QoS might be seen as an unnecessary service to be considered because the need for queuing is minimal or almost not required as compared to the WAN and Internet edge, where queuing is a primary function to enhance the service quality. Although this statement is valid to some extent, the need for QoS is not only limited to perform queuing functions.

The unified marking and accurate traffic classification (as close to the source as possible) QoS can offer, when enabled cross the campus LAN, also enables policing across the campus LAN to provide the flexibility and control to network operators to manage traffic usage based on different fields of traffic flows, such as ToS values. It can also be used as a protective mechanism in situations like DoS attacks, to mitigate their impact. Therefore, it is recommended that QoS be enabled across the campus LAN to maintain a seamless DS domain design in which classification and marking policies establish and impose trust boundaries, while policers help to protect against undesired flows at the access edge and across the LAN.

Enterprise Edge

Enterprise edge (WAN, extranet, or Internet) is the most common place that traffic flow aggregation occurs (where more or a larger number of traffic flows usually arrive from the LAN side and need to exit the enterprise edge, which is usually provisioned with lower capacity). For instance, the LAN side might be provisioned with Gigabit/10 Gigabit, whereas the WAN has only 10 Mbps of actual available bandwidth. Therefore, QoS is always one of the primary functions considered at the enterprise edge to achieve more efficient bandwidth optimization, especially for enterprises that are converging their voice, video, and data traffic. Logically, the enterprise edge represents the DS domain edge where mapping and profiling of traffic flows to align with the adjacent DS domain is required to maintain a seamless QoS design. For instance, Figure 10-37 shows an example of a 12-class to 4-class QoS model mapping at the enterprise WAN edge router (CE) toward the SP edge (PE) to achieve end-to-end consistent QoS policies.

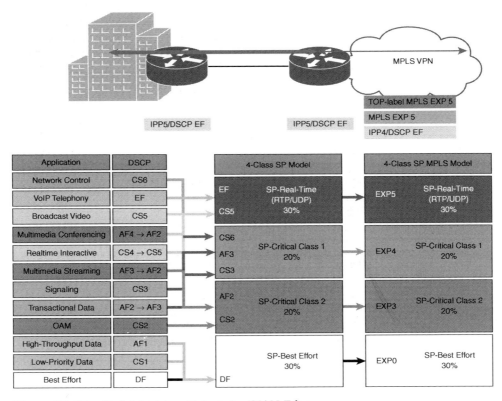

Figure 10-37 *QoS Mapping: Enterprise WAN Edge*

Note   The allocated bandwidth percentage in this figure is only for the purpose of the example and based on the best practices recommendations. However, these values technically must be allocated based on the SLA between the SP and the enterprise customer.

Note It is common that SPs offer their CoS based on IP Precedence marking only. As a result, the enterprise marking based on DSCP and deployed with the 8- or 12-class model may encounter inconsistent end-to-end markings. For instance, if there is a video RTP stream sent out from one site and its packets are marked with DSCP value of "DSCP 34" or AF41 (in binary, 100010), it will convert to IPP 4 (in binary, 100). In turn, it will come back as DSCP 32 (binary, 100000) at the other remote site. Therefore, a re-marking is required in this case at the other side (receiving) in the ingress direction to maintain a unified QoS marking end to end. Also, the used "MPLS DiffServe Tunneling mode" and its impact on the original DSCP marking across the SP network is covered later in this chapter.

IP Tunneling QoS Design Considerations

As discussed earlier in this book, the attractive pricing drives many enterprises to consider deploying different VPN solutions as either alternative solutions to the private WAN transport or as redundant paths to the private WANs. In addition, some enterprises have to comply with their security policy that dictates considering a secure IP transport across the WAN/MAN, even if it is private, in which case the enterprise may consider IPsec, secure DMVPN, or GETVPN to protect the communication over the WAN or MAN transport.

One primary concern is the impact of increased packet overhead on the existing applications, because each VPN solution will add additional IP and ESP headers, as shown in Figure 10-38. In addition, VPN brings a serious concern about bandwidth consumption. For instance, at Layer 3, a G.711 VoIP RTP stream needs 80 kbps. When this stream is sent over a GRE tunnel encrypted with IPsec, the total required bandwidth increases to ~112 kbps, which is an almost 40-percent bandwidth increase to transport the encrypted VoIP call. Therefore, bandwidth consumption with VPN is an essential point network designers need to consider, because it will usually impact the overall supported number of simultaneous voice calls or application sessions based on the actual available bandwidth.

In addition, the following factors with regard to QoS design should also be taken into account by network designers when considering any VPN solution:

- Additional packet delay caused by the encryption and decryption functions.

- Pre-crypto queuing.

- The unforeseen impact of QoS packet reordering (prioritization) that may lead the IPsec anti-reply mechanism to drop legitimate but out-of-sequence packets.

- ToS value preservation.

- Maximum transmission unit (MTU) issues.

- Original flow information by default will be hidden for outbound QoS policies. (Cisco's QoS preclassify feature helps in this case.)

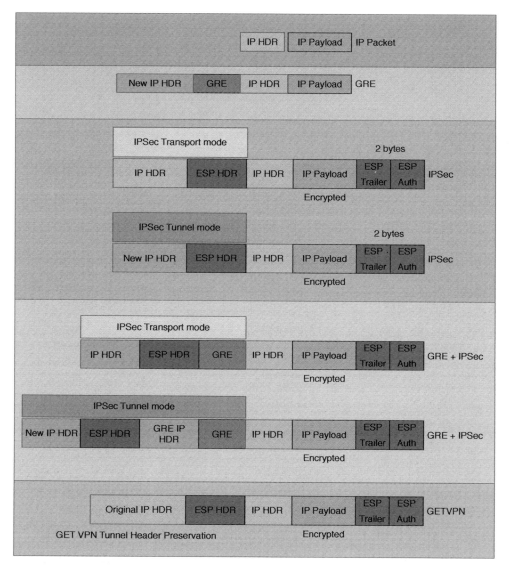

Figure 10-38   *IP Packet Overhead with VPN Solutions*

■ Traffic flow with regard to the VPN logical topology versus the underlying IP transport topology. For instance, adding an overlay solution based on DMVPN phase 1 over an MPLS L3VPN WAN will transform the topology from any to any to hub and spoke for traffic sent over the DMVPN cloud.

Furthermore, extending enterprise converged services, such as voice and video over an overlay (VPN) solution, requires overlaying QoS techniques and tools over the enterprise VPNs to satisfy the different service levels for voice, video, and other data business applications.

In general, the following QoS toolset forms the foundation of QoS design with VPN solutions:

- **Hierarchical QoS:** As discussed earlier, HQoS helps in scenarios where QoS policies have to be applied on an interface with a sub-line rate. Similarly, with VPN and tunneling, the tunnel might use a fraction of the line rate of the interface, in which HQoS helps to optimize per tunnel QoS.

- **CBWFQ queuing:** This is required when different traffic treatment is required.

- **Admission control:** To provide per-child QoS class admission control.

- **WRED:** Helps to further optimize TCP-based applications.

With the typical point-to-point VPN, whether it is a classic IPsec or GRE (combined with IPsec or not), traffic flow is more deterministic because it always between two points or sites over the VPN tunnel. However, because the nature of this type of VPN is based on point-to-point tunneling, it has high level of operational complexities and scalability limitations in large deployments. (For example, network operators need to maintain manual QoS polices per tunnel at the central or hub site, which makes any simple update a nightmare for the operations teams.) In contrast, DMVPN introduces a challenge with regard to QoS design here because DMVPN works in a hub-and-spoke topology and offers the ability to route traffic directly between the spoke sites, in which traffic flow is directed between spokes as well (not to mention the scale of remote site DMVPN support, where tens of hundreds of spokes can be easily added and integrated with the DMVPN cloud). This adds operational complexity to managing and maintaining seamless QoS where the hub normally has a single big pipe with higher bandwidth that can easily congest the spokes. Adding QoS policy per spoke at the hub site is a nonscalable and inflexible option.

The per-tunnel QoS feature with DMVPN will promote a zero-touch hub design that supports NHRP groups to dynamically provision QoS polices on a per-spoke basis at the DMVPN hub node facilitated by the NHRP group feature. Remote sites (spokes) can be profiled based on the provisioned WAN or Internet bandwidth and then automatically assigned QoS policy per spoke at the hub mGRE tunnel during the spoke tunnel registration (as shown in Figure 10-39), in which it will shape the traffic from the hub (higher-bandwidth side) toward the spoke (lower-bandwidth side) to be always aligned with the spoke's maximum download rate.

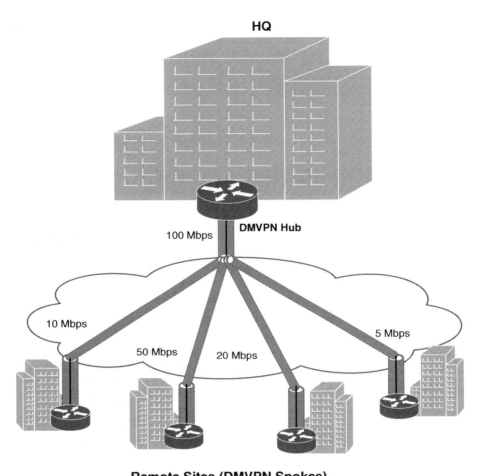

Figure 10-39   *DMVPN per Tunnel QoS*

> **Note**   At the hub site, network operators still need to define a policy to shape the traffic
> of the interface to match the actual provisioned sub-line rate of bandwidth. Spokes,
> however, should follow the typical HQoS deployment per site, where the bandwidth of
> the Internet/WAN link must be shaped to the maximum upload provisioned capacity.
> This means direct spoke-to-spoke traffic streams will be controlled by the HQoS polices
> defined at the spokes level

One key issue network designers must be aware of when considering per-tunnel QoS for
a DMVPN solution is that GRE, IPsec, and the L2 overhead must be considered when
calculating the required bandwidth for QoS shaping and queuing, because these headers

will be included as part of the packet size. This is because queuing and shaping, technically, is executed at the outbound physical interface of the DMVPN mGRE tunnel.

GETVPN, in contrast, preserves the entire original IP packet header (source and destination IP addresses, TCP and UDP port numbers, ToS byte, and DF bit) simply because QoS is applied at each GETVPN group member because no tunnels are used. This makes GETVPN design and deployment simpler, and the same standard WAN QoS design can be applied, with the exception that packet size will be increased and therefore must be considered as part of QoS bandwidth calculations.

Service Provider QoS Design

In modern SP networks, QoS is becoming a primary requirement because transporting Internet traffic, voice, video, cellular traffic, and MPLS VPN business traffic over a common IP backbone, each with different SLA expectations, will without any doubt introduce significant implications for both network design and operations. These implications are associated with many challenges, because each type of traffic has different bandwidth, jitter, and latency requirements. Failing to meet these requirements or an inability to satisfy the agreed SLAs will probably impact the SP business negatively, such as paying an expensive penalty, not to mention the impact on its reputation in the market. Therefore, QoS consideration in today's SPs is almost a must.

However, the consideration of QoS does not mean always to deploy QoS end to end (hop by hop). For instance, there might be an SP core network overprovisioned with high bandwidth where QoS will not practically add any value and network architects or designers may consider basic QoS only to protect important traffic flows in situations like double-failure scenarios within the core network. In fact, network designers, during the planning and design phase, can decide what QoS model, strategy, and tools are required to meet the SP business goals and priorities with regard to the offered services along with the utilized infrastructure, taking into consideration current traffic volume and the projected growth in the future.

All concepts, strategies, and methodologies covered earlier in this chapter are applicable. Therefore, this section covers only the considerations that are more specific to the SP style of network; all other concepts discussed earlier should be considered where applicable.

Traffic Marking Strategy

In SP types of networks and in large enterprise networks where the core is MPLS enabled while the edge of the network is non-MPLS such as the typical PE-CE connectivity model or an enterprise that has an MPLS core to interconnect multiple regional non-MPLS (native IP) networks (as shown in Figure 10-40), architects and network designers may need to consider different end-to-end traffic treatment with regard to marking based on the type of network, organization's objective, and application requirements. The following are the primary marking strategies (as defined in RFC 3270), also known as *MPLS DiffServe tunneling modes*. The selection of any mode or strategy will drive the overall QoS traffic marking and policy application. Therefore, they are the primary and most commonly used strategies to achieve a seamless end-to-end QoS with regard to the marking of IP traffic flowing across a single or multiple networks (DS domains), which in turn will influence the design and application of QoS queuing and admission control at the DS domains' boundaries.

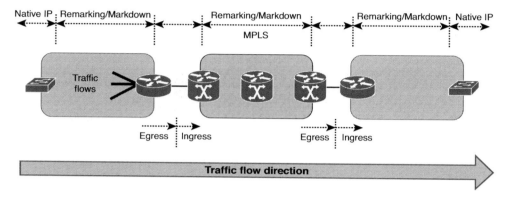

Figure 10-40   *Multiple DS Domains with MPLS Enabled in the Core*

Uniform Mode

With this mode, the first 3 bits of the IP ToS field (IP Precedence bits) will automatically be mapped to the MPLS EXP bits at the demarcation point between native IP and MPLS domains in the ingress direction and vice versa. This means that unified end-to-end marking values will be maintained across all the domains in a dynamic manner. In other words, both native IP and MPLS domains will be considered as a single DS domain.

If a re-marking is performed on a traffic flow that is out of contract within the MPLS domain, for example, this in turn will be reflected on the IP ToS value at the egress edge of the MPLS domain, as shown in Figure 10-41. This is an easy and simple-to-enable solution. However, from the design point of view, this might not be practically acceptable in scenarios like an MPLS L3VPN provider offering SLA with differentiated services, where customers normally need their traffic marking to be maintained end to end. In contrast, this mode can be a suitable option for enterprises that deploy their own core MPLS and traffic marking values and re-marked values that should be maintained intact end to end.

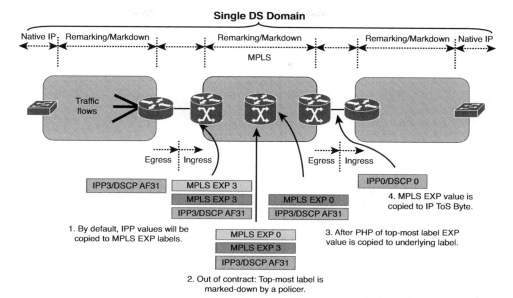

Figure 10-41 *MPLS QoS: Uniform Mode*

Pipe Modes

This mode consists of two flavors: the short and long modes. In general, both modes divide the QoS design with regard to the sample network in Figure 10-41 (native IP with MPLS core) into two DS domains. A typical example here is an MPLS VPN provider and its customers. With this mode (pipe), any re-marking that happens to the MPLS EXP is limited to MPLS EXP, without impacting the underlying IP packet's ToS byte. As a result, the MPLS core, such as the MPLS VPN provider, will have the flexibility to re-mark (mark down) out-of-contract traffic and apply its own policies across the MPLS cloud without impacting the original IP marking set by the customer side. This, in turn, will offer MPLS VPN customers, at the same time, a seamless end-to-end IP marking to maintain their own end-to-end QoS policies in a more simplified way (where minimal or no need for traffic re-mark is required at the remote CEs in the ingress direction to align with the enterprise marking model). In addition, MPLS EXP is not mapped automatically from the IPP and is required to be defined explicitly on the ingress direction of the MPLS DS domain to align with its QoS policies or the agreed SLA.

The short and long pipe modes, however, differ in the way they define the demarcation boundary between MPLS EXP marking and IP IPP/DSCP marking at the egress edge (PE) of the MPLS DS domain. With the short pipe mode, the egress QoS policies at the PE node facing the CE are based on IPP or DSCP values, as illustrated in Figure 10-42.

Note   The "long pipe mode" is sometimes referred to as "pipe mode."

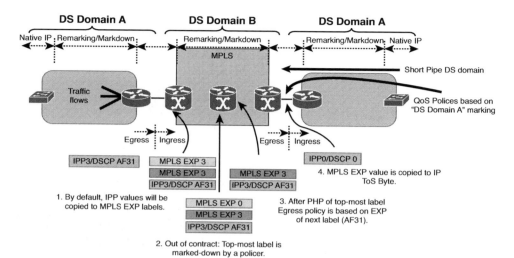

Figure 10-42 *MPLS QoS: Short Pipe Mode*

In contrast, the long pipe mode is based on the MPLS DS domain's explicit markings and re-markings of EXP values, as shown in Figure 10-43.

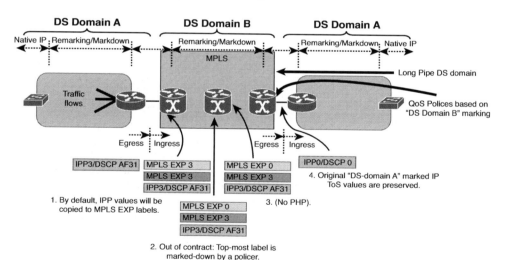

Figure 10-43 *MPLS QoS: Long Pipe Mode*

From a design point of view, the short pipe offers more desirable end-to-end QoS policies that align with the customer's (IP DS domain) if the scenario is a typical MPLS VPN. However, the short pipe mode may not be the right option if the design is a large-scale enterprise organization with MPLS core and the design goal is to treat out-of-profile or -contract traffic flows based on their re-marked EXP values when they exit the MPLS DS domain. (For example, a traffic flow marked as EXP 5, then re-marked to EXP0, should be treated as EXP0 by the QoS policy at the MPLS egress edge.) In other words, no one option is better than others; it all depends on the design requirements and how to align the QoS policies with design and strategy to offer a seamless scalable and flexible design.

> **Note**   Managed CE is one of the common services operators (such as MPLS VPN providers) offer to their customers. In offering this service, the MPLS VPN providers are responsible for configuring and operating the CE nodes. In this type of scenario, some operators prefer to reduce some of the QoS complexity, such as marking and re-marking from their PE nodes and moving it to the managed CE nodes, where the operator usually can define the QoS policies with the agreed bandwidth allocation and marking. With regard to marking, it is always preferred to keep it as simple and consistent end to end as possible. Therefore, MPLS EXP marking is the preferred marking at those managed CEs. However, the challenge here is that the majority of the PE-CE connectivity is based on native IP (non-MPLS). At the same time, the operator must not impact any IP DiffServ markings set by the customer. Pipe mode MPLS DiffServ tunneling, with an Explicit Null LSP, can resolve this challenge (RFC 3032), where a label is assigned for customer traffic going toward the PE. This label is used only to preserve the MPLS VPN operator's MPLS EXP markings across the CE-to-PE link; the original customer IP marking is kept intact.

DiffServ MPLS-TE (DS-TE)

As discussed earlier in Chapter 5, MPLS-TE introduces intelligence to the headend network node (source) to forward traffic based on multiple predefined criteria such as available bandwidth, link affinity attributes (like low-latency links), and SRLG considerations (a behavior known as *constraint-based routing*). DiffServ MPLS-TE (DS-TE) extends MPLS-TE to offer advanced class-based constraint routing of *guaranteed* traffic, in which MPLS-TE allows network operators to define two separate pools per link/path. Typically, the global pool reflects the overall available bandwidth over a given link (DS-TE), and the subpool reflects a subset of the available bandwidth for certain class such as EF (LLQ) class. It is important for the network designer to distinguish here between the standard DiffServ behavior discussed earlier in this section (such as CBWFQ and LLQ) and DS-TE, because DS-TE here can provide the control plane capability to book bandwidth at queue level (such as LLQ). Also, ideally it should align with the configured DiffServ LLQ bandwidth that provides the forwarding plane in this case.

In other words, DiffServ and DS-TE can complement each other (ideally). However, they are neither identical mechanisms, nor must they be enabled together. With DS-TE, network designers can achieve very advanced DiffServ-aware traffic engineering. For example, besides the standard ability of MPLS-TE to select a link to route traffic through based on certain criteria such as available bandwidth, DS-TE allows network designers to guarantee that the selected path can offer the available bandwidth at a class level, such as voice class. It also offers the ability to reroute traffic if a downstream node is experiencing congestion or has a limited available bandwidth to satisfy this class, which is impossible with the typical DiffServ to achieve because it is a per-hop mechanism (reactive local mechanism).

In addition DS-TE provides the ability to enable preemption priorities among DS-TE classes, where classes with higher priority can take precedence over those with lower priority during LSP signaling for the primary or backup MPLS-TE tunnel when there is not enough bandwidth available (tunnel preemption). Therefore, with MPLS DS-TE, SPs and large enterprises can offer end-to-end advanced QoS capabilities based on signaled rather than provisioned QoS to meet strict SLA requirements.

Note   With regard to MPLS DS-TE bandwidth constraints, there are two primary models: maximum allocation model (MAM) and Russian dolls model (RDM), as defined by IETF. The network designer may consider both models at the same time at different places across the network. However, this approach will increase design and operational complexity and will reduce the end-to-end level of consistency and reliability of the solution.

Setting up the MPLS-TE LSPs (tunnels) is half the job because traffic will not ride the TE tunnel automatically. There are multiple mechanisms to route traffic inside the TE tunnel, such as autoroute, forwarding adjacency (FA), static route, and policy-based routing. As covered in Chapter 5, each has its strengths and weaknesses. Technically, all these mechanisms are valid options to be used to route traffic down the MPLS DS-TE tunnels. However, the class-based tunnel selection (CBTS) mechanism offers a more flexible, scalable, and optimized TE solution when it is combined with MPLS DS-TE because it requires minimum configuration to dynamically route traffic over the desired DS-TE tunnels that takes into consideration the EXP marking of the traffic flows.

In addition, CBTS offers the ability to support multiple TE tunnels of a given tunnel bundle to exit the headend node via different interfaces based on the assigned CoS (MPLS EXP value) to take different paths. For instance, traffic marked with EXP 5 can be sent out an interface that crosses a path with lower latency than others, as shown in Figure 10-44.

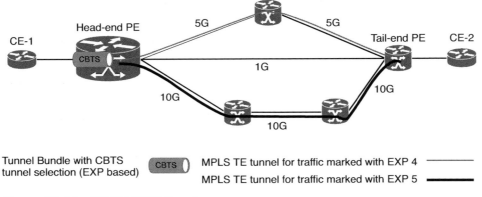

Figure 10-44   *DS-TE CBTS Based*

Note   *Tunnel bundle* refers to a group of normal TE or DS-TE tunnels that are sourced and destined from the same headend node to the same tail-end node. Typically, each can carry different MPLS EXP value.

Furthermore, one MPLS-TE primary design consideration discussed in Chapter 5 is whether to set up the TE tunnel PE to PE or provider (P) to P, which depends on the targeted environment and the desired goal to achieve. Setting up a full mesh of PE-to-PE MPLS-TE tunnels can be a complex solution to plan, design. and operate in large-scale networks. Nonetheless, to offer a true end-to-end service differentiation with regard to DS-TE, it is desirable for the coverage of the TE tunnel and path optimization to be end to end. However, this does not mean every single TE tunnel has to be PE to PE. Instead, network designers can selectively decide which TE tunnels (such as DS-TE enabled only) should protect certain type of traffic flows to be set up PE to PE (outer-mesh based).

The critical point with regard to QoS design across MPLS-based networks (regardless of whether it is an SP or large enterprise network) is which design direction should be used, such as best effort, end-to-end DiffServ QoS, DS-TE based, or a combination. Obviously, no one can answer this question other than the designer who is aware of the different design and application requirements and the underlying network architecture. However, the following foundational questions help network designers to direct the design strategy toward the right path during the planning phase:

- Is the targeted environment an SP or enterprise network? (Commonly, but not always, SP networks tend to have higher expectations in terms of traffic volume and network coverage and different SLA requirements.)

- Is the network bandwidth overprovisioned? (If yes, you may enable basic DiffServ QoS model.)

- Are there any sensitive applications that require strict SLA such as VoIP, video or any other mission/business-critical applications? If yes, if you fail to meet the end-to-end SLA for this traffic, will any penalty accrue, or will there be a business-critical impact? (Here you may decide to consider DS-TE [perhaps with MPLS-TE FRR] combined with a DiffServ model, if failing to meet the SLA has direct cost to or impact on the business.)

- Is MPLS-TE already enabled across the network? (If yes, this can simplify enabling DS-TE if required.)

- Does any inter-AS link require QoS considerations? (MPLS-TE over an inter-AS link can be a complex option to consider.)

- Is there any SRLG across the core?(If yes, MPLS-TE/DS-TE can overcome this design concern if an alternate path exists.)

As covered in Chapter 1, design simplicity and avoiding gold plating are vital principles to be considered in every design. Therefore, keep in mind that the more protocols and features there are enabled across the network, the more complex the network is to design and operate.

Further Reading

"Enterprise Medianet Quality of Service Design 4.0—Overview," http://www.cisco.com

"DiffServ—The Scalable End-to-End QoS Model," http://www.cisco.com

"IPsec VPN QoS Design," http://www.cisco.com

RFC 4124, *Protocol Extensions for Support of Diffserv-Aware MPLS Traffic Engineering*, http://www.rfc-base.org

RFC 3644, *Policy Quality of Service (QoS) Information Model*, https://tools.ietf.org

Network Security Design

Today's converged networks carry much business-critical information across the network (whether it is voice, video, or data), which makes it extremely important for that information to be secured and protected for two primary reasons. The first reason is for information security and privacy purposes. The second reason is to maintain business continuity at the desired level, such as protecting against distributed DoS (DDoS) attacks, regardless of whether this protection is within the internal network or between the different sites over an external network. Therefore, the design of a network infrastructure and network security must not be performed in isolation.

In other words, the holistic design approach discussed earlier in this book is vital when it comes to network security design considerations. No network should be designed independently from its security requirements. A successful network design must facilitate the application and integration of the security requirements by following the top-down approach, starting from the business goals and needs, to compliance with the organization's security policy standards, to a detailed design and integration of the various network technologies and components.

This section covers the different security aspects that network designers need to consider when planning, designing, or optimizing IP networks to a achieve a self-healing, secure network infrastructures that can mitigate and operate with an acceptable level of performance during security breaches or network attack situations and that can offer the required level of information security across the network transports.

Note Although the CCDE exam is not a security-focused exam, infrastructure security and the integration of security principles and methodologies with the network design are important aspects that every network designer must take into account to produce a successful design. In addition, one common challenge when optimizing an existing design is that network and security components are integrated in a way that either does not scale or does not provide the desired level of performance. Nonetheless, network designers are expected to identify the limitations in the design and optimize it in a way that meets the business and functional requirements. In other words, although the CCDE candidate is not expected to produce deep-level security design, the candidate should know how to produce a secure network design by integrating multiple security principles in a way that does not break the network design goals while at the same time not compromising security requirements. Therefore, this section only covers network security design principles, approaches, and considerations that can impact the network design and the overall network design objective. It focuses mainly on how to achieve an integrated secure network design.

Network Security Design Fundamentals

This section discusses the primary design principles and considerations that network designers must take into account when designing or validating an existing network design from a network security point of view.

Top-Down Design

As discussed earlier in this book, to achieve a successful business-driven design, network architect and designers must always consider this approach to build the foundation or the roadmap of the design. With regard to security, in particular network security, network designers should consider the following questions when designing a new network design or when evaluating an existing network design to help them draw the high-level picture of the design direction with regard to the security aspects:

- What are the business objectives and goals?

- What is the targeted industry (manufacturing, financial services, retail)? (This helps to identify industry-specific standards.)

- Is there any security policy and standards the design must comply with? (This is specific to the identified industry, such as Payment Card Industry Data Security Standard [PCI DSS] compliance.)

- What is a must and what is desirable to be protected (priorities)?

- What is the impact of a failure to protect the intended systems/networks on the business (such as cost or reputation)?

- Will security services or appliances break any mission-critical applications? If yes, how can this risk be avoided or mitigated?

- Are there any capital expenditure (capex) or operational expenditure (opex) concerns with regard to network security?

Security Policy Considerations

To secure any system or network, there must be predefined goals to achieve and specifications to comply with to ensure that the outcomes are measurable and always meet the organization standards. Therefore, to achieve this, organizations almost always develop security standards, policies, and specifications that all collectively aim to achieve the desired goal with regard to information security. This is what is commonly known as a *security policy*. A security policy is a formal statement of the rules by which people who are given access to an organization's technology and information assets must abide. It should also specify the mechanisms through which these requirements can be met and audited for compliance with the policy [86].

As a result, a good understanding of the organization's security policy and its standards is a crucial prerequisite before starting any network design or optimizing an existing design. This understanding ensures that any suggested solution will comply with the security policy standards and expectations of the business with regard to information security.

For instance, you may suggest redesigning an existing 1G dark fiber (owned by the organization) to a virtual leased line (VLL) solution (L2VPN based) that offers the same quality with lower cost. However, the security policy may dictate that any traffic traversing any network that is not owned by the organization must be encrypted. By taking this point into consideration, the network architect or designer here can add IPsec or MACsec to the proposed solution to provide an encrypted VLL, to ensure the suggested design supports and complies with the organization's security policy standards.

Holistic Approach Considerations

The integration of network infrastructure and network security (including security components such as firewalls and configurations such as infrastructure access control lists ACL [iALCs]) can be seen as a double-edged sword. This is because on the one hand, security will offer privacy, control, and stability to the network (for example, protect against DDoS attacks and unauthorized access). On the other hand, if both the network infrastructure and the security components are designed in isolation (siloed approach), then when they integrate together at some point, there will be a mix of the following issues:

- Complex integration
- Traffic drop
- Reduced performance
- Redesign or major design changes

For instance, in Figure 10-45, the network infrastructure of the Internet edge was designed to provide Internet access for the enterprise. Based on this, the network designer considered Enhanced Interior Gateway Routing Protocol (EIGRP) as the internal dynamic routing protocol and external Border Gateway Protocol (eBGP) to provide the edge routing to provide end-to-end connectivity.

However, after this design was reviewed by the security team, they suggested that a pair of firewalls in routed mode has to be introduced into this design, and remote-access VPN sessions have to be terminated on these firewalls to comply with the enterprise security standards, as shown in Figure 10-46. In addition, the added firewalls support only static routing.

Although it seems to be a simple change to introduce the firewalls into the original design, this simple change requires review of the entire design (IGP, BGP, inbound and outbound traffic flow, and policies to avoid asymmetrical routing, NAT setup on the edge routers to allow users' remote-access VPN sessions to terminate at the firewalls, in addition to whether these firewalls have any impact on the traffic flows of mission-critical applications passing through it). Therefore, it is important to adopt a holistic approach to promote an optimal, integrated, and secure network design that is flexible enough to achieve the intended goals with minimal operational and design changes.

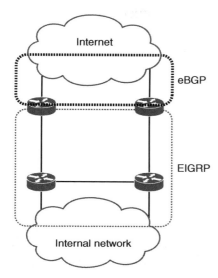

Figure 10-45 *Network Design Before Inserting Security Devices*

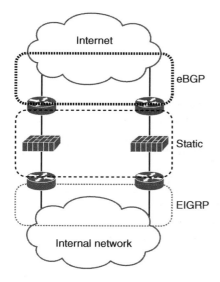

Figure 10-46 *Network Design After Inserting Security Devices*

Divide-and-Conquer Approach

To simplify the overall security design in a more controlled manner, a structured modular approach should be used by splitting the network into multiple domains. This approach helps to introduce *chokepoints* between the different domains to enforce structured control between these domains. Each domain should be given a level of trust based on the security requirements to facilitate controlling who and what is allowed to pass between the different domains by using various mechanisms such as packet filtering with iACLs or specialized security appliances (physical or virtual) such as a firewalls and intrusion prevention systems (IPS) to be positioned at each chokepoint (domain boundary point) between the different security domains.

Furthermore, security requirements sometimes dictate that within each security domain there must be subdomains where each should have its own specific security policies and access restrictions among other subdomains. In this case, network designers can introduce what is commonly known as *zones*. For example, a data center can be placed under a single security domain. Normally, inside the data center various services and applications require different levels of security enforcement between them, like web servers that can be placed in their own zone, database servers in different zones, and so on. With this approach, network designers can facilitate the security control to a large extent and optimize its manageability, as shown in Figure 10-47.

Note In Figure 10-47, the core block was not placed in its own domain to illustrate one of the recommended and proven design considerations that offloads any additional processing from the network core, such as security policies. However, some design requirements require the core to be treated as separate security domain.

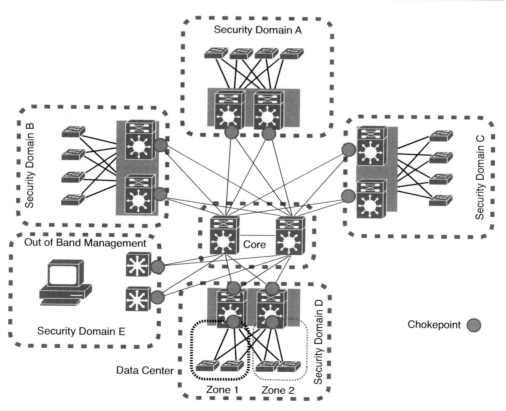

Figure 10-47 *Security Domains and Zones*

Security devices are almost always placed at the chokepoints (domains or zone boundary points). However, the type of security devices and roles can vary based on the domain or zone to be protected and its location in the network. For example, in Figure 10.47, a firewall is placed at the network management zone boundary to fulfill packet filtering and inspection requirements for OAM traffic flows in both directions, while at the public demilitarized zone (DMZ), there are multiple specialized security nodes such as web application firewall data loss prevention and IPS.

Nevertheless, it is critical that network architects and designers consider the type of the targeted network and its high-level architecture in terms of whether it is an SP network or enterprise network. Each of these networks (irrespective to its detailed design) has different traffic flow characteristics. For instance, enterprise networks always define chokepoint boundaries such as the Internet edge or connections to extranet networks where traffic is always controlled by strict and confined rules. In contrast, as covered earlier in Chapter 5, SP networks are transit types of network where traffic should be allowed to traverse the SP network between different customers' remote sites or peering ISPs in different directions.

By taking these high-level traffic pattern differences and applying the domains or zoning concept to each of these networks, it is obvious that SP networks have many external connections. This translates into many domain boundary points, usually with either very limited or no specialized security devices positioned at these boundary points with their customers. For example, with MPLS VPN providers who offer L3VPN and L2VPN, the top priority for them is usually to forward the high volumes of their customers' traffic with the least possible latency.

Enterprise networks, however, normally have limited domain boundary points to other domains (outsides domains, such as Internet and links to business partners). Usually these domain boundary points are controlled by several network security devices, with each focusing on a different security layer and function. In other words, although the concept of domains and zoning is applicable to every network, the type of the targeted network influences how this concept can be applied to a large extent.

Security Triad Principle (Confidentiality, Integrity, and Availability)

Confidentiality, integrity, and availability, also known as *CIA*, are considered the fundamentals of information security. In other words, these elements help to construct secure systems that protect information and resources (devices, communication, and data) from unauthorized access, modification, inspection, or destruction. Therefore, any breach to any of these three elements can lead to serious consequences. Consequently, network designers must be aware of these elements and how each impacts the network design, and at the same time how the network design can accommodate these principles as an integral part of it. Table 10-14 summarizes the characteristics of each of these elements and the common mechanisms used to achieve them.

Table 10-14   *Confidentiality, Integrity, and Availability*

CIA Triad Security Element	Characteristic	Mechanisms to Achieve
Confidentiality	Protect against unauthorized access to information to maintain the desired level of secrecy of the transmitted information across the internal network or public Internet (in other words, identifying who should have access to this information).	Cryptography, encryption, user ID and password (two-factor authentication is more common today) or security tokens. Cryptography can provide data confidentiality by modify the data into a format that can be understood only by the authorized entity.
Integrity	Maintain accurate information end to end by ensuring that no alteration is performed by any unauthorized entity.	Cryptography, data checksum. Cryptography enables the receiving entity to verify whether there was any alteration to the original, such as hashing.
Availability	Ensure that access to services and systems is always available and information is accessible by authorized users when required. Also, in modern networks, availability is not only measured by network or service up or down, but also by its quality. (For example, malicious traffic may increase latency in the network, which leads to a degraded VoIP quality [users might not be able to make voice call even though the voice system and the network are up]).	Systems designed with high availability at different levels (network, storage, compute, application) and that protect against attacks such as a DoS that attempts to stop access to resources.

Network Infrastructure Security Considerations

Securing today's modern networks is one of the most complicated tasks. Mobility and communication over the Internet are becoming one of the primary (de facto) methods of communications and essential requirements for many businesses. Therefore, to address these trends and requirements, sophisticated security countermeasures are required. Typically, a good security design follows a structured approach that divides the network into domains and applies security in layers, with each layer focusing on certain types of security requirements and challenges. This is also known as *defense in depth*, where multiple layers of protection are strategically located across the network and where a failure of one layer to detect an attack or malicious traffic flow will not leave the network at risk. Instead, the multiple security layers work in a back-to-back manner to detect the attack or malicious flow in the network [99]. Figure 10-48 summarizes the common security aspects that can be applied in a layered approach.

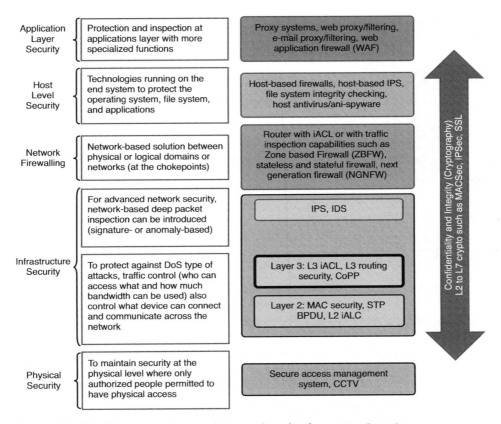

Figure 10-48   *Elements of Layered Network and Information Security*

This section covers infrastructure security and network firewall considerations, in brief, focusing on the integration and impact with regard to network design.

Network Device Level Security

Securing network devices is the first and essential consideration to protect any network. For instance, even though you may have a very secure control plane and network edge design and policies, if one or two network devices are compromised, the network can be taken down easily by introducing black-holing routes, generating a large amount of malicious traffic that is technically sourced from an internal (trusted) network device, or the attacker can even take advantage and access other internal zones that are not accessible externally. In addition to that, if someone can access a network device, it means all the traffic passing through this device can be sniffed and copied. This is dangerous for an organization that has sensitive information, such as credit card numbers or people's personal information. Therefore, protecting network devices is a fundamental requirement to achieving a secure network design.

To approach device-level protection in more structured manner, as a network designer you need to understand the following types of traffic that network devices normally handle, as summarized in Figure 10-49. Understanding the different traffic types passing through any network will help to identify how each traffic type can impact the device and the possible countermeasures for each.

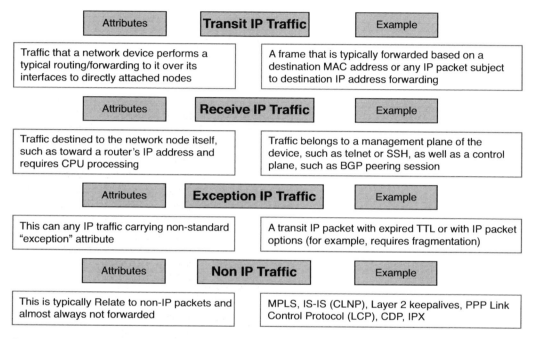

Figure 10-49 *Types of Traffic Handled by Network Devices*

The different traffic types listed in Figure 10-49 each has impact in terms of overloading network devices with regard to the IP traffic planes covered in Table 10-15 and Figure 10-50, because each has its own attributes and security considerations, based on Cisco's Network Foundation Protection (NFP) framework [100, 120].

Table 10-15 *IP Traffic and Device Planes*

Device Plane	Security Concern Example
Data plane	Responsible for controlling fast forwarding of traffic passing through a network device. However, this plane is normally limited to a certain number of packs per second (pps) based on the hardware platform's throughput. iACL, QoS toolset, remotely triggered black hole (RTBH), and Unicast Reverse Path Forwarding (uRPF) are common mechanisms to protect this plane.

Table 10-15 *continued*

Device Plane	Security Concern Example
Control plane	As discussed earlier in this book, the control plane is like the brain of the network node; it usually controls and handles all Layer 3 functions. Therefore, any control plane-related issues such as a flapping session with a BGP peer that advertises an extremely large number of prefixes will not only impact the network stability, but also the device itself will be impact because of high CPU spikes in this case. iACL, routing protection, and control plane policing (CoPP) are common mechanisms to protect this plane.
Management plane	As the name implies, this plane relates to the management traffic of the device, such as device access, configuration, troubleshooting, and monitoring. Therefore, its criticality is equal to the other planes described earlier. Any unauthorized access can lead to a device and network-wide crisis, such as injecting a black-holing route into the control plane or flooding the network with malicious traffic, which will ultimately impact all the hosts and users transiting though the network in general and this network device in particular. CPU and memory thresholding, AAA (authentication, authorization, and accounting), and CoPP are common mechanisms to protect this plane.

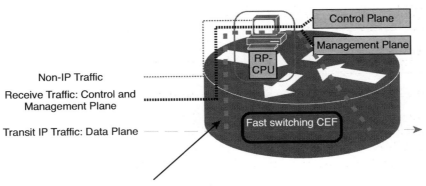

Figure 10-50 *Traffic Handling Within a Router*

Taking the different traffic types and how each is mapped into the relevant plane for processing in a structured manner, the following points should be considered as general and foundational guidance to achieving the desired level of device hardening and security level.[13] Consider that these points should not conflict or breach the security policy or company standards.

13. "Cisco Guide to Harden Cisco IOS Devices," http://www.cisco.com

- **Physical security:** The first basic security consideration is that network devices be placed physically in a secure place, where only authorized people can access them.

- **Authentication, authorization, and accounting:** Network devices must be accessible only by authorized people. Ideally, the access privileges must be multilevel role-based access (authorization level "who can do what") combined with a reliable accounting (logging) to keep track of who has access the devices and what has been done.

- **Secure the device management plane:** Ideally, the management sessions and activities of the network devices must be performed over protected protocols such as Secure Shell (SSH), Secure Sockets Layer (SSL), Secure File Transfer Protocol (SFTP), or IPsec. Also, it is always advised that an out-of-band management access to network devices be provisioned to offer secure, guaranteed direct access to critical network devices in situations where the network might be facing a DDoS attack (because in-band management access will be almost impossible).

- **Protect the hardware resources:** Maintaining a device hardware recourse is the foundation to maintaining traffic flow through the device. Therefore, protecting hardware resources such as CPU is an essential countermeasure to be considered with regard to device hardening, such as CoPP to protect the CPU from spikes because of excessive control plane traffic. Control plane protection (CPPr) also helps to protect from other types of traffic, such as exception and transit traffic.

- **Disable unused services:** A network node does not usually use every single service it has; normally, the device role and function within the network dictate which required services need to be turned on. In general, unused services should be disabled to limit the chances that an intruder or hacker can compromise one of these unused services to generate malicious traffic or DoS attacks.

- **Monitoring:** Network security is dynamic and always evolving and changing in response to the continuous technology and design developments and changes. As a result, there are always new system vulnerabilities, breaches, and intrusion developments. Therefore, to keep track of what is going on in terms of device utilization (bandwidth or hardware resource) and whether it is within the normal (baseline) limits, network and device monitoring helps network operators to always optimize device security either proactively or in a fast, reactive approach. Simple Network Management Protocol (SNMP) and NetFlow are the most common protocols used for this purpose, but not the only ones.

Although the device-level security considerations covered earlier are considered generic and standard foundational guidelines, the consideration of these guidelines will vary based on some other factors. Figure 10-51 identifies the primary influencing factors with regard to device-level security.

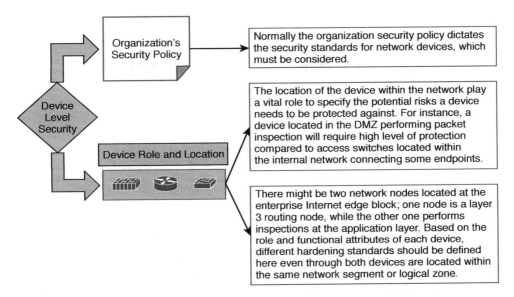

Figure 10-51 *Influencing Factors on Device-Level Security*

Layer 2 Security Considerations

Securing Layer 2 or data link layer communication is as critical as other higher layers in the network. One of the common practices is that network designers or operators focus more on securing higher layers across the network, such as the Layer 3 control plane, protocol, and session layers, without giving Layer 2 enough focus to secure it. As covered in multiple sections in this book, a building constructed with a weak foundation will not be able to deliver the promised value or end result and will be more vulnerable to damage.

Similarly, a highly secure network on the higher layer, such as network and application layers, can be easily taken out of service by simple Layer 2 flooding across its switched network. Therefore, it is critical to secure the network in a bottom-up manner to achieve a reliable and self-healing network security design. Layer 2 compared to other OSI layers is the simplest with regard to security considerations and one of the most dangerous at the same time. For instance, if a hacker compromises a data center switch, he can easily sniff all the traffic passing through this switch that might carry critical data. At the same time, this hacker can simply take the data center switched network down by flooding the ternary content-addressable memory (TCAM) table of the switch or sending malicious Layer 2 traffic storms. In addition, IPv6 raises a number of first-hop security (FHS) concerns that were not present in IPv4. Layer 2 security can be categorized as the following to produce a structured and flexible Layer 2 security design:

■ **Authentication and authorization:** Normally, the Layer 2 switched network is the network edge or boundary where end users and hosts connect. Typically, it is the edge where rogue and unauthorized endpoints can be connected. Therefore, only authorized devices must be permitted to connect to the network at the switch port level. This normally can be achieved by using different mechanisms and features, such as authentication with IEEE 802.1X, which can integrate with a network admission control system to authenticate users and their endpoints, port ACL (routed ALC, MAC ACL, VLAN ACL), DHCP snooping, and other port security features. (One or a combination of these mechanisms or features can be used based on the security goals, standards, and supported features. Also, IPv6 router advertisement (RA) guard, DHCPv6 guard, and IPv6 snooping help to mitigate IPv6 FHS concerns. Furthermore, the IEEE 802.1AE standard known as *MACsec* can be used to satisfy some security specifications that require protecting the data traversing an Ethernet LAN such as between the Layer 2 DCI edge nodes of a secure data center in which MACsec offers the ability of authenticating and encrypting packets between the two MACsec-capable devices at the DCI edge of the interconnected data centers.

■ **VLAN design:** Although one of the primary goals of VLANs is to provide separation at Layer 2, the design of these VLANs can sometimes lead to security concerns. For example, if an extended VLAN across two data centers over a DCI is compromised, this may lead to a major impact and risk to both data centers. Therefore, it is always recommended that Layer 2 domains should be contained to a limited range within the network (smaller failure domain); this also avoids issues such as Address Resolution Protocol (ARP) or unicast flooding. However, practically this is not always achievable because the reality is that application requirements dictate how the network should be designed. Accordingly, protective features and policies have to be considered in scenarios like this, such as defining rate limiting along the path and mitigating the impact of the traffic flooding. In addition to the typical separation VLANs provide to the design, private VLANs (PVLANs) offer a more advanced level of a controlled traffic separation between VLANs and between endpoints that reside within the same VLAN. Furthermore, the use of VLAN Trunking Protocol (VTP) can introduce a high risk to the switched network because inserting a switch that takes over the VTP server role will rewrite VLANs set up across the entire switched network under the same VTP domain. Therefore, securing VTP or considering VTP in transparent mode is always recommended to avoid its impact in situations like this.

■ **Layer 2 control plane:** As discussed earlier in this book, Layer 2 control protocols, such as Spanning Tree Protocol (STP), provide protective mechanisms against Layer 2 loops. However, STP is considered a double-edged sword because in the case of misconfiguration, with any security weakness any attacker can simply bring down the switched network or change its logical design. This is because no reliable authentication capability is built in to the STP. Therefore, if someone attaches a switch to the existing switched network that has better attributes than the other switch to make it the network root bridge, the network first will be unstable for a while during the election process of the new root bridge. Second, after this rogue switch is considered as the root, a disaster will probably occur in this network because of performance issues, and may introduce traffic black-holing at Layer 2. To further exacerbate the situation, most of the traffic will pass through this new root switch in which anyone can sniff the traffic or take it or copy or it. Moreover, this behavior can be dangerous to metro Ethernet providers if one of their customer switches become the root bridge. Therefore, protecting the Layer 2 control protocols used is an essential consideration to secure Layer 2 switched networks, such as protecting the root bridge by denying any other switch in the network from participating or sending a rogue message to be elected as a root bridge and filtering Layer 2 bridge protocol data unit (BPDU) messages at the network edge as well.

Layer 3 Control Plane Security Considerations

The Layer 3 control plane is the intelligence over the network that steers traffic toward reaching its intended destination. This means any wrong information can lead to traffic black-holing and the eventual dropping of packets. In addition, in a network with unprotected routing, anyone can easily bring it down by either flooding a large number of prefixes (legitimate or not) by inserting a rogue router or redirecting traffic a black-holing next hop or a sniffer. Therefore, securing the Layer 3 control plane is a must. However, the question here is this: Where is securing a control plane a must, and where is it just something beneficial to have? Although there is no one standard answer to this generic question, the following can be considered as general rules with regard to Layer 3 control plane security:

- Secure the control plane against rogue Layer 3 peers by authenticating routing sessions. This is a recommended practice to be considered across the entire routed domain and strongly recommended when peering with an external routing domain.

- Device protection with regard to Layer 3 control plane functions is a primary element to be considered. For example, if a router that is not supposed to receive and process prefixes receives a large number of them, this node might run out of memory. In all likelihood, its CPU will be overloaded, and this will result in a malfunctioning node in the routing path, which will introduce instability (because the routing session will probably keep going up and down in this case). A large percentage of traffic will also be dropped. Therefore, it is important to limit the maximum number of routes to be accepted by the node. This is common in MPLS L3VPN SP design, where normally the PE nodes limit the maximum number of prefixes per VRF/VPN.

- Accept only the routes that are expected to be received. This is common in MPLS L3VPN and ISPs, where the ISP, for example, will only permit the Provider Assigned "PA" or Provider Independent "PI" address space the customer has to advertise with the agreed subnet length, sometimes combined with uRPF check. For instance, a customer who owns /24 IPv4 public ranges will not normally be allowed to divide it and advertise it in the format of host routes (/32) unless it is agreed with the ISP. This is because the ISP always tries to protect their PE nodes from being overloaded with extra thousands or even can reach hundreds of thousands of extra routes.

■ Advanced BGP techniques such as QoS policy propagation with BGP (QPPB) and remote black-holing trigger can be used in SP-style networks to offer a more dynamic, flexible, controlled, and secure control plane design that is almost impossible to be achieved with the typical static filtering mechanisms, such as using ACLs or prefix lists.

■ QoS has powerful features that help to optimize Layer 3 control plane security design, usually by guaranteeing a minimum amount of bandwidth during congestion situations. This ensures the routing session will not be torn down, and it limits the amount of bandwidth to a predefined maximum allowed bandwidth. This protects the network from undesirable behavior such as DoS attacks by a rogue router, for example, that generates a large amount of traffic using the same control plane marking or even TCP/UDP port. To take advantage of this QoS as a protective mechanism here, it ideally should be applied across the entire routing domain and not only at the edge of the network.

■ CoPP, as covered earlier, should be considered on every network node to relax the impact of control plane flooding and protect network nodes from CPU spikes by blocking unnecessary or DoS traffic.

Note Although CoPP uses modular QoS CLI (MQoC), the QoS considerations earlier provide network-wide treatment on a per-hop basis for Layer 3 control plane traffic flows, whereas CoPP is focused only on a device level. As covered earlier, marking down the DSCP value of packets that are out of profile can impact how these packets will be treated by other nodes across the network.

Remote-Access and Network Overlays (VPN) Security Considerations

The most common and proven mechanisms for providing secure remote access for remote users and remote sites over the public Internet is the overlaid virtual private network (VPN). One common misconception is that the term *VPN* is always seen as a synonym for IPsec. In fact, IPsec offers cryptography at the network layer, whereas VPN can take different forms, such as MPLS L3VPN, MPLS L2VPN, SSL VPN, DMVPN, and so on. Therefore, it is important that network architects and designers distinguish between VPN and IPsec. Having said that, secured VPN with IPsec is the most common and proven combination that is used to protect the various types of VPN solutions. Table 10-16 compares the most common overlay VPN solutions from different design aspects.

Table 10-16 *Overlay VPN Solutions Comparison*

	IPsec	GRE	DMVPN	GETVPN	Remote Access (Client Based)
Standard	Yes	Yes	No (Cisco proprietary)	No (Cisco proprietary)	Yes
Overlay transport	P2P IPsec tunnel	P2P GRE	mGRE	Tunnel-less	P2P IPsec tunnel
Protection model	Peer to peer	Peer to peer with IPsec	Peer-to-peer with IPsec	Group protection (RFC 3547)	Peer to peer
IP routing	Static routing	Tunneled dynamic routing	Tunneled dynamic routing	Standard IP WAN dynamic routing	Reverse-route injection
Offers a protected VPN over public Internet	Yes	Yes, with IPsec	Yes, with IPsec	No	Yes
Offers a protected VPN over the IP WAN transport	Yes	Yes, with IPsec	Yes, with IPsec	Yes	Yes
Requires some changes to the existing Layer 3 routing design when used over the WAN	Yes	Yes	Yes	No	Yes*
Requires additional network equipment	No	No	No	Yes, such as key server	No
Support NATing	Yes	Yes	Yes	No (NAT must be performed before encryption or after decryption.)	Yes

*This VPN is commonly used to provide connectivity over the Internet.

One main consideration with regard to an enterprise VPN is whether to enable the VPN across the enterprise WAN. The typical answer to this depends on the business requirements, security policy, and the functional requirements. One must consider the impact on the business-critical applications because of the increased packet overhead by the VPN tunneling, especially when VPN is combined with IPsec, as shown previously in Figure 10-38. Besides, it is common that security devices in the path such as firewalls with NATing add a layer of design and operational complexity to the VPN solution.

In addition, introducing a VPN across the WAN can increase the design and operational complexity in scenarios where dual WAN connectivity is required (either dual routers or links). In these cases, the routing redundancy design will be moved from the typical IGP or BGP to IPsec redundancy, which might not be a suitable option for some design requirements. Therefore, GETVPN is becoming the most common and desirable secure VPN solution of the WAN because GETVPN by nature offers tunnel header preservation, which facilitates routing encrypted packets using the underlying network routing infrastructure. There is no need to consider any redundancy design at the VPN level, such as dual hubs or stateful IPsec high availability.

Even though securing IP traffic across the WAN will introduce a new layer of complexity, secure IP communication is a top priority for some businesses, like those in financial services environments. Sending internal traffic across the WAN will be seen by the business as trusting SP setup, security, employees, and even contractors and third parties who work and integrate with this SP not to perform any malicious activity. Therefore, for this type of business, it is common that IPsec, such as secure DMVPN or GETVPN, is deployed across the WAN.

In other words, enabling secure IP communication over the WAN is not a common practice because it is seen as adding an unnecessary layer of complexity and may impact the performance of some business applications, whereas for those business that are concerned most about security, secure IP communication over the WAN is essential. Therefore, the decision of whether to enable secure IP communications across the WAN is almost always based on the business type, priorities, and impact on the overall network and application performance, in addition to operational complexity.

Network-Based Firewall Considerations

Technically, a firewall is not a device built to perform routing or switching. Instead, it is a device that is primarily intended to perform security functions such as packet filtering, inspection, and VPN termination. Although almost all the firewalls nowadays support static and dynamic routing, the nature of these devices almost always impacts the network design. This impact varies based different factors and attributes. The following are the primary and most common and influencing factors that network designers must always consider whenever there is a firewall in the network path:

- **Stateful versus stateless firewall:** Typically, stateless firewalls deal with traffic in a static manner where traffic flows are only monitored and filtered (allowed or blocked) based on static information such as IP source, IP destination, or port numbers. This behavior from a network design point of view can introduce limitations and operational complexities because every single traffic flow needs to be included in both directions (ingress and egress) as part of the firewall entry rules. Stateless firewalls are also not very friendly with applications that automatically negotiate ports, such as RTP (UDP) ports, which are normally automatically negotiated during the signaling and establishment of a VoIP or video call. Stateful firewalls, in contrast, offer traffic monitoring and filtering that is more aware of traffic flows to overcome the limitations of the stateless firewalls, especially with applications that require dynamic port negotiation to establish their session, such as FTP, VoIP, and video RTP media streams.

- **Stateful versus stateless firewall failover:** Even though some Firewalls work in active-standby mode are stateful firewalls from a traffic handling perspective, the way these firewalls fail over from the active to the standby can take two forms, either stateless failover or stateful failover. With the stateless failover, the state table is usually not replicated to the standby peer firewall. This means in the event of active firewall failure, the active role will be moved to the standby firewall. The issue here is that after the failover happens, all the connections (active flows) have to be reinitiated. In contrast, stateful failover offers the ability to replicate the state table between the active and the standby firewalls to avoid reinitiation of the active session following a failover event. The impact of a session's reinitiation might not be an issue for some applications and businesses, but it can be a serious issue for others. Therefore, the decision whether to use stateless or stateful failover should ideally be driven by the design and application requirements.

- **Routed versus transparent firewall modes:** The other important factor that has a direct impact on network design with regard to firewalls, apart from the operational attributes of the firewalls (stateful or stateless), is that firewalls can operate as a Layer 3 or Layer 2 node. Technically, from a network design point of view, introducing a Layer 3 node into a routed network means that there will be a need to change IP addressing or a need for new IPs in the area where this firewall will be added, in addition to considerations about whether the firewall supports dynamic routing. For instance, if a firewall is added to an Intermediate System-to-Intermediate System (IS-IS) routed domain and the firewall does not support IS-IS, in this case static routing will be considered. This means a redesign of the routing will be required. Firewalls operating in Layer 2, however, will not introduce these challenges and can be inserted transparently into the routing domain. This is commonly known as *transparent mode* because there is no change required to the existing routing, IP addressing, or host default gateways. Furthermore, when a firewall operates in a transparent mode, it often loses some of its functions or features, such as providing VPN termination. However, this is completely vendor and device model dependent and can vary from one to another to a large extent. Remember that the CCDE exam is not hardware or vendor dependent. Therefore, if something relates to nonstandard software or hardware specification, it should be provided as part of the design scenario.

Based on the multiple sections and security layers discussed briefly in this section, Figure 10-52 provides a summarized list of some common network attacks and risks, along with the possible countermeasures and features that can be used to protect the network infrastructure and mitigate the impact of these attacks at different layers.

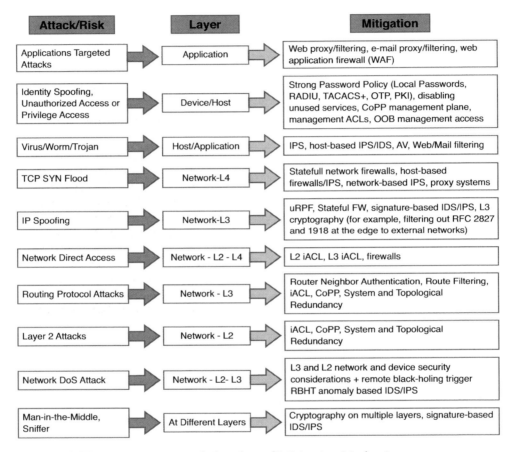

Figure 10-52   *Common Network Attacks and Mitigation Mechanisms*

Further Reading

RFC 6480, *An Infrastructure to Support Secure Internet Routing*, http://www.ietf.org

RFC 2725, *Routing Policy System Security*, http://www.ietf.org

RFC 7416, *A Security Threat Analysis for the Routing Protocol for Low-Power and Lossy Networks (RPLs)*, http://www.ietf.org

RFC 4272, *BGP Security Vulnerabilities Analysis*, http://www.ietf.org

RFC 7454, *BGP Operations and Security*, http://www.ietf.org

RFC 3948, *UDP Encapsulation of IPsec ESP Packets*, http://www.ietf.org

"Cisco Guide to Harden Cisco IOS Devices," http://www.cisco.com

"Cisco SAFE Reference Guide," http://www.cisco.com

Network Management

As discussed earlier in this book, today's modern networks carry multiple business-critical applications over one unified infrastructure such as voice, video, and data. In addition, in today's competitive telecommunications market, SPs always aim to satisfy their customers by meeting strict SLA requirements. As discussed earlier, various technologies, protocols, architectures, and constraints all collectively construct an operational network. However, designing and deploying a network using a business-driven approach will not guarantee the quality of the solution as well (that is, if the network is really operating as expected or not).

Moreover, traffic requirements in terms of pattern and volume can change over time as a natural result of business organic growth, merger and acquisition, and the introduction of new applications. This means that the network may end up handling traffic flows that it was not designed for. The question here is this: How can IT leaders and network operators know about what is going on? If the network is facing performance issues that need to be taken care of, how can the change and alteration be performed in a tracked and structured manner? In fact, configurations and changes are more of a concern compared to other aspects because any error can lead to either a downtime or a degraded performance, and based on recent studies such as the one conducted by ZK Research in 2013 with regard to network management, 37% of network downtimes are caused by human error, which makes its impact the biggest compared to other influencing factors, as shown in the Figure 10-53 [118,119].

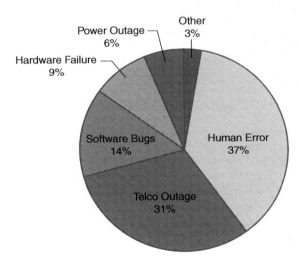

Figure 10-53 *Causes of Network Downtime Based on ZK Research, 2013*

Consequently, there must be a set of procedures and mechanisms capable of measuring and providing real-time and historical information about every single activity across the network to help the IT team take action in a more proactive manner instead of relying on only the reactive approach to be able to effectively, and in a timely manner, identify and fix issues or abnormal behaviors in which the mean time to repair (MTTR) needs to be kept as short as technically possible. Furthermore, the action taken by IT should also be performed in a controlled and structured manner to be tracked and recorded, also combined with some automation with regard to configuration and changes to help reduce the percentage of human errors. For the IT to achieve this, they need a network management solution that controls operation, administration, maintenance, and provisioning [88].

There are several industry standards and frameworks in the area of network management. This section discusses the ITU-T standard (FCAPS).

Fault, Configuration, Accounting, Performance, and Security

FCAPS is a network management framework defined by the International Organization for Standardization (ISO) to help organizations classify the objectives of network management into the following five distinct layers or categories:

- **Fault management:** This management layer aims to minimize network outages by employing a set of procedures and activities to detect and isolate network issues, along with the appropriate corrective actions to overcome current issues and prevent them from occurring again. Alarms, fault isolation, testing, and troubleshooting are example of fault management functions.

- **Configuration management:** This management layer aims to maintain a current inventory of network equipment, with its configurations to be used for planning, installation, and provisioning of new services and network equipment.

- **Accounting management:** It is implied by the name that this layer aims to ensure that each user or entity is billed or allocated an appropriate cost reference on the activities and utilization performed across the network. This can be measured based on various elements, such as a given service usage or bandwidth utilization. Usage management, pricing, auditing, and profitability analysis are examples of accounting management functions.

- **Performance management:** This layer aims to monitor and keep track of any performance issues, such as network bottlenecks, by continuously collecting and analyzing statistical information to monitor, correct, and optimize any reduced responsiveness across the network. This will potentially lead to enhanced capacity planning and quality measurement. Quality assurance, performance analysis, and monitoring are examples of the functions of this management layer.

- **Security management:** Typically, this layer focuses on the security of the management solutions (all the different layers above) in terms of access control, data confidentiality, and integrity with regard to network alarms, events, and reports. In addition, this layer sometimes refers to the monitoring and management of the network with regard to the security aspects such as unauthorized access, traffic spikes (DoS attacks), and targeted applications attacks.

Network Management High-Level Design Considerations

Network management is an extensive and large topic. In addition to that, network management is defined and approached differently based on the entity or organization that creates the standards and the aim of the standards or framework, such as FCAPS versus ITIL. Therefore, it is impossible to cover such a large and extensive topic in a single section or chapter. This section covers the primary points and considerations at a high level to help network designers to drive the considerations around network management in the most suitable direction. Typically, there can be more than one right direction or approach.

The answers to the following questions help to form the foundation of the network management solution:

- What is the targeted environment (such as enterprise, MPLS VPN SP, application SP, cloud-hosting SP)?

- Is there any existing network management solution? If yes, does the solution follow any standard approach or framework such as FCAPS?

- Is the solution to be added to overcome an existing challenge or for enhancement purposes?

- Are there any business-related constraints, such as budget?

- What is the goal of the solution (for example, monitoring and fault management, capacity planning, billing, monitoring for security purposes, or a combination of these goals)?

- Are there any security constraints with regard to enabling network management, such as only out-of-band management, or can secure in-band management protocols be used?

After all or most of these questions have been answered, network designers should have a good understanding about the high-level targeted network management solution and should be able to start specifying its detailed design, which should answer at least the following questions:

- What information or events do network management solutions need to collect or monitor?

- Where is the best place to gather the intended information or report the relevant events?

- Where should this information or these events be sent after the collection process?

- What is the degree of detail required and is full or partial data collection is required?

- Is the underlying transport network secure (internal) or untrusted (public Internet)?

- How is confidentiality and integrity of the polled or exported information maintained?

- What are the supported protocols and versions by the elements to be monitored and managed for the purpose of network management, such as SNMP or NetFlow?

Taking these questions into consideration, network designers can drive the solution selection and can specify which features and protocols are required and where they should be enabled. For example, an MPLS SP decided to offer VoIP service to their customers to make voice calls to public switched telephone network (PTSN) numbers across the SP IP backbone, in addition to Internet Session Initiation Protocol (SIP) VoIP applications using Cisco Unified Border Element (CUBE) as a SIP gateway, as shown in Figure 10-54.

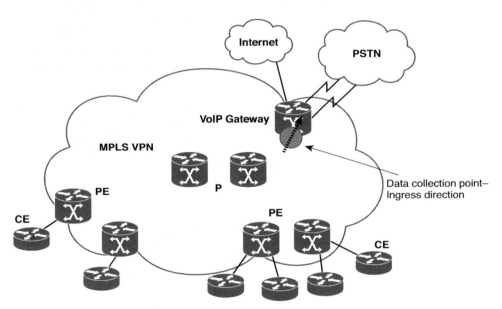

Figure 10-54   *MPLS VPN SP Sample Network*

According to the nature of this network, solution goals, and architecture, an accounting management needs to be considered here to measure the utilization of the service. In this example, VoIP calls usually require a collection of the actual usage in terms of duration and destination number, which is normally an endpoint IP or another voice gateway IP or CUBE (such as to another SIP URI or PSTN number, local or international), and then a correlation between the collected information and pricing needs to be performed to generate a billing per VPN customer/user per call. By enabling NetFlow at the centralized CUBE, this SP can export VoIP call usage to the NetFlow collector to obtain the desired reports for the billing purposes.

In this particular example, the main question is where to enable data collection. Is it better at the SP edge (PEs), SP core (P), or at the CUBE (voice gateway)? Based on the nature of the service and the traffic flow described, voice calls will be from customer sites toward the services edge gateway, and no VoIP calls are made: neither directly between the different VPN customers nor between sites of the same VPN customer across the MPLS VPN provider backbone. This means that every VoIP traffic flow will pass through the voice gateway, where the SP can perform ingress accounting per VoIP call flow in a centralized manner.

Another example is an enterprise with hundreds of remote sites connected over a single WAN network that carries different types of traffic, including VoIP, video, and data applications, as shown in Figure 10-55. This enterprise needs a network management solution that monitors WAN link utilization and reports any link that exceeds the available WAN bandwidth with regard to the traffic sourced from each remote site LAN. Based on these simple requirements, it is obvious that a performance management solution is required for the WAN links, where SNMP, for example, can be enabled per WAN link for the network management system (NMS) to collect the relevant Management Information Bases (MIBs) with regard to the utilization of each remote site WAN link. SNMP MIB polling also offers the ability to perform the polling based on a predefined time interval to retrieve the required information only when needed, to reduce the impact on the nodes' CPU and WAN performance.

However, if this enterprise requested that the utilization reports have to specify the top five protocols or applications using the WAN link during peak hours and the sources and destinations of these top five traffic flows during peaks hours, in this case egress accounting on the WAN links with NetFlow (IPFIX) is required to provide this level of visibility (per application, per session, or flow utilization).

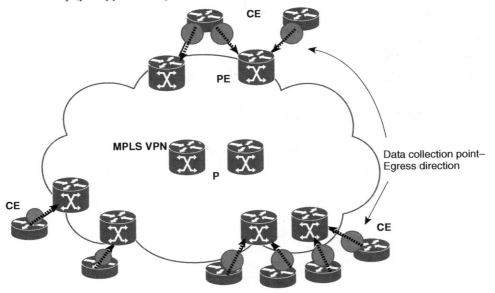

Figure 10-55 *Enterprise Network Sample for Network Management*

In this example, there are two primary design considerations worth analyzing. The first is the location of the data collection. Based on this scenario's requirements, a performance management solution is required to measure remote site WAN link utilization. This means a distributed data collection model is required here to measure and report the performance of the WAN link per remote site.

The second design consideration is in what direction the data or flows should be metered (ingress versus egress). Technically, in this particular example, to measure a CE router WAN link utilization for traffic sourced from the LAN side, in addition to identifying traffic types and top talkers over this link using different network management protocols (such as SNMP interface counters or NetFlow), measuring traffic in the egress direction will be an optimal choice. In addition, if the link measurement is considered at the egress direction in this example, it is recommended not to consider ingress data collection at the same node for the same purpose, to ensure that there will be no data duplication reported to the NMS.

From these two scenarios, it is obvious that the top-down approach is the most appropriate approach to developing and proposing a network management solution, starting from business goals and working toward the network management protocols.

Multitier Network Management Design

In general, it is proven that integrating and structuring multiple management systems and tools in a hierarchical manner offers a more flexible and efficient network management solution when multiple elements and managements are present. For instance, this layered approach helps to reduce the number of alerts seen by network operations support staff, only presenting filtered and relevant information and alerts. However, to achieve this in a large-scale network, a considerable amount of structured integrations are required between multiple management systems and tools in a layered approach. As shown in Figure 10-56 [89], this approach is recommended by Cisco systems because it offers the following benefits:

- Proactively identifies and corrects potential network issues before they become problems

- Offer optimized IT solution productivity by reducing and eliminating network connectivity loss to a minimum

- Focuses on the solution instead of the problem, which helps to reduce downtime duration (MTTR)

This multitier network management approach is based on bottom-up communication flow between the different management systems and tools using various protocols, including NetFlow, syslog, and SNMP. In fact, in a large network, it is almost always impossible to cope with the number of events reported from each network element to the NMS at the higher layers. In addition, in certain situations, a failure or fault in specific areas within the network can impact multiple devices. Typically, each device will independently alert the NMS. As a result, there will be duplicate instances of the same problem in this case.

With this architecture, the network management tier (NMT) receives the input from multiple elements and applications, and then performs root-cause analysis by correlating the original information received from multiple sources and identifying the event that has occurred. This level of abstraction for event correlation provided by the NMT offers a simplified and efficient network management and operation solution. Network operators will be presented with the event deemed to be the most relevant and important, associated with the deduplication capabilities of network events, to reduce the number of unnecessary messages presented to the operations personnel. The service management tier in this approach provides an added intelligence and automation to the filtered events by the NMT and event correlation for more optimization, which will help network operators to move from complicated element management (per alert) to managing network events and identified problems [89]. The level of automation and intelligence provided by this approach helps network operators avoid the classic network management approach also known as *box by box*, where the network operator or administrator needs to visit every single network node and manually configure, manage, and monitor each device separately.

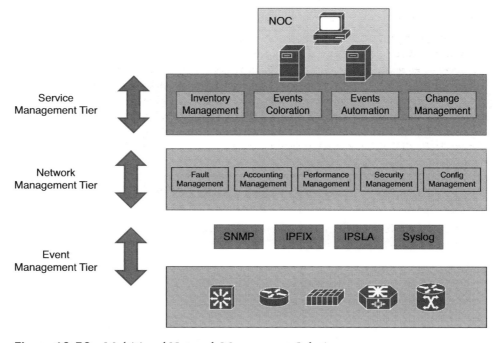

Figure 10-56 *Multitiered Network Management Solution*

Further Reading

RFC 6632, *An Overview of the IETF Network Management Standards*, http://www.ietf.org

RFC 4377, *Operations and Management (OAM) Requirements for Multi-Protocol Label Switched (MPLS) Networks*, http://www.ietf.org

Information Technology Infrastructure Library (ITIL) Foundation, https://en.wikipedia.org/wiki/ITIL

Summary

This chapter covered various advanced IP topics and services that are part of any network design. To avoid design defects, network designers need to always incorporate these in an integrated holistic approach rather than designing in isolation. Moreover, considering the top-down design approach is a fundamental requirement to achieving a successful business-driven design (for example, ensuring that the design complies with the organization's security policy standards). This chapter also emphasized the importance of considering the business priorities and design constraints in which network design ideally must adopt the "first things first" approach, which takes into consideration existing limitations, which may include staff knowledge, budget, or supported features and technologies.

Appendix

References

1. "IT Certifications and Career Paths, CCDE," http://www.cisco.com
2. R. White, D. Slice, and A. Retana. *Optimal Routing Design* (Cisco Press).
3. M. Medard, *Network Reliability and Fault Tolerance* (MIT).
4. "Gold Plating (Software Engineering)," http://www.wikipedia.com
5. "Data Center Access Layer Design," http://www.cisco.com
6. "The Evolution of the Next Generation Network," http://www.ciscolive.com
7. "Network Models and the Network Architect," http://www.ciscolive.com
8. *Scalable Routing Design Principles*, RFC 2791, http://www.ietf.org
9. "The Journey from CAPEX through TCO to Business Value," http://www.cisco.com
10. "Enterprise Campus 3.0 Architecture: Overview and Framework," http://www.cisco.com
11. "Cisco Data Center Business Continuity Planning Service," http://www.cisco.com
12. P. Oppenheimer. *Top-Down Network Design*, Second Edition (Cisco Press).
13. "OSPF Deployment in Modern Networks," http://www.ciscolive.com
14. "OSPF Design Guide," http://www.cisco.com
15. "OSPF Not-So-Stubby Area," http://www.cisco.com
16. "Enhanced Interior Gateway Routing Protocol (EIGRP)," http://www.cisco.com
17. "R&S Business Benefits," http://www.cisco.com
18. "High Availability Campus Network Design—Routed Access Layer Using EIGRP or OSPF," http://www.cisco.com
19. "EIGRP Design and Deployment," http://www.ciscolive.com
20. "Enhanced Interior Gateway Routing Protocol," http://www.cisco.com
21. "What Are OSPF Areas and Virtual Links," http://www.cisco.com
22. *OSPF Version 2*, RFC 2328, http://www.ietf.org
23. "IS-IS Mesh Groups," RFC 2973, https://tools.ietf.org/html/rfc2973
24. "BGP Case Studies," http://www.cisco.com
25. "BGP Peer Groups," http://www.cisco.com
26. "The Accumulated IGP Metric Attribute for BGP," https://tools.ietf.org
27. "Scalable Routing Design Principles," RFC 2792, https://tools.ietf.org
28. "Next Generation Enterprise WAN," http://www.cisco.com

29. "Network Services Virtualization," http://www.cisco.com
30. "Enterprise Campus 3.0 Architecture: Overview and Framework," http://www.cisco.com
31. "WAN Architectures and Design Principles," http://www.ciscolive.com
32. "Cisco Validated Designs for Enterprise WAN," http://www.cisco.com
33. *Experience with the BGP-4 Protocol*, RFC 4277, https://tools.ietf.org
34. "Configuring BGP Additional Paths," http://www.cisco.com
35. *BGP MULTI_EXIT_DISC (MED) Considerations*, RFC 4451, http://www.ietf.org
36. "Ethernet VPN (EVPN) and Provider Backbone Bridging-EVPN: Next Generation Solutions for MPLS-Based Ethernet Services," http://www.cisco.com
37. "Implementing BGP on Cisco IOS XR Software," http://www.cisco.com
38. "Cisco Dynamic Fabric Automation," http://www.cisco.com
39. "Distributed Virtual Data Center for Enterprise and Service Provider Cloud," http://www.cisco.com
40. "Overlay Transport Virtualization for Geographically Dispersed Virtual Data Centers - Improve Application Availability and Portability Solution Overview," http://www.cisco.com
41. "Active - Active Data Centre Strategies," http://www.ciscolive.com
42. "Cisco FabricPath Technology and Design," http://www.ciscolive.com
43. "IP NGN Carrier Ethernet Design: Powering the Connected Life in the Zettabyte Era," http://www.cisco.com
44. "Cisco IP Solution Center Carrier Ethernet and L2VPN User Guide," http://www.cisco.com
45. "Implementing Point to Point Layer 2 Services," http://www.cisco.com
46. "Deploying MPLS-Based Layer 2 Virtual Private Networks," http://www.ciscolive.com
47. *Pseudowire Setup and Maintenance Using the Label Distribution Protocol (LDP)*, RFC 4447, http://www.ietf.org
48. "Layer 2 Virtual Private Networks Using BGP for Auto-Discovery and Signaling," http://www.ietf.org
49. "Ethernet VPN (EVPN) and Provider Backbone Bridging-EVPN: Next Generation Solutions for MPLS-Based Ethernet Services," http://www.cisco.com
50. "Advanced Virtual Private LAN Service," http://www.cisco.com
51. "Overview of Provider Backbone Bringing and Integration Alternatives with VPLS," http://www.cisco.com
52. "BGP Techniques for Internet Service Providers," Cisco Systems, http://www.nanog.org
53. "Cloud and DC Architecture Evolution for Service Providers," http://www.cisco.com
54. "Cisco Virtualized Multiservice Data Center (2.3, 3.0.1), Design Guide," http://www.cisco.com
55. "Massively Scalable Data Center (MSDC), Design and Implementation Guide," http://www.cisco.com
56. "BGP/MPLS IP Virtual Private Networks (VPNs)," RFC 4364, http://www.ietf.org
57. *Virtual eXtensible Local Area Network*, RFC 7348, http://www.ietf.org
58. *Carrying Label Information in BGP-4*, RFC 3107, http://www.ietf.org
59. "Enterprise Multi-Homed Internet Edge Architectures," http://www.ciscolive.com
60. "Layer 2 Everywhere: Overcoming Overlay Transport Virtualization (OTV) Site Limitations Within and Between Data Centers," http://www.cisco.com

61. "draft-lapukhov-bgp-routing-large-dc-07," http://www.ietf.org
62. I. Hussain. *Fault-Tolerant IP and MPLS Networks* (Cisco Press).
63. "MPLS Traffic Engineering—Fast Reroute Link and Node Protection," http://www.cisco.com
64. J. Guichard, F. Faucheur, and J. Vasseur. *Definitive MPLS Network Designs* (Cisco Press).
65. "BGP PIC Edge for IP and MPLS-VPN," http://www.cisco.com
66. K. Lee, F. Lim, and B. Ong. *Building Resilient IP Networks* (Cisco Press).
67. "Financial Services Design for High Availability," http://www.cisco.com
68. L. Lobo and U. Lakshman. *MPLS Configuration on Cisco IOS Software* (Cisco Press).
69. "Enterprise QoS Solution Reference Network Design Guide," http://www.cisco.com.
70. "Cisco Globally Resilient IP," http://www.cisco.com
71. "Redundancy Mechanisms for Carrier Ethernet Networks and Layer 2 VPN Services," http://www.ciscolive.com
72. "VMDC DCI Design 1.0" http://www.cisco.com
73. E. Osborne and A. Simha. *Traffic Engineering with MPLS* (Cisco Press).
74. "Routed Fast Convergence and High Availability," http://www.cisco.com
75. "Data Center Overlay Technologies," http://www.cisco.com.
76. "Overlay Transport Virtualization for Geographically Dispersed Virtual Data Centers - Improve Application Availability and Portability Solution Overview," http://www.cisco.com
77. "rtgwg-bgp-routing-large-dc-xx," IETF draft, http://www.ietf.org
78. "design goals: availability," http://www.msdn.microsoft.com
79. "I-AS MPLS Solutions," http://www.ciscolive.com
80. *RSVP-TE: Extensions to RSVP for LSP Tunnels*, RFC 3209, http://www.ietf.org
81. "Metro Ethernet Services," http://www.cisco.com
82. "LISP Host Mobility," http://www.cisco.com
83. "Medianet WAN Aggregation QoS Design 4.0," http://www.cisco.com
84. "Cisco Application Centric Infrastructure Fundamentals," http://www.cisco.com
85. S. Convery. *Network Security Architectures* (Cisco Press).
86. *Site Security Handbook*, RFC 2196, http://www.ietf.org.
87. "Cisco Group Encrypted Transport VPN Data Sheet," http://www.cisco.com
88. A. Clemm. *Network Management Fundamentals* (Cisco Press)
89. "Network Management Systems Architectural Leading Practice," http://www.cisco.com
90. "QoS For IPSec VPNs" http://www.ciscolive.com
91. "IPv6: How to Get Started," http://www.cisco.com
92. "Per-Tunnel QoS for DMVPN," http://www.cisco.com.
93. "NewsRoom," http://www.gartner.com/newsroom/id/2636073
94. "Medianet QoS Design Strategy," http://www.cisco.com
95. *An Architecture for Differentiated Services*, RFC 2475, http://www.ietf.org
96. "Enterprise Medianet Quality of Service Design 4.0," http://www.cisco.com
97. "MPLS Traffic Engineering—DiffServ Aware (DS-TE)," http://www.cisco.com
98. G. Schudel. *Router Security Strategies* (Cisco Press).
99. "Cisco SAFE Solution Overview," http://www.cisco.com
100. "Control Plane Protection," http://www.cisco.com

101. http://whatis.techtarget.com/definition/Confidentiality-integrity-and-availability-CIA
102. "Cisco Network Foundation Protection Framework," http://www.cisco.com
103. "Cisco Network Foundation Protection Overview," http://www.cisco.com/c/dam/en/us/products/collateral/security/ios-network-foundation-protection-nfp/prod_presentation0900aecd80313fe3.pdf
104. "Market Data Network Architecture (MDNA) Overview," http://www.cisco.com
105. "Cisco SAFE Reference Guide," http://www.cisco.com
106. "Using MSDP to Interconnect Multiple PIM-SM Domains," http://www.cisco.com
107. "Control Plane Security Overview in Cisco IOS Software," http://www.cisco.com
108. "Advanced Topics in IP Multicast Deployment," http://www.ciscolive.com
109. "Comparing Traffic Policing and Traffic Shaping for Bandwidth Limiting," http://www.cisco.com
110. "IPvMulticasts Deployment and Configuration Guide," http://www.cisco.com
111. "IP Multicast Technology Overview," http://www.cisco.com
112. A. Martey. *Integrated IS-IS Routing Protocol Concepts* (Cisco Press).
113. "Network Functions Virtualization (NFV)," http://www.cisco.com
114. "Data Center Interconnect: Layer 2 Extension Between Remote Data Centers," http://www.cisco.com
115. "Deploying MPLS Traffic Engineering," http://www.ciscolive.com
116. "IPv6 Multicast Deployment and Configuration Guide," http://www.cisco.com
117. "Cisco IOS Quality of Service Solutions Configuration Guide," http://www.cisco.com
118. "Network Management Study, 2013," http://www.zkresearch.com
119. "Cisco APIC Enterprise Module Simplifies Network Operations," http://www.cisco.com
120. "Control Plane Policing Implementation Best Practices," http://www.cisco.com
121. "L3 Network Virtualization Design Concepts for the WAN," http://www.ciscolive.com
122. "Scaling Inter-Domain Routing-A View Forward," http://www.cisco.com
123. *Experience with the BGP-4 Protocol*, RFC 4277, http://www.ietf.org
124. "Deploying a Virtualized Campus Network Infrastructure," http://www.ciscolive.com
125. "Minimizing Packet Loss," http://www.ciscolive.com
126. The Cisco Certified Design Expert," http://www.ciscolive.com
127. "Advancements in L3 VPN over IP in the WAN," http://www.ciscoive.com
128. "HSRP Aware PIM," http://www.cisco.com
129. *Campus Network for High Availability Design Guide*, http://www.cisco.com
130. *Enterprise Campus Design: Multilayer Architectures and Design Principles*, http://www.ciscolive.com
131. *Campus Network for High Availability Design Guide*, http://www.cisco.com
132. *MPLS VPN Inter-AS with ASBRs Exchanging IPv4 Routes and MPLS Labels*, http://www.cisco.com
133. *Intermediate system-to-intermediate system protocol ISIS Deployment in Modern Networks*, http://www.ciscolive.com

Made in the USA
San Bernardino, CA
04 March 2017